Berlitz®

Croatian
Pocket Dictionary

Croatian – English
English – Croatian

Berlitz Publishing

New York · Munich · Singapore

Original edition edited by the
Langenscheidt editorial staff

Inset cover photo: © Punchstock/Medioimages

Neither the presence nor the absence of a designation indicating that any entered word constitutes a trademark should be regarded as affecting the legal status thereof.

Printed in Germany
ISBN-13: 978-981-246-942-7
ISBN-10: 981-246-942-7

1. 2. 3. 4. 5. 10 09 08 07 06

Contents

Abbreviations

adj	*adjective*, pridjev
adv	*adverb*, prilog
AERO	*aeronautics*, zrakoplovstvo
AGR	*agriculture*, poljoprivreda
Am	*American English*, američki engleski
ANAT	*anatomy*, anatomija
ARCHIT	*architecture*, arhitektura
ASTR	*astronomy*, astronomija
BIOL	*biology*, biologija
BOT	*botany*, botanika
Br	*British English*, britanski engleski
CHEM	*chemistry*, kemija
coll	*colloquial*, kolokvijalno
COM	*commerce*, trgovački
comp	*comparative*, komparativ
CUL	*culinary*, kulinarstvo
derog	*derogative*, preziran
eccl	*ecclesiastical*, crkveni
EL	*electricity*, elektricitet
etc	*et cetera*, *and so on*, i tako dalje
fam	*familiar*, familijarno
fig	*figurative*, figurativno
FILM	*film*, *cinema*, film
gen	*genitive*, genitiv
GEOGR	*geography*, geografija
GEOL	*geology*, geologija
GEOM	*geometry*, geometrija
GRAM	*grammar*, gramatika
hist	*historically*, povijesno
inf	*infinitive*, infinitiv
JUR	*jurisprudence*, plavo
konj	*conjunction*, veznik
MAR	*maritime term*, moreplovstvo
MATH	*mathematics*, matematika
MED	*medicine*, medicina
MIL	*military*, vojnički
MIN	*mineralogy*, mineralogija
MOT	*motoring*, motoristika

MUS	*music*, glazba
n	*noun*, imenica
OPT	*optics*, optika
p	*person*, lice
PAINT	*painting*, slikarstvo
PARL	*parliament*, parlament
pej	*pejorative*, pejorativno
PHOT	*photography*, fotografija
PHYS	*physics*, fizika
pl	*plural*, množina
poet	*poetical*, poezija
POL	*politics*, politika
pp	*past participle*, particip prošli
prep	*preposition*, prijedlog
pret	*preterite*, preterit
PRINT	*printing*, tiskarstvo
pron	*pronoun*, zamjenica
RADIO	*radio*, radio
REL	*religion*, religija
RLW	*railway*, željeznica
sg	*singular*, jednina
sl	*slang*
SPORT	*sports*, sport
TECH	*technology*, tehnika
TEL	*telephony*, telefon
TENNIS	*tennis*, tenis
THEAT	*theatre*, kazalište
th	*thing*, stvar
ugl	*uglavnom*, chiefly
UNIV	*university*, sveučilište
v	*verb*, glagol
VET	*veterinary medicine*, veterina
ZOOL	*zoology*, zoologija

Croatian – English

A

a and; **~?** what? eh?
abeced|a alphabet, ABC; ***po ~i*** in alphabetical order; **~irati** alphabetize
adapt|acija adaptation (*prostorija*); conversion; **~irati** adapt; convert
administra|cija administration; **~tivan** administrative
admiral admiral
adres|a address; **~ar** address book; directory; **~irati** address (to)
adut trump (card)
advokat attorney, lawyer; solicitor; barrister
aero|dinamičan streamlined; **~drom** airfield; (*međunarodni*) airport
afektirati be affected
afinitet affinity
afirm|acija recognition; **~irati se** win recognition
afrički African
Afrika Africa
afroamerički African-American
agencija agency
agent agent
agres|ija aggression; **~ivan** aggressive; **~or** aggressor
agronom agronomist
ah! oh!
ajde! come on!
akadem|ija academy; **~ik** academician; **~ski** academic(al)
akcija action; v. **dionica**
ako if
akrobacija acrobatics
akrobat acrobat; **~ski** acrobatic
akt (*umjetnički*) nude; v. **spis, čin**
aktiv|an active; **~irati** activate; **~nost** activity
aktuelan topical, current
akumulator (storage) battery
akustika acoustics *pl*
akutan acute
akuzativ accusative
akvarel water-colour
akvarij aquarium
akviziter *Am* solicitor
alarm, ~irati alarm
alat tool(s); implement(s)
album album
alergi|čan allergic (to); **~ja** allergy (to)
alfabet alphabet
ali but
alimentacija alimony
alkohol alcohol
alkohol|an alcoholic; ***~no***

piće alcoholic drink; **~ičar** alcoholic; **~izam** alcoholism
Alpe the Alps
alt MUS alto
alternativa(n) alternative
aludirati allude to, hint (at)
aluminij aluminium, *Am* aluminum
aluzija allusion (to), hint (at)
amater(ski) amateur(ish)
ambalaža packing, container(s)
ambasad|a embassy; **~or** ambassador
ambici|ja ambition; **~ozan** ambitious
ambijent ambiance, surroundings
ambulanta out-patient department
američki American
Amerika America; **~nac** American
amnesti|ja, ~rati amnesty
amo here, this way; ***~ tamo*** back and forth
amonijak (*plin*) ammonia; (*tekućina*) ammonia water
amputirati amputate
analfabet illiterate, analphabet; **~ski** illiterate, analphabetic
anali|tički analytical; **~za** analysis (*pl* ~es); **~zator** analyst; **~zirati** analyse
analogija analogy
ananas pine apple
anarhija anarchy
anarhist (~ički) anarchist
anatom|ija anatomy; **~ski** anatomic
anđeo angel; ***~ čuvar*** guardian angel
anemi|čan an(a)emic; **~ja** an(a)emia
anestezija an(a)esthesia
angaž|irati engage; **~man** engagement
angina tonsillitis; (*gnojna*) quinsy
anket|a poll; **~irati** poll
ansambl troupe, ensemble
antena aerial
antibiotik antibiotic
antifriz anti-freeze
antikvarijat second-hand bookshop
antilop suede
antipati|čan unlikable; **~ja** dislike, antipathy
aparat apparatus; (*za kućanstvo*) appliance
apartman suite
aperitiv aperitif
apetit appetite
apoteka chemist's; *Am* drug store
april April
apsolutan absolute
Arabija Arabia
arak (double) sheet
Arapin Arab
arhiv archives *pl*
arija tune
arogantan arrogant
asfalt asphalt
asistent assistant
astma asthma
atentat (assassination) attempt

aterirati land
atlas atlas
atlet|a athlete; **~ika** athletics; **~ski** athletic
atom atom; **~ski** atomic
august August
Australija Australia
Austrija Austria
austrijski Austrian
auto car, automobile; **~bus** bus; coach
automat automaton; ***~ za cigarete*** cigarette machine; **~ski** automatic
auto|mehaničar car mechanic; **~mobil** (moto-)car; **~mobilist** motorist; **~put**, **~strada** motorway; *Am* superhighway
autor author
autostop hitchhiking; ***putovat ~om*** hitch-hike
avet ghost; spook
avijacija aviation
avijatičar flier, aviator
avion (aero)plane; *Am* airplane; **~om** by plane, by air
Azija Asia

B

babica midwife
bacati (baciti) throw, cast, fling; ***~ u zrak*** blow up
bačva barrel, cask; (*za benzin*) drum
badava free (of charge); gratis
badem almond
Badnjak Christmas Eve
bager dredger; excavator
bagrem acacia
bahat arrogant
bajka fairy-tale
baka grandmother
bakalar cod (-fish); (*sušen*) stock-fish
bakar copper
baklja torch; **~da** torch-light parade
bakrorez copperplate; etching
bal ball
bala bale; roll
balast ballast
balavac whipper-snapper
balon baloon
Baltičko more the Baltic
balkon balcony
balvan beam
balzam bal(sa)m; **~irati** embalm
banana banana
bančiti carouse
banda band, gang
banka bank
banknota (bank-)note, *Am* bill
bankomat ATM
bankrot bankruptcy; **~irati** become (go) bankrupt
banja = **kupka, toplice**
bar[1] at least, at any rate, if only
bar[2] night club; bar(-room),

coctail lounge
bara pool, pond
baraka hut, shack, shed
barem = **bar**[1]
barka boat
barikada barricade
barometar barometer
baršun velvet
barun baron
barut (gun-) powder
bas bass; (*pjevač*) bass(o)
baš just, exactly, quite, precisely
baštin|a inheritance; heritage; **~ik** heir; **~iti** inherit
batak leg
baterija battery; (i MIL)
batin|a club, stick; **~e** *pl* beating
baviti se occupy oneself with; engage in, deal with
baza base (i MIL); basis
bazen (swimming) pool
bdjeti keep vigil; watch (over)
beba doll; (*dijete*) baby
bedak fool, ninny, simpleton
bedast foolish, silly
bedem wall, rampart
bedro thigh
bek back
beletristika fiction
Belgija Belgium
benzin petrol; *Am* gas(oline)
benzin|ski: ***~ska stanica*** filling petrol station
Beograd Belgrade
berba vintage
besanica insomnia
besciljan aimless
beskamatan interest-free
beskarakteran spineless, unprincipled
besklasni classless
beskompromisan uncompromising
beskoris|tan useless; **~nost** uselessness
beskraj|an endless; **~nost** endlessness
beskrupulozan unscrupulous
besmisao absurdity, nonsense; **~len** absurd, nonsensical
besmrt|an immortal; **~nost** immortality
besperspektivan unpromising
besplat|an, **~no** free, gratuitous, gratis; ***~na ulaznica*** free ticket
besposl|en idle, unemployed; **~ičiti** loaf, idle
bespravan rightless
besprijekoran impeccable; irreproachable
besprimjeran unexampled, matchless, unprecedented
besprincipijelan unprincipled
besraman shameless
bešćutan callous, emotionless
bešuman noiseless
beton concrete; ***armirani ~*** reinforced concrete
bez without
bezazlen artless; harmless; **~ost** artlessness; harmless-

ness
bezbojan colourless
bezbolan painless
bezbožan godless
bezbrižan carefree
bezbroj countless number; **~an** countless
bezdan abyss
bezduš|an heartless; **~nost** heartlessness
bezobrazan impudent
bezobzir|an reckless, regardless, inconsiderate; ***~no postupati*** be ruthless
bezglav brainless, confused
bezgraničan infinite, boundless
bezimen nameless
bezizražajan lacking expression, expressionless
bezličan lacking individuality; impersonal
beznačajan insignificant
beznadan hopeless
bezopasan harmless
bezuspješan abortive, unsuccessful
bezuvjetan unconditional
bezvoljan apathetic, languid
bezvrijedan worthless, valueless
bežičan wireless
biber pepper
biblija the Bible
biblioteka library; **~r** librarian
bicikl bicycle; **~ist** cyclist
bič whip; **~evati** whip, flog, lash
biće being, creature
bide bidet
bife bar, snack-bar, buffet
bijeda misery, poverty, want
bijedan wretched, miserable, poor
bijeg flight, escape
bijel white; **~ac** white (man); **~iti** bleach; paint white, whitewash
bijes fury, rage; **~an** furious; (*pas*) mad
bik bull
bilanca balance (sheet)
bilijun billion; *Am* milliard
bilo pulse; (*gorsko*) crest, ridge
biljar billiards *pl*
biljeg (revenue), duty stamp; *fig* mark; **~ovati** affix a revenue stamp to
bilješka note; *coll* memo
biljež||iti take notes, note down; record; **~nica** exercise book, note book; **~nik** (**javni ~nik**) notary (public); parish clerk; town clerk
bilj|ka plant; **~ni** vegetable
birač voter
biran choice, formal
birati choose, select; elect
birokra|cija bureaucracy; **~tski** bureaucratic
biser pearl; (*umjetno uzgojen*) cultured pearl; (*umjetni*) imitation pearl; **~nica** pearl-oyster
biskup bishop; **~ija** diocese; bishopric
biskvit (sweet) biscuit
bist|ar clear, limpid; **~rina**

clarity; **~riti** clarify; **~riti se** clear up
bit essence; **~an** essential
bitanga good-for-nothing
biti be; exist; ***nije bilo vremena*** there was no time
bitka battle
bitno essentially
bivol (water) buffalo
bivši former, one-time
bizon bison
bižuterija costume jewellery
bjegunac fugitive; ***vojni ~*** deserter
bjelan|ce white (of egg); **~čevina** albumen; protein
bjelilo bleach
bjelina white(ness)
bjelokost ivory
bjelogorica leaf forest
bjeloočnica white (of eye)
bjelouška ring snake
bjesnoća (*kod pasa*) rabies; madness
bjesnjeti rage; storm
bježati run away, escape
blag mild, gentle
blagajn|a (*u dućanu*) paying counter; (*ured*) pay office; (*za ulaznice*) box-office; (*za vozne karte*) booking-office, ticket-office; **~ica**, **~ik** cashier, booking clerk; (*bankovni*) teller; (*društva*) treasurer
blagdan holiday
blago hoard livestock, animals, cattle
blagodat boon, advantage, blessing
blagonaklon benevolent
blagoslov blessing; **~iti** bless
blagost mildness, gentleness
blagostanje prosperity, welfare; comfort; wealth
blagotvoran beneficial
blagovaonica dining-room
blagovremeno in time
blajhan dyed (blonde)
blam|aža disgrace; **~irati se** disgrace oneself
blanja plane; **~ti** plane
blat|an muddy; **~o** mud; **~obran** mudguard; *Am* fender
blažen blessed, blissful; beatified; **~stvo** bliss, beatitude
blebetati blab, prattle
blef, ~irati bluff
blenuti gape
blesa|n, ~v imbecile
blezgarija drivel
blijed pale
blijes|ak, ~kati flash glare, dazzle
bliskost closeness, nearness
blistati glitter, sparkle, dazzle
blistav glittering dazzling; *fig* brilliant
blitva Swiss chard, mangel
blizak close (to), near
blizanac twin
bliz|ina nearness, closeness; **~u** near, close
bliži nearer
bližnji fellow man (creature)
bludnica harlot, strumpet, prostitute
bluza blouse
bljedilo, **bljedoća** pallor,

paleness
bljutav flat, tasteless; *fig* insipid
bljuvati vomit; *coll* throw up; *fig* belch
bljuzgavica slush
bob broad-bean; **~ica** berry
boca bottle; **~čica** vial
bočni lateral
bod stich; (*poen*) point
bodar brisk, spirited
bodež dagger
bodljika prick; spine; **~v** prickly, spiny; ***~va žica*** barbed wire
bodriti encourage, cheer up
bofl shoddy goods
bog god; ***hvala ~u!*** thank goodness!
bogalj cripple, invalid
bogat rich, wealthy; **~aš** rich man; **~aši** the rich; **~stvo** wealth
boginj|a goddess; **~e** MED small-pox
boj battle; **~ište** battlefield
boja colour; *Am* color; (*ličilačka*) paint; (*za tkanine*) dye; ***uljena ~*** oil paint
bojadisati paint; dye
bojati se be afraid (of), fear
bojazan fear, apprehension; anxiety
bojažljiv timid
bojkot, ~irati boycott
bojler water-heater, geyser
bok side, flank; hip
boks boxing; **~ač** boxer; **~ati** box
bol pain, ache; (*duševni*) anguish; **~an** painful, aching
boles|nik patient; **~t** sickness, illness; disease; (*laka*) indisposition; **~tan** sick, ill
bolešljiv sickly
bolni|ca hospital; **~čar** man-nurse, orderly; **~čarka** nurse; ***~čka kola*** ambulance
bolovanje: ***na ~u*** at sick-leave
bolovati be ill with, suffer from
bolje better
boljeti hurt, ache, pain; ***boli me glava*** I have a headache; my head hurts
bolji better
bomba bomb; ***ručna ~*** (hand) grenade
bombar|der bomber; **~dirati** bomb (*artiljerijski*) shell
bombon sweet; *Am* candy
bor pine
bora wrinkle, line
borac fighter; *fig* champion
borav|ak stay; **~iti** stay, dwell, reside
borba struggle, fight; MIL combat
boriti se struggle, fight
borna kola armoured car
borovnica blueberry
bos barefoot(ed)
bosti prick; (*nožem*) stab
botanički vrt botanical garden(s)
božanski divine
božica goddess
Božić Christmas; ***~no drvce*** Christmas-tree

božji divine
bračn|i matrimonial, conjugal; ***~i par*** married couple; ***~o putovanje*** wedding trip, honeymoon
braća brothers; brethren
brada beard; (*kost*) chin; **~t** bearded
bradavica wart; (*sise*) nipple
bradva broad ax
brak marriage, matrimony, wedlock
brana (high) dam; (*zaustava*) lock; (*drljača*) harrow; **~ti** harrow
branič SPORT back
branik MOT bumper
branilac defender; JUR counsel, barrister, attorney
braniti defend (oneself)
brašno flour
brat brother; **~ski** fraternal
brati gather, pick; pluck
bratić cousin
bratstvo fraternity
brav wether
brav|a lock; ***patent ~a*** latch; ***obiti ~u*** pick a lock; **~ar** locksmith
brazda furrow; (*iza broda*) wake
brazgotina scar
brblja|rija idle talk; **~ti** chat, chatter; **~v** chatty, talkative; **~vac** chatterer, chatterbox; **~vost** chattiness
brčići *pl* clipped moustache
brd|o moutain, hill; **~ovit** mountainous, hilly; **~ski** mountain
bređa big with young
breme burden, load, weight
breskva peach
breza birch
brežuljak hill, hillock, knoll
brid edge; **~ak** sharp, cutting
briga worry, trouble; care; ***nije me ~!*** I don't care
brigada brigade
brija|č barber; **~čnica** barber's (shop); ***aparat za ~nje*** safety razor; (*električni*) electric razor; **~ti** (give a) shave; **~ti se** (have a) shave
brijeg = **brdo**
briljant brilliant; **~an** brilliant
brinuti se worry (about), be worried (about); care (for); be responsible (for)
brisa|č wiper; **~ti** wipe; mop; (*gumicom*) erase
britva razor
brižljiv attentive, painstaking, careful; **~o** carefully, attentively; **~ost** care, carefulness
brk moustache
brkati confuse, mix
brklja barrier; toll-bar
brnjica muzzle
brod ship, vessel. *coll* boat; ***putnički ~*** passenger ship, (*veliki*) liner; ***teretni ~*** cargo ship; ***ratni ~*** warship; ***na ~u*** aboard
brodograd|ilište shipyard; **~nja** shipbuilding; ***inženjer ~nje*** naval architect

brodolom shipwreck; **~ac** shipwrecked person
brodovlasnik shipowner
brodsk|i: ***~e isprave*** ship's papers; ***~a agencija*** shipping agency; ***~i prostor*** freight space; ***~i tovar*** cargo; ***~i motor*** marine engine
broj number; numeral; figure; (*cipela i sl.*) size; ***rimski (arapski) ~*** Roman (Arabic) numeral; ***označavati ~em*** number; ***u punom ~u*** in full force
brojan numerous
brojčanik (*sata*) face; (*telefona*) dial
brojilo: ***električno (plinsko) ~*** electricity (gas) meter
brojiti count
brojka figure; digit
brojnik numerator
brokat brocade
brom bromine
bron|ca, **~čan** bronze
bronhitis bronchitis
broš brooch
broš|iran paper-bound; **~ura** brochure
brstiti browse
bršljan ivy
brtvilo TECH gasket
brucoš freshman
brujati drone, hum
brundati grumble
brus whetstone; grindstone; **~ač** (knife) grinder; **~iti** grind; sharpen; (*britvu*) hone
brusnica cranberry
bruto-težina gross weight
brvn|ara log-cabin; **~o** foot-bridge
brz quick, fast, rapid; (*odgovor*) prompt
brzaci *pl* rapids *pl*
brzin|a speed, rapidity, quickness; promptness; (TECH) velocity; ***~om od 100 km na sat*** at a speed (*ili* rate) of sixty miles an hour; ***najveća ~a*** top speed; ***svom ~om*** at full speed; ***na ~u*** in a hurry; MOT ***preći iz prve u drugu ~u*** change over from first to second gear (*ili* speed); MOT ***mijenjati ~u*** shift gear; ***voziti nedozvoljenom ~om*** speed
brzinomjer speedometer
brzojav wire, telegram; (*preko mora*) cable; **~iti** (send a) wire; cable
brzojavni: ***~ ured*** telegraph-office
brzoplet hasty, rash
brzovozna roba express goods
brže! hurry up!
bubamara ladybird
bubanj drum
bubnuti say something silly; blurt out
bubnj|ar drummer; **~ati** drum; **~ić** ear-drum
bubreg kidney
bubrežnjak loin; (*goveđi*) sirloin, *Am* tenderloin
bubulji|ca pimple; **~čav** pimply

bucmast chubby; plump
buča marrow
bučan noisy
bučiti make noise; boom; roar
bućkuriš weak wine; slops *pl*
budala fool, simpleton; **~st** foolish, silly; **~ština** foolishness, silliness
budan awake; *fig* alert; ***biti ~*** sit up (late)
budilica alarm (clock)
buditi (se) wake up
budnost alertness, vigilance
budući|i future; ***~i da*** as, since; **~nost** future
budžet budget
bugačic|a blotting-paper; ***osušiti ~om*** blot
Bugar|in Bulgarian; **~ska** Bulgaria; **~ski** Bulgarian
buha flea
bujan luxuriant, dense, thick; well-developed
bujati swell; (*bilje*) grow luxuriant, spring up
bujica torrent, flood
buka noise, racket
buknuti flare up; break out
buktinja torch
buktjeti blaze, flame
bukva beech
bukvalan = **doslovan**
buldog bulldog
buldožer bulldozer
bulevar boulevard
buljiti stare, gape, gaze
bumbar bumble-bee
buna rebellion, revolt, uprising; MIL mutiny
bunar well; ***~ na čabar*** draw--well
buncati be delirious; *fig* talk incoherently
bunda sheepskin coat
bundeva pumpkin
bunil|o delirium; ***u ~u*** delirious
buniti stir up; **~ se** rise, rebel, revolt; grumble
bunker MIL pill-box
bunovan drowsy
buntov|an, **~nički** rebellious, mutinous; **~nik** rebel, insurgent; mutineer
bura north-easter; storm; **~n** stormy
burz|a (stock-) exchange, stock-market; ***~ovni izvještaj*** stock-report; ***~a rada*** labour exchange, employment office; ***crna ~a*** black--market; **~ijanac** stock--operator, market-operator
burž|oazija bourgeoisie; **~uj(ski)** bourgeois
busen turf, sod
buši|lica driller; drilling machine; **~ti** drill, bore; pierce, perforate, punch
but leg, ham; thigh; (*goveđi*) round (of beef)

C

car emperor; **~evina** empire; **~ica** empress
carić wren
carin|a customs; *(pristojba)* duty; ***~ski pregled*** customs inspection; ***podložan ~i*** dutiable; **~arnica** custom(s) house; **~ik** customs officer
cars|ki imperial; ***~ki rez*** Caesarean section; **~tvo** empire
CD CD; **~-player** CD player; **~-ROM** CD ROM
cedar cedar (-tree)
cedulja note; slip
ceh guild
celer celery
celofan cellophane
celuloid celluloid
celuloza cellulose
cement(irati) cement
centar centre, *Am* center
centarfor Centre Forward
centarhalf Centre Half, Back
centimetar centimetre
central|a heardquarters; ***električna ~a*** electric power station, power plant; **~izirati** centralize
centrifug|a *(za rublje)* spind-drier; ***sušiti u ~i*** spin-dry
cenzur|a censorship; **~irati** censor
cerada tarpaulin
cerekati se simper
ceremonija ceremony; **~lan** ceremonial
ceriti se grimace
cesta road, highway; **~rina** toll
chat|line chatline; **~room** chat room
cic printed calico
cičati squeak, squeal
ciferšlus zip fastener
cigara cigar
cigareta cirette
cigla brick; **~na** brickyard
cijediti strain, filter; **~ se** drip, trickle
cijel|i whole, entire; MATH ***2 ~a 3*** (2,3) two point three
cijena price; ***nabavna ~*** purchase price; ***najviša ~*** top price; ***proizvodna ~*** production price; ***tržna ~*** market price
cijeniti esteem, appreciate, value
cijepati split; *(drva)* chop
cijepiti graft; MED vaccinate, inoculate; **~ljenje** vaccination, inoculation
cijev tube, pipe; *(gumena)* hose; *(oružja)* barrel; RADIO valve, *Am* tube
cik-cak zig-zag
cikla red beet, beetroot
ciklama cyclamen
ciklon cyclone
ciklostil cyclostile, duplicator
ciklus cycle

cilindar cylinder; (*šešir*) top hat
cilj object, aim, purpose; **~ati** aim (at); *fig* hint (at)
cimet cinnamon
cini|čan cynical; **~k** cynic; **~zam** cynicism
cink zinc
cipela shoe; (*niska*) low shoe; (*visoka*) boot; (*gojzerica*) heavy-duty boot; (*salonka*) court shoe, *Am* pump; ***trgovina*** **~** shoe shop
cirkul|acija circulation; **~irati** circulate
cirkus circus
ciroza cirrhosis
cisterna cistern; (*kamion*) tank car
cit|at quotation; **~irati** quote
civil civilian; ***u ~u*** civilian clothes
civilizacija civilisation
cjedilo strainer
cjelin|a whole, totality; ***u ~i*** as a whole
cjelokupan total
cjelovit integral, entire
cjenik price-list
cjenkati se haggle
cjepanica (split) log
cjepidla|čiti split hairs; **~ka** hair-splitter
cjepivo vaccine
cjevanica shin-bone, shank
cmizdriti pule, whine
crack (*droga*) crack
crijep (roofing-) tile
crijevni intestinal
crijevo intestine
crknuti die
crkva church
crkven ecclesiastical; **~jak** sexton, verger
crkvica chapel
crn black; ***u ~ini*** in mourning; **~ka** brunette
crno|gorac Montenegrin; **~gorica** conifers, coniferous wood; **~manjast** dark
crpsti draw, pump
crta line; **~č** draughtsman; **~ti** draw
crtež drawing
crv worm; **~otočan** worm-eaten
crven red; **~dać** robin; **~ilo** red(ness); **~jeti** redden; **~kast** reddish
curica little girl
curiti run, flow, trickle
cvasti bloom, flower; (*drveće*) blossom; *fig* flourish
cvat bloom; *fig* flowering
cvije|će flowers; **~t** flower
cviljeti whine
cvjećarna florist's
cvjetača cauliflower
cvoko|tati: ***on ~će*** his teeth are chattering
cvrčak cicada, cricket
cvrčati (*cvrčak*) chirp; (*na vatri*) sizzle
cvrkut(ati) twitter; (*melodiozno*) warble
cyber- cyber...

Č

čabar pail, bucket
čačkalica toothpick
čačkati: ~ ***zube*** pick one's teeth
čađa soot; **~v** sooty
čahura MIL case, shell, cartridge; ZOOL cocoon, chrysalis
čaj tea; **~nik** tea-pot; (*samo za vodu*) tea-kettle
čak even
čamac (row-) boat; ~ ***za spasavanje*** life-boat; ***motorni*** ~ motor-boat
čangrizav peevish, morose
čaplja heron; (*siva*) egret
čar charm; **~ati** cast spells; **~oban** magic; *fig* charming; **~obnjak** magician; **~olija** sorcery; charm
čarape *pl* socks; (*ženske*) stockings, nylons; (*hulahup*) tights; (*za gojzerice*) over-socks; (*dokoljenke*) knee-socks
čas moment, instant, minute
časni honourable
časopis periodical, journal, magazine
čast honour; **~an** honourable; **~iti** honour, repect; (*plaćati*) treat
častohlepan ambitious
čaša glass
čaška BOT calix
čavao nail
čavka (jack) daw
čed|an demure, modest; **~nost** modesty
čega: ***iz*** ~ out of what; ***od*** ~ of what
čegrt|uša ZOOL rattlesnake; **~ati** rattle
Čeh Czech
ček cheque, *Am* check; ***~ovna knjižica*** cheque book; ***~ovni račun*** cheque account
čekaonica waiting-room
čekati wait (na for); ~ ***u redu*** queue, *Am* line up
čekić hammer
čekinja bristle
čekrk winch
čeli|čan steel; **~čana** steel plant (works)
čelik steel; ***kaljeni*** ~ tempered steel; ~ ***koji ne rđa*** stainless steel
čel|o forehead; *fig* front; ***biti na ~u*** (be at the) head; **~ni** frontal
čeljust jaw
čempres cypress
čemu why?; ***na*** ~ on what; ***o*** ~ about what
čep stopper; (*od pluta*) cork
čepić MED suppository
čeprkati scratch; poke about
čerupati pluck
česma fountain, well
čest frequent; **~o** frequently,

often
čestica particle, fragment
čestit honest
čestit|ati congratulate; **~ka** greeting card; congratulation
češalj comb
češati (se) scratch (oneself)
češće pretty often
češer BOT cone
Češki Czech
češlja|ti (se) comb (one's hair); **~onica** hairdresser's (shop)
češljugar goldfinch
češnjak garlic
četa host, troop; MIL company
četiri four
četka brush; ***~ za kosu*** hairbrush; ***~ za odijela*** clothes-brush; ***~ za cipele*** shoe-brush; **~ti** brush
četkica: ***~ za zube*** tooth-brush; ***~ za brijanje*** shaving brush; ***~ za nokte*** nail-brush
četrdeset forty
četrnaest fourteen
četvero four persons; **~kut** quadrangle; **~noške** on all fours; **~nožac** quadruped; **~ struk** fourfold
četvor|ci *pl* quadruplets; **~ica** four
četvorni: ***~ metar*** square metre
četvrt (*gradska*) district; ***~ sata*** a quarter of an hour; **~ina** quarter; **~godišnji** quarterly
četvrtak Thursday; ***Veliki ~*** Maundy Thursday
četvrti fourth
četvrtinka MUS crotchet, *Am* quarter note
čeznut|i yearn, long; **~ljiv** yearning, longing
čežnja yearning. longing
čičak bur(r)
čiji? whose?
čik (cigarette-) stump
čil healthy, lively; (*starija osoba*) hale
čim as soon as
čime with what?; ***nad ~*** above what
čimpanza chimpanzee
čin act; MIL rank; THEAT act
činiti do, make, perform; **~ se** seem, appear, look like
činovnik office worker, clerk, employee
činjeni|ca fact; ***~čno stanje*** the (real) facts
čipka lace; **~st** lacy, lace-like
čir boil; ***~ na želucu*** gastric (stomach) ulcer; ***~ na dvanaestercu*** duodenal ulcer
čist clean; *fig* pure; (*olovo*) refined; ***~a zarada*** net profit; ***~i prepis*** fair copy
čistač(ica) cleaner
čistilište Purgatory
čistina clearing
čistionica: ***kemijska ~*** cleaner's
čistiti clean; *fig* purify; (*kemijski*) dry clean; (*luku*) dredge; (*pile*) dress
čistka purge

čistoća cleanness; purity (*fig i o zlatu*)
čistokrvan thoroughbred
čišćenje: ***dati na ~*** have it dry-cleaned
čitak legible; readable
čitalac reader
čitanka reader
čitaonica reading-room
čitati read
čitav intact, safe; complete, entire, whole
čizm|a (high) boot; (*jahaća*) riding boot; (*gumena*) wellington, *Am* rubber boot; **~ica** bootee, *Am* lined boot
član member; GRAM article; **~arina** (membership) due; **~stvo** membership
članak article; ***uvodni ~*** leading article, leader
čoban(in) shepherd, herd
čokolad|a chocolate; ***~ni bomboni*** chocolates
čopor pack, troop
čorba broth, soup
čovječ|an humane; **~anstvo** mankind; **~ji** human, man's; **~nost** humanity
čovjek man; ***~ se umori*** one gets tired; ***odrastao ~*** adult; ***poslovan ~*** businessman
črčkati scrawl, scribble
čučati squat
čudak eccentric
čudan strange, queer, odd
čudesan miraculous
čuditi se be surprised (at), wonder
čudo wonder, miracle; **~tvoran** miraculous
čudovište monster
čuđenje surprise
čujan audible
čulo sense
čun canoe
čunj skittle, *Am* pin; ***~evi kuglane*** ninepins
čupa|ti pull, pluck; **~v** shaggy, dishevelled
čuperak tuft; lock
čuti hear; ***krivo ~*** hear wrongly, misunderstand
čuvanje keeping, preservation, guarding, protection
čuvar keeper; guard; watchman
čuvati keep; protect; take care of; guard, watch; **~ se** take care (of oneself)
čuven renowned, well-known, famous
čuvenj|e: ***poznavati po ~u*** know by reputation
čuvstvo feeling
čvarci *pl* greaves *pl*, *Am* cracklings *pl*
čvor knot; ***željeznički ~*** railway junction
čvorak starling
čvorište RLW junction, railway hub
čvoruga = **kvrga**
čvrst firm; sturdy; **~oća** firmness; sturdiness; solidity

Ć

ćaskati chatter
ćela bald spot, *(potpuna)* bald head; **~v** bald; **~vac** baldhead(ed)
ćelija cell
ćilim carpet; rug
ćirilica Cyrillic script
ćorav one-eyed
ćorsokak blind alley
ćosav beardless
ćud temper, disposition
ćudljiv whimsical; capricious; moody
ćuk owl
ćup (earthenware) jar
ćuš|ka, ~nuti slap (in the face)

D

da yes; that; ***znam ~ znaš*** I know (that) you know; if; ***~ znam*** if I knew; ***želim ~ vidim*** I want to see
dabar beaver
dadilja nanny, nurse, governess
dah breath; ***bez ~a*** breathless, out of breath
dahtati pant, gasp
dakako to be sure; surely, of course, without doubt
dakle well; consequently, therefore, thus
daktilograf typist
dalek distant, remote, far-away; **~o** far (away)
dalekosežan far-reaching
dalekovidan far-sighted (*i fig*), hyperopic
dalekovod overhead line, long distance power line (pipeline)
dalekozor fieldglass, binoculars; *(operni)* opera glass
Dalma|cija Dalmatia; **~tinac, ~tinski** Dalmatian
dalje farther; *(ugl fig)* further; **~!** go on!
dalj|nji far; distant; next, further; **~rođak** distant relative; **~ina** distance; ***iz ~ine*** at a distance
dan day; daylight; ***dobar ~*** good morning!. *poslije ručka* good afternoon! ***svaki ~*** every day
Danac Dane
danak tribute, tax
danas to-day; nowadays; ***do ~*** to this day; ***~ ujutro*** this morning
današnji present(-day), to-day's
dangubiti loaf, idle, waste time

danju in the daytime, by day, during the day
Danska Denmark
danski Danish
dapače on the contrary; exactly; even
dar present, gift; **~ežljiv** generous; **~ost** generosity
darovati present (with), make a present (of); donate
darovit gifted, talented; **~ost** gift, talent(s)
daska board; (*debela*) plank
daščara board hut, shed, cabin
daščica thin piece of board; shingle
dati give; provide; supply; **~ na popravak** (*čišćenje*) have it repaired (cleaned); **~ se na** set about … ing
datirati date
datula date
datum date; ***koji je danas ~?*** what's the date today?
davalac giver, donor
daviti choke, strangle; **~ se** choke; (*u vodi*) drown
davni ancient; **~na** ancient times, antiquity
davno long ago
daždevnjak salamander
debat|a, ~irati debate
debe|ljko obese person; *coll* fatty; **~ljuškast** plump, stout; **~o** fat, obese, stout; thick
debil moron
debl SPORT doubles *pl*
deblo (tree) trunk
deblj|ati se fatten; put on weight; **~ina** fatness
decembar December
decenij decade
decentraliz|acija decentralization; **~irati** decentralize
decilitar decilitre
decimalni: ***~ razlomak*** decimal (fraction); ***~ zarez*** decimal point
dečko (»*simpatija*«) boy-friend
defekt defect; (*kvar*) breakdown; **~an** defective; (*duševno*) handicapped
defetist(ički) defeatist
deficit deficit
defile MIL march-past; AERO fly-past; parade
defini|cija definition; **~rati** define
definitivan definitive; final
deform|acija deformity, deformation; **~iran** deformed; **~irati** deform; **~irati se** become deformed; lose shape
degeneriran degenerate
degradirati degrade; (*oficira*) demote
deka blanket
dekan dean
deklamirati declaim, recite
deklar|acija declaration; (*carinska*) customs declarion; **~irati** declare
dekolt|e low-cut neckline; **~irana** in a low-cut dress
dekoncetrirati distract; **~ se** lose concentration
dekorat|er (interior) decora-

tor; **~ivan** decorative
dekret decree, order; (*o postavljenju*) certificate of appointment
dekubitus MED bed-sore
dekuražirati discourage
deleg|acija delegation; **~at** delegate; **~irati** delegate, nominate
delikat|an delicate; **~esa** delicacy; ***~esna radnja*** delicatessen; **~nost** delicacy
delirij delirium; ***u ~u*** delirious
demagog demagogue; **~ija** demagog(uer)y
demagoški demagogical
demantirati deny, refute; **~ se** contradict oneself
demižon demijohn, wicker flask
demobiliz|acija demobilization; **~irati** demobilize, discharge
demokra|cija democracy; **~t** democrat
demolirati demolish, wreck, tear down; smash
demonstr|ant demonstrator; picket; **~irati** demonstrate
demontirati dismantle, remove, strip, take apart
denunci|jant informer; **~irati** inform (against), denounce
deodorant deodorant
depilator hair-remover
deplasiran out of place, inappropriate
deponirati deposit
deprimira|n depressed; **~ti** depress
deran urchin
der|ati tear, pull apart, rip; **~ati se** tear; (*vikati*) yell, scream, bawl, howl; **~njava** yelling
derište brat
desant MIL landing (operation)
desen pattern, design
desert *Br* sweet, *Am* dessert
deset ten; **~i** tenth; **~ina** one-tenth
desetar MIL corporal; squad leader
desetkovati decimate
desni *pl* gums *pl*
desni right(-hand)
desni|ca the right hand; POL the Right; **~čarski** rightist
desno (to the) right
destil|acija distillation; **~erija** distillery; **~irati** distill
destimulirati discourage
dešifrirati decode, decipher
detalj detail; **~an** detailed; **~no** in detail
deterdžent detergent
deva camel
devedeset ninety; **~i** ninetieth
devet nine; **~i** ninth
devetnaest nineteen; **~i** nineteenth
deviz|e *pl* foreign currency; ***~ni račun*** foreign-exchange account
dezavuirati disown; repudiate, disavow; withdraw support from

dezen = **desen**
dezert|er deserter; **~irati** desert
dezinfekcija disinfection
dezodorant deodorant
dezorganiz|acija disorganization; **~irati** disorganize; **~irati se** become disorganized
dežur|an on duty, on call; **~stvo** duty
dići = **dignuti**
diferencijal MOT differential (gear)
difterija diphtheria
diftong diphthong
dignuti lift, raise, hoist, elevate; pick up; **~ se** rise, get up
dijagonala diagonal
dijagram diagram, chart
dijalekt dialect
dijalog dialogue
dijapozitiv slide
dijeliti divide, separate; (*s drugim*) share; **~ se** divide
dijeljenje division (i MATH)
dijet|a diet; ***držati ~u*** diet
dijete child
dikobraz porcupine
dikt|at dictation; **~irati** dictate
dilema dilemma
dim smoke; **~iti se** smoke
dimljen: ***~a riba*** smoked fish
dimnja|čar chimney-sweep; **~k** chimney; (*brodski*) funnel, smoke-stack
dinamičnost dynamism
dinamit dynamite
dinamo dynamo
dinastija dynasty
dinja musk melon
dio (*gen.* **dijela**) part, share; ***rezervni ~*** spare part; **~ba** division, partition
dioni|ca share; part; **~čar** shareholder, *Am* stockholder; ***~čka glavnica*** share capital; ***~čko društvo*** joint-stock company, *Am* stock corporation
diplom|a diploma, certificate; **~irati** graduate, receive (take) a (university) degree
diplomat diplomat; **~ski** diplomatic
dirati touch
direkcija headquarters, head office; management
direkt|an direct; **~no** direct(ly)
direktor manager, director; (*škole*) headmaster, principal
dirig|ent conductor; **~irati** conduct
dir|ljiv touching, moving; **~nuti** touch
disati breathe, respire
disciplin|a discipline; field, branch; **~iran** disciplined; **~irati** discipline
disk discus
diskretan discrete
diskusija discussion
diskutirati discus
diskvalificirati (se) disqualify (oneself)

dispanzer clinic, health centre
dišni respiratory
div giant
divan wonderful, admirable
diverzant commando
dividenda dividend
diviti se admire, wonder
divlj|ač game; **~ak** savage; **~i** wild; **~ina** wilderness
divljenje admiration
divokoza chamois
divota magnificence
dizal|ica crane, hoist; **~o** lift, *Am* elevator
djec|a children; ***bez ~e*** childless
dječak boy
dječji childlike
djed grandfather
djelatnost activity
djelo work; deed, act
djelokrug sphere, field; domain
djelomi|ce, **~čno** partly, partially
djelotvoran effective, efficient
djelovanje activity
djelovati work, perform, be active; take effect
djeljiv divisible
djetao woodpecker
djetelina clover
djetinj|arija childishness; **~ast** childish; **~stvo** childhood
djevi|ca, **~čanski** virgin
djevičanstvo viriginity
djevojčica (little) girl
djevojka girl; (*»simpatija*) girl(-friend); maid
dlaka hair; **~v** hairy; **~vost** hairiness
dlan palm
dlijeto chisel
dnevni daily; **~ca** per diem; **~k** diary
dn|o bottom; ***bez ~a*** bottomless; ***na ~u*** at the bottom
do till, up to; (*prostorno*) to, as far as
dob age
doba time, age, era, epoch, period
dobaciti throw (over)
dobar good
dobavljati get, obtain, acquire; supply, procure, provide
dobitak gain, profit
dobiti get, obtain, recive, gain; ***~ natrag*** recover
dobitnik winner
dobričina good-natured fellow
dobro well; *n* farm; ***za tvoje ~*** for your own good; ***opće ~*** common good
dobrobit wellbeing, welfare, benefit
dobročin|itelj benefactor **~stvo** benefaction
dobroćudan good-natured
dobrodoš|ao, **~lica** welcome
dobrohotan benevolent
dobronamjeran well-meaning
dobrota goodness
dobrotvor benefactor; **~an**

charitable; ***~na priredba*** charity, benefic

dobrovolja|c volunteer; **~n** voluntary; **~no** voluntarily; ***~no se javiti*** volunteer

docent senior lecturer, *Am* assistant professor

doček reception; **~ati** meet; receive

dočepati se get hold of, capture

dočuti hear, learn

doći come, turn up, arrive; ***dobro ~*** come in handy; ***~ po*** come for

dodatak addition; appendix; supplement; admixture; (*na plaću*) bonus; = **doplatak**

dodati add; (*rukom*) hand, pass

dodatan additional

dodija|ti be fed up with; **~vati** bother, pester

dodijeliti assign, allocate

dodir touch; **~ivati se** adjoin; **~nuti** touch

dodjela assignment, allocation

doduše to be sure

događaj event; experience; ***razvoj ~a*** developments

dogled = **dalekozor**; **~an**: ***u ~no vrijeme*** in the near future

dogma dogma; **~tičan** dogmatic

dogoditi se happen, occur, take place

dogorijevati burn down; go out

dogovor arrangement; consultation; ***prema ~u*** as arranged, as agreed, by appointment

dogovoriti se settle, arrange, fix, agree

dograditi add a wing (a story)

dohodak income

dohvat reach; ***na ~*** within reach; **~iti** reach; get hold of

doista indeed, really

dojaditi = **dodijati**

dojam impression; ***ostaviti ~*** make an impression

dojenče suckling, nurseling

doji|lja wet-nurse; **~ti** breast-feed, nurse

dojka breast; **~inja** wet-nurse

dojm|iti se to be impressed; **~ljiv** impressionable

dok MAR dock

dokaz proof, evidence; **~ati** prove; **~ivati** try to prove; ***~ni materijal*** evidence

dokle how long? how far? ***~ god*** as long as; as far as

dokoli|ca leisure; idleness; **~čar** idler

dokopati se come by; get hold of; reach

dokrajčiti put an end to

doktor doctor; ***~ filozofije*** Ph. D.; **~at** doctorate, doctor's degree; **~irati** get one's doctor's degree

doktrina doctrine

dokumentirati document

dolar dollar

dolaz|ak arrival; **~iti** = **doći**
doli|čan fitting; **~kovati** befit
dolina valley
doliti add, pour some more, fill up
dolje down; downstairs
dom home; club, centre; (*studentski*) (residence) hall, *Am* dormitory; (*ferijalni*) hostel; **~ *zdravlja*** health centre; ***stanovnik* ~*a*** inmate; ***Donji* ~** Lower House; (*britanski*) House of Commons; ***Gornji* ~** Upper House
domać|i home, domestic; **~*a hrana*** home-cooked food; **~*a životinja*** domestic animal
domaći|ca hostess; housewife; ***dobra* ~*ca*** good housewife; **~n** master of the house; host
domaćinstvo household; housekeeping
doma|k, ~šaj reach
domet range; ***na* ~** within range; ***izvan* ~*a*** out of range
domin|antan dominant; **~irati** dominate
domine dominees *pl*
domišljat inventive; **~i se** think hard, try to guess; **~ost** inventiveness
domoći se = **dokopati se**
domovina one's country, homeland
donedavn|i recent; **~o** until recently
donekle to a degree, in some measure
donijeti bring; fetch; **~ *sa sobom*** bring along; **~ *dolje* (*gore*)** bring down (up)
donosilac bearer
donji lower
dopa|dljiv attractive; **~sti se** like; attract; **~*da mi se vrt*** I like the garden
dopirati reach
dopis (official) letter; (*novinski*) report, story; **~ivanje** correpondence; **~ivati se** correspond; **~nica** postcard, *Am* postal card; **~nik** correspondent, reporter
doplat|a additional payment; **~ak** allowance; **~iti** pay the difference
dopodne in the morning
dopratiti escort; see home
doprem|a, ~iti supply; transport
doprijeti reach
doprin|ijeti contribute **(to)**; **~os** contribution **(to)**
dopun|a, ~iti supplement; **~ski** supplementary
dopust leave; ***na* ~*u*** on leave
dopu|stiti allow, permit; (*u diskusiji*) grant; **~stiv** permissible; **~štenje** permission
doputovati arrive, come
dorastao equal to, up to
doruč|ak, ~kovati breakfast
dosad(a) so far
dosad|a boredom; **~an** boring; **~*no mi je*** I am bored; **~iti** be fed up

dosadašnji past, last; to date
dosađivati bother, pester; **~ se** be bored
doseg = **dohvat**
dose|liti se move in; immigrate, settle; **~ljenik** immigrant, settler
dosije file
dosjet|iti se have an idea; understand; **~ka** witty remark, joke; **~ljiv** = **domišljat**
doskočiti solve; outwit
doskora shortly, soon, before long
doslov|an literal; **~ce** literally
dosljed|an consistent; **~no** consistently; **~nost** consistence
dospje|će (*mjenice*) maturity, expiration; **~ti** arrive; manage; (*mjenica*) become due, mature, expire
dosta enough; **~ *mi je*** I've had enough
dostav|a delivery; **~iti** deliver
dostići catch up with
dostignuće achivement
dostižan achievable
dostojan worthy; **~stven** dignified; **~stvo** dignity
dostup|an accessible; **~nost** accessibility
dosuditi award
došljak new-comer
dotacija grant; subsidy
dotad till then
dotaknuti touch
doticaj = **dodir**
dotičan concerned, in question
dotirati subsidize
dotjera|n well-groomed; **~ti** drive (up) to; **~ se** dress up; tidy oneself up
dotle till then; as far as; during that time
dotrajao finished, worn out
dotući finish (off)
doušnik informer
dovdje this far
dovesti bring (over); **~ se** come by car, drive over
doviđenja! good by!
doviknuti call to
dovinuti se reach, attain; solve
dovitljiv = **domišljat**
dovle this far
dovod supply (pipe)
dovolj|an sufficient; **~no** enough
dovoz transport; supply
dovratnik door-post
dovrš|iti finish, complete; **~enje** completion
dovući drag (up) to; **~ se** drag oneself (up) to
doz|a dose; (*za cigarete*) cigarette case; **~iranje** dosage; **~irati** dose
dozna|čiti (*novac*) remit; = **dodijeliti**; **~ka** voucher, coupon
doznati learn, find out, hear, understand
dozreti mature, ripen, grow ripe

dozvati call back; call to; send for
dozvol|a permission; (*pismena*) permit; **~iti** = **dopustiti**
doživ|jeti live to see; experience, meet with; **~ljaj** experience; adventure
doživotan lifelong; **~ *zatvor*** life imprisonment
drač weed, thorn-bush(es), bramble(s)
drag dear, sweet; (*kovina*) precious; **~ *kamen*** precious stone
draga, **~i** beloved, sweetheart; (*uvala*) cove, small bay
drago: **~ *mi je*** I am glad
dragocjen precious, costly; **~ost** preciousness
dragulj jewel, precious stone; (*brušen*) gem; **~ar** jeweller
dram|a drama, play; **~atičan** dramatic; **~atizirati** dramatize; **~ski** dramatic
drangulije *pl* odds and ends; gewgaws
drap beige
drap|erije drapery, hangings; **~irati** drape
drastičan drastic
draškati caress
draž(est) charm; **~estan** charming
dražb|a auction; ***iznijeti na ~u*** put up for auction; **~ovaonica** auction-room(s); **~ovatelj** auctioneer
dražiti irritate, provoke
dre|čati scream; (*djeca*) howl; **~čav** = **kričav**
drek|a howling, outcry; **~nuti** give a yell
dremljiv drowsy, sleepy
dremucka|nje nap; **~ti** take a nap
dren BOT dogwood(-tree)
dres|irati train; ***~irane životinje*** performing animals; **~ura** training
dretva twine, pack-thread
drevan ancient
drhta|ti shake, shiver, tremble; **~v** trembling; **~vica** shivers *pl*
dribl|ati SPORT dribble; **~er** dribbler
drijema|nje, **~ti** doze, nap, snooze
drlja|ča, **~ti** harrow
drmati (se) shake, jolt
drndati: **~ *po gitari*** strum a guitar; **~ se** jolt (along)
drobiti crush; **~ se** crumble, fall to pieces
drog|a drug, *sl* dope; ***uzimati ~e*** take drugs, be a drug-addict; ***uzimaje ~a*** drug-addiction
drogerija chemist's, *Am* drugstore
drolja slut
dronj|ak tatter; **~ci** *pl* rags, tatters
droplja bustard
drops (acid) drop
drozg (song-)thrush
drozga dross, slag
drskost impudence, inso-

lence, impertinence
drug, ~arica fellow, companion, mate; ~ ***N.*** comrade N.
drugars|ki comradely; **~tvo** companionship, comradeship
drugdje elsewhere; ***negdje ~*** somewhere else
drug|i another, other; (*po redu*) second; (*slijedeći*) next; **~o** second(ly); ***to je nešto ~o*** that's something else
drugorazredan second-rate
drukčij|e differently; **~i** different
druker snap-fastener
društven sociable; **~i** social; public, national; ***~a igra*** party game; ***~o veće*** social evening; **~ost** sociability
društv|o society; community; COM company, corporation; ***praviti (nekome) ~o*** keep (one) company; ***u ~u*** in company; at a party
družiti se keep company, associate
drvarnica wood-shed, coal shed; (*podrum*) wood-cellar, coal-cellar
drv|en (i *fig*), wood, wooden; **~o** tree; wood, timber, *Am* lumber; ***ogrevno ~o*** firewood
drvodjelac carpenter; timberman, *Am* lumberman
drvorez wood-carving; (*grafika*) woodcut; **~ac** wood-carver; (*grafičar*) wood-engraver
drvosječa logger, lumberjack
drzak impudent, insolent, impertinent
držak handle, grip
držalo pen-holder
držanje carriage, bearing; attitude; behaviour
držati hold; (*artikl*) stock, carry; ***~ pčele*** keep bees; **~ se** hold on to; act; ***dobro se ~*** hold one's own; bear one's age well; ***~ se načela*** stick to a principle
država state; country
državljan|in citizen; subject; ***strani ~ni*** alien; **~stvo** citizenship; nationality
državni government(al), state, public, national
državni|čki statesmanlike; **~k** statesman
dub|ina depth; **~ok** deep; ***~ok 2 m*** two metres deep
dubokoum|an profound; **~nost** profundity
dućan shop, *Am* store
dud mulberry (-tree)
duda dummy, comforter, *Am* pacifier; (*na bočici*) teat, *Am* nipple
duet MUS duet(t)
dug long; ***~ 10 m*** ten metres long
dûg debt; ***u ~u*** in debt
duga rainbow
dugme button; ***pritisnuti na ~*** push a button; ***rupica za ~*** buttonhole

dugo (for) a long time; long
dugogodišnji long time
dugoročni long-term
dugotrajan long-lasting; durable
dugova|nje indebtedness; ***~nje i potraživanja*** debit and credit; **~ti** owe (i *fig*)
duguljast elongated
duh spirit; (*priviđenje*) ghost; = **duhovitost**
duhan tobacco
Duhovi Whit Sunday
duhovit witty; **~ost** wit(tiness)
duhovni spiritual
dukat gold coin
dulji|ti: ***da ne ~m*** to make a long story short
Dunav the Danube
dunja quince
duo duo
dubin dolphin
dupkom: ***~ pun*** packed
dupli double; **~kat** duplicate
duplje burrow, hole
dupsti hollow (out), gouge
dur MUS major
duriti se sulk
duš|a soul; **~evni** mental, spiritual
dušak: ***na ~*** at a gulp
dušek mattres
dušik nitrogen
dušmanin enemy, foe
dušmanski violent(ly), savage(ly)
Dušni dan All Souls' Day
dušnik windpipe, larynx
duvački: ***~ orkestar*** brass band; ***~ instrument*** wind-instrument
duž (all) along
dužan in debt; obliged (to), bound (to)
dužin|a length; ***po ~i*** lengthwise
dužnik debtor
dužnost duty; post, office; ***po ~i*** in the line of duty; ***nastupiti ~*** take up a post
dva two
dvadeset twenty; **~i** twentieth
dvanaesnik ANAT duodenum; ***čir na ~u*** duodenal ulcer
dvanaest twelve; **~i** twelfth
DVD DVD; **~-ROM** DVD-ROM
dvije two
dvjesta two hundred
dvoboj duel; ***izazvati na ~*** challenge to duel
dvocijevka double-barreled gun
dvodomni: PARL ***~ sistem*** two-chamber system
dvojak of two kinds
dvojb|a doubt, suspicion; **~en** doubtful, uncertain
dvojci *pl* twins *pl*
dvoje two (persons); ***~ ~*** in a couple
dvojezičan bilingual
dvojica two (male persons)
dvojka (number) two; group of two; (*karte*) deuce
dvojni double; bipartite
dvojnik (one's) double
dvokatnica three-storey

house
dvoklik double-click
dvokratan two-time
dvokrilac AERO biplane
dvokrilna vrata double-door
dvoličan two-faced, false; **~nost** duplicity; falseness
dvomotorac twin-engine aircraft
dvonožac biped
dvopek biscuit; MAR hard tack
dvor court; ***na ~u*** at court
dvorac country seat, manor house; (*zamak*) castle
dvorana auditorium, hall
dvoredan double-breasted (jacket)
dvorište court yard; ***~na zgrada*** back building
dvoriti attend, wait on
dvorkinja charwoman, cleaner, daily help
dvosjed two-seater
dvosjekli two-edged
dvosmislen ambiguous; **~ost** ambiguity
dvostran two-sided, bilateral
dvostruk double, two-fold
dvotočka colon
dvoumiti se be in a dilemma

DŽ

džamija mosque
džemper sweater, pullover
džep pocket; **~ar** pickpocket; **~arac** pocket-money, allowance; ***~na lampa*** torch, flashlight
džez jazz
džigerica liver
džungla jungle

Đ

đak pupil, schoolboy
đavao devil
đon sole
đubre (*osoba*) cad; = **gnoj**
đumbir ginger
đurđica lily of the valley
đuture: ***u ~*** in the lump, indiscriminately

E

ebanovina ebony
efekt effect; **~an** striking
efektivan effective; actual
efikasan efficacious, effective; **~nost** efficacy, effectiveness

egzaltiran highly strung; hyper-sensitive
egzist|encija existence; **~irati** exist
egzotičan exotic
ej! hej! hello there!
ekcem MED eczema
ekipa team
eklatantan glaring, obvious
e-knjiga e-book
ekonom steward; **~ičan** economical; **~ija** (*privreda*) economy; (*nauka*) economics *pl*; (*dobro*) farm; **~ika** economy; **~izirati** economize; **~ist** economist; **~ski** economic
ekran screen
eks: ***na ~!*** bottoms up!
ekscentri|čan, **~k** eccentric
eksces outrage, excess
ekshibicija exhibition
ekskurzija excursion, trip; ***stručna ~*** study tour
ekspeditiv|an prompt; **~nost** promptitude
eksperimentalan experimental
ekspert, **~an** expert
eksploat|acija exploitation; **~ator** exploiter; **~irati** exploit
eksplodirati explode, go off
eksploziv explosive
eksponat exhibit
ekspon|aža *photo* exposure; **~irati** *photo* expose
ekspresn|i: ***~o pismo*** *Br* express letter, *Am* special delivery letter
ekstaza ecstazy
eksternalizirati outsource
ekstra special; extra
ekstravagant|an extravagant; **~nost** extravagance
ekstrem extreme; **~an** extreme; **~ist**, **~istički** extremist
ekvator equator
elaborat survey; development plan; presentation
elan enthusiasm
elastič|an elastic; *fig* flexible; **~nost** elasticity; *fig* flexibility; = **gumilastika**
elektrana power plant, power station
elektron electron; **~ičar** electronics engineer; **~ika** electronics *pl*; **~ski** electronic
elektrotehnik|a electrical engineering; ***inženjer ~e*** electrical engineer
elita, **~n** elite
emajl enamel; **~iran** enamelled
embrio embryo
emigr|acija emigration; émigrés; **~ant**, **~antski** emigrant, émigré; **~irati** emigrate
emi|sija broadcast; transmission; **~tirati** broadcast; transmit
emocionalan emotional
enciklopedija encyclop(a)edia
Engle|ska Britain, United Kingdom; (*uža*) England; **~ski** English; **~skinja** Eng-

lishwoman; **~z** Englishman
eno! there!; look!
ep epic poem; **~ski** epic
epilep|tički, ~tičar epileptic
epilog epilogue
e-pošta e-mail
epruveta test tube
erotski erotic
eskadra squadron
estetski aesthetic
etapa stage; step; SPORT lap, leg
eter ether; RADIO air
etičan ethical
etiketa label; (*ponašanje*) etiquette
eto! there!
evanđelje Gospel
eventual|an possible; **~no** possibly, perhaps
eviden|cija files *pl*, records *pl*; **~tirati** keep files (records), register, record
evo! here you are!; there!
Evropa Europe

F

fagot MUS basson
fakin scamp, rascal
faktičan actual
faktura invoice, *Am* bill
fakultet college, school, faculty
faliti lack, want
fanatičan fanatical
fantazija imagination
fanzine fanzine
farmaceut pharmacist
farovi *pl* MOT headlights
fasada front, facade
fascikl folder
faši|st(ički) Fascist; **~zam** Fascism
fata morgana mirage
faza stage, step, phase
fazan pheasant
februar February
federativan federative
fen hair-drier
fenjer lantern
ferije *pl* holidays *pl*; vacation
festival festival
figura figure; *derog* figure-head; **~tivan** figurative
fijukati whistle
fik|cija fiction; **~tivan** fictitious
fiksan fixed
filatelist philatelist, stamp collector; ***~ičko društvo*** stamp club
filc felt
filijala branch
film film; *coll* picture; ***kolor ~*** colour film; ***crtani ~*** cartoon (film); ***kaubojski ~*** western
filozofski philosophical
fin well-bred, good-mannered; fine; **~o** nicely; with good manners; ***~o!*** fine!; **~oća** good breeding, good manners; refinement
finale SPORT finals *pl*; ***polu-~***

semi-finals *pl*
fitilj fuse, wick
fizi|ka physics *pl*; **~čar** physicist; **~čki** physical
flaster MED sticking-plaster
flauta MUS flute
flegma phlegm; **~tičan** phlegmatic
fleš *photo* flash lamp, flash unit, flash-light
flota MIL fleet, navy; mercantile marine
foka ZOOL seal
folija foil
folklor folklore; ***~na grupa*** folk dancers
fond fund; pool
forma form; shape
formalan formal
formalnost formality
format size; format
formula formula
formular form
forsirati press, force the issue
fosfat phosphate
fosfor phosphorus
fotelja arm-chair, easy chair
fotograf photographer; **~ija** photograph; (*vještina*) photography; **~ski** photographic
frak evening dress, tails, *coll* white tie; ***kaput ~a*** tailcoat
frakcija fraction
franak franc
Francu|ska France; **~ski** French; **~z** Frenchman
frapantan striking
frapirati amaze
franjeva|c, **~čki** Franciscan
fratar monk, friar
fraz|a phrase; idiom; **~er** phrase-monger; **~irati** use empty phrases
frigati fry
friz|er hairdresser; ***~erski salon*** hairdresser's; **~irati** do one's hair; **~irati se** have one's hair done; **~ura** hair style, hair-do
frižider refrigerator
frotir: ***~ ručnik*** terry towel; **~ati se** rub oneself with a towel
frula (shepherd's) flute
fuj! shame!; boo!
funkcioner functionary, official
funta pound (*novac i težina*)
furnir, **~ati** veneer
futrola case
fuzi|ja COM merger; **~onirati (se)** COM merge

G

gać|e *pl* (under)pants, *coll* shorts; (*duge*) long (under-) pants; **~ice** *pl* panties; (*kupaće*) trunks
gad cad; **~an** disgusting; ***~i mi se*** it makes me sick (*i fig*)
gađati aim (at)

geđenje disgust, loathing
gajde *pl* bagpipes *pl*
gajiti cherish, nurse; breed
gajtan braid
gakati quack
galam|a noise, racket; **~iti** make a noise
galant|an gallant; open--handed; **~erija** fancy goods *pl*
galeb (sea) gull
galerija gallery; **~ *slika*** picture gallery, art gallery
galop, **~irati** gallop
galoše galoshes, *Am* rubbers
gamad vermin
gamaše *pl* spats *pl*
gangster gangster
ganu|će emotion; **~ti** move, touch; **~tljiv** moving, touching
garan|cija, **~tirati** guarantee
garda Guards *pl*
garderoba *Br* cloak-room, *Am* checkroom; (*odjeća*) wardrobe
garnitura set
garnizon garrison
garsonijera bachelor flat (*Am* apartment)
gas: ***dati* ~** step on the gas
gasiti (*vatru*) extinguish; (*svjetlo*) put out; switch off; (*plin*) turn off; (*žeđu*) quench thirst
gasmaska gas-mask
gat pier, wharf
gata|nje fortune-telling; **~ra** fortune-teller; **~ti** tell fortunes
gavran raven
gaz ford; (*broda*) draught
gaza gauze
gazda landlord, host; boss; **~rica** landlady; housekeeper
gaziti tread (on)
gdje where; **~gdje** here and there; **~god** no matter where
generalštab headquarters *pl*
generator EL generator
genijalan: **~ *čovjek*** man of genius
geode|t (land) surveyor; **~zija** (land) surveying
geometrij|a geometry; **~ski** geometrical
geril|ac guer(r)illa; ***~ski rat*** guer(r)illa warfare
geslo motto, slogan
gestikulirati gesture
giba|k flexible, pliant; nimble; **~nje** motion; **~ti** move
gimnasti|cirati do gymnastics; **~čar** gymnast
gimnazija secondary school, grammar school, *Am* high school; **~lac** secondary--school (*Am* high-school) student
ginekolo|g gyn(a)ecologist; **~gija** gyn(a)ecology; **~ški** gyn(a)ecological
ginuti be killed, perish
gipkost flexibility; nimbleness
gips plaster (of Paris); ***noga u ~u*** leg in a cast
gitarist guitarist

glača|lo, **~ti** iron
glad hunger; (*opća*) famine; **~an** hungry; **~ovati** suffer hunger, starve
gladak smooth
gladiti stroke; smooth
glagol verb
glas voice; reputation; vote; ***na zlu ~u*** notorious; having a bad reputation
glasa|č voter; **~ti** vote; **~nje** voting; ballot
glas|an loud; **~no** loudly, aloud
glasiti run, go
glasnice *pl* vocal cords *pl*
glasnik messenger, herald
glasovit famous
glatko smoothly; (*govoriti*) fluently
glav|a head; **~om** himself, herself; ***~om bez obzira*** head over heels
glavar head
glavčina TECH (wheel) hub
glavica knoll, mound; (*luka*) bulb
glavni main, chief, principal; ***~ grad*** capital
glavnica capital; principal
glavno the main thing
glavobolje headache
glazba music; ***vojna ~*** military band
gle! look!
gledalac spectator; looker-on
gledati look at, watch; ***soba gleda na jug*** the room faces south; ***~ ukočeno*** stare at
gledište standpoint
gležanj ankle
glib ooze, mud; (*nanos*) silt
glina clay
glista earth-worm; (*crijevna*) (intestinal) worm
glob|a fine, penalty; **~iti** fine
globalizacija globalization
globus globe
gloda|lica TECH milling-cutter; **~ti** gnaw; **~vac** ZOOL rodent
glog BOT hawthorn
glomazan unwieldy, bulky
gluh deaf; **~oća** deafness; **~onijem** deaf-and-dumb
glum|a acting; **~ac** actor; **~ica** actress; **~iti** act
glup stupid; foolish; *coll* dumb, silly; **~an** blockhead, fool, simpleton; **~ost** nonsense; a foolish thing; stupidity
gljiva mushroom
gm|az ZOOL reptile; **~izati** crawl, creep
gnijezd|iti se, **~o** nest
gnoj dung, manure; MED pus; **~an**, **~enje** festering; **~iti** manure; fertilize; **~iti se** fester; **~ivo** (*stajsko*) manure; (*umjetno*) fertilizer
gnuša|nje loathing; **~ti se** loathe
gnjav|ator bore; **~aža** nuisance, bore; **~iti** bother, pester; make a fuss; **~iti se** drudge (at), have a lot of trouble
gnje|cav sodden, clammy;

~**čiti** squash, squeeze
gnjev wrath; ~**an** wrathful
gnjida nit
gnjil = **gnjio**
gnji|o rotten; ~**lost**, ~**ti** rot
gnjur|ac ZOOL diver; plunger; ~**iti** dive; plunge
gnjusan loathsome
go = **gol**
godina year; ***koliko mu je ~?*** how old is he?; ***u ~ma*** elderly; ***Nova ~*** New Year's Day; ***Sretna nova ~!*** Happy New Year!
godišnj|i annual; ***~e doba*** season; ~**ica** anniversary
godi|šte year; ~**ti** give pleasure, please
gojiti cultivate
gojzerice *pl* heavy boots *pl*
gol naked, nude; bare
golem huge, enormous, immense
golman goalkeeper
golotinja nudity; nakedness
golub pigeon; ***~ pismonoša*** carrier-pigeon; ~**ica** dove
goljenica shin-bone
gomila crowd, mob; ~**ti (se)** crowd, pile up
gomolj BOT bulb, tuber
goniti chase, pursue, run after; (*stoku*) drive
gonoreja gonorrhea
gora mountain
gor|ak bitter (*i fig*); ~**čina** bitterness
gore above, up there, overhead; (*lošije*) worse
gorila gorilla
gorivo fuel
gorjeti burn
gorljiv ardent; eager, zealous; ~**ost** ardour, eagerness, zeal
gornji upper, top
gorovit hilly, mountainous
gorski: ***~ lanac*** mountain chain
gorštak mountaineer, highlander
gorući burning (*i fig*)
gorušica mustard
gospod|a gentlemen; fine folks; upper classes; ~**in** gentleman; ***~in X*** Mr. X; ***~ine!*** Sir!; ~**stvo** lordship; power, rule
gospodar lord, master; boss; ~**iti** manage; rule, govern; ~**ski** = **(poljo)privredni**; ~**stvo** management; farm(-ing)
gospođ|a lady; ***~a X*** Mrs. X; ***~o!*** Madam!; ~**ica** young lady, miss; ***~ice X!*** Miss X!
gost guest; THEAT guest artist; ***večeras imamo ~e*** we have company (party) tonight
gostioni|ca *Br* public house; *Am* saloon, bar; (*seoska*) inn; ~**čar** publican, *Am* saloon-keeper; inn-keeper
gostiti entertain, treat; ~ **se** feast (on)
gostoljubiv hospitable; ~**ost** hospitality
gostova|nje THEAT guest performance; THEAT ***~li su ...***

guest artists were...
gošća (lady) guest
got|ica Gothic type; **~ika**, **~ski** Gothic
gotov ready, done, finished; ***u ~om*** in cash; **~ina** cash, ready money; **~o** almost, nearly; ***~o odijelo*** ready-made suit
goved|a (bovine) cattle; **~ina**, **~ski** beef; **~o** cow, ox
govno shit; turd
govor speech; (*pozdravni*) address
govoriti speak; talk; ***~ loše engleski*** speak broken English
govor|ljiv talkative; **~nica** rostrum; lady speaker; *tel* call-box, booth; **~nički** rhetorical; **~nik** speaker; **~ništvo** rhetoric
gozba feast, banquet
grab BOT hornbeam
graba ditch
grabež robbery; **~ljiv** rapacious; ***~ljiva ptica (životinja)*** bird (beast) of prey (*životinja*) predatory; **~ljivost** rapacity
grabilica (*ptica*) bird of prey
grabiti grab, snatch
grablj|ati, **~e** rake
gracioz|an graceful; **~nost** grace
grad town; (*veliki*) city; ***stari ~*** Old Town
grȁd hail(-storm); ***zrno ~a*** hailstone
gradić small town; market town
gradilište (construction) site; (*parcela*) plot, *Am* lot
gradit|elj builder; **~i** build, construct
gradivo material
gradnj|a construction; ***na ~i*** at the site; ***u ~i*** under construction
gradonačelnik mayor
gradsk|i town, city, urban, municipal; ***~a četvrt*** district
građa (building) material; structure; (*tjelesna*) build; (*gradivo*) material
građan|in, **~ka** citizen; town dweller; townsman
građanski civic; ***~ rat*** civil war; ***~ stalež*** middle class
građanstvo citizens; public; townsfolk, townspeople
građen: ***lijepo ~*** well-built; (*žena*) with a good figure
građev|ina building; **~inar** civil engineer; **~inarstvo** civil engineering; ***~insko poduzeće*** construction firm; ***~ni poduzetnik*** building contractor, builder; ***~na dozvola*** building permit
grafi|čar typographical worker; graphic artist; **~čki** typographic; **~ka** graphic arts; drawing(s) and engraving(s); **~kon** graph, chart
grah bean; (*jelo*) beans
graja hubbub, noise, uproar
graktati croak, caw
gram gram(me)
gramati|čki grammatical;

~čar grammarian; **~ka** grammar
gramofon record player; gramophone, *Am* phonograph
gramofon|ski: ***~ska ploča*** record, disc
gramzljiv covetous
grana branch; (*deblja*) bough
granata MIL shell
grančica twig
grani|ca border(-line), frontier; *fig* limit, boundary; **~čar** border-guard; **~čiti sa** border on; *fig* verge on
granit, ~ni granite
grašak pea; (*jelo*) peas
grav|er engraver; **~irati** engrave; **~ura** engraving
grb coat of arms
grba hump, hunch; **~v** humpbacked, hunchbacked; uneven; **~vac** humpback, hunchback
grč cramp, spasm; convulsion; (*u želucu*) gripes *pl*; **~evit** convulsive; ***~evito uhvatiti*** clutch
Grčk|a Greece; **~i** Greek
grdi|ti scold; **~nja** scolding
grdoba monstrosity
grdosija monster; colossus
greben crag; (*morski*) cliff; (*podvodni*) reef; (*sedlo*) ridge
gred|a beam; (*krovna*) rafter; **~ica** (*lijeha*) bed
grepsti scratch
greš|an sinful; **~nik** sinner
grešk|a mistake; fault, error; **~om** by mistake
grgeč ZOOL perch
grgljati gargle
grickati nibble
grijalica heater; electric fire
grija|nje: ***centralno ~nje*** central heating; **~ti** warm (up); heat; **~ti se** keep warm
grije|h sin; **~šiti** sin; make mistakes
grimiz crimson
gripa influenza, *coll* 'flu; grippe
gristi bite; **~ se** *fig* fret
griva mane
griz semolina, creamed wheat
Grk Greek
grkljan larynx
grliti (se) embrace, hug
grlo throat
grm bush, shrub; **~lje** bushes, shrubs
grm|jeti, ~ljavina thunder
grob grave, tomb; **~ar** grave-digger; **~lje** churchyard, graveyard; (*gradsko*) cemetery; **~nica** tomb
grof count; (*engleski*) earl; **~ica** countess (*i engleska*)
grohot laughter; ***~om se smijati*** roar with laughter
groktati grunt
grom thunder; **~obran** lightning-conductor; lightning-rod
groza horror; **~n** horrible, terrible
grozd bunch (of grapes)
groziti se threaten, menace

grozni|ca fever; **~čav(o)** feverish(ly)
grozota horror
grožđe grapes *pl*; ***suho ~*** raisins *pl*
grožnja threat, menace
grub rude; (*na dodir*) rough; **~ijan** brute; **~ost** rudeness; roughness
gruda lump; (*snijega*) snowball; **~ti se** fight with snowballs
grudi *pl* chest; (*ženske*) breasts *pl*
grudica small lump, clot
grudnjak brassière, *coll* bra
grup|a, **~irati (se)**, **~ni** group
grušati se (*krv*) clot, coagulate; (*mlijeko*) curdle
guba MED leprosy; **~v** leprous; **~vac** leper
gubica muzzle, nose, snout
gubitak loss; ***~ vrijednosti*** depreciation
gubi|ti lose; **~ti se** vanish; ***~ se!*** be off with you!, *sl* beat it!
guda|lo bow; ***~čki orkestar*** string orchestra
gudura gorge, ravine
gukati coo
gulaš goulash
guli|koža extortioner; **~ti** peel; *kožu* skin; *fig* fleece; **~ti se** peel
gum|a rubber; (*na kotaču*) tire; (*unutrašnja*) tube; ***kvar na ~i*** flat tire; ***~a za žvakanje*** chewing gum; **~eni** rubber; ***~ica za brisanje*** rubber
gumb button; **~ašnica** pin
gunđa|lo grumbler; **~ti** grumble; mutter
gungula riot, tumult
gunj blanket
gurati push; **~ se** push (through), elbow
gurkati (*laktom*) nudge; **~ se** nudge each other
gurman gourmet, gourmand
gurta webbing (belt)
gusak gander
gusar pirate; ***~ski brod*** pirate (ship); **~stvo** piracy
gusjeni|ca caterpillar; (*tenkovska*) caterpillar, track, tread; **~čar** tracked vehicle
guska goose (*pl* geese); ***divlja ~*** wild goose
gust thick; dense; **~oća** thickness; density
guša MED goitre; **~v** goitrous
gušiti choke; *fig* suppress; **~ se** choke, suffocate
guštara thicket, shrubs
gušterača (*žlijezda*) pancreas
gušter(ica) lizard
gut|ati, **~ljaj** swallow; gulp
guvernanta governess
guverner governor
gužva crush; *fig* trouble; **~ti** crumple; **~ti se** wrinkle, crease
gvozden iron, made of iron
gvožđe iron; ***kovano ~*** wrought iron; ***liveno ~*** cast iron; ***sirovo ~*** pig-iron; ***staro ~*** scrap-iron

H

hajduk outlaw
hajka (*u lovu*) battue; chase; *fig* persecution
halabuka hubbub, uproar, tumult
half SPORT half back
halo! (*na telefonu*) hello, hallo
halter (*široki*) girdle; (*uski*) suspender belt, *Am* garter
halucinacija hallucination
haljina dress; frock; (*duga*) gown
ham (horse) collar
hambar barn, granary
hap|siti, **~šenje** arrest
harati devastate; (*bolest*) rage, be rife
harem harem
harf|a harp; **~ist** harpist
haringa herring
harmoni|čan harmonious; **~ja** harmony
harmonika accordion; (*usna*) mouth organ; **~š** accordionist
hasura straw-mat, rush-mat
hauba MOT bonnet, *Am* hood; (*frizerska*) hair drier
hazard *fig* gamble; **~er** gambler; **~irati** gamble; ***~ne igre*** games of chance
heftati baste
hej! hey!; hello there!
heksnšus stiff back (neck), crick in the back (neck)
helikopter helicopter
heljda buckwheat
hemung inhibition; ***imati ~e*** be inhibited
here|tički, **~tik** heretic; **~za** heresy
hermafrodit hermaphrodite
hermetički zatvoren airproof, air-tight; waterproof
hidrauličan hydraulic
hidroavion seaplane; (*bez papuča*) flying boat
hidrocentrala hydro(-electric) power plant (station)
hidrogen hydrogen; ***~ska bomba*** H-bomb
higijen|a hygiene; **~ski** hygienic
hihot, **~ati** giggle
hijena hyena
hijerarhija hierarchy
hijeroglifi *pl* hieroglyph(ic)s *pl*
hiljada thousand
himna (national) anthem
hipnotizirati hypnotize
hipodrom racecourse, *Am* racetrack
hipofiza ANAT pituitary gland
hipohondar hypochondriac
hipoteka mortgage
hipoteza hypothesis (*pl* -eses)
hir caprice, whim; **~ovit** capricious, whimsical
histeri|čan hysterical; ***dobiti***

~čan napadaj go into hysterics; **~ja** hysteria; hysterics *pl*
hitac shot
hitan urgent, pressing
hlač|e *pl* trousers *pl*; (*kratke*) shorts *pl*; ***crta* („*bug*") *na* ~*ama*** crease
hlad shade; **~an** cold (*i fig*); ***~an obrok*** cold fare
hladetina jelly
hladiti cool; **~ se** (*jelo*) grow cold
hladnoća cold; *fig* coldness
hladnokrv|an cool; **~nost** coolness
hladnjača cold storage, refrigerator
hladnjak MOT radiator
hlađenje cooling
hlap|iti evaporate; **~ljiv** volatile
hljeb loaf
hmelj hop; (*plod*) hops *pl*
hobi hobby
hobotnica ZOOL octopus
hod walk; ***način ~a*** gait
hodati walk; march; (*vel. koracima*) stride
hodoča|snik pilgrim; **~stiti** go on a pilgrimage
hodža Moslem priest
hohštapl|er elegant fraud; show-off; **~irati** show off
homoseksuala|c, ~n homosexual
honorar fee; ***raditi ~no*** have a part-time job; work for a fee
horizontala, ~n horizontal
hormon hormone
hostija *eccl* Host; wafer
hotel hotel
hoznttregeri *pl Br* braces *pl*, *Am* suspenders *pl*
hrab|ar courageous, brave; **~renje** encouragement; **~riti** encourage; **~rost** courage, bravery
hram temple
hramati limp, hobble
hrana food; ***stan i ~*** board and lodgings
hraniti feed; nourish; **~ se** feed (*čime* on); take meals
hranljiv nourishing; **~ost** nutritive value
hrapav rough; **~ost** roughness
hrast oak; **~ovina** oak (wood)
hrbat back; (*brda*) ridge
hrčak ZOOL hamster
hren horse-raddish
hridina crag; (*morska*) cliff
hripavac MED whooping-cough
hrkati snore
hrom lame
hrop|ac death rattle; **~tati** (breathe with a) rattle
hrp|a heap, pile; ***na ~i*** heaped (up), piled (up)
hrska|ti crunch; **~vica** cartilage; CUL gristle
hrt greyhound
hrušt ZOOL cockchafer, may-bug, may-beetle
Hrvat, ~ica, ≗ski Croat(ian); **~ska** Croatia

htjeti want; ***htio bih platiti*** I would like to pay; ***nisam to htio reći*** I did not mean that
huckati *fig* egg on; ~ ***psa na*** set a dog on
hučiti roar, boom
hujati sough; whistle
hul|a blasphemy; **~iti** blaspheme
hulja scoundrel, villain
humak knoll, hillock; (*grobni*) mound
humanost humaneness
humanističk|i: ***~e znanosti*** the humanities *pl*
humor humour (*Am* -or)
hunjavica head-cold
hura! hurrah!, hurray!
huška|č agitator; ***ratni ~č*** war-monger; **~nje** agitation; **~ti** agitate; egg on
hval|a thank you *pl*; ***~a!*** thanks!; ***~a lijepa!*** thank you very much; ***~e vrijedan*** praiseworthy
hvalisa|ti se boast, bragg; **~v** boastful, bragging; **~vac** boaster, braggart; **~vost** boastfulness, bragging
hvaliti praise; ~ **se** boast, bragg
hvat cord (of wood)
hvatati catch; snatch at, grasp; ~ **se** stick to, cling to

I

i and; ***i … i …*** both … and
iako although, though
ići go; walk; ~ ***po*** go for, fetch, collect; ***ne ide*** it's no good; ***to ne ide*** it isn't done
ideal ideal; **~ism** idealism; **~ist** idealist
ideja idea; POL cause
identitet identity
ideolo|g ideologist; **~ški** ideological
idiot|izam idiocy; **~ski** idiotic
idući next, following
igdje anywhere
igla needle
igra play; SPORT game; ~ ***riječima*** pun, play on words
igra|č player; **~čka** toy; **~lište** playground; SPORT field, ground, court; **~rija** child's play; **~ti** play
ikada ever
ikako at all, in any way
ikra (hard) roe, spawn
ilegal|ac underground fighter; **~an** underground; illegal; **~nost** underground; ***preći u ~nost*** go underground
ili or; ***ili … ili*** either … or
ilovača loam; (*glina*) clay
ilustracija illustration
ilustrator illustrator
ilustrirati illustrate
iluz|ija illusion; ***razbiti ~ije***

disillusion
imaginaran imaginary
imalo at all
imanje *veliko* estate; *seljačko* farm, holding
imati have; possess, own; **~ *na sebi*** have on; ***ima dva ulaza*** there are two entrances; ***ima li?*** is there?, are there?
ime name; (*knjige*, *djela*) title; (*za razliku od prezimena*) first name; ***po ~nu*** called
imela BOT mistletoe
imendan name-day, fête-day
imenica noun, substantive
imenik directory; register
imenjak namesake
imenova|nje appointment; **~ti** appoint
imetak fortune, property
imit|acija imitation; **~ator** imitator; artist impersonator; **~irati** imitate; impersonate; (*ropski*) ape
imovina fortune, property; COM assets *pl*
imperativ GRAM imperative
imperfekt GRAM past tense, preterite
imperijali|st, **~stički** imperialist; **~zam** imperialism
imponirati impress
impoten|cija impotence; **~tan** impotent
impozantan impressive
impregnira|n waterproof; **~ti** (water) proof
improviz|acija improvisation; **~ator** improviser; **~iran** improvised, makeshift; impromptu; **~irati** improvise
impulzivan impulsive
imućan well-to-do, well off, rich, wealthy
imunitet MED *i* POL immunity
inače otherwise; ***i ~*** anyway
inauguracija inauguration
inaugurirati inaugurate
indignirati make indignant; **~ se** become indignant
Indija India; **~c** Indian; **~nac** (red) Indian, Native American; **ᴤnski** Native American
indirekt|an indirect; **~no** indirectly
indisponirati indispose
individua|lizam individuality
indoktrin|acija indoctrination, brainwashing; **~irati** indoctrinate, brainwash
infinitiv GRAM infinitive
inform|ativan informative; **~irati** inform; **~irati se** find out, make inquiries
injekcija injection
inkas|ator collector; **~irati** collect
inkomodirati inconvenience
inozem|ni foreign; ***u ~stvu*** abroad
inscenirati *fig* stage
insistira|nje insistence; **~ti** insist (on)
instal|acija installation; **~ater** fitter; **~irati** instal, fit
instruk|cija instruction; *daku*

private lesson; **~tor** instructor; *đaka* tutor
intelektualac educated person; *visoki* intellectual
inteligen|cija intelligence; educated classes, intelligentsia; **~tan** intelligent
interes interest, curiosity
intern|acija internment; **~irati** intern
interpret|acija interpretation; **~irati** interpret
interpunkcija punctuation
interurban *Br* trunk-call, *Am* long-distance call
intiman intimate; **~ *prijatelj*** close friend
intriga intrigue, plot
intuitivan intuitive
invalid invalid, disabled person; **~itet** disablement; **~nina** disablement allowance
inven|cija inventiveness, imagination; **~tivan** inventive, imaginative
invent|ar inventory; **~ura** stock-taking; ***vršiti* ~uru** take stock
investi|cija investment; **~rati** invest; **~tor** investor
inžinjer diploma engineer; **~ija** MIL engineers
inje white frost
ipak nevertheless, however, still, just the same
Ir|ac Irishman; **~ska** Ireland; **~ski** Irish
iritirati irritate
ironi|čki ironical; **~ja** irony
iscijediti squeeze out
iscrp|an exhaustive, thorough, complete; **~ljen** exhausted; **~ljenost** exhaustion; **~sti** exhaust
iscuriti trickle out, leak out
iseliti evacuate; **~ se** emigrate; move out
iselj|avanje, ~enički emigration; **~enik** emigrant
ishlapiti evaporate
isisati suck out; *fig* bleed white
isjeckati chop (up), shred
iskaliti se take it out (on)
iskapa|nje (*arheološko*) dig; **~ti** dig out, excavate
iskapiti drain
iskaz statement; **~ati** say, express, state; **~ati se** distinguish oneself; **~nica** identity card; membership card
iskidati tear to pieces
iskititi decorate
isklesati chisel out, sculpture
isključ|enje exclusion; expulsion; **~iti** exclude; expel; *mogućnost* rule out; **~iv** exclusive
iskočiti jump out, jump off; *vlak* jump the track, run off the rails, derail
iskop(av)ati dig out, dig up, excavate
iskorijeniti root out
iskoristiti make use of, utilize
iskra spark
iskrca|ti unload; **~ti se** disembark; **~vanje** unloading;

disembarkment
iskrčiti clear (land)
iskren sincere, frank, open; **~ost** sincerity, frankness
iskrenuti turn upside down; turn inside out
iskriviti bend out of shape, (*i fig*) twist; **~ se** bend
iskrsnuti crop up
iskrvariti bleed to death; lose much blood
isku|san experienced; **~siti**, **~stvo** experience
iskušati try out, test
iskvariti corrupt
ismija| ti, **~vanje** ridicule
ispaćen care-worn
ispad excess, outrage
ispaliti fire, discharge
isparava|nje evaporation; **~ti se** evaporate; steam
ispasti come off, fall off; be omitted; ***dobro*** **~** come out well
ispavati se have some sleep; have a good night's rest
ispeći roast
ispijen wasted; (*lice*) haggard
ispira|nje rinse; **~ti** rinse
ispisati se withdraw (from)
ispit examination, *coll* exam; ***proći (pasti) na ~u*** pass (fail) an examination; **~(iv)ati** examine; investigate; interrogate; test; **~ivač** examiner
ispiti drink (up), drain; waste
isplahnuti rinse
isplat|a payment; **~iti** pay (off, up); **~iti se** pay, be worth while
isplaziti (*jezik*) stick out (one's tongue at)
isplivati come up
isploviti sail, leave port
ispljunuti spit out
ispod under, below, underneath
ispoljiti (se) show
isporuči|ti deliver; **~v** deliverable
isposlovati arrange (for), secure
ispostaviti draw up, make out; **~ se** turn out
ispovijed confession; **~ati se** confess
ispovjed|aonica confessional; **~nik** confessor
ispraćaj seeing off
isprati wash out; rinse; bathe
ispratiti see off
isprava document, papers
isprav|ak correction; emendation; **~an** right, correct; in working order; **~iti** correct; emend; **~iti se** correct oneself
ispraz|an vain, frivolous; **~niti (se)** empty
ispred before, in front of, ahead of
ispregnuti unharness
isprekidan broken, halting, interrupted
ispričati tell; excuse; **~ se** apologize; excuse oneself
isprika excuse; apology
isprobati try out, test; *odjeću* try on

ispružiti (se) stretch
isprva at first
ispuc|ati crack; **~an** cracked, chapped
ispumpati let the air out, deflate; **~ se** deflate, go down
ispuniti fill (up, out); *životinju* stuff; *obećanje, želju* fulfil; **~ se** come true
ispustiti drop; let go (of); let out; **~ *zrak*** deflate
ispušn|a cijev exhaust pipe; ***~i plin*** exhaust gas
istaći emphasize, stress, point out
istaknut prominent, outstanding
istaknuti point out, emphasize; **~ se** distinguish oneself, become prominent
iste|ći flow out, run out, leak out; *rok* expire; **~k** expiration
isti the same
isticanje emphasis
istin|a truth; **~it** true; **~itost** truth(fullness); **~ski** true
istisnuti squeeze out; oust, replace
istjerati drive out; expell
isto: **~ *tako*** likewise; **~ *toliko*** as much
istoimen of the same name
istok east; ***na ~u*** in the east; ***na ~*** eastward(s)
istovar unloading; **~i(va)ti** unload
istovjet|an identical; **~nost** identity
istovremen simultaneous; **~o** at the same time
istraga inquiry, investigation
istraž|ivač explorer; investigator; **~ivanje** investigation; GEOGR exploration; *naučno* research; **~ivati** investigate; explore; research; ***~na komisija*** commission of inquiry
istrčati run out; **~ se** *fig* stick one's neck out
istresti shake out; dump
istrgnuti snatch away; pull out; **~ se** wrench oneself free
istrijebiti exterminate
istrljati (se) rub (oneself)
istrošiti wear out; **~ se** wear oneself out; spend a lot
istrugati scrape off
istrunuti rot (away), decay
istući beat
istup stand, action; withdrawal (from); **~iti** take a stand; withdraw (from) (*nož*) blunt
isturiti thrust out, protrude
isuš|enje drainage, reclamation; **~iti** drain, reclaim
išarati cover with scrawls (*ili* daubs)
iščaš|enje dislocation, *lakše* sprain; **~iti** dislocate, sprain; ***~iti nogu*** sprain one's ankle
iščekivanje expectation; suspense
iščetkati brush (off)
iščupati pluck out, pull out
išćuškati slap (repeatedly)
išijas MED sciatica

išta anything
Italija Italy
itd. etc. (et cetera)
itko anyone
iver chip, splinter
iz out of, from
iza behind, after
izabrati chose, select; (*glasanjem*) elect
izaći = **izići**
izaslan|ik delegate; emissary; **~stvo** delegation; mission
izaz|ov provocation; challenge; **~ovan** provocative; **~(i)vati** provoke; challenge (*uzrokovati*) cause, bring about
izažeti wring (out)
izbaciti throw out; omit
izbaviti deliver, liberate, relieve
izbezum|iti drive crazy; **~iti se** be beside oneself; **~ljen** beside oneself
izbi(ja)ti drive out, knock out; spring up, break out
izbirljiv hard to please, fastidious; **~ost** fastidiousness
izbje|ći, **~gavati** avoid; **~gavanje** avoidance; **~glica** refugee
izboč|en projecting, sticking out; **~ina** bulge, protuberance, convexity
izbor choice, selection; **~i** election; **~ni** election, electoral
izbrbljati blab out
izbrisati wipe; erase
izbrojati count
izdahnuti exhale; (*umrijeti*) expire
izdaj|a treason; **~ica** traitor
izdaleka from a distance; from far away
izdanak shoot
izdanje edition; *bez promjena* impression, printing; publication
izdašan abundant, economical; sustaining, plentiful
izdatak expense
izdati publish, bring out; (*odati*) betray; **~ se** betray oneself, give oneself away
izdava|č publisher; **~nje** distribution, delivery; letting out; **~ti** give out, distribute, deliver, issue; let out (= **iznajmiti**); ***~ti se za*** pose as
izderati wear out
izdisaj: ***na ~u*** at one's last gasp
izdržava|nje, **~ti** support; ***~ti se sam*** make one's own living
izdržati stand, hold out
izdržljiv tough; **~ost** stamina, endurance
izdupsti hollow out
izdvojiti (se) separate
izgarati MOT *i fig* burn
izgladiti smooth; *fig* iron out
izglad|niti, **~njeti** starve, famish
izglasati vote
izgled appearance; prospect, outlook; ***na ~*** seemingly; **~ati** seem; look, appear;

kako ~aju? what do they look like?
izglodati gnaw; wear away
izgon banishment
izgorjeti burn (down, out)
izgovarati se excuse oneself
izgovor pronunciation; (*isprika*) excuse; **~iti** pronounce
izgrad|iti build, construct; develop; **~nja** building, construction; development
izgrditi scold
izgred disorderly conduct; **~i** riots
izgrepsti scratch out
izgristi bite (several times); CHEM corrode
izgubiti lose; **~ se** lose one's way
izići go out, get out, come out; get off
izigrati outwit
izjaloviti se fall through
izjasniti se declare oneself
izjav|a statement, declaration; **~iti** state, declare
izjednačiti equalize; make uniform
izjesti CHEM corrode; **~ se** fret
izjuriti rush out
izlaga|č exhibitor; **~ti** exhibit, display, show; expose; **~ti se** (*opasnosti*) expose oneself (to danger)
izlanuti blurt out
izlaz way out, exit; ***~ za nuždu*** emergency exit
izleći se be hatched
izlet outing, excursion; **~ište** excursion centre, weekend resort; **~nik** excursionist
izletjeti fly out; rush out
izliječiti cure
izlika pretence, excuse
izliti pour out, empty; (*kovina*) cast; **~ se** overflow (*rijeka*)
izliza|n threadbare; worn out; **~ti se** become threadbare; wear out
izlog shop-window; show-window
izlož|ba show, exhibition, **~iti** = **izlagati**, **iznijeti**
izlječiv curable
izljev outflow, discharge
izmak: ***na ~u*** running low; expiring; **~nuti** avoid; escape; **~nuti se** dodge
izmamiti coax (out)
između between; (*više od ovoga*) among
izmetina excrement(s), faeces *pl*
izmijeniti exchange; (*dijelove*) replace; (*promijeniti*) change
izmirenje reconciliation
izmiriti reconcile
izmi|sliti invent, make up; **~šljotina** fabrication, fiction, lie
izmjena exchange; replacement; change
izmjenjiv exchangeable; replaceable; **~ati se** take turns
izmjeriti measure
izmlatiti beat up

izmoriti tire out
izmožden wasted, drained
izmrcvariti mangle (i *fig*)
izmučiti torture, torment; wear out, tire; **~ se** have a lot of trouble; tire oneself out
iznad above; over
iznajmiti (*sam*) rent, hire; (*drugome*) let out
iznemog|ao exhausted; (*od starosti*) feeble; **~lost** exhaustion; feebleness
iznena|da suddenly; **~dan** sudden; **~diti**, **~đenje** surprise
iznevjer|enje betrayal; **~iti** betray
iznijeti take out; outline, set forth, present; bring up
izniman exceptional
izno|s amount, sum; **~siti** amount to, total; (*odijelo*) wear out; **~šen** worn out
iznova anew, afresh
iznu|diti extort; **~đivač** extortioner; **~đivanje** extortion
iznutra (from) inside
izobilje abundance
izoblič|enost distortion, deformity; **~iti** distort, deform; **~iti se** become distorted (*ili* deformed)
izobraz|ba training; **~iti** train
izol|acija isolation; EL insulation; EL ***~aciona traka*** insulating tape; **~irati** isolate; EL insulate
izopć|enje excommunication; **~iti** excommunicate
izosta|janje non-attendance; **~nak** absence; **~ti** stay away, fail to attend; fail to take place
izostav|iti omit, leave out, drop; **~ljanje** omission
izoštriti sharpen
izrabljiva|č exploiter; **~ti** exploit
izračunati calculate, compute
izrad|a workmanship; **~iti** make, manufacture; draw up, work out
izraniti wound all over
izras|lina excrescence; **~ti** grow up
izravan direct, straight
izravnati straighten; (*račun*) settle
izraz expression; **~it** marked, distinct; **~iti** express; **~iti se** express oneself
izražajan expressive
izre|ći say, utter; **~ka** saying
izrešetati riddle
izrez (*dekolte*) low neck; **~ak** (*novinski*) *Br* cutting, *Am* clipping; **~ati** cut out, carve out; cut to pieces
izričit explicit
izrod renegade; (*nakaza*) freak; **~iti se** degenerate
izroniti emerge, come out; (*podmornica*) surface
izrovati root up
izruč|enje delivery; extradition; **~iti** deliver; hand over, extradite, give up

izrugiva|nje, **~ti se** ridicule
izubijati se suffer bruises
izuč|en trained, skilled; **~avati** study; **~iti** learn (a trade); undergo training for
izum invention; **~itelj** inventor; **~iti** invent
izum|irati, **~rijeti** die out
izuti se take off one's shoes
izuze|tan exceptional; **~tak** exception; **~ti** except; (*oslobodíti*) exempt; **~tno** exceptionally; **~vši** except, excluding
izvad|ak extract, excerpt; **~iti** take out; remove
izvaliti prize out; = **bubnuti**; **~ se** sprawl
izvan out of, outside; ***~ sebe*** beyond oneself; **~a** from outside, on the outside
izvanred|an extraordinary, exceptional; special; ***~no zasjedanje*** emergency session; ***~ni troškovi*** extras
izvedba execution; performance
izvesti take out; deduce; execute, perform; (*vezom*) embroider; **~ se** go out for a ride (*ili* drive)
izvezen embroidered
izvid||jeti investigate, find out; **~nica** reconnaisance party
izviđa|č scout; **~iti** MIL reconnoitre; **~nje** reconnaissance
izvijestiti report, inform
izvin|iti excuse; ***~ite!*** excuse me!; **~iti se** apologize
izvinjenje apology
izvinuti twist; = **uganuti**
izvirati spring (i *fig*)
izviždati hiss down; boo
izvjesiti hang out; (*oglas*) put up
izvjestan a certain
izvje|stitelj reporter; **~štaj** report
izvještačen affected; **~ost** affectation
izvježba|n practised; trained
izvlačiti (*lutriju*) draw; = **izvući**; **~ se** = **zabušavati**
izvod certificate; deduction; **~iti** = **izvesti**
izvođenje deduction; v. **izvedba**
izvojevati win, secure
izvol|jeti deign, please; ***~ite kruha!*** have some bread! ***~ite ući!*** come in please!; ***što ~ite?*** what can I do for you?
izvor spring; *fig* source; **~ni** original
izvoz export(s); **~iti** export; **~nik** exporter
izvrgnuti (se) expose (oneself)
izvrnuti (se) overturn; = **iskrenuti**, **prevrnuti**
izvrstan excellent; (*okus*) delicious
izvrš|an executive; **~enje** performance, execution, carrying out; **~itelj** executor; **~iti** carry out, perform, execute; (*dužnost*) discharge; (*zločin*) commit

izvući draw out, pull out, get out, haul out; extract; (*iz škripca*) get out, extract; **~ se** get out, extricate oneself

J

ja I
jablan poplar
jabu|čica ANAT Adam's apple; **~ka** apple; apple-tree; **~kovača** *vino* cider; *rakija* apple-brandy
jač|anje strengthening; **~ati** strengthen; intensify; **~ina** strength, vigour, power
jad grief, distress; **~an** poor, miserable; **~ikovati** complain, lament; **~nik** poor man, wretch
jaglac primrose
jagmiti se scramble for
jagod|a strawberry; **~ica** ANAT cheek-bone
jaha|č rider; SPORT jockey; ***~čko odijelo*** riding outfit; ***~ći konj*** riding horse; **~nje** (horse) riding, ride; ride (on horseback)
jaje egg; ***tvrdo (meko) kuhano ~*** hard-(soft) boiled egg; ***~ na oko*** fried egg
jajnik ANAT ovary
jak strong, powerful; **~o** very; **~ost** strength, power
jakna jacket; ***kućna ~*** smoking jacket
jalov sterile; barren
jama pit, hole
jam|ac guarantee, guarantor; **~čevina** deposit, security; bail; **~čiti**, **~stvo** guarantee
jantar amber
januar January
janje, **~tina** lamb
jao! oh! ow!, ouch!, woe
Japan Japan; **~ac** Japanese; **⁓ski** Japanese
jarac he-goat
jarak ditch; trench
jaram yoke (i *fig*)
jarbol mast
jare kid
jarebica partridge
jarki bright; *fig* ardent
jaruga gully
jasan clear; obvious, evident
jasen ash-tree
jasika asp(en)
jasle *pl* manger
jasnoća clarity; obviousness
jastog lobster
jastreb hawk
jastu|čnica pillowcase, pillow slip; **~k** pillow; cushion
jašenje riding
jašiti ride
jato flock; *riba* school, shoal
jauk cry of pain, yell; **~ati** cry with pain, yell
jav|an public; ***~na kuća*** brothel; **~nost** public
javiti let know, notify; report; inform
javor maple(-tree)

jaz gulf, gap
jazav|ac badger; **~čar** dachshund
jazbina lair (i *fig*)
jecati sob
ječam barley
ječmenac sty(e)
jedać|i: ***~i pribor*** cutlery; ***~a soba*** dining room
jedan one; ***~ drugoga*** each other, one another; ***~ do drugoga*** side by side; ***~ preko drugoga*** over each other; ***~ za drugim*** one after another; ***~ po ~*** one by one
jedanaest eleven; **~i** eleventh; **~erac** SPORT penalty kick
jedanput once; ***na ~*** at one gulp; at one sitting
jedar fresh, vigorous
jedin|ac only child; **~i** the only; **~ica** unity (i MIL); **~o** only
jedinstv|en unique; unanimous; **~o** unity
jednačiti eqnalize
jednadžba equation
jednak equal; equivalent; alike, similar; **~o** equally; **~ost** equality
jednina GRAM singular
jedno one (thing); (*otprilike*) about, some
jednobrojan plain; self-coloured
jednoduš|an unanimous; **~no** unanimously; **~nost** unanimity, complete agreement, unity
jednoglasno unanimously
jednokatnica two-storey house
jednokratan one-time
jednokrilac AERO monoplane
jednolič|an monotonous; uniform; **~nost** monotony; uniformity
jednom once; (*jednoć*) once upon a time
jednomotorac AERO single-engine aircraft
jednoobraz|an uniform; **~nost** uniformity
jednook one-eyed
jednoredan single-breasted (jacket)
jednosmjeran MOT one-way (street)
jednostav|an simple; **~no** simply; **~nost** simplicity
jednostran one-sided; **~ost** one-sidedness
jednostruk single, one-fold
jednjak gullet, MED (o)esophagus
jedrenj|ak sailship, sailing-boat, sailing-ship; **~e** sailing; ***ići na ~e*** go sailing, go for a sail
jedrili|ca sailboat, sailing-boat; SPORT yacht; (*zračna*) glider, (*visinska*) sailplane; **~čar** (*na vodi*) yachtsman; (*zračni*) glider pilot; v. **modelar**; **~čarstvo** (*zračno*) gliding
jedrina freshness; vigour
jedriti sail; glide

jedro sail
jedva hardly, scarcely, barely
jeftin cheap (i *fig*), inexpensive; **~oća** low prices
jegulja eel
jek: ***u punom ~u*** in full swing; at its height, at the height of; **~a** echo
jel|a fir(-tree); **~ovina** deal, fir-wood, fir-timber
jelen deer; (*mužjak*) stag, hart; ***obični ~*** red deer
jelo dish; food; **~vnik** menu
jenjati abate, go down, slacken
jer because, as, for
jesen autumn, *Am* fall
jesetra sturgeon
jesti eat, take food; take one's meals; **~v** edible, eatable
jetr|a liver; ***~ena pašteta*** liver sausage, liverwurst
Jevrej|in Jew; **~ski** Jewish
jez|a shudder; ***hvata me ~a*** *coll* it gives me the creeps; **~iv** ghastly, eerie
jezero lake
jezgra nucleus, core, heart
jezič|ac (*vage*) pointer; **~av** sharp-tongued; **~ni** language, linguistic
jezik language; *u ustima* tongue; *na cipeli* tongue
jež hedgehog; *morski* sea urchin
jod iodine
jogunast prankish
joha alder(-tree)
jorgan quilt, *Am* comforter
jorgovan lilac
još still; ***~ ne radi*** he doesn't work yet; ***~ jednom*** once more; ***~ kruha*** (some) more bread; ***~ jučer*** only yesterday; as late as yesterday; ***~ 1900.*** as early as 1900; as late as 1900
jubilej jubilee; anniversary
jučer yesterday; ***~ ujutro*** yesterday morning
jug south; ***na ~u*** in the south; ***na ~*** southward(s); **~oistok** south-east; **~ovina** thaw; **~ozapad** south-west
Jugoslav|en *hist* Yugoslav; **~ija** *hist* Yugoslavia; **~enski** *hist* Yugoslav
juha soup; ***~ od povrća*** vegetable soup; ***kokošja ~*** chicken soup
juli July
juna|čki heroic, gallant; brave, bold; **~k** hero; **~kinja** heroine; **~štvo** heroism, gallantry
juni June
juriš MIL charge; ***osvojiti na ~*** take by storm; **~ati** charge, storm
juriti rush, dash; MOT speed
juta jute
jut|arnji, **~ro** morning; ***dobro ~ro!*** good morning!; **~ros** this morning
južni southern, south
južnjak south wind

K

k(a) to, toward(s)
kabanica coat, overcoat
kabao tub, pail, bucket
kabel EL cable
kabina MAR cabin; AERO (pilot's) cockpit; (*na kupalištu*) cabin, (*na samomžalu*) cabana; (*za probe*) fitting room
kabriolet MOT convertible
kaca vat; tun, tub
kaciga helmet
kad(a) when; if; ***bilo ~*** any time, no matter when; ***~ bih znao*** if I knew
kada bathtub
kad|ar (*filmski*) take; (*stručni*) **~rovi** trained personnel; *adj* able, apt
kadet cadet
kadionica censer
kadulja sage
kaiš belt
kajak SPORT kayak
kaja|nje remorse, repentance; **~ti se** feel remorse; regret
kajgana scrambled eggs
kajsija apricot, apricot-tree
kak|av what kind of; ***~va je torta*** what's the cake like?
kako how; ***~ to?*** how come?
kaktus cactus
kakvoća quality
kalaj tin
kalati (se) cleave, split
kalcij calcium
kaldrma cobbles *pl*
kalem spool, reel
kalendar calendar
kalež chalice
kalfa journeyman
kalij CHEM potassium
kaliti temper; *fig* harden; **~ se** harden oneself
kalorifer fan-heater
kaluđer monk; **~ica** nun
kalup (*ljevački*) mould; (*za cipele*) shoe-tree, (*postolarski*) last
kaljače galoshes, *Am* rubbers
kaljav dirty, muddy
kaljuža mud-hole, slush; *fig* quagmire
kamat|e *pl* interest; ***~na stopa*** rate of interest; ***~e na ~e*** compound interest
kamelhar camel hair
kameja cameo
kamen stone; rock; boulder; ***~o doba*** Stone Age; **~ac** MED calculus, stone(s); **~it** stony, rocky, craggy; **~olom** quarry
kamera (FILM) camera
kamgarn worsted
kamilica c(h)amomile (tea)
kamin fire-place
kamion *Br* lorry, *Am* truck
kamo where (to); ***~ bilo*** anywhere; ***a ~ li*** let alone
kamp camp, camping site,

camp(ing) ground; **~ovati** camp
kamufl|aža, **~irati** camouflage
Kana|da Canada; **~ski** Canadian; **~đanin** Canadian
kanafas backing, buckram
kanal (*prirodni*) channel; (*prokopani*) canal; (*kanalizacija*) sewer; ***otvori televizor na ~ 2*** tune it to channel 2; **~izacija** sewers *pl*; **~izirati** *fig* channel
kanape divan
kanarinac canary
kancelar chancellor; **~ija** office
kandid|at candidate; applicant; **~atura** candidacy; **~irati** nominate; **~irati se** run
kandža claw
kanonik canon
kanta can; (*za smeće*) (dust-) bin
kantina canteen
kao like, as; **~ da** as if
kao|s chaos; **~tičan** chaotic
kap drop; MED stroke; ***~ po ~*** drop by drop; ***udarila ga je ~*** he had a stroke; ***~i za nos*** drops
kapa cap; (*francuska*) beret; bonnet
kapak cover, lid; (*očni*) eye-lid; (*prozorski*) shutter
kapara earnest-money; deposit
kapati drop, drip
kapel|a chapel; band; **~an** chaplain; **~nik** band-master
kapetan MIL captain; MAR master, skipper
kapica (*na tubi*) cap
kapital capital; **~ist** capitalist; **~izam** capitalism
kapitul|ant defeatist; **~irati** surrender
kaplar = **desetar**
kapric caprice, whim; **~irati se** be difficult
kapsla cap
kapuljača hood
kaput coat, overcoat, topcoat; (*prelazni*) light (weight) coat
karakter character; ***~an čovjek*** man of character; **~ističan**, **~istika** characteristic
karamela *Br* toffee, *Am* taffy
karanfil carnation
karantena quarantine
karat carat
karavan caravan; (*automobil*) *Br* estate car, *Am* station waggon
karbon-papir carbon paper
karcinom MED carcinoma
karfiol cauliflower
karijer|a career; **~ist** careerist
karika link (i *fig*)
kariran checked
karlica ANAT pelvis
karneval carnival
karniša curtain rail
karoserija body
karta (*igraća*) card; (*vozna*) ticket; (*zemljopisna*) map; **~ti se** play cards; **~š**

card-player
karter MOT oil-sump, oil-pan
karton cardboard; (*kartoteke*) card
kas, **~ati** trot
kasa cash-box, money-box; cash-desk, checkout-counter; ***registar* ~** cash register
kasarna barracks *pl*
kasn|i late; **~ije** later, afterwards; **~iti** be late; **~o** late
kaš|a porridge, gruel; pulp; **~ica** pap
kaš|alj, **~ljati** cough; **~ljucati** hack
kat floor, stor(e)y; ***drugi* ~** *Br* second floor, *Am* third floor
katar MED catarrh
katastar land office
katastrofa disaster; **~lan** disastrous
katedra teacher's desk; lecture desk; UNIV chair
kategorija category
katkad sometimes, off and on, now and then
katran tar
kau|cija deposit; **~č** couch; ***~č za razvlačenje*** sofa-bed; **~čuk** caoutchouc
kava coffee; ***crna* (*turska*) ~** black (Turkish) coffee; **~na** café
kavalir (proper) gentleman; **~ski** chivalrous; **~ština** chivalry
kavez cage
kavga fight; brawl
kavijar caviar
kazališ|te theatre (*Am* theater); ***Narodno ~te*** National Theatre; **~ni** theatre, theatrical
kazalo index; table of contents
kazaljka (*sata*) hand; (*instrumenta*) pointer; (*velika*, *mala*) ***~ hour*** (minute) hand; ***~ za sekunde*** seconds hand
kazan MIL food-kettle; = **kotao**
kazati say; (*drugome*) tell
kazn|a punishment, penalty; ***novčana ~a*** fine; ***smrtna ~a*** corporal punishment; ***~eni udarac*** (*prostor*) SP penalty kick (area); **~ionica** prison, penintentiary; **~iti** punish; (*novčano*) fine
kažiprst forefinger, index-finger
kažnj|avan with a record; **~avanje** punishment; **~enik** convict; **~iv** punishable
kći daughter
kečiga sturgeon
kelj savoy (cabbage), kale
kemi|čar chemist; **~ja** chemistry; **~jski**, **~kalija** chemical
kengur cangaroo
kerami|čki ceramical; **~ka** ceramics *pl*
kesa bag; (*za novac*) purse
kesiti se grin; smirk
kesten chestnut
kicoš dandy; **~ki** dandyish
kičm|a backbone, spine; **~enjak** ZOOL vertebrate
kiće|n ornate; flowery; **~nje** decoration

kidati tear (apart); break; rend; **~ se** tear
kifla croissant
kihati sneeze
kijača cudgel, club
kikiriki peanuts
kikser gaffe
kila MED hernia; **~v** *fig* feeble, softy
kimati nod
kiml caraway (seeds)
kinin quinine
kin|o *Br* cinema, pictures; *Am* movies; ***ići u ~o*** go to the pictures (*Am* movies); ***u ~u*** at the pictures (*Am* movies)
kiosk kiosk
kip statue; **~ar** sculptor; **~arski** sculptural; **~arstvo** sculpture
kip|jeti boil, seethe, (*potiho*) simmer; **~ući** boiling hot
kirur|g surgeon; **~gija** surgery
kise|lina, **~o** acid; **~lo** *fig* wryly; ***~li krastavci (paprike)*** pickled gherkins (peppers)
kisik oxygen
kisnuti get drenched
kist brush
kiš|a rain; ***pada ~a*** it is raining; **~ica** drizzle; **~ni** rainy; ***~ni ogrtač*** raincoat; **~nica** rain-water
kišobran umbrella; ***stalak za ~e*** umbrella-stand
kit ZOOL whale; ***lov na ~ove*** whaling; ***lovac na ~ove*** whaler; **~olovac** (*brod*) whaler
kit (*prozorski*) putty; **~ati** putty up
kit|a bunch; **~ica** small bunch; (*pjesme*) stanza
kititi decorate, adorn
kivan resentful; grudging
klackalica seesaw
klada log
kladi|onica betting office; ***igrati (dobiti) na sportskoj ~onici*** play (win) the pools; **~ti se** bet
kladiv|o: ***bacanje ~a*** hammer-throwing
klanac (mountain) pass, gorge
klanjati se bow
klanje slaughter (i *fig*), massacre
klaonica slaughter-house, abattoir
klarinet clarinet
klas ear, spike
klatež scum
klati slaughter, kill
klavi|r piano; **~jatura** keyboard
kle|čati kneel; **~knuti** kneel (down)
klekovača geneva
klepetati rattle
klerikalac POL clerical
klesa|r stone mason; **~ti** dress stone
klet|i, **~va** curse, swear
klevet|a, **~ati** slander; **~nik** slanderer
klica *fig* germ; BOT shoot, sprout; **~ti** shoot, sprout;

(*glasom*) cheer
kliconoša MED carrier
klijent client; **~ela** clientele
kliješta *pl* pincers (i *fig*); (*za žicu*) (combination) pliers *pl*; (*rakova*) claws *pl*
klika clique
kliknuti cheer, yell
klima climate; ***~tsko liječenje*** rest cure; **~tizacija** air-conditioning; **~tiziran** air-conditioned
klimakterij MED climacterium, *coll* change of life
klimati (se) wobble, nod
klimav loose, shaky, wobbly
klin wedge; peg; MIL spearhead
klinčić (*začin*) clove
klip cob; TECH piston; **~an** big lout; **~sati** trudge
klistir MED enema; **~ati** give an enema
klisura crag, sheer rock, (*morska*) cliff
kliše cliché; (*tiskarski*) block
kliza|č(ica) skater; (*umjetni*) figure skater; **~k** slippery (i *fig*); **~lište** skating rink; **~ljka** skate
klizanje: ***~ na ledu*** skating
klizati slip; (*vozilo*) skid; (*na ledu*) skate
kliziti glide
klobučar hatter
klokotati gurgle
klon clone; **~iranje** cloning; **~irati** clone
klonu|lost, **~ti** collapse; ***~ti duhom*** become despondent
klopka trap (i *fig*)
klopotati rattle
klor CHEM chlorine; **~irati** chlorinate
klub club
klupa bench; (*školska*) desk; (*u crkvi*) pew
klupko ball (of wool, string)
kljaštriti prune (i *fig*)
kljenut palsy, paralysis
kljova tusk
kljucati peck
ključ key (i *fig*); MUS clef; ***~ od kuće*** street-door key; ***pod ~em*** *fig* under lock and key; **~anica** keyhole; ***~no pitanje*** key issue; ***francuski ~*** *Br* spanner, *Am* wrench
ključati stuff (i *fig*)
kljun bill; (*grabljivice*) beak
kljuse jade
kljuvati pick (out)
kmet surf; **~stvo** serfdom
kne|ginja duchess; **~z** duke; **~ževina** principality, dukedom
knjiga book; volume; ***glavna ~*** COM ledger
knjigoveža book-binder
knjigovo|dstvo bookkeeping; **~đa** bookkeeper
knjiški bookish
knjižar bookseller; **~a** *Br* bookshop, *Am* book store
književn|i literary; **~ik**, **~ica** writer; **~ost** literature
knjiži|ca booklet; **~ti** book, enter; (*u korist*) credit
knjižni|ca library; **~čar** li-

brarian
kob fate, destiny, fortune; **~an** fatal
kobac sparrow-hawk
kobasica sausage
kobila mare
kobilica Keel
kocka cube; (*igraća*) die (*pl* dice); **~r** gambler; **~ti se** play dice; gamble
kočija coach, carriage; **~š** coachman, driver
kočiti brake (i *fig*); **~ se** stiffen
kočnica brake
kod at; by; near; ***~ nas*** at our place; with us; in our case; ***~ toga*** at the same time; in doing so
kofer suitcase
koješta! nonsense!
koji which, (*osobe*) who; that
koket|a, **~irati** flirt
kokice popcorn *pl*
kokodakati cackle
kokosov: ***~ orah*** coconut; ***~a palma*** coconut-tree
kokoš hen; **~injac** hen-house
koks coke; **~ara** coke plant
koktel cocktail
kola cart, wag(g)on; **~r** cartwright
kolac pole, stake
kolač cake; tart; (*slastičarski*) pastry; **~ić** *Br* (sweet) biscuit, *Am* cooky
kola|nje circulation; **~ti** circulate
koleb|anje vacillation; hesitation; **~ati se** vacillate; waver; hesitate
koleg|a colleague; job-mate; (*student*) fellow-student; **~ijalan** comradely; helpful
kolektiv collective, staff; **~an** collective
kolera MED cholera
koliba hut
kolica hand-cart; (*dječja*) perambulator, pram; (*invalida*) wheel-clair
količina quantity, amount
kolijevka cradle, cot
kolik|i how large; what a; **~o** how much, how many; ***u ~o*** insofar
kolnik roadway
kolodvor railway station; (*autobusni*) **~** bus station
kolona MIL column
koloni|ja colony; **~zirati** colonize
kolonjska voda cologne
kolosalan splendid
kolosjek RLW ga(u)ge
kolotečina rut (i *fig*)
kolovođa ringleader
kolovoz August
koludrica nun
kolumba MAR drop-keel
kolut ring
koljač cut-throat, murderer
koljeno knee
komad piece; **~ić** (little) bit
komand|a, **~irati** command; **~ant**, **~ir** commander
komarac gnat, mosquito
kombajn combine harvester
kombinat complex, large plant

kombine slip; ***radnički ~zon*** overalls *pl*
komedija comedy
komemor|acija commemoration; **~irati** commemorate
koment|ar comment, commentary; **~irati** comment, make comments
komercijalan commercial
komesar commissary; POL commissar
komeša|nje commotion; **~ti se** stir
kometa comet
komfor modern conveniences *pl*; comfort; **~an** with modern conveniences
komisija commission
komoda chest of drawers, commode
komor|a COM *i* TECH chamber; PHOT ***tamna ~a*** dark room; ***~na muzika*** chamber music
komotan loose, comfortable; (*čovjek*) easy-going, indolent
kompaktni disk compact disk
kompanjon COM partner
kompar|ativ GRAM comparative; **~irati** compare (to, whit); collate
kompleks complex; (*psihički*) complex, inhibition; **~aš** inhibited person
komplet set
kompli|ciran complicated; **~kacija** complication
kompon|irati MUS compose; **~ist** composer
kompot stewed fruit; (*u konzervi*) canned fruit
kompozi|cija composition (i MUS); RLW train **~tor** MUS composer
kompromis, **~ni** compromise; ***učiniti ~*** compromise
kompromit|antan compromising; **~irati (se)** compromise (oneself)
komunal|an municipal, public; **~ije** *pl* public services *pl*
komunikacije *pl* communications *pl*; roads *pl*
komuni|st, **~stički** communist; **~zam** communism
konac thread; end
konač|an final, ultimate; **~no** finally
konačište lodgings *pl*; nn
koncept (rough) draft
koncern COM combine
koncert concert; (*kompozicija*) concerto
koncipirati draft
kondicional, **~an** GRAM conditional
kondolira|nje condolence, **~ti** condole, express sympathy (with)
kondukter conductor; (*željeznički*) *Br* guard, *Am* conductor
konfekcij|a ready-made clothes *pl*; ***industrija ~e*** garment industry
konferansje master of ceremonies
konferencija conference

konjunkt|iv GRAM subjunctive; **~ura** COM boom
konkret|an concrete; ***govoriti ~no*** speak to the point
konkuren|cija competition; **~t** competitor, rival; **~tan** COM competitive
konoba wine cellar; **~r** waiter; **~rica** waitress
konop rope, line, cord; (*debeli brodski*) hawser; **~lja** hemp; **~ljarka** linnet
konspira|cija secrecy; ***radi ~cije*** for security reasons; **~tivan** secrete
konstat|acija statement, remark, observation; **~irati** state, remark, observe
konstruirati design; construct
konstruk|cija design; GRAM construction; **~tor** designer; constructor
kontrabas MUS double bass
kontracepcij|a contraception, birth control; ***sredstva za ~u*** contraceptives
kontrapunkt MUS conterpoint
kontrarevolucija counterrevolution
kontrašpijunaža counterespionage
kontrol|a, **~irati** control check; **~or** controller; (*voznih karata*) inspector
kontura contour, outline
konvencija convention
konvenirati suit
konzerv|a, **~irati** *Br* tin, *Am i Br* can; ***tvornica ~i*** cannery
konzul consul; **~at** consulate
konj horse; (*teretni*) draft-horse; (*trkaći*) race-horse; (*šah*) knight; ***na ~u*** on horseback; **~anik** horse-rider; MIL cavalryman; **~ica** cavalry; **~ska** (*snaga*) horse-power; **~ušar** stable-boy; **~ušnica** stable
konjak cognac, French brandy
koordin|acija co-ordination; **~irati** co-ordinate
kopa|č diger; **~ti** dig
kopča clasp, buckle; **~ti** button (up)
kopi|ja copy, duplicate; (*tipkana*) carbon; PHOT print; **~rati** copy, duplicate; PHOT print; (*kroz papir*) trace
kopito hoof
kopkati bother
koplj|e spear; (*konjičko*) lance; SPORT ***bacanje ~a*** javelin-throwing
kopneni land
kopniti thaw, melt
kopno land
koprcati se struggle, kick
koprena veil
kopriva nettle
kora (*stabla*) bark; (*sira*) rind; (*kruha*) crust; (*krumpira*) skin (*oguljena* peel)
kora|cati walk, march; pace; **~čnica** march; **~k** step, pace
koral, **~ni** coral
korekt|an correct; **~or** proof-reader; **~ura** proof

korespondent correspondent
korice *pl* cover; (*noža*) sheath; (*sablje*) scabbard
korigirati correct
korijen root; ***iz ~a*** radically
koris|nik beneficiary, user; **~nost** usefulness; **~t** advantage, benefit; **~tan** useful; **~titi** be useful; serve; use; draw on
korištenje use, utilization
koriti scold; blame
korito trough; (*broda*) hull; (*riječno*) bed
korizma Lent
korjenit radical
kormil|ar helmsman; steersman; **~ariti** steer; **~o** helm; (*pod vodom*) rudder
kornjača turtle; (*morska*) tortoise
korota mourning
korov weed(s)
korumpiran corrupt
korupcija corruption, bribery
kos[1] ZOOL blackbird
kos[2] *adj* slanting, inclined
kosa scythe; **~c** mower; (*srpom*) reaper
kosati CUL chop; (*fino*) mince
kosina slope
kosit|er: ***~ren*** tin
kositi mow
kosmat hairy
kost bone (i *riblja*)
kostim suit, (*klasični*) tailored suit; THEAT costume; fancy dress
kost|obolja gout; **~ur** skeleton
koš waste-paper basket; **~ara** basket; **~arka** SPORT basketball
koščat bony
košnica beehive
koštac: ***uhvatiti se u ~*** *fig* tackle
koštan (of) bone
koštati cost; ***šta ~?*** how much is this?
koštica stone; (*sitna*) pip
košulja shirt
košuta ZOOL hind
kotač wheel
kotao kettle; TECH boiler
kotar district, county
kotiti se have young
kotlet chop; CUL cutlet
kotlina GEOGR hollow, depression; (*zavalje*) basin
kotrljati (se) roll
koturaljka roller-skate; ***voziti se na ~ma*** roller-skate
kova|č blacksmith; **~čnica** smithy; forge; **~k** malleable; **~ti** forge, hammer; (*novac*) mint
koverta envelope
kovčeg suit-case, trunk; chest, box
kovina metal
kovnica (*novca*) mint
kovrč|ast curly; **~ati**, **~ica** curl
koza goat
kozice smallpox
kozmetič|arka beautician;

~ki cosmetic
kozm|ički cosmic; **~os** cosmos
kož|a leather; (*ljudska*) skin; (*životinjska*) hide; **~ica** cuticle; membrane
krabuljni ples fancy-dress ball
kradljivac thief; (*u dućanu*) shop-lifter
krađa theft; shop-lifting
krafna doughnut
kraj end, close; (*predio*) country, area; *prep* beside by, next to, near
krajnik ANAT tonsil
krajnji extreme
krajolik landscape
krak leg (i *šestara*)
kralj king (i *šah*, *karte*); **~evina** kingdom, monarchy; **~evski** royal; **~ica** queen (i *šah*, *karte*)
kralježak ANAT vertebra; **~njaci** *pl* vertebrates
kramp pick
krasan wonderful, splendid; beautiful, handsome
krasta MED scab, crust
krastača ZOOL toad
krastavac cucumber; ***kiseli ~*** pickled gherkin
krasti steal
krat|ak short; (*vremenski*) short, brief; **~ica** abbreviation; **~koća** brevity; **~kotrajan** short-lived; **~kovidan** short-sighted (*i fig*)
krater crater
kraul crawl SPORT
krava cow; **~r** cow-boy, cow-herd
kravata necktie, tie; (*leptirka*) bow-tie
krcat *fig* packed; **~i** load
krčag jug, ewer
krčiti clear (land)
krčma *Br* (low) pub; *Am* (low) bar, saloon; **~r** = **gostioničar**
krdo herd
krea|cija (*modna*) design; **~tor** (*modni*) fashion designer
kreč = **vapno**; **~iti** whitewash
kreda chalk
kredenc kitchen cabinet, cupboard
kreirati design
kreketati croak
krema CUL filling, cream
kremen flint
krenuti move towards; (*na put*) set off
krepak sturdy; (*starac*) hale; (*obrok*) hearty
krepost virtue; **~an** virtuous
kresati strike (sparks)
kreštati screech
kretanje movement; MED exercise
kreten MED *i fig* cretin
kreton printed cotton
kreveljiti se make faces
krevet bed
krezub toothless; gap-toothed
krh|ak brittle, fragile; **~otina** fragment
kričav (*boja*) loud, gaudy

krigla beer-mug
krijepiti strengthen
krijes bonfire; **~nica** glow--worm
krijumčar smuggler; **~enje** smuggling; **~iti** smuggle; ***~ena roba*** smuggled goods *pl*
krik, **~nuti** scream, shriek
krilo wing (i *zgrade*, *vrata*)
krinka mask
kristal, **~an** crystal
kriška slice
kriterij criterion
kriti (se) hide
kritičan critical
kriv guilty; (*pogrešan*) wrong; (*nakrivljen*) awry, **~o** wrongly
krivac culprit
kriviti blame
krivnja guilt; fault, blame
krivotvor|en forged, counterfeit; **~ina** forgery; **~itelj** forger, counterfeiter; **~iti** forge, counterfeit
krivovjer|ac heretic; **~je** heresy
krivuda|v winding; **~ti** wind
krivulja curve
kriz|a crisis; **~antema** chrysanthemum; **~ma** REL confirmation
križ cross; **~a** *pl* ANAT small of the back; **~aljka** crossword (puzzle); **~ar** crusader; **~arski** (*pohod*) crusade; **~ati** cross through, eliminate; BOT ZOOL cross-bread; **~ati se** cross oneself
krma MAR stern; (*stočna*) fodder
krnj incomplete
kroj cut; (*na papiru*) pattern sheet; **~ač** tailor; **~ačica** dressmaker; **~iti** cut
krokodil crocodile
krom chromium; **~iran** chromium-plated
kroni|čan chronic; **~ka** chronicle
krošnja (tree) top
krot|ak meek; **~iti** tame
krov roof; ***~ne grede*** rafters
kroz through
krpa rag; (*kuhinjska*) dish--towel, tea-cloth; (*za prašinu*) duster; **~riti** *fig* plug holes, improvise, eke out; **~ti** mend, repair; (*čarape*) darn
krpelj ZOOL tick
krsni list birth certificate
krstari|ca MIL cruiser; **~ti** cruise
krstiti baptize, christen; = **križati**
Krš GEOGR Karst
kršćan|in, **~ski** Christian; **~stvo** Christianity
krš|enje violation; **~iti** violate
krštenje baptism, christening
krti|ca mole; **~čnjak** mole--hill
krug circle; ring; (*u trci*) lap
kruh bread; ***bijeli*** (***crni***) **~** white (brown) bread
kruliti rumble
krumpir potato; (*pire*) mashed potatoes; (*»pom-*

fri«) *Br* chips, *Am* French fries; (*pržene ploške*) *Br* crisps, *Am* chips
krun|a crown (*i zuba*); **~ica** REL rosary; **~isanje** coronation; **~isati** crown
krup|an big, large; **~ica** groats *pl*; = **griz**
kruška pear
krut stiff; (*ne tekuć*) solid; *fig* rigid, inflexible
krуž|iti circulate, rotate; **~nica** circle
krv blood; **~arenje** bleeding; **~ariti** bleed; **~av** bloody; **~avica** black pudding, blood sausage; **~nik** executioner; **~oločan** bloodthirsty; **~oproliće** bloodshed; **~otok** circulation
krzmati hesitate
krzn|ar furrier; **~o** fur
kržljav stunted; **~ost** stunted growth
kubi|st, **~stički** cubist; **~zam** cubism
kuca|ti knock; (*sat*) tick; (*srce*) beat; ***~nje srca*** heart-beats
kucnuti se clink glasses
kučina oakum
kuć|a house; (*velika stambena*) *Br* block of flats, *Am* apartment house; ***kod ~e*** at home; ***ići ~i*** go home
kućan|ica housewife, housekeeper; **~stvo** household; housekeeping
kućevlasnik house-owner
kućica little house; (*puževljeva*) shell
kućn|a: ***~a pomoćnica*** maid, help; ***~i posao*** housework
kuda where; which way
kuditi blame, scold, criticize; *coll* tell off
kudjelja tow, hemp
kudrav shaggy; curly
kuga plague
kugl|a ball; SPORT shot; ***bacanje*** (***bacač***) ***~e*** shot-putting (shot-putter); **~ana** *Br* skittle-alley, *Am* bowling alley; **~anje** *Br* skittles *pl*, *Am* bowling; ***~ični ležaj*** TECH ball-bearing
kuhača ladle
kuhalo cooker
kuhar cook; **~ica** cook; (*knjiga*) *Br* cookery book, *Am* cookbook
kuhati cook; (*u vodi*) boil
kuhinja kitchen
kuja bitch
kuk hip; hip-joint
kuka hook
kukac insect
kukast hooked; ***~i križ*** swastika
kukati wail; complain
kukavica coward; (*ptica*) cookoo
kukolj BOT cockle
kukuljica hood
kukurikati crow
kukuruz *Br* maize, *Am* (Indian) corn; ***klip ~a*** ear of corn, cob
kul|a tower; ***~e u oblacima*** castles in the air

kulis|e *pl* scenery, sets *pl*; ***iza ~a*** *fig* behind the scenes
kuljati pour out; gush
kum godfather; (*vjenčani*) best man; **~a** godmother; (*vjenčana*) matron of honour (*neudata* maid of honour); **~če** godchild; **~ovati** be godfather; ***~ovska slama*** Milky Way
kumir idol
kuna ZOOL marten
kundak (rifle) stock, butt
kunić rabbit
kunjati be droppy; = **drijemati**
kup heap, pile
kupac buyer, purchaser
kupač bather
kupać|e gaćice *pl* swim(-ming) trunks *pl*, bathing trunks *pl*; ***~i kostim*** swimsuit, bathing costume (*jednodjelni* one-piece swimsuit)
kupalište bathing place; (*mjesto*) seaside resort; (*toplice*) watering-place, spa
kupanje (*u kući*) bath; ***ići na ~*** go to the beach, go for a swim
kupaona bathroom
kupati give (one) a bath; **~ se** have a bath, take one's bath; (*na otvorenom*) bathe, have a swim
kupe RLW compartment
kupina blackberry
kupiti buy, purchase; = **skupljati**
kupke (*toplice*) spa
kupnj|a, kupovina purchase; ***ići u ~u*** go shopping
kupon coupon
kupus cabbage; ***kiseli ~*** sauerkraut
kura MED cure
kurir courier
kurje oko corn
kurs course
kurva whore
kurziv italics *pl*
kušati taste; try
kušnj|a test; ***staviti na ~u*** put to the test
kut corner; GEOM *fig* angle
kuta overalls *pl*
kutija box
kutlača big ladle
kutnjak molar, back tooth
kvačilo MOT clutch; ***ubaciti ~*** throw in the clutch
kvadr|at square; ***2 na ~at*** 2 squared, the second power of 2; **~irati** square
kvaka (door-) handle; (*okrugla*) (door) knob
kvalifi|cirani: ***~cirani radnik*** skilled worker; **~cirati** train; qualify; **~kacije** *pl* training
kvalitet quality; **~an** of good quality
kvantitet quantity
kvar breakdown, fault, (engine) trouble; ***biti u ~u*** be out of order
kvariti spoil; corrupt; **~ se** (*hrana, roba*) go bad, be perishable
kvartet quartet(te)

kvasac leaven, (*kupovni*) yeast
kvočka brood-hen
kvorum quorum
kvota quota
kvrga bump (*i na glavi*); (*u drvu*) knot; **~st** bumpy; knotty

L

labav loose (*i fig*)
labil|an unstable; **~nost** instability
labirint labyrinth
laboratorij laboratory, *coll* lab
labud swan
ladica drawer
lađa boat; ship, vessel; **~r** boatman
lafeta MIL gun-carriage
lagan light; easy; **~o** slowly; sofly, gently; easy, easily
lagati lie, tell lies
lai|k layman; **~čki** as a layman
laja|nje, ~ti bark; **~v** having a loose tongue
lak *adj* light; (*jednostavan*) easy; **~oća** lightness; facility
lakat elbow
lak *n*, **~irati** lacquer, varnish; ***~irane cipele*** patent-leather shoes
lakom greedy; **~ost** greediness
lakoum|an light-minded; **~nost** light-mindedness
lakovjeran credulous
lakrdija buffonery; **~š** buffoon
laktaš pusher; **~ki** pushing
lampa lamp
lampion Chinese lantern
lan flax
lanac chain (*i fig*)
lanč|anik (*bicikla*) chain; **~ić** chain
lane ZOOL fawn
lani last year
lansirati launch (*i fig*)
lanjski last-year, last year's
lasica ZOOL weasel
laska|nje flattery; **~ti** flatter; **~v** flattering; **~vac** flatterer
lastavica swallow
lastika elastic
lašti|lo polish; **~ti** polish, *coll* shine
latica BOT petal
latinica Latin characters
latiti se reach for; take up
lav lion; **~ica** lioness
lava (*vulkanska*) lava
lavina avalanche
lavež bark(ing)
lavirati steer a middle course
lavor (wash) bowl
laž lie, falsehood; **~ac** liar; **~an** false, fake; **~ljiv** lying
lebdjeti hover, float
leća BOT lentil; OPT lens
leći (*jaja*) lay; = **legnuti**
led ice; **~ana** ice works; **~en** ice-cold, icy; *fig* frigid;

(*piće*) iced; **~eno doba** Ice Age; **~enjak** (*glečer*) glacier; **~ište** freezing point; **~iti (se)** freeze; **~olomac** ice-breaker
ledina green; empty field; GEOGR heath
leđ|a back *sg*; ***za ~ima*** behind one's back; ***~no plivanje*** SPORT back stroke
legitim|acija card; (*osobna*) identity card; **~irati se** show one's identity card
legnuti lie down; go to bed
legura alloy
lekcija *fig* lesson
lektira reading; (*obavezna*) set books
lektor language instructor; language editor
lem, **~iti** TECH solder; **~ilo** TECH soldering iron
leopard leopard
lepeza fan
lepršati flutter
leptir butterfly; (*noćni*) moth
lesonit hardboard
leš: ***staza od ~a*** SPORT cinder--track, = **drozga**
leš, **~ina** corpse, (dead) body; **~inar** ZOOL vulture
let flight; ***pokusni ~*** test flight; ***u ~u*** in flight; on the wing; **~eći**, **~enje** flying; **~jeti** fly
letač flyer, flier; ***~ko osoblje*** air crew(s)
letak leaflet
letimi|ce cursorily; **~čan** cursory
letlampa TECH blowlamp
letva lath
lezbijka lesbian
ležlaj bed; TECH = **ležište**; **~aljka** deck-chair; (*za plažu*) chair-bed; **~ati** lie
ležećke lying
ležer|an relaxed; **~nost** relaxed manner
ležište TECH bearing, support
li: ***ideš ~?*** are you going? do you go?
libela ZOOL dragon-fly; *alat* level
libreto MUS libretto, book
lice face; person, party; ***glavno ~*** hero
licemjer hypocrite; **~an** hypocritical; **~je** hypocrisy
licitacija auction
liči|lac (house-) painter; **~ti** paint, varnish
ličinka ZOOL larva
ličn|i personal; **~o** personally; **~ost** personality
lift lift
liga league
lignit brown coal, lignite
lignja ZOOL cuttle-fish, squid
lihvar usurer; **~enje** usury; **~iti** practise usury; **~ski** usurious
liječ|enje treatment, cure; **~iti** treat, cure; **~iti se (od)** undergo treatment (for); **~nica** lady doctor; **~nik** doctor, physician
lijeha bed
lijek medicine, drug; *fig* remedy; ***~ za sve*** cure-all

lijen lazy; **~čina** lazy-bones; **~ost** laziness
lijep beautiful, handsome, nice, pretty, attractive; ***to je ~o od vas*** that is nice of you
lijepiti stick, glue, paste; **~ se** stick, be sticky
lijes *Br* coffin, *Am* casket
lijeva|k funnel; (*na posudi*) spout, beak; (*bombe*) crater; **~ti** pour; (*kovinu*) cast; ***~no željezo*** cast iron
lijevi, ~o left
lik figure; image; (*romana*) personage, character; ***~ovne umjetnosti*** visual arts; ***~ovni umjetnik*** artist
liker liqueur
likvidirati liquidate
lim (*materijal*) sheet metal; (*artikl*) sheet; **~ar** plumber; **~eni** sheet (-metal); ***~ena glazba*** brass band; ***~enka*** tin, can; ***bijeli ~enka*** tin plate
limun lemon; **~ada** lemonade
limuzina (*zatvorena kola*) *Br* saloon, *Am* sedan; (*luksuzna*) limusine
linčovati lynch
linija line; (*prometna*) line, service
linoleum linoleum
linjati se moult, lose hair; shed one's coat
lipa BOT lime-tree, linden
lipanj June
liposukcija liposuction
lirski lyric
lisica fox
lisičine *pl* handcuffs; ***staviti ~*** handcuff
lisnica wallet
list BOT leaf; (*papira*) sheet; (*na nozi*) calf; (*riba*) sole
list|a list; **~ati** turn over leaves; (*stablo*) come out in leaf; ***~ovni papir*** note-paper
listopad October
lišaj BOT lichen; MED eczema
lišavanje deprivation
lišće leaves *pl* foliage
liš|en deprived of; **~iti** deprive
litica sheer rock, crag
litra litre (*Am* liter)
livada meadow
lizati lick
logor, ~ovati camp; **~aš** detainee, internee, camp inmate; **~ovanje** camping
loj tallow; ***kao po ~u*** like clockwork
lojal|an loyal; **~nost** loyalty
lokal premises *pl*
lokati (*životinja*) lap (up)
lokomotiva engine, locomotive
lokot padlock
lokva puddle, pool
lom break; MED fracture; *fig* uproar
lomač|a (*pogrebna*) pyre; ***umrijeti na ~i*** die at the stake
lomiti (se) break
lomljava crash
lon|ac pot; **~čar** potter; ***~čar-***

ska roba pottery; **~čić** cup
lopat|a shovel; (*kopača*) spade; **~ica** ANAT shoulder-blade; (*dječja*) spade
lopoč BOT water-lily
lopov thief; *fig* rascal; **~luk** dirty trick; **~ski** rascally
lopta ball; **~ti se** play with ball
losos *riba* salmon
loš bad, inferior
lotati = **lemiti**
lotos BOT lotus
lov hunt, shoot(ing); ***ići u ~*** go hunting, go shooting; **~ac** hunter; ***igrati se ~ice*** play tag; **~iti** catch; *lov* hunt, shoot; (*ribu*) fish
lovor laurel; *fig* laurels *pl*
loza BOT vine
lozinka MIL password, *fig* motto
loža THEAT box
lož|ač stoker; RLW fireman; **~iti** stoke, fire; heat
lubanja skull
lubenica water melon
luckast having a screw loose, crazy
lučki port; ***~ grad*** port (town); ***~ radnik*** *Br* docker, *Am* longshoreman
lud crazy, mad, insane; **~ilo** craziness, madness, insanity; **~nica** lunatic asylum, (*i fig*) madhouse; **~orija** monkey business; **~ost** folly, foolishness; **~ovati** fool; be mad about
luđak madman
lugar *Br* forester, *Am* ranger
luk BOT onion; (*drobnjak*) chives *pl*; (*bijeli*) garlic
lûk ARCHIT arch; (*oružje*) bow
luka harbour (*Am* harbor), (*velika*) port
lukav crafty, cunning, sly; **~ost** craftiness, cunning, slyness; **~ština** trick
lukobran break-water
lukovica bulb
luksuz luxury; **~an** luxurious; luxury, de luxe, fancy
lula pipe
lumpati have a spree; *sl* be out on the town
lupa|nje banging; **~ti** bang, knock; (*nogama*) stomp
lupetati talk nonsense
lupina = **kora**, **ljuska**
luster light fixture, hanging lamp; (*kristalni*) chandelier
lutati wander, rove, roam
lut|ka doll; ***kazalište ~aka*** puppet theatre
lutrij|a lottery; ***dobiti na ~i*** win the lottery
lužina lye (*i* CHEM)

LJ

ljag|a blemish, blot, spot; ***bez ~e*** spotless
lječilište sanatorium; (*mjesto*) health-resort
ljekovit healing; ***~o bilje*** medicinal herbs; **~ost** healing property
ljenčariti loaf, idle
ljepak bird-lime; ***ići na ~*** *fig* take the bait
ljepenka cardboard
ljep|ilo (*uredsko*) gum, paste; (*stolarsko*) glue; (*univerzalno*) cement, adhesive; **~ljiv** sticky, adhesive; **~ljivost** stickiness
ljep|ota beauty; **~otica** beauty; **~uškast** pretty, charming
ljestv|e ladder *sg*; **~ica** scale
lješnjak hazel-nut
ljetina crops *pl*, harvest
ljetn|i summer; ***~a pozornica*** open-air stage
ljetnikovac summer cottage
ljeto summer; **~valište** summer resort
ljiljan lily
ljubak charming, lovable
ljubav love; ***meni za ~*** for my sake; ***~no pismo*** love letter; ***~ni par*** lovers *pl*; **~nica** lover, mistress; **~nik** lover
ljubaz|an kind, nice; **~nost** kindness
ljubi|ca BOT violet; **~čast** purple
ljubimac favourite
ljubitelj fan; ***~ konja*** horse lover
ljubiti love; (*poljubiti*) kiss
ljubomora jealousy; **~n** jealous
ljud|i people; **~ski** *adj* human; *adv* properly, soundly; humanely
ljudožder cannibal; (*životinja*) man-eater; **~stvo** cannibalism
ljulja|ška swing; **~ti (se)** swing, rock, sway
ljupkost charm
ljuska BOT husk, pod, shell; (*jajeta*) shell; (*riblja*) scale
ljušt|iti husk, shell; peel; **~ura** shell
ljut angry (**na** with); (*okus*) hot, pungent; **~ina** anger; (*okus*) pungency; **~iti** make angry, annoy; **~iti se** be angry

M

ma but; why!
maca BOT catkin
mač sword
mač|ak tom-cat; **~e** kitten; **~ka** cat
mačeva|lac fencer (*i* SP); **~nje** fencing; **~ti se** fence
maćeha step-mother
maćuhica BOT pansy
mada = iako
madež mole
madrac mattress; ***feder ~*** spring-mattress; ***luft ~*** air mattress
Madžar, Ꝏski Hungarian; **~ska** Hungary
mađioničar conjurer
magarac donkey; *fig* ass
magazin store-room; (*puške*) magazine
magistrala arterial road
magl|a fog; (*nad velikim gradom*) smog; (*jutarnja*) mist; **~ica** haze; **~ovit** foggy; *fig* nebulous
magnet magnet; MOT magneto; **~izirati** magnetize; **~ski** magnetic; ***~ska igla*** magnetic needle
magnetofon tape-recorder; ***snimiti na ~*** tape-record; ***~ska traka*** (magnetic) tape
mah: ***uzeti ~a*** gain ground, spread; ***na ~ove*** off and on
mahati swing; (*rukom*) wave, be frenzied; **~ost** frenzy
mahnuti beckon, motion
mahovina BOT moss
mahun|a BOT pod; **~e** *pl* green beans
maj May
majčin mother's; **~ski** motherly, maternal; **~stvo** motherhood
majica (*kratkih rukava*) T-shirt; (*gimnastička*) gym vest; (*potkošulja*) *Br* vest, singlet, *Am* undershirt
majka mother
majmun monkey; (*čovjekoliki*) ape
majoneza CUL mayonnaise; salad cream
major MIL major
majstor master; **~ija** clever trick; **~ski** *adj* masterly; *adv* skilfully; **~stvo** mastery
majur farmstead
mak BOT poppy; (*sjeme*) poppy seed
makar = iako, bar; ***pa ~*** even if
Makedon|ac Macedonian; **~ija** Macedonia; **Ꝏski** Macedonian
maketa (scale) model
maknuti (se) move
malaksa|o exhausted; **~ti** become exhausted; **~lost** exhaustion
malari|ja MED malaria; **~čan** malarial

malen small, little
malenkost trifle, small matter
mali small, little; MAR cabin-boy
malin|a raspberry; **~ovac** raspberry juice
mališan little boy; **~i** little children
malo a little; ***~ prije*** a minute ago; ***imati ~ novaca*** (*nešto*) have a little money, (*nedovoljno*) have little money; COM ***na ~*** retail
malodušan fainthearted
malograđan|in, **~ski** petty bourgeois; **~ština** petty bourgeois mentality
maloljet|an under age; **~nik** minor; **~nost** minority
maloposjednik smallholder
malter mortar
maltretirati maltreat
malverzacija malversation
malj sledge
mama mother, mamma, ma
mam|ac bait, lure; **~iti** lure, entice
mamlaz clot, slob
mamur|an drowsy; (*od pića*) hung over; **~luk** drowsiness; hangover
mamuza spur
man|a fault; flaw, defect; ***bez ~e*** faultless, flawless
manastir = **samostan**
mandarinka (*voće*) tangerine
manekena (fashion) model
mangup scamp, rascal
mansarda (*stan*) attic
manšet|a (*rukava*) cuff; (*hlača*) turn-up; ***dugme za ~u*** cuff-link
mantil overalls *pl*
manjak deficit; (*u težini*) short weight
manje less, fewer
manji smaller; *fig* minor; **~na** minority
manjka|ti lack; **~v** defective, deficient
mapa writing-case; album; GEOGR map
maratonac SPORT marathon runner
marcipan CUL marzipan
marelica apricot
margarin margarine
marionet|a, **~ski** puppet
mariti care (for)
marka (postage) stamp; COM make
markiz marquis; **~a** marquise, *Br* marchioness
marljiv diligent, hard-working; **~ost** diligence, hard work
marmelada jam; (*od naranče i sl.*) marmalade
marš march
maršal marshal
mart March
masa mass
mas|aža, **~irati** massage; **~er** masseur; **~erka** masseuse
mask|a mask; (*podvodna*) goggles *pl*; = **krabuljni ples**; **~irati** mask; **~irati se** disguise oneself

maslac butter; ***kruh s ~em*** bread and butter
maslačak BOT dandelion
maslina olive (-tree)
masnoće fats *pl*
mas|t (cooking) fat; (*svinjska*) lard; (*biljna*) vegetable fat; MED ointment; **~tan** greasy (*i hrana*)
mašin|a machine; **~erija** machinery (*i fig*)
mašiti se reach for
mašna bow, ribbon
mašta imagination; **~ti** (day-) dream
mat (*šah*) mate; (*boja*) dull; ***šah ~*** checkmate
mater|inski = **majčinski**; **~nica** ANAT uterus, womb
matica queen(-bee); TECH nut
matineja matinée
matirati checkmate
matovilac BOT corn salad
matrica stencil
maza coddle; ***mamina ~*** mother's pet
mazati smear, coat, spread
mazga mule
maz|ivo lubricant; **~ut** masoot
mažuran CUL marjoram
mećava snowstorm, blizzard
med honey; ***~eni mjesec*** honey-moon
medalj|a medal; **~on** locket
meduza ZOOL jelly-fish
medvjed bear; (*bijeli*) white bear; (*igračka*) teddy-bear
međa boundary, border, frontier
među between; among
među|čin entr'acte; **~gradski** interurban; **~igra** intermezzo; **~kat** mezzanine; **~narodni** international; ***~narodno pravo*** international law; **~palublje** between decks; **~soban** mutual, reciprocal; **~tim** however; meanwhile; **~vrijeme** meantime
mehaničar mechanic, mechanician
mehanizam mechanism
mek soft (*i fig*); (*meso*) tender
meka bait
meket, **~ati** bleat
mekinje bran, pollard
mekoća softness
mekšati soften
mekušac molly; ZOOL mollusc
melem balm (*i fig*)
mene, **meni** me
meniskus MED SPORT slipped (knee) cartilage
menstru|acija menstruation; **~irati** menstruate
menza (factory, student) restaurant
mes|ar butcher; **~nat** fleshy; **~nica** butcher's; **~o** meat; (*živo*) flesh; ***kosano ~o*** minced meat; ***sušeno ~o*** smoked meat
mesing = **mjed**
mesti sweep
meta target
metak cartridge

metal metal
metar metre (*Am* meter)
meter PRINT maker-up
metež confusion, chaos
metilj VET liver-fluke
metla broom
metnuti place, put, set
metoda method
metrički metric
metropola metropolis, capital
mi we; ***meni*** me
micati (se) move, stir
mig *fig* hint, wink; **~ati** blink; **~nuti** wink
migoljiti se wiggle
migrena MED migraine
mijaukati miaow
mijeh bellows *pl*
mijenja|nje change, modification, alteration; **~ti** change, modify, alter; vary; (*novac*) exchange; **~ti se** change; vary
mijesiti knead
miješa|n mixed; **~ti** mix; blend; (*žlicom*) stir; **~ti se** interfere
mikročip micro chip
mikser CUL mixer
milicija police; militia
milijarda *Br* milliard, *Am* billion
milion million
milina pleasure
milo = **drago**
milosr|dan merciful; **~đe** mercy
milost grace, favour (*Am* favor); mercy; **~inja** alms *pl*; **~iv** graceful; merciful
milova|nje caress(es), fondling; **~ti** caress, fondle; **~ti se** caress
milja mile; MAR knot
miljenik favourite (*Am* favorite); *dijete* darling, pet
miljokaz mile-stone
mimo past; except; **~ići** pass by; overlook, neglect; **~ići se** miss each other
min|a charge; MIL mine; (*za penkalu*) refill; **~er** dynamiter; **~irati** blast, dynamite; *fig* undermine; MIL mine; **~obacač** MIL mortar; **~olovac** MIL minesweeper; **~onosac** MIL mine-layer
minsk|i: ***~o polje*** minefield
mio = **drag**
mir peace; quiet; calm; ***pustiti na ~u*** leave alone; **~an** peaceful; quiet; calm; (*nepomičan*) still
miraz dowry
miris smell; (*ugodan*) fragrance; **~an** fragrant; **~ati** smell (*i nosom*); (*ugodno*) smell sweet (fine *etc.*)
miriti (se) make peace; conciliate
mirodija spice
miroljubiv peaceful
mirova|nje rest; immobility; **~ti** rest; keep still; TECH be idle
mirovni: ***~ pregovori*** peace talks; ***~ ugovor*** peace treaty
misa mass; (*protestantska*) service

mis|ao thought; idea; **~liti** think; mean; ***nisam to ~lio*** I didn't mean that
miš mouse (*pl* mice); **~olovka** mouse-trap
mišić ANAT muscle; **~čav** muscular
mišljenje opinion, view
mit myth
miteser blackhead
miting POL (mass) rally, meeting
mit|o bribe, *Am* graft; **~iti** bribe; corrupt
mitraljez heavy machine-gun
mizeran = **bijedan**
mjed brass
mjehur bubble; (*mokraćni*) bladder; (*opeklina*) blister; ***~ sapunice*** soap bubble
mjenica bill (of exchange), draft
mjenjačnica exchange office
mjer|a measure; ***zapreminska ~a*** measure of capacity; ***~a za težinu*** measure of weight; ***površinska ~a*** superficial measure; ***po ~i*** made to measure; ***u velikoj ~i*** to a large extent
mjer|enje measurement; **~ilo** criterion; **~iti** measure; (*težinu*) weigh; **~odavan** competent, authoritative
mjesec month; (*planeta*) moon; ***mladi ~*** new moon; ***puni ~*** full moon
mjesečar sleep-walker
mjesečina moolight, moonshine
mjesečn|i, ~ik, ~o monthly
mjesni local
mjestimice in places
mjesto place (*i naselje*), spot; (*sjedalo*) seat
mjesto instead of
mješa|nac half-breed; half-caste; (*pas*) mongrel; **~vina** mixture
mješina wine-skin
mješovit mixed; ***trgovac ~om robom*** grocer; ***trgovina ~om robom*** *Br* grocer's, *Am* grocery
mještanin townsman (*pl* townspeople); *iz istog mjesta* fellow-townsman
mlad young; ***~i krumpir*** new potatoes *pl*
mlada bride
mlade|nački youthful; **~nci** bride and bridegroom; newly-weds *pl*; **~ž** young people, the youth
mladi|ca BOT shoot; **~ć** boy, young man
mlad|o young; ***imati ~e*** have young; **~olik** youthful; **~ost** youth; **~oženja** bridegroom
mlak lukewarm (*i fig*)
mlatiti (*žito*) thresh; = **tući**
mlaz jet; ***~ svjetlosti*** beam of light; ***~ni avion*** jet plane
mliječ (*riblji*) milt; (*matični*) royal jelly; **~ni** milk; ***~ni proizvodi*** dairy products; ***~na staza*** Milky Way
mlijeko milk; (*kiselo*) sour milk; (*mlačenica*) butter-milk

mlin mill
mlinac: *~ za kavu* coffee grinder
mlinar miller
mlinski: *~ kamen* millstone
mlitav limp; (*fizički*) flabby; *fig* languid
mlohav flabby
mljaskati smack one's lips
mljekar milkman; (*proizvođač*) dairyman; **~a** dairy; **~ica** milkmaid; (*muzilja*) dairymaid; **~stvo** dairy, milk-shop; (*privreda*) dairy farming, dairy industry
mlje|ti grind; ***grubo (fino) ~ven*** rough (fine) ground
mnijenje opinion; ***javno ~*** public opinion
mnog|i many; **~o** a lot, a great deal
mnogo|brojan numerous; **~stran** *fig* versatile
mnoštvo (large) crowd
množ|enje multiplication (*i razmnožavanje*); **~ina** plural; **~iti (se)** multiply
mobitel cell phone
močiti wet; (*namakati*) soak
močvara swamp; **~n** swampy
moć power, might; **~an** powerful, mighty; **~i** be able; *n pl* REL relics *pl*; ***mogu*** I can; ***ne mogu*** I cannot, I can't
mod|a fashion, vogue; ***po ~i*** fashionable
modar azure, (dark) blue
modelar model-maker; **~stvo** model-making
moderan modern, up-to-date; (*po modi*) fashionable
modistica milliner
modni fashion
modrica bruise
modus way
moguć possible; **~nost** possibility
moj my; mine; **~i** my family; ***to je ~e*** this is mine
mokar wet; damp
mokr|aća urine; ***~aćni mjehur*** bladder; **~enje** urination; **~iti** urinate
mol MUS minor
molb|a request; (*jača*) imploration; (*pismena*) application; ***podnijeti ~u*** apply; ***podnosilac ~e*** applicant
molećiv pleading
moliti ask, beg, request; (*jače*) implore; (*boga*) pray; ***~m!*** (*nakon Hvala!*) *Br* not at all, *Am* you're welcome; ***~m?*** (beg your) pardon; **~ vas** please; **~ti se** pray
molitv|a prayer; **~enik** prayer-book
molo MAR mole, pier
moljac (clothes-) moth; ***izjeden od ~a*** moth-eaten
moljakati importune
mom|ački bachelor; **~ak** lad; = **mladić**; (*neženja*) bachelor; **~čad** SPORT team; (*veslačka*) crew; **~čić** young lad
monah monk
monden *adj* fashionable; *n* playboy; jet-setter
mont|aža fitting, putting up,

instalation; (*filmska*) editing; **~ažni** prefabricated; **~er** fitter; **~irati** fit (on), put up, instal; edit
moped moped
mora nightmare
morati have to; ***moram*** I must
mor|e sea; ***na ~u*** at sea; (*ljetovanje*) at the seaside; **~eplovac** seafarer
mornar sailor; **~ica** *ratna* navy; *trgovačka* merchant navy
morsk|i sea, maritime; ***~a bolest*** sea-sickness (*bolestan od nje* sea-sick); ***~i pas*** shark
moruna *riba* sturgeon
morž ZOOL walrus
most bridge (*i kapetanski, zubarski*); ***viseći ~*** suspension bridge
mostić foot-bridge
mostobran MIL bridge-head
mošt must
motati wind (up); **~ se** hang about; meddle
motel motel
motik|a hoe; ***kopati ~om*** hoe
motka pole
motocikl motorcycle; ***prikolica ~a*** sidecar; ***voziti se na ~u*** ride a motocikl; **~ist** motor cyclist
motor engine; ***električni ~*** (electric) motor; ***vanjski ~*** (*za čamac*) outboard motor (engine)
motorn|i: ***~i čamac*** motor-boat; (*s kabinom*) cruiser; ***~a pila*** power saw
motriti watch, observe
mozaik mosaic
mozak brain; ***mali ~*** cerebellum; ***potres mozga*** brain concussion
možda perhaps, maybe
moždina: ***koštana ~*** bone marrow; ***leđna ~*** spinal cord
mračan dark
mrak dark(ness)
mramor, **~ni** marble
mrav ant; **~injak** ant-hill
mraz frost; ***ofuren od ~a*** frost-bitten
mrcvariti mangle (*i fig*), torture
mrena MED cataract
mreškati (se) ripple
mreža net (*i* SPORT); (*za tržnicu*) shopping bag, string bag; (*za ležanje*) hammock; (*internet*) net; ***cestovna ~*** road network
mrežnica (*oka*) retina
mrgoditi se sulk, pout; frown, scowl
mrijest, **~iti se** spawn
mrk frowning, sullen
mrkva carrot
mrlj|a, **~ati** spot, stain; ***masna ~a*** grease spot; ***očistiti ~u*** remove a spot
mrmljati mumble; grumble, mutter
mrsko: ***~ mi je*** I hate to …
mrša|viti lose weight; **~v** thin, *coll* skinny; *fig* meagre
mrt|av dead; **~vi** the dead;

~vac dead man
mrtvačk|i: ***~a glava*** death's head, (*s kostima*) skull and cross bones; ***~a kola*** hearse
mrt|vačnica mortuary, (*policijska*) morgue; **~vilo** lethargy; **~vorođen** still-born; **~vorođenče** still-born child
mrvi|ca crumb; **~ce** CUL bread crumbs; **~ti (se)** crumble
mrz|ak hateful; **~iti** hate; **~ovolja** surliness; **~ovoljan** surly
mržnja hatred
mucati stutter, (*i fig*) stammer
mučan painful, embarrassing; very hard
muče|nik martyr; **~nje** torture (*i fig*)
mučiti torture; *fig* torture, torment; **~ se** suffer; = **gnjaviti se**; ***muči nas glad*** we are suffering from hunger
mučn|ina nausea; ***~o mi je*** I feel sick
mućkati shake
mud|ar wise; **~rac** wise man; **~rijaš** wiseacre; **~rolija** smart stuff; **~rost** wisdom; **~rovati** speculate
mudo ANAT testicle
muha fly; (*boks*) fly weight
muk|a torture, torment; *fig* drudgery, nuisance; ***staviti na ~e*** (put to the) torture
mukao hollow, dull
mukati low, moo
muktaš sponger, parasite
mulj silt, ooze; mud
multikulturalan multicultural
mumija mummy
mumljati mumble
municija ammunition
munj|a lightning; **~evit** quick as lightning; **~evito** with lightning speed
Musliman, **≗ski** Moslem, Muslim
musti milk (*i fig*)
mušica midge; = **hir**
mušk|arac man, male; **~i** male, masculine; **~obanja** tomboy
mušterija customer
mut|an turbid, muddy; *fig* vague; **~iti** trouble
mutav tongue-tied (*i fig*)
mutiranje cracking of the voice
muraza milch-cow
muzi|cirati play, perform; **~čar** musician; **~kalije** musical supplies *pl*
muž husband; **~evan** manly, virile; **~evnost** virility; **~jak** male

N

na on; at; ~ ***koncertu*** at the concert; ***dvaput ~ dan*** twice a day; ~ ***metre*** by the metre; ~ ***to*** after this; to that
nabaciti throw in; suggest
nabasati run into
nabav|a purchase, acquisition; supply; **~ljač** supplier; buyer; **~ljati** purchase, acquire; supply
nabiti tamp, ram; (*oružje*) load; EL charge; (*koljeno*) hit, hurt, bruise
nabor fold; **~ati (se)** wrinkle
nabosti spear; **~ se** prick oneself
nabra|janje listing; **~jati** list; **~ti (se)** fold; wrinkle; shrink
nabreknuti swell
nabujati swell; *rijeka*, *tijesto* rise
nabusit gruff; hot-tempered; surly
nacifran all dressed up
nacigan frilled; shirred
nacija nation; ***Ujedinjene nacije*** the United Nations
nacional|an national; **~ist** nationalist; **~izacija** nationalization; **~izirati** nationalize
nacrt plan, design; drawing; (*dokumenta*) draft; (*tekst*) draft; ~ ***ugovora*** draft contract; ~ ***zakona*** bill
načelnik (department) head; = **gradonačelnik**
načelo = **princip**
načeti cut into; (*i fig*) broach
način way, manner; ***na taj ~*** in this way; **~iti** make; do; commit
načitan well-read
načuti hear; get wind of
naći find; **~ se** meet; find oneself; ***~ se pred*** be faced with
naćuliti: ***~ uši*** prick up one's ears (*i fig*)
nad above, over
nada hope; (*izgled*) prospect
nadahnu|će inspiration; **~ti** inspire
nadalje further
nadaren gifted, talented
nadasve above all; first of all
nadati se hope
nadbiskup archbishop
nadčovje|čan superhuman; **~k** superman
nadglasati outvote
nadgledati inspect, control, supervise
nadglednik overseer; foreman; inspector
nadgrobni: ***~ spomenik*** tombstone
nadimak nickname; (*od milja*) pet name
nadira|nje advance, invasion, penetration; **~ti** advance, invade, penetrate

nadje|nuti CUL stuff; **~v** CUL stuffing
nadlaktica upper arm
nadlež|an competent; **~nost** competence
nadmašiti surpass; excel
nadmeta|ti se compete; (*na dražbi*) (out)bid; ***javno ~nje*** invitation of tenders; bidding
nadmoć|an superior; **~nost** superiority
nadmudri|ti outwit; **~vati se** quibble
nadnaravan supernatural
nadni|ca (day's) wage; **~čar** labourer
nadobudan promising; ambitious; naive
nadoći rise
nadograd|iti add a wing (storey etc.); **~nja** wing; addition
nadoknada compensation
nadovezati tie on; add
nadraž|aj stimulus; irritation; **~iti** chafe, irritate
nadreali|st, **~stički** surrealist; **~zam** surrealism
nadstojnik caretaker
nadu|t bloated, inflated; *fig* arrogant; **~ti** inflate, bloat; **~ti se** become bloated; **~tost** MED flatulence; *fig* arrogance
nadvikivati se try to outshout one another
nadvisiti surpass in height, be higher
nadvladati overcome
nadvožnjak overpass
nadzirati inspect, control, supervise
nadzor inspection, control, supervision; **~ni** supervisory; **~nik** supervisor, inspector
nadživjeti outlive
naft|a petroleum, *coll* oil; **~alin** naphthalene, mothballs *pl*; **~ovod** oil pipeline
nag naked, nude; bare
nagađa|nje guesswork; **~ti** guess
nagao sudden; rash; *narav* short-tempered
nagaziti step on
nagi|b inclination; **~njati** incline; = **nagnuti**
naglas|ak stress; *strani* accent; **~iti** stress (*i fig*)
naglavce head foremost; *fig* headlong; upside down; ***skočiti ~*** dive
naglo rashly; **~st** rashness; hot temper
nagluh hard of hearing
nagnut inclined, tilted; **~i** incline, tilt; **~i (se)** incline, tilt; lean over
nagod|ba settlement, agreement; **~iti se** come to terms, reach an agreement
nagomila(va)ti (se) accumulate
nagon instict; impulse; ***po ~u*** instinctively
nagovarati persuade; urge
nagovijestiti announce; hint (at); herald
nagovještaj announcement;

hint
nagovor persuasion; address; **~iti** persuade; *osloviti* address
nagrad|a reward; (*novčana*) prize; **~iti** reward
nagradni: **~ *natječaj*** prize competition
nagrditi make ugly
nagrizati CHEM corrode
nagrnuti crowd into; rush forward
nahoče foundling
nahraniti feed
nahuškati egg on, urge
naići: **~ *na*** come across
naime that is to say; namely
naivan simple-minded, ingenuous; naïve
naivčina *sl* sucker
naizmjence by turns
najam rent; hire; **~nina** rent (-al)
najaviti announce; **~ se** announce one's visit
najbolj|e best; ***sve* ~e** best wishes; **~i** the best
najdalje farthest, furthest
najdraži dearest; favourite
najednom suddenly, at once
najesti se eat one's fill; have enough
najezda invasion
naježiti se get goose-pimples (goose-flesh)
najgor|e worst; **~i** the worst; **~nji** the uppermost, the topmost
najkasnije: **~ *za tjedan*** in a week at the latest
najlon nylon; **~ke** nylons *pl*
najmanje the least; at the least; ***ni* ~** not at all
najmiti take on lease; hire, rent
najmodavac lessor
najmoprimac lessee
najniži bottom(most), lowest
najnoviji the latest
najprije first
najradije: **~ *bih*** I should like best to
najuriti throw out
najviše most; **~ *sat*** one hour at the most
nakaz|a monster; freak; **~an** monstrous; deformed; **~nost** monstrosity; deformity
nakit jewellery
naklad|a: ***u* ~i** published by; **~nik** publisher
naklapati gossip, tattle
naklon bow; **~ost** favour; inclination
naknad|a compensation; **~a *štete*** indemnity, damages *pl*; **~iti** compensate, make up for
naknadno subsequently, later on
nakon after
nakostriješiti se bristle up
nakovanj anvil
nakrcati load; pack
nakr|enuti, **~iviti** tilt, cock, set awry
nakup|ac buyer; **~iti (se)** accumulate, amass
nakupovati buy

nalaz finding
nalazište: ~ ***ugljena*** coal deposit; coal field
nalaz|iti se be situated; **~nik** finder
nalegnuti lean heavily against
nalet onrush; **~jeti** crash into
naličje reverse (side)
nalijepiti stick on
naliti pour
nalivpero fountain pen
nalo|g, ~žiti order, decree
naljepnica sticker
nama (to) us
namet rate; **~nuti** impose; **~nuti se** intrude; *pitanje* arise; **~ljiv** intrusive; **~ljivac** intruder; busybody; **~nik** parasite
namignuti wink (at)
namijeniti design, intend; set apart
namirisati (se) perfume (oneself)
namiriti settle
namirnice provisions *pl*
namjena purpose
namjer|a intention; **~avati** intend; **~no** on purpose
namjestiti set; fix, mount; (*sobu*) furnish; (*zaposliti*) employ; **~ se** take a job
namješt|aj furniture; **~en** employed; = **usiljen**; ***sve je to ~eno*** *fig* it's all rigged; **~enik** employee; **~enje** employment, job
namočiti dip, wet; soak
namotati wind up
namrgoditi se frown
namrštiti se frown
nanijeti deposit; wash ashore; (*na kartu*) plot
naniže downward(s)
nanos deposit, drift
nanula wooden-soled sandal
nanjušiti smell; *fig* find out
naoblač|en overcast, cloudy; **~iti se** become overcast (cloudy)
naobra|zba education; schooling; **~ziti se** educate; **~žen** educated
naočale glasses *pl*, spectacles *pl*; *za sunce* sun glasses; (*zaštitne*) goggles
naočarka ZOOL cobra
naočigled svih in sight of everybody
naoko seemingly
naokolo around; ***svuda ~*** all around
naopak(o) upside-down; reverse(ly); wrong; inside-out
naoruža|n armed; **~nje** weapons *pl*; armament; **~ti (se)** arm
napad attack; (*zračni*) (air) raid; **~ač** attacker; aggressor; **~aj** MED attack, seizure; **~an** striking, conspicuous; **~ati** attack
napakostiti spite
napamet by heart
napast temptation; ***dovesti u ~*** tempt
napasti attack
napastovati molest
napatiti se suffer much

naperiti aim (at)
napet tight; (*puška*) cocked; (FILM) gripping; (*živci*) tense; **~i** make tight, tigten; cock; tense; **~i se** become tight, become tense; **~o** intently; **~ost** tightness; tension, suspense
napipati touch; find by groping
napisati write
napit|ak drink; **~i se** drink one's fill; get drunk
naplakati se cry one's heart out
naplat|a charge; collection; **~iti** charge; collect
napoj (i *fig*) slops *pl*
napoj|iti (*stoku*) water; **~nica** tip
napokon finally
napola half
napomen|a, ~uti remark, note
napon EL tension; ***visoki ~*** high tension
napor effort; **~an** strenuous, gruelling, exhausting
naprasan *smrt* sudden
naprasit short-tempered, hot-headed
naprašiti powder
naprava device, contraption; = **sprava**
napraviti do, make, commit
naprečac off-hand; at once
napred|ak progress; growth, development; **~an** progressive; **~ovanje** progress; MIL advance; (*u službi*) promotion; **~ovati** make progress, get on; grow, develop; MIL advance; (*u službi*) be promoted; (*u rastu*) thrive
naprezati exert, strain; **~ se** exert oneself, make efforts, struggle
naprijed forward, ahead; ***~!*** come in!
naprotiv on the contrary
naprstak thimble
napršnjak (*dječji*) bib; (*za jelo*) feeder
naprt|iti burden with shoulder; **~njača** knapsack
napuhati inflate
napuk|ao cracked; **~lina, ~nuti** crack
napumpati pump up
napuniti fill (up); stuff
napu|stiti abandon, give up, withdraw (from); **~štanje** abandonement, withdrawal
naramenice *pl Br* braces *pl*, *Am* suspenders *pl*
naranča, ~st orange
nara|sti grow (up); **~štaj** generation
narav nature; ***u ~i*** in kind; **~an** natural; **~no** of course
narcisa BOT daffodil
nared|ba, ~iti order; decree; **~nik** sergeant
narezak: ***hladni ~*** cold meats *pl*, cold cuts *pl*
narječje dialect
narko|man drug addict; **~manija** drug addiction; **~tizirati** narcotize
naročit special; **~o** specially

narod people, nation; **~an** national; ***~ne pjesme*** folk songs; country songs; **~nost** nationality
naručaj armful; = **zagrljaj**
naru|čen on order, ordered; **~čiti** order; (*portre*) commission; **~džba** order; commission; ***otkazati ~džbu*** cancel an order; **~džbenica** order form
narukvica bracelet
narušiti disturb
nas us
nasadi *pl* floral displays *pl*, gardens *pl*, beds *pl*; **~ti** (*kokoš*) set; (*alat*) helve
nasamariti fool, cheat, deceive; **~ se** miscalculate, overreach oneself, be duped
nasamo in private; ***govoriti ~*** have a word in private
nase|liti (se) settle; ***gusto ~ljen*** densely populated; **~lje** settlement; (*stambeno*) housing estate, housing development; **~ljenik** settler
nasil|an violent; **~nik** bully; **~no** by force; violently
nasilje violence
nasip dike, (i RLW) embankment
nasititi se eat enough, fill one's stomach
nasjesti be duped, take the bait
naslada, ~đivati se delight, relish, thrill (to)
naslaga layer
naslijediti inherit, (*nekoga*) succeed
naslikati paint
naslon back; support; **~niti (se)** lean against; **~njač** arm-chair
naslov title, heading; (*novinski*) headline; ***~na strana*** title page
naslućivati have a presentiment; (*zlo*) forebode
nasljed|an hereditary (i MED), inheritable; **~nica** heiress; **~nik** heir, inheritor; (*prijestolja, dužnosti*) successor; **~stvo** inheritance; ***ostaviti u ~stvo*** leave by will; *fig* bequeathe
nasmij|ati make one laugh; **~ati se** laugh; **~ešiti se** smile
nasred in the middle of
nasr|nuti rush (at); **~taj** onrush; **~tljiv** aggressive
nastamba quarters *pl*
nasta|niti accommodate, put up; **~niti se** find quarters; settle; **~njen** occupied; populated; ***~njen u*** resident of
nasta|ti begin, originate; come, fall, set in; **~nak** beginnings *pl*, origin, rise
nastav|a instruction, teaching; ***sutra nema ~e*** there are no classes tomorrow
nastav|ak continuation; (*prekinutog*) resumption; (*romana*) instalment; (*produžetak*) extension; GRAM ending, suffix; **~iti** go on,

continue carry on, resume; **~it će se** to be continued
nastavnik teacher, instructor, tutor
nastavno: **~ osoblje** teaching staff
nastoja|nje endeavour (*Am* -vor), effort; **~ti** endeavour, make efforts, try
nastradati have (meet with) an accident
nastran eccentric, peculiar, odd; deviating; **~ost** eccentricity, oddity; deviation
nastup appearance; (*držanje*) bearing, poise; **~ službe** taking up a post; **~ati** appear; bear oneself, come on; take up; MIL advance; (*noć, razdoblje*) set in
nasukati (se) run aground *i fig* strand
nasumce at random
nasuprot opposite
nasuti lay, cover; fill up (*holes*)
naš our, ours; **~i** our group; our people; our troups; **to je ~e** this is ours
naširoko far and wide; = **opširno**
naškoditi harm, damage, injure; cause (do) harm
nat (*čarapa*) seam; **čarape bez ~a** seamless stockings
nataknuti put on; stick (on); pierce (with)
natalitet birth rate
natapa|nje impregnation; = **navodnjavanje**, **namakanje**; **~ti** irrigate
natašte on an empty stomach
nate|čen swollen; **~ći** swell
nategnuti tighten; *fig* stretch
natenane leisurely; in great detail
natezati se romp, scuffle; *fig* wrangle
natikača mule, scuff
natjeca|nje competition; SPORT contest, event; **~telj** competitor; contestant; (*za namještenje*) applicant; COM tenderer; **~ti se** compete; apply (for a job); COM tender (for a contract)
natječaj competition; = **nadmetanje**; **nagradni ~** prize competition; **raspisuje se ~ za** applications (COM tenders) are invited for
natjerati compel, force; **~ na smijeh** make one laugh
natmur|en sullen, gloomy; (*dan, nebo*) overcast; **~iti se** become sullen (overcast)
natovariti load; pile high; *fig* burden with
natpis inscription; (*firma*) sign(board)
natprosječan above-the-average
natra|g back, backwards; **~ške** backwards
natražnja|čki, **~k** reactionary
natrij CHEM sodium
natrpati stuff, cram
natucati speak a little
natući = **nabiti**

natuknuti hint (at)
natur|a: ***u ~i*** in kind
naučan scientific; research; ***~ni rad*** research work; ***~ni radnik*** research worker; = **naviknut**; **~enjak** scholar, scientist, learned man; **~iti** learn; (*drugoga*) teach, instruct; **~nik** apprentice
nauk apprenticeship; **~a** science
nauljiti oil
naušnica ear-ring; (*knipsa*) ear-clip
nava|la attack; *fig* crush, rush; ***vođa ~le*** SPORT centre forward; **~ljivati** attack, urge, pester
navečer in the evening; ***danas ~*** tonight; ***sutra ~*** tomorrow night
navesti induce, make; list, specify; quote
navija|č SPORT supporter; **~ti** wind (up); SPORT root for, support
navijestiti announce
navik|a habit; custom; **~nuti** accustom; **~nuti se** become accustomed to, get used to **~kao** used to, accustomed to
naviše upwards (of)
navlaka cover
navod allegation, statement; quotation; **~iti** quote, state **~ni** alleged; reputed; **~nici** quotation marks; **~no** allegedly; reputedly
navodnjava|nje irrigation; **~ti** irrigate
navođenje inducement; quotation
navoj EL coil
navorati (se) wrinkle
navratiti drop in, look in
navrat time, occasion; ***~ nanos*** helter-skelter; ***u više ~a*** several times
navršiti: ***~la je 18 god*** she is turned 18
navući pull on, slip over; *fig* incur; MED catch
nazad|ak, **~ovati** decline; **~an** backward; reactionary
nazdrav|iti toast; drink to one's health; ***~lje!*** here's to you!
nazepsti catch a chill (cold)
naziv name; term; **~ati** name, call, denominate, **~nik** MATH denominator
naznačiti mark, denote
nazoč|an present; **~nost** presence
nazor idea, view, opinion
nazovi would-be, pseudo-
nazvati call, name, term; (*telefonski*) call, ring up
nažalost unfortunately
naždarati se cram oneself
nažuljati make sore, chafe; **~ se** get sores, get blisters
ne no; not; ***~ mići se*** don't move
neafirmiran unestablished
neaktivan inactive
neartikularan inarticulate
nebes|a heavens (*pl*); **~ki** heavenly

nebitan unessential
nebo sky; REL heaven; ***pod vedrim ~m*** in the open, open-air, out-door(s); **~der** sky-scraper
nebriga lack of care
nebrojen countless
nečastan dishonourable
nečiji someone's
nečist dirty; impure; filthy; **~oća** dirtiness; impurity; filth
nečitljiv illegible
nečovječan inhuman
nečujan inaudible
nečuven unheard-of, extraordinary
nećak nephew; **~inja** niece
nećka|nje reluctance; **~ti se** be reluctant
nedaća set back, adversity, misfortune
nedaleko nearby; **~ *od*** not far from
nedarovit untalented
nedav|an recent; **~no** not long ago; recently
nedisciplina indiscipline
nedjelo misdeed, crime
nedjelj|a Sunday; weekend; week; ***dvaput ~no*** twice a week; **~om** on Sundays
nedjeljiv indivisible
nedobronamjeran malevolent
nedogledan immense, boundless
nedokučiv *fig* inscrutable, inconceivable
nedolazak failure to come, absence
nedoličan unseemly, indecent
nedonošče abortive child; *fig* abortion
nedopu|stiv inadmissible; **~šten** prohibited, forbidden
nedorađen lacking finish, unfinished
nedorastao immature
nedorečen under-stated; **~ost** understatement
nedosljed|an inconsistent; **~nost** inconsistency
nedosta|jati lack; **~tak** lack; shortcoming, drawback, defect; ***u ~tku*** for want of
nedostatan insufficient, inadequate
nedostižan unattainable, out of reach; matchless
nedostojan unworthy
nedotjeran badly groomed; unfinished
nedoumica dilemma
nedovoljan insufficient, inadequate
nedovršen unfinished, incomplete
nedozreo immature; unripe
nedozvoljen forbidden, prohibited
nedruštven unsociable
nedužan innocent, guiltless
nedvojben certain, beyond doubt
nega|cija negation; **~tivan** negative
negdje somewhere
negirati negate, negative, re-

ject
nego than; ***tko ~ ti?*** who but you?
negodova|nje disapproval (of), displeasure (at); **~ti** express one's disapproval
negostoljubiv inhospitable
nehaj indolence, indifference, lack of interest
nehoti|ce by accident; **~čan** unintentional
neimaština want, poverty
neimenovan unnamed
neiscrpan inexhaustible
neishranjen undernourished; **~ost** malnutrition
neiskorišten unused
neiskorjenjiv ineradicable
neiskren insincere, false
neiskusan inexperienced
neispavan in need of sleep
neisplaćen unpaid
neisprav|an faulty, out of order; false, incorrect; improper; **~nost** fault, malfunction
neispunjen unfulfilled; unfilled; blank, unused
neistin|a untruth; **~it** untrue
neistražen unexplored, uninvestigated
neizbjež|an inevitable; **~nost** inevitability
neizbrisiv indelible
neizdržljiv lacking stamina; unbearable, intolerable
neizgrađen *fig* immature, undeveloped
neizlječiv incurable
neizmijenjen unchanged, unaltered
neizmjeran immense, infinite
neizostavno infallibly
neizgrađen rough, crude, unrefined
neizravan indirect
neizreciv unspeakable, unutterable
neizvediv impracticable, unfeasible
neizvjes|tan dubious, uncertain; **~nost** dubiousness, uncertainty; suspense
neizvježban untrained, unpracticed
nejasan not clear, indistinct; *fig* vague
nejednak unequal; uneven; **~ost** inequality
neka: **~ *uđu*** let them come in
nekada formerly, long ago, in old days, once upon a time; **~šnji** former; ancient
nekako somehow
nekamo somewhere
nekažnjen unpunished; **~o** with impunity
neki a, some, a certain, any
neknjiževan non-standard
nekoliko a few, some, any, several
nekorektan incorrect
nekoristan useless
nekretnine real estate, immovable property
nekuda somewhere, anywhere
nekulturan uncultured
nekvalificiran unskilled, un-

qualified
nekvalitetan inferior
nelagod|an uneasy; **~nost** uneasiness
nelogič|an illogical; **~nost** lack of logic
nelojalan disloyal
neljubazan unkind
neljudski inhuman
neman monster
nemar indolence; **~an** indolent
nem|ati lack; be without; ***~a vode*** there is no water; ***~a na čemu*** = **molim**
nemilosrdan merciless, pitiless
nemilost disfavour (*Am* -vor); ***u ~i*** out of favour
nemio deplorable
nemir unrest, restlessness; (*duševni*) anxiety; **~i** riots; **~an** restless; *fig* troubled
nemoć helplessness; infirmity; **~an** helpless; feeble
nemoguć impossible
nemoj do not; don't
nemoral immorality; **~an** immoral
nenadmašiv matchless
nenadoknadiv irretrievable
nenametljiv unobtrusive
nenamjeran unintentional
nenastanjen uninhabited
nenormalan abnormal
neobvezan not obligatory; (*šk. predmet*) *Br* optional, *Am* elective
neobič|an unusual; ***~no brz*** remarkably (*ili* very) fast
neobjašnjiv inexplicable
neobljubljen unpopular, disliked
neoboriv irrefutable
neobrađen uncultivated, waste; crude
neobrazovan uneducated
neobuzdan unrestrained
neobziran inconsiderate
neočekivan unexpected
neodgojen ill-mannered, rude; **~ost** bad manners
neodgovor|an irresponsible; **~nost** irresponsibility
neodložan urgent, pressing
neodluč|an indecisive; ***~an rezultat*** SPORT draw; ***igrati ~no*** SPORT draw; **~nost** indecision
neodređen indefinite; vague
neodrživ untenable
neograničen unlimited; absolute
neokaljan spotless
neokretan awkward; unresourceful
neokrnjen whole, intact
neonska reklama neon light
neopasan harmless; safe
neopažen unnoticed
neophodan indispensable
neopisiv indescribable
neopravdan unjustified
neopredijeljen uncommitted
neoprezan incautious
neoprostiv unpardonable, inexcusable
neorganski inorganic
neosiguran uninsured; not secured

neosjet|an imperceptible; **~ljiv** unfeeling; numb; **~ljivost** lack of feeling; numbness
neoskvrnjen inviolate
neosnovan groundless
neosporan indisputable
neostvariv unrealizable, impracticable
neosvojiv unconquerable
neotesan boorish, churlish, ill-mannered
neotporan delicate; having low resistance
neotuđiv inalienable
neovlašten unauthorized
neozbilj|an not serious, frivolous; **~nost** frivolity, levity
neoženjen single
neparan odd
nepatvoren genuine, true
nepažljiv inattentive; absent-minded; (*neobziran*) inconsiderate; **~ost** inattention; absence of mind; lack of consideration
nepce palate
nepismen illiterate (i kao *n*); **~ost** illiteracy
neplaćanje non-payment
neplodan fruitless
nepobitan irrefutable
nepobjediv invincible
nepodmitljiv incorruptible
nepodnosiv unbearable, intolerable
nepoduzet|an unenterprising; **~nost** lack of enterprise
nepogoda bad weather, storm; **~n** unsuitable
nepogrešiv infallible
nepokolebljiv unshakable, imperturbable
nepokoran insubordinate, disobedient
nepokretan motionless, still; fixed; *fig* unenterprising
nepomirljiv implacable
nepopravljiv irreparable; (*osoba*) incorrigible
nepopularan unpopular
nepopunjen unfilled, vacant; ***~o radno mjesto*** vacancy
nepopustljiv unyielding; inexorable; relentless
neposlu|h disobedience; **~šan** disobedient
neposredan direct, immediate
nepostojan inconstant
nepostojeći non-existing
nepošt|en dishonest; unfair; **~enje** dishonesty; **~ivanje** disrespect; disregard
nepotpun incomplete
nepotreban unnecassary
nepouzdan unreliable
nepovjer|enje distrust **~ljiv** distrustful
nepovoljan unfavourable
nepovrediv inviolable
nepozna|t unknown; **~vanje** ignorance (of)
nepoželjan undesirable
nepraktičan unpractical
neprav|da injustice; **~edan** unjust
nepravilan irregular (i GRAM); incorrect

nepredviđen unforeseen
nepregledan immense, vast; (*tekst*) badly laid out
neprekidan continuous, incessant, uninterrupted, unbroken
neprelazan GRAM intransitive
neprestano continuously, incessantly
nepresušan in exhaustible
nepretenciozan unpretentious
neprihvatljiv unacceptable
neprijatan unpleasant, disagreeable; embarassing
neprijatelj enemy; **~ski** hostile, unfriendly, enemy; **~stvo** hostility, enmity
neprijazan unkind, unfriendly
neprikladan unsuitable
neprilika trouble
neprimjetan unobservable, imperceptible
neprirodan unnatural; (*usiljen*) affected
nepristoj|an impolite; indecent, dirty; **~nost** impoliteness; indecency
nepristran impartial
nepristupačan inaccessible; (*osoba*) aloof
neprobojan bullet-proof; *fig* impenetrable
neprocjenjiv priceless; *fig* invaluable
neprohodan impassable, impenetrable, rugged
neprolazan (ever-)lasting, imperishable
neprometan quiet
nepromišljen thoughtless, rash
nepromjenljiv unchangeable, fixed
nepromočiv waterproof
nepropisan irregular, contrary to regulations
nepropustan air-tight, water-tight, hermetic
neprovediv impracticable
neproziran opaque, non-transparent
nepušač non-smoker; ***kupe za ~e*** non-smoking compartment
nerad idleness; **~o** unwillingly, reluctantly
neranjiv invulnerable
neraspolože|n in a bad mood; **~nje** bad mood
nerast boar
nerastopiv insoluble
neravan uneven
nerazborit unwise
nerazderiv tear-proof
nerazdvojan inseparable
nerazgovjetan unintelligible
nerazjašnjiv inexplicable
nerazoriv indestructible
nerazrješiv insoluble
nerazum|an unreasonable, not sensible; **~ijevanje** lack of understanding; **~ljiv** incomprehensible; unintelligible
nerazvijen undeveloped (i *photo*); ***~e zemlje*** underdeveloped countries; **~ost** underdevelopment

nerđajući rust-proof; **~ čelik** stainless steel
nerealan unrealistic
nered disorder; **~i** riots, rioting
neredovit irregular
nerentabilan unprofitable
nerješiv insoluble
nerodica crop failure
nerotkinja barren woman
nerv|čik high-strung person; **~irati** make nervous; annoy; **~oza** nervousness; **~ozan** nervous
nesagoriv incombustible
nesamostalan dependent on others, lacking independence
nesanica MED insomnia
nesavjestan unconscientious, perfunctory
nesavladiv unsurmountable; invincible
nesavršen imperfect; **~ost** imperfection
nesebič|an unselfish; **~nost** unselfishness
neseser dressing case
neshva|ćanje lack of understanding; **~ćen** misunderstood; unrecognized; **~tljiv** incomprehensible, inexplicable
nesiguran unsafe; unsteady; uncertain
nesklad disharmony; discrepancy; disproportion; **~an** disharmonious, discrepant; disproportionate
nesklon disinclined, reluctant
neskroman immodest
neslaganje disagreement
neslan unsalted, saltless
neslavan inglorious, infamous
nesloga discord
neslomljiv unbreakable
nesložan discordant
neslućen undreamt of, unsuspected
nesmiljen merciless
nesmisao absurdity
nesmotren = **nepažljiv**
nesnalažljiv unresourceful
nesnosan unbearable, intolerable
nesnošljiv intolerant
nesolidan unreliable; inferior
nespavanje lack of sleep; insomnia
nespojiv incompatible
nesporazum misunderstanding
nesposob|an incompetent; incapable; MIL a reject; ***proglasiti ~nim*** MIL reject
nespreman unready
nespretan clumsy
nesrazmjer disproportion; **~an** disproportionate
nesre|ća bad luck; unhappiness; ***prometna ~ća*** road accident; **~tan** unlucky; unhappy; ***~tan slučaj*** accident; **~tnik** poor man, wretch
nesređen unsettled, unstable, unbalanced
nestalan inconstant, unsta-

ble, fluctuating
nesta|nak disappearance; **~ti** disappear; **~li** missing
nestaš|an playful; **~luk** prank
nestašica shortage
nesti lay eggs
nestrpljiv impatient; **~ost** impatience
nestručan inexpert; unskilled; non-technical; **~njak** non-expert, layman
nesuđen not destined
nesuglasica disagreement
nesumnjiv doubtless, undoubted
nesuvisao incoherent
nesuvremen old-fashioned
nesvijest unconsciousness, swoon; ***u ~i*** unconscious; **~an** unaware
neškodljiv harmless
neškolovan uneducated; untrained
nešto something
netaktičan tactless
netaknut untouched, intact
netko somebody, someone
neto COM net
netočan incorrect, inaccurate
netolerantan intolerant
neubrojiv not sound of mind
neučtiv impolite
neudata single
neudoban uncomfortable
neuglađen unpolished, rough-mannered
neugledan plain, drab
neugodan unpleasant, disagreeable; embarassing
neugodnost trouble; ***imati ~i*** have trouble; be embarrassed
neujednačen uneven
neuk uneducated, ignorant
neukrotiv untamable
neukus bad taste; **~an** tasteless
neuljepšan plain, unvarnished
neuljudan impolite
neumjeće lack of skill
neumjeren immoderate
neumjes|tan, **~no** out of place; **~nost** impropriety
neumoljiv inexorable, merciless
neumoran tireless, indefatigable
neumrli deathless; immortal
neuništiv indestructible
neunosan unprofitable
neupotrebljiv unserviceable, useless, unsuitable
neupućen uninitiated; uninformed
neuputan inadvisable
neuravnotežen unbalanced; **~ost** lack of balance
neuredan untidy
neusiljen unaffected
neuslužan unobliging
neuspje|h failure; setback; **~šan** unsuccessful
neusporediv incomparable
neustrašiv fearless
neutaživ unquenchable
neutješan disconsolate, broken-hearted

neutrt untrodden
neuvažavanje disregard
neuviđavan inconsiderate
nevažeći invalid
neveseo cheerless
nevezan (*razgovor*) informal
nevidljiv invisible
nevin innocent; virgin; ***proglasiti ~im*** JUR acquit; **~ost** innocence; (*spolna*) virginity
nevjeran unfaithful
nevjerojat|an incredible; **~no** incredibly
nevjesta bride; (*snaha*) daughter-in-law; (*bratova žena*) sister-in-law
nevješt unskilled
nevolja trouble
nevrijeme bad weather; storm
nezaboravan unforgettable
nezadovolj|an dissatisfied, discontented; **~nik** malcontent; **~stvo** dissatisfaction, discontent
nezahval|an ungrateful; *fig* thankless; **~nost** ingratitude
nezainteresiran not interested; **~ost** lack of interest
nezakonit illegal; (*dijete*) illegitimate
nezamjenljiv irreplaceable
nezanimljiv uninteresting
nezapaljiv nonflammable, uninflammable
nezapamćen unprecedented
nezapažen unnoticed
nezaposlen unemployed, out of work; **~ost** unemployment
nezasitan insatiable, greedy
nezavidan unenviable
nezavis|an independent; **~nost** independence
nezbrinut unprovided (for)
nezdrav unhealthy
nezgoda accident; trouble; **~n** inconvenient; embarrassing; (*osoba*) difficult; ***dovesti u ~n položaj*** embarrass
nezgrapan ungainly, awkward
nezna|lica ignorant person, ignoramus; **~nje** ignorance
neznatan negligible, insignificant
nezreo unripe; *fig* immature
neženja bachelor
ni: **~ ... ~** neither ... nor; ***~ ti nisi došao*** you did not come either
ničice prostrate
ničij|i nobody's, no one's; (anybody's, any one's); ***~a zemlja*** no man's land
nigdje nowhere (anywhere)
nijans|a shade, nuance; **~irati** shade
nijedan none, (*od dvojice*) neither (any, either)
nijednom not once
nijeka|nje denial, mute; **~ti** deny; negate
nijem dumb, mute; *fig* speechless, dumbfounded
Nijemac German
nikada never (ever)
nikakav no, none, no one

(any)
nikako not at all, in no way (at all, in any way)
nikamo, **nikuda** nowhere (anywhere)
niknuti spring up (*i fig*)
nilski konj ZOOL hippopotamus, *coll* hippo
nimalo not a bit (a bit)
niotkuda from nowhere
nipošto = **nikako**
nisko low; (*podlo*) basely; **~st** low height; baseness
nišan (*puške*) sight; target; **~iti** (take) aim
ništa nothing (anything); ***~ za to*** never mind; **~rija** good-for-nothing; scoundrel; **~van** trifling
nit thread
nitko nobody, no one (anybody, any one)
nitkov scoundrel, villain
nivelirati level
niz row, series; **~ati** produce in succession; (*bisere*) string (up); **~ati se** follow each other
nizak low; (*osoba*) short; (*podao*) base, mean
nizbrd|ica (downward) slope; **~o** downhill
nizina plain, lowlands *pl*
Nizozemsk|a the Netherlands, Holland; **≗i** Dutch
nizvodno downstream
no but; ***~?*** well?
noć night; ***preko ~i*** overnight; **~u** at night, by night; ***laku ~!*** good night!
noć|as this night; **~iti** spend the night
noć|ni: ***~ni čuvar*** night watchman; ***~ni lokal*** night spot; night club; ***~na košulja*** night shirt; ***~na posuda*** chamber pot; ***~ni ormarić*** bedside cabinet
noga leg; (*stopalo*) foot; (*stola*) leg; ***s krivim („o") ~ma*** bow-legged; ***s „o" ~ma*** knock-kneed
noga|ri trestle; tripod; **~vica** trouser leg
nogomet football, *coll* soccer; **~aš** footballer
noj ostrich
nokat (finger) nail
nokaut SPORT knock-out; **~irati** SPORT knock out
norm|a norm; (*radna*) quota (*i fig*); **~irati** set quotas; standardize
nos nose
nosač (*prtljage*) porter; TECH support; ARCHIT girder; ***~ aviona*** aircraft carrier
nosi|la stretcher; **~lac** bearer, (*nagrade*) holder; **~ti** carry; (*odjeću*) wear; TECH support; **~vost** carrying capacity
nosorog ZOOL rhinoceros
nošnja costume; ***narodna ~*** folk costume
nota MUS POL note
notes memo-pad
notoran notorious
nov new; *fig* novel; ***~ novcat*** brand new

novac money; ***kovani ~*** coins
novajlija tiro (tyro), beginner, new hand (at)
novč|an monetary, financial; ***~ana uputnica*** money order; **~anica** (bank-)note, *Am* i bill; **~anik** purse; wallet; **~ić** (small) coin, *fig* penny
novela short story
novembar November
novin|ar journalist; **~arski** journalistic; **~arstvo** journalism; **~e** newspaper, *coll* paper
novitet novelty
novogradnja newly-built house; house under construction; *Br* block of flats, *Am* apartment house
novoizabran newly elected
novorođenče new-born child
novost news *pl*; novelty
novotarija novelty, *derog* new-fangled thing
nozdrva nostril
nož knife; ***ubosti ~em*** stab, knife
nudi|st nudist, naturist; **~zam** nudism
nuditi offer, bid
nukati encourage, urge
nuklearan nuclear
nul|a zero; *fig* nobody; ***10 ispod ~e*** ten below (zero); SPORT ***2 : 0*** two to nil
numerirati number
nusprostorije (usual) offices
nusproizvod by-product
nutkati press, urge
nuzzarada incidental earnings on the side
nuž|an necessary; **~da**, **~nost** necessity

NJ

njakati bray, hee-haw
njedra bosom, breast
njega nursing; care
njegov his; its
njegovat|elj(ica) nurse; **~i** nurse; look after; *fig* cultivate
Njem|ačka Germany; **&ački** German; **~ica** German
njezin her, hers; **~i** her family; ***to je ~o*** this is hers
njež|an tender; delicate; **~nost** tenderness; delicacy
njiha|lo PHYS pendulum; **~ljka** swing; **~ti (se)** swing, rock, sway
njihov their, theirs; **~i** their family; ***to je ~o*** this is theirs
njiva (cultivated) field
nju her
njuh sense of smell
njušiti smell, sniff
njuška muzzle, *coll* nose; **~lo** Nosy Parker; **~ti** *fig* nose (after, for)

O

o! oh!
o about
oaza oasis
oba both
obad gad-fly
obal|a (*rijeke*) bank; (*mora*) shore; **~ni** coastal
obamr|ijeti become numb, become lethargic; **~lost** numbness, lethargy
obao round; spherical
obara|č trigger; **~ti** = **oboriti**
obas|ipati, **~uti** shower, heap, flood
obasjati light up
obavez|a obligation, engagement; ***izvršiti ~u*** meet one's obligation; **~an** obliged; **~ati** put under obligation; **~ati se** oblige oneself, commit oneself
obavijati wind round
obavijest information; **~iti** inform, notify, let know
obav|iti, **~ljati** do, perform, carry out; see to
obavještaj|ac intelligence officer; ***~na služba*** intelligence service
obaz|irati, **~reti se** take into consideration; look around; ***ne ~irati se na*** disregard; **~riv** considerate
obdanište (day) nursery, kindergarten
obdukcija post mortem
obeća|nje promise; ***održati*** (***prekršiti***) ***~nje*** keep (break) a promise; **~(va)ti** promise; *fig* show promise; ***koji mnogo ~va*** promising
obeshrabriti discourage
obezbjediti = **osigurati**
obeščastiti dishonour; (*djevojku*) ravish
običaj custom; = **navika**
obič|an ordinary, common; usual; **~no** usually
obići = **obilaziti**
obijeliti whitewash
obijest wantonness; **~an** wanton, spoilt
obilan abundant
obilaz|ak tour, round; **~iti** go round; look up; make a tour of, tour; make one's rounds
obilovati abound (in)
obilje abundance
obiljež|iti mark; **~je** mark, stamp
obim = **opseg**, **obujam**
obistiniti se = **ostvariti se**
obiti (*bravu*) pick
obitelj, **~ski** family
objasniti explain
objašnj|avanje wrangle, scene; **~avati se** wrangle, make a scene; **~enje** explanation
objav|ljivanje announcement; proclamation; publication; release; **~iti** an-

nounce; proclaim; (*knjigu*) publish; (*podatke*) release
obje both
objekt object (i GRAM); (*građevina*) facility, plant, building, project; (*plovni*) vessel, craft
objektiv OPT objective; **~an** objective; **~nost** objectivity
objelodaniti make public, disclose
objeručke wholeheartedly, eagerly
objesiti hang (up); (*čovjeka*) hang; **~ se** hang oneself
obla|čan cloudy, overcast; **~k** cloud; ***olujni ~k*** storm cloud
oblast district
obletjeti fly round
oblijepiti paste over; plaster over; cover, coat
oblik shape, (i GRAM) form; ***poprimiti ~*** take a form; **~ovati** shape, form
oblina roundness
obliz(iv)ati lick; **~ se** *fig* lick one's chops
obližnji surrounding, neighbouring, nearby
oblog MED compress; ***staviti ~*** apply a compress; **~a** lining, coat, casing
obložiti coat, cover, overlay, line; face
oblutak pebble
obljetnica anniversary
obljubljen popular; **~ost** popularity
obman|a delusion; **~uti** delude; = **prevariti**
obnov|a reconstruction; renewal, restoration; revival; **~iti** reconstruct; renew, restore; revive
oboa MUS oboe, hautboy
obod (*šešira*) brim
obogatiti make rich; **~ se** become rich
obojak foot-rag, foot-cloth
oboj|e, ~ica both
obojen coloured; dyed; painted; stained
obolje|nje = **bolest**; **~ti** become (fall) ill
obor (*ovčji*) (sheep) fold; (*konjski*) paddock; (*transportni*) cattle-pond
oborine *pl* precipitation
oboriti strike down; overturn; (*avion*) shoot down, bring down
obostran mutual, reciprocal
obožavat|elj admirer; worshipper; **~i** adore, worship
obožava|nje adoration, worship; admiration; **~telj** worshipper; admirer, fan; **~ti** adore, worship; admire
obračun showdown; COM settlement; **~ati** calculate; settle; *fig* settle accounts with
obraće|nje REL conversion; **~nik** REL convert
obrad|a processing; (*teme*) treatment; (*zemlje*) cultivation, tillage; ***~iva zemlja*** arable land; **~iti** process; treat; cultivate, till
obradovati delight, make happy, please

obramben defensive
obran|a defence (*Am* defense); **~iti** defend (successfully); = **braniti**; ***~iti naslov prvaka*** SPORT retain championship
obrasti overgrow; be overgrown
obrat|an reverse; contrary; **~no** reversely, the other way round; contrary; ***i ~no*** and vice versa
obrati (*mlijeko*) skim; (*voćku*) pick
obratiti REL convert; **~ se** contact, apply to; REL become a convert
obratnik GEOGR tropic
obraz cheek; *fig* good name, honour
obrazac form
obrazložiti argument, motivate; explain
obrazova|n educated; **~nost** education; **~ti** educate; form
obred, **~ni** ritual
obrez|ati trim; REL circumcise; **~ivanje** REL circumcision
obrijan shaved
obris outline, contour
obrisati = **brisati**
obrlatiti bring around; get around one
obrnut = **obratan**; **~i** reverse; (*naglavce*) turn upside-down
obrok meal; = **rata**
obronak hill-side, slope
obrt handicraft; ***umjetni ~*** applied art; **~nica** trade licence; **~nik** craftsman, artisan
obrub = **porub**
obruč ring; (*dječji, bačvarski*) hoop; MIL encirclement, pocket
obrva eyebrow
obučavati train
obučen dressed; trained
obuć|a footwear; **~i (se)** dress
obuhvaćati include, cover
obuj|am circumference; **~miti** clasp, encircle
obuka training
obustav|a suspension; discontinuance; **~iti** suspend; discontinue
obuv|ati se put (*ili* pull) on shoes; **~en** with one's shoes on, in one's shoes
obuzdava|nje restraint, control, curb; **~ti** restrain, (keep under) control, curb; subdue; **~ti se** restrain oneself
obuzeti seize, overcome; (*zaokupiti*) absorb
obveznica COM bond, obligation
obzir regard, consideration; ***~om na*** in view of; ***bez ~a na*** regardless of; ***uzeti u ~*** take into consideration (*ili* account); make allowances for; **~an** considerate
ocari|niti clear (through the customs); impose (*ili* collect) duty on; **~njenje** (cus-

toms-) clearance
ocat vinegar; ***vinski ~*** wine vinegar
ocijeniti evaluate, assess; (*đaka*) mark, grade
ocjena evaluation, assessment; mark, grade
ocrniti defame
ocrta(va)ti outline
ocva|o BOT *i fig* run (*ili* gone) to seed; *fig* past its prime; (*žena*) passée, faded; **~sti** run (*ili* go) to seed; be past its prime; (*žena*) fade
očaj, ~avati despair; **~an** desperate
očarati fascinate, enchant, thrill
očekiva|nje expectation; **~ti** expect
očenaš Our Father, Lord's Prayer
očetkati brush (off)
očevida|c eye-witness; **~n** = **očit**
oči *pl* eyes; ***podići ~*** raise one's eyes; ***oboriti ~*** lower (*ili* cast down) one's eyes; ***upada u ~*** it is noticeable
očica (*na čarapi*) *Br* ladder, *Am* run
očigled: ***meni na ~*** in my sight; **~an** = **očit**
očijukati ogle (one), make eyes (at)
očins|ki fatherly; **~tvo** paternity
očistiti = **čistiti**
očit evident, obvious; **~ovati se** manifest itself
očnjak canine tooth, eye-tooth
očuh step-father
očuvati = **sačuvati**
od of; from; ***brži ~ mene*** quicker than me; ***~ danas*** from today; ***~ 1950*** since 1950; ***~ ... do*** from ... to; ***roman ~ Faulknera*** novel by Faulkner
odab(i)rati select, pick out, choose
odahnuti = **odlanuti**
odakle from where(?); ***~ste?*** where are you from? ***~znate?*** how do you know?
odan devoted, loyal; **~ost** devotion, loyalty
odande from there
odapeti squeeze off; (*strijelu*) let fly, shoot
odar: ***ležati na odru*** lie in state
odasvud from everywhere, from all sides, *coll* from all over (the place)
odašiljač (RADIO) transmitter
odatle from there
odavanje disclosure; betrayal
oda(va)ti: ***~ tajnu*** disclose; (*osobu*) betray; (*umor*) indicate, reveal; **~ se** betray oneself, *coll* give oneself away
odavde from here
odavna (for) a long time
odaz(i)vati se call back; *fig* respond to
odbaci|ti throw off; *fig* dis-

card, reject; (*optužbu*) repudiate, deny; (*glasanjem*) defeat; **~vanje** rejection; repudiation, denial
odbi|janje refusal, rejection; MATH subtraction; deduction; **~(ja)ti** refuse; turn down; (*prijedlog*) reject, discard; MATH subtrack; (*od iznosa*) deduct, take off; (*napad*) repel, beat off; (*svijetlost*) reflect; **~(ja)ti se** lopta rebound, bounce off; (*svijetlost*) reflect
odbitak deduction; ***uz ~*** deducting
odbojan repulsive
odbojka SPORT volley-ball
odbor committee; ***upravni ~*** managing board, managing committee; **~nik** committeeman
odbrusiti snap back
odcijep|iti se split off, secede; **~ljenje** split, secession
odčepiti uncork, unstopper
oderati (*kožu*) skin
odgađanje = **odgoda**
odgod|a delay, postponement; MIL deferment; **~iti** put off, delay, postpone
odgoj upbringing; ***bez ~a*** bad-mannered; **~itelj** (youth) councellor; kindergarten teacher; **~iti** bring up
odgonetnuti decipher, solve
odgovara|jući suitable, adequate; corresponding; **~ti** suit; be adequate; be responsible; = **odgovoriti**
odgovor|(iti) answer, reply; = **odvratiti**; **~an** responsible; **~nost** responsibility
odgristi bite off
odgurnuti push away
odigrati se take place
odijeliti = **odvojiti**
odijelo (*muško*) suit; (*odjeća*) clothes *pl*
odio department; division, section
odjaviti check out; **~ se** (*s računala*) log out
odjeća clothes *pl*
odjednom suddenly; all at once, at one go
odjedriti sail away
odjek echo, *fig* repercussion; **~nuti** echo, reverberate
odjel = **odio**
odjuriti rush away
odlagati = **odgoditi**, **odložiti**
odlanuti be (*ili* feel) relieved
odlaz|ak departure; **~iti** go away; **~i!** go away!
odlediti defrost
odletjeti fly away
odležati be bedridden; spend
odličan excellent
odlijepiti unstick; pull off
odlik|a distinction, characteristic; **~aš** top-pupil, straight A scholar; **~ovanje** medal; **~ovati** decorate, give a medal; **~ovati se** distinguish oneself
odliti pour off; (*u kalupu*) cast
odlom|ak fragment; (*teksta*) paragraph; **~iti** break off

odložiti = **odgoditi**; put down; lay aside
odluč|an determined, resolute; **~iti (se)** decide, make up one's mind; **~nost** determination, resolution
odluka decision; (*sudska*) verdict
odlutati wander away
odljev (*za vodu*) sink; (*odljevak*) cast(ing)
odljutiti se cool down
odmah at once, immediately, straight away
odmaknuti (se) move away, move over, shift
odmamiti lure away; head off
odmara|lište (*dom*) holiday home, rest home; (*mjesto*) health resort; **~ti** rest; **~ti se** (take) rest
odmazda retaliation, reprisal
odmet; ***nije na ~*** it can't hurt; **~nik** outlaw; rebel; **~nuti se** become an outlaw; rebel against
odmicati get away; (*vrijeme*) pass; = **odmaknuti**
odmjer|en *fig* deliberate, measured; **~iti** measure; (*pogledom*) look one up and down, give one a mean look
odmoći harm
odmor rest; relaxation; (*pauza*) break; **~an** rested; **~iti** rest; ***dobro se ~iti*** have a good rest
odmotati unwrap
odmrznuti (se) thaw off
odnekle from somewhere
odnijeti carry away, take away
odnos relation; connection; **~an** in question, particular; **~iti se** apply (to); concern; treat; **~no** or; respectively
odnošaj (sexual) intercourse
odobrava|nje approval; acclamation; **~ti** approve; acclaim; ***ne ~ti*** disapprove
odobrenje permission; approval
odobriti approve; authorize; grant
odojak suckling pig
odoljeti resist
odostraga from behind
odoz|do from below; **~go** from above
odračunati deduct
odraditi work off
odrast|ao grown up, adult; **~i** grow up
odraz reflection; **~iti** reflect; **~iti se (od)** reflect from; (na) effect, show in
odreći se give up, renounce; resign (from)
odred MIL detachment, force
odredba decree, order; (*ugovora*) provision
odredi|šte destination; **~ti** determine, lay down; fix; assign
određen definite; particular; certain
odreknuće renunciation
odrešenje discharge, acquit-

tal
odreza|k (*mesa*) steak; (*novinski*) cutting; **~ti** cut off (*i fig*)
odricanje renunciation; sacrifice
odriješiti untie; acquit
odrješit bluff
odrod renegade
odron land-slide; **~iti se** slide down, come down
odrpan tattered
odrubiti: **~ *glavu*** behead one
održa|nje = **opstanak**; **~ti** (*riječ*) keep; (*sastanak*) hold; **~vanje** maintenance, upkeep; care; servicing; observance; **~vati** maintain, keep up; care for; service; observe; **~(va)ti se** hold one's own; survive; take place, be held
odsada from now on
odseliti se move (away), go to live (in)
odsjaj reflection
odsjeći cut off (*i fig*)
odsjek department; section
odsjesti put up (at), stay (at)
odsjev reflection
odskočiti jump back, jump aside; rebound; *fig* stand out
odskoč|ni: **~*na daska*** SPORT spring-board; *fig* stepping-stone
odslužiti serve (one's term, one's time)
odspavati (have some) sleep
odstojanje = **daljina**, **razmak**
odstra|niti remove, clear; get out of the way; **~niti se** withdraw; **~njenje** removal
odstup|anje surrender; skretanje departure; MIL retreat; **~ati**, **~iti** give up, surrender; depart (from); MIL retreat; **~nina** compensation; (*za stan*) key money
odsukati refloat
odsustvo MIL leave; **~vati** be absent
odsut|an absent; **~*an duhom*** absent-minded; **~nost** absence
odsvirati play; finish playing
odsvuda from everywhere
odšarafiti unscrew; **~ se** come loose, come off
odšetati stroll away; **~ *do*** go for a walk to
odškrinuti leave ajar
odštet|a compensation; JUR damages *pl*; **~iti** compensate
odšuljati se sneak away
odšutjeti hold one's tongue
odučiti = **odviknuti**
odudarati contrast (with), clash (with)
odugovlačiti hesitate, delay
oduljiti se linger, drag on
odumirati wither away; die out
oduprijeti se resist
oduran = **odvratan**
odustati give up, withdraw, decide against
odušak outlet, vent
odušev|iti make enthusiastic;

enrapture; **~ljen** enthusiastic; **~ljenje** enthusiasm; rapture

oduvijek always; from times immemorial

oduz|et paralyzed; **~eti** take away; strip off; MATH subtract; **~imanje** subtraction

odužiti se repay; = **oduljiti se**

odvagnuti weigh (*i fig*)

odvajanje separation; removal; (*sredstava*) appropriation

odvaliti pry loose, prize off; (*svršiti*) get it over with

odvaž|an daring; **~iti se** dare; take courage; take one's chance; **~nost** daring

odverglati rattle off

odvesti take (to); take away; transport, remove; (*autom*) drive, give one a lift; **~ se** drive (to), ride (to); drive away

odvezati untie, undo; **~ se** get untied

odvija|č screw-driver; **~ti** unwind, unroll; reel off; unscrew; **~ti se** run, take place, be in progress

odviknuti break one of a habit; **~ se** lose a habit; give up

odviše too much

odvod, **~đenje** disposal, removal; discharge; drainage; **~diti** = **odvesti**; **~dnjavanje** drainage

odvoj|ak branching road; RLW siding; **~iti** separate; remove; (*sredstva*) appropriate

odvoz transport; removal; **~iti** transport, remove

odvraćanje dissuasion, discouragement

odvrat|an disgusting, repulsive; **~iti** dissuade, discourage, warn against, talk out of; **~nost** disgust

odvrnuti turn off; unscrew

odvući draw away, drag off; **~ se** drag oneself off

odzdraviti greet in return

odzvanjati reverberate

ofuriti scald; **~ se** get scalded

ogavan = **odvratan**

ogladnjeti become hungry

oglas notice; (*novinski*) advertisement, *coll* ad

oglas|ni: ***~na ploča*** bulletin-board, notice-board; ***~ni zavod*** advertising agency

oglasnik: ***mali ~*** classified advertisements

oglasiti announce; advertise

oglav (horse) collar

ogled inspection; trial; ***poslati na ~*** send on approval

ogleda|lo mirror, looking-glass; **~ti se** look round; be mirrored (in); *fig* be reflected (in); come to grips (with)

ogledni experimental; model

ogluh|a JUR default; ***iz ~e*** by default

oglušiti become deaf; ***~ se na*** turn a deaf ear to

ognjište fire-place
ogoliti lay bare
ogoljeti become bare
ogorč|en (em)bitter(ed); **~enje** bitterness; **~iti** embitter
ogovara|nje backbiting; (*trač*) gossip; **~ti** backbite; gossip
ograd|a fence; (*željezna*) railing; (*od žice*) wire netting; **~iti** fence in; enclose; **~ se** fence oneself (from)
ogranak branch; chapter
ograničen (*duševno*) dim-witted; **~enost** dim-wittedness; **~enje** restriction, limitation; **~iti** restrict, limit; ***~iti se na*** restrict oneself to
ogre|botina, **~psti** scratch; **~psti se** scratch oneself
ogriješiti se sin (against); violate
ogrjev fuel; firewood
ogrlica collar; (*nakit*) necklace
ogrnuti (se) slip (a coat)on; wrap (in)
ogroman huge; vast
ogrozd gooseberry
ogrtač cloak; = **kaput**, **kuta**; ***kućni ~*** (*muški i ženski*) dressing-gown, *Am i* (bath) robe; (*kraći ženski*) house-coat
oguliti peel; (*koljeno*) graze; **~ se** peel
oh! oh!
ohla|diti cool; **~diti se** *fig* cool off; **~đenje** *fig* estrangement
ohol haughty; **~ost** haughtiness
ohrabr|enje encouragement; **~iti** encourage; **~iti se** take courage
ojačati become strong(er); = **pojačati**
okajati make amends for
okaljati *fig* dirty, sully
okameniti (se) petrify
okaniti se give up
okapa|nje *fig* trouble; **~ti** bank up
oki|dač trigger; **~nuti** pull the trigger
oklad|a bet, wager; **~iti se** (make a) bet
oklijeva|nje hesitation; **~ti** hesitate
okliznuti se slip
oklop armour; (*viteški*) suit of armour, plate
oklop|ni: ***~ni vlak*** (***kola***) armoured train (car); ***~ne jedinice*** armour
okno (*rudarsko*) shaft, pit
oko eye; (*mreže*) mesh
oko (a)round; ***~ 10 sati*** about 10 o'clock
okoli|ca neighbourhood, surroundings *pl*; **~na** environment
okoliša|ti beat about the bush; ***bez ~nja*** bluntly
okolnost circumstance; ***olakotna*** (***otežavajuća***) **~** extenuating (aggravating) circumstance
okolo around, about

okomi|ca, **~t** vertical
okomiti se attack
okončati end, terminate
okorio inveterate
okosnica *fig* skeleton, framework
okov|ati chain; provide with fittings; **~i** *pl* chains, fetters; (*metalni*) fittings
okrajak remnant; stub, end
okrasti steal from; rob
okrečiti whitewash
okre|nuti (se) turn; **~tati se** turn (round), revolve, rotate, spin
okrepa refreshment
okret turn; revolution, rotation; **~an** agile, nimble; **~nost** agility, nimbleness
okrhnuti chip
okrijepiti (se) refresh (oneself)
okrilje shelter; patronage
okriviti blame; accuse
okrnjiti infringe; injure
okrstiti name; dub
okršaj skirmish
okrug district; **~ao** round; **~lica** CUL dumpling
okruniti (se) crown (oneself)
okrutan cruel; **~nost** cruelty
okružiti surround
okrznuti graze
oktobar October
okupator occupier
okupiti (se) gather
okus, **~iti** taste
okuša|n tried; **~ti se** try one's hand at
okvir frame; *fig* ***u ~u*** under; as part of
olabaviti slacken, loosen; **~ se** relax
olako: ***uzeti ~*** take lightly
olakš|anje relief; **~ati** facilitate; **~ica** privilege
oličenje embodiment
ološ rabble, scum
olov|ka pencil; ***kemijska ~ka*** ballpoint; **~an**, **~o** lead
oltar altar
oluj|a storm; **~ni** stormy
oluk gutter; drain-pipe
olupina wreck (*i fig*)
omaknuti se let slip
omalovažava|nje belittling; ***s ~njem*** slightingly; **~ti** belittle
omam|a daze; **~iti** stun, daze
omaška slip, oversight
omč|a noose; ***čvor ~e*** slip-knot
omeđiti *fig* delimit
ometati hamper; thwart; (*emisiju*) jam
omiljen popular; **~ost** popularity
omjer ratio, proportion
omladina young people, youth
omogućiti make possible
omorika spruce
omot wrapping; cover; (*knjige*) = **ovojnica**; **~ati** wrap
omražen hated
on he; ***~ sam*** he himself
ona she; ***~ sama*** she herself; **~j** that; ***~j koji*** he who
ona|j that; ***~j koji*** he who; **~kav**, **~ko** = **takav**, **tako**; ***i***

~ko anyway; **~mo** = **tamo**
onda then; ***pa šta ~?*** so what?
ondje = **tamo**
one they; those
onemogućiti make impossible; frustrate; **~ se** disqualify oneself
oneraspoložiti put in a bad mood; depress; **~ se** become depressed
onesposobiti disable; knock out
onesvije|stiti se faint; **~šten** unconscious
oni they; those; that lot
ono it; that thing; ***~ što*** that which; **~liko** = **toliko**
onuda there, that way
opačina depravity, black deed, vicious act
opada|nje decrease, decline, falling off; **~ti** = **opasti**
opak wicked; vicious
opal|iti burn, singe; (*oružje*) fire; (*sunce*) burn, tan; **~jen** = **preplanuo**
opametiti bring to reason; **~ se** come to reason, learn sense
oparati undo, unstitch
opasač belt
opas|an dangerous; **~ati** girdle, belt; **~ka** note; footnote; **~nost** danger; **~ti** decrease, decline, fall off
opat abbot; **~ica** abbess; nun; **~ija** abbey
opaziti observe, notice
opažanje observation
općenit general; vague; **~o** generally
općenje intercourse (*i spolno*)
opći general; common; underlying
općin|a district; municipality; (*gradska*) borough; (*zgrada*) townhall; **~ski** municipal
općiti have intercourse with (*i spolno*)
opeći (se) burn (oneself)
opeka brick
opeklina burn
oper|a opera; **~eta** operetta
operacija *fig* MIL operation; MED operation, surgery
opera|cioni: ***~ciona dvorana*** (operating) theatre; **~ter** MED operator; *kino* projectionist
operirati operate (*i fig*)
opet again; **~ovano** repeatedly
opip (sense of) touch; **~ljiv** tangible
opir|anje, **~ati se** = (*pružati*) **otpor**
opis description; **~(iv)ati** describe
opismeniti make literate
opiti make drunk; **~ se** get drunk
opjevati praise in verse (*ili* song)
opkoliti surround
opkop trench; (*oko zamka s vodom*) moat
oplak(iv)a|ti lament, mourn;

(*more*) lap, wash; **~nje** lamentation
oplata board lining, planking; (*sobna*) panelling, wainscot; (*za betoniranje*) forms, form boards
oplemeniti ennoble; refine; improve
opločen (*keram. pločicama*) tiled; (*mramor*) marble-faced; (*hrastovom oplatom*) oak-panelled
oplod|iti fertilize; **~nja** fertilization; ***umjetna ~nja*** artificial insemination
oploviti sail around
opljačkati rob (*i fig*), hold up
opna membrane
opoj|an: ***~no sredstvo*** drug; MED narcotic
opomen|a warning; **~uti** warn
oponaša|nje imitation; mimicking; **~ti** imitate; mimic
opor (*okus*) tart; (*vino*) dry; *fig* harsh
oporav|ak recovery, convalescence; rest cure; **~iti se** get better, convalesce
oporezovati tax
oporuka (last) will, testament
opovrgnu|će refutation; denial; **~ti** refute; deny
opoz|iv, **~vati** recall; repeal; (*narudžbu*) cancel; cancellation
oprašiti dust, powder
oprati wash
opravda|n justified, legitimate; **~nje** justification; **~ti** justify; clear; **~vati se** justify oneself, make excuses
opre|čan contradictory; **~ka** contrast
opredijeliti se take sides, commit oneself
oprem|a equipment; (*knjige*) design, get-up; **~iti** equip; fit (out)
oprez caution; ***biti na ~u*** be on one's guard; **~an** cautious
oproban tried
oprost REL indulgence; (*od poreza*) exemption; **~iti** forgive, pardon; **~iti se** take one's leave, part
opršt|aj leave-taking, parting, farewell; ***~en od poreza*** tax exempt, free from taxes
opršnjak bib, feeder
opruga spring
opsada siege, blockade
opseg degree, measure; = **obujam**; **~žan** extensive
opsjed|ati besiege (*i fig*), blockade; **~nut** *fig* possessed
opskrb|a supply, provisioning; **~ljivati** supply, provide, furnish; **~ljivati se** supply oneself, get (in supplies)
opskrbni: ***~ centar*** shopping centre
opsta|nak existence; survival; **~ti** exist; survive
opšir|an detailed, circumstantial; **~no** at length in de-

tail
opšiti edge; hem
optere|ćenje load, strain; *fig* burden, liability; ***nasljedno ~ćenje*** (hereditary) taint; **~titi** load, strain; burden
opticaj circulation
optuž|ba accusation, charge; **~enik** defendant; **~iti** accuse (of), charge (with)
opunomoć|enik authorized person; **~iti** authorize
opustiti relax; **~ se** chill out
opust|jeti become deserted; **~ošiti** devastate
opušak cigarette stub
ora|č ploughman; **~nica** (plough-) field; **~ti** plough, *Am* plow
orah walnut
oranžada (*prirodna*) *Br* orange squash, *Am* orangeade; (*umjetna*) orange pop, orange soda
ordin|acija *Br* consulting room, *Am* (doctor's) office; ***~ira od 3—5*** his hours are 3–5
orgija orgy
orgulj|aš organist; **~e** *pl* organ
orhideja orchyd
orijentirati orientate; **~ se** orientate oneself; ***~ se na*** concentrate on, adopt the course towards
oriti se resound
orkan hurricane
orkestar orchestra
ormar (*za odjeću*) wardrobe; (*s policama*) cupboard; (*za knjige*) book-case; (*ugrađen*) closet
ormarić: ***garderobni ~*** locker; ***kuhinjski ~*** kitchen cabinet, kitchen unit
oronuo decrepit; (*zgrada*) dilapidated
orositi se (*staklo*) fog up; (*zid*) sweat
ortak partner; accomplice
oruđe implement(s), (*i fig*) tool
oruž|je arms, weapons; ***hladno ~je*** cold steel; ***vatreno ~je*** fire-arms; ***bez ~ja*** unarmed
oružni: ***~ list*** gun licence, gun permit
osa wasp
osakatiti cripple
osam eight; **~deset** eighty
osam|a: ***na ~i*** secluded; **~ljen** lonely; **~ljenost** loneliness
osamnaest eighteen
osamostaliti se become independent
osebujan peculiar
osedlati saddle
oseka low tide
osigura|č EL fuse; ***pregorio je ~č*** a fuse has blown; **~nje** insurance; ***životno ~nje*** life insurance; ***~nje od požara*** fire insurance; **~(va)ti** insure; *fig* secure, make sure, make provision for; **~(va)ti se** insure; *fig* provide against, play safe
osijediti turn grey, get grey

hair

osim besides, except, in addition to; ~ ***toga*** moreover; apart from this

osinjak wasp nest

osip rash; eczema

osiromašiti become poor; impoverish

osjeća|j feeling, emotion; **~jan** sensitive, emotional; **~ti** feel; ***dobro se ~ti*** feel well

osjetan marked, substantial

osjet|ilo sense; **~iti** feel; **~ljiv** susceptible; sensitive; touchy; **~ljivost** susceptibility; sensitiveness; touchiness

oskoruša service (berry)

oskud|an scanty, meagre; **~ica** scarcity; lack; **~ijevati** feel lack (of); suffer privation

oskvrnuti desecrate

oslabiti weaken

oslić silver hake

oslijepiti become blind; (*nekoga*) blind

oslobo|diti (make) free, liberate; set free; exempt (from); **~diti se** become free; free oneself; feel more at ease; **~đenje** liberation; exemption

oslon|ac support; **~iti se** lean (on); *fig* rely on

osloviti address

osluškivati eavesdrop; listen

osmi|jeh, ~jehnuti se smile

osmrtnica notice of death

osniva|č founder; **~nje** foundation; **~ti** base; **~ti se** rest on

osnov|a basis; foundation; GRAM stem; ***u ~i*** basically, in substance; at the root; ***na ~u*** on the basis (*ili* strength) of; in terms of; in view of; **~ati** found, establish; **~an** well-grounded; **~ati** found, establish, set up; **~ni** fundamental, basic, elementary, underlying

osoba person

osobi|na characteristic; **~t** special; **~to** particularly, especially

osoblje personnel, staff

osobn|i personal; **~o** personally

osoran harsh, gruff

osovina TECH axle; GEOM axis

ospice measles *pl*

osporavati dispute, challenge, question, contest

osposob|iti fit; train, qualify; make usable, repair; **~ljavanje** training, qualification; rehabilitation; repair

osramotiti (se) disgrace (oneself)

osrednji average; mediocre

ostali the others; ***između ~og*** among other things

ostarjeti grow old

ostat|ak remnant; **~i** remain; ***~i miran*** keep one's temper; ***~i bez (soli)*** run out of (salt); ***~i pri*** stick to, insist

on
ostava store-room; broom--closet
ostaviti leave; give up; (*u nasljedstvo*) bequeath; (*oporučno*) leave by will; (*momka, djevojku*) throw over
ostavk|a resignation; ***dati ~u*** resign
ostavština inheritance
osti trident
ostriga oyster
ostruga spur
ostrugati scrape (off); scrape clean
ostvar|enje realization; **~iti** realize; **~iti se** be realized; **~iv** feasible
osud|a JUR sentence; *fig* condemnation; **~iti** sentence; condemn
osujetiti frustrate, thwart
osumnjičiti suspect
osušiti dry (up); mop (up); **~ se** dry up; wither
osuti se get (*ili* break out in) a rash
osvaja|č conqueror; (*žena*) lady-killer; **~nje** conquest; **~ti** conquer
osvet|a, **~iti** revenge; **~iti se** revenge oneself; **~ljiv** vindictive; **~nik** avenger
osvjestiti se come to; *fig* come to reason
osvijetliti light up; *fig* shed light on; PHOT expose
osvit daybreak
osvjedočiti = **uvjeriti**
osvetljenje lighting
osvjež|enje refreshment; (*ponavljanje*) brushing up; **~iti (se)** refresh (oneself) brush up
osvojiti conquest; take; win
osvr|nuti se look back; *fig* take into consideration; take note of, deal with, refer to, review; **~t** reference, review
ošamariti slap (one's face)
ošinuti lash (i *fig*)
ošišati cut one's hair, give one a haircut; **~ se** have one's hair cut, get a haircut
oštar sharp; *fig* severe, harsh
ošte|ćenje, **~titi** damage; **~titi se** be (*ili* get damaged)
oštri|ca cutting edge; **~lo** (pencil) sharpener; **~na** sharpness; *fig* severity, harshness; **~ti** sharpen
oštriga oyster
oštrokondža shrew
oštroum|an shrewd; **~nost** shrewdness
otac father
otada since (then), from that time
otcijepiti se split off; secede
otčepiti (*bocu*) uncork, unstop(per); (*sudoper*) unstop; **~ se** open (up)
oteći run off, drain; MED swell
otegnuti protract; **~ se** drag on
oteklina swelling
oteti grab (*ili* wrench) from, take (away) from, carry

off; ~ **se** break free
otezanje protraction; delay
otežati make more difficult, impede
othraniti raise, bring up
othrvati se withstand
oticanje flow-off, run-off, drain
otići go away; leave, depart
otimačina robbery (*i fig*)
otipkati type (up)
otirač (*za noge*) door-mat
otis|ak print(ing), imprint; (*prsta*) fingerprint; **~nuti** print (off); imprint; **~nuti se** push off
otjerati chase away; send packing
otkad since; ***~?*** since when? how long?
otkako as long as; since
otkaz notice; ***dati ~*** (*sam*) give notice, quit; (*drugome*) give notice, dismiss; **~ati** give notice, quit; cancel, call off; fail
otkinuti break off, tear off, rip away; ~ **se** break off, tear loose, come off
otklanjanje elimination, removal; deviation, refusal
otkloniti eliminate, remove; decline; (*zlo*) ward off
otključati unlock
otkočiti uncock
otkopati dig up; uncover
otkopčati undo, unbutton; ~ **se** come unbuttoned
otkriće, **~vanje** discovery; (*spomenika*) unweiling; **~ti** discover; uncover; unveil; reveal; track down
otkuda from where(?)
otkup ransom; redemption; buying off, purchase; **~iti** ransom; redeem; buy off, purchase; **~nina** ransom
otmi|ca abduction; kidnapping; **~čar** abductor; kidnapper
otmjen distinguished; stylish, elegant; **~ost** distinction; elegance
otok island; MED swelling
otopi|na solution; **~ti (se)** melt; thaw
otorinolaringolog ear-nose--throat specialist
otpa|d drop-out rate; wastage; **~dak**, **~ci** waste, refuse, litter; **~danje** falling-off; *fig* defection, desertion; **~dati**, **~sti** fall off, come off; drop out; defect, desert; ***10% ~da na uvoz*** imports account for (*ili* cover) 10%
otpiliti saw off
otpirač skeleton-key
otpisati *fig* write off
otpla|ta payment(s); ***na ~tu*** *Br* on hire purchase, *Am* on the instalment plan; **~ćivati**, **~titi** pay off (by instalments)
otploviti sail (off)
otpor resistance, opposition; ***pružati ~*** resist, oppose; **~an** resistant, hardy, tough; ***~an na rđu*** rust-resistant, rust-proof; **~nost** resistance

otpratiti see off (to), see (*ili* walk) home
otprem|a shipping, forwarding; **~iti** send off, ship, forward; **~nik** forwarding agent; **~nina** severance pay; **~ništvo** forwarding; forwarding agency
otprije from before
otprilike about, approximately, roughly
otpustiti dismiss; discharge
otpuštanje dismissal; discharge
otputovati leave, depart
otraga behind, at the back
otrca|n shabby; **~ti se** become shabby
otrčati run off, run away
otres|it bluff, curt; **~ti** shake (down); shake off; **~ti se** get rid of; (*na nekoga*) snap at
otrgnuti tear off, break off, wrench loose; **~ se** break away, break loose
otrijezniti (se) sober up
otrov poison; **~an** poisonous; **~anje** poisoning; **~ati** poison; **~ati se** take poison
otrpa(va)ti dig out
otuda from there; *fig* hence
otuđiti se grow apart
otup|iti dull; **~jeti** become dull
otvor opening; **~en** open; *fig* frank, outspoken; (*bazen, kino*) outdoor, oper-air; ***na ~enom*** in the open, out of doors; **~eno** frankly; openly; **~enje** opening, inauguration, dedication; **~iti** open; (*plin*, RADIO) turn on; (*svečano*) inaugurate, dedicate; ***~iti sastanak*** call a meeting to order; **~iti se** open
otvrdnuti harden
ovacija ovation
ovaj this (one)
ovak|av such; **~o** like this, this way
ovamo (over) here
ov|an ram; (*uškopljen*) wether; **~ca** sheep; (*ženka*) ewe; **~čar** shepherd; sheepfarmer; (*pas*) sheep-dog (*njemački*) Alsatian, German shepherd; **~čarstvo** sheep-farming; ***~čje mlijeko*** ewe's milk
ovdašnji local; of this town
ovdje here
ovi these, this lot
ovi(ja)ti wind round
ovis|an dependent; **~iti** depend (on); **~nost** dependence
ovjekovječiti immortalize
ovjer|a notarization; verification; **~(ov)iti** notarize; verify
ovladati master
ovlast = **ovlaštenje, punomoć**; **~iti** authorize, empower; license
ovlaštenje authority, powers *pl*
ovlažiti moisten
ovo this
ovogodišnji this year's

ovoj bandage; **~nica** (*knjige*) dust jacket
ovolik so big; **~o** so much
ovratnik collar
ozakoniti legalize
ozbilj|an serious; **~nost** seriousness; ***misliš li ~no?*** are you serious? do you mean it?
ozdrav|iti get well, recover; **~ljenje** recovery
ozeblina chilblain
ozepsti freeze; catch a cold
ozlijediti injure, hurt; **~ se** hurt oneself
ozljeda injury
ozlogla|siti bring into disrepute; **~šen** disreputable
ozlojediti exasperate
ozlovoljiti annoy
ozna|čiti mark, designate; characterize; **~ka** mark, designation; characteristic
oznoj|en sweating; **~iti se** be sweating; break into a sweat
ozvučiti wire for a sound; (*prisluškivati*) bug
ožalostiti sadden; distress
ožbukati (coat with) plaster
ožednjeti become thirsty
ože|niti (se) marry; get married; **~njen** married
ožeti wring out
ožigosati *fig* brand
ožiljak scar
oživ|iti bring to life, revive; enliven; **~jeti** come to life, revive; become animated

P

pa and; well
pačati se interfere (in); meddle (with)
pače even; moreover; (*mala patka*) duckling
pad fall; tumble; decline; drop; **~ati** fall; drop; decline; sink; **~ež** GRAM case
pado|bran parachute; **~branac** parachutist
pahuljica flake, fluff
pak then; again
pak|ao hell; **~lina** pitch
paket parcel, package
pakirati pack
paklen hellish, infernal
pakost malice; **~an** malicious, spiteful
pakovati pack
palac thumb
palača palace
palačinka pancake
pal|enje ignition; burning; **~ikuća** incendiary, arsonist, *coll* fire-bug; **~iti** burn; ignite; fire (a gun); brand; MED cauterize
palma palm
paluba deck, board
paljba fire; discharge; volley
pamćenje memory
pamet mind; wits; intelligence; **~an** sensible; clever; wise

pamtiti remember, memorize
pamuk cotton
pandža claw
panika panic
panj stump; block
papa pope
papak hoof
papar pepper
paparazzo paparazzo
papiga parrot
papir paper; ~ ***za pakovanje*** brown (wrapping) paper; ~ ***za precrtavanje*** tracing paper; ~***nat novac*** (bank-) notes; *Am* bills; ~**nica** stationer's shop
paprat fern
papr|ena metvica pepper-mint; ~**iti** season with (red) pepper
papuča slipper
par pair; couple
par|a steam, vapour; smallest coin; penny; ***pun*** ~***e*** vaporous; damp
parati rip, tear open; unstitch
parket parquet; ~**iranje** parqueting; ~**irati** parquet
parkirati park
parn|i, ~**o** grijanje steam heating; ~***i kotao*** steam boiler; ~***a kupelj*** steam bath
parnica law-suit
parobrod steamboat, steamship
pas dog; ***morski*** ~ shark
pâs belt; girdle; (*struk*) waist; ~**ati** girdle; belt
pasmina breed; stock; race
pasoš passport
pasti = **padati**
pastir shepherd; herdsman
pastrva trout
pastuh stallion
pasulj beans
paš|a pasture, pasturage; ~**njak** common; pasture ground
patisak reprint
patiti suffer
patka duck
patnja suffering; pain; agony
patuljak dwarf
patvor|en counterfeit; false; artificial; ~**ina** forgery; counterfeit; ~**iti** counterfait; forge
paučina (cob) web
pauk spider
paun peacock
pazikuća caretaker
paziti (keep) watch; take care; be careful; mind; look out (for)
pazuh armpit
pažljiv careful; attentive; considerate
pažnj|a attention; care; consideration; ~***u pobuditi*** draw attention (to)
pčela bee
pec|ati angle; fish; ~**nuti** prick; sting
pecivo rolls
pečat seal; stamp; signet; ~**iti** seal; ~***ni vosak*** sealing-wax
pečen baked; roast(ed); ~***i krumpir*** fried potatoes; ~***a teletina*** roast veal; ~**ka** roast meat

pečenje roasting; baking; roast meat
pečurka mushroom
peć stove; oven; ***visoka*** ~ blast furnace; **~i** bake; roast; (*sunce*) burn
pećina cave; cliff; rock
pećnica oven
pedeset fifty
pegla iron; **~ti** iron; press
pehar jug
pekar baker; **~na** bakery
pekmez jam; (*od naranča*) marmelade
pelene diapers (*pl*)
pelivan acrobat; rope-dancer
penja|ti se climb; **~čica** climbing-plant, creeper
pepe|lnica Ash-Wednesday; **~ljara** ash-tray; **~ljika** pot-ash; **~o** ashes
perad poultry; fowls
peraja fin
perčin pig-tail
perec German Brezel
periferija outskirts
perika wig
periš pen-knife; pocket-knife
perivoj park; gardens
perje feathers; plumage
pero feather; (*za pisanje*) pen
peron platform
peršin parsley
perunika iris
perušati pluck
perut dandruff; scurf
pes|t, **~nica** fist
pet five
peta heel
petak Friday; ***veliki*** ~ Good Friday
peteljka stalk; stem
petlja loop; noose; **~ti** fumble
petnaest fifteen
petrolej petroleum; kerosene oil
piće drink, beverage
pidžama pyjamas, pajamas (*pl*)
pijan drunk, intoxicated; **~ac**, **~ica** drunkard; boozer; **~čevati** drink; tipple; **~ka** spree; drinking-bout; **~stvo** drunkeness; boozing
pijavica leech; *fig* usurer
pijesak sand
pijetao *Br* cock; *Am* rooster
pijuckati sip
pijukati cheep; chirp
pila saw; **~na** saw-mill
pile chicken; **~tina** chicken
piliti saw
pilot pilot
pilotina = **piljevina**
piljar fruit-monger; hawker; **~ica** market-woman
piljevina saw-dust
piljiti stare, gaze
PIN broj PIN number
pionir pioneer
pipa *Br* tap; *Am* faucet; **~c** tap
pipati feel, touch
pir wedding
pirjati stew
pisac writer; author
pisaći writing; ~ ***pribor*** stationery; ~ ***stol*** desk; ~ ***stroj*** typewriter

pisak mouthpiece
pisaljka pencil; slate-pencil
pisanka copy-book; note--book
pisar scribe; clerk; **~na** office
pisati write
piskati pipe; whistle
piskutati squeak
pism|en written; (*čovjek*) literate; **~o** letter; (*rukopis*) handwriting
pištati fizzle; hiss
pištolj pistol
pita pie
pit|ak drinkable; ***~ka voda*** drinking water
pita|nje question; **~ti** ask; question
piti drink
pitom tame; **~iti** tame
pivara brewery
pivni|ca (wine) cellar; **~čar** wine cellar keeper
pivo beer; **~vara** = **pivara**
pizma malice; spite
pjega spot; freckle; **~v** spotty; freckled
pjen|a foam; froth; (*od sapuna*) lather; **~iti se** foam; froth; **~ušac** champagne; **~ušav** foaming; sparkling (wine)
pjesma poem; song; **~rica** song-book
pjesni|k poet; **~štvo** poetry
pješa|čiti go on foot; tramp; **~k** pedestrian
pješadija infantry
pješčan sandy; ***~i brijeg*** sand dune; ***~a ura*** sand--glass
pješ|ice, **~ke** on foot
pjeva|č singer; **~čica** (female) singer; **~nje** singing; **~ti** sing
plač weeping; cry(ing)
plaća salary; wages; payment; **~nje** payment, paying; **~ti** pay; reward; *fig* atone for
pladanj plate; dish; (*taca*) tray
plah shy, timid; **~ost** shyness, timidity
plahta sheet
plakati cry, weep
plamen flame; ***u ~u*** aflame; on fire
plam|sati flare; **~tjeti** flame; blaze
plan plan; **~irati** plan; make plans
plandovati idle; dally; be at leisure
planina mountain; **~r** mountaineer; **~renje** mountain climbing, mountaineering
plantaža plantation
planuti catch fire; *fig* burst out in anger
plaš|iti frighten, scare; alarm; **~ljiv** timid; afraid
plašt mantle; cloak
platina platinum
plati|ti pay; **~v** payable
platno linen
plav blue; fair, blonde
plavac pumice (-stone)
plaviti overflow; flood
plaziti crawl, creep

pleća shoulders; back
pleme tribe; clan; **~nit** noble
plem|ić nobleman; aristocrat; **~stvo** nobility; aristocracy
ples dance, ball; **~ač** dancer; **~ačica** (girl-) dancer; **~ati** dance
plesti knit; braid
pletenica plait; tress
plet|er wicker(work); hurdle; **~ivo** knitting; network
pličina shallow
plijen prey; booty; **~iti** plunder
plijesan mould
plima high tide
plin gas; **~ara** gasworks; **~omjer** gasmeter; **~ovod** gas-pipe
plin|ski: ***~ska glavna cijev*** gas main; ***~ska rasvjeta*** gas light
plitak shallow
plitica plate; platter
pliva|č swimmer; **~ti** swim
plivaći: ***~ bazen*** swimming pool
ploč|a slab; plate; board; (*gramofonska*) disc, record; **~ica** (*za pisanje*) slate; tile; **~nik** pavement; *Am* sidewalk
plod fruit; **~an** fertile; fruitful; **~nost** fertility; fruitfulness
ploha surface
plomb|a filling; **~irati** stop
plosnat flat; level
ploška slice
plot fence; enclosure
plov|an navigable; **~idba** navigation; **~iti** navigate; sail; float
pluća lungs (*pl*); **~ni** pulmonary; lungs
plug *Br* plough, *Am* plow
pluta|ča buoy; **~ti** float
pluto cork
plužiti plough
pljačka robbery; **~š** robber; plunderer; **~ti** rob; plunder
pljesak applause
pljeska|nje applause; **~ti** applaud
plјesniv mouldy; musty; **~iti** mould; grow musty
pljunuti spit
pljusak shower
pljus|ka slap (in the face); **~nuti** box one's ears; slap one's face
plju|vačka spittle; **~vati**, **~nuti** spit; **~vačnica** spittoon
po about; after; on; along; during; at; by; ***~ tome*** after that
pobacati throw off one by one
poba|citi miscarry; **~čaj** miscarriage
pobija|nje refutation; **~ti** refute; dispute; argue
pobijediti conquer, defeat; win
pobirati collect; pick up; (*porez*) raise (tax)
pobiti = **pobijati**; kill off; slaughter
pobjeći run away; flee; es-

cape
pobjed|a victory; **~nik** victor; winner; **~onosan** victorious; triumphant
pobjeđivati = **pobijediti**
pobjesniti become furious; (*pas*) become rabid
poblijediti turn pale
pobliže in detail; closely
pobočnik adjutant
poboljša|nje improvement; **~ti** improve
pobornik defender; advocate
pobož|an religious; pious; **~nost** piety
pobrati = **pobirati**
pobrinuti se take care of; see to
pobrka|n confused; mixed up; **~ti** mix up; confuse
pobrojiti count up (out)
pobu|da incentive; stimulus; impulse; incitement; **~diti**; **~đivati** arouse; stimulate; incite
pobun|a riot; rebellion; **~iti** stir up mutiny; **~iti se** rebel against
pocrnjeti (*od sunca*) get tanned (sunburnt)
pocrvenjeti blush; turn red
počast honours; homage; **~iti** honour; pay homage; (*pogostiti*) treat one to
počekati wait for
počelo element; rudiments (*pl*)
počešati (se) scratch (oneself)
počešljati comb; **~ se** do one's hair; comb
počet|ak beginning; start; origin; outset; ***iz ~ka*** anew; over again; **~an** initial; preliminary; **~i** begin, start; commence; ***~i parnicu*** institute proceedings; **~nik**, **~nica** beginner
počevši od beginning with
počinak rest
počinit|elj committer; **~i** commit; do
počinuti se rest; repose
počinjati = **početi**
počistiti clean up; clear up
počivati = **počinuti se**
počupati se scuffle
poći set off; ***~ po*** fetch
pod under, below; ***~ svaku cijenu*** at any price; ***~ izgovorom*** under the pretence
pod floor; (*tlo*) ground
podanik subject
podao infamous; wicked
podast|irati, **~rijeti** submit
podatak datum (*pl* data); piece of information
podatan pliable, flexible
podati se give oneself up to; (*užitku*) indulge in; become addicted to
pod|badati, **~bosti** spur on; instigate
podbočiti prop up; support
podbradak double chin
podc|ijeniti, **~jenjivati** underrate; undervalue
podcrta|ti, **~vati** underline; (*fig*) emphasize
podčiniti subordinate; sub-

ject to
podera|n torn; **~ti** tear; rend
podesan suitable; appropriate
podgrijati warm up
podi|ći, **~gnuti** raise; lift; erect; build; put up (a price); set up; raise (a protest; money); ***~ći oči*** raise one's eyes; **~ći se** rise; get up
podijeliti divide; distribute; share
podivljati grow wild; run wild
podjza|nje erection; raising; **~ti** = **podići**
podjarm|iti, **~ljivati** subjugate; enslave; **~ljivanje** subjugation
podje|la division, distribution; **~ljivati** = **podijeliti**
podlaktica forearm
podleći succumb
podlo|ga base; ground; **~žan** subject (to)
podlost baseness; vileness
podložan subject to; subordinate
podmazati grease (under)
podmetnuti put under (below)
podmi|ćivati, **~titi** bribe
podmiri|ti, **~vati** settle, square
podmladak offsprings; the rising generation
podmor|nica submarine; **~ski** submarine
podmuk|ao underhand; perfidious; **~lost** perfidy; foul play
podnajam sub-lease
podne noon, midday; ***poslije ~*** (in the) afternoon; ***prije ~*** (in the) morning
podn|ijeti, **~ositi** bear, endure, stand; hold out; suffer; **~ošljiv** bearable; tolerable
podnož|je (*planine*) foot; **~nik** footstool
podražaj stimulus, incentive; irritation
podre|diti, **~đivati** subordinate; subject to; **~đen** subordinate; accessory
podrezati trim, cut
podrigivati se belch, retch
podrijetlo origin; descent; stock
podroban minute; detailed; in detail
podrovati undermine
podrtina ruin; wreck
područje territory; province; district
podrug|ivati se mock; ridicule; **~ljiv** mocking; disdainful
podrum (wine-)cellar
podružnica branch(-office)
podsje|ćati, **~titi** remind
podstav|a lining; **~iti** line
podsticat|elj instigator; **~i** instigate, incite; stir up; rouse
podstrići crop, clip
podsvijest subconsciousness
podučavati teach

podudarati se conform; correspond
poduka instruction
podup|irati, ~rijeti prop up; support; patronize
poduz|eće enterprise; firm; undertaking; **~etan** enterprising; **~eti, ~imati** undertake; venture; **~etnik** contractor
podval|a deception; **~iti** cheat, swindle
podvezica garter; suspender
podviknuti shout
podvlačiti underline
podvodan swampy; marshy
podvor|ba service; **~iti** serve; attend; **~nik** attendant
podvostručiti double; duplicate
podvožnjak underpass; railway bridge
podvr|ći, ~gnuti subjugate; submit
podvući = **podvlačiti**
podzem|an underground; ***~ne vode*** subterranean waters; **~lje** underground
pogađati guess; **~ se** bargain; haggle
pogan foul; excrements (*pl*); **~in** heathen
pogasiti put out fire; extinguish
pogaziti trample down; run down (over); (*riječ*) break one's word
pogibao = **pogibelj**
pogibati perish; die; ***~ od gladi*** starve; ***~ od žeđi*** die with thirst
pogibelj danger; risk; ***u životnoj ~i*** in danger of life; **~an** dangerous
poginuti = **pogibati**
pogladiti stroke; caress
poglavica chieftain; chief
poglavlje chapter
pogled look; gaze; glance; glimpse; view; ***u ~u*** in view of; with regard to; **~ati** look at; cast a glance at
pognut bent; stooping; **~i se** bend; stoop
pogodan favourable
pogod|ba condition; agreement; **~iti** guess; (*cilj*) hit the mark
pogon motive; drive; works
pogon|ski: ***~sko kolo, ~ski kotač*** driving wheel; ***~ski remen*** belt; ***~ska sila*** (***snaga***) motive power; driving power
pogoršati make worse; aggravate
pogostiti entertain; treat a p to
pogovor epilogue
pograbiti seize, grab; snatch
pogrda insult, abuse; **~n** abusive, insulting
pogreb funeral; burial
pogreš|an wrong; defective; mistaken; **~ka** error; mistake; (*tiskarska*) misprint; **~no** by mistake
pogriješiti make a mistake; (*u pravopisu*) misspell
pogub|an perilous, danger-

ous; **~iti** kill; behead; execute
pohaban worn out; shabby
poharati ravage; lay waste
pohlepa greed; avidity; lust; **~n** avid; greedy
pohoditi call (up)on; visit
pohota lust; sensuality; **~n** lustful; sensual
pohraniti deposit; store for safe-keeping
pohrliti hurry to; run to
pohvala praise; **~n** praiseworthy
poimence by name; ***pozivati* ~** call the roll
pojača|ti, **~vati** reinforce; strengthen; **~lo** amplifier
pojam notion; idea; concept
pojas belt, girdle; zone; (*tijela*) waist; ***~ za spasavanje*** lifebelt
pojav|a appearance; **~iti se** appear
pojedin|ac single person; individual; **~ce** singly; one by one; **~i**, **~ačan** single; **~ost** detail; particular(s)
pojednostaviti simplify
pojeftiniti become cheaper
pojesti eat up; finish one's meal
poji|lo, **~šte** watering-place; **~ti** give drink to; water
pojmiti understand; grasp
pojuriti rush; dash on
pokaj|ati se repent; be sorry for; **~nički** repentant
pokapati bury
pokaz|ati, **~ivati** show, demonstrate; display; ***~ ati se tačnim*** prove true
pokisnuti get wet
poklade carnival; shrove-tide
poklanjati = **pokloniti**
poklati slaughter
poklik shout, cry; exclamation
poklisar ambassador; envoy
pokliznuti slip; slide; skid
poklon bow; curtsey; (*dar*) gift, present; ***~-bon*** gift card; **~iti se** bow down (before); (*fig*) pay homage
poklopac lid
pokoj rest, repose; ***~ mu vječni*** may he rest in peace
pokojni the late; deceased; dead; **~k**, **~ci** the deceased
pokolj slaughter; massacre
pokoljenje generation
pokop burial; **~ati** bury
pokor|a penitence; **~an** obedient; submissive; **~avati**, **~iti se** obey; **~enje** subjection; **~nost** obedience
pokraj beside; close to; by
pokrajina province; country(side)
pokrasti steal
pokratiti shorten
pokrečiti whitewash
pokrenuti move; set in motion; start (the engine)
pokret movement; motion; **~an** movable; **~ni most** swing-bridge; ***~na imovina*** movables (*pl*); ***~na ploča*** turn-table; **~ati** = **pokrenuti**
pokri|će cover(ing); security;

~ti, **~vati** cover; **~vač** cover; blanket; ***~vač krova*** tiler; slater
pokroviteIj protector; patron; **~stvo** patronage
pokrpati mend; darn
pokrstiti christen; baptize
pokucati knock
pokućstvo furniture
pokuditi blame
pokunjen downcast
pokupiti collect; gather; pick up
pokus trial; test
pokusn|i: ***~a vožnja*** trial drive
pokuša|j attempt; **~ti** try; attempt; ***~ti sreću*** take one's chance
pokvar|en (*moralno*) corrupt; bad; spoiled; (*mast*) rancid; **~enost** corruption; **~iti** corrupt; spoil; ruin; **~ljiv** (*hrana*) perishable
pokvasiti wet; moisten
pol pole; ***Sjeverni*** (***Južni***) **~** North (South) pole
pol(a) half
polag close to; near
polagan slow; **~o** slowly
polaga|nje: ***~nje temelja*** laying the foundations; **~ti** lay, set, place; deposit; (*zakletvu*) take an oath; (*račun*) render account; (*ispit*) sit for an examination
polako = **polagano**
polarn|i polar, arctic; ***~a zvijezda*** polar star; **~ica** polar star
polaskati flatter
polaz|ak start, departure; setting out (off); **~iti** start, set out (off); depart; leave
poledica hard frost; ice; *Am* glaze
polet dash; animation; zeal
polica shelf
polic|ajac policeman; **~ija** police
polijeva|nje watering; ***kola za ~nje*** watering lorry; **~ti**, **politi** water; pour on; sprinkle
polovica half
položaj situation; position; condition; stand
položen laid; placed; situated
pol|ožiti = **~agati**; ***~ožiti ispit*** pass the exam; ***~ožiti oružje*** lay down arms
polubrat step-brother; foster-brother
poludjeti go mad (crazy)
poluga lever; (crow-)bar; ***~ mjenjača*** MOT gear-lever
polu|krug semicircle; **~kugla** hemisphere; **~mjer** radius; **~mjesec** half-moon; crescent; **~otok** peninsula; **~sestra** step-sister; foster-sister; **~vrijeme** SPORT half-time
poljana plain; field
polje field; *fig* range; scope; line
poljepšati embellish, beautify
poljodjel|ac farmer; peas-

ant; **~ski** agricultural; **~stvo** agriculture, farming
poljoprivreda agriculture
Polj|ska Poland; **Ŝski** Polish
poljub|ac kiss; **~iti** kiss
poma|ći = **~knuti**
pomaga|lo help; tool; **~nje** help; assistance; relief; **~ti** = **pomoći**
pomaknuti move; shift; (*uru*) **~ *naprijed*** put forward; **~ *natrag*** put back
pomanjkanje want; lack; shortage
pomast ointment
pomesti sweep up
pom|icati = **~aknuti**, **~aći**; **~ičan** mobile; movable
pomilovati caress; stroke; grant an amnesty
pomiriti (se) reconcile; make it up
pomi|sliti, **~šljati** think (of)
pomla|diti, **~đivati** rejuvenate
pomnožiti multiply
pomnj|a care; attention; **~iv** attentive, careful, pedantic
pomoć help, aid, assistance
pomoć|i help, aid, assist; **~nik** assistant; **~u** by means of
pomoliti se appear, crop up; (*moliti*) pray
pomorac seaman
pomor|ski: **~*ska sila*** naval power; **~stvo** navigation, seamanship
pomrčina (solar) eclipse
pomrsiti entangle; *fig* confuse
ponajviše mostly, chiefly
ponaša|nje behaviour; manners; conduct; **~ti se** behave, conduct
ponavlja|nje repetition; **~ti** repeat; revise
ponedjeljak Monday
ponekad sometimes; off and on
ponijeti take (along)
poništ|en cancelled; **~enje** annulment; cancellation; **~iti** annul; cancel
poniz|an humble; meek; **~iti** humble; humiliate; **~iti se** humble oneself; **~nost** humility
poniženje humiliation
ponoć midnight
ponor abyss; precipice
ponos pride; **~an** proud; **~iti se** be proud of
ponov|iti = **ponavljati**; **~o** again
ponud|a offer; bid; **~iti** offer; **~iti se** offer one's services; volunteer
ponjava sheet
pooštriti intensify
pop priest
popaliti burn down
popečak steak
popeti se climb; clamber up
popis list; inventory; **~ *stanovništva*** census; **~ati** make an inventory
popiti drink out (up)
poplašiti frighten; startle
poplav|a flood; overflow;

deluge; **~iti** flood; overflow; submerge
popločiti pave; (*drvom*) panel
poplun quilt
popodne afternoon
poprav|ak repair; mending; **~iti, ~ljati** repair; mend; improve; reform; (*greške*) correct
popreč|an oblique; transversal; ***~ni presjek*** cross section
poprijeko across; diagonally
poprilici about; approximately
poprsje bust
poprskati (be)spatter; sprinkle
popular|an popular; **~nost** popularity
popuniti fill, fill out, complete; replenish
popust reduction; discount; allowance; **~iti** reduce; yield; give in; give way; **~ljiv** indulgent; yielding; **~ljivost** yielding; indulgence
popušiti smoke (out); finish smoking
popuštati = **popustiti**
poput like; similar; ***biti ~*** look like
popuznuti slide down
pora pore
poraba use; usage
porast increase; growth; **~i** grow up; increase
poratni post-war
poravnati level; smoothe; (*spor*) make up
poraz defeat; overthrow; **~an** crushing; annihilating; **~iti** defeat
porazdijeliti distribute
porazgovoriti have a talk
poražen defeated; beaten
porculan porcelain; china
poreći = **poricati**
pored beside; (*također*) besides; as well
poredak order
poredati put in order; arrange in rows
poremetiti put out of order
porez tax; taxation
porezni: ***~ obaveznik*** tax-payer; **~k** tax-collector
poricati deny; dispute; revoke
porijeklo = **podrijetlo**
poriluk leek
porinuće launching
poriv impulse; impetus
porod birth; delivery
porodica family
porođaj = **porod**
porok vice
porot|a jury; **~nik** juror; member of the jury; juryman
Portu|gal Portugal; **♀giški** Portuguese
porub hem; border; **~iti** hem; turn down
poručnik lieutenant
porug|a mockery; scorn; **~ljiv** mocking; scornful
posada crew
posaditi plant; set

posao work; job; employment; business
posavjetovati se consult (with)
poseb|an special; separate; particular; **~no** particularly; specially; **~no *izdanje*** special edition
poseći, posegnuti reach out (for); seize
posijati sow
posijedjeti grow white
posin|iti adopt (as son); **~jenje** adoption
posipati strew; sprinkle; **~ *šljunkom*** gravel
posjećen visited; frequented
posjeći (*drvo*) fell; cut down; (*šumu*) clear; deforest
posjećivati visit, frequent
posjed property; (*imanje*) estate; landed property; **~nik** owner; proprietor; **~ovati** own; possess
posjet visit; call; **~ilac** visitor; **~iti** = **posjećivati**; **~nica** visiting-card
poskakivati hop; skip
poskupiti become dearer; raise the price
poslagati arrange in order
poslan|ik ambassador; delegate; **~stvo** embassy; legation
poslastica sweet; delicacy; titbit
poslati send; dispatch; **~ *natrag*** return; **~ *po*** send for
poslije after; afterwards; **~ *podne*** (in the) afternoon
poslodavac employer
poslov|an business; businesslike; **~no *pismo*** business letter; **~ni *prijatelj*** business partner; **~ni *promet*** commerce; trade; **~no *vrijeme*** office hours
poslovanje doing business; management
poslovica proverb
poslovnica office; bureau
poslovođa head (chief) clerk; manager
posluga service; attendance
poslu|h obedience; **~šan** obedient; docile; **~šati** obey, listen to; **~šnost** = **posluh**
poslužavnik tray
posluž|iti serve; attend (to); wait upon; **~iti se** help oneself to; **~itelj** attendant; porter
posljedica consequence; result; effect
posljednji the last; final
posmatrati watch; observe
posmrtn|i posthumous; **~o *slovo*** obituary (notice)
posoliti salt
pospan sleepy; **~ac** sleepyhead
pospješi|ti, ~vati hasten; accelerate
posprdan mocking; ironical
pospremati put in order, tidy up; (*sobu*) do the room; (*stol*) clear away
posramiti make ashamed
posrebriti silver; coat with

silver; silver-plate
posred in the middle of
posrednik mediator; go-between
posred|ovanje mediation; intervention; **~ovati** mediate; intervene
posr|nuti, ~tati stumble; stagger
postaja station; stop; ***krajnja*** ~ terminus
posta|jati, ~ti become; grow; get; originate
postajkivati linger; stop
postanak origin
postar oldish; advanced in years
postarati se take care of; attend to; (*postati star*) age
postav|iti put, place, set
postelj|a bed; **~ina** bedding; bed-clothes
postepen gradual; progressive
postići attain; achieve
postiti fast
postizati = **postići**
posto per cent
postojan steady; constant; stable; ***~a boja*** fast colour
postoja|nje being; existence; **~ti** exist; be; live
postojeći existing; present
postola shoe; **~r** shoe-maker; ***~rska radnja*** shoe-repairs
postolje stand
postotak percentage
postradati suffer injury (damage; loss)
postrance sideways; aside; out of the way
postrijeljati shoot down (off)
postrojenje formation; (*tvornica*) plant
postup|ak procedure; proceeding; **~ati, ~iti** treat, deal with; behave towards
posuda vessel; container
posudben: ***~a knjižnica*** lending library
posuditi (*drugom*) lend; (*od drugoga*) borrow
posuđe dishes
posuđivati = **posuditi**
posumnjati suspect; doubt
posušiti dry (up)
posuti = **posipati**
posvaditi se quarrel; fall out with
posve entirely; fully; quite
posvećivati consecrate; devote; dedicate
posvet|a consecration; dedication; **~iti** = **posvećivati**
posvjedočiti attest; certify; affirm
posvojiti adopt
posvuda everywhere; all over
pošast plague; epidemic
pošiljka shipment; parcel
poškakljati tickle
poškropiti sprinkle
pošta post, mail; post-office; ***glavna*** ~ General Post-Office
poštansk|i post, postal; ***~i brod*** mail-boat; ***~i činovnik*** post-office clerk; ***~i ček*** postal order; ***~a kola*** mail-car; ***~i***

pretinac post-office box; ***~a pristojba*** postage; ***~i sanduk*** letter-box; pillar-box; ***~a uputnica*** money order; ***~i ured*** post-office
poštar postman; **~ina** postage
poštedjeti spare
pošte|n honest; fair; just; upright; ***na ~nu riječ*** upon my word; **~nje** honesty; honour; fairness
poštivati esteem; respect; estimate
pošto? how much?
pošto after; when
poštova|n respected; esteemed; honoured; ***~ni gospodine!*** (*u pismu*) Dear Sir; **~nje** respect; homage; esteem; ***s ~njem*** respectfully; (*u pismu*) Yours faithfully; Yours truly; **~ti** = **poštivati**
pošumiti afforest
pota|ći, ~knuti animate; stimulate; inspire
potajno secretly, surreptitiously
potamniti destroy; kill off
potam|niti obscure; darken; **~njeti** grow dark
pota|nko in detail; minutely; **~nje** more detailed
potapati sink; put under water
potapšati tap
potegnuti pull
potencija power
poteškoća difficulty; trouble
potez line; move; ***~ pera*** stroke; **~ati** = **potegnuti**
pothvat enterprise; undertaking
potica|j impulse; incentive; **~ti** = **potaći**
potiljak nape
potis|kivati, ~nuti press (push) back
potišten depressed; **~ost** depression
potjecati originate; be derived from
potjera chase; pursuit; **~ti** drive (chase) away
potkapati undermine
potkivati shoe (a horse)
potkopati = **potkapati**
potkova horse-shoe; **~ti** = **potkivati**
potkresati cut off
potkrijepiti corroborate
potkrovlje loft
potkupiti bribe
potlačiti oppress; press down; crush; subdue
potočnica forget-me-not
potok brook
potom|ak descendant; offspring; **~stvo** posterity; descendants (*pl*)
potonuti sink; go down
potonji the latter
potop deluge; flood; **~iti** sink
potpaliti set fire to; light
potpetica heel
potpis signature; **~an** signed; **~ati** sign; **~nik** the undersigned; subscriber
potplat sole

potplatiti bribe
potpom|agati, **~oći**, **~ognuti** support; aid; assist
potpora support; relief; (*dotacija*) subsidy; **~nj** prop; pillar
potporučnik sub-lieutenant
potpredsjednik vice president
potpukovnik lieutenant-colonel
potpun complete; full; **~iti** complete; fill up; **~ost** completeness; integrity
potraga search; pursuit
potrajati last; continue
potratiti waste
potraži|ti look up (for); search; **~vanje** demand; claim; reclamation; **~vati** claim; reclaim
potražnja demand
potrčati run; start running
potreb|a necessity; want; need; ***u ~i*** in case of need; **~an** necessary; needed
potrepštine requirements, accessories
potres earthquake; concussion; **~ti** shake
potrga|n torn; **~ti** tear
potrostručiti treble; triple
potroš|ač consumer; **~ak** consumption; expenditure; expense; **~iti** spend; **~nja** consumption
potruditi se take pains; give oneself the trouble
potucati se live a vagabond's life; wander about
potući se come to blows
potužiti se complain
potvr|da confirmation; certificate; (*primitka*) receipt; **~diti** confirm; ratify; certify; attest
potvrdni affirmative
poubijati kill off; massacre; slaughter
pouč|avati teach; instruct; coach; **~an** instructive; **~iti** teach; instruct; **~ljiv** teachable; apt to be taught
pouka instruction; tuition
pouzda|n reliable; trustworthy; **~nik** confidant; reliable person; **~nje** confidence; trust; ***pun ~nja*** full of confidence; trusting; **~ti se** rely on; trust; have confidence in
pouzeće cash on delivery
povećа|lo magnifying glass; **~nje** enlargement; increase; growth; **~ti** enlarge, magnify; **~ti se** increase; become enlarged
povelja charter; bull
povenuti wither
povesti take; lead
povez bandage; **~ati** bind; bandage
povi|jati; **~ti** bandage; swaddle up
povijest history; **~an** historical
povijuša climbing plant; creeper
povik cry; outcry; exclamation; **~nuti** exclaim; cry out

povi|siti heighten; (*cijenu*) raise, put up; **~šenje** increase, rise; elevation; **~šica** rise
povjeravati se unbosom oneself to; confide in
povjer|enik commissioner; confidant; **~eništvo** commission; committee; **~enje** confidence; trust; **~iti** confide; entrust (with); **~ljiv** trustful; confidential
povjerovati believe (in)
povjetarac breeze
povlačiti drag along; trail; (*novac*) withdraw; **~ se** (*vojska*) retreat
povlađivati acclaim; applaud; approve
povla|stica privilege; **~šten** privileged
povod motive; cause
povoda|n swampy; flooded; **~nj** flood
povoditi se imitate
povodom on the occasion of
povoj bandage; (*djeteta*) diaper, swaddling-clothes
povoljan favourable; propitious; convenient
povorka procession; ***svečana ~*** festive procession; parade
povraćati vomit
povratak return
povrat|an, ***~na karta*** return ticket; ***~na zamjenica*** reflexive pronoun
povratiti return; give back; (*bacati*) vomit, throw up; **~ se** return; go (come) back
povrće vegetables (*pl*)
povreda violation; offence; (*ozljeda*) injury
povremen periodical
povrh besides; over, above
povrijediti injure, hurt; wrong; (*zakon*) violate, break
površ|an superficial; **~ina** surface; (*tlo*) area; **~inski** surface; **~nost** superficiality
povučen reserved, unsociable; **~ost** seclusion; privacy
povući = povlačiti
pozabaviti se amuse oneself; have a good time
pozadina background
pozajm|ica loan; **~iti** (*drugome*) lend, give a loan; (*od drugoga*) borrow
pozdrav greeting; salute; **~iti** greet; salute
pozelenjeti become (turn) green
pozirati pose
pozitivan positive, definite; affirmative
poziv call; summons; (*zvanje*) vocation; **~ati** invite; summon; call; ***~ati natrag*** recall, summon back; ***~ati u pomoć*** call for help; **~ati se** refer to
pozivnica invitation card
pozla|ćen gold-plated, gilt; **~ćivati**, **~titi** gild, plate with gold
poznanik acquaintance; **~stvo** acquaintance

pozna|t known, well-known; ***opće ~t*** well-known; **~ti**, **~vati** know, be acquainted with; **~valac** expert, connoisseur; **~vanje** knowledge
pozno late
pozor attention; ***stati ~*** stand at attention; **~an** attentive
pozorište = **kazalište**
pozornica stage
pozornost attention; ***privući ~*** draw attention to
pozvati = **pozivati**
pozvoniti ring
požaliti regret
požar fire; ***siguran od ~a*** fireproof
požderati eat up greedily; gobble up
poželj|an desirable; **~eti** wish; crave for
požeti reap
požrtvov|an self-sacrificing; unselfish; **~nost** self-denial, devotion
požuda lust; desire; **~n** greedy; lustful; avid
požuriti hurry, hasten; rush; **~ se** hurry up; make haste
požut|iti make yellow; **~jeti** become (turn) yellow
prababa great-grandmother
praćakati se splash about, (*riba*) thrash
praćka sling
pradjed great-grandfather
prag threshold; door-step; (*pruge*) sleeper
prah dust; powder; ***puščani ~*** gun-powder
prak|sa practice; (*rad*) practical work; **~tičan** practical
pralja washerwoman
pramac bow
pramen tuft; lock
pranje washing
praonica wash-room; laundry
praporac (little) bell
pras|ac, **~e** pig; **~etina** pork
pras|ak report, explosion, detonation; **~kati** crack, pop; explode; detonate
prasica sow
praskozorje dawn
praš|ak powder; (*biljke*) pollen; **~an** dusty; **~ina** dust; ***brisati ~inu*** dust
prašnik pistil
praštati pardon, forgive
prašuma virgin forest
prati wash; **~ se** wash (oneself)
prat|ilac escort, companion; **~iti** (*kući*) see home; (*na vlak itd.*) see off; accompany; **~nja** escort; suite
praunučad great-grandchildren
praunuk great-grandson; **~a** great-granddaughter
prav just, right; proper; genuine; real; actual
pravac direction
pravda justice; **~ti se** quarrel
praved|an just; (*nepristran*) impartial; fair; **~nost** justice
pravi the right one; true; original; authentic
pravica justice; right

pravič|an right, fair, just; **~nost** justice, righteousness
pravil|an regular; **~nost** regularity; **~o** rule, principle; standard; regulation
praviti make, produce, manufacture; create; form
pravni legal, judicial; **~k** lawyer; **~čki** legal
pravo right; justice; law; **~doban** opportune; **~dobno** in (on) time; **~kut** rectangle; **~kutan** rectangular; **~kutnik** rectangle; **~moćan** valid; **~pis** spelling; orthography; **~rijek** verdict; sentence; **~slavan** Orthodox
praz|an empty, vacant; **~nik** holiday; **~nina** emptiness; ***~no mjesto*** vacancy; **~niti (se)** empty
praznovjer|an superstitious; **~je** superstition
prčkati fumble
prćija dowry
prčiti (*usta*) pout
pre- (*previše*) too
prebaciti overturn; (*preko ramena*) throw over (the shoulder)
prebira|č sorter, picker; **~ti** select, pick out
prebiva|lište home; residence; **~ti** live, reside
prebje|ći run over; desert; **~g(lica)** deserter; runaway
preboljeti get over, get well
prebrojiti count
precijeniti overrate, overestimate
preciz|an precise, accurate; **~nost** preciseness
precrtati oss out, cancel, (*prerisati*) copy, trace over
prečac short cut
prečaga = **prečka**
preči more important
prečka rung; bar
prečuti not catch; ignore
pred before; in front of; ***~ 8 dana*** eight days ago
preda|ja delivery; (*neprijatelju*) surrender; capitulation; (*usmena*) tradition; **~nje** lecture; **~ti** deliver; give up; hand over; **~ti se** surrender, capitulate; **~telj** deliverer; sender; **~vač** lecturer; **~vati** (*uručiti*) deliver; lecture
predbaci|ti, **~vati** reproach
predbilježba (advance) subscription; booking; **~iti** subscribe (register) in advance
predbroj|iti se subscribe (to); **~ka** subscription
predgovor preface; introduction
predgrađe suburbs; outskirts
predigra prelude
pred|io, **~jel** region
predi|onica spinning-mill; cotton-mill; **~vo** yarn
predlaga|č proposer, promoter; **~ti** suggest; propose
predložiti = **predlagati**
predmet object; subject; theme
predmnijevati suppose; presume

prednost preference; advantage; privilege; ***dati ~*** favour; prefer
prednjačiti lead the way; *fig* take the lead
prednj|i front; leading; ***~a četa*** avantguard; ***~a strana*** foreground
predočiti show; produce; ***~ sebi*** form an idea; figure oneself; imagine
predodžba idea; notion; conception
predomisliti se change one's mind
predosjećati have a foreboding
predrasuda prejudice; bias
predsjedni|štvo chairmanship; presidentship; **~k** president, chairman
predsoblje hall
predstav|a performance; show; **~iti** introduce; **~ništvo** representation; **~nik** representative
predstoj|ati be forth coming; **~nik** head, principal; manager
predstraža advance-guard
predujam advance
preduslov prerequisite
predusresti prevent; anticipate
preduvjet = **preduslov**
preduzimati undertake
predvečerje eve
predvesti bring (lead) before; bring in
predvi|djeti foresee; envisage; **~đanje** foreseeing; anticipation; **~đen** foreseen; anticipated
predvoditi lead the way; go ahead
predvorje vestibule; entrance-hall
pređa yarn
prefrigan shrewd, clever; cunning
pregača apron; pinafore
pregaziti run down (over); (*vodu*) wade over
pregibati bend
pregled review, survey; synopsis; examination; **~an** synoptic; **~ati** look over; examine; survey; revise; (*ne opaziti*) overlook; **~avač** examiner; inspector; surveyor
pregorjeti (*vatra*) burn through; get over (a loss, etc)
pregovara|č negotiator; mediator; **~nje** negotiations; **~ti** negotiate
pregovori negotiations (*pl*)
pregra|da compartment; partition; MAR bulkhead; **~diti** partition off; reconstruct
pregršt handful; armful
prehlad|a cold; **~iti se** catch a cold
preina|čiti alter; remodel; reconstruct; **~ka** alteration; modification
prekapati dig up; rummage
preki|d interruption; break; ***~d vatre*** cease-fire; ***bez ~da*** continually; cease-

lessly; ***na ~de*** on and off; **~dač** switch; **~dati**, **~nuti** interrupt; discontinue; disconnect; break off
prekipjeti boil over
prekjuče(r) the day before yesterday
preklani the year before last
preklinjati implore
preklop|iti fold over; ***~ni stolac*** folding-chair
preko across; over; on the other side; ***~ dana*** during the day; ***~ reda*** out of one's turn
prekobaciti se turn a summersault
preko|brojan supernumerary; odd; **~mjeran** immoderate; excessive; **~mjernost** excess; **~morski** oversea(s)
prekopati dig up; turn over the ground
prekoračiti overstep; (*kršiti*) transgress; (*račun*) overdraw; (*nadmašiti*) exceed
prekoriti blame; find fault with; rebuke
prekosutra the day after tomorrow
prekrasan wonderful; magnificent
prekrca|ti trans-ship; **~vanje** trans-shipment
prekretnica turning-point
prekriti cover (with)
prekrižiti se cross oneself
prekrstiti give another name; (*ruke*) cross one's arms
prekrš|aj offence; breach; transgression; **~iti** break; transgress; trespass
preksinoć the evening before yesterday
prekuhati boil (over again)
prekupac middleman
prelaz crossing; transit; (*preko pruge*) level crossing; **~iti** cross; go over; exceed
preletjeti fly over
prelijevati se overflow; flood
prelomiti break in two
preljub adultery; **~nica** adulteress; **~nik** adulterer
prema toward(s); against; (*nasuprot*) opposite to; ***~ tome*** consequently; accordingly
premalo too little; ***~ plaćen*** underpaid
premašiti exceed; surpass
premazati smear; coat (all over)
premda (al)though
premetačin|a search; ***nalog za ~u*** search-warrant
premijera first-night
preminuti die, pass away
premišljavati consider, think over; hesitate
premjer|avati, **~iti** measure; survey; (*okom*) look one up and down (from top to toe)
premje|stiti remove; transfer; **~štenje** removal; transference
premlatiti beat all over; thrash

premoć predominance; superiority; overweight; **~an** superior; predominant
premor|enost overwork; **~iti se** get tired; overwork
premostiti bridge over; span with a bridge
prenagliti se act rashly
prenapeti stretch too tightly; overstrain
prenapuč|iti over-populate; **~enost** over-population
prenatovariti overload
prenatrpan overcrowded
prenemagati se affect
prenera|ziti astound; stupify; stagger; **~žen** dumbfounded; staggered
prenijeti bring (carry) over; convey; MATH carry forward
prenoćiti spend the night
prenositi = **prenijeti**
prenosiv transferable
prenuti se wake up
preoblačiti (se) change clothes
preobući = **preoblačiti**
preokrenuti turn over; turn upside down
preokret revolution; sudden change
preopteretiti overburden; overload
preorati plough up
preosta|li remaining; left over; **~tak** remnant; remains (*pl*); **~ti** remain over, be left
preoteti snatch away (from); **~ *maha*** gain ground; spread
prepasti startle; frighten
prepatiti suffer; endure pain
prepečenica double distilled brandy
prepelica quail
prepeličar spaniel
prepiliti saw through, saw up (in two)
prepir|ati se quarrel; argue; **~ka** quarrel; dispute
prepis|ati copy; **~ka** correspondence
preplanuo suntanned
preplašiti frighten, scare; **~ se** get frightened (scared)
preplaviti overflow, flood
preplivati swim across
prepoloviti halve, divide in two
prepona obstacle; (*utrke*) hurdle
preporod renaissance, revival
preporu|čen recommended; (*pismo*) registered; **~čiti** recommend; (*pismo*) register; **~ka** recommendation
prepotentan presumptious; overbearing
prepoznati recognize
prepreden crafty, cunning
prepreka obstacle
spriječiti prevent; obstruct
preproda|ja re-sale; **~vač** retailer; huckster; **~vati** retail; re-sell
prepun too full; overcrowded; **~iti** overfill
prepu|stiti leave (to); cede
preračunati convert

prera|dba remodelling; alteration; manufacture; **~diti** re-make; manufacture
preran too early; premature
prerasti outgrow
prerez section; **~ati** cut through
prerisati copy a drawing
prerušiti (se) disguise (oneself)
presa|diti transplant
presahnuti dry up
prese|liti move; **~ljenje** removal
presene|ćen staggered; surprised; **~titi** surprise; stagger
presijecati traverse, cross
presipa|ti shoot into another container
presjeći = **presijecati**; cut
presk|akivati keep jumping (over); **~očiti** jump over
preslušа|nje (cross-)examination; hearing; trial; **~ti** (cross-)examine; interrogate
preso|liti over-salt; **~ljen** over-salted
prestan|ak discontinuance; end; ***bez ~ka*** ceaselessly
prestati cease; stop; finish; ***~ raditi*** stop work
presti spin; (*mačka*) purr
presti|ći, **~gnuti** overtake; surpass
prestrašiti frighten; scare; startle; **~ se** get frightened
prestupna godina leap-year
presud|a judgement; sentence; **~an** decisive; **~iti** pass judgement on; judge; bring a verdict
presušiti dry up; run dry
presvijetao too bright; most illustrious
presvlačiti change (clothes)
presvlaka (*jastuka*) slip
presvući = **presvlačiti**
preša press; (*žurba*) hurry; **~n** pressed; (*hitan*) pressing, urgent; **~ti** press
preštampati reprint
prešutjeti keep secret; conceal
pretakati pour out into another vessel; (*u boce*) bottle
preteći outrun; overtake; (*nadmašiti*) outdo; surpass
preteg|a overweight; **~nuti** outweigh
pretek abundance; ***imati na ~*** abound in
prete|zati = **~gnuti**; predominate; **~žan** predominant; outweighing; **~žnost** overweight; predominance
prethod|an preliminary; previous; **~iti** precede; lead the way
pretinac pigeon-hole; locker; drawer; ***poštanski ~*** post-office box
pretio fat
pretis|ak re-print; **~kati** re-print
pretjecati overtake
pretjera|n exaggerated; **~nost** extravagance; exaggeration; **~ti** exaggerate;

overdo
pretočiti = **pretakati**
pretovariti overload; transship
pretplaćen subscribed to
pretplat|a subscription; **~iti se** subscribe to
pretpostav|ka hypothesis; supposition; presumption; **~iti** suppose, presume; **~ivši** supposing
pretprodaja advance-sale; advance booking
pretraga search
pretra|žiti search; scan; **~živanje** scan; **~žnik** scanner
pretrčati run across
pretres|ati, ~ti discuss
pretrpjeti undergo; endure; suffer
pretvarati se pretend, feign, simulate
pretvoriti transform; turn into
preudati remarry
preudesiti alter, change; re-arrange
preuranjen premature
preure|đenje alteration; re-arrangement; **~diti** alter; re-arrange
preuveliča|ti exaggerate
preuzet|an presumptious; assuming; arrogant; **~nost** presumption; arrogance; **~i** take over
preuzima|nje taking over; **~ti** = **preuzeti**
prevađati = **prevoditi**
prevag|a overweight; **~nuti** turn the scale
prevaliti (*srušiti*) overthrow, overturn; upset; (*put*) cover a distance, travel; **~ se** topple over (down)
prevar|a fraud; deception; swindle; **~iti** cheat; deceive; swindle (out of); **~iti se** be mistaken; mistake, be wrong
prevejan cunning, crafty; **~ac** crafty fellow
preve|sti (~dem) translate; render into
preve|sti (~zem) carry over; transfer; take over
previ|jati, ~ti fold, bend; (*ranu*) dress
previnuti turn down; bend
previše too much
prevlačiti pull over; cover
prevlada|ti prevail, win; overcome
prevlaka slip, case; cover; (*tanka*) film; GEOGR isthmus
prevlast predominance; supremacy
prevodi|lac translator; interpreter; **~ti** translate; interprete
prevoz transport; freight; **~iti** transport; transfer
prevrat revolution; subversion
prevr|nuti, ~tati overthrow; overturn; upset; **~nuti se** tumble (topple) down; **~tljiv** fickle, inconstant, changeable
prevući = **prevlačiti**

prezime surname, family name
prezimiti spend the winter; (*životinje u snu*) hibernate
prezir, **~anje** disdain, scorn, contempt; **~an** contemptible, scornful; **~ati**, **prezreti** contempt, scorn, look down upon
preživjeti survive; outlive
prhak crisp; (*zemlja*) loose
prhut dandruff, scurf
pri at, by, near; **~ *svemu tome*** for all that
prianjati adhere; cling to; stick to
pribada|ča safety-pin; pin; **~ti** pin; tack
pribaviti supply (with); provide; obtain
pribi|jati, **~ti** nail (to)
približa|n approximate; **~vanje** approach(ing); **~vati (se)** approach; draw near
pribor accessories (*pl*); outfit; trimings (*pl*); appliances (*pl*); **~ *za jelo*** cutlery; silverware
pribrajati add up (together); sum up
priča story; tale; **~ti** tell a story; narrate
priče kati wait for
pričiniti se appear, seem
pričuva reserve; **~ti** reserve for; save
pričvrstiti fasten; attach
prići come up to; approach
pridavati add; attribute
pridjev adjective
pridobiti win over; talk over
prido|ći, **~laziti** come (arrive) later on; **~šlica** newcomer
pridružiti (se) join
pridržati keep (back); not let go; (*pravo*) reserve (right)
prigibati (se) bend; stoop; bow
prignuti = **prigibati**
prignječiti press down; crush
prigod|a opportunity; occasion; chance; **~om** on the occasion of
prigov|arati reproach; blame; find fault with; **~or** objection; criticism
prigrijati warm up; re-heat
prigušiti smother; suffocate; (*glas*) subdue
prihod income; revenue; profit
prihvat|iti accept; seize; **~ljiv** acceptable
prijašnji former; previous
prijat|an pleasant; agreeable; **~elj** friend; **~eljski** friendly; **~eljstvo** friendship; **~i** suit; be to one's taste
prijav|a denunciation; report; **~iti** report; denounce
prijavni: **~ *ured*** registry (office); **~ca** registration form
prijaz|an kind, amiable; friendly; **~nost** kindness, amiability
prije before; ago; formerly; previously; **~ *ili kasnije*** sooner or later; **~ *svega*** first of all; ***što ~ to bolje*** the sooner the better

priječiti hinder; prevent, stop (from)
prejeći = **prelaziti**
prijedlog proposal; suggestion; *gr* preposition
prijekor reproach
prijelaz crossing; passage; (*pruge preko ceste*) level crossing
prijelom break; fracture; rupture
prijem reception; admittance
prijemnik (wireless, television) set
prijenos transfer(ence); transport; MATH carrying over
prijepis copy; transcription
prijeporan disputable; questionable
prijesto, **~lje** throne; **~lnica** metropolis, capital
prijet|iti threaten; **~nja** threat; menace
prijevara fraud, cheat; deception; swindle
prijevod translation
prijevoz transport; (*brodom*) shipping
prijevoz|an: ***~no sredstvo*** vehicle; conveyance
prikaz account; review; **~ati** represent; present; expose; THEAT perform; **~ivanje** (re)presentation; show; performance
prikladan suitable, convenient; fit; proper; appropriate
prikloniti se lean to; show inclination for
priključ|ak connection; **~iti** join to; connect
prikolica (*motocikla*) side car; (*automobila*) caravan; trailer
prikopčati buckle to; button up; fasten
prikovati rivet
prikratiti (*koga*) not give one his due; (*vrijeme*) pass the time
prikriti hide; cover
prikupiti collect
prilago|diti accommodate to; adapt; **~diti se** get accustomed to; adapt oneself to
prilaz access; way to; **~iti** approach; draw near
priličan fair; considerable; **~no** rather; fairly; considerably
prilijepiti glue, paste, stick on; ***~ ćušku*** box one's ears; **~ se** adhere; stick
prilik|a opportunity, chance; occasion; **~e** conditions; circumstances; ***od ~e, po prilici*** about, approximately, roughly
priliv inflow; flux
prilog supplement; contribution; GRAM adverb; ***u ~u*** enclosed; ***govoriti u ~*** speak in favour of
prilož|en enclosed; added; **~iti** enclose; add
priljepčiv contagious; infectious
priljubiti se cling to; snuggle to

prima|ći (se), ~knuti (se) draw nearer; move closer
primalac receiver, recipient
primalja midwife
primam|iti lure; attract; tempt; **~ljiv** attractive; alluring
primanje acceptance; reception; admittance; ***soba za ~*** drawing-room
primati accept; receive; (*plaću*) draw
primicati se = **primaći se**
primijeniti apply (to)
primijetiti notice; observe
primirje armistice
primit|ak receipt; acceptance; **~i** = **primati**
primitivan primitive
primjećivati = **primijetiti**
primjedba remark: comment; note
primje|na application; use; **~nljiv** applicable; **~njivati** apply (to)
primjer example, instance; ***na ~*** for instance, for example; **~ak** copy; specimen; sample; **~an** model; exemplary; **~en** fair; adequate; appropriate
primjesa mixture; ingredient
primka receipt
primorati force, compel
primorje seaside; littoral; coast
princip principle; ***iz ~a*** on principle
prin|esti, ~ositi contribute; give one's share
prinud|a compulsion; **~an** compulsory; **~iti** force; compel
prionuti tackle (work); work hard; (*prilijepiti se*) cling to; adhere
priopć|enje communication; announcement; **~iti** announce; inform
pripadati belong; appertain to
pripasati girdle on; buckle on
pripasti = **pripadati**
pripaziti look after; keep an eye on
pripis|ati make a note; (*uzrok*) ascribe to; put down to; (*u zaslugu*) put to one's credit
pripit tipsy
pripitomiti tame
pripoj|enje annexation; **~iti** annex
pripom|agati, ~oći help, assist, aid; **~oć** help, aid, assistance
pripov|ijedati tell, narrate; **~ijetka, ~ijest** story, tale; **~jedač** story-teller, narrator
priprav|a preparation; **~an** ready; handy; **~nost** readiness; **~iti** prepare; make (get) ready
priprem|a preparation(s); **~ati** prepare
priprost simple, homely; primitive
pripu|stiti admit; let in; **~štanje** admittance, admission

prirast increase; growth; **~i** grow together
prire|dba show; performance; **~diti**, **~đivati** prepare, arrange
prirez additional tax, surtax
prirod crop, produce
prirod|a nature; ***mrtva ~a*** still life; **~opis** natural history (science); **~oslovac**, **~oznanac** naturalist
priruč|an: ***~a knjižnica*** reference library
priručnik reference book; textbook
prise|ći, **~gnuti** swear, take an oath; **~ga** oath; (*kriva*) perjury
prisiliti compel, force
prisizati = **priseći**
priskrbiti procure; obtain
prisloniti (se) lean to (against)
prisluškiva|č eavesdropper; **~ti** eavesdrop
prispjeti arrive; get to; ***~ na vrijeme*** arrive in due time
prispodoba comparison
prista|janje fitting, fit; (*pristanak*) agreement; **~jati** fit; suit; go well with; (*brod*) land; **~nak** consent; agreement; **~nište** quay, pier; (*zračno*) airport, airfield
pristao handsome; neat
pristaša partisan; follower
pristati = **pristajati**; agree, consent
pristoja|n decent; proper; polite; courteous; **~ti se** be proper (decent)
pristojba duty; fee(s)
pristojnost decency; propriety; politeness
pristran partial; biassed; **~ost** partiality; bias
pristup admission; access; ***~ zabranjen!*** no admittance; **~ačan** accessible; within reach; **~iti** approach; come up to; join, enter; (*na internet*) log in
prisustvo presence; **~vati** be present; attend
prisutan present; ***biti ~*** be present at; attend
prisutnost = **prisustvo**; ***~ duha*** quick wit
prisvojiti usurp; claim
prišapnuti whisper into one's ear
prišarafiti screw up
prišiti sew on; stitch on
prišt pimple; **~av** pimply
prištedjeti save; economize
pritegnuti tighten
pritis|ak pressure; oppression; **~kati**, **~nuti** press (down); oppress; weigh heavily on
pritjecati flow into
pritok tributary
pritrčati run up to
prituž|ba complaint; **~iti se** complain
priuč|iti se get accustomed (used) to
priuštiti (*nekome*) not grudge one; ***ja si to ne mogu ~*** I cannot afford it

privatan private
privezati fasten, tie; bind; (*psa na lanac*) chain
privid|an apparent; **~no** seemingly; apparently; **~nost** illusion; pretence; make-believe
priviđenje hallucination; apparition
priviknuti se get accustomed (used) to
privilegij privilege
privinuti embrace, hug
privjesak pendant; (*na kovčegu*) tag
privlačan = **privlačiv**
privlač|iti attract, draw; appeal to one; **~iv** attractive; **~ivost** attraction
privo|la consent; **~ljeti** give one's consent, consent; agree
privreda economy; **~n** economic; business
privremen temporary; provisional
privrijediti earn, make money
privržen attached (devoted) to
privući attract, draw
prizemlje ground floor; *Am* first floor
priziv appeal
prizna|nje acknowledgement; recognition; confession; **~vati** acknowledge, recognize; confess, admit
prizor sight; spectacle; scene
prizvuk accompanying sound
prkos spite; obstinacy; **~an** obstinate; spiteful; **~iti** defy; be obstinate
prlja|ti dirty; **~v** dirty; foul; filthy; **~vština** dirt; squalor; filth
prnj|a rag; **~av** tattered; **~e** rags, tatters (*pl*)
proba trial; test; THEAT rehearsal
probadati pierce; stitch
probati try; test; (*jelo*) taste; THEAT rehearse
probav|a digestion; ***loša ~a*** indigestion; **~iti** digest; **~ljiv** digestible
probijati penetrate; break through; **~ se** cut (fight) one's way (through)
probisvijet vagabond; good-for-nothing
probitačan profitable; advantageous
probiti = **probijati**
problem problem; **~atičan** problematic
problijediti turn (become) pale
proboj|an piercing; not proof to; **~nost** penetrability
probosti = **probadati**
probuditi wake up; awake; **~ se** wake (up)
probušiti pierce; perforate; (*kartu*) punch
procedura procedure
proces process; legal action
procesija procession
procijediti filter; strain

procijeniti evaluate; estimate
procje|na estimate; **~njivati** = **procijeniti**
procuriti leak (out)
procvasti begin to bloom; *fig* flourish
pročelnik head; chief; principal
pročelje façade; front
pročistiti clean; purify; purge
pročitati read (through)
proći go (pass) by; (*nestati*) disappear; (*na ispitu*) pass (the exam)
proda|ja sale; ***u ~ji*** on sale; **~ti**, **~vati** sell; vend; **~vač** seller; salesman; shop-assistant; vendor; **~vačica** salesgirl, saleswoman; shop-assistant
prod|irati, **~rijeti** penetrate; break in (through)
prodoran piercing
prodrmati shake up
produbiti deepen; hollow out
producirati produce; manufacture
produk|cija production; **~t** product; **~tivan** productive; **~tivnost** productivity
produ|ljiti, **~žiti** lengthen; prolong; extend
prođa sale
profanirati profane
profesor teacher; (*sveučilišni*) professor
profil profile
proganjati persecute; chase
proglas proclamation; manifesto; **~iti** proclaim; issue a manifesto
progna|n exiled; banned; banished; **~nik** exile; expatriate; outlaw; **~ti** exile; banish
prognoza forecast
progon persecution; pursuit; **~iti** = **proganjati**; **~stvo** exile; banishment
progovoriti begin to speak; break silence
program program(me)
progres progress; advancement; **~ivan** progressive
progresija progression
progristi bite (gnaw) through
progunđati mutter
progurati push through
progutati swallow
prohodan passable
prohtjeti se have a mind (longing) after
proigrati gamble away
proizaći originate from; result from, follow
proizvađač producer
proizvesti = **proizvoditi**
proizvod product; produce; **~iti** produce; **~nja** production
projekt project
projicirati project
projuriti rush past; speed by
prokl|et damned; cursed; **~eti**, **~injati** damn, curse
prokopati dig through
prokrčiti clear; ***~ si put*** force

one's way through, break one's way through
prokulica Brussels sprouts (*pl*)
prolaz passage, thoroughfare; transit; arcade; **~an** passing; transient; transitory; **~iti** pass by, go by; traverse; **~nik** passer-by
proleter proletarian
proli|jevati, ~ti spill; (*krv, suze*) shed
prolistati put forth leaves; turn (over) the leaves (of a book), skim through
prolom oblaka cloud-burst
proljeće spring
proljev diarrhoea
promaknu|će promotion, advancement; **~ti** promote, advance
promaš|aj failure; **~iti** miss, fail; make a mistake
promatra|č observer; onlooker; **~ti** observe, watch
promećuran enterprising, pushing
promet traffic; (*novca*) circulation; (*poslovanje*) trade, business; (*robe*) turnover; ***teretni ~*** goods traffic; ***putnički ~*** passenger traffic; ***zračni ~*** air traffic; ***povući iz ~a*** withdraw from circulation
promet|an: ***~na nezgoda*** road accident
promicati further, promote, advance
promijeniti change, alter; (*novac*) change
promiješati mix (up); stir (up)
promi|sliti consider, think over; **~šljen** deliberate; cautious; **~šljenost** deliberation; consideration
promje|na change; alteration; **~nljiv** changeable; (*vrijeme*) unsettled; (*ćud*) inconstant; unstable
promjer diameter
promjeriti measure; (*koga okom*) look one up and down
promocija conferring of the degree; graduation
promoči|ti soak through; **~v** not waterproof
promrmljati mutter; mumble
promuk|ao hoarse, husky; **~lost** hoarseness, huskiness
pronaći find out; discover; invent
pronevjer|enje embezzlement; **~iti** embezzle
pronicav sharp, keen; clever; **~ost** insight, intuition; sagacity
proniknuti penetrate; see through one
propa|danje decay, decline; (*zgrade*) dilapidation; **~dati, ~sti** decay, decline; (*zgrada*) dilapidate; (*tlo*) sink; **~st** decline, ruin, catastrophe
propagirati propagate
propelo crucifix
propeti se rear (rise) on hind

legs
propiliti saw through
propinjati se = **propeti se**
propis rule, regulation; **~ati** regulate; (*lijek*) prescribe
propitkivati se gather information; enquire about
propovijed sermon; **~ati** preach, deliver a sermon; **~aonica** pulpit
propovjednik preacher
propuh draught; ***tu je ~*** it is draughty here
propusnica pass, permit to pass
propust negligence, omission; **~iti** omit; neglect (fail) to do; miss
proputovati travel all over
proračun estimate; calculation; **~ati** estimate; calculate
proreći foretell, predict, forecast, prophesy
prorez (*rupa*) slot, slit; (*ploha*) section
proricati = **proreći**
proro|čanstvo prophecy; **~k** prophet; **~kovati** = **proreći**
prosac suitor, wooer
prosijati sieve, sift
prosijecati cut through, intersect
prosijed greyish; grizzled
prosinac December
prosipati waste; scatter; spill
prositi ask, beg; (*djevojku*) woo, propose
prosja|čiti beg, live by begging; **~k** beggar
prosje|čan average, ordinary; **~k** the average; (*ploha*) section
proslav|a celebration, festival, commemoration; **~iti** celebrate; **~iti se** become famous
proslijediti forward
proso millet
prost rude, vulgar, common; ***~ od*** free from; ***~ narod*** mob; **~ak** vulgar (rude) person; boor; **~aštvo**, **~ota** vulgarity; dirty (foul) speech; obscenity
prostirač mat, doormat; rug
prostirati (*stol*) lay
prostitutka prostitute
prostoduš|an naive, straightforward; sincere; **~nost** artlessness; naivety; sincerity
prostor space, room; ***zrakoprazan ~*** vacuum; **~ija** room; (*radna*) premises (*pl*)
prostota vulgarity
prostran spacious, wide
prostrijeliti shoot through
prostrijeti = **prostirati**
prosuditi form a judgement (opinion)
prosuti = **prosipati**
prosvjećivati educate, enlighten
prosvjed protest; objection; **~ovati** protest, object
prosvjeta education, enlightment; educational system; **~n** educational
prošao past, by-gone; (*zad-*

nji) last; *(nedavan)* recent
prošetati take a walk, go for a walk
proširiti widen, stretch; expand
prošiti sew through, stitch through
prošli = **prošao**
prošlogodišnji last year's
prošlost past, past time
prošuljati se creep (steal) through
prošupljiti perforate, puncture
proteći flow by; *(vrijeme)* pass by; expire
protegnuti se stretch
proteza artificial limb
protezati se = **protegnuti se**
protiv against
protiv|an contrary; opposite; *(nesklon)* opposed; **~no** on the contrary; ***~na stranka*** the opposition; **~iti se** oppose; object to; **~nik** adversary, antagonist; opponent; **~nost** opposition; the opposite; contrast
protjecati = **proteći**
protjerati expel; drive away; banish
protkati interweave; streak with
protrčati run by (through)
protrljati rub, massage all over
protumačiti explain
protu|mjera reprisal, countermeasure; **~napad** counterattack; **~otrov** antidote; **~pravan** unlawful, illegal; **~slovan** contradictory; opposing; **~sloviti** contradict; oppose; **~slovlje** contradiction; **~staviti se** be opposed to; resist; **~teža** counterpoise; counter balance; **~ustavan** unconstitutional; **~vrijednost** equivalence; **~zakonit** illegal, unlawful
proučavati study, research; investigate
prouzro|čiti, **~kovati** cause; bring about
prova bow, prow
proval|a eruption; outburst; *(u kuću)* breaking in, burglary; **~ija** abyss; **~iti** break in(to); burst into; erupt; **~nik** burglar
provesti *(vrijeme)* spend; *(izvršiti)* carry out; **~ se** *(vožnja)* go for a drive (ride); *(zabava)* enjoy oneself
providan transparent
providnost providence
provincija province; the provinces
provizija commission
provizoran provisional; temporary
provjeriti examine, check
provjetriti air; ventilate
provocirati provoke
provodadžija matchmaker
provoditi = **provesti**
proza prose; **~ičan** prosaic
proziran transparent; clear
proziv|anje, **~ka** roll-call; **~ati** call the roll

prozor window; ***staklo ~a*** window-pane; ***krilo ~a*** casement; ***gledati kroz ~*** look out of the window
prozračiti = **provjetriti**
prozreti look through, see through
proždrljiv greedy, gluttonous; **~ost** greediness, gluttony
prožet imbued, permeated; **~i** imbue, permeate
prsa breast, bust, bosom
prska|lica sprayer; **~ti** spray, sprinkle, splash
prsluk waistcoat
prsnuti explode, burst
prst finger; (*nožni*) toe
prste|n ring; **~njak** ring finger
pršut smoked ham
prtljag|a luggage; *Am* baggage; ***kola (vagon) za ~u*** luggage van
prtljati bungle; fumble
prtljažnik *Br* boot; *Am* trunk
pruće brushwood
prud dune, sandbank
pruga (railway-)line; stripe, streak; **~st** striped, streaky
prut twig, rod; thin stick
pruž|ati, **~iti** offer, hand to; pass; **~ati se** stretch; extend
prvak SPORT champion
prvenstvo priority; SPORT championship; ***~ svijeta*** world championship
prvi (the) first
prvo first, firstly, in the first place; **~bitan** original, primary; **~razredan** first-class, first-rate
prvorođen first-born
prž|en roasted; (*na roštilju*) grilled; **~iti** roast, fry, grill; (*sunce*) burn
pržolica roast beef
pset|ance puppy, doggie; **~o** dog
psov|ati scold, rebuke; blame; *coll* tell off; **~ka** oath, curse
pšenica wheat
ptica bird; ***~ selica*** migratory bird
publika public, audience
publikacija publication
puca|nj shot; **~ti** shoot, fire (a gun); (*staklo*) crack
puce button
pucketati crackle, pop; (*jezikom*) click (smack) one's tongue
pucnjava shooting, firing, explosion
pučanstvo population; inhabitants
pučina high seas
pučk|i popular; ***~a škola*** elementary (primary) school
pući = **pucati**
puhati blow; puff, pant
puk common people; populace
puki mere
puknuti = **pucati**
pukotina crack, fissure, crevice; rift, gap
pukovni|ja regiment; **~k** colonel

pumpa pump; **~ti** pump
pun full, filled; ***~a žlica*** (***košara***) a spoonful (a basketful)
punica mother-in-law
puniti fill up; stuff
puno much, a lot of, a great deal; **~glavac** tadpole; **~ljetan** of age; ***postati ~ljetan*** come of age; **~moć** authorization; mandate; COM procuration
pup bud
pupak navel
pup|ati bud, put forth buds; **~oljak** bud
pura turkey-hen; **~n** turkey--cock
pust waste; deserted
pusten felt, made of felt
pustinja desert; **~k** hermit
pustiti leave, let go; abandon; ***~ na slobodu*** set free; ***~ na miru*** leave alone; ***~ unutra*** admit, let in
pustolov adventurer; **~an** adventurous; **~ina** adventure
pustoš waste; **~iti** devastate, lay waste
puš|ač smoker; **~iti** smoke
pušk|a gun, rifle; **~arnica** loop-hole; **~omet** range
puštati = **pustiti**
put way; path; trail; (*putovanje*) travel, trip, journey, voyage; (*puta*) time; ***jedam~*** once; ***dva~*** twice; ***tri~*** three times
pùt complexion, skin; ***tamne ~i*** dark-coloured; **~en** sensual, carnal
putanja orbit
putn|i travel, travelling; ***~a karta*** ticket; **~ica** passport; **~ik** passenger, traveller; ***trgovački ~ik*** commercial traveller, salesman
putokaz sign-post
putopis travel-book; travels (*pl*)
putova|nje travelling, trip, journey; (*morem*) voyage; **~ti** travel
puzati crawl, creep
puž snail; (*bez kućice*) slug
pužev: ***~a kućica*** shell of a snail

R

rabat discount
rabin rabbi
rab|iti use, be used; **~ljen** used, secondhand
racija raid
racionirati ration
račun account, calculation; bill; *come* invoice; ***položiti ~*** render an account; ***otvoriti ~*** open an account; ***stroj za ~anje*** adding-machine, calculating machine; **~ati** calculate, do sums; **~ovodstvo** accountancy; **~ovođa**

accountant
računati se fork, bifurcate
rad work, labour; job
radi because of, on account of; ~ ***nas*** for our sake
radije rather, sooner
radin industrious, diligent, hard-working; **~ost** industry, diligence
radionica workshop
raditi work; do; labour; ***radi se o*** it is a question of
radn|i working; ***~i dan*** work-day, working day; ***~a soba*** study; ***~o vrijeme*** working hours; **~ik** worker, workman
radnja action; work; (*dućan*) shop
rado gladly, willingly
radost joy, delight; cheerfulness; **~an** glad, gay, joyful
radovati se be glad (of), rejoice (in); (*unaprijed*) look forward to
radozna|o curious, inquisitive; **~lost** curiosity, inquisitiveness
rađati give birth to, bear
rafin|erija refinery; **~irati** refine
rahitis rickets (*pl*)
raj paradise
rajčica tomato
rak crab; (*slatkovodni*) crayfish; (*bolest*) cancer
raka grave, tomb, sepulchre
raketa rocket
rakija brandy
ralica plough; (*za snijeg*) snowplough
ralje jaws (*pl*)
rame shoulder
ran early; **~ije** earlier; (*prije*) formerly, previously; **~o** early
ran|a wound, sore; injury; **~iti** wound, inflict wound; hurt
ranjav sore; **~ost** vulnerability
ranjen wounded; **~ik** wounded person
ranjiv vulnerable
rap (*glazba*) rap
rapsodija rhapsody
rasa race
rasadnik nursery(-garden)
rascijepati split, chop
rascvasti se burst into bloom (blossom)
rashla|diti chill; **~diti se** cool down (off); **~đivanje** cooling, chilling
rashod expenditure, expenses (*pl*)
rasip|an extravagant, wasteful; **~ati** waste, squander, be wasteful; **~nik** spendthrift
rasje|ći cut up; split up; **~klina** cleft, fissure, rift
raskalašen dissolute, lascivious; **~ost** debauchery; lasciviousness
raski|nuti pull to pieces; tear asunder
raskliman shaky, rickety
raskol split; (*politički*) secession; (*vjerski*) schism, heresy
raskomadati break into

pieces; ~ **se** disintegrate, fall to pieces
raskopčati unbutton, undo
raskoračiti se stand astride
raskoš luxury; splendour; pomp; **~an** luxurious, sumptuous; profuse
raskrinkati expose, unmask
raskrstiti se break off relations (with)
raskršće cross-roads; crossing; intersection
raskuštrati dishevel, rumple
raskužiti disinfect
raskvašen sodden, soaked through
rasol pickle, brine
raspad crumbling, decay; **~ati se** crumble, fall to pieces; dilapidate
raspakovati unpack
raspaliti inflame with passion; stir up flames; make one's blood boil
rasparati unstitch, slit, rip
raspasti se = **raspadati se**
raspe|će crucifix; **~ti** crucify, nail to the cross
raspiriti stir up
raspit|ati se, **~ivati se** make enquiries, inquire after; **~ivanje** making enquiries
rasplakati se burst into tears
raspli|nuti se fade away, dissolve; **~njivač** MOT carburettor
rasplod breeding; **~iti se** breed, multiply
raspodjela distribution
raspojasa|n dissipated; **~ti se** dissipate
raspolagati dispose of, have at one's disposal
raspoloviti halve, divide (split) in two
raspoložen disposed; (*dobre volje*) in a good mood; ***loše*** ~ in a bad mood
raspoloženje temper, mood; (*dobro*) high spirits; (*loše*) low spirits
raspoloživ available
raspon span; range
raspored scheme, programme); plan; ~ ***sati*** time-table; **~iti** arrange, sort out
rasporiti rip open (off); (*šav*) unstitch
raspoznati recognize; discern; tell one from another; identify
rasprav|a debate, discussion; (*sud*) trial; (*pismena*) treatise, paper; **~ljati** discuss, debate
raspremati clear away; dismantle
rasproda|ja (clearance) sale; **~n** sold out; (*knjiga*) out of print; **~ti** sell out, sell off; clear out stock
rasprostirati se spread, extend
rasprostra|niti spread out (far and wide); **~njen** wide-spread
rasprsnuti (se) explode, burst, blow up
raspršiti (se) dissipate, scat-

ter; disperse
raspu|can cracked, split; **~cati**, **~knuti** crack, split; burst
raspu|stiti dismiss; **~šten** dismissed; undisciplined, wild
rasrditi make angry, anger; **~ se** get angry
rast growth; **~i** grow
rasta|janje parting, taking leave; **~jati**, **~ti se** part with, take leave
rastaliti melt; (*rudaču*) smelt; (*snijeg*) thaw
rastanak parting, taking leave
rastapati melt, dissolve; (*rudaču*) smelt; **~ *se od milja*** be in raptures
rastav|a divorce; **~iti** take to pieces; dismantle; separate; **~iti se** get (obtain) a divorce; divorce; **~ljen** divorced
rastegnuti stretch; draw
rasteretiti disburden, disencumber, relieve of burden
rastez|ati stretch, extend; **~ljiv** elastic, tensile
rasti grow
rastjerati drive away, scatter, dispel
rastopi|ti dissolve; melt; thaw; **~v** soluble
rastovariti unload
rastres|en absent-minded; distracted; **~enost** absent-mindedness; **~ti** distract; **~ti se** amuse oneself, relax
rastrgati tear to pieces
rastrijezniti se sober (down)
rastrojen deranged; shattered
rastrošan extravagant; wasteful
rastužiti sadden, distress
rastv|arati decompose; dissolve
rastvoriti open, push open; gape
rasu|lo dissolution, decadence; falling to pieces; ruin; **~ti** scatter, spill; (*imetak*) squander, waste
rasvijetliti light up, illuminate; brighten up
rasvjeta light(ing), illumination
raščlaniti divide into joints (sections); dismember
raščupati ruffle, dishevel
raširiti widen, broaden; extend, expand
rašlj|ast forked; **~ati se** bifurcate; fork; **~e** fork; (*vilinske*) divining-rod, dowsing-rod
raštrkati scatter, disperse
rat war
rata instalment
ratar farmer; ploughman; tiller; **~ski** agricultural; **~stvo** agriculture; tillage
ratnik warrior; fighter
ratoboran militant; aggressive
ratova|nje warfare, war campaign; **~ti** make war (upon), be at war (with)
ravan level, flat; (*smjer*) straight, right; (*uspravan*)

upright; ***njemu*** **~** his equal
ravan plain, plateau
ravnalo ruler
ravnatelj head-master, director; principal
ravnati straighten, make even; **~ se** follow one's example; conform to the rule
ravni|ca plain; **~na** plane
ravno straight, direct; **~dušan** indifferent, calm, unconcerned; **~dušnost** indifference; **~pravan** enjoying the same rights; **~teža** equilibrium, balance
razab(i)rati discern, make out
razan different, diverse, various
razapet stretched; (*na križ*) crucified; **~i** stretch; (*na križ*) crucify; (*šator*) pitch; (*jedra*) spread
razapinjati = **razapeti**
razara|č destroyer; **~nje** destruction, devastation; **~ti** destroy, demolish, devastate
razaslati send out
razbacati throw (cast) about
razbaštiniti disinherit
razbibriga pastime
razbi|(ja)ti break in pieces, smash, shatter; **~ti se** (*brod*) be shipwrecked, suffer shipwreck
razbjesniti infuriate, madden; **~ se** get mad (enraged)
razbludan lascivious, sensual; immoral
razboj loom
razbojnik robber, bandit
razboljeti se become (fall) ill
razbor common sense, reason; **~it** sensible, reasonable; **~itost** common sense
razdera|n torn; **~ti** tear (to pieces), rend
razdijeliti divide, separate; distribute
razdioba distribution, division
razdjeljak (kose) parting
razdoblje period, era
razdor dissension, discord; split
razdragan overjoyed; delighted
razdraž|iti irritate, exasperate; provoke; **~ljiv** irritable; **~ljivost** irritability
razdv|ajati, **~ojiti** separate
razglasiti spread (news)
razglasni: **~ *uređaj*** public address system
razgled|ati view, look at; (*grad*) see the sights; **~avanje** sightseeing; **~nica** picture postcard
razgov|arati (se) talk, converse; discuss; **~or** talk, conversation; **~orljiv** talkative, communicative
razgranati se ramify, branch out
razgraničiti fix the boundaries
razi|ći se, **~laziti se** disperse, separate; break up
razina level
razjaditi se lose one's tem-

per
razjariti enrage, infuriate; **~ se** get enraged (furious); lose one's temper
razja|sniti explain; **~šnjenje** explanation
razlaga|nje exposition, explanation; **~ti** explain, expound
različak corn-flower
različ|an, ~it different, various; **~itost** diversity, variety
razlijegati se resound, re-echo
razli(jeva)ti se overflow; brim over
razlik|a difference; **~ovanje** distinction, differentiation; **~ovati** distinguish, differentiate; **~ovati se** differ, vary
razlog reason; ground; cause
razlomak fraction
razl|ožiti = ~agati
razlupati break; crash; smash
razljutiti anger, make angry; annoy; (*jako*) enrage; **~ se** get angry
razmak distance; interval
razmatra|ti consider; contemplate; view; **~nje** consideration
razmazati spread (on, over)
razma|ziti spoil; **~žen** spoiled
razmet|ati se show off, brag; **~ljiv** showing off, bragging
razmijeniti change, exchange
razmirica disagreement, dispute, quarrel
razmi|sliti consider; think over; meditate; **~šljanje** consideration; ***bez ~šljanja*** without hesitation
razmjena exchange
razmjer proportion; **~an** proportional, proportionate
razmnožiti se multiply
razmotati unfold, unpack; undo
raz|motriti = ~matrati
razmrsiti disentangle; unravel
razmrskati shatter, smash; fracture
raznolik various, diverse; heterogeneous; **~ost** variety, diversity
raznos|iti deliver; run errands; **~ač** errand-boy; deliverer
raznježiti se be moved; become effeminate
razočara|n disappointed; **~ti** disappoint; **~ti se** be disappointed
razonoda pastime; leisure
razoriti destroy, demolish
razoružati disarm
razotkriti disclose; expose; uncover
razraditi work out in detail
razred form; *Am* grade; (*soba*) classroom; (*vlak*) ***prvi ~*** first class
razrediti classify, arrange; sort
razrez slit, cut; **~ati** cut up, carve
razrijediti dilute
razriješiti unravel, unknot, solve; absolve; acquit

razrok cross-eyed; squint-eyed; **~o gledati** squint
razrušiti pull down; wreck, demolish
razularen unbridled, unrestrained
razum intellect, reason, sense; **zdrav ~** common sense; **~an** reasonable, sensible
razum|jeti understand, comprehend; **krivo ~jeti** misunderstand; **~ijevanje** understanding, comprehension
razuzdan dissipated; unrestrained; **~ost** dissipation
razvali|na ruin, wreck; **~ti** wreck, pull down
razvedriti se clear up; brighten up
razveseliti cheer up; give joy; gladden; **~ se** be glad; cheer up
razvesti se divorce
razvezati untie, unbind, undo
razvi(ja)ti develop
razvlačiti draw out, extend; (*tijesto*) roll out
razvod divorce
razvodniti water, dilute
razvoj development, progress
razvrat corruption, immorality, debauchery; **~an** rakish, dissipated; **~nik** rake
razvr|ći, ~gnuti dissolve; (*brak*) divorce; (*ugovor*) annul, cancel
razvrstati classify; arrange
razvući draw out, stretch; extend
raž rye
ražalostiti make sad, sadden, afflict; **~ se** become sad (distressed)
ražanj spit; barbecue
ražar|en red-hot, white-hot; **~iti se** become red-hot; glow
ražestiti se fly into a rage; lose one's temper
ražnjići slices of meat roasted on a skewer
rđa rust; **~ti** rust; **~v** rusty; corroded by rust
realan real; realistic; practical
rebro rib
recenz|ent critic, reviewer; **~ija** review, criticism
recept (*za jelo*) recipe; (*liječnički*) prescription
recidiva relapse
recipročan reciprocal
recit|acija recitation; **~irati** recite
rečen said, expressed; **~ica** sentence; clause
reći say, tell; utter
red order; row; file; string; range; series; **na meni je ~** it's my turn; **po ~u** by turns; **vozni ~** time-table
redak line; (*stih*) verse
redar keeper of order; policeman; **~stvo** police
redatelj (*filmski*) director; (*kazališni*) producer
redati arrange in rows
rediti put in order; tidy up

redni: ~ ***broj*** ordinal number
redom one after another, successively, by turns
redov|an, **~it** regular, ordinary; **~no**, **~ito** regularly, normally; **~itost** regularity
redovni|ca nun; **~k** monk, friar
ređati = **redati**
reflektor spot-light
reform|a reform; **~irati** reform
regenerirati regenerate
regent regent
regetati (*žaba*) croak
registrirati register
regrut recruit; **~irati** recruit; enlist recruits
regul|aran regular; **~irati** regulate; control
reklam|a publicity; advertisement; advertising; ***praviti ~u*** advertize
rekonvalescent convalescent
rekord record; ***potući ~*** break the record
rektor vice-chancellor; (*počasni*) chancellor; *Am* president; (*u Škotskoj*) rector
rekvirirati requisition
rekviziti requisites
relativ|an relative, comparative; **~nost** relativity
religi|ja religion; **~ozan** religious
relikvija relic
remek-djelo master-piece
remen strap; belt; (*za britvu*) strop
remorker tug(boat)
renesansa renaissance; revival
rentgen (*zrake*) X-rays; ***~ aparat*** X-ray (apparatus); **~izirati** X-ray; take an X-ray; **~ski** X-ray
renovirati renovate, restore
rep tail; (*povlaka*) train; (*red ljudi*) queue
repa turnip; (*šećerna*) sugar-beet
repatica comet
repatrirati repatriate
repertoar repertoire, repertory
represalije reprisals
reprezent|acija representation; **~ant** representative; **~irati** represent
reprodu|cirati reproduce; **~kcija** reproduction
republika republic; **~nac** republican
reputacija reputation
resa fringe; tassel; tuft
resiti adorn; decorate
restauracija restaurant; (*obnova*) restoration
restaurirati restore
restrikcija restriction
restringirati restrict
rešetati sift; riddle
rešetka grate, grating; wire-netting
rešeto sieve, riddle
retuširati retouch
reuma rheumatism
revan eager, keen; dilligent
revati bray

revidirati revise
revija review
revnost eagerness, zeal
revolucija revolution; **~onar** revolutionary; **~onaran** revolutionary; **~onirati** revolutionize
revolver revolver; gun
rez cut, gash, slash; incision
rezak sour, tart, biting
rezati cut, slice; carve
rezbarija carving; engraving; **~ti** carve; engrave
rezervacija reservation, booking
rezervat reservation
rezervirati reserve; book
rezervni spare; **~ *dijelovi*** spare parts
rezervoar reservoir, water-tank
rezidencija residence
rezignacija resignation; **~iran** resigned
rezolucija resolution
rezultat result; effect; consequence
režati snarl, growl
režija (*troškovi*) overheads, overhead expenses; FILM directed by; (*kazalište*) production; **~ser** FILM director; (*kazalište*) producer
riba fish; **~r** fisherman; **~renje** fishing, fishery; **~riti** catch fish, go fishing; **~rstvo** fishing trade
ribati scrub
ribič angler
ribnjak fish-pond
ribolov fishing
ricinus (*ulje*) castor oil
ridati sob
riđ reddish, ginger; **~okos** ginger-haired; red-haired
rigati vomit; belch; (*vulkan*) erupt
riječ word; term; expression; ***časna* ~** word of honour
rijedak rare, scarce; thin
rijeka river, stream; ***uz* ~u** upstream; ***niz* ~u** downstream
riješiti solve; settle; attend to; **~ se** get rid of, rid oneself of; (*odlučiti*) make up one's mind
rijetko rarely, seldom; **~st** rarity
rikati roar
rilo trunk
rima rhyme
rimokatolički Roman Catholic; **~k** Roman Catholic
rimski Roman
ris lynx
risač draftsman, designer; **~ti** draw; **~rija** drawing
riskantan risky
ritam rhythm
ritati se kick; struggle
ritmički rhythmical
riziko risk; hazard
riznica treasury; **~čar** treasurer
riža rice
rječit eloquent; fluent; talkative; **~ost** eloquence
rječnik dictionary; vocabulary; lexicon

riješavati = **riješiti**
rješenje solution; decision
rob slave; **~lje** slaves; ***trgovac ~ljem*** slave-trader
roba goods (*pl*); merchandise; ware
robija hard labour
robiti rob, plunder, loot
robn|i: ***~a kuća*** department store
robo|vanje slavery; ***~vati*** slave
rod (*spol*) sex; GRAM gender; ***u ~u*** related, akin
roda stork
rodan fertile; fruitful
rodbina relations, relatives, kin
rodilište maternity hospital (ward)
roditelj parent; **~i** parents
roditi bear, give birth to
rodni native; ***~ grad*** native town; ***~ list*** birth certificate
rodoljub patriot; **~iv** patriotic; **~lje** patriotism
rodom a native of
rodoslovlje genealogy, family tree; pedigree
rođak relation, relative, kinsman; **~inja** relative, kinswoman
rođen born; **~dan** birthday
rođenje (child)birth, delivery
rog horn; (*jelena*) antler; **~at** horned; (*jelen*) antlered
rogoboriti clamour (against), storm
rogoz bull-rush; **~ina** rush-mat
roj swarm, flock; **~iti se** swarm; teem (*fig*)
rok term, time-limit; ***u ~u od*** within
roktati grunt
roman novel; ***~ u nastavcima*** serial; **~tičan** romantic
rominjati (*kiša*) drizzle; (*potok*) murmur, babble
roni|lac diver, plunger; **~ti** dive, plunge
ropkinja female slave
ropotar|ija scrap, lumber; **~nica** lumber-room
ropski slavish
rosa dew
roštilj grill, gridiron
rotkv|a (*crna*) black radish; **~ica** radish
rov shaft; (*rudnik*) gallery, pit; **~ati** dig up, root up, undermine
rovariti plot, scheme, conspire, intrigue
rovaš tally, score
rožnica cornea
rt cape, promontary
rub edge; rim; margin; border; (*porub*) hem
rubac handkerchief; kerchief, scarf
rubin ruby
rublje underwear; linen; (*prljavo*) washing; laundry
rubrika section; heading
ruča|k dinner, lunch; **~ti** dine, have dinner (lunch)
ruč|ica small hand; small handle; **~ka** handle
ručni manual, hand; ***~ rad***

handicraft; needlework; ~ ***sat*** wrist-watch
ručnik towel
ruda, **~ča** ore, mineral; **~r** miner; (*ugljena*) collier, coalminer; **~rstvo** mining
rudast curly
rudnik mine, pit; (*ugljena*) colliery
rudo shaft, pole
rudokop mine
rugati se mock, make fun of, scoff
rugoba monster; scarecrow; (*nakaznost*) ugliness, monstrosity
ruho clothes, garments, attire
ruin|a ruin, wreck; **~irati** ruin, wreck
rujan September
ruka hand; (*do ramena*) arm; (*šaka*) fist
rukav sleeve
rukavica glove
rukomet volley-ball
rukopis handwriting; manuscript
rukovati handle, operate; **~ se** shake hands
rukovet handful
rukovodi|ti manage, guide, direct; **~lac** manager; high official
rulja mob, rabble
rum rum
rumen red, reddish, flushed; **~ilo** blush, flush; red colour; **~iti se** blush, get red
rumunjski Roumanian
runo fleece
rupa hole; gap; puncture; (*na brodu*) scuttle
rupčić handkerchief
rupičav full of holes, perforated
ruski Russian
ruš|enje pulling down, demolition; **~evan** dilapidated; **~evina** ruin; **~iti** pull down, demolish, destroy; overturn; **~iti se** fall down; collapse; tumble down
rutav shaggy; hairy
ruža rose
ružan ugly, plain; nasty
ružičast rosy; pink
ružiti abuse, call names
ružmarin rosemary
rva|č wrestler; **~nje** wrestling; **~ti se** wrestle
rzati neigh

S

s, sa with
sabira|č collector, gatherer; **~ti** collect, gather
sablast ghost, spectre, phantom; spook; **~an** ghostly, weird
sabla|zan scandal; blasphemy; **~zniti se** be schocked; **~žnjiv** shocking, outrageous, scandalous

sablja sabre
sabor parliament, congress; (*crkveni*) synod
sabotira|ti sabotage; **~nje** sabotage
sabra|n gathered; (*duhom*) concentrated; **~ti** gather; **~ti se** concentrate
sačinjavati form part of
sačuvati preserve, conserve; keep (from)
saće honey-comb
sad, **sada** now, at present, at the moment
sadašnj|i present, current, present-day; **~ost** the present time
sad|iti plant; **~nica** seedling
sadra plaster
sadreni: **~ *ovoj*** plaster-cast
sadrž|aj contents; substance; summary; **~avati** contain; hold; comprise; include; **~ina** volume
sađenje planting, setting
safir sapphire
sag carpet, rug
sagibati (se) bend
sagnut bent; **~i se** bend
sagnjiti rot, decay
sagraditi build, erect, construct
sagriješiti sin, commit a sin
sahran|a burial; **~iti** bury
saj|am fair, market; ***mjesto* *~ma*** fair grounds; **~amski** fair; of the fair; **~mište** fair grounds
sakat crippled, mutilated; **~iti** mutilate, maim
sakriti hide, conceal
saksonski Saxon
sakup|iti, **~ljati** gather, assemble, collect
salama salami
salamura pickle
salata salad; (*glavatica*) lettuce
saldo balance
salitra saltpetre
saliven cast
salutirati salute
sam alone; sole; only; **~ac** (*neženja*) bachelor, single man; **~o** only; just; merely; **~oća** solitude, loneliness
samljeti grind
samoglasnik vowel
samo|ljublje egoism, selfishness; **~obrana** self-defence; **~pouzdanje** self-confidence; **~prijegor** self-denial, self-sacrifice; **~pregoran** self-denying, self-sacrificing; **~stalan** independent, emancipated; self-supporting; **~stan** monastery, friery; (*ženski*) nunnery, convent; **~ubojstvo** suicide; ***počiniti ~ubojstvo*** commit suicide; **~uprava** autonomy, home-rule; **~voljan** arbitrary; self-willed; obstinate
san sleep; slumber; dream
sanatorij sanatorium, *Am* sanitarium
sandala sandal
sanduk trunk, chest, case; ***mrtvački ~*** coffin; ***poštanski ~*** letter-box, pillar-box

sanen sleepy, drowsy
sani|rati sanify, improve; **~taran** sanitary
sankcija sanction
santa iceberg
sanjar|enje day-dreaming; **~ski** dreaming; **~iti** day-dream
sanjati dream
sanjiv sleepy, drowsy
sanjkati se sleigh, sledge
saobraćaj traffic, transportation, communication; intercourse; **~ac** traffic policeman
saon|e, ~ice sleigh, sledge; toboggan
saopć|enje communication; announcement; **~iti** communicate; announce; make known
sapet tightened; (*svezan*) bound, tied; uncomfortable; **~i** tighten; bind, tie
sapun soap; **~ati** soap; lather; **~ica** soap-suds; lather
sardina sardine
sarka|stičan sarcastic; **~zam** sarcasm
sarma rolled leaf of sour cabbage stuffed with minced meat and rice
sasjeći cut up, cut in pieces; chop up
saski Saxon
saslušа|ti lend an ear to; listen to; hear; **~nje** hearing; audience; trial
sasta|jati se meet regularly; **~nak** meeting; appointment; **~ti (se)** meet, encounter
sastav composition; structure; **~ak** composition; essay; draft, sketch; **~iti, ~ljati** compose; construct; put together; join; draw up; **~ni** component, integral
sastojati se consist (of)
sastojina ingredient; component part
sasuti shoot out; (*na*) shower upon
sasvim entirely, completely; quite; fully
sašiti sew up (together)
sat clock; (*ručni*) watch, wrist-watch; (*vrijeme*) hour; (*obuka*) lesson, class, period; ***svaki ~*** every hour; ***~ zaostaje*** watch is slow; ***~ ide naprijed*** watch is fast
satelit satellite
satira satire
satnica time-table
satrti crush; break into pieces
saučesnik participant; (*krivac*) accomplice
saučešće condolence; sympathy
sav all, all the…, whole, entire
savez alliance, union; association; confederation; **~ni** federal, allied, federative; united; **~nički** allied; **~nik** ally; **~ništvo** alliance, confederacy
savijati bend, curve; roll;

fold; wind; ~ **se** bend
savjest conscience, consciousness; **~an** conscientious, scrupulous
savjet piece of advice; (*općenito*) advice, counsel; (*ljudi*) council; **~nik** counsellor, member of a council, councillor; adviser; **~ovati** advise; give a piece of advice; counsel
savladati conquer, overcome
savršen perfect, matchless; **~stvo** perfection
sazidati build, erect, construct
saz(i)vati convene, call together, summon
sazreti ripen, mature
saža|lan pitiful, sympathizing; **~liti** pity, have pity on, be sorry for; **~ljenje** compassion, pity
sažeti contract; compress; condense; ~ ***ramenima*** shrug one's shoulders
scena scene; (*pozornica*) stage
scenarij scenario
se myself, yourself, himself, herself, itself, ourselves, yourselves, themselves; ***oni*** ~ ***vole*** they love each other (one another)
sebe oneself; myself, yourself, himself, herself, itself, ourselves, yourselves, themselves; ***on je izvan*** ~ he is beside himself (with)
sebeljublje egoism
sebi to oneself; ***imati na*** ~ wear, have on; ***doći k*** ~ recover, come to
sebič|an selfish; **~nost** selfishness, egoism
secirati dissect
sedam seven; **~deset** seventy; **~naest** seventeen
sedef mother-of-pearls
sedl|ar saddler; **~ati** saddle; **~o** saddle
sedmi seventh
sedmi|ca week; **~čno** weekly
sekcija section
seksual|an sexual; **~nost** sexuality
sekta sect
sekunda second
selica, ***ptica*** ~ migratory bird
seli|dba moving, removal; **~ti** move; change one's residence; (*ptica*) migrate
selo village; (*suprotno od grada*) the country
selja|čki peasant, rustic; **~k** peasant, farmer; countryman; **~kinja** peasant-woman, country-woman; **~štvo** peasantry; country people; farmers
semafor traffic lights, semaphore
senat senate
sendvič sandwich
senzaci|ja sensation; **~onalan** sensational
seoba = **selidba**
seoski village, country; ~ ***dvor*** country-house, country-residence

septembar September
serija series
servil|an servile; **~nost** servility
sestr|a sister; ***časna ~a*** nun; **~ična** cousin; **~ić** cousin; **~inski** sisterly
sezati reach; stretch out
sezon|a season; **~ski** seasonal
sfera sphere
sfinga sphinx
shema scheme; outline; plan
shodan suitable, proper, convenient; appropriate
shrva|n overpowered; crushed; broken; **~ti** overwhelm, overpower, crush
shvaća|nje comprehension, understanding; (*nazor*) view, idea; ***krivo ~nje*** misunderstanding; **~ti** comprehend, understand
shvatiti = **shvaćati**
si = **sebi**
sibirski Siberian
siciljanski Sicilian
sići descend, get down (off)
sićušan tiny, very small, minute
sidro anchor; ***pustiti ~*** drop anchor
siga stalactite, stalagmite
signal signal; **~izirati** signal, make signals
sigur|an sure, safe, secure; certain; **~nost** safety; certainty
sijalica (electric) bulb
sijamski Siamese
sijati (*svijetlo*) shine, glitter; (*sjeme*) sow; disseminate; spread
siječanj January
sijed grey, grey-haired; **~jeti** become (grow) grey
sijelo meeting; (*sjedište*) seat
sijeno hay
sijevati lighten, flash
siktati hiss
sila force; (*nasilje*) violence; vehemence; strength; intensity; ***konjska ~*** horsepower; **~n** powerful, strong, mighty
silaz|ak descent, coming down; **~iti** = **sići**
siledžija tyrant, oppressor, bully
siliti force, compel, make one do
silnik = **siledžija**
silno powerfully, violently, tremendously
silom by force
silovati rape, violate
silovit violent, brutal, tyrannical; **~ost** violence, brutality
simbol symbol, sign; **~ičan** symbolical
simetri|čan symmetrical; **~ja** symmetry
simfonij|a symphony; **~ski** symphonic
simpati|čan nice, attractive, likable; **~ja** liking, sympathy
simulirati simulate, feign, pretend
sin son

sindikat syndicate, trade union
sinoći ast night, yesterday evening
sinovac nephew
sinu|ti shine, flash; **~*lo mi je*** it dawned upon me; it occurred to me
sipa cuttle-fish
sipati strew, litter, spill
sipljiv asthmatic
sir cheese
sirena siren
siroče orphan
siroma|h poor man, beggar; **~si** the poor; **~šan** poor, needy; (*jadan*) miserable, wretched; **~štvo** poverty, neediness; misery
sirot|a, **~ica** poor woman; **~ište** orphanage
sirov raw, uncooked; **~ina** raw material
sirup syrup
sisa breast, bosom, bust; (*vrh*) teat, nipple
sisa|ljka sucker; pump, suction pump; **~ti** suck; **~vac** mammal
sistem system, **~atičan** systematic; **~atizirati** systematize
sit full; satiated; (*fig*) fed up with, sick of, tired of
sitan minute, tiny; petty, trivial
sitni|ca trifle; **~čav** pedantic, hair-splitting; **~š** change; petty cash
sito sieve, riddle
sitost satiety, fill
situacija situation
siv grey; **~kast** greyish
sjaj radiance, brilliancy, brightness, shine; splendour; **~an** shining, radiant, brilliant
sjati (se) shine, blaze, beam; glitter
sjecište intersection, junction
siecka|ti mince; hash; chop; **~*no meso*** minced meat
sjeća|nje memory; recollection; **~ti se** remember, recall, recollect
sjeći chop; (*rušiti*) fell (down)
sjed|alo seat; **~ište** seat; residence; (*glavno*) headquarters; **~iti** sit, be seated; **~nica** sitting, session; meeting; conference
sjediniti unite, join
sjekira axe, hatchet
sjeme seed; **~nje** seeds
sjemenište seminary
sjemenka grain of seed
sjena (*predmeta*) shadow; (*hladovina*) shade
sjenica (*ptica*) titmouse; (*vrtna*) bower
sjenik hay-loft, hay-barn
sjenilo (*lampe*) lamp-shade
sjenovit shady
sjesti sit down, take a seat, be seated
sjeta melancholy; sadness; low spirits; **~n** melancholic, moping, blue

sjetilo sense
sjetiti remind one of; **~ se** remember
sjetva sowing; sowing-time
sjever the north; **~ni** north, northern, northerly; **~njača** Pole-star; **~njak** north wind
sjevero|istočan north-east, north-eastern; **~istok** north-east; **~zapad** north-west; **~zapadan** north-western
skaka|ti jump, spring, leap, hop; **~vac** grass-hopper, locust
skakutati hop, skip
skala scale
skameniti se stand petrified; be rooted to the ground
skandal scandal; **~izirati** scandalize; **~izirati se** be shocked; **~ozan** scandalous, shocking
skandinavski Scandinavian
skandirati scan
skanjivati se hesitate
skapavati starve; perish with (cold, hunger, thirst)
skela ferry, ferry-boat
skele scaffolding
skelet skeleton
skeptičan sceptical
skic|a draft, sketch; **~irati** sketch, make a sketch; make a rough draft
ski|dati, **~nuti** take down; (*odjeću*) take off; remove; (*teret*) unburden
skij|anje skiing; **~aš** skier; **~ati (se)** ski; **~e** skis (*pl*)
skit|alac, **~nica** vagabond, tramp; **~ati se** tramp, stroll; (*lutati*) wander, roam
sklad harmony, proportion; uniformity, concordance; **~an** harmonious; **~atelj** composer; **~ati** compose; **~ba** composition, piece of music
skladište warehouse, store-house; depot
sklanjati decline
sklapati fold; (*ruke*) clasp; (*oči*) shut, close; (*ugovor*) make
skliza|č skater; **~k** slippery, smooth; **~lište** skating-rink; **~ljka** skate; **~nje** skating; **~ti se** skate; slide; **~v** slippery
sklon favourable; (*nekome*) favouring; well-disposed towards
skloni|šte shelter; **~ti se** shelter; take refuge
sklonost favour; inclination
sklop complex
sklopiti = **sklapati**
skočiti jump, leap, spring
skok jump, leap; **~ *uvis*** high jump
skopčati clasp, button, hook
skorbut scurvy
skoro soon, in a short time, in the near future; (*prošlost*) lately; recently; (*gotovo*) almost, nearly
skorojević upstart
skoroteča messenger
skorup cream
skraćenica abbreviation;

~ivati = **skratiti**
skratiti shorten; abbreviate
skrb care; worry; **~iti se** take care; look after; worry; **~nik** guardian; tutor; **~ništvo** guardianship, tutorship
skrenuti turn; diverge, deviate
skretnica switch, point
skrivati hide, conceal
skrivi|ti be guilty; cause; ***on je to ~o*** it is his fault
skrižaljka table; schedule
skrlet scarlet fever
skrojiti cut out
skrom|an modest, humble; **~nost** modesty, humility
skrovi|šte hiding-place; shelter; **~t** hidden, secret
skroz through
skrš|en broken-hearted, heart-broken; **~iti** crush, shatter, overcome
skrupul|a scruple; **~ozan** scrupulous
skrušen penitent, repentant; humble; **~ost** repentance; humility
skrutiti se congeal; coagulate; stiffen
skucati scrape together
skuč|en cramped (up); restrained; restricted; **~iti** cramp up; restrain; restrict
skuhati boil; prepare; make
skulptura sculpture; (*kip*) statue
skup[1] group; assembly
skup[2] expensive, dear, costly
skupa together; jointly
skupan collective; joint, common
skupina group; cluster
skup|iti, ~ljati gather, collect; assemble; (*novac*) raise
skupocjen precious, valuable
skupoća expensiveness, costliness; high cost of living
skupština meeting; assembly; gathering; congregation; convention
skuša mackerel
skvrčiti se shrivel, shrink; wrinkle
slab weak, faint, feeble; **~ašan** weakly; **~ina** flank, loins; **~iti** weaken; grow weak (feeble)
slabo poorly, weakly, badly; slightly; **~krvan** anaemic; **~krvnost** anaemia; **~st** weakness, faintness, frailty; **~uman** feeble-minded, half-witted, imbecile
slad malt
slad|ak sweet; **~iti** sweeten, sugar
slado|kusac gourmet; **~led** ice-cream
slaga|r type-setter, compositor; **~rna** printing-house; **~ti** (*tisak*) set type; (*na hrpu*) pile (heap) up; (*urediti*) put in order; (*smotati*) fold up; (*reći laž*) tell a lie; fib; **~ti se** agree with; harmonize; get along with; ***ne ~ti se*** disagree with

slam|a straw; (*na krovu*) thatch; **~nat** straw; **~nati krov** thatched roof; **~njača** straw mattress, pallet
slan salted, salt; **~a** (*mraz*) hoar-frost
slanina bacon
slap waterfall
slast delight; sweet
slastičar confectioner; **~na** confectionery, cake-shop
slati send, dispatch
slatkiš sweet, sweetmeat
slatkovodan fresh-water
slava fame, glory; renown, popularity, reputation; **~n** famous, renowned
slavenski Slavonic, Slavic
slavina tap, cock, *Am* faucet
slav|iti glorify; (*svečanost*) celebrate; **~lje** triumph; festivities (*pl*)
slavo|dobitan triumphant; **~hlepan** ambitious; longing for fame; **~luk** triumphal arch
slavuj nightingale
sle|ći, ~gnuti ramenima shrug one's shoulders
slediti se freeze
sleđ herring
slezena spleen
slič|an similar, like, alike, resembling; **~iti** resemble, be like (similar); **~nost** similarity, resemblance, likeness
slijed sequence, succession, continuity; **~eći** the following; **~iti** follow, come after
slijep blind; ***~i miš*** bat; **~ac** blind man
slijepiti glue (paste, stick) together
slijevati se flow into
slika picture; image; (*uljena*) painting; (*crtež*) drawing; **~r** painter, artist; **~rstvo** painting; **~ti** paint (*fig*) depict, portray
slikov|it picturesque; figurative; **~nica** picture-book
slina saliva; (*pljuvačka*) spittle; **~v** slobbery
slitina alloy
slobod|a freedom, liberty; **~an** free; ***~ni mislilac*** free-thinker; ***~no vrijeme*** spare time, leisure
slog syllable
sloga harmony, concord
sloj layer
slom fracture; break; crash; (*živaca*) breakdown; (*zdravlja*) collapse; **~iti** break; fracture; crash
slon elephant; ***~ova kost*** ivory
slovački Slovak
slovenski Slovene
slovo letter; ***veliko ~*** capital letter
slož|an harmonious; unanimous; **~iti** = **slagati**; **~iti se** come to an agreement, come to terms
slučaj chance, case; incident; (*nesretan*) accident; **~an** accidental
sluga man-servant, boy; valet

sluh hearing; ear
slušač|č hearer, listener; student; **~lica** (*telefona*) receiver; ***objesiti ~licu*** ring off; **~lice** ear-phones, head-phones; **~teljstvo** audience, public; **~ti** listen to; (*pokoravati se*) obey
sluškinja maid(-servant); woman servant
slut|iti have a presentiment; (*zlo*) forebode; **~nja** presentiment, forboding
sluz slime; (*iz nosa*) snot; **~av** slimy; snotty
služavka = sluškinja
služb|a service; employment; post; situation; (*božja*) service, mass; **~en** official; formal; ***~eno putovanje*** business (official) trip; **~enik** employee; official; clerk
služinčad servants (*pl*)
služiti serve; attend; wait upon; **~ se** make use of, use; (*kod stola*) help oneself to
služnik porter
sljedbenik follower
sljepić blind-worm
sljepočica temple
sljepoća blindness
smaknu|će execution; **~ti** execute, put to death
smalaksati weaken, lose strength, become exhausted
smanjiti diminish, lessen, reduce; restrict
smaragd emerald
smatrati consider, think, look upon as
smeće rubbish, litter, garbage; ***kanta za ~*** dustbin, ashcan; ***lopatica za ~*** dust-pan
smeđ brown; (*od sunca*) suntanned, sunburned
smekšati soften, mellow
smesti confuse, bewilder
smet|ati disturb, intrude; be in the way; (*priječiti*) hinder; (*dodijavati*) annoy; (*prekidati*) interrupt; **~en** embarrassed, confused, perplexed; **~nja** disturbance, interruption, interference; hindrance; (RADIO) atmospherics (*pl*)
smežura|n wrinkled; shrivelled; **~ti se** wrinkle; shrivel up
smicalica trick
smijati se laugh; (*grohotom*) roar with laughter
smijeh laughter, laugh; ***prasnuti u ~*** burst out laughing
smiješak smile
smiješan funny, ridiculous, comical, amusing; (*glup*) silly, absurd
smiješati mix up
smiješiti se smile
smijuckati se giggle, chuckle
smilovati se feel pity on
smion brave, courageous, daring, bold; **~ost** courage, bravery
smirak emery-cloth, emery-paper
smir|en appeased, quiet,

calm; **~iti** appease, calm
smisao sense; meaning; (*sklonost*) turn, taste
smjel = **smion**; **~ost** = **smionost**
smjena shift
smjer direction, course; trend; **~ati** trend; tend towards; (*ciljati*) aim at; **~nica** trend; directive
smjesa mixture; blend; alloy
smjesta at once, immediately
smje|stiti lodge, accommodate, house; place; **~stiti se** settle down; **~štaj** position, situation; accommodation
smjeti be allowed (permitted), may; (*usuditi se*) dare
smočiti wet, moisten, make wet; drench
smočnica pantry, larder
smokva fig; fig-tree
smola resin; bitumen, pitch; **~st** resinous; pitchy
smota|k bundle, roll; scroll; **~ti** fold; roll up (in); wrap up
smotra review, inspection; muster
smračiti se darken, become dark
smrad bad smell (odour); stench
smrdjeti stink, smell badly
smrdljiv stinking, foul-smelling
smrkavati se = **smračiti se**
smrskati crush, smash
smršati lose weight, slim; grow thin
smrt death; **~an** deadly, fatal; ***~na kazna*** capital punishment; ***~ni slučaj*** (*nesreća*) casualty; **~nik** mortal; **~onosan** lethal, deadly, fatal; **~ovnica** death certificate
smrviti pound, crumble; crush
smrzavati se freeze; turn to ice
smrznuti se freeze to death; die by frost
smušen muddleheaded, confused
smut|iti confuse, bewilder; **~ljivac** trouble-maker, intriguer; **~nja** intrigue, mischief, trouble
snabdijevati supply, provide
snaći se find one's way; orientate oneself
snaga strength; power; force
snaha daughter-in-law
snalaziti se = **snaći se**
snast (*broda*) rigging
snažan strong, vigorous, powerful
snebivati se be shocked
snesti (*jaje*) lay (egg)
snijeg snow; ***~ pada*** it snows
snijeti = **snesti**
snim|ati photograph, take a photograph; (FILM) shoot; **~ka** snapshot; photograph
sni|ziti lower; reduce; cut down; **~ženje** reduction
snop sheaf; bundle
snositi bear, stand, suffer,

endure
snošljiv tolerant, indulgent; **~ost** tolerance
snovati plan; devise; plot, scheme
snovi dreams
snubiti (*djevojku*) woo; propose; (*glasove*) canvass, solicit votes
snužd|en depressed, dejected, in low spirits; **~iti se** become depressed; brood
sob reindeer
soba room, chamber; **~ *za goste*** spare room; **~ *za primanje*** reception-room, drawing-room; ***radna* ~** study; **~rica** chamber-maid
sobica small room, closet
sobovina sable (fur)
socija|lan social; **~list** socialist; **~listički** socialistic; **~lizam** socialism
sociolog sociologist; **~ija** sociology
sočan juicy
sok juice; (*biljke*) sap; (*pečenke*) gravy, dripping
soko(l) falcon, hawk
sokoliti encourage
sol salt; **~ana** (*uz more*) salt-pan; salt-works; **~enka** salt-cellar
solidan real; sound, reliable; (*život*) regular
solidarnost solidarity
solika sleet
soliti salt, add salt
sotona satan, devil
sovjetski *hist* Soviet; **♀ Savez** *hist* the Soviet Union
sova owl
spajati join together, put together, connect, combine
spaliti burn down; cremate
spam (*e-poštom*) spam
spar|an close, sultry, oppressive; stuffy; **~ina** sultriness, closeness
spas salvation; liberation; **~avati**, **~iti** save, rescue, deliver; ***pojas za ~avanje*** lifebelt; **~itelj** rescuer; Redeemer; **~onosan** salutary, beneficial; **♀ovo** the Ascension
spavać|i sleeping; ***~a kola*** sleeping car, sleeper; ***~a soba*** bedroom; (*za više ljudi*) dormitory
spavaćica nightdress
spavati sleep, be asleep; (*zimskim snom*) hibernate
speci|fičan specific; **~jalan** special, particular
spekulirati speculate
spiker announcer; news reader
spilja cave
spirala spiral; **~n** spiral
spis document, official paper; **~atelj** writer, author
spiskati squander, waste
splasnuti deflate
splav raft; **~ar** rafter
splesti knit; plait
spletka intrigue, plot; **~riti** intrigue, plot
sploštiti flatten
spočitavati reproach

spodoba figure
spoj combination, joining; (*veza*) connection; ***kratki ~*** short circuit; **~iti** join; connect; combine; **~ka** tie, copula; **~nica** (*riječi*) hyphen; (*za papir*) paper clip
spokoj|an calm, tranquil; **~nost** tranquility, calm
spol sex; **~ni** sexual; ***~ni organi*** genitals
spolja outside, from outside; **~šnost** the exterior, the outside
spomen (*sjećanje*) remembrance; (*predmet*) souvenir, keepsake; ***nije vrijedno ~a*** not worth mentioning; ***~-ploča*** memorial tablet; **~ik** monument; **~ut** mentioned, above-mentioned; **~uti** mention
spominjati = **spomenuti**
spona copula; tie, clasp
spor slow; (*duhom*) slow-witted; ***~ čovjek*** sluggard, slow-coach
spor confflict, disagreement; dispute; **~an** controversial, disputable
sporazum agreement, understanding, settlement; **~an** agreeing to, consenting; ***biti ~an*** agree to, consent; **~jeti se** come to an agreement, come to terms
spored|an secondary, subordinate; ***~na ulica*** side street
sport sport; **~aš** sportsman; **~ski** sport(s)
sposob|an capable, fit for, able; **~nost** ability, capability; skill; efficiency
spota|ći se, **~knuti se** trip over, stumble
spozna|ja cognition; awareness; **~ti** become aware, comprehend
sprat = **kat**
sprava apparatus; appliance; gadget
sprd|ati se ridicule, mock, make fun of; **~nja** ridicule, mockery
sprečavati = **spriječiti**
sprema readiness; (*znanje*) qualification; (*stvari*) equipment; **~n** prepared; ready; (*voljan*) willing
sprem|ati prepare, get ready; put in order, tidy; (*sobu*) do the room; **~ati se** prepare oneself, get ready; (*na neki čin*) be about to; (*zalihu*) store; **~ište** warehouse, store-room; **~nost** readiness
spretan skilful, clever
spreza|nje conjugation; **~ti** conjugate
sprijateljiti se make friends with
spriječiti prevent, hinder, obstruct
sprijeda in front of, before, ahead
sprov|esti (*vrijeme*) spend, pass; (*pratiti*) accompany, escort; (*život*) lead a life
sprovod funeral
sprovodni: ***~ list*** bill of lad-

ing
sprtljati bungle
sprud sand dune
spržiti broil, roast; (*prejako*) overdo; (*opržiti*) burn; scald
spustiti let down; drop; **~ se** come down, descend; sink
spušta|nje sinking, falling, descending; **~ti** = **spustiti**
sputa|ti, **~vati** bind, fetter, chain
spužv|a sponge; ***brisati ~om*** sponge
sram shame; **~ežljiv** shame-faced; (*plah*) shy, timid; **~iti se** be ashamed, feel ashamed; **~ota** disgrace; scandal; shame; **~otan** shameful, disgraceful; **~otiti** put to shame, disgrace; discredit
srasti se grow together, grow into one
srav|niti make level; (*sa zemljom*) raze; (*usporediti*) compare
sraz collision, crash; **~iti se** collide; clash
Srbi|ja Serbia; **Ꝣjanski** Serbian; **~n** Serb
srce|e heart; ***lupanje ~a*** palpitation
srčan of the heart, heart; (*hrabar*) brave, bold; **~ost** courage, bravery
srdač|an hearty, cordial, affectionate; kind; **~nost** cordiality, amiability
srdit angry, cross; **~i** make angry, annoy; **~i se** be angry, get angry
srdžba, **srditost** anger
srebro silver
sreć|a (*u duši*) happiness; (*slučaj*) (good) luck; **~om** luckily, fortunately; ***na ~u*** luckily; (*nasumce*) at random; **~ka** lottery-ticket
sred in the middle of
sredina middle, centre, (*Am* center) midst
središ|nji central, middle; **~njica** head office; headquarters; **~te** centre, middle; headquarters
srednji middle; medium; ***~ vijek*** Middle Ages; ***~ rod*** neuter
Sredozemno more the Mediterranean
sredst|vo means; medium; instrument; ***bez ~ava*** resourceless, lacking means
sređen (*čovjek*) sedate, serious; (*uređen*) settled; classified
sresti meet, encounter, come across
sret|an happy; lucky, fortunate; ***~no!*** good luck!
sricati spell
srijeda Wednesday; ***čista ~*** Ash Wednesday
srkati sip
srn|a doe, roe; **~dač** buck, roe-buck; **~etina** venison
srod|an akin; related; **~nik** kinsman, relative; **~nost** relationship, kinship
srok rhyme

srozati se collapse, topple down
srp sickle
srpanj July
srpski Serbian
srušiti pull down, demolish, fell; upset, knock down, overturn; **~ se** fall down; collapse
srž core, pith
stabil|an stable, firm; **~nost** stability
stab|lo tree; (*deblo*) trunk; **~ljika** stalk, stem
stadij stage
stadion stadium
stado (*goveda*) herd; (*ovaca, itd.*) flock
staja stable; cowshed; (*svinjac*) pigsty
stajalište stop; station; (*pogled*) view-point, standpoint
stajati stand; (*cijena*) cost
stakl|ar glazier; **~en** glass; (*pogled*) glazed; **~enik** greenhouse, hothouse; **~enina** glass-ware; **~o** glass; (*prozora*) window-pane; **~ovina** broken glass
stalak stand; (*kipa*) pedestal; (*slikarski*) easel
stal|an stable, steady, permanent; **~ež** estate, order, class; **~nost** stability, permanency, continuity
staložiti se settle, be deposited
stambeni housing, residential
stan flat; *Am* apartment; lodging; **~ar** tenant, lodger; **~arina** rent
stanica station; ***željeznička* ~** railway station
staniol tin-foil
stanka pause; interval; break; intermission
stanodavac landlord
stanovati live, reside
stanovište standpoint, point of view
stanovit certain, particular
stanovni|k inhabitant, dweller, resident; **~štvo** population, inhabitants
stanj|e state, condition; situation; ***biti u ~u*** be able; (*sredstva*) afford to; ***ona je u drugom ~u*** she is pregnant, she is with child, she is in the family way
stapa|nje amalgamation; merging; **~ti** amalgamate, merge; blend
star old, aged; ***~i vijek*** antiquity; ***~o željezo*** scrap iron
star|ac old man; **~ački** of an old man; senile; **~ci** the old
staratelj guardian, tutor, trustee; **~stvo** guardianship, tutorship
starati se take care; attend to; see to; look after
staretinar old-clothes man; junkman; **~na** junkshop
starica old woman
stariti age, get (grow) old
starin|a antique; **~ski** antique; ancient; old-fashioned

starješina superior; senior; chief
staromodan old-fashioned; out of date
staro|sjedilac aboriginal, indigene; **~slavenski** old Slavonic
starost old age
stas stature; **~it** tall
stati stand; (*uspravno*) stand upright; (*prestati*) stop, halt; (*imati mjesta*) hold, have place; ***u ovu sobu stane 100 ljudi*** this room seats 100 people
statisti|čki statistical; **~ka** statistics
stativa (*nogomet*) goal-post
statu|s status, rank; **~t** statute
stav attitude; **~ak** MUS movement
staviti put, place; lay; ***~ na kocku*** risk; ***~ u nepriliku*** embarrass; ***~ na stranu*** put aside; ***~ na raspoloženje put*** at the disposal of; ***~ u pokret*** set (put) in motion; start
stavljati = **staviti**
stavka item; paragraph
staza path; trail; track
stečaj bankruptcy; insolvency; ***pasti pod ~*** go bankrupt
steći acquire, win, get, obtain
stega discipline; strictness
stegno thigh
stegnut drawn tight, tightened; **~i** tighten; draw tight; contract; (*obuzdati*) restrain
stenograf stenographer, shorthand writer; **~ija** shorthand; stenography; **~irati** take down in shorthand
stenjati moan, groan
stepen = **stupanj**
stepeni|ca step; stair; (*ljestava*) rung; **~ce** stairs, steps; **~šte** staircase, stairway
sterati se stretch; extend
sterilan sterile; barren
stez|anje contraction; tightening; (*grčenje*) cramp; *fig* restriction; **~ati** = **stegnuti**; **~nik** corset; girdle
stići arrive, come, reach, get to; (*dostići*) catch up with; (*zadesiti*) strike
stid shame; ***~ me je*** I am ashamed; **~ljiv** bashful; shy; shamefaced
stih verse, line; **~otvorac** versifier; (*podrugljivo*) rhymester
stijeg banner; standard; flag
stijena rock, cliff
stijenj wick
stil style; manner; **~istički** stylistic; **~istika** theory of style (writing), stylistics
stimulirati stimulate, rouse
stipendija scholarship, fellowship; bursary
stis|ak pressure, squeeze; **~ka** crush, press, jam; (*neprilika*) pinch; fix; **~kati** press, squeeze; (*gnječiti*) quash; (*šaku*) clench; **~nut** compressed, pressed, squeezed; **~nuti** = **~kati**; **~nuti se** (tkanina) shrink

stišati quiet, calm
stizati = **stići**
stjeca|nje acquisition; gaining, winning; **~ti** acquire, gain, get, earn
stjenica (bed-)bug
sto a hundred
stô = **stol**
stočar cattle-breeder; rancher; **~stvo** cattle-breeding
stog stack; (*sijena*) hay-stack
stoga therefore, consequently
stogodišnji centenary; **~ca** hundredth anniversary, centenary
stoječke standing, erect
stoka cattle, live stock
stol table; **~ac**, **~ica** chair; (*bez naslona*) stool; **~ar** joiner, carpenter; (*za pokućstvo*) cabinet-maker; **~arija** joiner's workshop
stol|ni: ***~na crkva*** cathedral; ***~no suđe*** crockery; **~njak** table-cloth
stoljeće century
stonoga centipede
stopa (*mjera*) foot; (*trag*) foot-print, trace; **~lo** foot, sole
stopiti se melt; weld; unite
stotina a hundred
stovari|šte = **skladište**; **~ti** unload; discharge; dump
stožac (*sijena*) rick, stack; (GEOM) cone
stradati suffer
straga behind, at the back of, in the rear
strah fear, fright
straho|počitanje awe; reverence; respect; **~ta** horror, terror; **~vit** dreadful, terrible, horrible, frightful
stramputic|a side-track; wrong way; ***poći ~om*** go astray; take to evil courses
stran strange; (*inozeman*) foreign; outlandish
stran|a side; (*knjige*) page; ***jaka ~a*** strong point; ***slaba ~a*** weak point; ***s jedne ~e*** *fig* on one hand; ***s druge ~e*** *fig* on the other hand; ***s moje ~e*** as to me, on my part; ***šalu na ~u*** joking apart; ***sa svih ~a*** on all sides, from everywhere; ***držati se po ~i*** remain neutral, not take sides
stranac stranger; (*inozemac*) foreigner; alien
stranica page
stranka party; faction; (*na sudu*) party
strast passion; (*spolna*) sensuality, lust; **~ven** passionate; lustful, erotic
straš|an terrible, horrible, dreadful, frightful; **~ilo** scarecrow, fright; **~iti** frighten, scare, alarm; **~iti se** be frightened (scared); **~ljiv** timid, fainthearted
strateg strategist; **~ija** strategics
stratište scaffold
straž|a watch, guard; (*vojnička*) sentinel, sentry; (*na*

brodu) mast-head watch; ***izmjena ~e*** changing the guard; **~ar** policeman, constable; **~arnica** sentry-box; watch-tower; **~ariti** keep watch, be on sentry-go
stražnji back, rear; **~ca** backside, buttocks, bottom
streha roof; eaves
strel|ica arrow; **~ovit** quick as lightning
strelja|na shooting gallery; rifle-range; **~ti** shoot; ***~čka vještina*** marksmanship
stremen stirrup
strep|iti be anxious about, fear for; (*drhtati*) tremble; **~nja** fear, anxiety, worry
stres|ti, **~ati** shake (off); **~ti se** shiver, shudder
strg|ati, **~nuti** tear (pull) off; (*masku*) unmask
stric uncle
stričak BOT thistle
strići shear, clip; crop; ***~ ušima*** prick one's ears
strijel|a arrow; ***tobolac za ~e*** quiver; **~ac** shooter; archer; ***dobar ~ac*** good marksman, good shot
strijeljati shoot; fire
strina aunt
strka rush; scramble
strm, **~enit** steep; **~ina** slope
strmoglaviti (se) precipitate (oneself)
strn stubble; **~ište** stubble-field
strog strict, severe, harsh; **~ost** severity, strictness
stroj engine, machine; ***parni ~*** steam engine; ***pisaći ~*** typewriter; ***~ za pranje rublja*** washing machine; **~ar** engineer, machinist; (*kože*) currier; **~arnica** engine-room
strojiti (*kožu*) tan; curry
strojnica machine-gun
strojovođa engine-driver; *Am* engineer
strop ceiling
strp|jeti se be patient, have patience; **~ljiv** patient; **~ljenje**, **~ljivost** patience
stršiti protrude, project, stand (jut) out
stručak stalk of flower; sprig
struč|an professional, expert; skilled; **~njak** specialist, expert; connoisseur
strug lathe; plane; **~ati** scrape, grate; plane
struja (*vode*) stream; current; **~ti** stream, circulate, flow
struk waist; = **stručak**
struka line; branch of business (knowledge); profession
struna string; chord; (*konjska*) horse-hair
strunuti rot, decay; putrify
strunjača mattress
strvina carrion; carcass; **~r** vulture
stub|e stairs; ***niz ~a*** flight of stairs; **~ište** staircase
stu|cati, **~ći** pound; **~ći se** get bruised

studen cold; chill; (*hladan*) cold, chilly; **~i** November
student student; **~ *medicine*** medical student
stup (*drven*) post; (*zgrade*) column, pillar; **~ac** column; paragraph
stupanj degree, grade
stupati march, pace, stride
stupica trap, pitfall, snare
stupiti make a step, step, tread; **~ *na snagu*** become valid, come into force
stupnjevati grade; compare
stvar thing; matter, object; stuff; **~an** real, actual; **~ati** create; form; make; **~no** actually, really, in fact; **~nost** reality, actuality
stvor, **~enje** creature, being, man; **~itelj** creator; originator; **~iti** create, form, make; **~iti se** appear suddenly
subot|a Saturday; **~om** on Saturdays
subvenci|ja subsidy, grant; **~onirati** subsidize
sučelice facing, opposite to
sućut sympathy; condolence; ***izraziti*** **~** express sympathy, condole
sud law-court, court of justice; tribunal; (*nazor*) judgement, opinion; (*posuda*) container; **~ac** judge, justice; magistrate; (*nogomet*) referee; (*tenis*) umpire
sudar collision, crash; **~iti se** collide, crash, smash
sudben court, judicial, legal; **~*i postupak*** legal proceedings
sudbina fate, destiny; fatality
sudbonosan fatal, ominous
sudionik participant; partner
suditi (*na sudu*) try; sit in court; hear the case; give (pass) judgement; (*prosuditi*) consider; judge; estimate
sudjelova|nje taking part, participation; **~ti** take part, participate
sudnica courtroom, court
sudnji dan REL doomsday
sudoper sink
sudsk|i court, judicial, juridical; **~*a rasprava*** hearing, trial; **~*i nalog*** warrant; **~*i praznici*** court vacation
suđe dishes; vessels; kitchen utensils; (*porculan*) crockery
suđenje trial
suge|rirati suggest; **~stija** suggestion; **~stivan** suggestive
suglas|an agreeing with; agreeable to; **~iti se** agree, be agreeable to; **~nik** consonant; **~nost** agreement, consent, accord
sugrađanin fellow-citizen
suh dry; (*uveo*) withered, shrivelled; (*čovjek*) thin, lean, slender; **~*o zlato*** pure gold; **~*o meso*** smoked meat; **~oparan** dry, dull; monotonous
sujeta vanity, conceit; **~n**

vain, conceited
sujevjer|an superstitious; **~je** superstition
sukno cloth, woolen fabric
suknja skirt
sukob conflict, clash; collision; **~iti se** conflict, clash, collide
sukrivac accomplice, accessory
sulica lance, spear
sumnj|a suspicion, doubt; **~ati** doubt, suspect; **~ičav** suspicious, doubting; **~iv** suspect, suspected; dubious
sumor|an sombre, dull, gloomy; **~nost** gloom, depression
sumpor sulphur, brimstone; **~an** sulphuric
sumračan dusky
sumrak twilight, dusk; ***~ se hvata*** night falls
sunarodnjak fellow-countryman, compatriot
sunc|e sun; sunshine; **~obran** sunshade; **~okret** sunflower
sunča|n sun, sunny; ***~na pjega*** freckle; **~nica** sun-stroke; **~nje** sun-bathing, lying in the sun; **~ti se** sunbathe, lie in the sun
suoč|enje confrontation; **~iti** confront, meet (bring) face to face
suparni|k rival, competitor; (*neprijatelj*) enemy, adversary, opponent; **~štvo** rivalry, antagonism
supotpisati countersign
suprot|an contrary, opposite; **~nost** the opposite, the contrary
suprotstaviti se oppose, withstand, resist
suprug husband; **~a** wife
suptil|an subtle; **~nost** subtlety
suputnik fellow-traveller
surad|nik collaborator; co-operator; **~nja** collaboration
surađivati collaborate, co-operate
surla trunk
surogat substitute
surov rude, brutal, gross; **~ost** brutality
susjed neighbour; **~an** neighbouring, next-door; **~stvo** neighbourhood
susre|sti meet, come across, encounter; **~t** meeting, encounter; **~tljiv** obliging, helpful
sustati become tired; slacken off
sustav system; method; **~an** systematic, methodical
sustići catch up with
suš|a drought; want of rain; dryness; (*sjenik*) shed, barn; **~en** dried; (*na dimu*) smoked; **~ica** consumption, tuberculosis; **~ičav** consumptive; **~iti** dry; (*meso*) smoke
suština essence, substance
suton twilight, dusk

sutra tomorrow; **~dan** the next day; **~šnji** tomorrow's
SUV SUV (sport utility vehicle)
suvislo coherently; **~st** coherence
suviš|ak surplus, excess; **~an** superfluous; **~e** too much, in excess, excessively; **~nost** superfluity, excess
suvremen contemporary; modern, present-day, current; **~ik** contemporary
suza tear
suzbi|jati, **~ti** beat back; repulse; withstand, resist
suziti shed tears, run with tears; (*opseg*) make narrower; limit; (*odijelo*) take in
sužanj captive; prisoner; slave; **~stvo** captivity; slavery
svadba wedding; marriage
svadben|i: ***~o putovanje*** honeymoon
svad|iti se quarrel; fall out; **~ljiv** quarrelsome
svađa quarrel; dispute; discord; row; **~ti se** = **svaditi se**
svagda always, ever; ***za ~*** for good; **~šnji** every day; daily
svagdje everywhere
svakakav all kinds of; various
svak|ako at any rate; by all means; (*sigurno*) certainly; **~i** every; each; ***u ~o doba*** at any time; **~idašnji** everyday; **~odnevni** everyday, daily; **~ojaki** of all kinds, various; **~uda** everywhere; in all diretions
sva|liti, **~ljivati** topple down; overturn; ***~liti krivnju na*** lay the blame on
svanu|će dawn; break of day, daybreak; **~ti** dawn
svariti stew; brew; (*kovinu*) weld
svašta all kinds
svat wedding guest
svatko everyone, everybody
sve all, everything
svečan solemn, festive; **~ost** festivity; feast; celebration
svećen|ik priest; clergyman; **~stvo** clergy
svejedno nevertheless; all the same; still
sve|kar father-in-law; **~krva** mother-in-law
svemir universe; space
svemoć omnipotence, almightiness; **~an** omnipotent, almighty
svemoguć = **svemoćan**
svesrdan cordial
svesti deduce; attribute
svestran manysided; versatile; universal; **~ost** versatility; universality
svet saint, holy, sacred; ***~o pismo*** the Bible; the Scriptures; ***~o trojstvo*** Holy Trinity; **~ac** saint, holy man; (*zaštitnik*) patron saint; (*blagdan*) holiday; **~inja** sacred thing; **~ište**

shrine, sanctuary; **~kovati** celebrate; observe a holiday; **~kovina** holiday; **~ost** sanctity; holiness
sveučilište university
sveukupan total, entire, whole
sveza connexion; association; **~k** volume; **~ti** bind, tie, fasten
svežanj bundle; parcel
svi all; everbody
svibanj May
svibanjsk|i: ***~o drvo*** May-pole
sviđati se like; please; ***to mi se sviđa*** I like it
svijati bend, ply, curve
svijeć|a candle; **~njak** candlestick
svijest consciousness; ***izgubiti ~*** faint (away); **~an** conscious, aware
svijet world; the universe; (*ljudi*) people
svijet|ao bright, light; **~liti** shine; cast light; **~lo** light; (*dnevno*) daylight; ***sjeverno ~lo*** Northern lights
svil|a silk; (*umjetna*) rayon, artificial silk; (*sirova*) raw silk; **~en** silk; silky; ***~ena buba*** silk-worm
svinuti = **svijati**
svinj|a pig, hog, swine; **~ac** pigsty; **~arija** filthiness, dirty mess; (*riječi*) obscenity; (*postupak*) shameless (mean) treatment (trick); **~etina** pork
svira|la pipe; flute; **~ti** play
Svisveti All Saints's Day
svita suite
svitak roll, coil
svitati dawn
svizac marmot
svjedočiti bear witness to, give evidence
svjedodžba (*školska*) report; (*isprava*) certificate, testimonial
svjedok witness; (*očevidac*) eye-witness
svjetiljka lamp; lantern; (*džepna*) torch
svjetina mob, populace, rabble
svjetionik lighthouse; beacon
svjetl|ost light; daylight; (*sjaj*) brightness; **~ucati** glitter, glimmer, sparkle twinkle
svjetov|an secular, lay, wordly; **~njak** layman
svjetsk|i world, world-wide; universal; cosmopolitan; ***on je ~i čovjek*** he is a man of the world; ***~i rat*** World War; ***~o prvenstvo*** world championship; ***~a trgovina*** world trade; ***~o tržište*** world market
svjež fresh; new; (*hladan*) cool, chilly; **~ina** freshness; coolness, chill
svlačiti (se) undress; take off clothes
svladati conquer, vanquish, beat, overcome; **~ se** keep

one's temper
svod vault; (*luk*) arch, arcade
svodnik procurer
svoj one's own
svojatati claim unjustly; usurp
svojeglav obstinate, stubborn, wilful; **~ost** obstinacy
svojevoljan arbitrary; (*rado*) voluntary
svojina property, possession
svojstv|o characteristic, trait, property, quality; **~en** characteristic, distinctive, peculiar
svota sum, total; amount; ***okrugla ~*** lump sum
svrab itch; scab
svraćati divert; (*pozornost*) call (draw) attention; **~ se** = **svratiti se**
svraka magpie
svratište inn; hotel
svratiti se drop in, come to see; call on (at)
svrbjeti itch
svrdlo bore
svrgnuti (*s prijestolja*) dethrone; depose
svrh|a purpose, aim, object, end; ***bez ~e*** with no purpose; aimless(ly)
svrš|avati, **~iti** end, finish, complete, conclude; **~etak** end, finish completion, close
svući = **svlačiti**
svuda everywhere, all over, throughout
svukuda = **svuda**

Š

šablona stencil; model; pattern
šah chess
šahovsk|i: ***~a ploča*** chessboard; ***~a figura*** chessman
šaka fist
šakal jackal
šal scarf, shawl
ša|la fun, joke, jest; **~liti se** joke, jest, crack jokes; **~ljiv** humorous, funny
šalica cup
šampanjac champagne
šampionat championship
šampon shampoo; ***prati ~om*** shampoo
šanac trench; (*oko utvrde*) moat
šapa paw
šap|at whisper; **~nuti** whisper; **~tati** whisper; THEAT prompt; **~tač**, **~talac** prompter
šara hue, tinge
šaraf screw; **~iti** screw
šaran carp
šaren multi-coloured
šarka hinge
šarlah scarlet fever
šaš reed, bulrush

šašav crazy
šator tent
šav seam
ščepati seize, grab, grip, catch hold of
šćućuriti se crouch, squat
šećer sugar; **~ana** sugar refinery; **~iti** sugar, sweeten
šećern|i: ***~a repa*** sugar-beet; ***~a trska*** sugar-cane
šegrt apprentice; **~ovati** be apprenticed to
šenut crazy, mad; **~i** go mad, become insane
šepa|ti limp; **~v** lame, limping
šepiriti se strut about, swagger
šeprtlja bungler, fumbler
šesnaest sixteen
šest six; **~i** the sixth
šest|ar, **~ilo** pair of compasses
šešir hat
šet|ač, **~alac** walker, stroller; **~alište** promenade, walk; **~ati se** walk, stroll; **~nja** walk, stroll; ***ići na ~nju*** go for a walk
ševa (sky-)lark
šezdeset sixty
šib|a rod, birch; **~ati** flog, birch; **~ica** match; **~lje** brushwood; (*za pletenje*) wicker
šifra code, code-letter; cipher
šija nape
šikara coppice, underwood, thicket
šiknuti gush forth, squirt
šilo awl
šilja|k point, end; peak; **~st** pointed
šiljiti sharpen, point
šindra shingle
šinja rail
šipak hip; haw
šipka rod; bar; ingot
šir|enje spreading; expansion; **~ina** width, breadth; stretch; **~iti (se)** spread, propagate; (*proširiti*) extend, expand; widen; **~ok** wide, broad; **~okogrudan** liberal, broad-minded
širom (*otvoren*) wide open
šiša|nje (*kose*) hair-cut; (*ovaca*) shearing; clipping, cropping; **~ti** cut hair; crop; shear; clip
šišmiš bat
ši|ti, **~vati** sew, stitch
šiva|ći: ***~ća igla*** sewing-needle; ***~ći stroj*** sewing-machine; **~nje** sewing
škaklj|ati tickle; **~iv** ticklish
škare a pair of scissors (shears)
šilj|av squinting, cross-eyed; **~avost** squint; **~iti** squint, be cross-eyed
škod|a damage, harm; **~iti** damage, do harm, be harmful; **~ljiv** injurious, harmful
škola school; **~rina** tuition fee, school fee
školova|nje schooling; **~ti** school, teach; train; **~ti se** receive one's education

školjka shell
škopiti castrate, geld
Škot Scot, Scotsman; **~ska** Scotland; **~ski** Scottish
škrebetaljka rattle
škrga gill
škrgutati grind one's teeth
škriljevac slate
škrinja chest
škripa|c scrape, fix, pinch; ***natjerati u ~c*** corner, press hard; **~ti** creak, crunch; (*cipele*) squeak
škrlet scarlet fever
škrob starch; **~iti** starch
škropi|lo sprinkler; **~ti** sprinkle; spray
škrt mean, stingy; miserly; **~ac** miser; **~ost** stinginess
škulja hole, gap
škver ship-yard, dockyard
šljaka dross, slag
šljem helmet
šljiv|a plum; (*suha*) prune; (*stablo*) plum-tree; **~ovica** plum-brandy
šljuka snipe
šljunak gravel, pebbles (*pl*)
šminka make-up; **~ti** make-up
šmrkav snotty
šofer driver, chauffeur
šogor brother-in-law; **~ica** sister-in-law
šojka jay
šopati cram, stuff
špaga string
Špan|ija Spain; **~jolac** Spaniard; **~jolski** Spanish
šparga asparagus
šperploča plywood
špijun spy; **~aža** espionage
špilja cave, cavern, grotto
špinat spinach
šta = **što**
štafeta relay race
štagalj barn, shed
štaka crutch; (*visoka*) stilt
štakor rat
štala stable; cow-shed
štampa press; printing-press; **~r** printer; typesetter; **~rija** printing-house; **~ti** print
štand stand
štap stick; walking-stick; **~ić** baton
štaviti tan
šted|ionica savings bank; (*kutija*) savings-box; **~jeti** save, economize; **~ljiv** saving, thrifty, economical; **~ljivost** thriftiness, economy; **~nja** saving, economy
štednjak kitchen range
štektati yelp
štene puppy, young dog
šteta damage; harm; ***kakva ~!*** what a pity! **~n** harmful; (*po zdravlje*) unwholesome
štet|iti damage, harm, hurt; **~ovati** suffer damage (loss)
štićenik protégé, favourite
štipati pinch; nip
štirka starch; **~ti** starch; stiffen with starch
štit shield; **~iti** protect; shield; defend, guard; **~onoša** shield-bearer
štivo reading-matter
što what; **~ (*prije*) *to* (*bolje*)**

the (sooner) the (better); **~god** whatever, whatsoever
štoperica stop-watch
štošta all kinds of things
štova|lac admirer; **~n** respected, esteemed; **~nje** esteem, respect, regard; **~telj** = **~lac**; **~ti** respect, esteem, honour
štrajk strike; walk-out; **~aš** striker; **~ati** strike
štrca|ljka syringe; sprinkler; atomizer; **~ti** spurt, jet; sprinkle
štropot clatter, noise
štuca|ti hiccup; **~vica** hiccup
štuka pike
štula stilt
šubara fur-hat (cap), busby
šuga mange; scab; **~v** mangy; scabby
šuljati se sneak; slink
šum noise, murmur; rustle
šuma wood(s); (*velika*) forest; **~r** forester; **~rstvo** forestry
šumjeti make a dull noise; rustle; roar
šumovit wooded, afforested; **~ *kraj*** woodland
šunka ham
šupa shed
šup|alj hollow; (*zub*) rotten, decayed; *fig* empty, shallow; **~ljikav** porous; perforated; **~ljikavost** porosity; **~ljina** hollow, cavity, pit
šurjak brother-in-law; **~inja** sister-in-law
šurovati plot, scheme
šuš|anj rustle, rustling; **~kati** rustle; (*šaptati*) whisper
šut|jeti be silent, hold one's tongue; **~ljiv** quiet, reserved, taciturn; **~nja** silence
Šve|dska Sweden; **⁐dski** Swedish; **~đanin** Swede
šve|lo sewing; needlework; **~lja** dressmaker; seamstress
Švicar|ac Swiss; **~ska** Switzerland; **⁐ski** Swiss
švrljati loiter, stroll

T

ta well, why, still; this
taban sole
tabela list, tabulated list; schedule
tabl|a board; (*školska*) blackboard; **~ica** plate
tabor camp, encampment
tabu taboo
tačan exact, accurate; punctual, precise
tačk|a stop, full stop; dot; (*decimalna*) point; ***~a i zarez*** semicolon; ***dvije ~e*** colon
tačnost punctuality; exactness; precision
tada then, at that time; in that case; **~šnji** the then,

of that time
taj this
taj|an secret; underhand; **~no pismo** code, cipher; **~ni agent** plainclothes man, secret agent
tajanstven mysterious
tajiti keep secret; conceal
tajna secret, mystery
tajni|ca, **~k** secretary; **~čki** secretarial; **~štvo** secretary's office, secretariate
tajnost secrecy
takav such (a); like that, that sort of
takm|ac rival, competitor; **~ičiti se** compete, contest
taknuti touch, feel
tako so, thus, in this way; **~ da** so that; **~ reći** so to speak
također also, too; besides, in addition to
taksa due; tax; rate
taksi taxi, cab
takt tact; (MUS) time, measure; bar; **~ičan** tactful; tactical; **~ika** tactics, strategy, policy
talac hostage
talas wave; billow; surge; **~ati se** wave, undulate; swell
talent talent, gift; **~iran** talented, gifted
Talijan Italian; **~ski** Italian
tali|onica smelting works, smeltery; **~šte** melting-point; **~ti** melt; *(rudaču)* smelt
talo|g sediment, grounds, dregs; **~žiti (se)** settle, leave sediment
tama darkness, dusk; night; **~n** dark, obscure, dusky, dim
tamaniti destroy, exterminate
tamjan incense
tamnica prison, jail, gaol, dungeon
tamo there, in that direction; **amo ~** to and fro, back and forth; **~ preko** over there, across; **~šnji** living there, local
tanak thin; slender; slim; frail
tane bullet
tank tank; **~er** tanker
tankoćutan sensitive
tantijema royalty
tanjiti thin, make thin
tanjur plate; **~ić** saucer
tapati grope for (after)
tapeta wall-paper; **~r** upholsterer
tapkati patter
tarac pavement, paved walk; **~ati** pave
tarifa tariff
tast father-in-law
tašt vain, conceited; **~ina** vanity, conceit
tašta mother-in-law
tat thief; *(đepar)* pick-pocket
tat|a, **~ica** dad, daddy
tava (frying-)pan
tavan attic; garret; loft
tavanski: **~ prozor** dormer-window
te and; besides

tečaj course; circulation; (*novca*) rate of exchange
teč|an savoury, appetizing; **~nost** savouriness, flavour; relish; (*glatkoća*) fluency
teći run, flow, stream
tegl|enje towing, hauling, tugging; **~iti** tow, haul, tug, drag
tegoba difficulty, hardship; toil; **~n** difficult, hard, toilsome
tehni|čar technician; **~čki** technical; **~ka** technology; technique
tek[1] only, not earlier than, not until, as late as
tek[2] appetite; (*okus*) taste, flavour; ***bez ~a*** tasteless
teklić runner, messenger, courier; errand-boy
tekst text; (*predmet*) subject, theme; words
tekstil textile, fabrics
tekući running; fluent, flowing, current; ***~ račun*** current acount; **~na** liquid
telad calves (*pl*)
tele calf
telefon telephone; **~irati** telephone; ring up; call up
telefonsk|i: ***~a govornica*** telephone booth, call-box
telegraf telegraph; **~irati** send a telegram (a wire), wire
telegram telegram, wire; cable
teletina veal
televiz|ija television, TV; **~or** television set, TV set
teliti se calve
tema theme
temelj foundation, basis, base; substructure; ***na ~u*** on the ground of, based on, on the basis of; **~an** fundamental, basic; **~it** thorough; fundamental; **~iti** base upon, found on; **~ito** thoroughly; radically, completely
temperament temperament; (*živahnost*) vivacity, animation; **~an** full of temperament
temperatur|a temperature; ***mjeriti ~u*** take one's temperature
tempo rate; ***ovim ~m*** at this rate
tenda awning
tendencija tendency, trend
tenis tennis
tenk tank
teor|etski theoretical; **~ija** theory
tepati babble; (*mucati*) stammer
tepih carpet, rug
terasa terrace
teret burden, load; cargo, freight; weight; **~iti** press heavy upon; weigh down heavily; oppress
teret|ni: ***~ni brod*** cargo boat; ***~ni vlak*** freight train, goods train; **~njak** lorry, truck
teritorij territory
termofor hotwater bottle

tesa|r carpenter; **~ti** hew, trim (a log)
testament last will, testament
teško heavily; hard; severely, badly; (*jedva*) hardly, scarcely; **~ća** difficulty, hardship; ***praviti ~će*** raise difficulties
teta aunt; **~k** uncle
tetiva tendon; sinew, ligament
tetka = **teta**
tetošiti pamper, coddle, pet
tetrijeb grouse
teturati totter, stagger
teza thesis, dissertation
teža gravitation
težak[1] farm hand, field labourer
težak[2] heavy, weighty; (*naporan*) hard, difficult
teži|na weight; load; **~ti** weigh; **~šte** gravity centre
ti you; (*arch*) thou
ticalo feeler, antenna
ti|cati touch, feel; **~cati se** border on, touch, adjoin; ***mene se ~če*** I am concerned; ***što se ~če*** with regard to, as regards, regarding
tifus typhoid (fever)
tig|ar tiger; **~rica** tigress
tih still, quiet, silent; **~o** still, quietly; softly
tijek course, flow; circulation
tijelo body; constitution; ***raditi dušom i ~m*** put his heart and soul into the work
tijesak press
tijesan tight; narrow; close
tijesto dough, pastry
tik close by, next to
tikva pumpkin; gourd; (*glava*) noddle, pate; **~n** blockhead, imbecile
tili: ***u ~ čas*** in a jiffy
tim(e) with this, in this way; ***~ više*** the more so
tinta ink; **~rnica** ink-pot, inkstand
tinjati smoulder
tip type, character; **~ičan** typical, characteristic
tipka key
tipka|č, **~čica** typist; **~ti** type
tipograf type-setter
tirani|n tyrant; **~ja** tyranny
tirkiz turquoise
tisak tipography, print, printing; ***kosi ~*** italics; ***masni ~*** heavy (bold) type
tiska throng; squeeze; crowd
tiskanica form
tiska|r printer; **~ra** printing-house; printing-works; **~ti** print; (*gnječiti*) squeeze, press
tisuća thousand
tišina quiet, silence, stillness
tištati press; pinch; weigh down; oppress
titrati oscillate, vibrate; (*svjetlo*) flicker
titula title
tjed|an week; ***dva ~na*** a fortnight; ***dva puta na ~an*** twice a week; ***konac ~na*** weekend; **~nik** weekly;

~no weekly; a week
tjeles|an bodily, corporal, physical; ***~na kazna*** corporal punishment; ***~na straža*** bodyguard
tjelovježba gymnastics, physical training
tjeme crown of head, top of head
tjeralica warrant of apprehension
tjerati drive; chase; pursue
tjeskoba anxiety; **~n** anxious, uneasy
tjesnac strait; gorge; ***natjerati u ~*** corner, press hard
tjestenina noodles; pastry
tješiti console, comfort; **~ se** find comfort in
tkalac weaver
tkalački: ***~ stan*** loom
tka|nina fabric, cloth; **~ti** weave
tkivo tissue; fabric
tko who; **~god** whoever, whosoever
tlač|enje oppression, pressure; **~itelj** oppressor, despot; **~iti** press, squeeze; oppress, tyrannize
tlak pressure; **~omjer** pressure gauge
tlapnja illusion, delusion, fancy
tlo ground, earth, soil; ***plodno ~*** rich soil; ***gubiti ~*** lose ground; **~crt**, **~ris** ground-plan
tmina darkness, dusk
tmuran gloomy, dull, sombre, overcast
to this, it, that; ***~ jest*** that is; ***k ~me*** besides, moreover
toaleta toilet; (*odjeća*) dress
toaletni: ***~ stolić*** toilet-table, dressing-table; ***~ papir*** toilet-paper
tobogan toboggan, slide
tobolac quiver
tobož|e ostensibly; under the pretence; **~nji** ostensible; quasi, would-be; pretended
točak wheel
točan exact; punctual; accurate, precise
točiti pour out
točk|a (full) stop; dot; point; (*stavka*) item; (*ugovora*) clause; ***~a zarez*** semicolon; ***dvije ~e*** colon
točno punctually; exactly; **~st** punctuality; exactness
tok course; flow, stream; ***u ~u*** in the course of
tokar turner; **~iti** turn (wood)
tolerantan tolerant
tolik such a; of such size; **~o** so much, so many
toljaga club, cudgel
ton tone, sound, note; (*boje*) shade, tint
tona ton; **~ža** tonnage
tonuti sink, go to the bottom
top gun, cannon
top|ao warm; ***~lo mi je*** I am warm
topi|onica smeltery, smelting works; **~ti se** melt; dissolve; ***snijeg se topi*** it is thawing
toplice watering-place, spa

topl|ina, **~ota** warmth; **~omjer** thermometer
topništvo artillery
topola white poplar
toptati tramp, trample, stamp
tor pen; (sheep-)fold; ***zatvoriti u ~*** pen, fold
toranj tower; (*šiljast*) spire, steeple
torba bag; kitbag; **~r** pedlar; vendor; **~riti** peddle
torbica (*ženska*) handbag, purse
torped|irati torpedo; **~o** torpedo
torpiljarka torpedo-boat
torta cake
tovar load, cargo, freight, shipment; **~iti** load, freight
tovarni: ***~ list*** (*brodski*) bill of lading; (*željeznički*) way-bill
toviti fatten
trabunjati talk incoherently, drivel
tračak beam, ray
tračati gossip
tračnica rail; track
tradici|ja tradition; **~onalan** traditional
trafika tobacconist's (shop)
trag track, trace, trail; (*stopa*) footprints; ***bez ~a*** without a trace; **~ati** track, follow the track, trace
trag|edija tragedy; **~ičan** tragical
traj|an lasting, durable, permanent, continual; **~anje** duration; **~ati** last; continue; be permanent; **~nost** durability, permanence
trak, **~a** band, strip, ribbon; tape; ***~ svijetla*** beam, ray
trakavica tapeworm
traktor tractor
traljav shabby, poor
tralje rags, tatters
tram beam
transmisija transmission
transport transport, transportation; **~er** conveyor belt; **~irati** transport
tranzit transit
trapiti se mortify
tratina lawn, turf
tratinčica daisy
tratiti waste, squander, dissipate
trav|a grass; pasture; **~anj** April; ***prvi ~nja*** All Fool's Day; **~ka** grass-blade; **~nik** pasture-land, meadow
tražen looked for, demanded, asked, applied for; **~enje** searching, seeking, looking for; **~ilac** searcher; applicant; **~iti** look for, seek, search; (*zahtijevati*) claim; (*moliti*) request, apply for
trbuh belly, abdomen
trčati run, race; rush, dash
trebati need, be in need of, require; ***on treba da to učini*** he must do it; ***treba mi 10 minuta da to svršim*** it takes me 10 minutes to finish it
treći the third; **~na** one third

tref club
tren, **~utak** instant, jiffy, moment; ***u ~ oka*** in a jiffy, in no time; **~utačan**, **~utan** momentary, instantaneous
tren|er coach, trainer; **~irati** coach, train
trenuti wink, bat
trenje friction, rubbing
trepavica eye-lash
treperiti flicker, twinkle; flutter
trep|et fright, trepidation, fear, panic; (*svijetla*) twinkle; **~tati** wink, blink; twinkle, quiver
tresak bang, slam, crash
treset peat; **~ište** peat-bog
tres|kati, **~nuti** slam, bang; fall with a thud, thud
tresti shake; agitate; **~ se** tremble, shake, shiver
trešnja cherry; (*stablo*) cherry-tree; (*drmanje*) shaking, vibration
trezvenjak abstinent, teetotaller
trg market; square; (*sajam*) fair
trgati tear off, pluck; (*brati*) pick, gather
trgnuti (*mač*) draw the sword; **~ se** start, be startled; (*natrag*) recoil, pull back, shrink
trgovac shopkeeper, dealer; (*na malo*) retailer, tradesman; (*na veliko*) merchant, wholesale dealer
trgovačk|i commercial, merchant, trade, mercantile; ***~i brod*** merchant ship, merchant man; ***~i putnik*** commercial traveller; ***~i pomoćnik*** shop-assistant, salesman; ***~i ugovor*** trade agreement, contract; ***~a komora*** chamber of commerce; ***~a kuća*** firm, business; ***~a mornarica*** merchant marine
trgovati trade, do business, deal in, bargain
trgovina trade, commerce, traffic; (*na malo*) retail business; (*na veliko*) wholesale trade; (*dućan*) shop, store; ***slobodna ~*** free trade; ***~ mješovitom robom*** grocer's (shop), grocery
trgovište market town
tri three; ***~ puta*** three times
tribina grand stand, platform
trice trifles
tričav petty, insignificant, trivial
trideset thirty
trijem porch; cloister; arcade; portico
trije|ska wooden splinter, chip; **~šće** splinters, chips
trijez|an sober; **~nost** sobriety
trinaest thirteen
triumf triumph; **~alan** triumphal; triumphant; **~irati** triumph, exult over
trivijal|an trivial; **~nost** triviality
trka running, race; **~č** runner,

racer; (*konj*) race-horse; **~lište** race-course, race-track
trljati rub, massage
trn thorn
trnci pins and needles; ***~ me prolaze*** (*od strave*) it makes my flesh creep; it gives me the shivers
trnokop pick(-axe)
trnovit thorny, spiny
trnuti become numb
trnje brambles, thorny bushes
trofej trophy
trojci triplets
Trojstvo Trinity
trokut triangle; **~an** triangular
trolejbus trolley-bus, trolley-car
trom sluggish, slack, slow
tromjesečni quarterly
tromost slowness, sluggishness
tronožac tripod
tronut deeply moved
trop|i tropics (*pl*); **~ski** tropical
troska slag, dross
trostruk threefold, triple
trošak expense, cost, expenditure; ***putni ~*** travelling expenses; ***na moj ~*** at my expense; ***pogonski troškovi*** overhead expenses
trošan in bad repair, dilapidated; shabby
trošiti spend; (*uporabom*) use, wear out; (*tratiti*) waste
troškovnik estimate
trošnost dilapidation, tumbledown state
trouglast three-cornered
trova|nje poisoning; **~ti** poison
trpak bitter
trpati cram, stuff, press into
trpjeti suffer; endure, stand, bear; (*dopustiti*) tolerate, put up with
trs (grape-)vine
trsiti se take pains, try hard
trs|ka reed, cane; **~tika** reed
trti rub, chafe; massage
trtica rump
truba trumpet; bugle; **~č** trumpeter; bugler
trubiti trumpet, blow trumpet
trud pains; effort, trouble; ***dati si ~a*** take pains
trud|an tired; **~na** pregnant, with child; **~nica** pregnant woman; **~noća** pregnancy; **~ovi** childbed pains, throes
truditi se take pains, endeavour, take trouble
trul rotten; **~ež** rot, rotteness, decay
trun bit; mite; grain; mote
trunuti rot, decay; putrify, decompose
trup trunk; stem; (*broda*) hull; **~lo** corpse, dead body; carcass
trza|j jerk, twitch; **~ti** jerk, twitch; **~vica** convulsion; agitation, perturbation
tržište market, trade centre

tržnica market-hall
tu here, in this place
tuberkuloza tuberculosis, consumption; **~n** consumptive
tucati pound, crush
tuce(t) dozen
tuča hail; **~ *pada*** it hails
tučnjava row, brawl, fight
tući beat, strike; **~ se** fight
tuđ strange, foreign; **~inac** stranger; foreigner; alien
tug|a sorrow, sadness, grief; ***~a za zavičajem*** homesickness, nostalgia; **~ovati** sorrow, mourn (for over), grieve
tulipan tulip
tuliti howl; hoot, yell, boo
tumač interpreter; **~enje** interpretation, explanation; **~iti** interpret, explain; ***krivo ~iti*** misinterpret
tumarati roam, ramble, stray
tunel tunnel
tup blunt, dull; *fig* stupid, dense; **~ost** dullness, bluntness
tur buttocks, backside, bottom
tur|ati, ~iti push, shove
turbina turbine
Turčin Turk
turi|st tourist; **~stički** tourist; **~zam** tourism, tourist trade
turnir tournament, contest
turoban sad, melancholy; gloomy, depressed
turpija file, rasp
Tursk|a Turkey; **2i** Turkish
tuš (*tinta*) Indian ink; shower; **~irati se** take a shower
tut|anj roar, thunder, boom; **~njiti** boom, thunder, roar
tutor guardian, tutor; **~ski** tutorial; **~stvo** tutorship, guardianship
tužan sad, sorrowful
tuž|ba accusation; complaint; prosecution; report; denouncement; **~en** accused; **~ilac, ~itelj**, plaintiff; prosecutor; ***javni ~lac*** public prosecutor; **~iti** accuse (of); charge (with); sue; prosecute; **~iti se** complain (of)
tvar matter, stuff; substance; material
tvoj your; yours
tvor skunk, polecat
tvor|ac creator, maker; **~ba** formation, creation; **~evina** product; creation; make; **~nica** factory; mill; plant; works; **~nički** manufactured; factory produced
tvrd hard; solid; rigid
tvrd|iti affirm, assert; maintain; **~nja** assertion, affirmation, statement
tvrdoća hardness; firmness; solidity
tvrdoglav obstinate, stubborn, opinionated; **~ost** obstinacy, stubborness
tvrdokor|an obstinate, persistent; hardened; obdurate; **~nost** obstinacy, obdu-

racy
tvrđava fortress, stronghold; citadel
tvrtka firm; house

U

u in, at; by; into; ~ ***to*** at that moment; ~ ***tom smislu*** to this effect; ~ ***njegovo ime*** on his behalf
ubav sweet, pretty, nice, charming
ubica = **ubojica**
ubi|ti kill, murder, slay; assassinate; **~stvo** murder; assassination
ublaž|enje soothing, alleviation; (*kazne*) mitigation; **~iti** soothe, alleviate; mitigate
ubod sting, stab; bite
ubog poor, needy; wretched, miserable
uboj|ica murderer, killer; **~it** murderous, deadly; **~stvo** = **ubistvo**
ubosti sting, prick; bite
ubrajati include, comprise
ubrati pick, gather
ubrojiti = **ubrajati**
ubrus serviette, napkin
ubrzati accelerate, quicken, speed up, increase speed
ubuduće in future
ucijeniti blackmail
ucjena blackmail
učen learned, erudite, scholarly; **~ica** pupil, schoolgirl; **~ik** pupil, schoolboy; disciple; **~jak** scholar; scientist; learned man; **~ost** erudition, learning
učes|nik participant; **~tvovati** participate, take part in
učešće participation, taking part in
učin|ak effect; **~iti** make, do; commit
učionica schoolroom, classroom
učita|ti download; **~vanje** download
učit|elj teacher, schoolmaster; instructor; **~i** (*drugoga*) teach; learn, study
učtiv polite, civil, courteous; **~ost** politeness, courtesy, civility
učvrstiti make firm, fix, fasten
ući enter, come in, get in
udahnuti breathe in, inhale
udaja marriage
udaljen far, distant, remote, out-of-the-way; **~ost** distance, remoteness
udalji|ti se go (get) away
udar stroke; coup; ***državni*** ~ coup d'état
udara|c blow, stroke; (*nogom*) kick; (*lagan*) tap, rap; **~ti** keep beating (striking, hitting)
udariti strike, hit, kick,

knock; ~ ***o*** hit (strike, bump) against; ~ ***u oči*** strike one; ~ ***u plač*** burst into tears
udarnik shock worker
udati marry; ~ **se** get married
udaviti strangle
udebljati se get fat
udes fate, destiny
ude|siti arrange; manage
udic|a angle, fish-hook; ***loviti ~om*** angle
udijeliti grant, give; confer upon
udio share, allotment
udisati breathe (in), inhale
udjenuti (*konac*) thread a needle
ud|o limb, member; ***spolni ~ovi*** privy parts
udob|an comfortable, cosy; **~nost** comfort, cosiness
udomaćiti domesticate; ~ **se** feel oneself at home
udomiti se settle down; feel oneself at home
udostojati se condescend
udov|a, **~ica** widow; **~ac** widower; **~ištvo** widowhood
udovoljiti satisfy, comply with; fulfil a requirement; (*želji*) humour
udruž|enje association, union; society; **~iti se** unite, enter into partnership; associate
udubina recess, niche
udušiti suffocate, stifle, smother, choke
udvarati court, pay court to
udvor|an polite, courteous; gallant; obliging; **~nost** politeness, courtesy, civility
udžbenik textbook
ufa|nje hope; **~ti se** hope
ugađati (*glazbalo*) tune; humour one, try to please one
ugalj = **ugljen**
uganuti sprain, dislocate
ugao corner; angle
ugasiti put out, extinguish; (*svijetlo*) turn off; (*žeđ*) quench; ~ **se** go out
ugaziti stamp down, tread down, trample down
uglađen refined, courteous, well-mannered; **~ost** politeness, good manners
uglat angular
uglaviti fix, agree to, determine
uglavnom mainly, chiefly
ugled reputation, renown, prestige; **~an** respected, distinguished, eminent
ugledati set eyes upon, see; ~ **se** follow somebody's example
ugljen coal; ***drveni*** ~ charcoal; ***kameni*** ~ hard coal, anthracite; **~okop** coal-mine, colliery, coal-pit
ugljič|an carbonic; ***~na kiselina*** carbonic acid
ugljik carbon
ugnjetavati oppress, tyrannize
ugod|an pleasant, agreeable; **~iti** please
ugojiti fatten; ~ **se** get fat,

put on weight
ugovarati negotiate
ugovor contract, agreement; (*državni*) treaty, pact; **~iti** make an agreement
ugrabiti snatch, grab, seize; (*dijete*) kidnap
ugraditi build in
ugrijati heat, warm
ugristi bite
ugriz bite
ugro|ziti, **~žavati** threaten, jeopardize, imperil
ugušiti suffocate, smother, choke; (*bunu*) put down
uhađati shadow
uhititi arrest, apprehend
uho ear; (*igle*) eye of a needle
uhod|a spy; **~iti** shadow; practise espionage
uhvatiti catch, seize, capture, catch hold of
uistinu really, truly
ujak uncle
ujed bite; **~ati** bite; sting
ujedi|niti unite; **~njenje** union
ujedljiv biting, sarcastic, bitter; **~ost** sarcasm
ujesti = **ujedati**
ujna aunt
ujutro in the morning; ***sutra* ~** tomorrow morning
ukazati point out (at), show
uki|dati, **~nuti** cancel, annul; abolish; do away with
ukiseliti pickle; **~ se** turn sour
ukl|anjati, **~oniti** remove, do away with; **~oniti se** go out of the way, avoid
uključi|ti include, comprise; **~vo** inclusively, including
uknjižiti register, make an entry, enter in books
ukoč|en stiff, rigid; **~iti** stiffen, make stiff; **~iti se** become stiff, stiffen
ukonačiti accomodate, put up
ukopati bury
ukor reprimand, blame, rebuke; **~iti** blame, reprimand, scold; tell off
ukorijeniti take root; become rooted
ukosnica hair-pin
ukras ornament, decoration; trimming; **~iti** decorate, ornament; **~ni** ornamental, decorative
ukrasti steal, pilfer
ukratko in short, in a nutshell
ukrcati se embark, board, go aboard
ukrotiti tame; (*konja*) break in; bridle, subdue
ukućanin inmate
ukuha|n preserved; **~ti** preserve (fruit)
ukup|an total, whole, entire; ***~na svota*** sum total; **~no** totally, entirely, wholly, all together
ukus taste; flavour; ***bez ~a*** tasteless; **~an** tasteful, savoury
ulagati (*novac*) deposit; in-

vest; (*u drvo*) inlay
ulagivati se toady, fawn (up)on
ulaz entrance; admission, entry; **~ak** entry; **~iti** enter; **~nica** ticket, admission-ticket; **~nina** entrance-fee
ulediti freeze
uleknuti se sag, curve, subside
ulica street; (*mala*) lane; (*slijepa*) blind alley
uličnjak ragamuffin, vagabond, bum, loafer
ulijeniti se grow lazy
uli|jevati, ~ti pour in(to); *fig* inspire, instil
ulizi|ca toady; **~vati se** = **ulagivati se**
ulog deposit
uloga role, part
ulomak fragment; passage
uloviti catch, catch hold of; seize
ulozi gout
uložiti = **ulagati**
uludo in vain; foolishly
ulje oil; **~n** oily, oiled
uljepšati beautify, embellish, adorn
uljiti oil, lubricate
uljud|an courteous, civil, polite; **~nost** courtesy, politeness, civility
uljuljati rock; lull; **~ *u san*** rock to sleep
um reason, intellect; mind; ***palo mi je na ~*** it occurred to me; an idea struck me
uma|ći, ~knuti escape
umak sauce; (*sok od pečenke*) gravy; **~ati** dip (into)
umalo nearly, almost
umanjiti lessen, diminish, reduce; **~ se** diminish; (*zaliha*) run short
umarati fatigue, tire, weary, exhaust
umekšati soften, mellow; **~ se** soften; relent
umet|ak insert; inset; **~ati, ~nuti** insert, set in, interpolate
umijeće skill, art
umijesiti knead (into)
umiješa|ti mix (blend) into; intermingle; involve; ***biti ~n*** be involved in
umilja|t sweet, lovable; **~vati se** ingratiate oneself with
umirati die slowly, be dying
umiriti calm down; pacify; appease
umiroviti send into retirement; pension off
umišlj|ati si be conceited; fancy; **~en** conceited, vain; **~enost** conceit, vanity
umi|ti, ~vati se wash; **~vaonik** washbasin
umjeren moderate; reasonable; medium; **~ost** moderateness, frugality
umjestan appropriate, suitable, fit; tactful
umjesto instead (of)
umjetan artificial; artistic
umjeti know how to; be skilled; be able
umjetn|ički artistic(al); ***~ičko***

djelo work of art; **~ik** artist; **~ina** work (object) of art; **~ost** art; artistry
umnožiti multiply
umobol|an insane, mad; **~nost** insanity, madness
umočiti dip into
umor fatigue, exhaustion, weariness; **~an** tired, weary, exhausted
umoriti tire, exhaust; (*ubiti*) murder, kill; **~ se** get tired
umorstvo murder, homicide; assassination
umotati wrap up; envelop
umrijeti die, pass away; (*od gladi*) starve (to death)
umrljati smear, soil, stain
umrtviti deaden, benumb
umuknuti stop speaking, remain speechless; (*od zaprepaštenja*) be struck dumb
unakrs|ni: ***~na vatra*** cross-fire; ***~no ispitivanje*** cross-examination; **~t** crosswise
unapređ|enje advancement promotion; **~ivati** = **unaprijediti**
unaprijed in advance; beforehand; **~iti** advance, promote, further
unatoč in spite of; nevertheless
unatrag backwards
unča ounce
unesrećiti make unhappy; ruin; **~ se** be hurt (injured)
uniforma uniform
unija union
unijeti carry into; (*upisati*) enter, make an entry; register, record
uništ|avati, **~iti** destroy, demolish, ruin, wreck; **~enje** destruction, ruin, demolition
univerzitet university
unosan profitable
unositi = **unijeti**
unovačiti recruit, enlist
unovčiti convert into money; sell
unu|čad grandchildren; **~če** grandchild; **~k** grandson; **~ka** granddaughter
unutar within; inside; **~nji** internal, interior; (*zemlja*) inland
unutra inside; indoors; **~šnji** = **unutarnji**
uobičajen usual, customary, habitual
uobraž|avati si be conceited; **~en** conceited, vain
uoči on the eve of
uokviriti frame
uopće generally, in general, altogether; **~ ne** not at all
uostalom after all
upada|n conspicuous; **~ti** sink into; (*u riječ*) cut in, interrupt; (*u oči*) strike one's eyes, be conspicuous
upadica incident; interruption
upala inflammation; ***~ pluća*** pneumonia; ***~ slijepog crijeva*** appendicitis
upaliti set fire to; light; (*električno svijetlo*) turn on; **~ se**

catch fire; become inflamed
upaljač lighter
upaljiv inflammable; **~ost** inflammability
upamtiti remember, memorize; bear (keep) in mind
upasti = **upadati**
upijati absorb; suck in; soak
upirati se lean against
upis registration, enrolment; (*zapis*) entry, record; **~ati** register, enrol, enlist; record; **~nina** registration-fee
upit inquiry, question; **~ati** ask, question, inquire, make inquiry
upiti = **upijati**
upitni: **~ *arak*** questionnaire
upitnik question mark, mark of interrogation
upla|ćivati, **~titi** pay in
uplaš|en frightened, scared; **~iti** frighten, scare; **~iti se** get frightened (scared)
uplat|a payment; (*rata*) instalment; **~iti** pay in
uplesti interweave, intertwine; involve, entangle
uple|tati, **~sti se** meddle, interfere
uplitati = **upletati**
upliv influence; **~isati** influence
upljesniviti se become musty (mouldy), mould
uporab|a use, usage; employment; **~iti** use, employ
uporan persistent; stubborn
upored|an parallel; **~iti** parallel; compare; **~o** by the side of, along with
upoređiva|nje comparison; **~ti** = **uporediti**
uporište foothold, footing
upornost persistence, stubbornness
uposl|en employed; **~iti** employ
upotpuniti complete
upotreb|a use, usage; **~iti**, **~ljavati** use; make use of; employ
upoznati get to know, get acquainted with; meet
upozor|enje warning; **~iti**, **~avati** warn, caution; draw one's attention to
uprav|a administration, management; **~itelj** manager, director; (*škole*) headmaster; **~ljati** manage; direct; run; operate
upravni administrative; governing, ruling; **~ *govor*** direct speech
upravo just, directly; exactly
upregnuti harness
uprijeti (*pogled*) fix one's eyes upon; **~ se** exert oneself; make an effort
uprljati dirty, soil
upropastiti ruin, wreck
uprskati spatter, bespatter
uprtiti (*na se*) shoulder (a burden, etc.)
upu|ćen informed, acquainted with, initiated; **~ćivati**, **~titi** instruct, direct; (*na nekoga*) refer to
upu|ta instruction, direction;

~tan advisable, opportune; ~titi = ~ćivati; ~titi se start, set off; (*u nešto*) get the knack of, become skilled in
uputnica money-order
ura (*vrijeme*) hour; clock; (*ručna*) (wrist-)watch; ***sunčana ~*** sun-dial
uračunati take into account; comprise
uraditi do, make; commit; ***uradi sam*** DIY (do it yourself)
uraniti rise (get up) early
urar watchmaker
ureći (*sastanak*) make (an appointment), fix the time; (*začarati*) cast a spell on
ured office; bureau
uredan tidy, neat, orderly
uredba regulation; act
urediti put in order; arrange; regulate; (*spremiti*) tidy
uredni|k editor; (*glavni*) editor in chief; ***~čki odbor*** editorial board; **~štvo** editor's office; (*služba*) editorship
uredovn|i: ***~o vrijeme*** office-hours, working-hours
uređ|aj arrangement, equipment; **~enje** arrangement, putting in order; establishment; (*računa*) settling; **~ivati** put in order; (*časopis*) edit
ures ornament, decoration; trimming; **~iti** ornament, adorn, decorate; trim; garnish
urezati incise; notch; make a cut; engrave
urlati howl, roar, bellow, yell
urna urn
urnebes uproar, hullabaloo; **~an** uproarious, thundering
urod crop, yield; **~iti** bear (yield) fruit
urođen indigenous, native, aboriginal; inborn; **~ički** aboriginal; **~ik** native, indigene, aboriginal
uroniti dive, plunge
urot|a conspiracy, plot; **~iti se** conspire, plot; **~nik** conspirator
uruč|enje handing in, delivery; **~iti** hand; deliver
usaditi fix into, insert; embed; implant; *fig* instil
usahnuti wither, die, shrivel up
usavrš|avati, ~iti perfect, improve
useknuti se blow one's nose
useliti se move in(to); immigrate
useljenik immigrant, settler, colonist
ushi|ćen enthusiastic, delighted, elated; **~ćenje, ~t** delight, rapture, enthusiasm; **~titi** enrapture, delight
usidjelica spinster, old maid
usidriti anchor; **~ se** cast anchor
usijan red-hot, white-hot; ***~a glava*** hothead
usiljen constrained, forced, unnatural
usiriti se curdle, set

usisati suck in, absorb
usisivač: *~ za prašinu* vacuum cleaner
usitniti chop, hash up
usjeći cut in, incise, indent
usjev crop(s)
uskladiti bring into harmony, harmonize
uskličnik mark of exclamation
usklik exclamation, shout, cry; **~nuti** cry out, exclaim, call out
uskomešati se get agitated, make a fuss, be in a flutter
uskoro soon, before long, shortly
uskotračan narrow-gauge
uskra|ćivati, **~titi** refuse, deny; grudge
Uskrs Easter, Easter Sunday
uskrsnu|će resurrection; **~ti** bring (come) back to life; resurrect
uslijed because of, owing to; *~ toga* as a result, because of that, as a consequence
uslišati grant; give ear (audience) to
uslov condition; *pod ~om* on condition that
uslu|ga favour, service, a good turn; **~žan** obliging, kind, helpful; **~žnost** kindness, helpfulness
usmen oral; verbal
usmjeriti aim, head
usmrtiti kill; put to death
usn|a, **~ica** lip; *zečja ~a* harelip
usnuti fall asleep, drop off
usoliti put in salt, pickle
usov avalanche
uspava|nka lullaby; **~ti** lull (to sleep)
uspeti se climb; rise
uspijevati succeed; prosper, be successful; thrive
uspinjača funicular
uspinjati se = **uspeti se**
uspje|h success; **~šan** successful; prosperous; efficient; **~šnost** efficiency
uspjeti succeed, be successful; manage; *ne uspje i* fail
usplahiren agitated, in a flutter; **~ost** agitation, flutter, fluster
uspomena memory, reminiscence; (*predmet*) souvenir
uspon climb; rise; ascent
uspored|an parallel; **~ba** comparison; **~iti** compare; **~o** side by side, along with
usporiti slow down; slacken
uspostav|iti, **~ljati** restore, rehabilitate
usprav|an upright, erect, vertical; **~iti** set upright, erect; **~iti se** stand (sit) upright; hold oneself upright
usprkos despite, in spite of, for all
usprotiviti se resist, object to, oppose; be against
usput by the way, on the way
usrećiti make happy
usred amidst, in the middle of, among
usredotočiti (se) concen-

trate
usta mouth
usta|liti se become settled; **~ljen** settled, established, stable
ustanak uprising, rebellion
ustanov|a institution, establishment; **~iti** establish, found, create
ustati rise, get up; stand up; (*buna*) rise up in arms
ustav constitution; **~an** constitutional
ustav|a dam; **~iti** stop; hold up
ustavotvoran constituent
uste|gnuti, ~zati deduct, take away; **~gnuti se** hold back, refrain from, abstain from
ustoličiti install, place in office, inaugurate
ustraj|an persistent, persevering; steadfast; **~ati** persevere, persist; **~nost** persistence
ustrijeliti shoot, kill
ustrojiti (*kožu*) tan, dress; organize
ustručava|nje hesitation, reluctance; **~ti se** hesitate; shrink from; be reluctant
ustuknuti give in, yield
ustup|ak concession; **~ati, ~iti** concede; give up, cede; renounce
usud fate, destiny
usuditi se dare, venture, have the courage
ususret towards
usvojiti adopt
uš louse
ušančiti se dig oneself in, entrench (oneself)
ušće mouth of river
ušećeriti preserve in syrup (sugar)
ušiti sew in
uškopiti castrate, geld
ušljiv lousy
uštap full moon
ušte|da savings; **~djeti** save
uštinuti pinch; nip
uštipak doughnut
uštrcati inject; squirt into
uštrojiti castrate, geld
ušuljati se sneak in, steal in, slip in
ušutjeti stop speaking, become silent
ušutkati silence
utaboriti se encamp, pitch camp
utajiti embezzle; suppress
utakmica match, contest, competition
utaman in vain; **~iti** destroy, exterminate
utamničiti imprison
utažiti soothe; (*žeđu*) quench; (*glad*) satisfy
uteći run away, escape, flee
uteg weight
utemelji|ti found, establish; **~telj** founder, creator
utihnuti become still (silent)
utirati tread down, stamp, beat
utis|ak impression; **~nuti** impress, stamp, imprint, indent

utišati silence, quiet, appease
utjeca|j influence; impact; **~ti** influence; (*rijeka*) flow into
utjeha consolation, comfort, solace
utjeloviti embody, incorporate
utjer|ati, ~ivati drive into; (*dug*) enforce payment
utješiti comfort, console, give comfort
utkati weave into, interweave
utočište refuge, shelter, recourse
utopiti se be (get) drowned
utorak Tuesday
utovariti load; ship
utrk|a race; **~ivati se** race, run a race; *fig* compete
utrnuti extinguish; go out
utroba intestines (*pl*); bowels (*pl*); (*majčina*) womb
utrošiti spend, expend
utrpati cram (squeeze) into
utrt beaten; **~a staza** beaten track; **~i** beat, tread down
utržak proceeds (*pl*)
utvara phantom, spectre, apparition, ghost
utvarati si be conceited
utvr|da fortification, fort, fortress, stronghold; **~diti, ~đivati** fortify, strengthen; (*činjenicu*) establish a fact
uvala bay, gulf; cove; (*dolina*) valley
uvaž|avati, ~iti take into consideration; alow for; appreciate; esteem, respect
uveče in the evening
uveća|ti, ~vati increase, enlarge, magnify
uvenuti fade, wither, droop, wilt
uvesti introduce, let in, bring in; import
uvez binding; **~ati** bind
uvid insight, inspection
uvi|djeti, ~đati realize, comprehend, be aware of; **~đavan** considerate, tolerant, understanding
uvijek always; ***za ~*** for good, for ever; ***još ~*** still
uvjer|avanje assurance; **~avati, ~iti** assure, convince, persuade; **~iti se** make sure, convince oneself; **~enje** conviction, persuasion; (*svjedodžba*) certificate; **~ljiv** convincing, persuasive
uvjet condition, term; ***pod ~om*** on condition, provided that; **~an** conditional; **~ovati** condition; stipulate
uvježbati drill, train, practise
uvod introduction; **~iti** introduce; **~nik** editorial, leading article, leader
uvojak lock, curl
uvoz import; **~iti** import
uvred|a offence, insult, outrage; **~ljiv** insulting, abusive
uvrijediti offend, insult, give offence to, hurt; **~ se** take offence
uvrijeđen offended, insulted
uvriježiti se take root
uvrstiti insert, interpolate
uz(a) along with; near, by, be-

side; ~ **to** besides, in addition to, moreover
uzajaman mutual, reciprocal
uzajmiti (*drugome*) lend; (*od drugoga*) borrow
uzak narrow; (*tijesan*) tight
uzalud in vain, uselessly; **~an** useless, futile
uzao knot
uzastopce one after another; at a stretch
uzbrd|ica slope, rise; **~o** uphill
uzbu|diti, **~đivati** excite, agitate, thrill; **~dljiv** exciting, thrilling; **~đen** excited; **~đenje** excitement, agitation, thrill
uzbun|a alarm; commotion, disturbance; ***dati znak za ~u*** sound an alarm; **~iti** alarm, sound an alarm; agitate; cause commotion
uzburkan stormy, rough
uzda rein, bridle
uzdah sigh; **~nuti** sigh
uzdati se rely upon, trust
uzdi|ći, **~gnuti** lift up, raise, elevate
uzdisati sigh
uzdizati = **uzdići**
uzdrmati shake, give a shock
uzdržati se abstain from, restrain oneself
uzdržavanje keep, maintenance; support, alimentation
uzdržavati keep, support; **~se** = **uzdržati se**
uzduh air
uzduž along, alongside
uzemlj|enje earthing; **~iti** earth
uzet paralyzed
uzeti take; ~ ***pod svoje*** adopt; ~ ***slobodu*** take a liberty; ~ ***zajam*** raise (take) a loan; ~ ***u obzir*** take into consideration
uzetost paralysis
uzgajati bring up, rear; (*voćke*) grow; (*stoku*) breed, raise
uzglavlje head of bed; pillow
uzgoj breeding, raising; growing, cultivation
uzgred by the way, incidentally; **~an** incidental; unimportant
uzica line, string, lead
uzići ascend, rise
uzimati take
uzjahati mount a horse
uzlaz ascent, ascension; **~an** rising; **~iti** rise, ascend, climb
uzletjeti take off; rise in the air
uzma|k retreat; **~knuti**, **~ći** retreat, withdraw, fall back
uzmanjkati run short of
uzmicati = **uzmaknuti**
uznemiren alarmed, uneasy, anxious, agitated
uznemiri|ti, **~vati** disturb, trouble; alarm, worry
uzni|čar gaoler, jailer; **~k** prisoner
uznojiti se perspire, sweat
uzor model, ideal; **~ak** pat-

tern, design; sample; **~an** ideal, model, perfect
uzrast stature; growth; **~i** grow up
uzrečica saying, proverb
uzročan causative
uzrok cause, reason, ground; source; **~ovati** cause, bring about
uzruja|n agitated, excited, nervous; **~nost** excitement, agitation; **~ti se** get agitated
uzurpirati usurp
uzvanik guest
uzvik exclamation, cry; **~nuti, ~ivati** shout, exclaim
uzvišen exalted, sublime
uzvra|ćati return, repay; **~t** return; ***za ~t*** in return
uzvrpoljiti se fidget; get fidgety
užaren red-hot; white-hot, glowing
užas horror, terror; **~an** horrible, terrible, dreadful; **~nuti se** be horrified
uže rope, cord
užežen rancid
užina tea, high tea; light meal
uži|tak pleasure, delight, treat; **~vati** enjoy, find pleasure in
užurban hasty, hurried

V

vabiti allure, entice, tempt, attract
vadičep corkscrew
vaditi take out, pull out, extract
vaga balance, scale; weighing-machine; **~ti** weigh; balance
vagon carriage, coach, car
vajar = **kipar**
vakcina vaccine
val wave; billow, surf; ***zvučni ~*** sound wave; ***dužina ~a*** wavelength; **~ovit** wavy, undulating; ***~ovit lim*** corrugated iron
valuta currency
valjak roller; (*parni*) steam-roller; (*za rublje*) mangle
valjan good; proper; valid; convenient; **~ost** validity
valjaonica rolling-mill
valjati (*vrijediti*) be valid; be good; ***to ne valja*** this is not right; (*željezo, itd.*) roll
valjda perhaps, maybe; probably
valjušak dumpling
vam(a) (to) you
vampir vampire
van out, out of doors
vanbračan illegitimate
vani out, out of doors, outside
vanilija vanilla
vanredan extraordinary
vanjsk|i outside, outdoor, exterior; ***~a trgovina*** foreign

trade
vanjština exterior; appearance
vap|aj cry (for help); **~iti** cry (for help)
vapnen chalky, chalk; lime; **~ac** limestone
vapno lime; ***živo ~*** quicklime; ***gašeno ~*** slaked lime
vara|lica impostor, cheat, swindler; **~ti** cheat, swindle; (*obmanuti*) deceive; **~ti se** be mistaken, be deceived; **~v** = **varljiv**
varijanta variant
variti boil; digest; (*zavarivati*) weld
varivo (boiled) vegetables
varjača ladle
varka deceit, trick, stratagem
varljiv deceitful, misleading
varnica spark
varoš town
vas you
vaš your, yours
vašar fair, market
vatr|a fire; flame; **~en** fiery; ardent, passionate; ***~eno oružje*** fire-arms; **~enost** ardour; fieriness
vatrogas|ac fireman; **~ci** fire-brigade
vatrogasn|i: ***~a kola*** fire engine
vatro|met fireworks (*pl*); **~stalan** fire-proof
vaza vase
vazal vassal
važ|an important; **~iti** be valid, signify, matter, weigh, carry weight; **~nost** importance; significance
večer evening; eve
večera dinner; supper
večeras this evening; tonight
večerati have dinner (supper)
već already
većina majority, the greater part, most
većinom mostly; mainly; (*obično*) usually
vedar serene; clear; (*veseo*) cheerful
vedriti se clear up
vedro pail, bucket
velegrad large town, big city
veleizdaja high treason
velesila great power
veličanstv|en magnificent, grand, glorious, gorgeous, splendid; **~o** majesty
velič|ati extol, exalt; **~ina** magnitude, greatness; size; dimension
velik large, big; great
velikaš aristocrat, lord, peer, nobleman
velikoduš|an generous; **~nost** generosity, magnanimity
velo = **veo**
veljača February
vena vein
Venecija Venice; **~nski** Venetian
ventil valve; ***sigurnosni ~*** safety valve
ventil|acija ventilation; **~irati** ventilate

venuti wilt, wither, droop
veo veil
veoma very, very much, greatly
vepar wild boar
veranda veranda
verati se climb
verbalan oral, verbal
veresija credit, loan
verglec barrel-organ
vertikalan vertical, upright
verzija version
verziran versed (in), skilled (in)
vese||liti se be glad, rejoice; be merry; **~lje** gaiety, joy, delight; (*zabava*) merry-making; **~o** cheerful, gay, merry
vesl|ati row; paddle; **~o** oar; paddle
vesti embroider
veterina veterinary medicine; **~r** veterinary, veterinarian, vet; **~rski** veterinary
veto veto; ***uložiti* ~** put a veto
vez embroidery, fancy-work
veza connection; (*odnos*) relation; (*na internetu*) link; **~n** bound, tied; **~ti** bind, fasten, tie; (*spajati*) link, connect
vezivo embroidery, fancy-work, needle-work
veznik conjunction
veža doorway, porch
vi you
vibrirati vibrate, oscillate
vičan accustomed, used to
vid (eye-)sight
vidik view; vista
vidjelo: ***doći na* ~** come to light; ***iznijeti na* ~** bring to light
vidjeti see
vidljiv visible; prominent, conspicuous; **~ost** visibility
vidokrug horizon
vidra otter
viđenj|e seeing, meeting; ***do* ~*a!*** see you on ...; see you soon; I'll be seeing you; so long; ***po* ~*u*** by sight
vihor whirlwind, gale
vijadukt viaduct
vijak screw
vijavica blizzard, snowstorm
vijeća|nje consultation, conference; **~ti** confer, discuss
vijeć|e council; **~nica** town hall; **~nik** councillor, alderman, senator
vijek century; age; ***novi* ~** modern times; ***srednji* ~** the Middle Ages; ***stari* ~** ancient times
vijenac wreath
vijesnik messenger
vijest news; tidings (*pl*); information
vijoriti se flutter; wave
vijuga|st winding, devious, meandering; **~ti** wind, meander
vika shouts (*pl*), outcry; **~ti** shout, cry; yell, howl
vila[1] fairy, fay, nymph
vila[2] (*zgrada*) villa; country-house; (*mala*) cottage
vile hay-fork, pitchfork

vil|ica, **~juška** fork
vilica (*čeljust*) jaw
vime udder
vinara wine-shop
vino wine; ***bijelo* ~** white wine; ***crno* ~** red wine; **~grad** vineyard; **~gradar** winegrower; **~gradarstvo** wine-growing
vinov: ***~a loza*** grapevine
vinuti se soar up, fly up
violina violin
vir whirlpool, eddy
viriti stick out; (*gledati*) peer, peep
virtuoz virtuoso; **~nost** virtuosity
virus (*na računalu*) virus
viseći: ***~ most*** suspension bridge
visibaba snowdrop
visina height, altitude
visjeti hang (down)
viso|k high, tall; **~ravan** plateau, table-land
višak surplus, excess; (*u težini*) overweight
više more, plus; higher; ***~ manje*** more or less; ***~ puta*** several times, repeatedly; ***nikad ~*** never more; **~struk** manifold
višezadaćni: ***~ rad*** multitasking
višnja sour cherry
višnji almighty, omnipotent
vitak slim, slender
vitalan vital; active
vitao windlass
vite|ški chivalrous, gallant, knightly; **~štvo** chivalry, knighthood; **~z** knight
viti wind, twist; **~ se** twine, intertwine; **~ca** lock, curl; (*biljke*) tendril
vitlati brandish, flourish, swing
viza visa
vizija vision, apparition
vječ|an eternal, everlasting; **~nost** eternity
vjeđa eyelid
vjenča|n married; ***~ni list*** marriage certificate; ***~ni prsten*** wedding ring; **~nje** wedding; **~ti** marry, wed; **~ti se** get married
vjera religion, belief, faith
vjeran faithful, loyal, true
vjeren engaged; **~ik** fiancé; **~ica** fiancée
vjeridba engagement; **~ti se** get engaged
vjernici congregation
vjernost fidelity, loyalty, faithfulness
vjerodajnica credentials (*pl*)
vjerodostojan credible; authentic; reliable
vjeroispovijest religion, faith
vjerojat|an probable, likely; **~no** probably, likely; **~nost** probability, likelihood
vjeroloman faithless, disloyal
vjeronauk cathechism
vjerovati believe
vjerovnik creditor
vjerski religious

vješa|la gallows; **~lica** hanger; **~ti** hang (up)
vješt skilled, skilful, adroit; efficient; **~ak** expert; **~ina** skill; proficiency
vještica witch
vjet|ar wind; (*lagan*) breeze; **~renjača** windmill; **~robran** windscreen; **~rovit** windy
vjeverica squirrel
vježba exercise, drill, practice; training; **~ti** drill, exercise, practise, train
vježbenica exercise-book; textbook
vlada government, rule; (*uprava*) administration; **~r** ruler; sovereign; **~ti** rule, reign, govern; dominate; **~ti se** behave
vlaga humidity, moisture, dampness
vlak train; ***brzi ~*** express; fast train; ***direktni ~*** through train; ***putnički ~*** passenger train; ***teretni ~*** goods (freight) train
vlakn|ast fibrous; **~o** fibre
vlakovođa guard, locomotive driver; *Am* engineer
vlas hair; *fig* hair's breadth; **~i** hair
vlasac (*luk*) chive
vlasni|k owner, proprietor; **~štvo** ownership, property, possession
vlast power, might; authorities (*pl*); command
vlastel|a landed gentry, estate-owners; **~in** estate-owner, squire; lord of the manor
vlastit one's own; **~o ime** proper name
vlastoručan written in one's own handwritting; autographic
vlasulja wig, periwig; **~r** wig-maker, hairdresser
vlat blade
vlažan damp, moist, wet, humid
vô = **vol**
voć|arna fruit-shop; **~arstvo** fruit growing; **~e** fruit; **~ka** fruit-tree; **~njak** orchard
vod EL lead; line; (*ljudi*) squad
vod|a water; ***uz ~u*** upstream; ***niz ~u*** downstream
vodeći leading
voden watery; (*razvodnjen*) diluted; ***~i konj*** hippopotamus; ***~a boja*** water-colour; ***~i znak*** water mark; **~ica** water-mill
vodič guide; (*knjiga*) guide-book
vodik hydrogen
voditi guide; lead, take the lead; (*upravljati*) direct; manage, run; (*okolo*) take round, show round; ***~ pregovore*** negotiate, carry on negotiations
vodnik sergeant
vodo|mjer water-gauge; **~pad** waterfall; **~ravan** horizontal, level; **~skok** fountain; **~staj** water-level;

~vod water-supply
vodstvo guidance; leadership
vođa leader
voj|arna barracks; **~evati** war, carry on war
vojni military, army; ~ ***sud*** court martial; **~čki** military, army; soldierlike, soldierly; **~k** soldier; private
vojsk|a army; **~ovođa** general, army leader, commander in chief
vojvo|da duke; **~dina** dukedom; **~tkinja** duchess
vokal vowel
vol ox
volonter volunteer
volumen volume
volj|a will; (*raspoloženje*) mood, temper; ***on je dobre*** (***zle***) ***~e*** he is in a good (bad) mood; ***imati ~e za*** be in the mood for; ***po ~i*** at will; **~an** willing; ready
voljeti like, love, be fond of; ~ ***više*** prefer, like better
vonj smell, odour; **~ati** smell
vosak wax
vošt|anica (wax-) candle; **~iti** wax, polish with wax
voz train; waggon, cart
voza|č driver; motorist; **~rina** fare; freight
vozi|lo vehicle; **~ti (se)** drive, ride
vozn|i: ***~i red*** time-table; ***~a cijena*** fare; ***~a karta*** ticket; ***~i park*** rolling stock
vožnja ride, drive
vrabac sparrow
vrača|ra fortune-teller; **~ti** tell fortune
vraćati return; give back; restore; ~ **se** return, come back
vrag devil, satan
vrago|lija prank, practical joke, roguery; **~ljan** rogue; **~ljast** roguish, mischievous
vrana crow
vrat neck
vrata door; gate; ***ulazna ~*** front door; **~r** doorkeeper; *Am* janitor; SPORT goalkeeper
vratiti se = **vraćati se**
vratnica door-post
vratobolja sore throat
vratoloman reckless, foolhardy
vražji devilish, diabolical
vrba willow; (*za pletenje*) osier; ***tužna ~*** weeping willow
vrcati (MED) extract (honey); (*iskre*) sparkle; ~ **se** fidget
vrč jug, pitcher; mug, jar; (*s poklopcem*) tankard
vrebati lurk, spy upon, lie in ambush; watch for
vreć|a sack, bag; **~ica** paper bag
vrelište boiling-point
vrelo well, spring, source
vremenski time; ~ ***izvještaj*** weather report
vremešan old, aged, advanced in years
vrenje boiling; fermentation;

seething
vreo boiling, boiling hot
vreti boil; ferment; seethe; (*lagano*) simmer
vreva crowd, throng, crush
vrganj mushroom
vrh top, summit, peak
vrhnje cream; ***tučeno ~*** whipped cream
vrhovni supreme; highest; ***~ zapovjednik*** commander-in-chief
vrhunac = **vrh**; *fig* culmination
vrijed|an worth; worthy; (*marljiv*) diligent, industrious; ***~no je*** it's worth while
vrijediti be worth, be valuable, be of value
vrijednost value, worth; ***bez ~i*** valueless, worthless; ***gubitak ~i*** depreciation
vrijeđati offend, insult, give offence to, hurt
vrijeme time; (*meteorološko*) weather; (*gramatičko*) tense; ***na ~*** on (in) time; ***krajnje ~*** high time; ***cijelo ~*** all the time
vrijesak heather
vriskati scream, shriek
vrištati = **vriskati**
vrlet crag, cliff; **~an** craggy, rugged, rocky
vrlina virtue
vrlo very, most
vrpca ribbon, tape, band
vrpoljiti se fidget, be restless
vrst(a) sort, kind; species; **~an** capable, competent; excellent
vršak tip, point; top; peak
vršenje practice, execution; (*žita*) threshing
vršiti perform, execute, practise; (*žito*) thresh
vršilica threshing-machine
vrt garden; (*povrtnjak*) kitchen garden; (*cvjetnjak*) flower garden
vrtati bore, drill
vrtjeti turn (spin) round, rotate, revolve; ***vrti mi se u glavi*** I feel dizzy
vrtlar gardener; **~ija** nursery
vrtlog whirlpool, eddy
vrtoglav dizzy, giddy; **~ica** dizziness, giddiness
vrtuljak merry-go-round
vruć hot; **~ica** fever; **~ina** heat
vrvjeti teem, swarm
vucibatina vagabond; good-for-nothing
vučjak Alsatian
vući drag, pull, haul; (*tegliti*) tow, tug
vuk wolf; **~odlak** vampire
vulgar|an vulgar; **~nost** vulgarity, coarseness
vulkan volcano; **~ski** volcanic
vun|a wool; **~en** wool, woollen

Z

za for; ***dan ~ danom*** day after day; ***~ čas*** in a moment; ***~ uvijek*** forever, for good
zabaciti reject; dismiss
zabačen rejected; off the map, remote; out-of-the--way
zabadati pin into; (*dražiti*) tease
zabadava free, gratis, free of charge; (*uzalud*) in vain
zabasati lose one's way, go astray
zabašuriti hush up
zabat gable
zabava (*društvo*) party; merry-making; entertainment, amusement; fun; **~n** amusing, funny, entertaining
zabav|ljati, ~iti amuse, entertain; **~ljati se** have a good time, have fun, amuse oneself; **~iti se** occupy oneself with
zabezeknut dumbfounded, struck dumb; **~i** strike dumb, dumbfound
zabijati hammer, drive in(to)
zabilježiti make a note, jot down; mark
zabitan out-of-the-way, remote, secluden
zabiti = **zabijati**
zablatiti soil; muddy; (*odjeću*) bedraggle
zabliještiti dazzle; flash
zablud|a delusion, misconception, fallacy; **~iti** lose one's way, go astray
zaboljeti cause pain, hurt; grieve
zaborav oblivion; **~an** forgetful; **~iti** forget
zabran|a prohibition, ban; **~iti, ~jivati** forbid, prohibit, interdict, ban
zabrinut anxious, worried, concerned; **~i se** become anxious, worry; **~ost** anxiety, worry, concern
zabun|a mistake, misunderstanding; confusion, bewilderment; **~iti se** make a mistake, be mistaken; **~om** by mistake
zabušavati shirk
zabušiti se run into, collide with, crash into
zacijeliti heal
zacijelo surely, certainly, no doubt
zacrvenjeti become red, redden; **~ se** blush, redden
začarati cast a spell on, bewitch
začepiti stop (up), plug, cork (up)
začet|i conceive, become pregnant; **~nik** originator, creator
začin seasoning, spice, dressing; **~iti** season, spice

začuditi surprise, astonish; **~ se** be surprised (astonished)
začuđen astonished, surprised, amazed
zaći (*sunce*) set
zadaća task; (*domaća*) homework
zadatak = **zadaća**; (*matematički*) problem
zada|ti set (a problem); ***~ti bol*** inflict pain, hurt; ***~ti muke*** cause trouble
zadaviti strangle; choke
zadesiti happen (to); befall
zadiha|n out of breath, breathless; **~ti se** be out of breath, gasp
zadijevati tease, annoy
zadim|ljen smoky, filled with smoke; **~iti** fill with smoke
zadirkiva|ti tease; **~nje** teasing
zadnji last, latest, final; terminal
zadnjica buttocks, bottom, backside
zadobiti get, receive
zadovolj|an content, satisfied, happy, pleased; **~avajući** satisfactory; **~avati, ~iti** satisfy; **~iti se** be satisfied (with); **~stvo** satisfaction; **~ština** satisfaction; amends
zadrijemati drop off, fall asleep, doze
zadruga community; cooperative
zadrža|ti, ~vati keep back; retain, hold back; hold up; delay; **~ti se** be delayed, get held up
zadubljen absorbed in (thought)
zadupsti se be absorbed in (thought)
zadušiti se suffocate, choke
zaduž|iti se run into debt; **~nica** promissory note, I O U (= I owe you)
zaga|diti (*zrak*) pollute; **~đen** polluted; **~đivanje** (*zraka*) polution
zaglušiti deafen
zagnjuriti plunge, dive; immerse
zagonet|an puzzling, mysterious; **~ka** puzzle, riddle, mystery, enigma
zagorčiti embitter
zagov|arati intercede, plead with a p. for; **~or** pleading, intercession
zagrad|a bracket, parenthesis; **~iti** fence in
zagrijati warm (up); **~ se** *fig* become enthusiastic about
zagristi bite in(to)
zagrižljiv biting, sarcastic, bitter
zagr|liti embrace, hug; **~ljaj** embrace, hug
zagroziti se threaten, menace
zagušiti (se) suffocate, choke
zagušljiv stuffy, stifling
zahod lavatory, toilet, water-closet
zahrđati get rusty, rust

zaht|ijevati demand; claim; require; **~jev** demand, requirement, claim
zahva|la thanks, acknowledgement; **~lan** grateful, obliged; thankful; **~liti**, **~ljivati** thank; **~lnost** gratitude; **~ljujući** thanks to, owing to
zahvat hold, grip, clutch; **~iti** catch hold of; grip, clutch
zainteresiran interested in
zaista really, indeed, truly, of course
zajam loan; advance
zajamčiti guarantee, warrant; vouch for
zajašiti mount a horse
zajedljiv sarcastic, bitter
zajedn|ica community, co-operative; union; **~ički** common; joint; **~o** together; in common; jointly
zajutrak breakfast
zaka|sniti be late; **~šnjenje** coming (being) late; delay
zakazati fix (time)
zaklada foundation
zaklati kill, slaughter, butcher
zaklet sworn; **~i se** swear, take an oath; **~va** oath; ***kriva ~va*** perjury
zaklinjati implore, beseech; **~ se** = **zakleti se**
zaklon shelter; screen, shield; **~iti** shelter; shield, screen; **~iti se** take shelter
zaključ|ak conclusion; resolution; **~an** conclusive; final
zaključati lock up
zaključiti conclude, draw a conclusion; resolve
zakon law; act of parliament; **~ik** code; **~it** lawful, legal; **~ito** legally, lawfully; **~itost** lawfulness; **~odavac** legislator; **~odavan** legislative; **~odavstvo** legislature; **~ski** legal; statutory
zakopati bury
zakopčati button up
zakoračiti step (into)
zakovati rivet
zakrabuljiti se disguise oneself
zakračunati bolt
zakrčiti block the way, obstruct; bar, jam
zakre|nuti, **~tati** turn; swerve; twist
zakri|lje protection; patronage; **~liti** shield, protect; patronize
zakrpa patch; **~ti** darn; patch up; mend
zakržljati stunt; be stunted
zakulisan underhand; secret
zakup lease; rent; **~iti** lease, rent; **~nik** lease-holder; tenant
zakuska snack
zakvačiti hook up; clasp; fasten
zalaga|onica pawn-shop; pawnbroker's; **~ti** pawn; **~ti se (za)** plead for, speak in favour of
zalajati start barking
zalaz sunset; **~iti** set; (*nekamo*) frequent, haunt

zalediti se freeze up
zaletjeti se dart, rush forward; (*izbrbljati*) blab, go too far
zaliha supply, stock, store
zalijeniti se grow lazy
zalijepiti stick (together), glue, paste
zalijevati water, irrigate
zalisci whiskers
zaliti = **zalijevati**
zalog pawn, pledge; mortgage
zalogaj morsel, bite, snack
založiti pawn; pledge; mortgage; (*jesti*) have a snack
založnica pawn-ticket
zaludjeti infatuate, fascinate
zalupiti bang; (*vratima*) slam (the door)
zalutati stray, go astray, lose one's way
zaljev bay, gulf
zaljubiti se fall in love with
zamah swing; ***u punom ~u*** in full swing; **~nuti** swing, brandish
zamak castle
zamalo nearly; (*vremenski*) in a short time
zamamljiv tempting, alluring
zamašnjak fly-wheel
zamatati wrap, envelop
zamaza|n dirty, filthy, grimy; **~ti** dirty, soil
zametak embryo
zametnuti mislay
zamijeniti exchange; (*nekoga s nekim*) mistake for
zami|sao idea; conception; **~sliti** imagine, fancy; conceive; **~šljen** thoughtful
zamjen|a exchange; **~ica** pronoun; **~ik** substitute, deputy, proxy
zamjenjivati = **zamijeniti**
zamjer|avati, **~iti** take offence, resent, bear a grudge
zamka trap, snare, pitfall
zamoliti ask, beg; ask a favour
zamoriti tire, fatigue, exhaust
zamota|k parcel, package, packet; bundle; **~ti** wrap up, do up
zamračiti obscure, dim, darken
zamrljati soil, stain, smear
zamr|siti entangle; (*kosu*) ruffle; **~šen** entangled; intricate; complicated
zamuknuti become silent, be speechless (dumb-founded); (*zvuk*) fade away
zanat trade, craft, handicraft; **~lija** craftsman, artisan
zanemari|ti, **~vati** neglect; omit; fail to do
zanese|n carried away; exalted, enthusiastic; **~njak** fanatic; dreamer
zanijekati deny
zanijemiti remain speechless, be dumb-founded
zanijeti carry away; enrapture; (*žena*) conceive, become pregnant; **~ se** be carried away; become enraptured

zanima|nje interest; (*zvanje*) profession, vocation, occupation; **~ti (se)** be interested in, take an interest in; (*baviti se*) be engaged in
zanimljiv interesting
zanos enthusiasm; rapture; ecstasy; **~iti se** = **zanijeti se**
zanovijetati nag, grumble
zao bad, wicked, naughty, evil
zaobi|ći, ~laziti go round; *fig* circumvent
zaogrnuti wrap, cloak
zaokrenuti turn (round); swerve
zaokružiti round off; surround
zaokupiti absorb; engage, occupy
zaosta|lost backwardness; **~o** behindhand; in arrears; (*duševno*) backward; **~ti** fall (lag) behind; be behindhand with; (*plaćanje*) be in arrears with
zaoštriti sharpen
zaova sister-in-law
zapad west; (*sunca*) sunset; **~ni** west, western, westerly
zapadati (*sunce*) set, go down; (*trošak*) cost, have to pay
zapad|no west, westward(s); **~njak** westerner; (*vjetar*) west wind
zapaliti set fire to, set on fire, ignite, light; (*svijetlo*) turn on (the light); **~ se** catch fire
zapaljenje = **upala**
zapamtiti remember, memorize
zapa|njen astounded, amazed, dumbfounded; **~njiti** astonish, dumbfound, strike dumb
zapapriti pepper, season with pepper
zapa|sti = **~dati**
zapaziti = **opaziti**
zapečatiti seal up
zapeti get (be) stuck
zapis note; entry; **~ati** write (jot) down; make a note; **~ničar** person taking the minutes; **~nik** minutes (*pl*)
zapitati ask, question, inquire
zapjevati start singing
zaplakati start crying; burst into tears, burst out crying
zaplašiti frighten, scare, startle
zaplesti entangle; confuse; **~ se** get involved; (*zbuniti se*) get confused
zaplet, ~aj entanglement, complication; plot; **~ati** = **zaplesti**
zaplijeniti confiscate; capture
zaploviti set sail, start sailing
zapljesniviti become musty (mouldy)
započeti begin, start; initiate
zapomagati cry for help
zapor catch, bar, bolt; **~ka** bracket
zaposjed|nuti, ~ati occupy,

take possesion of
zapo|sjesti = **~sjednuti**
zaposliti employ; make busy
zapostav|iti, **~ljati** neglect, disregard, slight
zapovijed order, command; **~ati** order, command; rule, give orders
zapovjediti = **zapovijedati**
zapovjed|ni: ***~ni način*** imperative; **~nički** commanding; **~nik** commander, commandant; (*vrhovni*) commander in chief; **~ništvo** command, authority, leadership
zaprašiti cover with dust; powder
zapravo as a matter of fact, in reality
zapreg|a team; **~nuti** harness
zapreka obstacle, hindrance; ***utrka sa ~ma*** hurdle-race
zaprem|ati, **~iti** occupy; **~ina** capacity; (*brodska*) tonnage
zaprepastiti frighten, scare, alarm; **~ se** be alarmed (scared, panic-stricken)
zaprepašte|n frightened, terrified, panic-stricken; **~nje** consternation, panic, fright
zapriječiti hinder, prevent from, obstruct
zaprijetiti (se) threaten, menace
zaprlja|n dirty, soiled; **~ti** soil, dirty, stain
zaprositi ask in marriage
zapt discipline
zapučak button-hole
zapu|stiti, **~štati** neglect; (*napustiti*) abandon; **~stiti se** become careless; become slovenly; **~šten** neglected, uncared-for; deserted, abandoned
zaračunati charge; **~ *previše*** overcharge
zara|da earnings (*pl*); (*dohodak*) income; **~diti** earn, make money
zarasti heal (up)
zaratiti se make war, declare war
zara|za infection, epidemic; **~zan** infectious, contagious, epidemic, catching; **~ziti** infect (with)
zarđa|o rusty, corroded by rust; **~ti** rust, become corroded by rust
zarez cut, incision, score; (*znak*) comma; **~ati** cut into, incise, notch
zarob|iti capture, make (take) a prisoner, enslave; **~ljenik** prisoner, captive; **~ljeništvo** captivity
zaroniti dive, plunge; dip
zaruč|en engaged; **~nica** fiancée; **~nik** fiancé; **~iti se** get engaged
zaruke engagement
zarumenjeti se blush, become red
zasaditi plant
zaseban separate
zaselak hamlet
zasićen saturated, fed up, satiated; **~ost** saturation,

surfeit
zasijati sow (with)
zasipa|ti, **~vati** fill up holes (ditches)
zasititi se satiate, surfeit, be fed up
zasjati brighten up, emit light; shine
zasjed|a ambush; ***biti u ~i*** lie (be) in ambush; ***pasti u ~u*** fall into an ambush
zasjeda|nje session, sitting, meeting; **~ti** be in session, sit
zasjeniti shade, screen
zaskočiti take by surprise, take unawares
zasladiti sweeten
zaslijepiti blind, dazzle; (*prevariti*) deceive
zaslon screen; **~iti** screen, shade
zaslu|ga merit, credit; **~žan** meritorious, praise-worthy
zasluži|ti, **~vati** earn; deserve; be worthy of; be entitled to
zasnovati plan, scheme, project
zaspati fall asleep, drop off, go to sleep
zasram|iti shame, make ashamed; **~ljen** ashamed
zastar|io out of date, obsolete; old-fashioned, outmoded; **~jelost** obsoleteness; **~jeti** become obsolete; lose validity
zastati halt, stop
zastav|a flag, banner, colours (*pl*), standard; **~nik** ensign, standard-bearer
zastidjeti se become ashamed; blush
zastirati veil, screen; hide from view
zastoj standstill; jam
zastor curtain; blind
zastra|niti, **~njivati** deviate, diverge; wander; digress; **~njivanje** deviation, digression
zastraši|ti, **~vati** frighten, scare; alarm; intimidate
zastr|ijeti, **~ti** veil, screen, curtain
zastup|ati represent; **~nik** representative, deputy, agent; **~stvo**, **~ništvo** representation; agency
zasukati roll up, tuck up; ***~ rukave*** *fig* set to work
zasun bolt, bar; **~uti** bolt, bar
zasuti fill up (holes); bury
zasušiti (se) dry up
zasvijetliti light up, flash
zašarafiti screw up
zašećeriti sweeten, sugar
zašiljiti sharpen, point
zašiti sew up
zaštedjeti save
zašti|ćivati = **~titi**
zaštit|a protection; screen; **~iti** protect, shelter, screen, shield
zaštit|ni: ***~ni znak*** trade-mark; **~nik** protector, patron
zašto? why?, what for?; ***~ ne?*** why not?

zatajiti conceal; keep secret; (*zabašuriti*) hush up
zateći come upon (across); (*na djelu*) catch red-handed
zate|gnuti, **~zati** pull tight, tighten; (*odgoditi*) delay
zatiljak nape
zatim then, after that
zatišje lull, quiet period
zato therefore; consequently
zatom|iti, **~ljivati** suppress; cork up
zaton bay, gulf
zatražiti demand, ask for, claim; apply for
zatrovati poison, envenom
zatrpati fill (up), stop
zat|rti, **~irati** exterminate; destroy; eradicate
zatv|arati, **~oriti** shut, close; (*u zatvor*) imprison; (*pipu*) turn off; **~or** prison, jail, gaol
zaudarati stink
zaustav|iti, **~ljati** stop, put a stop to, halt, check; **~iti se** stop; come to a standstill
zaušnica slap, box on the ears
zauvijek forever, for good
zauzdati bridle, check, curb
zauz|eće capture, conquest, taking possession of; **~eti**, **~imati** capture; take by assault, take possession of; **~eti se** (*za nekoga*) intercede (for, on behalf of), plead
zavad|a dispute, quarrel; **~iti se** quarrel, fall out
zavesti seduce; mislead
zavezati bind, tie (up)
zavežljaj bundle
zavičaj native country (place); ***čeznuti za ~em*** be homesick; ***čežnja za ~em*** homesickness
zavi|dan envious, jealous; **~djeti**, **~đati** envy, be envious
zavijati (*zamatati*) wrap up; (*cesta*) wind, curve; (*tuliti*) howl, whine
zaviknuti cry out, shout
zaviri|ti, **~vati** peer, peep (into)
zavis|an dependent; **~iti** depend (on)
zavist envy, jealousy
zaviti wrap up
zavitlati brandish, swing
zavjer|a conspiracy, plot; **~enik** conspirator, plotter; **~iti se** conspire, plot
zavjesa curtain; blind
zavjet vow, pledge; **~ovati se** make a vow
zavlačiti delay, procrastinate
zavod institution, establishment, institute
zavod|iti = **zavesti**; **~ljiv** tempting, alluring, seductive; **~nik** seducer
zavoj bend, curve, serpentine; (*povoj*) bandage; **~nica** spiral
zavoljeti grow fond of, take a fancy to; fall in love with
zavor brake
zavrijediti deserve, merit, be

worth
zavrnuti roll up, tuck up; twist, turn
završ|an final, last; **~en** finished, completed; **~etak** end; **~iti** finish, end, complete
zavrtati = **zavrnuti**
zavrtje|ti spin, turn round, revolve; ***~lo mi se*** I felt giddy
zazidati wall in
zazirati shrink from, have an aversion to
zazivati invoke; (*pomoć*) call for help
zazoran objectionable, shocking, offensive
zazubic|a: ***rastu mi ~e*** my mouth waters
zbaciti throw off, cast off
zbijati jam; compress; nail together; ***~ šalu*** make fun of, poke fun at
zbijen compact, packed; massive, thickset
zbilja reality, actuality; really, truly, indeed
zbir sum, total
zbirka collection
zbi|ti se, ~vati se happen, take place, occur
zbog because of, owing to, due to; ***~ toga*** therefore
zbogom goodbye
zbor meeting, gathering, assembly, convention; (*pjevački*) choir; ***nastavnički ~*** teaching staff
zbornik miscellany, collection; (*zakona*) code
zbrajati sum up; add
zbrka confusion, mess, muddle, chaos; **~ti** confuse, muddle, make a mess
zbroj sum, addition, total; **~iti** = **zbrajati**
zbu|niti embarrass, confuse, puzzle, bewilder; **~njen** confused, embarrassed, puzzled, bewildered
zdenac well
zdepast thick-set, stocky, squat, dumpy
zdjela dish, bowl
zdrav healthy, well, in good health; **~ica** toast; **~lje** health; ***u vaše ~lje!*** to your health!
zdravo! hello!
zdravstven health, sanitary; ***~a služba*** health service
zdrobiti crush; pound; crumble
združiti (se) unite, ally (to)
zdušan conscientious; eager
zdvajati despair, be desperate
zdvoj|an desperate, despairing; **~iti** = **zdvajati**; **~nost** despair
zeba finch
zebnja anxiety
zebra zebra
zec hare; (*kunić*) rabbit
zele|n green; **~nilo** greens (*pl*); greenery, verdure; **~nkast** greenish; **~njeti (se)** become green
zelje cabbage
zemaljsk|i earth, earthly; ***~a***

kugla globe
zemlja earth, globe; (*kopno*) land; (*tlo*) soil, ground; (*država*) country
zemljak countryman
zemljan earthen; ***~o posuđe*** earthenware
zemljište piece of land; plot, site
zemljopis geography
zemljoradnik farmer, agricultural worker
zemljotres earthquake
zemljovid map
zepsti be cold, freeze; (*drhtati*) shiver with cold
zet son-in-law
zgaziti crush, trample down
zglavak = **zglob**
zglob joint; (*prstiju*) knuckle
zgnječiti crush, squash, press
zgoda opportunity, chance, occasion; event; **~n** favourable; suitable; (*zabavan*) amusing; (*lijep*) handsome, nice
zgoditak lucky hit; prize
zgoditi se happen
zgotoviti complete, finish
zgrabiti catch, seize, get hold of, grab
zgrada building
zgražati se be shocked, be disgusted, feel disgust at
zgrbljen bent, stooping
zgrčiti (*šaku*) clench; cramp, contort; **~ se** be contorted (cramped)
zgrijati warm (up), heat; **~ se** get warm, warm oneself
zgroziti se = **zgražati se**
zgr|tati, **~nuti** shovel (up); (*novac*) hoard (up)
zgrušiti se curdle, coagulate, clot
zgusnuti (se) thicken, condense
zgužvati (se) crease, crumple, wrinkle
zibati rock, swing
zid wall; **~ar** bricklayer, mason, stone-mason; ***slobodni ~ar*** freemason
zid|arski: ***~arska žlica*** trowel; **~ati** build; **~ine** walls
ziherica safety-pin
zijevati yawn
zim|a winter; (*hladnoća*) cold, chill; **~ski** winter, wintry
zimzelen evergreen
zjapiti gape
zjenica pupil
zlat|an gold; golden; **~ar** goldsmith; **~ica** buttercup; **~nik** gold coin; **~nina** jewelry; **~o** gold
zlikovac criminal
zlo evil, harm, mischief
zloba malice, spitefulness; **~n** malicious, spiteful; wicked
zločest naughty, wicked
zločin crime; **~ac** criminal
zloća wickedness
zlo|ćudan ill-natured, malevolent; **~duh** evil spirit; **~glasan** notorious, infamous, scandalous; **~koban** ominous, ill-omened; **~namjeran** malicious; **~rabiti**

abuse, misuse; **~radost** = **zloba**; **~stavljati** ill-treat, maltreat; abuse; **~sutan** ominous, foreboding; **~tvor** = **zločinac**; **~upotreba** misuse, abuse; **~volja** ill (bad) temper; sulleness; **~voljan** bad-tempered, sullen

zmaj dragon; (*dječji*) kite

zmija snake; (*otrovna*) viper

značaj character; **~an** characteristic; significant, notable; **~ka** characteristic, trait, feature; **~nost** significance

znač|enje meaning, sense; significance; **~iti** mean; signify; matter; **~ka** badge

znak sign, symbol, mark; (*zaštitni*) trade-mark

znamen mark, sign; (*na koži*) mole

znamenit famous, well-known, prominent; **~ost** importance; **~osti** sights (*pl*); ***razgledavati ~osti grada*** go sightseeing; see the sights

znamenka figure; = **znamen**

znan|ac acquaintance; **~ica** acquaintance

znanost science; ***prirodne ~i*** natural sciences

znanstven scientific; **~ik** scientist

znanje knowledge; (*učenost*) erudition, learning

znatan considerable, remarkable, substantial

znati know

znatiželja curiosity, inquisitiveness; **~n** curious, inquisitive

znoj sweat, perspiration; **~an** perspiring; **~iti se** perspire, sweat

zob oats (*pl*)

zobati peck

zona zone, belt

zoolo|g zoologist; **~gija** zoology

zoološki: ***~ vrt*** zoological garden, zoo

zor|a dawn, daybreak; ***u ~u*** at dawn

zov call

zrač|an airy, air; ***~na pošta*** air mail; ***~na pruga*** airline, airway; ***~na sisaljka*** air-pump; ***~ni napad*** air-raid; ***~ni ventil*** air-valve; **~iti** air; MED radiate

zrak air; ***nepropustljiv za ~*** airtight; ***dignuti u ~*** blow up

zrak|a ray; ***rentgenske ~e*** X-rays

zrakoplovstvo aviation; (*vojno*) air force; ***Britansko ~*** the Royal Air Force

zrcalo mirror, looking-glass

zrelost maturity, ripeness; ***ispit ~i*** school leaving examination

zre|o ripe, mature; **~ti** ripen, mature

zrn|ast granular, granulated; **~at** grainy; **~o** grain; (*tane*) bullet

zub tooth (*pl* teeth); ***izvaditi ~*** extract (pull out) a tooth;

~ac tooth, cog; (*vilice*) prong; **~alo** set of teeth; (*umjetno*) denture; **~ar** dentist
zub|ni: **~ni *kamenac*** tartar; **~*no meso*** gums
zubobolja toothache
zujati buzz, hum
zumbul hyacinth
zupč|anik cog-wheel; **~ast** indented; **~ati** indent
zvaničan official
zvanje profession, vocation, walk of life
zvati call; **~ se** be called; ***kako se on zove?*** what is his name?
zveč|ati sound, clink; **~ka** rattle
zveketati = **zvečati**
zvijer beast
zvijezda star; **~ *repatica*** comet
zvižd|ati whistle; **~uk** whistle
zvjer|injak zoological garden; **~ski** beastly, brutal; savagely; **~stvo** brutality, atrocity
zvjezdarnica observatory
zvon|ak resonant; **~ar** sexton, sacristan; **~ce** small bell; **~ik** belfry, bell-tower; **~iti** ring (a bell); toll; **~o** bell
zvrk top
zvrkast foolish, crazy
zvuč|an sonorous, resonant; *fig* high-sounding; **~ati** sound, resound; **~nik** loudspeaker; **~nost** sonority
zvuk sound

Ž

žab|a frog; (*krastača*) toad; **~ica** (*praskavica*) cracker
žacati se be reluctant, shrink from
žal beach, shore
žalac sting
žal|ba complaint; **~iti** regret, deplore; **~iti se** complain
žalost sorrow, sadness; ***biti u ~i*** be in mourning; **~an** sad; **~iti** sadden, distress; **~iti se** be sad (distressed), grieve at
žalovati mourn, be in mourning
žaljenje regret, grievence; pity
žamor din, murmur
žao harm, wrong; **~ *mi je*** I am sorry; ***učiniti na ~*** do harm, hurt
žaoka = **žalac**
žar glow; (*žeravica*) live coal; *fig* ardour, enthusiasm
žara urn; (*izborna*) ballot-box
žar|ač poker; **~ište** focus; **~iti (se)** glow; be glowing hot; **~ki** glowing, red-hot; *fig* ardent
žarulja electric bulb
žbica spoke (of wheel)

žbuka mortar, plaster; **~ti** mortar, plaster
žderati gorge oneself with, eat greedily
ždral crane
ždrijebe foal
ždrijelo throat; gullet; (*ponor*) gorge, chasm
žedan thirsty
žeđa thirst; **~ti** be thirsty, suffer thirst
žega sweltering heat
želud acorn
želudac stomach
želj|a wish, desire; longing; **~eti** wish, desire
željez|an iron; **~arija** hardware shop, ironmongery; **~ara** ironworks
željezni|ca railway; *Am* railroad; ***podzemna ~ca*** underground railway, the Tube; *Am* subway; **~čar** railwayman
željezni|čki: ***~čka stanica*** railway station; ***~čki prag*** railway sleeper; ***~čka nesreća*** railway accident; ***~čka pruga*** railway line
željezo iron; ***staro ~*** scrap iron; ***liveno ~*** cast iron; ***kovano ~*** wrought iron
željno eagerly
žemička, **žemlja** roll
žena woman; (*supruga*) wife
ženi|dba marriage; (*vjenčanje*) wedding; **~ti (se)** marry, get married
ženka female
ženskar lady-killer, womanizer
ženski female; feminine, womanly, women's; **~nje** womenfolk
žeravica live coal
žesta alcohol; spirit
žest|ina violence, vehemence, intensity; **~iti se** be angry, lose one's temper, rage; **~ok** violent, vehement; severe; ***~oka pića*** spirits
žet|elac reaper; **~i** reap; **~va** harvest
žezlo sceptre; mace
žganci corn mush
žgaravica heartburn
ži|ca wire; MUS chord, string; **~čan** wire; ***~čana mreža*** wire-netting; **~čara** cable-railway, cable-car
židak liquid, running
Židov Jew; **~ka** Jewess; **Ꙩski** Jewish
žig brand; (*na zlatu*) hall-mark; stamp; (*poštanski*) postmark
žigic|a match; ***zapaliti ~u*** strike a match
žigosati brand, stamp; (*zlato*) hall-mark
žila vein, artery
žilav tough, muscular, sinewy; **~ost** toughness, stamina
žilet razor blade
žir acorn
žir|ant endorser; **~irati** endorse
žitarica cereal

žitelj inhabitant; **~stvo** population, inhabitants; ***popis ~stva*** census
žitnica granary
žito corn, grain, cereals (*pl*)
živ living, alive, live; (*živahan*) lively
živa quicksilver, mercury
živac nerve
živad poultry, fowls
živah|an lively; **~nost** liveliness, vivacity
živalj = **žiteljstvo**
živčan nerve, nervous; ***~i sustav*** nervous system; ***~i slom*** nervous breakdown
živež provision, victuals
živežne namirnice = **živež**
živica hedge
živin|a animal; **~ski** beastly
živio! long live! cheers!
živjeti live, exist, be alive
življenje living, life, existence
život life, existence
životinj|a animal, beast; **~ski** animal, beastly; **~stvo** zoology, fauna
životn|i life; ***~a snaga*** vital force; ***~i standard*** standard of life
životopis biography, (*vlastit*) autobiography; **~ac** biographer
žli|ca spoon; **~čica** teaspoon
žlijeb gutter, spout
žlijezda gland
žmiriti blink
žnjeti reap
žohar cockroach
žrtv|a sacrifice; offering; **~ovati** sacrifice; **~ovati se** sacrifice oneself, devote oneself to
žrvanj grindstone
žubor murmur; **~iti** murmur; babble
žuč gall
žučni: ***~ kamenac*** gall stone
žudjeti long for, yearn after
žulj blister, callus; **~evit** callous; (*ruka*) horny
žuma|nce, **~njak** yolk
žuna woodpecker
žup|a parish; **~nik** vicar, parson
žur|an urgent, hasty, quick, fast; **~ba** haste, hurry, urgency; **~iti se** hurry, make haste, hasten
žurnal (*kino*) newsreel
žustar brisk, lively, agile
žut yellow; **~ica** jaundice; **~jeti** turn (become) yellow
žvaka|ti chew; ***~ća guma*** chewing-gum

A

a [ei, ə] neodređeni član; jedan, neki
aback [ə'bæk] otraga; *coll* ***taken ~*** zapanjen, preneražen
abandon [ə'bændən] odreći se; napustiti; **~ed** odbačen
abash [ə'bæʃ] posramiti
abate [ə'beit] smanjiti (se); **~ment** popust
abbey ['æbi] opatija
abbreviat|e [ə'bri:vieit] skratiti; **~ion** kratica; pokraćenje
abdicat|e ['æbdikeit] odreći se; abdicirati; **~ion** odricanje; abdikacija
abdomen ['æbdəmen] (donji) trbuh
abduct [əb'dʌkt] oteti; **~ion** otmica
abed [ə'bed] u krevet(u)
abet [ə'bet] podbadati
abeyance [ə'beiəns] neriješenost
abhor [əb'hɔ:] gnušati se; **~rence** gnušanje; **~rent** gnusan
abide [ə'baid] ostati; ustrajati
ability [ə'biliti] sposobnost
abject ['æbdʒekt] bijedan, prezren
abjure [əb'dʒuə] odreći se pod zakletvom
able ['eibl] sposoban; valjan; **~-bodied** fizički sposoban
abnegate ['æbnigeit] poreći, zanijekati
aboard [ə'bɔ:d] na brodu; ***all ~!*** *Am*, RLW polazak!
abode [ə'boud] boravak; prebivalište
abolish [ə'bɔliʃ] ukinuti
abolition [æbə'liʃən] ukidanje
abomina|ble [ə'bɔminəbl] odvratan; **~tion** mrskost
abortion [ə'bɔ:ʃən] pobačaj
abound [ə'baund] obilovati (čime), imati u izobilju
about [ə'baut] oko, okolo; otprilike; o
above [ə'bʌv] (iz)nad; gore; ***~ all*** prije svega
abreast [ə'brest] usporedo; ***keep ~ of*** ići u korak s
abridg|e [ə'bridʒ] pokratiti; **~(e)ment** skraćena verzija
abroad [ə'brɔ:d] u inozemstvo(u)
abrogat|e ['æbrəgeit] ukinuti; **~ion** ukinuće
abrupt [ə'brʌpt] iznenadan; osoran

abscess ['æbsis] apsces
absence ['æbsəns] odsutnost; pomanjkanje
absent ['æbsənt] odsutan; **~-minded** rastresen
absolute ['æbsəlu:t] apsolutan; **~ly** potpuno
absolve [əb'zɔlv] osloboditi, odriješiti
absor|b [əb'sɔ:b] upiti; **~ption** upijanje
abstain [əb'stein] uzdržati se; **~er** apstinent
abstemious [æb'sti:miəs] umjeren
abstention [æb'stenʃən] uzdržavanje
abstinen|ce ['æbstinəns] apstinencija; **~t** koji apstinira
abstract ['æbstrækt] apstraktan; rezime, sažetak
absurd [əb'sə:d] apsurdan; smiješan; **~ity** besmislenost
abdundan|ce [ə'bʌndəns] (izo)bilje; **~t** obilan
abus|e [ə'bju:z] zlorabiti; [ə'bju:s] zloupotrena; **~ive** pogrdan
abut [ə'bʌt] graničiti; **~ter** susjed
abyss [ə'bis] bezdan
academ|ic [ækə'demik] akademski; **~ician** akademik; **~y** akademija
accelerat|e [æk'seləreit] ubrzati; MOT dati gas; **~ion** ubrzanje; **~or** pedala gasa
accent ['æksənt] naglasak; **~uate** naglasiti; **~uation**, naglašavanje
accept [ək'sept] prihvatiti; **~able** prihvatljiv; **~ance** prihvaćanje; **~or** COM prihvatnik (mjenice)
acces ['ækses] pristup; MED napadaj; **~ible** dostupan (***to***)
accessor|y [æk'sesəri] pripadan; *pl* **~ies** pribor; pripaci
accident ['æksidənt] slučaj; nesretan slučaj; **~ *insurance*** osiguranje protiv nesretnog slučaja; **~al** slučajan
acclamation [æklə'meiʃən] klicanje, aklimacija
acclimatize [ə'klaimətaiz] aklimatizirati
acclivity [ə'kliviti] uzbrdica
accommodat|e [ə'kɔmədeit] prilagoditi; smjestiti; **~ing** uslužan; **~ion** prilagođavanje; smještaj; ***seating* ~ion** broj sjedala; **~ion train** *Am* lokalni vlak
accomp|animent [ə'kʌmpənimənt] pratnja; **~any** pratiti
acoomplice [ə'kɔmplis] sukrivac, ortak
accomplish [ə'kɔmpliʃ] izvršiti; **~ed** obrazovan; **~ment** izvršenje; postignuće; *ugl pl* sposobnosti
accord [ə'kɔ:d] **1.** slagati se; **2.** **~ance** podudaranje; **~ing to** u skladu
accordion [ə'kɔ:diən] harmonika
accost [ə'kɔst] osloviti
account [ə'kaunt] račun; ob-

račun; konto; prikaz; razlog; ***on no ~*** nikako; ***on ~ of*** zbog; ~ ***for*** razjasniti; SPORT postići; **~able** odgovoran; **~ant** knjigovodstveni revizor; **~-book** knjiga računa
accoutrements [ə'kuːtəmənts] *pl* oprema
accredit [ə'kredit] akreditirati
accretion [æ'kriʃən] prirast
accrue [ə'kruː] izrasti (*from*); narasti
accumulat|e [ə'kjuːmjuleit] nakupiti (se); **~ion** nakupljanje, akumulacija
accura|cy ['ækjurəsi] tačnost; **~te** tačan
accursed [ə'kəːsid] (pro)klet
accus|ation [æklu'zeiʃən] optužba; **~e** optužiti; **~er** tužilac
accustom [ə'kʌstəm] priviknuti (***to*** na); **~ed** priviknut
ace [eis] as
acerbity [ə'səːbiti] jetkost
acet|ate ['æsitit] CHEM acetat; ***alumina ~ate*** aluminijev-acetat; **~ic acid** ocetna kiselina; **~ify** zakiseliti (se); **~one** aceton; **~ylene** acetilen
ache [eik] boljeti; bol
achieve [ə'tʃiːv] postići; provesti; **~ment** dostignuće; izvršenje
aching ['eikiŋ] bolan
acid ['æsid] kiseo; kiselina; **~ity** kiselost; **~-proof** otporan na kiseline; **~ ulous** kiselkast
acknowledg|e [ək'nɔlidʒ] priznati; potvrditi (prijem); **~(e)ment** priznanje
acme ['ækmi] vrhunac; kriza
acorn ['eikɔːn] BOT žir
acoustics [ə'kuːstiks] akustika
acquaint [ə'kweint] upoznati; **~ance** poznanstvo; znanac
acquiesce [ækwi'es] pomiriti se (***in*** sa)
acquire [ə'kwaiə] steći; **~ment** (s)tečevina, stjecanje
acquisition [ækwi'ziʃən] stjecanje; (s)tečevina; nabavka
acquit [ə'kwit] osloboditi (***of*** od); **~tal** oslobođenje; **~tance** namira
acre ['eikə] jutro, ral (40, 46 ara)
across [ə'krɔs] preko; u promjeru; ***come ~*** nabasati na
act [ækt] djelovati; ponašati se; THEAT glumiti; čin, akt; **~ing** postupak; THEAT gluma; **~ion** akcija, postupak, djelovanje; tužba, sudski postupak; **~ionable** kažnjiv
activ|e ['æktiv] aktivan; okretan; marljiv, **~ity** aktivnost; živahnost; marljivost
actor ['æktə], **actress** glumac(-ica)
actual ['æktʃuəl] pravi, stvaran; **~ity** stvarnost, zbilja
acute [ə'kjuːt] oštar (*bol*,

sluh); oštrouman
A. D. ['ei'di:] = **Anno Domini** ljeta gospodnjeg
adapt [ə'dæpt] prilagoditi; **~ability** prilagodivost; **~able** prilagodiv
add [æd] dodati; pribrojiti, zbrojiti; **~ *up*** zbrojiti
adder ['ædə] riđovka
addition [ə'diʃən] dodatak; zbrajanje; ***in ~ to*** osim
address [ə'dres] adresirati; osloviti; adresa; nastup; **~ *oneself*** obratiti se; **~ee** naslovnik(-ica)
adept [ə'dept] upućen, vješt
adequa|cy ['ædikwəsi] adekvatnost; **~te** adekvatan
adhere [əd'hiə] (***to***) prianjati; držati se (čega), pristajati (uz); **~nt** koji se drži čega; pristaša
adhesive [əd'hi:siv] ljepljiv; ljepivo
adit ['ædit] hodnik u rudniku
adjacen|cy [ə'dʒeisənsi] graničenje; susjedstvo; **~t** susjedni
adjoin [ə'dʒɔin] graničiti (sa)
adjourn [ə'dʒə:n] odgoditi; prekinuti (zasjedanje)
adjudge [ə'dʒʌdʒ] dosuditi (***to*** nekome)
adjudication [ə'dʒu:di'keiʃən] presuda (u nečiju korist)
adjunct ['ædʒʌŋkt] dodatak; (uredski) pomoćnik
adjure [ə'dʒuə] preklinjati
adjust [ə'dʒʌst] popraviti, namjestiti; TECH podesiti (***to***); **~ment** podešavanje; ispravljanje; pomirenje, izravnanje
administ|er [əd'ministə] upravljati; **~er *an oath*** zakleti (*koga*); **~ration** uprava; **~rator** administrator; izvršitelj oporuke
admira|ble ['ædmərəbl] izvrstan, zadivljujući; **~ tion** divljenje
admiss|ible [əd'misəbl] dopustiv; **~ion** primamanje, pristup; priznanje; **~ion ticket** ulaznica
admit [əd'mit] dozvoliti pristup; priznati; **~tance** pristup; ***no ~!*** ulaz zabranjen!
admixture [əd'mikstʃə] primjesa
admoni|sh [əd'mɔniʃ] opomenuti; **~tion** opomena
ado [ə'du:] buka; skanjivanje
adopt [ə'dɔpt] posvojiti; usvojiti; **~ion** posvajanje; usvajanje
ador|able [ə'dɔ:rəbl] divan; **~ation** obožavanje; **~e** obožavati
adorn [ə'dɔ:n] ukrasiti; **~ment** ukras
adroit [ə'drɔit] spretan; **~ness** spretnost
adulat|ion [ædju'leiʃən] ulagivanje; **~or** dodvorica
adult ['ædʌlt] odrastao; odrasla osoba
adulter|ate [ə'dʌltəreit] patvoriti; **~ation** patvorenje; **~er**, **~ess** preljubnik (~ica);

~y preljub
advance [əd'vaːns] napredovati; prodrijeti; dati predujam; napredak, napredovanje; predujam; **~ment** unapređenje
advantage [əd'vaːntidʒ] prednost; **~ous** povoljan
adventur|e [əd'ventʃə] pustolovina; **~er** pustolov; **~ous** pustolovan; uzbudljiv
advers|ary ['ædvəsəri] protivnik; **~e** nepovoljan; **~ity** nedaća
advert [əd'vəːt]: **~ *to*** upozoriti na
advertis|e ['ædvətaiz] oglasiti; **~ement** reklama; **~er** oglašivač; **~ing film** reklami film; **~ing space** prostor za reklamu
advice [əd'vais] savjet(i); **~-boat** izvidnički brod
advisable [əd'vaizəbl] uputan; **~ness** uputnost
advis|e [əd'vaiz] savjetovati; posavjetovati se (***with*** sa); **~ed** razborit; **~ory board** savjetodavna komisija
advoca|cy ['ædvəkəsi] zagovaranje; **~te** ['~it] zagovornik; ['~eit] zagovarati
aerial ['ɛəriəl] zračni; RADIO antena
aero... ['ɛərou] zračni; **~drome** uzletište; **~gram** radiogram; **~naut** zrakoplovac; **~plane** avion
afar [ə'faː] (*ugl* **~ *off***) daleko
affab|ility [æfə'biliti] prijaznost; **~le** prijazan
affair [ə'fɛə] posao; prilika; stvar
affect [ə'fekt] djelovati na; škoditi (zdravlju); pretvarati se; **~ation** prenemaganje; **~ed** afektiran; **~ion** ljubav; čuvstvo; **~ionate** privržen
affidavit [æfı'devit] izjava pod prisegom
affiliat|e [ə'fılieit] pripojiti; **~ion** primanje, pripajanje; pripadnost
affinity [ə'fıniti] srodnost
affirm [ə'fəːm] potvrditi; **~ation** tvrdnja; iskaz; **~ative** potvrdan
affix [ə'fıks] pričvrstiti
afflict [ə'flikt] ožalostiti; ***~ed with*** koji pati od; **~ion** tuga; nedaća
affluen|ce ['æfluəns] obilje; **~t** pritok
afford [ə'fɔːd] pružiti; ***I can't ~ it*** ne mogu sebi priuštiti
affront [ə'frʌnt] uvrijediti; uvreda
afield [ə'fıːld] u polje(u)
afloat [ə'flout] koji plovi; u pokretu; u opticaju
afoot [ə'fut] pješke; koji se odvija
aforesaid [ə'fɔːsed] već spomenut
afraid [ə'freid] uplašen; ***be ~ of*** bojati se od
afresh [ə'freʃ] iznova
African-American [ˌæfrikən'əmerikən] afroamerički; Afroamerikanac, Afroame-

rikanka

after ['a:ftə] nakon; poslije; **~birth** ANAT posteljica; **~-crop** pabirčenje **~-effect** naknadno djelovanje; **~-glow** večernje rumenilo; **~noon** poslijepodne; **~wards** kasnije, zatim

again [ə'gein] opet, ponovo; ***now and ~*** tu i tamo; ***~ and ~*** opetovano, neprestano

against [ə'geinst] protiv

age [eidʒ] dob, starost; ***of ~*** punoljetan; ***under ~*** maloljetan; **~d** postariji

agen|cy ['eidʒənsi] agencija; **~t** agent, zastupnik

agglomerat|e [ə'glɔməreit] zgrudati (se); **~ion** nakupina

aggrandize ['ægrəndaiz] povećati

aggravat|e ['ægrəveit] otežati; pogoršati; **~ion** pogoršanje; *coll* razljućivanje

aggregat|e ['ægrigeit] nakupiti (se); **~ion** nakupina

aggress|ion [ə'greʃən] napad; **~ive** agresivan; borben; **~or** napadač

agil|e ['ædʒail] okretan, agilan; **~ity** agilnost

agitat|e ['ædʒiteit] uzburkati; rovariti; **~ion** burkanje; uzbuđenje; **~or** agitator

ago [ə'gou]; ***a year ~*** prije godinu dana; ***long ~*** davno

agon|izing ['ægənaiziŋ] bolan; **~y** bol; agonija

agrarian [ə'grɛəriən] zemljoradnik; zemljoradnički

agree [ə'gri:] složiti se; pristati; prijati; uskladiti; **~able** prijatan; sporazuman (***to*** sa); **~ment** sporazum; slaganje; sklad

agricultur|al [ægri'kʌltʃərəl] poljoprivredni; ratarski; **~e** poljoprivreda; **~ist** poljoprivrednik

ague ['eigju:] groznica

ahead [ə'hed] naprijed; ***straight ~*** pravo

aid [eid] pomoći; pomoć

ail [eil]: ***what ~s you*** što te tišti?; **~ing** bolešljiv; **~ment** bolest

aim [eim] ciljati (***at*** na); *fig* ***~ at*** težiti za; cilj; svrha; **~less** besciljan

air [ɛə] zrak; povjetarac; prozračiti; izraz lica; izgled; napjev; ***in the open ~*** na otvorenom; *Am* ***on the ~*** uključen za emitiranje; *Am* ***a show is on the ~*** program se emitira; **~base** zračno uporište; **~-conditioned** s klima uređajem; **~-cooled** na zračno hlađenje; **~craft** avion(i); **~craft carrier** nosač aviona; **~-cushion** zračni jastuk; **~-force** vojno zrakoplovstvo; **~ing** provjetravanje; šetnja; **~-jacket** prsluk za spasavanje; **~-lift** zračni most; **~-liner** putnički avion; **~-mail** avionska pošta; **~man** letač; **~-passenger** putnik u avionu; **~-pipe**

cijev za zrak; **~plane** *Am* avion; **~-pocket** razrijeđeni zračni prostor; **~-raid** zračni napad; **~raid shelter** sklonište od zračnog napada; **~ship** cepelin; **~-tight** hermetičan; **~-tube** zračnica; **~y** zračan; lakomislen
ajar [ə'dʒa:] pritvoren, otškrinut
akin [ə'kin] srodan (***to*** kome)
alarm [ə'la:m] uzbuna; strah; alarmirati; uznemiriti; **~-clock** budilica
alas [ə'la:s] jao! avaj!
alcohol ['ælkəhɔl] alkohol; **~ic** alkoholni
alcove ['ælkouv] alkoven; niša
alderman ['ɔ:ldəmən] vijećnik
ale [eil] svijetlo englesko pivo
alert [ə'lə:t] budan; ***on the ~*** na oprezu
alien ['eiliən] stran; stranac; **~ate** otuđiti; **~ation** otuđenje
alight [ə'lait] zapaljen; osvijetljen; sići, izići; AERO spustiti se
alike [ə'laik] sličan
aliment ['ælimənt] hrana; **~ary** prehrambeni; **~ation** prehrana; uzdržavanje
alive [ə'laiv] živ; živahan
all [ɔ:l] svi; sve; cijeli; ***not at ~*** nikako; nema na čemu!; ***for ~ I care*** što se mene tiče; ***~ the better*** utoliko bolje; ***~ right*** u redu! dobro!
allegation [æle'geiʃən] navod; tvrdnja
allege [ə'ledʒ] navesti; tvrditi
allegorical [æle'gɔrik(ə)l] alegoričan
alleviat|e [ə'li:vieit] olakšati; **~ion** olakšanje
alley ['æli] aleja; uličica
All Fools' Day Prvi april
alliance [ə'laiəns] savez
all-in sveukupni
allopathist [ə'lɔpəθist] alopat
allocution [ælə'kju:ʃən] besjeda
allot [ə'lɔt] dodijeliti; **~ment** dodjela; parcela
allow [ə'lau] dopustiti; odobriti; uračunati, uzeti u obzir; **~able** dopustiv; **~ance** dozvola; džeparac; doplatak; popust
alloy ['ælɔi] legura; [ə'lɔi] legirati
all-round svestran
All Saints' Day Svisveti; **~ Souls' Day** Dušni dan
allude [ə'lu:d] aludirati (***to*** na)
allure [ə'ljuə] namamiti; **~ment** mamljenje; privlačnost
allustion [ə'lu:ʒən] aluzija
ally [ə'lai] sklopiti savez sa; udružiti se; ['ælai] saveznik
allmight|iness [ɔ:l'maitinis] svemoćnost; **~y** Svemogući
almond ['a:mənd] badem
almost ['ɔ:lmoust] skoro
alms [a:mz] *sg ili pl* milosti-

nja
aloft [ə'lɔft] gore, visoko
alone [ə'loun] sam; ***let*** (*ili* ***leave***) ***a person ~*** pustiti nekoga na miru
along [ə'lɔŋ] duž, niz; ***all ~*** od početka, skroz
aloof [ə'lu:f] dalek(o); po strani
aloud [ə'laud] glasno
alp [ælp] gorski vrh; **≈s** Alpe; **Alpine sun** visinsko sunce
already [ɔ:l'redi] već
Alsace ['ælsæs] Elzas
also ['ɔ:lsou] također; nadalje
altar ['ɔ:ltə] oltar
alter ['ɔ:ltə] promijeniti (se); popraviti; **~ation** popravak (konfekcije)
altercation [ɔ:ltə:'keiʃən] rječkanje
alterna|te [ɔ:l'tə:nit] naizmjeničan; ['~neit] izmjenjivati (se); **~ting current** izmjenična struja; **~tion** izmjena; **~tive** alternativa; ***I have no ~tive*** nemam izbora
although [ɔ:l'ðou] premda
altitude ['æltitju:d] visina; **~ flight** visinski lijet
altogether [ɔ:ltə'geðə] ukupno; potpuno
alum ['æləm] stipsa
always ['ɔ:lwəz] uvijek
am [æm] (je)sam *vidi* **be**
a. m. ['ei'em] = **ante meridiem** dopodne
amalgamat|e [ə'mælgəmeit] stopiti (se); **~ion** stapanje; fuzija
amass [ə'mæs] nakupiti, zgrnuti
amaz|e [ə'meiz] (jako) začuditi; **~ement** iznenađenje; **~ing** koji iznenađuje
ambassador [æm'bæsədə] ambasador, izaslanik
amber ['æmbə] jantar
ambigu|ity [æmbi'gjuiti] dvosmislenost; **~ous** dvosmislen, nejasan
ambitio|n [æm'biʃən] ambicija; **~us** ambiciozan
ambulance ['æmbjuləns] bolesnička kola; **~ station** stanica za hitnu pomoć
ambuscade [æmbəs'keid], **ambush** ['æmbuʃ] zasjeda; napasti iz zasjede
amend [ə'mend] popraviti (se); **~ment** ispravak, amandman; **~s** *pl* odšteta
amiab|ility [eimjə'biliti] ljubaznost; **~le** ljubazan
America [ə'merikə] Amerika; **~n** Amerikanac (-ka); američki
amicable ['æmikəbl] prijateljski; miroljubiv
amid(st) [ə'mid(st)] između
amiss [ə'mis] krivo; loše; ***take ~*** zamjeriti
amity ['æmiti] prijateljski odnosi
ammonia [ə'mounjə] amonijak; ***liquid ~*** salmijak
ammunition [æmju'niʃən] municija

amnesty ['æmnesti] amnestija; pomilovati
among(st) [ə'mʌŋ(st)] između
amorous ['æmərəs] zaljubljen (*of* u)
amortiz|ation [əmɔ:ti'zeiʃən] amortizacija; **~e** amortizirati
amount [ə'maunt] (*to*) iznositi; iznos, zbroj
ample ['æmpl] prostran; opsežan; obilan; **~ness** opsežnost
amplification [æmplifi'keiʃən] proširavanje; pojačavanje
amplif|ier (valve) ['æmplifaiə vælv] RADIO pojačalo; **~y** pojačati; proširiti
amputate ['æmpjuteit] amputirati; istrgnuti
amuse [ə'mju:z] zabavljati; nasmijavati; **~ment** zabava
an [æn, ən] neodređeni član; jedan, neki
anaemi|a [ə'ni:miə] anemija; **~c** slabokrvan
anaesthetic [ænis'θetik] anestetik
analog|ic(al) [ænə'lɔdʒik(əl)] analogan, sličan
analog|ous [ə'næləgəs] analogan; **~y** ['-ədʒi] analogija
analys|e ['ænəlaiz] analizirati, raščlaniti; **~is**, *pl* **~es** [ə'næləsis, -i:z] analiza, raščlanjivanje
anarchy ['ænəki] anarhija
anatom|ist [ə'nætəmist] anatom; **~y** anatomija
ancest|or ['ænsistə] praotac; predak; **~ry** preci
anchor ['æŋkə] sidro; usidriti se; **at ~** usidren
anchovy [æn'tʃouvi] inćun, sardela
ancient ['einʃənt] drevan, nekadašnji; **~ly** od davnine
and [ænd] i; a
anew [ə'nju:] iznova
angel ['eindʒəl] anđeo
anger ['æŋgə] ljutnja; gnjev; razgnjeviti
angle ['æŋgl] kut; ugao; (*for*) pecati, *fig* loviti
Anglo-Saxon ['æŋglou'sæksən] Anglosas; anglosaski
angry ['æŋgri] ljutit
anguish ['æŋgwiʃ] bol, patnja, tjeskoba
angular ['æŋgjulə] uglat
animadversion [ænimæd'və:ʃən] prigovor, kritika, osuda
animal ['ænimәl] životinja; životinjski
animat|e ['ænimeit] oživiti, obodriti; **~ion** oživljavanje; živost
animosity [æni'mɔsiti] neprijateljstvo
anise ['ænis] anis
ankle ['æŋkl] gležanj
annals ['ænəlz] *pl* ljetopis; anali
annex [ə'neks] dodati; priključiti; ['æneks] dodatak; depandansa, krilo; **~ation** aneksija

annihilate [ə'naiəleit] uništiti
anniversary [æni'vəːsəri] godišnjica
annotat|e ['ænouteit] popratiti opaskama; **~ion** opaska
announce [ə'nauns] najaviti; oglasiti; **~ment** najava; oglas; **~r** RADIO spiker (-ica)
annoy [ə'nɔi] ljutiti; dodijavati; **~ance** ljutnja; smetanje; **~ing** dosadan, koji smeta
annual ['ænjuəl] godišnji
annuity [ə'njuiti] anuitet
annul [ə'nʌl] poništiti; **~ment** poništenje
anon [ə'nɔn] odmah; ubrzo; ***ever and ~*** neprestano
anonym|ity [ænə'nimiti] anonimnost; **~ous** anoniman
another [ə'nʌðə] drugi; još jedan
answer ['aːnsə] odgovoriti; odgovarati; ***~ the bell*** otvoriti vrata kuće (stana); odgovor (***to*** na); **~able** odgovoran
ant [ænt] mrav
antagonist [æn'tægənist] protivnik (-ica)
ante|cedents [ænti'siːdənts] raniji život; **~chamber** predsoblje; **~date** antedatirati; **~diluvian** pretpotopan, staromodan
antelope ['æntiloup] ZOOL antilopa
ant-hill mravinjak
anti ... ['ænti] protu ...
anti-aircraft-gun protuavionski top
anticipat|e [æn'tisipeit] **~ion** predusretanje; predviđanje; predosjećaj
anti-dazzle (shield) MOT štitnik nad farovima
antidote ['æntidout] protuotrov
anti-freeze MOT antifriz
antipathy [æn'tipəθi] antipatija (***against, to*** prema)
antiquar|ian [ænti'kwɛəriən] antikni; **~y** antikvar
antiqu|e [æn'tiːk] antikni, star; **~ity** davnina, stari vijek
antiseptic [ænti'septik] antiseptik
anti-tank gun protutenkovski top
antlers ['æntləz] rogovlje
anus ['einəs] ANAT čmar
anvil ['ænvil] nakovanj
anxiety [æŋ'zaiəti] tjeskoba; uznemirenost
anxious ['æŋkʃəs] zabrinut (***for, about*** zbog); nestrpljiv
any ['eni] itko, bilo tko (koji); svatko; **~body**, **~one** bilo tko; **~how** bilo kako; u svakom slučaju; **~thing** išta, bilo šta, sve; **~way** = **~-how**; **~where** bilo gdje (kamo)
apart [ə'paːt] na stranu; posebno; ***~ from*** osim; **~ment** soba; *Am* stan
apath|etic [æpə'θetik] apatičan; **~y** ['æpəθi] bezvoljnost
ape [eip] (čovjekoliki) majmun; majmunisati

aperient [ə'piəriənt] sredstvo za otvaranje
aperture ['æpətjuə] otvor
apiary ['eipiəri] pčelinjak
apiece [ə'pi:s] po komadu, svaki
apish ['eipiʃ] majmunski (*i fig*)
apolog|ist [ə'pɔlədʒist] branilac; **~ize** ispričati se (***for*** zbog); **~y** izvinjenje
apople|ctic [æpə'plektik]; **~ctic fit** kap; **~xy** kap, izljev krvi
apostroph|e [ə'pɔstrəfı] apostrof; obraćanje; **~ize** obratiti se
appal [ə'pɔ:l] zapanjiti
apparatus [æpə'reitəs] aparat
apparel [ə'pærəl]: ***wearing ~*** odjeća
apparent [ə'pærənt] očit; naizgled, prividan
appeal [ə'pi:l] apelirati (***to*** na); obratiti se; priziv; umoljavanje; **~ing** koji umoljava; primamljiv
appear [ə'piə] pojaviti se; nastupiti; **~ance** pojava; nastup; vanjština; izgled
appease [ə'pi:z] umiriti; utažiti
append [ə'pend] dodati; **~icitis** [~di'saitis] upala slijepog crijeva
appertain [æpə'tein] pripadati (***to*** kome, čemu)
appeti|te ['æpitait] apetit (***for*** za); **~zing** privlačan, ukusan
applau|d [ə'plɔ:d] odobravati; pljeskati; **~se** [~z] aplauz, odobravanje
apple [æpl] jabuka; **~-pie** pita od jabuka
appliance [ə'plaiəns] sprava; kućanski aparat
applicable ['æplikəbl] primjenjiv (***to*** na)
applicant ['æplikənt] molilac
application [æpli'keiʃən] premazivanje, oblaganje; primjena; molba (***for*** za); marljivost
apply [ə'plai] staviti; primijeniti (***to*** na)
appoint [ə'pɔint] odrediti; imenovati; **~ment** dogovor; imenovanje
appraise [ə'preiz] procijeniti; **~ment** procjena; **~r** procjenitelj
appreciat|e [ə'pri:ʃieit] cijeniti; poštovati; ***I fully ~e it*** potpuno sam svjestan toga; duboko to cijenim; **~ion** poštivanje; razumijevanje
apprehen|d [æpri'hend] uhapsiti; shvatiti; bojati se; **~sible** shvatljiv; **~sion** hapšenje; shvaćanje; **~sive** zabrinut (***of*** zbog, za)
apprentice [ə'prentis] naučnik, šegrt; dati u nauk; **~ship** nauk
apprise [ə'praiz] obavijestiti
approach [ə'proutʃ] približiti se; *fig* pristupiti; približavanje; pristup; **~able** pristu-

pačan
approbation [æprə'beiʃən] odobrenje
appropriat|e [ə'proupriit] primjeren; [-ieit] prisvojiti; odvojiti; **~ion** prisvajanje; odvajanje (sredstava)
approv|al [ə'pru:vəl] odobrenje; ***on ~al*** na ogled; **~e** odobriti; **~ed** prokušan
approximate [ə'prɔksimit] približan
appurtenances [ə'pə:tinənsiz] *pl* pripaci; pribor
apricot ['eiprikɔt] kajsija, marelica
April ['eipril] travanj, april
apron ['eiprən] pregača
apt [æpt] prikladan; sklon (***to do***); okretan (***at*** u)
aptitude ['æptitju:d] sposobnost, dar za
aquatic [ə'kwɔtik] vodeni; **~s** *pl* vodeni sportovi
Arab ['ærəb] Arapin; **~ia** [ə'reibjə] Arabija; **~ian** arapski; Arapin (-kinja) **~ic** ['ærəbik] arapski; gum **~ic** gumirabika, ljepilo
arbitra|riness ['a:bitrərinis] proizvoljnost; **~ry** proizvoljan; samovoljan
arbitrat|e ['a:bitreit] presuditi; **~ion** arbitraža; **~or** arbiter
arbour ['a:bə] sjenica
arc [a:k] luk
arcade [a:'keid] arkada
arch [a:tʃ] luk; svod; vragoljast
archaeolog|ist [a:ki'ɔlədʒist] arheolog; **~y** arheologija
arch|bishop ['a:tʃ'biʃəp] nadbiskup; **~duchess** nadvojvodkinja; **~duke** nadvojvoda
archipelago [a:ki'peligou] arhipelag
architect ['a:kitekt] arhitekt; **~ure** ['-ktʃə] ararhitektura
archives ['a:kaivz] *pl* arhiv
archness ['a:tʃnis] vragolanstvo
arc-lamp ['a:klæmp] lučna lampa
arctic ['a:ktik] arktički, sjeverni, polarni
ardent ['a:dənt] vatren, gorljiv, strastven
ard|our ['a:də] vatrenost, gorljivost; revnost; **~uous** naporan; ustrajan
are [a:] si, smo, ste, su
area ['ɛəriə] površina, ploha; ***danger ~*** opasno područje; ***prohibited ~*** zabranjena zona
Argentine ['a:dʒəntain] argentinski; Argentinac (-ka); ***the ~*** Argentina
argue ['a:gju:] dokazivati; raspravljati; rezonirati
argument ['a:gjumənt] argument; rasprava; **~ation** argumentacija
arid ['ærid] suh, spržen; **~ity** [æ'riditi] suša
aright [ə'rait] *adv* pravo, dobro

arise [ə'raiz] dizati se (***from*** iz)
aristocra|cy [æris'tɔkrəsi] aristokracija; **~t** aristokrat; **~tic(al)** aristokratski
arithmetic [ə'riθmətik] aritmetika; **~al** [æriθ'metikl] aritmetika; aritmetički
ark [aːk] arka, korablja
arm [aːm] ruka; oslon za ruke; oružje (*ugl pl*); *pl* grb; naoružati (se); **~ament industry** industrija za naoružavanje
armature ['aːmətjuə] armatura; EL rotor, kotva
arm|chair ['aːmtʃɛə] naslonjač; **~ful** naramak
armistice ['aːmistis] primirje
armlet ['aːmlit] narukvica; traka oko rukava
armour ['aːmə] oklop; oklopne jedinice; oklopiti; **~ed train** oklopni vlak; **~er** oružar; **~y** oružana
armpit ['aːmpit] pazuho
army ['aːmi] vojska (i *fig*); armija; **~ command staff** komanda vojske
aroma [ə'roumə] aroma; **~tic** [ærə'mætik] aromatičan
around [ə'raund] oko(lo)
arouse [ə'rauz] probuditi; potaknuti
arrange [ə'reindʒ] urediti; dogovoriti; organizirati; **~ment** aranžman; dogovor
array [ə'rei] (borbeni) poredak; poredati; odjenuti
arrear [ə'riə] zaostatak
arrest [ə'rest] hapšenje; obustava; uhapsiti; zaustaviti
arriv|al [ə'raivəl] dolazak; došljak; *pl* brodovi (vlakovi) u dolasku; COM dospjela roba; **~e** doći; prispjeti; ***~e at*** doći do (zaključka)
arrogan|ce ['ærəgəns] arogancija; **~t** arogantan
arrow ['ærou] strijela
arsenal ['aːsinl] arsenal
arsenic ['aːsnik] arsen
arson ['aːsn] palež
art [aːt] umjetnost; umijeće; ***Master of* ≗*s, M. A.*** magistar humanističkih znanosti; ***applied ~s, ~s and crafts*** primjenjena umjetnost, umjetni obrt
arter|ial [aː'tiəriəl] arteterijski; ***~ial road*** prometna arterija; **~iosclerosis** arterioskleroza; **~y** ['aːtəri] arterija
artful ['aːtful] lukav, prepreden; **~ness** lukavost
artichoke ['aːtitʃouk] artičoka
article ['aːtikl] artikl; članak; stavak; odlomak
articulat|e [aː'tikjuleit] artikulirati; **~ion** artikulacija; raščlanjivanje
artificial [aːti'fiʃəl] umjetan; **~ silk** umjetna svila
artisan [aːti'zæn] obrtnik
artist ['aːtist] umjetnik (-ca); **~ic** umjetnički
artless ['aːtlis] naravan, prostodušan

as [æz] kao; kada; pošto; ~ ***good*** ~ dobar kao i; ~ ***it were*** tako reći; ~ ***well*** ~ kao i
ascen|d [ə'send] uspeti se; vinuti se; **~dancy** nadmoć, prevlast (***over*** nad); **♀sion (Day)** Spasovo, Uzašašće; **~t** uspon
ascertain [æsə'tein] ustanoviti
ascetic [ə'setik] asketski; asket; **~ism** askeza
ascribe [əs'kraib] pripisati
ash [æʃ] pepeo; **♀ Wednesday** Pepelnica
ashamed [ə'ʃeimd] postiđen; ***be/feel*** ~ ili/stidjeti se (***of*** čega)
ash-can *Am* kanta za smeće
ashore [ə'ʃɔ:] na obali (u)
ash-tray pepeljara
Asia ['eiʃə] Azija; ~ **Minor** Mala Azija
Asian-American [ˌeiʃn-'əmerikən] azijskoamerički; Amerikanac azijskog porijekla
Asiatic [eiʃi'ætik] azijatski; Azijat(-kinja)
aside [ə'said] na stranu; po strani; postrance
ask [a:sk] pitati; moliti (***for*** za); pozvati; zahtijevati (***for*** nešto)
asleep [ə'sli:p] u snu; ***to be*** ~ spavati
asparagus [əs'pærəgəs] šparga
aspect ['æspekt] pogled; izgled; stanovište
aspen ['æspən] jasika; ~ **leaf** jasikov list
asperse [əs'pə:s] poškropiti
aspire [əs'paiə] težiti (***to***, ***after*** za)
aspirin ['æspirin] aspirin
ass [æs] magarac
assail [ə'seil] napasti; salijetati; **~ant** napadač
assassin [ə'sæsin] atentator; plaćeni ubojica; **~ate** izvršiti atentat; **~ation** atentat
assault [ə'sɔ:lt] napadaj; juriš; jurišati; napasti
assembl|age [ə'semblidʒ] sastavljanje; montaža; **~e** sastaviti, sakupiti (se); **~er** monter; **~y** skupština; montaža (stroja); **~y line** *Am* tekuća vrpca
assent [ə'sent] pristanak; pristati
assert [ə'sə:t] ustvrditi; **~ion** izjava
assess [ə'ses] oporezovati; procijeniti; **~ment** procjena; **~or** prisjednik
assets ['æsets] *pl* aktiva; imovina
assid|uity [æsi'djuiti] ustrajnost, marljivost; **~uous** [ə'sidjuəs] marljiv
assign [ə'sain] doznačiti; **~able** doznačiv; prijenosan; **~ee** [æsi'ni:] opunomoćenik; JUR povjerenik
assist [ə'sist] pomagati; **~ance** pomoć; **~ant** pomoćnik (-ica)

assizes [ə'saiziz] *pl* porotni sud
associat|e [ə'souʃieit] asociirati; udružiti (se); [˷iit] drug; **˷ion** udruživanje, društvo
assort [ə'sɔːt] sortirati; **˷ment** asortiman, izbor
assuage [ə'sweidʒ] ublažiti; utažiti
assum|e [ə'sjuːm] pretpostavljati; poprimiti; preuzeti (vlast); **˷ption** pretpostavka, preuzimanje; drzovitost
assur|ance [ə'ʃuərəns] osiguranje; garancija; samopouzdanje; sigurnost; **˷e** osigurati
asthm|a ['æsmə] astma; **˷atic** [æs'mætik] astmatičan; astmatičar
astir [əs'təː] u pokretu
astonish [əs'tɔniʃ] iznenaditi, zapanjiti; **˷ing** zapanjujući
astound [əs'taund] zapanjiti
astray [əs'trei] zalutao; ***go ˷*** zalutati; dospeti na krivi put
astride [əs'traid] raširenih nogu (***of*** preko); objahavši, opkoračivši
astringent [əs'trindʒənt] koji steže (sredstvo) opor
astro|loger [əs'trɔlədʒə] astrolog; **˷nomer** astronom; **˷nomy** astronomija
asunder [ə'sʌndə] na komade, raskidan, razdvojen
asylum [ə'sailəm] azil
at [æt] na, u, kod; ***˷ the door*** na vratima; ***˷ a ball*** na plesu; ***˷ table*** za stolom; ***˷ school*** u školi; ***˷ the age of*** u starosti od; ***˷ a blow*** jednim udarcem; ***˷ five o'clock*** u pet sati; ***˷ home*** kod kuće
Athens ['æθinz] Atena
athlet|e ['æθliːt] atlet; **˷ic(al)** [˷'letik(əl)] atletski; **˷ics** *pl* atletika
at-home dan za primanje posjeta
ATM [eitiː'em] = **automated teller machine** bankomat
atmosphere ['ætməsfıə] atmosfera; **˷ics** [˷'feriks] radio atmosferske smetnje
atom ['ætəm] atom; **˷ic** [ə'tɔmik] atomski; **˷ bomb** atomska bomba; **˷ energy** atomska energija; **˷izer** ['ætəmaizə] raspršivač, sprej
atone for [ə'toun] dati odštetu; okajati
atroci|ous [ə'trouʃəs] grozan; **˷ty** [ə'trɔsiti] grozota; zvjerstvo
at-seat TV [ət'siːt,tiːviː] TV uz sjedalo
attach [ə'tætʃ] pripojiti, pričvrstiti; *fig* pridodati; ***˷ oneself*** pridružiti se; **˷ed** pričvršćen (***to*** kome); **˷ment** privrženost
attack [ə'tæk] napasti; zadesiti; napad(aj)
attain [ə'tein] postići (***to*** nešto); dočepati se; **˷ments** *pl* znanje; dostignuća

attempt [ə'tempt] pokušati; pokušaj, nastojanje; atentat
attend [ə'tend] pratiti; posluživati; polaziti, pohađati; pobrinuti se; **~ance** posluživanje; posjećivanje; pohađanje; publika; ***hours of ~ance*** uredovno vrijeme; **~ant** sluga; poslužitelj
attent|ion [ə'tenʃən] pažnja; **~ive** pažljiv
attenuate [ə'tenjueit] oslabiti
attest [ə'test] potvrditi, posvjedočiti; **~ation** potvrda; svjedočanstvo
attic ['ætik] potkrovlje
attitud|e ['ætitju:d] stav; držanje; AERO položaj aviona u letu; ***~e of mind*** gledanje na, nazori; **~inize** pozivati, izvještaćeno se držati
attorney [ə'tə:ni] odvjetnik
attract [ə'trækt] privlačiti; **~ion** privlačnost, atrakcija; **~ive** privlačan; lijep; **~iveness** privlačnost
attribut|able [ə'tribjutəbl] pripisiv; **~e** [ə'tribju:t] pripisivati; ['æt~] atribut, značajka; **~ion** [ætri'bju:ʃən] pripisivanje, pridavanje
attrition [ə'triʃən] trošenje; zator
auburn ['ɔ:bən] crvenkasto-kestenjav
auction ['ɔ:kʃən] dražba; **~eer** dražbovatelj
audaci|ous [ɔ:'deiʃəs] smion, drzak; **~ty** [ɔ:'dæsiti] smionost, drskost
audible ['ɔ:dəbl] čujan
audience ['ɔ:djəns] audijencija; publika
auditor ['ɔ:ditə] knjigovodstveni revizor
auditorium [ɔ:di'tɔ:riəm] gledalište; dvorana
aught [ɔ:t]: ***for ~ I care*** što se mene tiče
augment [ɔ:g'ment] povećati (se); **~ation** povećanje, prirast
August ['ɔ:gəst] kolovoz, august; **~** [ɔ:'gʌst] uzvišen, slavan
aunt [a:nt] tetka, strina
aurist ['ɔ:rist] specijalist za ušne bolesti
aurora [ɔ'rɔ:rə] rumenilo zore, zora
auspices ['ɔ:spisiz] *pl* okrilje
auspicious [ɔ:s'piʃəs] povoljan
auster|e [ɔ:s'tiə] strog, opor; **~ity** [~'teriti] strogost, štednja
Austria ['ɔ:striə] Austrija; **~n** austrijski, Austrijanac (-ka)
autar|chy, **~ky** ['ɔ:ta:ki] autarhija
authentic [ɔ:'θentik] autentičan; **~ate** provjeriti
author|(ess) ['ɔ:θə(ris)] pisac, autor; začetnik; **~itative** [~'θɔriteitiv] autoritativan; **~ity** autoritet; vlast; stručnjak; punomoć; ***on good ~ity*** iz pouzdanog vrela; **~ize** ovlastiti, opunomoćiti;

~ship autorstvo
auto ['ɔːtou] *Am coll* automobil
autogenous [ɔː'tɔdʒinəs]: **~ welding** autogeno zavarivanje
auto|giro ['ɔːtoudʒaiərou] AERO autožiro; **~graph** autogram; **~matic(ally)** automatski; **~nomous** autonoman; **~psy** autopsija
autumn ['ɔːtəm] jesen; **~al** [ɔː'tʌmnəl] jesenski
avail [ə'veil] pomoći; ***~ oneself of*** poslužiti se; **~able** raspoloživ; koga ima
avalanche ['ævəlaːnʃ] lavina
avaric|e ['ævəris] gramzljivost; **~ious** [ævə'riʃəs] gramzljiv
avenge [ə'vendʒ] osvetiti; **~r** osvetnik
avenue ['ævinjuː] aleja; *Am* avenija
average ['ævəridʒ] prosjek; havarija; ***on an ~*** u prosjeku; ***~ person*** prosječan čovjek; izračunati prosjek; iznositi u prosjeku
aver|se [ə'vəːs] nesklon (***to, from***); **~sion** averzija; **~t** odvratiti
aviat|e ['eivieit] AERO letjeti; **~ion** avijacija; ***~ion ground*** uzletište; **~or** pilot, avijatičar
avocation [ævə'keiʃən] uzgredno bavljenje; hobi
avoid [ə'vɔid] izbjegavati
avow [ə'vau] priznati; izjaviti; **~al** očitovanje
await [ə'weit] očekivati
awake [ə'weik] budan; ***be ~ to a danger*** biti svjestan opasnosti; ***wide ~*** potpuno budan; probuditi se; **~n** probuditi
award [ə'wɔːd] nagrada; presuda; dodijeliti
aware [ə'wɛə]: ***be ~ of*** biti svjestan čega; znati; ***become ~ of*** postati svjestan čega, primijetiti
away [ə'wei] odatle; na stranu
aw|e [ɔː] strahopoštovanje; ***~e-struck*** pun strahopoštovanja; **~ful** strašan; **~fully** *coll* vrlo
awhile [ə'wail] načas, na neko vrijeme
awkward ['ɔːkwəd] nespretan; nezgodan; **~ness** nespretnost
awning ['ɔːniŋ] platneni krov (čamca, dućana, kavane)
awry [ə'rai] naopako, naheren(o); naopak(o) (i *fig*)
axe [æks] sjekira; odsjeći; *coll* otpustiti
ax|is *pl* **~es** ['æksis, -iːz] osovina; **~le** osovina kotača
ay(e) [ai] da!, razumijem!
azure ['æʒə] azuran; nebesko plavetnilo

B

B. A. ['biː 'ei] = **Bachelor of Arts** osoba koja ima diplomu (drugog stupnja) na filozofskom fakultetu
babble [bæbl] tepati; blebetati; blebetanje; **~r** blebetalo
baby ['beibi] malo dijete, beba; **~hood** najranije djetinjstvo
bachelor ['bætʃələ] neženja; **~ girl** neudata djevojka
back ['bæk] leđa; pozadina; naslon; natrag, otraga; poduprati; indosirati; kladiti se na; **~-bite** ogovarati; **~bone** kičma; **~coupling** feedback; **~door** stražnja vrata; **~ground** pozadina; **~-hand(er)** bekhend; **~stairs** stražnje stubište; **~ward** natraške; zaostao; **~wardness** zaostalost
bacon ['beikən] slanina
bacteri|um *pl* **~a** [bæk'tiəriə(m)] bakterija
bad [bæd] loš, pokvaren, zao; ***he is ~ly off*** loše mu ide; ***want ~ly*** jako željeti, nužno trebati
badge [bædʒ] značka
badger ['bædʒə] jazavac
badness ['bædnis] pokvarenost
baffle ['bæfl] osujetiti
bag [bæg] torba, vreća; **~gage** MIL ili *Am* prtljaga; **~gage check** *Am* potvrda iz garderobe; **~gy** vrećast; **~pipe** gajde; **~-snatcher** otimač tašni
bail [beil] jamstvo; jamac; jamčiti
bailiff ['beilif] nadzornik sudnice
bait [beit] meka; mamac
bak|e [beik] peći; **~er** pekar; **~ery** pekara; **~ing powder** prašak za pecivo
balance ['bæləns] vaga; ravnoteža; bilanca; saldo; (iz-) balansirati (se)
balcony ['bælkəni] balkon (i THEAT)
bald [bɔːld] ćelav; **~ness** ćelavost
bale [beil] bala
balk [bɔːk] greda; balvan; zapreka; spriječiti
ball [bɔːl] ples, bal; lopta; klupko; tane, zrno; TECH **~-and-socket** kuglični zglob
ballast ['bæləst] balast
ball-bearing kuglični ležaj
ballet ['bælei] balet; **~ dancer** balerina, baletni plesač
balloon [bə'luːn] balon
ballot ['bælət] glasačka kuglica ili listić; tajno glasati; **~-box** glasačka kutija
balm [baːm] melem
balsam ['bɔːsəm] balzam
Baltic ['bɔːltik] baltički; **~**

(***Sea***) Baltik
balustrade [bæləs'treid] balustrada
bamboo [bæm'buː] bambus
ban [bæn] zabrana; zabraniti
banana [bə'naːnə] banana; RADIO ~ **plug** banana utikač
band [bænd] vrpca, traka; orkestar, glazba, družina
bandage ['bændidʒ] povez, zavoj
band|box kutija za šešire; ~(-)**master** dirigent, kapelnik
bang [bæŋ] prasak; udariti; zalupiti
banish ['bæniʃ] prognati; ~**ment** progonstvo
banisters ['bænistəz] *pl* ograda stepenica
bank [bæŋk] obala; banka; uložiti (novac) u banku; AERO nagnuti se u zavoju; ~(**ing**) **account** bankovni račun; ~-**bill** bankovna mjenica; *Am* novčanica; ~**er** bankar; ~**ing** bankarstvo; ~**ing-house** bankovna kuća; ~-**note** novčanica ~-**rate** diskontna stopa; ~**rupt** bankrot; ~**ruptcy** stečaj; ~**rupt's estate** stečajna masa
banns [bænz] *pl* crkveni ozivi za vjenčanje
banquet ['bæŋkwit] banket gozba; gostiti se
banter ['bæntə] zadirkivanje; zadirkivati
bapti|sm ['bæptizəm] krštenje; ~**st** baptist; ~**ze** ['bæptaiz] krstiti
bar [baː] šipka; prečka; greda; šank; JUR odvjetnički stalež; zakračunati, sprečavati
barb [baːb] kuka (strelice i sl); ~**ed wire** bodljikava žica
barbar|ian [baː'bɛəriən] barbar; ~**ous** ['baːbərəs] barbarski
barber ['baːbə] brijač; ~'**s shop** brijačnica
bare [bɛə] gol; prazan; bez dlaka; otkriven; ~**faced** besraman; ~-**footed** bos(onog); ~-**headed** gologlav; ~**ness** golotinja; oskudnost
bargain ['baːgin] jeftina kupnja; pogodba; cjenkati se
barge [baːdʒ] teglenica
bark [baːk] kora drveta; lavež; lajati
bar-keeper gostioničar
barley ['baːli] ječam
barm [baːm] kvasac, vinska pjenica
barmaid pipničarka
barn [baːn] hambar, štagalj
barometer [bə'rɔmitə] barometar
baron ['bærən] barun; ~**ess** barunica
barracks ['bærəks] *pl* kasarna
barrage ['bæraːʒ] brana; MIL baraža; ~ **baloon** baražni balon
barrel ['bærəl] bačva; bubanj; cijev od puške; ~-**organ** orguljice, vergle
barren ['bærən] jalov
barri|cade [bæri'keid] bari-

kada; dići barikadu; **~er** barijera; zapreka; RLW peronska ograda
barrister ['bæristə] (viši) odvjetnik
bartender *Am* pipničar
barter ['ba:tə] trgovanje zamjenom robe; tako trgovati; **~ (*away*)** zamijeniti
base [beis] nizak; podao; osnovica; baza (i CHEM, MIL); temeljiti; AERO sletjeti; ***be ~d on*** temeljiti se na; **~ball** bejzbol; **~less** neosnovan; **~ment** postolje; suteren; **~ness** niskost, podlost
bashful ['bæʃful] stidljiv, plah
basin ['beisn] umivaonik; lavor; bazen
bask [ba:sk] sunčati se
basket ['ba:skit] košara
bass [bæs] grgeč; brancin; [beis] bas (glas)
bast [bæst] liko drveta
bastard ['bæstəd] nezakonit; nezakonito dijete
baste [beist] zalijevati (pečenje) vlastitom masti; privremeno prošiti, "heftati"; *coll* izlupati
bat [bæt] šišmiš; kriket palica
bath [ba:θ] kupanje; **~robe** *Am* ogrtač za kupanje; **~-room** kupaona; **~(ing)--tub** kada za kupanje
bathe [beiθ] kupanje; kupati se na otvorenom
bathing-cap ['beiðiŋkæp] kapa za kupanje; **~-costume** kupaći kostim; **~-drawers** kupaće gaćice; **~-gown** ogrtač za kupanje; **~ suit** *Am* kupaći kostim
batsman ['bætsmən] kriket branič (s palicom)
batter ['bætə] udarati; oštetiti, istrošiti
battle ['bætl] bitka; boriti se; **~ plane** borbeni avion
battue [bæ'tu:] hajka
Bavaria [bə'vɛəriə] Bavarska; **~n** bavarski, Bavarac
bawl [bɔ:l] derati se; urlati; plakati
bay [bei] zaljev, zaton; lovor; lajati; riđan (konj)
be [bi:] biti; ***there is, are*** ima; **~ *reading*** upravo čitati; ***I am to ~*** moram (treba da ...)
beach [bi:tʃ] žal, plaža
beacon ['bi:kən] svjetionik
bead [bi:d] (stakleno i dr) zrno ogrlice
beak [bi:k] kljun
beam [bi:m] greda; zraka svjetla; sjaj; **~ aerial** usmjerena antena
bean [bi:n] grah
bear [bɛə] medvjed; COM bessist
bear [bɛə] podnositi; nositi; roditi; **~ *to the right*** držati desno; **~ *up*** ustrajati
beard [biəd] brada; **~ed** bradat; **~less** golobrad
bear|er ['bɛərə] nosač; donosilac (mjenice); **~ing** nošenje; podnošenje; držanje orijentacija; TECH, *ugl pl* le-

žaj; ***take one's ~ing*** orijentirati se (***about*** u pogledu)
beast [bi:st] zvijer; blago; **~ly** zvjerski; grozan
beat [bi:t] (is)tući; udarati; prestići; udar; kucaj; revir
beauti|ful ['bju:təful] lijep; **~fy** uljepšati
beauty ['bju:ti] ljepota; ljepotica; **~ shop**, *Am* **~ parlor** kozmetički salon; **~-spot** umjetni madež; mjesto s lijepom prirodom
beaver ['bi:və] dabar; dabrovina
because [bi'kɔz] jer; ***~ of*** zbog
beckon to ['bekən] dozvati (koga) migom
become [bi'kʌm] postati; doličiti; pristajati (šešir itd.); **~ing** pristao; doličan
bed [bed] krevet; lijeha; podloga; **~-clothes** *pl* posteljina; stelja; **~ fellow** drug u spavanju; **~-linen** posteljina (bez pokrivača); **~-pan** noćna posuda (za krevet); **~rid(den)** prikovan uz krevet; **~room** spavaća soba; **~side lamp** lampa na noćnom ormariću; **~side rug** prostirač pred krevetom; **~spread** (ukrasni) prekrivač za krevet; **~stead** okvir kreveta; **~tick** inlet; **~time** vrijeme za spavanje
bee [bi:] pčela; *Am* moba; *coll* ***have a ~ in one's bonnet*** imati fiksnu ideju
beech [bi:tʃ] bukva
beef [bi:f] govedina; **~ eater** stražar u londonskom Toweru; **~steak** biftek; **~-tea** bujon
beehive ['bi:haiv] košnica; **~-keeper** pčelar; **~-keeping** pčelarstvo; **~-line** zračna linija; *coll* ***make a ~-line for*** krenuti ravno prema
beer [biə] pivo
beet [bi:t] repa; ***red ~*** cikla
beetle ['bi:tl] kukac
beetroot ['bi:trut] repa; **~ sugar** šećer od šećerne repe
befall [bi'fɔ:l] zadesiti, dogoditi se
befit [bi'fit] pristojati se
befool [bi'fu:l] nasamariti
before [bi'fɔ:] prije; ranije; ispred; **~hand** unaprijed (i ***- with***)
befriend [bi'frend] sprijateljiti se s nekim; štititi
beg [beg] moliti, umoljavati (***of***); COM ***I ~ to state*** slobodan sam primijetiti
beget [bi'get] začeti; roditi
beggar ['begə] prosjak; *coll* prijan
begin [bi'gin] početi; **~ner** početnik; **~ning** početak
begrudge [bi'grʌdʒ] zavidjeti
beguile [bi'gail] zavarati; kratiti (vrijeme)
behalf [bi'ha:f]: ***on*** (ili ***in***) ***~ of*** u ime; u korist
behav|e [bi'heiv] ponašati se, vladati se; **~iour** ponašanje

behead [bi'hed] odrubiti glavu
behind [bi'haind] iza; straga
behold [bi'hould] ugledati
beige [beiʒ] drap (boja)
being ['bi:iŋ] biće; postojanje
belay [bi'lei] MAR omotati konop oko klina
belch ['beltʃ] podrigivati se; rigati
belfry ['belfri] zvonik
Belgi|an ['beldʒən] belgijski; Belgijanac; **~um** Belgija
belie [bi'lai] poricati; iznevjeriti
belie|f [bi'li:f] vjerovanje; **~vable** vjerojatan; **~ve** vjerovati; **~ver** vjernik
bell [bel] zvono, zvonce; **~-flower** zvončić; ljevač zvona; **~-glass** stakleno zvono; **~-boy** lift boj
bellows ['belouz] *pl* ***(a pair of ~)*** mijeh
bell|-pull povlak za zvonce; **~-push** dugme za zvono; **~-wiring** žice za zvonce
belly ['beli] trbuh
belong [bi'lɔŋ] pripadati (to kome, čemu); **~ings** imovina
beloved [bi'lʌvd] voljen; **~** ['-id] voljeno biće
below [bi'lou] dolje, ispod, niže
belt [belt] pojas; pogonski remen; opasati
bemoan [bi'moun] oplakivati
bench [bentʃ] klupa; sud
bend [bend] zavoj, okuka; savinuti (se); pokoriti se
beneath [bi'ni:θ] = **below**
benefact|ion [beni'fækʃən] dobročinstvo, blagodat; **~or**, **~ress** dobročinitelj
benefi|cence [bi'nefisns] dobrotvornost; **~cent** dobrotvoran; **~cial** koristan; **~t** koristiti; blagodat; THEAT dobrotvorna priredba; ***for the ~t of*** u korist
benevolen|ce [bi'nevələns] dobrohotnost; **~t** dobrohotan
benign [bi'nain] dobrostiv; blagonaklon; MED neopasan; **~ity** [bi'nigniti] dobrostivost
bent: **~ *on*** odlučan, nakanio; sklonost
benumb [bi'nʌm] otupiti, umrtviti
benz|ene, **~ine** ['benzi:n] benzin (za mrlje)
benzol|(e) ['benzɔl], **~ine** benzol
bequ|eath [bi'kwi:θ] oporučno ostaviti; **~est** ostavština
bereave [bi'ri:v] lišiti
berry ['beri] boba
berth [bə:θ] MAR sidrište; brodski ležaj; *fig* (dobar) položaj
beseech [bi'si:tʃ] zaklinjati; **~ing** molećiv
beside [bi'said] pokraj; **~s** osim
besiege [bi'si:dʒ] opsjedati
besom ['bi:zəm] metla od

pruća
besprinkle [bi'spriŋkl] poštrcati
best najbolje; nešto najbolje; ~ ***man*** vjenčani kum; ***Sunday*** ~ nedeljno odijelo; ***make the*** ~ ***of a bad job*** spašavati situaciju
bestir [bi'stə:]: ~ ***oneself*** pokrenuti se
bestow [bi'stou] dati, podijeliti; **~al** darivanje
bet [bet] oklada; kladiti se; **~ting** klađenje
betake [bi'teik]: ~ ***oneself*** poći, obratiti se (***to*** kome)
bethink [bi'θiŋk]: ~ ***oneself*** sjetiti se (***of*** na)
betimes [bi'taimz] rano, navrijeme
betray [bi'trei] iznevjeriti; izdati; **~al** izdaja; **~er** izdajica
betroth [bi'trouð] zaručiti se (***to*** za); **~al** zaruke
better ['betə] bolje; nešto bolje; ***get the*** ~ ***of*** savladati; ***so much the*** ~ utoliko bolje; ***you had*** ~ ***go*** bilo bi bolje da odeš
between [bi'twi:n] između; ~ ***you and me*** među nama rečeno; **~-decks** potpalublje
bevel ['bevəl] kosina; ukositi; TECH **~-wheel** čunjasti zupčanik
beverage ['bevəridʒ] napitak
bevy ['bevi] jato; društvo (žena)
bewail [bi'weil] oplakivati
beware [bi'wɛə] čuvati se
bewilder [bi'wildə] zbuniti; **~ment** zbunjenost
bewitch [bi'witʃ] očarati (i *fig*)
beyond [bi'jɔnd] tamo daleko; preko; ***it is*** ~ ***me*** ne ide mi u glavu; ~ **measure** pretjerano
Bible ['baibl] Biblija
bicarbonate [bai'ka:bənit]: ~ ***of soda*** soda bikarbona
bicycl|e ['baisikl] bicikl; voziti bicikl; **~ist** biciklist
bid nalog; ponuda; pokušaj; narediti; ponuditi; ~ **farewell** reći zbogom
bier [biə] mrtvačka nosila; odar
big velik; krupan; ***talk*** ~ praviti se važan
bigamy ['bigəmi] bigamija
bight [bait] uvala
bigness ['bignis] krupnoća
bigot ['bigət] bigot
bigwig ['bigwig] *coll* velika zvjerka
bike [baik] *coll* bicikl
bilberry ['bilbəri] BOT borovnica
bil|e [bail] žuč; gnjev; **~ious** ['biljəs] žučljiv
bill [bil] kljun; lista; zakonski prijedlog; mjenica (i ~ ***of exchange***); račun; ~ ***of fare*** jelovnik; ~ ***of loading*** brodski tovarni list
billet ['bilit] doznaka za konačište; ukonačiti
billfold *Am* lisnica
billiard ['biljəd] biljarski;

~**-cue** štap za biljar; ~**s** *pl* biljar
billow ['bilou] veliki val; talasati se; ~**y** uzburkan
bill-sticker ljepitelj oglasa
bi-motored dvomotorni
bin sud, posuda
bind [baind] (za-, pri-)vezati; obavezati; ~**ing** obavezan
binoculars [bi'nɔkjuləz] *pl* dvogled
biograph|er [bai'ɔgrəfə] životopisac; ~**y** životopis
biplane dvokrilac
birch [bəːtʃ] breza
bird [bəːd] ptica; ***~'s eye view*** ptičja perspektiva
birth [bəːθ] rođenje; porod; ~**day** rođendan; ~**place** rodno mjesto
biscuit ['biskit] keks
bissextile year [bi'sekstailjəː] prestupna godina
bit komadić; TECH šiljak svrdla; žvale
bit|e [bait] ugriz; zagristi; peći (papar); štipati (studen); ***~e at*** otresti se na; ***once bitten twice shy*** tko se jednom opeče i na hladno puše; ~**ing** oštar
bitter ['bitə] gorak; gorko pivo; ~**ness** ogorčenost; ~**s** *pl* gorki liker
black [blæk] crn; taman; mračan; laštiti (cipele); ~**berry** kupina; ~ **eye** modrica na oku; ~**head** sujedica; mitteser; ~**ing** crno laštilo za cipele; ~**leg** štrajkolomac; ~**market(eer)** šverc(er); ~ **sheep** *fig* crna ovca; ~**smith** kovač
bladder ['blædə] mjehur
blade [bleid] oštrica; pločica; vlat
blam|e [bleim] krivnja; okrivljavanje; okrivljavati; ~**(e)able**, ~**eworthy** pokudan, vrijedan prijekora; ~**eless** nedužan
bland [blænd] blag
blank [blænk] neispisan; bezizražajan; bez rime; praznina
blanket ['blæŋkit] pokrivač, deka
blasphem|e [blæs'fiːm] huliti (***against*** na); ~**y** ['blæsfimi] hulenje
blast [blaːst] zapuh (nalet) vjetra; trubljenje; TECH jaki mlaz zraka; uništiti; dići u zrak; ~**-furnace** visoka peć
blaze [bleiz] plamen; plamsati; buktjeti
blazer ['bleizə] "blejzer" (sportski kaput od vune)
bleach [bliːtʃ] bijeliti
bleak [bliːk] gol, pust; surov
bleat [bliːt] blejati
bleed [bliːd] krvariti
blemish ['blemiʃ] mrlja; ljaga; nagrditi
blend (po)miješati; mješavina
bless [bles] blagosloviti; hvaliti; ~**ed** blagoslovljen, usrećen (***with***)
blessing ['blesiŋ] blagoslov

blind [blaind] slijep; (*fig* ***to*** za); ~ **alley** slijepa ulica; ~ **flying** letenje po instrumentima; ~ **gut** slijepo crijevo; ~ **shell** MIL granata koja zataji; zaslijepiti; platnena žaluzina; ~**fold** **1.** zavezanh očiju; **2.** zavezati oči; ~**ness** sljepoća
blink treptanje; bljesak; treptati; ~ ***the facts*** zatvoriti oči pred činjenicama
bliss blaženstvo; ~**ful** blažen, presretan
blister ['blistə] mjehur
blizzard ['blizəd] mećava
bloat [blout] naduti; ~**er** dimljen slani sleđ
block blok; panj; zapreka; ~ ***up*** zapriječiti, blokirati; ~**ed account** blorani račun; ~**ade** blokada; ~**head** budala; ~**-system** RLW blok sistem
blood [blʌd] krv (*i fig*); ~**-blister** krvavi žulj; ~**less** beskrvan (*i fig*); ~**-poisoning** otrovanje krvi; ~**-pressure** krvni pritisak; ~**shot** zakrvavljen; ~**-vessel** krvni sud
bloom [blu:m] cvijet; cvat; (pro)cvasti
bloomer ['blu:mə] *coll* greška
blot mrlja (i *fig*); ~ ***out*** precrtati; ~**ter** upijač; ~**ting-pad** podloga od bugačice; ~**ting paper** bugačica
blouse [blauz] bluza
blow [blou] udarac (i *fig*); ***come to*** ~***s*** potući se; puhati; izgoriti (osigurač); ~ ***in*** *coll*, *fig* banuti; ~ ***over*** proći; ~ ***one's nose*** useknuti se; ~ ***up*** dići (odletjeti) u zrak; eksplodirati (i *fig*); ~**er** vratašca peći; ~ **fly** muha zujara
blue [blu:] plav, modar; plavetnilo; modrina; ~ **bottle** različak; muha zujara; ~**jacket** mornar; ~**print** plan
bluff [blʌf] strm; otvoren; strma obala; blef(irati)
bluish ['blu:iʃ] plavkast
blunder ['blʌndə] greška; pogriješiti
blunt [blʌnt] otvoren; bez uvijanja; ~**ness** otvorenost
blurb [blə:b] *Am* reklama na ovojnici
blurt [blə:t]: ~ ***out*** izlanuti
blush [blʌʃ] crvenilo; pocrvenjeti
bluster ['blʌstə] razmetljivost; huka
boar [bɔ:] vepar; nerast
board [bɔ:d] daska; karton; stol; košta; uprava; ministarstvo; komisija; *Am* ukrcati se; pokriti daskama; kuhati za; ~ ***of Trade*** ministarstvo trgovine; *Am* privredna komora; ~**er** osoba na hrani; ~**ing house** pansion; ~**ing school** internat
boast [boust] hvalisanje; hvalisati se
boat [bout] čamac; brod; ~**ing** vožnja čamcem;

~swain [bousn] noštromo
bob [bɔb] uteg njihala; ljuljati se; poskakivati; **~bed hair** potkraćena (ženska) kosa
bobbin ['bɔbin] kalem; **~-lace** čipka na batiće
bobby ['bɔbi] *sl* policajac
bodice ['bɔdis] prslučić; košuljac; gornji dio haljine
bodily ['bɔdili] tjelesni
bodkin ['bɔdkin] šilo; debela igla za navođenje
body ['bɔdi] tijelo; trup; (***dead***) ~ leš; karoserija; skup
bog [bɔg] močvara; **~gy** močvaran
bogus ['bougəs] lažan
Bohemia [bou'hi:mjə] Češka; **~n** Čeh; boem
boil [bɔil] kipjeti; ključanje; čir; **~er** (parni) kotao
boisterous ['bɔistərəs] bučan, neobuzdan
bold [bould] smion; **~ness** smionost
bolster ['boulstə] jastuk (na kauču); podloga; poduprijeti
bolt [boult] klin; zasun; zakračunati; juriti; naglo gutati; plašiti se (konj); ***a ~ from the blue*** grom iz vedra neba
bomb [bɔm] bomba; ***incendiary ~*** zapaljiva bomba; bombardirati; ***~ed out*** beskućnik zbog bombardiranja; **~er** bombarder; **~-proof** siguran od bombi
bond veza; *pl* okovi; obveznica; ***in ~*** pod carinskom zabranom; ***~ed warehouse*** konsignaciono skladište; **~age** ropstvo
bone [boun] kost
bonfire ['bɔnfaiə] krijes
bonnet ['bɔnit] šeširić
bonus ['bounəs] premija; posebna dividenda; doplatak
bony [bouni] košćat
booby-prize ['bu:bi-praiz] *coll* nagrada zadnjemu
book [buk] knjiga; svezak; knjižiti, upisati; rezervirati (karte); ***be in a person's good*** (***bad***) ***~s*** dobro (loše) stajati kod nekoga; **~-binder** knjigoveža; **~-case** ormar za knjige; **~-end** potporanj za knjige; **~ing office** blagajna za vozne karte; **~-keeper** knjigovođa; **~-mark** znak u knjizi (da se zapamti mjesto); **~-seller** knjižar; **~-shelf** polica za knjige
boom [bu:m] konjunktura; nagli razvoj; imati veliki komercijalni uspjeh
boon [bu:n] blagodat
boost [bu:st] *Am coll* reklamirati; stimulirati
boot [bu:t] visoka cipela, čizma; prostor za prtljagu; **~-jack** izuvač za čizme; **~s** *pl* sluga u svratištu
booty ['bu:ti] plijen
booze [bu:z] *coll* piti; piće; pijančevanje; **~r** pijanac
border ['bɔ:də] rub; granica; lijeha; obrubiti; graničiti

(***upon*** sa)
bore [bɔː] plimni val
bore [bɔː] bušiti; *coll* gnjaviti; *coll* gnjavator; **~dom** dosada
boric ['bɔːrik]: **~ *acid solution*** MED borna voda
borough ['bʌrə] trgovište; (***municipal***) **~** gradska općina
borrow ['bɔrou] posuditi (od)
bosh [bɔʃ] *coll* glupost
bosom ['buzəm] grudi; njedra
boss izbočina; *coll* poslodavac, gazda, šef
botan|ical [bə'tænikəl] botanički; **~ist** botaničar; **~y** botanika
botch [bɔtʃ] pokvariti
both [bouθ] oba, obje, oboje; **~ *of them*** oba, obje, oboje; **~ *... and*** i ... i, kako ... tako
bother ['bɔðə] gnjavaža; gnjaviti se
bottle ['bɔtl] boca; puniti u boce; **~*d beer*** pivo u bocama
bottom ['bɔtəm] dno; uzrok; **~less** bez dna
bough [bau] grana
bounce [bauns] poskočiti, odskočiti; poskok, odskok
bound [baund] obavezan; ***be ~ to do*** morati učiniti, sigurno učiniti; na putu; ograničiti; skočiti; **~ary** granica; **~less** bezgraničan; **~s** *pl fig* granica
boun|tiful ['bauntiful] obilan; darežljiv; **~ty** darežljivost; premija
bouquet ['bukei] kita cvijeća; aroma (vina)
bovril ['bɔvril] bujon od ekstrakta
bow [bou] luk; mašna; [bau] naklon; nakloniti se
bowels ['bauəlz] *pl* utroba
bowl [boul] zdjela; glava lule; kugla; kotrljati; kuglati se; **~er** polucilindar
box kutija; šimšir; sanduk; THEAT loža; kočijaševo sjedalo; TECH kučište; boksati; **~ *on the ear*** zaušnica; **~ *a person's ear*** ćušnuti nekoga; **~er** boksač; **~-keeper** vratar loža; **~-office** kazališna blagajna; **~room** ostava
boy dječak; mladić; **~hood** dječaštvo; **~ish** dječački; **≈ Scouts** skauti
brace [breis] spona; **~s** *pl*, naramice; proteza; osvježiti
bracelet ['breislit] narukvica
bracket ['brækit] konzola; zagrada; staviti u zagrade
brag [bræg] hvalisanje; hvalisati se; **~gart** ['~gət] hvalisavac
braid [breid] pletenica; gajtan; (o)plesti
brain [brein] mozak; razum; ***rack*** *ili* ***puzzle one's ~s*** razbijati glavu; **~less** bez pameti, nepromišljen; **~-wave** *coll* ideja; **~-worker** intelektualni radnik
brake [breik] kočnica; kočiti

bran [bræn] mekinje
branch [bra:ntʃ] grana; ogaranak; struka; podružnica; ~ (*out*) granati se; ~**line** odvojak pruge; ~**-office** podružnica
brand [brænd] glavnja; zaštitni znak; vrsta; užeći
brand-new nov novcat
brandy ['brændi] konjak; rakija
brass [bra:s] mjed; ~**band** duvačka glazba
brassiere ['bræsiə] grudnjak
brave [breiv] hrabar; prkositi; ~**ry** hrabrost
brawl [brɔ:l] glasna svađa; svađati se
brawn [brɔ:n] mišice
brazen ['breizn] mjeden; drzak; ~**ness** drskost
Brazil-nut [brə'zil'nʌt] brazilski orah
breach [bri:tʃ] prekid; prekinuti; ~ ***of contract*** povreda ugovora; ~ ***of peace*** javni izgred
bread [bred] kruh; ~ ***and butter*** kruh s maslacem
breadth [bredθ] širina
break [breik] prelom; slom; stanka, odmor; ~ ***of day*** osvit; ~ ***down*** oboriti, slomiti se; zaplakati; ~ ***up*** raskomadati, rastjerati, razići se raspasti se; ~**able** loman; ~**-down** slom; MOT kvar; ~**fast** doručak; doručkovati; ~**-neck** vratoloman
breast [brest] grudi; ~**-pin** igla za kravatu; ~**-stroke** prsno plivanje
breath [breθ] dah; ***below one's*** ~ šaptom; ~**e** [bri:ð] disati; ~**ing** disanje; ~**less** bez daha; ~**taking** zapanjujuć
breeches ['britʃiz] *pl* livrejske hlače; jahaće hlače
breed [bri:d] pasmina; izleći; uzgajati
breez|e [bri:z] povjetarac; ~**y** lahorast
brevity ['breviti] kratkoća
brew [bru:] variti (pivo); kuhati (kavu); spremati se (oluja i *fig*); ~**age** svareni napitak; ~**er** pivar; ~**ery** pivara
bribe [braib] mito; podmititi; ~**ry** podmićivanje
brick [brik] opeka; ~**layer** zidar; ~**-works** *pl* ciglana
bridal ['braidl] svadbeni
bride [braid] mlada; ~**groom** mladoženja; ~**smaid** djeveruša
bridge [bridʒ] most; bridž (kartaška igra)
bridle ['braidl] uzda; (za)uzdati; ~**-path** jahačka staza
brief [bri:f] kratak; ~**ness** kratkoća
brig brig (jedrenjak s dva jarbola)
brigand ['brigənd] razbojnik
bright [brait] svijetao, sjajan, blještav; pametan; ~**en** oživiti, razvedriti se; ~**ness** sjas; vedrina, inteligencija

brillian|cy ['briljənsi] sjaj; visoka inteligencija; **~t** briljantan, vrlo inteligentan
brim rub; obod
brimstone ['brimstən] sumpor
bring [briŋ] donijeti; **~ *an action*** podići tužbu; **~ *about*** izazvati; **~ *along*** donijeti; **~ *forth*** roditi, stvoriti; **~ *out*** iznijeti; istaknuti; **~ *up*** uznijeti; odgojiti; **~er** donosilac
brink rub; obala
briquette [bri'ket] briket
brisk žustar; brz
brisket ['briskit] prsa (meso)
bristle ['brisl] čekinja; **~ *up*** nakostriješiti se
Brit|ain ['britən] (Velika) Britanija; **~ish** britanski; **~on** Britanac
brittle ['britl] krhak
broatch [broutʃ] ražanj; načeti (bačvu, temu)
broad [brɔ:d] širok, prostran; **~-axe** bradva; **~cast** emisija; emitirati; **~cast(ing)-station** radio stanica; **~day** bijeli dan; **~-minded** širokogrudan, tolerantan
broil [brɔil] peći
broker ['broukə] mešetar, posrednik
bronze [brɔnz] bronca, brončan
brooch [broutʃ] broš
brood [bru:d] leglo; izleći
brook [bruk] potok; **~let** potočić
broom [brum] metla; **~stick** držak metle
Bros. ['brʌðəz] = **brothers** (u naslovu poduzeća)
broth [brɔθ] juha od mesa i povrća
brother ['brʌðə] brat; **~hood** bratstvo; **~-in-law** šurjak
brow [brau] obrva; čelo
brown [braun] smeđ; crn (kruh); **~ paper** pak-papir
bruise [bru:z] modrica; ostaviti modricu
brush [brʌʃ] četka; kist; (o)četkati; **~ *up*** obnoviti, osvježiti; **~wood** guštara
Brussels ['brʌslz] Bruxelles; **~ sprouts** prokulice
brut|al ['bru:tl] brutalan; **~ality** [ž'tæliti] brutalnost; **~e** životinjski; *fig* životinja
bubble ['bʌbl] mjehur(ić); tlapnja; varka
buck [bʌk] ZOOL mužjak
bucket ['bʌkit] kablica, vedro
buckle ['bʌkl] kopča; zakopčati
buckram ['bʌkrəm] kruto platno
bud [bʌd] pupoljak; pupati
budge [bʌdʒ] maknuti se
budget ['bʌdʒit] budžet
buff [bʌf] meka goveđa koža
buffer ['bʌfə] odbojnik vagona
buffer ['bʌfıt] udarac; bife (serviranje); udarati; boriti se sa
buffoon [bə'fu:n] lakrdijaš
bug [bʌg] stjenica; *Am* ku-

kac; **~aboo**, **~bear** strašilo; **~gy** stjeničav
bugle-horn ['bju:glhɔ:n] lovački rog
build [bild] graditi; osloniti se (***upon*** na); **~ *in*** ugraditi; **~ *up*** izgrađivati; **~er** graditelj; **~ing** zgrada; **~ing trade** graditeljstvo, građevinarstvo
bulb [bʌlb] lukovica; žarulja
bulge [bʌldʒ] izbočina; izbočiti se
bulk [bʌlk] obujam; glavnina; **~y** opsežan; glomazan
bull [bul] bula; bik; mužjak; COM hosist (špekulant); **~dog** buldog; **~et** tane, zrno; **~etin** bilten
bullion ['buljən] zlato (srebro) u šipkama
bullock ['bulək] vol
bull's-eye ['bulzai] centar mete
bumble-bee ['bʌmblbi:] bumbar
bump [bʌmp] udarac; čvoruga; udariti u; **~ *off*** *Am sl* ucecati, ubiti
bumper ['bʌmpə] čaša puna do ruba; MOT branik
bun [bʌn] žemička (s grožđicama)
bunch [bʌntʃ] svežanj; grupa
bundle [bʌndl] zavežljaj; smotati
bung [bʌŋ] vranj (čep) bačve; **~alow** prizemni ljetnikovac; **~-hole** rupa u bačvi za vranj (čep)
bungle [bʌŋgl] loš posao; pokvariti
bunion ['bʌnjən] MED oteklina prvog zgloba na nožnom palcu
bunk [bʌŋk] ugrađen ležaj; ležaj na kat
bunker ['bʌŋkə] brodsko spremište za ugljen
bunk(um) ['bʌŋk(əm)] *Am coll* blebetanje, glupost
buoy [bɔi] plutača; **~ancy** sposobnost plutanja; **~ant** koji ne tone; poletan
burden ['bə:dən] teret, tovar, breme; **~some** tegotan, neugodan
burglar ['bə:glə] (noćni) provalnik; **~y** provala
burgundy ['bə:gəndi] burgundac (vino)
burial ['beriəl] pogreb; **~-ground** groblje
burlesque [bə:'lesk] burleskan; lakrdija
burn [bə:n] opeklina; (iz)gorjeti; spaliti; **~er** plamenik; **~ing** gorući; **~ish** polirati, laštiti; **~t gas** ispušni plin
burst [bə:st] prsnuće; provala; raspuknuti se, eksplodirati; **~ *out laughing*** prasnuti u smijeh
bury ['beri] pokopati; sakriti
bus [bʌs] autobus; ***miss the* ~** zakasniti na autobus; *fig* propustiti priliku
busby ['bʌzbi] visoka gardijska šubara
bush [buʃ] grm; šikara; TECH metalna obloga ležaja

bushel [buʃl] mjera za žito (35 l)
bushy ['buʃi] čupav
business ['biznis] posao (i *fig*); poslovi; stvar; ***on ~*** poslovno; *pl* **~es** lokali; **~-like** poslovan
bus-stop ['bʌs'stɔp] autobusna stanica
bust [bʌst] poprsje
bustle ['bʌsl] žurba, vreva; užurbati se
busy ['bizi] zaposlen; prometan; ***~ oneself*** zaposliti se
but [bʌt] ali; nego; osim; samo; ***all ~*** skoro, gotovo; ***~ now*** tek sada
butcher ['butʃə] mesar; **~y** mesnica
butler ['bʌtlə] pivničar; glavni sluga
butt [bʌt] kundak; meta (i *fig*); ***~ in*** *coll* umiješati se
butter ['bʌtə] maslac; namazati maslacem; **~fly** leptir
button ['bʌtn] dugme; ***~ up*** zakopčati; **~-hole** rupica za dugme
buy [bai] kupiti; **~er** kupac, nakupac
buzz [bʌz] zujanje; zujati; došaptavati; **~er** *tel* zujalo
by [bai] kraj; uz; pomoću; mimo; ***~ day*** danju; ***~ far*** daleko; ***~ itself*** (samo) po sebi; ***~ rail*** željeznicom; ***day ~ day*** dan za danom; ***~ twos*** po dvoje; ***~ the ~*** uzgred govoreći; ***go ~*** proći mimo; **~gone** minuo; **~-name** drugo ime; nadimak; **~-product** nusproizvod; **~ stander** promatrač; **~-street** sporedna ulica; **~-way** sporedni put

C

cab fijaker; taksi
cabbage ['kæbidʒ] kupus; **~-lettuce** salata glavatica
cabby ['kæbi] *coll* fijakerist; taksist
cabin ['kæbin] koliba; kabina; **~-boy** "mali" na brodu
cabinet ['kæbinit] ormarić; kabinet; radio kutija aparata; **~ council** ministarsko vijeće; **~-maker** model-stolar
cable ['keibl] kabl; poslati kablogram; **~gram** kablogram
cab|man fijakerist; taksist; **~-stand** stajalište za taksije
cackle ['kækl] kokodakanje; kokodakati
cadeverous [kə'dævərəs] mrtvački blijed
caddy ['kædi] nosač golf palica
cage [keidʒ] (zatvoriti u) kavez; MIN teretno dizalo
cajole [kə'dʒoul] laskati; **~ry** laskanje
cake [keik] kolač(ić); torta; komad

calamit|ous [kə'læmitəs] zlosretan; **~y** nesreća
calcify ['kælsifai] ovapneniti (se)
calcula|ble ['kælkjuləbl] izračunljiv; **~te** (iz)računati; *Am coll* misliti; **~ting machine** računski stroj; **~tion** računanje
calendar ['kælində] kalendar
calf, *pl* ***calves*** [ka:f, -vz] tele; list (na nozi)
calibre ['kælibə] kalibar (i *fig*)
calico ['kælikou] šareno platno
call [kɔ:l] poziv; uzvik; THEAT poziv pred zavjesu; posjeta; ***on ~*** COM na opoziv; zvati; nazvati; pozvati; posjetiti (***at***, ***on*** koga); ***~ for*** doći po; ***~ up*** pozvati u vojsku; **~-box** i **~-office** telefonska govornica; **~ing** poziv; zvanje
callo|sity [kæ'lɔsiti] žuljavost; **~us** ['kæləs] žuljav; bešćutan
calm [ka:m] miran, spokojan; bezvjetrina; ***~ down*** smiriti se
calorie ['kæləri] kalorija
calumn|iate [kə'lʌmnieit] klevetati; **~y** kleveta
cambric ['keimbrik] batist
camel ['kæməl] deva
camera ['kæmərə] fotoaparat
camomile ['kæməmail]: **~ tea** čaj od kamilice
camp [kæmp] logor; **~-bed** poljski krevet; **~-stool** lovački stolac; logorovati
campaign [kæm'pein] pohod
camphor ['kæmfə] kamfor
can [kæn] moći; limena kutija; *Am* konzerva; **~ned goods** *Am* konzerve; **~ opener** *Am* otvarač konzervi
canal [kə'næl] kanal (*umjetni* i MED)
canary [kə'nɛəri]: ***~ (bird)*** kanarinac
cancel ['kænsəl] ukinuti; otkazati
cancer ['kænsə] MED rak; **~ous** kancerozan
candit ['kændid] iskren
candidate ['kændidit] kandidat
candied ['kændid] ušećeren
candle ['kændl] svijeća; **~ power** svijeća (mjera); **~stick** svijećnjak
candour ['kændə] iskrenost
candy ['kændi] kandis (šećer); *Am* bombon(i); ušećeriti
cane [kein] trska; štap
canister ['kænistə] limena kutija
cannery ['kænəri] *Am* tvornica konzervi
cannon ['kænən] top(ovi); (biljar) karambol
cannot ['kænɔt] ne mogu
canoe [kə'nu:] indijanski kanu
canon ['kænən] kanon; kanonik

canopy ['kænəpi] baldahin
can|t [kænt] žargon; licemjerstvo; **~teen** kantina; **~ter** kratki kas, galop
canvas ['kænvəs] jedrenina; ulje (slika); **~s** agitirati; agitiranje
cap [kæp] kapa; poklopac
capa|bility [keipə'biliti] sposobnost; **~ble** ['žəbl] sposoban, u stanju
capacious [kə'peiʃəs] prostoran, opsežan
capacit|ate [kə'pæsiteit] osposobiti; **~y** kapacitet
cape [keip] rt; pelerina
caper ['keipə] kapar; skok u vis
capital ['kæpitl] kažnjiv smrću; izvrstan; glavni grad; kapital; veliko slovo; **~ism** kapitalizam; **~ist** kapitalist; **~ist(ic)** kapitalistički; **~ization** kapitalizacija; **~ize** kapitalizirati
capitulat|e [kə'pitjuleit] kapitulirati; **~ion** kapitulacija
capon ['keipən] kopun
capric|e [kə'pri:s] hir; **~ous** [kə'priʃəs] mušičav; **~iousness** hirovitost
capsize [kæp'saiz] prevrnuti (se) (brod)
captain ['kæptin] kapetan; zapovjednik
caption ['kæpʃən] *Am* natpis; film prijevod
captivate ['kæptiveit] zarobiti; očarati
captiv|e ['kæptiv] uhvaćen; zarobljenik; **~e *baloon*** vezani balon; **~ity** sužanjstvo
capture ['kæptʃə] hvatanje; plijen; uhvatiti; zaplijeniti
car [ka:] kola; auto; **~ lift** garažna dizalica
caravan [kærə'væn] karavan; prikolica
caraway ['kærəwei] kumin, kiml
carbide ['ka:baid] karbid
carbine ['ka:bain] karabin
carbohydrate ['ka:bou'haidreit] ugljični hidrat
carbolic [ka:'bɔlik]: **~ acid** karbolna kiselina
carbonic [ka:'bɔnik]: **~ acid** ugljična kiselina
carbon ['ka:bən] ugljik; kopija; **~ paper** karbon papir
carbuncle ['ka:bʌŋkl] tvrd, bolan čir
carburrettor ['ka:bjuretə] rasplinjač
card [ka:d] karta; ***throw up one's ~s*** otkriti karte; **~board** karton
cardinal ['ka:dinl] kardinal; **~ number** glavni broj
card|-index, ~ registry kartoteka; **~ sharper** varalica na kartama; **~ table** stol za kartanje
care [kɛə] briga; **~ *of* (*c/o*) ...** kod; ***take ~*** čuvati se; paziti; ***take ~*** brinuti se (***of*** za); **~ *for*** brinuti se za; ***I don't ~ for*** (ili ***about***) ***it*** svejedno mi je; ne volim; ***with ~*** brižljivo, oprezno!

career [kə'riə] karijera
care|ful ['kɛəful] pažljiv (***about*** sa); **~less** bezbrižan; nemaran
caress [kə'res] milovanje; milovati
care|taker ['kɛəteikə] pazikuća; **~worn** izmučen od briga
cargo ['ka:gou] teret
caricature ['kærikə'tjuə] karikatura; karikirati
caries ['kɛərii:z] truljenje zubi
carman ['ka:mən] vozar
carmine ['ka:main] karmin
carnation [ka:'neiʃən] karamfil
carnival ['ka:nivəl] karneval
carol ['kærəl]: ***Christmas ~*** božićna pjesma
carouse [kə'rauz] pijančevati
carp [ka:p] šaran; čangrizati; ***~ at*** gunđati na
carpenter ['ka:pintə] tesar; stolar
carpet ['ka:pit] tepih; **~ing** sagovi (na metar); **~-sweeper** aspirator
carpool ['ka:pu:l] voziti se na posao i sl. u skupini
carriage ['kæridʒ] prijevoz; vagon, kočija; prevoznina; držanje; **~-free**, **~-paid** uz besplatan dovoz
carrier ['kæriə] prevoznik, otpremnik
carrot ['kærət] mrkva
carry ['kæri] nositi; donijeti; ***~ away*** odnijeti; ***~ on*** nastaviti; ***~ out*** provesti
cart [ka:t] kola; ***put the ~ before the horse*** *fig* početi naopako; kirijašiti; **~age** vozarina; **~er** vozar; **~-grease** kolomaz
cartoon [ka:'tu:n] nacrt; karikatura; crtani film
cartridge ['ka:tridʒ] metak
carve [ka:v] (raz)rezati; gravirati; klesati
carving ['ka:viŋ] rezbarija; **~-knife** nož za rezanje pečenog mesa
cascade [kæs'keid] slap(ovi)
case [keis] kutija; futrola; sanduk; slučaj; ***in ~*** u slučaju; ***in any ~*** u svakom slučaju
casement ['keismənt] prozorsko krilo
cash [kæʃ] gotovina; unovčiti; ***~ down*** polog; ***~ on delivery*** pouzećem; **~ payment** plaćanje u gotovom; **~-register** regisar kasa
cashier [kæ'ʃiə] blagajnik; [kə'~] otpustiti uz lišenje čina
cashmere [kæʃ'miə] kašmir
casing ['keisiŋ] navlaka
casino [kə'si:nou] kasino
cask [ka:sk] bačva; **~et** kutija za nakit; *Am* lijes
cast [ka:st] bacanje; odljev; *fig* kov; (iz-, od-) baciti; TECH lijevati; **~ iron** lijevano željezo; **~ steel** lijevani čelik
castaway ['ka:stəwei] brodolomac

caste [ka:st] kasta; **~-feeling** kastinski duh
castigate ['kæstigeit] kazniti
castle ['ka:sl] dvorac; zamak; (*Šah*) kula; roširati
castrol-oil ['ka:stər'ɔil] ricinusovo ulje
casual ['kæʒjuəl] slučajan, prigodan; **~ty** nesreća; **~ties** MIL gubici
cat [kæt] mačka
catalogue ['kætəlɔg] katalog; popis
cataract ['kætərækt] vodopad; brzaci
catarrh [kə'ta:] katar; hunjavica
catastroph|e [kə'tæstrəfı] katastrofa; **~ic** [kætə'strɔfık] katastrofalan
catch [kætʃ] ulov; plijen; uloviti; uhvatiti; zateći; **~ *on*** imati uspjeha **~ing** zarazan; **~penny** bazarski artikl; **~word** krilatica, natuknica
caterpillar ['kætəpilə] gusjenica; **~ tractor** gusjeničar
catgut ['kætgʌt] MED katgut, niti od ovčjih crijeva
cathedral [kə'θi:drəl] katedrala
Catholic ['kæθəlik] katolički; katolik
cattle ['kætl] stoka; **~-show** izložba stoke
caucus ['kɔ:kəs] sastanak pred izbore (glasanje)
cauldron ['kɔ:ldrən] kotao
cauliflower ['kɔliflauə] cvjetača
causal ['kɔ:səl] uzročni; **~ity** uzročnost
cause [kɔ:z] uzrok; proces; pouzročiti, izazvati; **~less** bezrazložan
caustic ['kɔ:stik] sredstvo za izjedanje; *fig* zajedljiv
cauterize ['kɔ:təraiz] ispaliti (ranu)
cauti|on ['kɔ:ʃən] oprez(-nost); opomena; upozoriti; **~ous** oprezan
cave ['keiv] špilja
cavil ['kævil] tražiti prigovore (***at, about*** čemu)
cavity ['kæviti] šupljina
caw [kɔ:] graktanje
cayman ['keimən] ZOOL kajman (vrsta krokodila)
CD [si:'di:] = **compact disc** CD; **~-player** CD-player; **~ ROM** CD-ROM
cease [si:s] prestati; **~less** neprestan
cede [si:d] ustupiti, prepustiti
ceiling ['si:liŋ] strop; AERO maksimalna visina; *fig* gornja granica; **~ price** najviša cijena
celebrat|e ['selibreit] slaviti; **~ed** glasovit; **~ion** proslava
celebrity [si'lebriti] slavna osoba
celerity [si'leriti] brzina
celery ['seləri] celer
celestial [si'lestjəl] nebeski
celibacy ['selibəsi] celibat; neženstvo
cell [sel] ćelija; *phone* mobitel; **~ar** podrum; pivnica

cellophane ['seləfein] celofan
cellphone ['selfoun] mobitel
cellul|oid ['seljulɔid] celulojd; **~ose** celuloza
cement [si'ment] cement; ljepilo
cementery ['semitri] groblje
censor ['sensə] cenzor; cenzurirati; **~ship** cenzura
censure ['senʃə] kritika; osuditi
census ['sensəs] popis stanovništva
cent [sent]: ***per ~*** posto
centennial [sen'tenjəl] stogodišnji (-ca)
central ['sentrəl] središnji; **~ heating** centralno grijanje; **~ office** (EL **~ station**) centrala; **~ization** centralizacija; **~ize** centralizirati
centre ['sentə] centar; **~ forward** vođa navale; **~ half** centarhalf; koncentrirati se
century ['sentʃuri] stoljeće
CEO [si:i:'ou] = **chief executive officer** generalni direktor, generalna direktorica
cereal ['siəriəl] žitni, žitne pahuljice; **~s** žitarice
cerebral ['seribrəl] mozgovni
ceremon|ial [seri'mounjəl] svečan; ceremoniozan; **~y** ceremonija
certain ['sə:tən] siguran; izvjestan; **~ty** sigurnost
certificat|e [sə'tifıkit] svjedodžba; **~ion** posvjedočenje
certi|fy ['sə:tifai] posvjedočiti; **~tude** sigurnost
cession ['seʃən] odstup
cesspool ['sespu:l] zahodna jama
CFO [si:ef'ou] = **chief financial officer** financijski direktor, financijska direktorica
chafe [tʃeif] trljati; upaliti; bjesnjeti
chaff [tʃa:f] pljeva; trica
chain [tʃein] lanac; okovati lancima
chair [tʃɛə] stolica; **~man** predsjednik
chalk [tʃɔ:k] kreda; ***~ up*** označiti kredom
challenge ['tʃælindʒ] izazov; prigovor; poticaj; teškoća; izazvati; osporiti
chamber ['tʃeimbə] soba; ***~ of Industry and Commerce*** privrednotrgovačka komora; **~lain** komornik; **~maid** sobarica
chamois ['ʃæmwa:] divokoza
champagne [ʃæm'pein] šampanjac
champion ['tʃæmpjən] pobornik; prvak; **~ship** prvenstvo
chance [tʃa:ns] slučaj; sreća; prilika; ***by ~*** slučajno
chancellor ['tʃa:nsələ] kancelar
chandelier [ʃændi'liə] veliki luster
change [tʃeindʒ] promjena; mijenjanje; sitniš; promije-

niti; RLW presjesti; **~less** nepromjenljiv; **~able** promjenljiv
channel ['tʃænl] kanal; ***official ~s*** službeni put(evi)
chap [tʃæp] momak, čovjek; ispucana koža
chapel ['tʃæpəl] kapelica
chaplain ['tʃæplin] kapelan
chapter ['tʃæptə] poglavlje
character ['kæriktə] slovo; karakter; lik; (doba) glas; karakteristika; **~istic** karakterističan (***of*** za); **~ize** karakterizirati
charcoal ['tʃa:koul] drveni ugalj
charge [tʃa:dʒ] punjenje; naboj; zaduženje; briga; služba; ***~s*** *pl* troškovi; ***free of ~s*** besplatan; napuniti; zaračunati; povjeriti; optužiti; **~able** pripisiv; podložan
charit|able ['tʃæritəbl] dobrotvoran; **~y** ljubav prema bližnjemu; dobrotvornost; ***~y begins at home*** najprije je bog sebi bradu stvorio
charlotte ['ʃa:lət] vrst torte od jabuka
charm [tʃa:m] čarolija; draž; šarmirati
chart [tʃa:t] pomorska karta
charter ['tʃa:tə] povelja; najmiti; **~-party** ugovor o brodskom najmu
charwoman ['tʃa:wumən] dvorkinja
chase ['tʃeis] lov; progon; loviti; progoniti
chasm ['kæzəm] ponor
chassis ['ʃæsi] šasija
chaste [tʃeist] krepostan; čist
chasti|se [tʃæs'taiz] kazniti; **~ty** djevičanstvo
chat [tʃæt] čavrljanje; čavrljati; **~line** chatline; **~ room** chat room; **~ter** klepetati; cvokotati; **~terbox** klepetalo
cheap [tʃi:p] jeftin (*i fig*); **~en** pojeftiniti; **~ness** jeftinoća
cheat [tʃi:t] prevara; varalica; prevariti
check [tʃek] šah (u šahu); zapreka; *Am* ček; sprečavati; provjeriti; **~ed** kockast; **~er** nadglednik; **~mate** šahmat; **~-room** *Am* garderoba; **~-up** *Am* kontrola, pregled
cheek [tʃi:k] obraz; *coll* drskost; **~y** *coll* drzak
cheer [tʃiə] raspoloženost; klicanje; ***three ~s!*** triput hura! razveseliti klicati nekome; (i **~ *up***) razveseliti se; **~ful** veseo; **~less** neveseo
cheese [tʃi:z] sir; **~-monger** prodavač sira
chemical ['kemikəl] kemijski; **~s** *pl* kemikalije
chemise [ʃi'mi:z] košuljac
chemist ['kemist] kemičar; apotekar; **~ry** kemija
cheque [tʃek] ček; **~-book** čekovna knjižica; **~red** kockast; šaren
cherish ['tʃeriʃ] voljeti, njegovati
cherry ['tʃeri] trešnja

chess [tʃes] šah; **~-board** šahovska ploča; **~man** šahovska figura
chest [tʃest] sanduk; grudi; **~ of drawers** komoda
chestnut ['tʃestnət] kesten; kestenjast
chew [tʃu:] žvakati
chewing-gum guma za žvakanje
chicken ['tʃikin] pile; **~-pox** MED kozice
chief [tʃi:f] glavni; glavar; šef; **~tain** poglavica
chilblain ['tʃilblein] ozeblina
child [tʃaild] *pl* ***~ren*** ['tʃildrən] dijete; **~hood** djetinjstvo; **~ish** djetinjast, djetinji
chill [tʃil] studen; zimnica; ***take the ~ off*** smlačiti (tekućinu); **~ed meat** meso iz frižidera; **~(i)ness** hladnoća; **~ out** opustiti se; **~y** hladan; ***feel ~y*** zepsti
chime [tʃaim] skladna zvonjava; odbijati (sat); *fig* složiti se
chimney ['tʃimni] dimnjak; **~-sweeper** dimnjačar
chin [tʃin] brada (kost)
china ['tʃainə] porculan; **~ware** porculansko posuđe
chine [tʃain] hrptenjača
Chinese [tʃai'ni:z] kineski; Kinez(i)
chink [tʃink] pukotina
chip [tʃip] komadić; okrhnuti; odrezati; *coll* ***~s*** ili; ***~ped*** (ili ***chip***) ***potatoes*** pržene ploške krumpira
chirp [tʃə:p] cvrkutati
chirrup ['tʃirəp] coktati; cvrčati
chisel ['tʃizl] dlijeto; klesati
chivalr|ous ['ʃivəlrəs] viteški; **~y** viteštvo
chlor|ine ['klɔ:ri:n] klor; **~oform** kloroform; kloroformirati
chocolate ['tʃɔkəlit] čokolada
choice [tʃɔis] izbor; izabran; **~ness** odabranost
choir ['kwaiə] (pjevački) zbor; kor (dio crkve)
chok|e [tʃouk] (u)gušiti; gušenje; EL **~ing** coil prigušnica
choler|a ['kɔlərə] kolera; **~ic** koleričan
choose [tʃu:z] izabrati; odlučiti se za
chop [tʃɔp] udar; kotlet; sjeći; **~-house** restoran; **~per** mesarska sjekirica; **~py** nestalan (vjetar); uzburkan (more)
chord [kɔ:d] struna, akord
chorus ['kɔ:rəs] kor; zbor; refren
christen ['krisn] krstiti; **~ing** krštenje
Christian ['kristjən] kršćanski; **~-name** krsno ime; **~ity** kršćanstvo
Christmas ['krisməs] Božić; **~-box** Božićni poklon
chromatic [krə'mætik] kromatski
chromium ['kroumiəm]:

~-plated kromiran
chromo (litograph) ['kroumou('liθəgra:f)] višebojna litografija
chronic ['krɔnik] kroničan; **~le** kronika
chronological [krɔnə'lɔdʒikəl] kronološki
chuck [tʃʌk] *coll* otpuštanje; **~ *out*** izbaciti
chuckle ['tʃʌkl] smijuljiti se
chum [tʃʌm] drug
church [tʃə:tʃ] crkva; **~-service** služba božja; **~yard** groblje
churl [tʃə:l] neotesanac; **~ish** neotesan
churn [tʃə:n] bućkati (maslac); zapjeniti se
cicatrize ['sikətraiz] zarasti
cider ['saidə] jabukovo vino
cigar [si'ga:] cigara; **~-box** kutija za cigare; **~-case** etui za cigare; **~-cutter** nožić za cigare; **~-holder** cigarluk
cigarette [sigə'ret] cigareta
cinder ['sində] žeravica; troska, šljaka
cinema ['sinimə] kino; **~-show** kino predstava
cipher ['saifə] nula; šifrirati
circle ['sə:kl] krug; THEAT ***dress ~*** mezanin; ***upper ~*** balkon; okružiti
circuit ['sə:kit] strujni krug; kružni let; ***short ~*** kratki spoj
circula|r ['sə:kjulə] kružni; ***~r letter*** okružnica; ***~r railway*** kružna pruga; ***~r saw*** kružna pila; **~te** kolati; **~tion** kolanje
circum|ference [sə'kʌmfərəns] obujam; **~navigate** oploviti; **~scribe** opisati; **~stance** okolnost; **~stantial** podroban
circus ['sə:kəs] cirkus; okrugli trg
cistern ['sistən] cisterna
cite [sait] citirati; pozvati (na sud)
citizen ['sitizn] građanin; **~ship** državljanstvo
city ['siti] grad; poslovni dio grada
civil ['sivil] građanski; uljudan; **~ ceremony** civilno vjenčanje; **~ity** [si'viliti] uljudnost; **~ization** civilizacija; **~ize** civilizirati
clad [klæd] odjeven; odjenut
claim [kleim] pravo; zahtjev na; zahtijevati; tvrditi
clamber ['klæmbə] verati se
clammy ['klæmi] hladan i znojan, hladno vlažan
clamour ['klæmə] vika; bučiti
clamp [klæmp] spona; štip
clandestine [klæn'destin] potajan
clang [klæŋ] zveka; zvečati; odjekivati
clap [klæp] udarac; pljeskati
claret ['klærət] crno (trpko) vino
clash [klæʃ] sukob; zveket; sukobiti se
clasp [kla:sp] kopča, spona;

zakvačiti; zakopčati; **~-knife** nož na sklapanje
class [kla:s] klasa; razred; **~ *with*** svrstati sa
classic ['klæsik] klasik; *pl* mrtvi jezici; **~*(al)*** klasičan
classi|fication [klæsifɪ'keiʃən] klasifikacija; **~fy** ['~fai] klasificirati razvrstati
class|-struggle, **~-war** klasna borba
clause [klɔ:z] klauzula; GRAM (kratka) rečenica
claw [klɔ:] kandža; pandža; (rakova) kliješta; grepsti
clay [klei] glina; ilovača; **~ey** glinen
clean [kli:n] čist; čistiti; **~liness** ['klenlinis] čistoća; **~ly** čist; **~se** čistiti
clear [kliə] jasan; bistar; netto; **~ *(up)*** razvedriti (se); razjasniti (se); očistiti ***(of)***; **~ance** razjašnjenje; TECH slobodan prostor; carinjenje; carinska potvrda; ***~ance sale*** rasprodaja
Clearing| House obračunski zavod; **≈ arrangement** klirinški sporazum
clearness ['kliənis] jasnoća; razumljivost
cleave [kli:v] raskoliti; *fig* prionuti ***(to)***
cleft [kleft] pukotina; rascjep
clemency ['klemənsi] blagost
clench [klentʃ] stegnuti; stisnuti (*zube, šaku*)
clergy ['klə:dʒi] svećenstvo; **~man** svećenik
clerical ['klerikəl] svećenički; činovnički
clerk [kla:k] činovnik; *Am* trgovački pomoćnik
clever ['klevə] okretan; pametan; **~ness** spretnost; pamet
click [klik] škljocaj; škljocnuti
client ['klaiənt] klijent
cliff [klif] greben; hridina
climate ['klaimit] klima
climb [klaim] (po)peti se; **~er** alpinist; penjačica; **~ing iron** *pl* dereze
clinch [klintʃ] učvrstiti; COM perfektuirati; **~er** *coll* nepobitan argument
cling [kliŋ]: **~*(to)*** priljepiti se uz
clinic ['klinik] klinika; **~al** klinički; ***~al thermometer*** toplomjer
clink [kliŋk] zveket; **~ glasses** kucnuti se
clip [klip] štipaljka; kvačica; striženje; ***fountain-pen* ~** zakvačka nalivpera; ***(paper)* ~** spojnica; ***tie-*~** igla za kravatu; odrezati; bušiti (kartu); **~per** *Am* veliki putnički avion; **~pers** *pl* mašina za šišanje; **~pings** odresci; novinski izresci
cloak [klouk] ogrtač; **~-room** garderoba; RLW prtljažna garderoba
clock [klɔk] veliki (zidni i sl) sat; ukrasni uzorak na čara-

pi sa strane; **~wise** u smjeru kazaljke na satu
clod [klɔd] gruda (zemlje)
clog [klɔg] panj; klompa; sputati
clon|e [cloun] klon; klonirati; **~ing** kloniranje
close [klous] zatvoren; skriven; diskretan; uzak; tijesan; zbit; prigušen; [klouz] svršetak; ***~ by, ~ to*** blizu, pokraj; **~-up** FILM snimak izbliza; **closing time** vrijeme zatvaranja lokala; redarstveni sat
closet ['klɔzit] kabinet, ormar
closure ['klouʒə]: PARL ***motion for ~*** zahtjev za zaključenje debate
cloth [klɔθ], *pl* **~s** štof; stolnjak; ***dish~*** krpa za suđe; ***face~*** mali ručnik za pranje lica; ***lay the ~*** prostrijeti stol
cloth|e [klouθ] obući; zaodjeti; **~s** *pl* odjeća; odijela; rublje; posteljina; **~es-basket** košara za prljavo rublje; **~es-peg** štipaljka; **~es-press** ormar za odjeću rublje; **~ier** prodavač tekstila; **~ing** odjeća
cloud [klaud] oblak; naoblačiti (se); **~y** oblačan
clove [klouv] klinčić (mirodije)
clover ['klouvə] BOT djetelina
clown [klaun] klaun
club [klʌb] toljaga; klub; udruženje
clue [klu:] *fig* ključ; trag
clump [klʌmp] gruda
clums|iness ['klʌmzinis] nespretnost; **~y** nespretan; nezgrapan
cluster ['klʌstə] grozd; skup
clutch [klʌtʃ] zahvat; MOT kvačilo; zgrabiti
Co. [kou] = **Company**
c/o = **care of**
coach [koutʃ] kočija; vagon; trener; voziti kočiju; trenirati; **~-box** kočijaševo sjedalo; **~man** kočijaš
coagulate [kou'ægjuleit] zgrušati se
coal [koul] (kameni) ugljen; **~-pit** rudnik ugljena; **~-scuttle** kanta za ugljen
coarse [kɔ:s] grub; sirov; **~ness** grubost
coast [koust] obala; *Am* sanjkalište; sanjkati se; **~er** brod obalne plovidbe
coat [kout] kaput(ić), ogrtač; prevlaka; premaz; zaodjeti; pokriti, premazati; ***cut one's ~ according to one's cloth*** pružati se prema pokrivaču; ***~ of arms*** grb; **~ing** pokrivač, prevlaka, premaz
coax [kouks] laskati
cobble ['kɔbl] kocka za popločivanje; krpati cipele; **~r** postolar
cobweb ['kɔbweb] paučina
cock [kɔk] pijetao; **~-chafer** hrušt; **~-crowing** kukurikanje; **~-fight(ing)** borba pijetlova; **~ney** rođeni Londo-

nac; **~pit** pilotska kabina; **~roach** žohar; **~scomb** pijetlova krijesta; **~-sure** *coll* samouvjeren; **~tail** koktel
cocoa ['koukou] kakao
coco-nut ['koukənʌt] kokosov orah
cod [kɔd] bakalar; ***dried ~*** sušeni bakalar
cod-liver oil bakalarevo (riblje) ulje
coefficient [koui'fiʃənt] koji zajedno djeluje; ***~ of safety*** koeficijent sigurnosti
coerc|e [kou'ə:s] prisiliti; **~ion** prisila, prinuda
coexist ['kouig'zist] postojati istodobno; **~ence** koegzistencija, istovremenost
coffee ['kɔfi] kava; **~-bean** zrno kave; **~-grounds** kavin talog; **~-pot** lonac za kavu; **~room** mala blagovaonica (osobito u hotelu)
coffin ['kɔfin] lijes; staviti u lijes
cog [kɔg] TECH zub na zupčaniku
cogitate ['kɔdʒiteit] razmišljati; smišljati
cognac ['kounjæk] konjak
cognition [kɔg'niʃən] spoznaja
cog-wheel TECH zupčanik
coheir ['kou'ɛə] subaštinik; **~ess** subaštinica
cohere [kou'hiə] biti suvisao; **~nce, ~ncy** suvislost; **~nt** suvisao
coil [kɔil] navoj; EL svitak; ***~ up*** smotati (se); krivudati
coin [kɔin] (kovani) novac; kovati; ***~ed money*** kovani novac; **~age** kovanica; **~(-box) telephone** javna telefonska govornica
coincide [kouin'said] podudarati se
coincidence [kou'insidəns] podudaranje
coiner ['kɔinə] krivotvoritelj novca
coke [kouk] koks; koksirati
Col. = **colonel** ['kə:nl]
cold [kould] hladan; hladnoća; prehlada; ***~ meat*** hladni naresci; ***catch ~*** prehladiti se
colic ['kɔlik] kolika
collaborat|e [kə'læbəreit] surađivati; **~or** suradnik
collapse [kə'læps] (doživjeti) slom
collar ['kɔlə] ovratnik; ulaz; ščepati; **~-bone** ključna kost
collation [kɔ'leiʃən] uspoređivanje; laki obrok
colleague ['kɔli:g] kolega
collect ['kɔlekt] kratka molitva; [kə'lekt] skupiti; pridignuti; naplatiti; **~ion** zbirka; ***forcible ~ion*** utjerivanje; **~or** sakupljač; primalac
college ['kɔlidʒ] koledž; fakultet
collide [kə'laid] sudariti se (***with***)
collie ['kɔli] škotski ovčarski pas
collier ['kɔliə] kopač ugljena

collision [kə'liʒən] sudar
colloquial language [kə'loukwiəl] razgovorni jezik
colonel ['kə:nl] pukovnik
coloniz|ation [kɔlənai'zeiʃən] kolonizacija; **~e** kolonizirati, naseliti (se)
colony ['kɔləni] kolonija
colour ['kʌlə] boja; rumen (lica); izlika; **~s** *pl* zastava; bojiti; uljepšati; pocrveniti; **~ed** obojen; crnački; nebijelački; **~less** bezbojan
colt [koult] ždrijebe
column ['kɔləm] stup; stupac; rubrika
comb [koum] češalj; češljati
combat ['kɔmbət] borba; boriti se protiv
combination [kɔmbi'neiʃən] kombinacija; **~s** *pl* gaće i potkošulja u jednom
combine [kəm'bain] spajati, sjediniti; ['kɔmbain] *Am* COM savez trust; kombajn
combusti|ble [kəm'bʌstəbl] zapaljiv; **~s** *pl* gorivo, MOT pogonsko gorivo; **(internal) ~on** [kəm'bʌstʃən] **engine** motor s unutrašnjim sagorijevanjem
come [kʌm] doći; **~ *to*** budući; **~ *along*** pridružiti se; požuri!; **~ *by*** proći pokraj; **~ *for*** doći po; **~ *in*** ući; **~ *up to*** biti ravan, odgovarati; **~ *up with*** dostići; **~-back** *coll fig* povratak; spreman odgovor
comedian [kə'mi:diən] komičar; **~y** ['kɔmidi] komedija
comely ['kʌmli] pristao
comestibles [kə'mestiblz] *pl* jestvine
comfort ['kʌmfət] udobnost; utjeha; tješiti; **~able** udoban; **~er** (topli) šal
comic ['kɔmik] komičar; **~ paper** humoristički časopis; **~ strip** strip
command [kə'ma:nd] zapovjedništvo; zapovijed; ***at*** (ili ***by***) **~ *of*** po naređenju; **~er** zapovjednik; **~er-in-chief** vrhovni zapovijednik; **~ment** REL zapovijed
commemorat|e [kə'meməreit] komemorirati; **~ion** komemoracija
commence [kə'mens] započeti; **~ment** početak
commend [kə'mend] preporučiti; **~able** preporučljiv
comment ['kɔmənt] komentar; **~ *on*** komentirati; **~ary** komentar
commerc|e ['kɔmə:s] trgovina; promet; **~ial** komercijalan; trgovački; **~ialize** komercijalizirati; iznijeti na tržište
commission [kə'miʃən] nalog; provizija; komisija; naložiti; **~er** opunomoćenik, komesar
commit [kə'mit] povjeriti; počiniti; angažirati; **~tee** odbor
commod|e [kə'moud] ko-

moda; bolesnička stolica za obavljanje nužde; **~ity** roba, artikl
common ['kɔmən] zajednički, uobičajen, opći; **♀** ***Council*** općinsko vijeće; **~ law** običajno pravo; ***the British ♀wealth*** Britanska zajednica naroda; **~er** neplemić; član Donjeg doma; **~place** otrcana fraza; banalan; **~ sense** zdravi razum; **~s** *pl* pučani; ***House of ♀s*** Donji dom
commotion [kə'mouʃən] uzbuđenje; komešanje
communal ['kɔmjunl] zajednički; općinski
communica|te [kə'mju:nikeit] saopćiti; održavati vezu, komunicirati (***with***); **~tive** razgovorljiv; **~tion** saopćenje, komunikacija
commun|ion [kə'mju:njən] općenje; pričest; **~ism** komunizam; **~ity** zajednica; zajedništvo
compact ['kɔmpækt] sporazum; [kə'~] kompaktan, sažet; **~ disc** kompaktni disk
companion [kəm'pænjən] pratilac; kompanjon; **~ship** društvo
company ['kʌmpəni] društvo; kompanija;
compar|able ['kɔmpərəbl] usporediv; **~ative** [kəm'pærətiv] komparativan; relativan **~e** usporediti; **~ison** usporedba; GRAM komparacija
compartment [kəm'pa:tmənt] odjelak; kupe
compass ['kʌmpəs] opseg; kompas; **~es** *pl* šestar
compassion [kəm'pæʃən] saučešće; **~ate** sućutan
compatible [kəm'pætəbl] spojiv, koji se podnosi
compatriot [kəm'pætriət] zemljak
compel [kəm'pel] prisiliti
compendious [kəm'pendiəs] skraćen; sažet
compensat|e ['kɔmpenseit] nadoknaditi; odštetiti; izjednačiti; **~ion** nadoknada; odšteta; izjednačenje
compete [kəm'pi:t] natjecati se (***for***); takmičiti se; **~nce** nadležnost; sposobnost; **~nt** nadležan, sposoban
competit|ion [kɔmpi'tiʃən] takmičenje; konkurencija; **~or** takmičar, konkurent
complacent [kəm'pleisnt] spokojan
complain [kəm'plein] žaliti se (***about, of***); potužiti se; **~t** žalba; bolest
complaisant [kəm'pleizənt] uslužan
complet|e [kəm'pli:t] potpun; završiti; **~ion** izvršenje; dopuna
complex|ion [kəm'plekʃən] ten, boja lica; **~ity** zamršenost
compliance [kəm'plaiəns] udovoljenje; ***in ~ with***

prema, u skladu sa
complicate ['kɔmplikeit] komplicirati
compliment ['kɔmplimənt] kompliment; pozdrav; ['₋ment] učiniti kompliment, čestitati
comply [kəm'plai] udovoljiti, poslušati (***with***)
component [kəm'pounənt] sastavni dio
compos|e [kəm'pouz] sastaviti; napisati; umiriti; **₋er** kompozitor; **₋ition** sastavljanje; kompozicija (školski) sastav; **₋itor** slagar; **₋ure** [₋'pouʒə] sabranost
compound ['kɔmpaund] složen; **~ interest** kamate na kamate; **~ fracture** MED komplicirani prelom
comprehen|d [kɔmpri'hend] shvatiti; **₋sible** shvatljiv; **₋sion** shvaćanje; **₋sive** opsežan
compress [kəm'pres] sažeti; ['kɔm₋] oblog; **₋or** TECH kompresor
comprise [kəm'praiz] obuhvaćati, uključivati, sadržati
compromise ['kɔmprəmaiz] kompromis; kompromitirati
compuls|ion [kəm'pʌlʃən] prinuda; **₋ory** obabavezan; ***₋ory expropriation*** prisilno razvlaštenje
compute [kəm'pju:t] (iz)računati; procijeniti (***at***)
comrade ['kɔmrid] drug
concave ['kɔn'keiv] konkavan; **~ mirror** udubljeno ogledalo
conceal [kən'si:l] zatajiti; sakriti
concede [kən'si:d] prepustiti; priznati
conceit [kən'si:t] uobraženost; **₋ed** umišljen; **₋edness** umišljenost
conceive [kən'si:v] zamisliti; začeti
concentr|ate ['kɔnsentreit] koncentrirati (se); zgusnuti; **₋ation camp** koncentracioni logor; **₋ic** koncentričan
conception [kən'sepʃən] predodžba, koncepcija
concern [kən'sə:n] briga; stvar; važnost; ticati se; zanimati; **₋ing** što se tiče, u vezi sa
concert ['kɔnsət] koncert; [kən'sə:t] uskladiti
concession [kən'seʃən] ustupak; dozvola
conciliat|e [kən'silieit] pomiriti; **₋ory** pomirljiv
concise [kən'saiz] sažet
conclu|de [kən'klu:d] zaključiti; završiti; **₋sion** [₋ʒən] zaključak; **₋sive** zaključan; uvjerljiv
concord ['kɔŋkɔ:d] sloga; **₋ant** u skladu
concrete ['kɔnkri:t] konkretan; beton
concur [kən'kə:] sastati se; slagati se; pridonijeti
concussion [kən'kʌʃən] po-

tres
condemn [kən'dem] osuditi; **~ation** [kɔndem'neiʃən] osuda
condense [kən'dens] zgusnuti (se); **~r** kondenzator
condescend [kɔndi'send] udostojati se; **~ing** milostiv
condition [kən'diʃən] stanje; položaj; uvjet; ***~s*** *pl* prilike, okolnosti; **~al** uvjetni, ovisan (***upon***)
condole [kən'doul] izraziti saučešće; **~nce** saučešće
conduc|e [kən'dju:s] voditi, pridonijeti (***to***); **~ive** koji pridonosi
conduct ['kɔndəkt] ponašanje; [kən'dʌkt] voditi; vladati se; **~ing** sprovodni; **~ion** vođenje; **~or** kondukter; EL vodič; dirigent
conduit ['kɔndit] provodna cijev; kanal
cone [koun] stožac; češer
confection|er [kən'ʃekʃənə] slastičar; **~ery** slastice; slastičarna
confedera|cy [kən'fedərəsi] savez; **~te** udružen; saveznik; **~tion** savez
confer [kən'fə:] podijeliti; vijećati; **~ence** konferencija
confess [kən'fes] priznati; **~ion** priznanje; ispovijed; **~or** ispovjednik
confid|ant(e) [kɔnfi'dænt] pouzdanik; **~e** [kən'faid] povjeriti (se); **~ence** povjerenje; samopouzdanje; **~ential** povjerljiv
confine [kən'fain] ograničiti (***to***); ***be ~d*** ležati kao porodilja; **~ment** ograničenje; zatvor; porod
confirm [kən'fə:m] potvrditi; **~ation** potvrda; REL krizma
confiscat|e ['kɔnfiskeit] konfiscirati; **~ion** konfiskacija
conflagration [kɔnflə'greiʃən] (veliki) požar
conflict ['kɔnflikt] borba; sukob; [kən'~] sukobiti se (***with***)
confluence ['kɔnfluəns] stjecište; spajanje
conform [kən'fɔ:m] prilagoditi; ravnati se (***to***); **~ity** sklad; ***in ~ with*** prema
confound [kən'faund] pobrkati; smesti
confront [kən'frʌnt] suočiti (***with***); suprostaviti se
confus|e [kən'fju:z] pobrkati; zbuniti; **~ion** zbrka; zabuna
confute [kən'fju:t] pobiti (tvrdnju)
congenial [kən'dʒi:niəl] srodan (po duši)
congestion [kən'dʒestʃən] navala krvi; zakrčenost
conglomerate [kɔn'glɔmərit] zgrudan; konglomerat; [~reit] zgrudati (se)
congratulat|e [kən'grætjuleit] čestitati; **~ion** čestitanje
congregat|e ['kɔŋgrigeit] sa-

kupiti (se); **~ion** zbor; vjernici, pastva
congress ['kɔŋgres] kongres; **~man** *Am* član Kongresa
conic|(al) ['kɔnik(əl)] čunjast; **~ section** presjek stošca
conjecture [kən'dʒektʃə] nagađati
conjunct|iva [kɔndʒʌŋk'taivə] očna spojnica; **~ivitis** konjunktivitis; **~ure** stjecaj okolnosti
conjur|ation [kɔndʒu'reiʃən] zaklinjanje; **~e** ['kʌndʒə] zaklinjati; **~ *up*** prizvati; dočarati
conne|ct [kə'nekt] povezati (se); ***be well ~cted*** imati dobre veze; **~cting rod** TECH radilica; **~ctive tissue** vezivno tkivo; **~xion** veza; spoj
conquer ['kɔŋkə] pobijediti; osvojiti; **~or** osvajač; pobjednik
conquest ['kɔŋkwest] osvajanje; pobjeda
conscien|ce ['kɔnʃəns] savjest; **~tious** [~ʃi'enʃəs] savjestan
conscious ['kɔnʃəs] svjestan; **~ness** svijest
conscription [kən'skripʃən] opća vojna obaveza
consecrate ['kɔnsikreit] posvetiti; blagosloviti
consecutive [kən'sekjutiv] konsekutivan; za redom
consent [kən'sent] pristanak; dozvola; pristati
consequen|ce ['kɔnsikwens] posljedica; ***of no ~ce*** nevažan; ***in ~ce of*** uslijed; **~tly** dakle; prema tome; kasnije
conserva|tion [kɔnsə:'veiʃən] očuvanje; **~tive** konzervativan [kən'sə:vətiv]
consider [kən'sidə] razmatrati; smatrati; **~able** znatan; priličan; **~ate** obziran; **~ation** razmatranje; obzir
consign [kən'sain] poslati; **~ment** pošiljka; **~ee** naslovnik, primalac; **~or** pošiljač
consist [kən'sist] sastoji se ***(of, in)***
consisten|cy [kən'sistənsi] čvrstoća, gustoća; dosljednost; **~t** dosljedan; u skladu sa, spojiv
consol|ation [kɔnsə'leiʃən] utjeha; **~e** [kən'soul] tješiti
consolidat|e [kən'sɔlideit] učvrstiti; sjediniti; **~ion** konsolidacija
consort ['kɔnsɔ:t] suprug (a)
conspicuous [kən'spikjuəs] upadan; ***be ~ by one's absence*** odsutnošću pokazati svoju vrijednost
conspir|acy [kən'spirəsi] zavjera; **~ator** urotnik; **~e** [~'spaiə] urotiti se
constable ['kʌnstəbl] policajac
constan|cy ['kɔnstənsi] postojanost; **~t** stalan; vjeran, postojan

consternation [kɔnstə:'neiʃən] zaprepaštenje
constituen|cy [kən'stitjuənsi] birači; izborni kotar; **~t** sastavni dio
constitut|e ['kɔnstitju:t] sačinjavati; predstavljati; osnovati; postaviti; **~ion** sastav; konstitucija; ustav
constrain [kən'strein] prisiliti; **~t** prinuda
construct [kən'strʌkt] (sa-)graditi; **~ion** (iz)gradnja; **~or** graditelj
consul ['kɔnsəl] konzul; **ⵒ General** generalni konzul
consult [kən'sʌlt] posavjetovati se; potražiti (u knjizi); **~ing hours** vrijeme ordiniranja; **~ing room** liječnička ordinacija
consume [kən'sju:m] potrošiti; **~r** potrošač; **~r goods** roba široke potrošnje
consummate [kən'sʌmit] savršen; ['kɔnsʌmeit] dovršiti
consumption [ken'sʌmpʃən] potrošnja; MED sušica
contact ['kɔntækt] dodir; kontakt; [kən'tækt] naći, kontaktirati
contagio|n [kən'teidʒən] zaraza; **~us** zarazan
contain [kən'tein] sadržavati; **~er** posuda; ambalaža
contemplat|e ['kɔntempleit] razmatrati; **~ion** razmatranje; **~ive** kontemplativan
contemporary [kən'tempərəri] suvremen; suvremenik
contempt [kən'tempt] prezir; **~ible** prezira vrijedan; **~uous** preziran
content [kən'tent] zadovoljan; zadovoljiti; ***to one's heart's ~*** do mile volje; **~s** ['kɔntents] *pl* sadržaj; **bone of ~ion** kamen smutnje; **~ment** zadovoljstvo
contest ['kɔntest] borba; [kən'test] osporavati; **~able** prijeporan
context ['kɔntekst] kontekst
continent ['kɔntinənt] kontinent; **ⵒ** Evropa; **~al** kontinentalan
continu|al [kən'tinjuəl] neprekidan; stalan; **~ance** trajanje, nastavljanje; **~ation** nastavak; ***~ation school*** produžna škola; **~e** nastaviti; zadržati; ***to be ~ed*** nastavak slijedi; **~ous** neprekidan; **~ous current** istosmjerna struja
contour ['kɔntuə] kontura
contraband ['kɔntrəbænd] krijumčaren; krijumčarena roba
contract [kən'trækt] stisnuti (se); navući (bolest); ugovoriti; ['kɔn~] ugovor; **~ing party** ugovorna strana; **~or** poduzetnik; **~ual** ugovorni
contradict [kɔntrə'dikt] protusloviti; **~ion** protuslovje; **~ory** protuslovan
contrary ['kɔntrəri] suprotan; nepovoljan; ***on the ~***

naprotiv
contrast ['kɔntræst] oprečnost; [kən'træst] kontrastirati; odskakivati
contravention [kɔntrə'venʃən] kršenje
contribut|e [kən'tribju:t] pridonijeti; **~ion** doprinos; **~or** suradnik; **~ory** doprinosni
contrite ['kɔntrait] skrušen, pokajnički
contriv|ance [kən'traivəns] izum; domišljatost; naprava; **~e** izumiti; postići; **~er** domišljata osoba
control [kən'troul] nadzor; vlast nad; ***Government ~, State ~*** državni nadzor; ***foreign ~*** strana uprava; ***remote*** ili ***distant ~*** teledirigiranje; RADIO ***volume ~*** regulator zvuka; nadzirati; **~** ***(oneself)*** obuzdati (se); **~ler** kontrolor; nadglednik; MOT vozareva kočnica
controversy ['kɔntrəvə:si] spor(no pitanje)
contus|e [kən'tju:z] nabiti, ostaviti; modrica; **~ion** naboj, modrica
convalesce [kɔnvə'les] oporavljati se; **~nce** oporavljanje; **~nt** koji se oporavlja
convenien|ce [kən'vi:njəns] pogodnost; ***at your earliest ~ce*** što prije moguće; **~t** pogodan
convent ['kɔnvənt] samostan; **~ion** kongres; **~ional** konvencionalan
convers|ation [kɔnvə'seiʃən] razgovor; **~e** razgovarati; **~ion** pretvaranje; obraćanje; prelaženje
convey [kən'vei] prenijeti; prevesti; **~ance** otpremanje; odvoz; priopćenje; **~or (belt)** konvejer, tekuća vrpca
convict ['kɔnvikt] kažnjenik; robijaš; [kən'-] osuditi ***(of*** na)
convince [kən'vins] uvjeriti ***(of*** u)
convocation [kɔnvə'keiʃən] sazivanje
convoy ['kɔnvɔi] pratnja; pratiti
convulsion [kən'vʌlʃən] grčevi; *fig* potres
cook [kuk] kuhanje; kuhar(ica); kuhati
cool [ku:l] prohladan; hladnokrvan; ohladiti se; **~ness** hladnoća; svježina
coolie [ku:li] kuli
cooper ['ku:pə] bačvar; badnjar
co-operat|e [kou'ɔpəreit] surađivati; **~ion** suradnja; **~ive** spreman na suradnju; ***~ive society*** potrošačka zadruga; ***~ive store*** zadružna prodavaonica
cop [kɔp] *sl* policajac
cope [koup] ogledati se; biti dorastao ***(with*** čemu)
copious ['koupjəs] obilan; razvučen

copper ['kɔpə] bakar; bakreni sitniš; ~ **plate (engraving)** bakrorez
copy ['kɔpi] kopija; prijepis; uzorak; primjerak (*knjige*); broj (*novina*); ***fair*** ~ čistopis; ***rough*** ~ koncept; prepisivati, kopirati; **~-book** bilježnica; **~ing-ink** tinta za kopiranje; **~ing-press** tijesak za kopiranje; **~right** autorsko pravo
coral ['kɔrəl] koralj
cord [kɔ:d] špaga; konop; vezati; ***~ed*** rebrast (tkanina); **~age** užad; užarska roba
cordial ['kɔ:diəl] srdačan; želučani liker
corduroys ['kɔ:dərɔiz] *pl* hlače od kordsamta
core [kɔ:] srž; srčika
cork [kɔ:k] pluto; (za)čepiti; **~screw** vadičep
corn [kɔ:n] žito; *Am* kukuruz; kurje oko; usoliti; **~ed beef** konzervirana govedina; **~-cob** *Am* klip kukuruza
corner ['kɔ:nə] ugao; kut; **~-house** kuća na uglu
cornet ['kɔ:nit] MUS kornet; tuljac
Cornish ['kɔ:niʃ] kornvalski; iz Cornwalla
coron|ation [kɔrə'neiʃən] krunidba; **~er** ['-nə] mrtvozornik; **~et** ['-it] dijadem
corpor|al ['kɔ:pərəl] tjelesni; kaplar, desetar; **~ation** korporacija; *Am* dioničko društvo
corpse [kɔ:ps] lešina
corpulen|ce ['kɔ:pjuləns], **~cy** debljina; **~t** debeo
corpus ['kɔ:pəs] korpus, zbirka, tijelo; **♀ Christi** Tijelovo
corral [kɔ'ra:l] obor (za stoku)
correct [kə'rekt] tačan, ispravan; ispraviti, popraviti; korigirati; CHEM razblažiti; **~ion** popravak, ispravak; kazna; **~ness** ispravnost
correspond [kɔris'pɔnd] odgovarati (***to*** čemu); dopisivati se; **~ence** podudaranje; dopisivanje; **~ent** korespondent; **~ing** odgovarajući
corridor ['kɔridɔ:] hodnik; **~-train** vlak s hodnikom koji spaja vagone
corrigible ['kɔridʒəbl] ispravljiv
corroborate [kə'rɔbəreit] potvrditi
corro|de [kə'roud] izjedati; nagrizati; **~sive** TECH sredstvo koje nagriza; **~sion** nagrizanje
corrugate ['kɔrugeit] narebriti; nažlijebiti; **~d iron** valoviti lim
corrupt [kə'rʌpt] pokvaren; pokvariti; podmititi; **~ion** pokvarenost; podmitljivost
corset ['kɔ:sit] steznik
cosiness ['kouzinis] udobnost
cost [kɔst] cijena; trošak; ***I***

learnt it to my ~ naučio sam to na vlastitoj koži; koštati; COM izračunati cijenu koštanja
costermonger ['kɔstəmʌŋgə] ulični prodavač
cost|ly ['kɔstli] skup; dragocjen; **~-price** cijena koštanja; nabavna cijena
costume ['kɔstjuːm] odjeća; odjenuti
cosy ['kouzi] prijatan; poklopac za čajnik
cot [kɔt] poljski krevet; kolijevka
cottage ['kɔtidʒ] kućica; vikendica
cotton ['kɔtn] pamuk; pamučno platno; pamučni
couch [kautʃ] ležaj; ležaljka; kauč; prilegnuti; čučnuti; **~ potato** rob televizije
cough [kɔf] kašalj; kašljati
council ['kaunsl] vijeće; **~lor** ['~silə] vijećnik
counsel ['kaunsəl] savjet; odvjetnik; savjetovati; **~lor** savjetnik
count [kaunt] brojenje; zbroj; grof; brojati; ***~ upon a p*** *fig* računati s nekim
countenance ['kauntinəns] lice; duševni mir
counter ['kauntə] brojilo; brojilac; žeton; tezga; protivno; uzvraćati udarac (u boksu); **~act** suzbijati; **~balance** protuteža; uravnotežiti; COM izravnati; **~clockwise** obratno od smjera kazaljke na satu; **~feit** ['~fit] patvoren; krivotvoren; **~feiter** krivotvorina; krivotvoren **~part** par(alela) duplikat; **~sign** supotpisati
countess ['kauntis] grofica
count|ing-house poslovnica; **~less** bezbrojan
countrified ['kʌntrifaid] seljački; neuglađen
country ['kʌntri] selo; predio; zemlja, domovina; **~man** seljak; zemljak; **~woman** seljanka; zemljakinja
county ['kaunti] grofovija
coupl|e ['kʌpl] par; spojiti; **~ing** TECH spojka
courage ['kʌridʒ] hrabrost; **~ous** [kə'reidʒəs] hrabar, odvažan
course [kɔːs] tok; MAR i COM kurs; hod; UNIV kolegij; jelo (po redu); utrka; trkalište; ***in due ~*** kad bude vrijeme; redovitim putem; ***of ~*** jasno, naravno
court [kɔːt] dvor; sud; udvarati se; **~eous** uljudan; **~esy** uljudnost; **~ier** dvorjanin; **~-martial** vojni sud; **~-plaster** ljepljivi melem; **~ship** udvaranje; **~yard** dvorište
cousin ['kʌzn] bratić; sestrična
cover ['kʌvə] pokrivač; poklopac; omot; pokrov; zaklon; zaštita; MOT vanjska guma (kod dvokolice);

stolni pribor za jednu osobu; pokriti; prevući; **~ing** pokrov, prevlaka; ***floor ~ing*** materijal za pod; **~let** prekrivač za krevet; **~t** skrovit; udata; skrovište; guštara
covetous ['kʌvitəs] gramzljiv; **~ness** gramzljivost
cow [kau] krava
coward ['kauəd] kukavica; plašljivac; **~ice** kukavičluk
cow|boy dječak koji čuva krave; *Am* kauboj; **~catcher** RLW *Am* plug (lokomotive)
cower ['kauə] čučati; zguriti se
cowhide ['kauhaid] goveđa koža
cox|comb ['kɔkskoum] kicoš; budala; **~swain** ['kɔks(-wei)n] kormilar
coy [kɔi] plah, bojažljiv
crab [kræb] rak; morski rak
crack [kræk] prasak; pukotina; *cocaine* crack; praskati; slomiti; skršiti; razbiti; ***~ a joke*** ispričati šalu; **~ed** napuknut; **~er** bombon praskalica; *Am* keks; **~le** pucketati; **~nel** tanki dvopek
cradle ['kreidl] kolijevka; položiti u kolijevku
craft [kra:ft] lukavost; obrt; vozilo; letalo, plovni objekt; **~sman** obrtnik; **~smanship** vještina; izrada; **~y** lukav, prepreden
crag [kræg] litica; **~gy** krševit
cram [kræm] nabiti; *coll* bubati
cramp [kræmp] grč; TECH spona
cranberry ['krænbəri] BOT brusnica
crane [krein] ždral; dizalica; ***~ one's neck*** kriviti vrat
crank [kræŋk] ručka; **~ (*up*)** MOT ručno pokrenuti; **~shaft** TECH koljenčasta osovina; radilica
crape [kreip] krep, flor
crash [kræʃ] slom; AERO pad aviona, udes; tresnuti; AERO srušiti se; **~-helmet** zaštitni šljem
crate [kreit] sandučić od letava; pletena košara; sanduk
crater ['kreitə] krater; rupa granate
crav|e [kreiv] usrdno moliti; čeznuti za; žudjeti; **~ing** čežnja, žudnja
crawl [krɔ:l] puzanje; gmizanje; puzati; gmizati; SPORT kraul
crayfish ['kreifiʃ] rak (potočni)
crazy ['kreizi] lud
creak [kri:k] škripati
cream [kri:m] vrhnje; krema; obirati vrhnje; ***cold ~*** krema za lice
crease [kri:s] nabor; pregib; ***well ~d trousers*** hlače s oštrom crtom
creat|e [kri:'eit] stvarati; THEAT kreirati; izazvati; **~ion** stvaranje; **~or** stvaralac; **~ure** ['kri:tʃə] stvor
credentials [kri'denʃəlz] *pl*

vjerodajnice, akreditivi
credib|ility [kredi'biliti] vjerodostojnost; **~le** ['-dəbl] vjerodostojan
credit ['kredit] povjerenje; vjerodostojnost; čast; kredit; ***letter of ~*** kreditno pismo; pripisati; kreditirati; **~able** vrijedan povjerenja; **~or** vjerovnik
credulity [kri'dju:liti] lakovjernost
creed [kri:d] vjera, vjerovanje
creek [kri:k] zaton; draga; *Am* rječica
creep [kri:p] puzati (i *fig*); ***my flesh ~s*** jeza me podilazi; **~er** penjačica; **~y** jeziv
cremat|ion [kri'meiʃən] spaljivanje (leša); **~orium**, *Am* **~ory** krematorij
crepuscular [kri'pʌskjulə] sumračan
crescent ['kresnt] polumjesec
crest [krest] kresta; kukma; perjanica; vrhunac; **~fallen** pokunjen
crevasse [kri'væs] raspuklina (u glečeru)
crevice ['krevis] pukotina
crew [kru:] posada, momčad
crib [krib] jasle; škola; skriveni prijevod
crick [krik] grč
cricket ['krikit] zrikavac; SPORT kriket; ***not ~*** nepošteno
crier ['kraiə] izvikivač; telal
crim|e [kraim] zločin; prestup; kriminal; **~inal** ['kriminl] prestupnički; kriminalac
crimson ['krimzn] grimiz(an); karmin; zagasitocrven
cringle [krindʒ] puzati pred (to)
cripple ['kripl] bogalj; osakatiti; *fig* onemogućiti
cris|is, *pl* **-es** ['kraisis, -i:z] kriza
crisp [krisp] svjež; hrskav; kovrčati se
criti|c ['kritik] kritičar; **~cism** kritika; **~cize** kritizirati; osuđivati
croak [krouk] graktati, kreketati; **~er** *fig* zloguki prorok
crochet ['krouʃei] kačkanje; kačkati
crockery ['krɔkəri] zemljano suđe
crocodile ['krɔkədail] krokodil
crooked ['krukid] kriv
crop [krɔp] guša; usjevi, prihod
cross [krɔs] križ; križanje; ljut (***with*** na); ***be at ~ purposes*** krivo se razumjeti; **~-beam** nosač; traverza; **~-examination** unakrsno ispitivanje; **~ing** križanje; **~-word puzzle** križaljka
crotchet ['krɔtʃit] kukica
crouch [krautʃ] čučnuti
croup [kru:p] MED krup,

gušobolja
crow [krou] vrana; graktati; **~-bar** željezna poluga
crowd [kraud] mnoštvo, gomila; gomilati (se); nabiti; vrvjeti
crown [kraun] kruna; okruniti
crucible ['kru:sibl] lonac za taljenje
crucifixion [kru:si'fikʃən] raspeće
crude [kru:d] sirov; nerafiniran
cruel ['kruəl] okrutan; nemilosrdan; **~ty** okrutnost
cruise [kru:z] krstariti; kružno putovanje (brodom); **~r** MAR krstaš, krstarica
crumb [krʌm] mrvica; **~le** (raz)mrviti (se)
crumple ['krʌmpl] (iz)gužvati (se); (z)gnječiti (se)
crusade [kru:'seid] križarska vojna
crush [krʌʃ] gužva; smrskati; zdrobiti
crust [krʌst] kora; okoriti se (snijeg); **~ed** pokrit kožicom (staro vino); uvriježen (običaj)
crutch [krʌtʃ] štaka
cry [krai] uzvik; dozivanje; vikati; plakati
crystal ['kristl] kristal; **~lize** kristalizirati
ct(s) = cents
CU ['si:ju:] = **see you** CU
cub [kʌb] mladunče (lava itd.)
cub|e [kju:b] kocka; **~ic root** kubni korijen
cuckold ['kʌkəld] rogonja; učiniti rogonjom
cuckoo ['kuku:] kukavica
cucumber ['kju:kəmbə] krastavac
cudgel ['kʌdʒəl] kijača, toljaga; **~ one's brains** razbijati glavu;
cue [kju:] štap za biljar; znak (riječ)
cuff [kʌf] manšeta, suvratak (rukava)
culminat|e ['kʌlmineit] kulminirati; **~ion** *fig* vrhunac, najviša tačka
culp|able ['kʌlpəbl] kriv; kažnjiv; **~rit** krivac; optuženik
cultivat|e ['kʌltiveit] kultivirati; obrađivati; njegovati; **~ion** kultiviranje *fig* njegovanje; **~or** zemljoradnik
cultur|al ['kʌltʃərəl] kulturan; kulturni; **~e** ['-tʃə] kultura; gajenje; **~ed** obrazovan
cumin ['kʌmin] BOT kumin, kim
cumulative ['kju:mjulətiv] koji se gomila
cunning ['kʌniŋ] lukav; lukavost
cup [kʌp] šalica; pehar; pokal; **~board** ['kʌbəd] kredenc, ormar za posuđe
curable ['kjuərəbl] izlječiv
curate ['kjuərit] kapelan

curbstone ['kə:bstoun] kameni rub pločnika
curd [kə:d] gruševina, skuta; **~le** zgrušati (se)
cure [kjuə] liječenje; lijek; liječiti; soliti
curio|sity [kjuəri'ɔsiti] radoznalost; raritet; **~us** ['~riəs] radoznao; čudan
curl [kə:l] uvojak; kovrčati; **~ing irons**, **~ing tongs** "brenšer", kovrčaljka (za kosu); kovrčav
currant ['kʌrənt] grožđica; ribiz
currency ['kʌrənsi] kolanje; valuta
current ['kʌrənt] struja; tok; tekući, sadašnji
curse [kə:s] prokletstvo; prokleti
curtail [kə:'teil] potkresati; skratiti (***of*** za)
curtain ['kə:tn] zastor; zavjesa; **~-lecture** "propovijed" žene mužu prije spavanja
curts(e)y ['kə:tsi] "kniks"; "kniksati"
curvature ['kə:vətʃə] **of the spine** iskrivljenost kičme;
curve ['kə:v] krivulja; (is)kriviti (se)
cushion ['kuʃən] (tvrd) jastuk; obložiti; ublažiti
custard ['kʌstəd] krema od jaja
custody ['kʌstədi] nadzor; zatvor
custom ['kʌstəm] navika; običaj; mušterije; **~s** carina; **~ary** uobičajen; **~er** kupac; ***queer ~er*** čudak; **~-house** carinarnica; **~-house officer** carinik
cut [kʌt] (od-, na-, ra-, pro-, pre-) sjeći, rezati; odrezak; porezotina; rezanje (igraćih karata); prekid; redukcija; (***short***) ~ prečac; ~ ***off*** *tel* prekinuti; ~ ***out*** EL isključiti; ~ ***short*** prekinuti; ***be ~ out for*** biti stvoren za; ***you have your work ~ out with him*** imat ćeš dosta posla s njim; **~ glass** brušeno staklo; **~ teeth** dobijati zube
cutler ['kʌtlə] nožar; **~y** jedaći pribor
cutlet ['kʌtlit] kotlet
cut|-out MOT zaklopac ispuha; **~ter** krojilac; MAR kuter; **~ting** zajedljiv; oštar; izrezak; odrezak
cwt. = **hundredweight**
cyber... [,saibə] CYBER-
cycl|e ['saikl] ciklus; bicikl; voziti bicikl; ***four-~e engine*** četverotaktni motor; **~ist** biciklist
cylinder ['silində] cilindar; valjak
cynic ['sinik] cinik; **~al** ciničan
Czech [tʃek] Čeh(inja); češki

D

dab [dæb] lupkanje; mrlja; (lako) dodirnuti
dabble ['dæbl] brljati; baviti se čim (amaterski)
daddy ['dædi] tatica
dagger ['dægə] bodež
daily ['deili] dnevni(o); dnevne novine
daint|iness ['deintinis] nježnost; izbirljivost; **~y** nježan; izbirljiv; slastan; poslastica
dairy ['dɛəri] mljekarstvo
daisy ['deizi] tratinčica
dam [dæm] brana; zagraditi branom
damage ['dæmidʒ] šteta; *pl* odšteta; oštetiti
damask ['dæməsk] damast
damn [dæm] proklinjati; osuditi
damp [dæmp] vlažan, pun pare; vlaga; (*Am* i **~en**) ovlažiti; prigušiti; **~er** prigušivač
danc|e [da:ns] ples; plesati; **~er** plesač(ica); **~ing room** plesna dvorana
dandy ['dændi] kicoš
Dane [dein] Danac, Dankinja
danger ['deindʒə] opasnost; **~ous** opasan
dangle ['dæŋgl] visjeti
Danish ['deiniʃ] danski
dapple|d ['dæpld] šaren, pjegav; **~-grey** zelenko (konj)
dare [dɛə] usuditi se; prkositi
daring ['dɛəriŋ] smion; odvažnost
dark [da:k] taman; mračan; ***leap in the ~*** skok u nepoznato; **~ *lantern*** svjetiljka sljepica; **~en** potamniti; **~ness** tama; **~-room** tamna komora
darling ['da:liŋ] dragi; ljubimac
darn [da:n] (po)krpati (čarape); ***~ing-needle*** igla za štopanje; ***~ing yarn*** konac za štopanje
dart [da:t] sulica; strelica; baciti; pojuriti
dash [dæʃ] jurenje; nalet; dodatak (ruma i sl.); povlaka; ***cut a ~*** *coll* ostaviti blistav dojam; zavitlati; razbiti; uništiti (nadu); srnuti; ***~ through*** projuriti; **~-board** blatobran; MOT ploča za instrumente; **~ing** vatren
date [deit] datum; vrijeme; rok; *Am coll* sastanak; datirati; ***out of ~*** zastarjeo; ***up to ~*** suvremen; ažuran
date [deit] datulja
daughter ['dɔ:tə] kći; **~-in-law** snaha
dauntless ['dɔ:ntlis] neustrašiv
dawdle ['dɔ:dl] *coll* dangubiti
dawn [dɔ:n] zora; svitati

day [dei] dan; rok; ***this ~*** danas; ***the other ~*** neki dan; ***~'s work*** dnevni posao; **~break** svitanje; **~light** dnevno svjetlo; **~ spa** rekreacijski centar
daze [deiz], **dazzle** ['dæzl] zabliještiti
dead [ded] mrtav; zamro; pust; nepokretan; dubok (san); neisporučiv (pismo); ***~ slow!*** najmanjom brzinom!; **~-beat** nasmrt umoran; **~en** umrtviti, prigušiti; **~lock**: ***reach a ~*** doći do mrtve tačke, zapeti; **~ly** ubitačan
deaf [def] gluh (***to*** za); zaglušiti; **~ness** gluhoća
deal [di:l] dio; količina; posao; (ras-, po-)dijeliti; postupati; ***~ with*** baviti se sa; ***a great ~*** mnogo; **~er** trgovac; **~ings** *pl* poslovi; kontakt
dear [diə] skup; drag
dearth [də:θ] nestašica
death [deθ] smrt; **~rate** smrtnost
debarkation [di:ba:'keiʃən] iskrcavanje
debase [di'beis] smanjiti vrijednost
debate [di'beit] debata; debatirati
debauch [di'bɔ:tʃ] raskalašenost
debenture [di'bentʃə] obveznica
debit ['debit] dugovanje; ***to the ~ of*** na teret; zadužiti; **~ card** debitna kartica
debt [det] dug; **~or** dužnik(-ca)
decadence ['dekədəns] propadanje
decanter [di'kæntə] brušena stolna boca
decapitate [di'kæpiteit] odrubiti glavu
decay [di'kei] propadanje; propadati; raspadati se
decease [di'si:s] smrt; preminuti
deceit [di'si:t] prevara; **~ful** prevaran
deceive [di'si:v] zavesti; obmanuti
December [di'sembə] prosinac, decembar
decen|cy ['di:snsi] pristojnost, doličnost; **~t** pristojan
deception [di'sepʃən] prevara
decide [di'said] odlučiti (se); **~d** odlučan
decipher [di'saifə] dešifrirati
decision [di'siʒən] odluka; **~ board** komisija za donošenje odluka
decisive [di'saisiv] odlučan, presudan
deck paluba; **~-chair** ležaljka
declaim [di'kleim] deklamirati; napadati
declaration [deklə'reiʃən] deklaracija
declare [di'klɛə] izjaviti; deklarirati
decline [di'klain] opadanje; slabljenje; opasti

decode [di'koud] dešifrirati
de|compose [di:kəm'pouz] raščlaniti; raspadati se; **~compressor** MOT dekompresor; **~control** ukinuti privredna ograničenja
decorat|e ['dekəreit] ukrasiti; odlikovati; **~ion** odlikovanje
decorous ['dekərəs] doličan
decrease ['di:kri:s] smanjivanje; [di:'kri:s] opasti
decree [di'kri:] dekret; naredba; donijeti naredbu
decry [di'krai] kuditi
dedicat|e ['dedikeit] posvetiti; **~ion** posveta; požrtvovnost
deduce [di'dju:s] zaključivati
deduct [di'dakt] odbiti, odračunati; **~ion** odbijanje
deed [di:d] djelo, čin; isprava, dokument
deem [di:m] smatrati
deep [di:p] dubok; dubina; **~en** produbiti (se); **~ness** dubina
deer [diə] jelen; jelenska divljač
deface [di'feis] nagrditi
defalcation [di:fæl'keiʃən] pronevjerenje
defame [di'feim] klevetati
defeat [di'fi:t] poraz; poraziti; osujetiti
defect [di'fekt] nedostatak; mana; **~ion** otpad; **~ive** manjkav
defen|ce [di'fens] obrana; **~celess** nezaštićen; **~d** braniti (se); **~dant** optuženik; **~sive** obramben
defer [di'fə:] odgađati
deference ['defərəns] pokoravanje; poštovanje
defian|ce [di'faiəns] prkos; neposluh; **~t** prkosan
deficien|cy [di'fiʃənsi] manjak; **~t** nedostatan
deficit ['defisit] manjak
defile ['di:fail] klanac; [di'fail] defilirati
defin|e [di'fain] definirati; odrediti; **~ite** ['definit] određen; **~ition** definicija; OPT oštrina; **~itive** definitivan
deflat|e [di'fleit] (balon itd.) ispuhati; smanjiti inflaciju; **~ion** deflacija (valute)
deform [di'fɔ:m] izobličiti, deformirati; **~ity** izobličenje, nagrđenost
defraud [di'frɔ:d] prevariti (***of***)
defray [di'frei] snositi (troškove), podmiriti
deft spretan, okretan
defy izazivati, prkositi
degenerat|e [di'dʒenəreit] izroditi se, degenerirati se; **~ion** degeneracija
degrad|ation [degrə'deiʃən] degradacija; **~e** degradirati
degree [di'gri:] stupanj (i *fig*); ***by ~s*** postepeno; ***in some ~*** donekle
deign [dein] udostojati se
delay [di'lei] odgoda; zakaš-

njenje; odgoditi
delegate ['deligeit] delegirati; ['~git] delegat
deliberate [di'libərit] namjeran; [~reit] vijećati
delica|cy ['delikəsi] poslastica; istančanost; **~te** nježan; slabašan
delicious [di'liʃəs] ukusan
delight [di'lait] uživanje; uživati u; **~ful** divan
delineate [di'linieit] opisati
delinquent [di'liŋkwənt] prekršitelj
deliver [di'livə] osloboditi; isporučiti; MED pomoći pri porodu; predati (poruku); održati (govor); dostaviti (poštu); **~ance** izbavljenje; **~y** dostava, isporuka; predaja; način predavanja; porod
delude [di'lu:d] varati; obmanuti
deluge ['delju:dʒ] poplava
delusi|on [di'lu:ʒən] zabluda; iluzija; **~ve** [~siv] varav
demagogue ['deməgɔg] demagog
demand [di'ma:nd] zahtjev; potražnja; zahtijevati; ***on ~*** na zahtjev
demeanour [di'mi:nə] ponašanje
demesne [di'mein] posjed, domena
demi ... ['demi] polu-
demilitariz|ation ['di:militərai'zeiʃən] demilitarizacija; **~e** demilitarizirati
demob(ilize) ['di:'mɔb(di:'moubilaiz)] demobilizirati
democra|cy [di'mɔkrəsi] demokracija; **~t** ['deməkræt] demokrat; **~tic** demokratski; **~tize** demokratizirati
demoli|sh [di'mɔliʃ] demolirati; **~tion** [demo'liʃən] razaranje
demon ['di:mən] demon; zloduh
demonstrat|e ['demənstreit] dokazati; pokazati; demonstrirati; **~ion** demonstracija; prikazivanje; dokazivanje
demur [di'mə:] oklijevanje
demure [di'mjuə] trijezan; smjeran
den jazbina; *coll* radna soba
denial [di'naiəl] nijekanje; demanti
denominate [di'nɔmineit] nazvati
denote [di'nout] označiti
denounce [di'nauns] tužiti
dens|e [dens] gust; zbit; **~ity** gustoća
dent [dent] ulupina
dent|ifrice ['dentifris] zubna pasta (prah); **~ist** zubar; **~ure** umjetno zubalo
denude [di'nju:d] ogoliti
deny [di'nai] zanijekati; demantirati
depart [di'pa:t] otputovati; odstupiti (***from*** od); **~ment** odjel; *Am* ***State* ~*ment*** ministarstvo vanjskih poslova; **~ment store(s)** robna kuća; **~ure** odlazak

depend [di'pend] **(up)on** ovisiti o; osloniti se na; ***it ~s*** to ovisi; **~ant** *Am* član obitelji (vojne osobe); **~ence** ovisnost
depict [di'pikt] ocrtati
depilatory [de'pilətəri] depilator
deplorable [di'plɔːrəbl] za osudu
depopulation ['diːpopju'leiʃən] opadanje (gubitak) stanovništva
deport [di'pɔːt] deportirati; **~ation** deportacija
depose [di'pouz] svrgnuti; dati izjavu
deposit [di'pɔzit] polaganje; CHEM taloženje; ulaganje (u banku); uplata; deponirati; taložiti (se)
depot ['depou] depo, skladište; *Am* ['diːpou] željeznička stanica
deprecat|e ['deprikeit] kuditi; **~ion** neodobravanje
depreciat|e [di'priːʃieit] sniziti vrijednost; omalovažavati; **~ion** omalovažavanje; COM amortizacija
depress [di'pres] pritisnuti; sniziti; deprimirati; **~ed** potišten; **~ion** potištenost; (***barometric***) **~*ion*** niski pritisak
deprive [di'praiv] lišiti
depth [depθ] dubina
deputy ['depjuti] zastupnik
derail [di'reil] iskočiti iz tračnica; **~ment** iskakanje vlaka
derange [di'reindʒ] poremetiti (i duševno)
derision [di'riʒən] izrugivanje
derive [di'raiv] izvesti; potjecati; (korist) izvlačiti (***from*** od)
derogate ['derəgeit] prikraćivati (***from***)
descend [di'send] sići, spustiti se; potjecati; MIN spustiti se u rov; **~ant** potomak
descent [di'sent] silaženie; potjecanje; MIN silaženje u rov; strmina
describe [dis'kraib] opisati, prikazati
description [dis'kripʃən] opis
desert ['dezət] pust; pustinja; [di'zəːt] napustiti; dezertirati; **~ion** napuštanje; dezertiranje
deserve [di'zəːv] zaslužiti, zavrijediti
design [di'zain] nacrt; uzorak; desen; TECH konstrukcija, izvedba; konstruirati; namijeniti; **~er** dizajner; konstruktor
designat|e ['dezigneit] označiti; **~ion** oznaka
desir|able [di'zaiərəbl] poželjan; ugodan; **~e** želja; željeti; **~ous** željan
desist [di'zist] odustati (***from***)
desk pisaći stol; školska klupa
desolat|e ['desəleit] opusto-

šiti; ['-lit] pust; ~ion opustošenje
despair [dis'pɛə] očaj; očajavati
desperate ['despərit] očajan
despise [dis'paiz] prezirati
despite [dis'pait] prezir; prkos; ~ ***of*** usprkos
despond [dis'pɔnd] očajavati; ~ency očaj
dessert [di'zə:t] slatko (voće) poslije jela, slatkiši
destin|ation [desti'neiʃən] odredište, cilj; ~e ['-tin] odrediti; ~y ['-tini] sudbina
destitut|e ['destitju:t] siromašan; lišen; ~ion oskudica; bijeda
destroy [dis'trɔi] razoriti; ~er razarač
destruct|ion [dis'trʌkʃən] razorenje; ~ive razoran
detach [di'tætʃ] odvojiti; odijeliti; ~ment odvajanje; odred
detail ['di:teil] potankost, pojedinost; potanko opisati; ~ed detaljan
detain [di'tein] zadržati, zaustaviti
detect [di'tekt] otkriti; ~ive detektiv; ~or radio detektor
detention [di'tenʃən] pritvor
deter [di'tə:] odvratiti
deteriorate [di'tiəriəreit] pogoršati se
determin|ate [di'tə:minit] određen; ~ation odlučnost; određenje; ~e odrediti; odlučiti
detest [di'test] osjećati odvratnost prema; ~able odvratan
detonation [detou'neiʃən] eksplozija; prasak
detract [di'trækt] kuditi
detriment ['detrimənt] šteta; uštrb
devaluat|ion [di:vælju'eiʃən] devalvacija; ~e devalvirati
devastate ['devəsteit] opustošiti
develop [di'veləp] razviti (se); ~er PHOT razvijač; ~ment razvoj
deviat|e ['di:vieit] zastraniti; ~ion devijacija
device [di'vais] naprava; sredstvo; crtež; geslo
devil ['devl] đavo; ~ish đavolji
devise [di'vaiz] izmisliti
devoid [di'vɔid] **(of)** lišen, bez
devolve [di'vɔlv] preći ***(upon)***
devot|e [di'vout] posvetiti; ~ed odan; ~ion odanost; pobožnost
devour [di'vauə] proždrijeti
devout [di'vaut] pobožan
dew [dju:] rosa; ~y rosan
dexter|ity [deks'teriti] spretnost; ~ous spretan
diabetes [daiə'bi:ti:z] šećerna bolest
diagnos|e ['daiəgnouz] MED postaviti dijagnozu; ~is, *pl* ***~es*** dijagnoza
dial ['daiəl] sunčana ura;

brojčanik telefona (sata); TEL birati broj
dialect ['daiəlekt] narječje
diameter [dai'æmitə] promjer
diamond ['daiəmənd] dijamant
diaphragm ['daiəfræm] ošit; *tel* membrana; OPT blenda
diarrhoea [daiə'riə] MED proljev
diary ['daiəri] dnevnik
dice [dais] *pl* kocke; kockati se; **~-box** čaša za kockanje
dictat|e [dik'teit] diktirati; propisivati; **~ion** diktat; **~or** diktator; **~orial** diktatorski; **~orship** diktatura
dictionary ['dikʃənri] rječnik
die, *pl* ***dice*** kocka; umrijeti; odumrijeti; **~ out** izumrijeti
diet ['daiət] dijeta; propisana hrana; sabor, skupština
differ ['difə] razlikovati se; razilaziti se; **~ence** razlika; razmimoilaženje nesuglasica; **~ent** različit
difficult ['difikəlt] težak, naporan; **~y** teškoća
diffuse [di'fju:z] proširiti
dig (is-)kopati
digest [di'dʒest] probaviti; ['daidʒest] sažeti; prikaz, pregled; **~ible** probavljiv; **~ion** probava
digital ['didʒitl] digitalni; **~ camera** digitalni fotoaparat; **~ photo** digitalna fotografija
dignif|ied ['dignifaid] dostojanstven; **~y** *fig* uzvisiti
dignity ['digniti] dostojanstvo
digress [dai'gres] udaljiti se od predmeta; **~ion** digresija
dike [daik] nasip; kanal; ograditi nasipom
dilate [dai'leit] raširiti (se)
diligen|ce ['dilidʒəns] marljivost; **~t** marljiv
dilute [dai'lju:t] razrijediti
dim taman; nejasan; MOT ***~ the headlights*** prigušiti farove
dimension [di'menʃən] opseg, dimenzija
diminish [di'miniʃ] smanjiti (se); spasti
diminution [dimi'nju:ʃən] smanjenje
dimple ['dimpl] jamica
din buka; galama
dine [dain] ručati, večerati
ding-dong zvonjava
dingy ['dindʒi] prljav; tmuran
dining|-car kola za ručanje; **~-room** blagovaonica
dinner ['dinə] glavni obrok dana (ručak ili večera)
dint: ***by ~ of*** pomoću, zahvaljujući
dip umočiti; potopiti; utonuti; uranjanje; kratko kupanje; nagibi
diphtheria [dif'θiəriə] difterija
diplomacy [di'plouməsi] diplomacija
dipper ['dipə] velika kuhača
direct [di'rekt] izravan; neposredan; **~ current** isto-

smjerna struja; ~ **hit** puni pogodak; direktno (i **~ly**); upravljati; usmjeriti; uputiti; nasloviti; **~ion** smjer; upravljanje; upućivanje; adresa; uprava;
director [di'rektə] direktor; ***board of ~s*** upravni odbor; **~y** adresar
dirigible ['diridʒəbl] upravljiv; cepelin
dirt [də:t] prljavština; zemlja; ***~ cheap*** za bagatelu; **~y** prljav; uprljati
disability [disə'biliti] nesposobnost
disable [dis'eibl] onesposobiti; osakatiti; **~d** invalid; ***~ ex-service-man*** ratni vojni invalid
disabuse [disə'bju:z] otvoriti oči (*fig*)
disadvantage [disəd'va:ntidʒ] nepovoljan položaj; **~ous** nepovoljan
disaffect [disə'fekt] otuđiti; **~ion** nezadovoljstvo
disagree [disə'gri:] ne slagati se; ne podnositi; **~able** neugodan; **~ment** neslaganje
disappear [disə'piə] nestati; **~ance** nestanak
disappoint [disə'point] razočarati; **~ment** razočaranje
disappro|bation, **~val** [disæprə'beiʃən, ~ə'pru:vəl] negodovanje; **~ve** ne odobravati
disarm [dis'a:m] razoružati (se); **~ament** razoružanje
disarrange ['disə'reindʒ] poremetiti; **~ment** poremećenje
disast|er [di'za:stə] katastrofa; **~rous** koban; katastrofalan
disavow ['disə'vau] zanijekati; odreći se; **~al** odricanje
disbelie|f ['disbi'li:f] nevjerovanje, sumnja; **~ve** ne vjerovati, sumnjati
disburse [dis'bə:s] isplatiti; izdati; **~ment** isplata; izdatak
discern [di'sə:n] razabrati; razlučiti; uvidjeti; **~ing** oštrouman; **~ment** oštroumlje
discharge [dis'tʃa:dʒ] rasteretiti; isprazniti; ispaliti; izvršiti (dužnost); namiriti (dug); otpustiti; rasterećenje; izvršenje; otpuštanje
disciple [di'saipl] učenik; sljedbenik
discipline ['disiplin] disciplina, stega; disciplinirati, kazniti
diclaim [dis'kleim] nijekati
disclos|e [dis'klouz] razoriti; odati; **~ure** razotkrivanje
dis|colour [dis'kʌlə] gubiti boju; **~comfort** neudobnost; nelagodnost; biti neugodan; **~compose** uznemiriti; **~concert** smutiti; osujetiti; **~connect** prekinuti vezu (***from***, ***with***); EL isključiti; TECH otkvačiti; **~consolate** neutješan

discontent ['diskən'tent] nezadovoljstvo; **~ed** nezadovoljan
discontinu|ance [diskən'tinjuəns] prekid; **~e** prekinuti; otkazati (novine)
discord(ance) [dis'kɔ:d (-əns)] nesklad, gloženje
discount ['diskaunt] popust; dati popust; **~able** odračunljiv; **~enance** osuditi
discourage [dis'kʌridʒ] obeshrabriti; destimulirati
discourse [dis'kɔ:s] govor; **~ on, upon, about** govoriti o
discover [dis'kʌvə] otkriti; **~er** pronalazač; **~y** otkriće
discredit [dis'kredit] loš glas; diskreditiranost; diskreditirati
discreet [dis'kri:t] diskretan
discretion [dis'kreʃən] diskrecija; razboritost; sloboda odlučivanja; ***at one's ~*** po volji (nahođenju)
discriminat|e [dis'krimineit] razlikovati od; **~ion** razlikovanje; diskriminacija
discuss [dis'kʌs] raspravljati; diskutirati; **~ion** [~'kʌʃən] diskusija
disdain [dis'dein] prezir; prezirati; omalovažavati
disease [di'zi:z] bolest; **~d** bolestan
disembark ['disim'ba:k] iskrcati (se)
disengage ['disin'geidʒ] osloboditi; **~d** slobodan; **~ment** oslobođenje; raskidanje zaruka
disentangle ['disin'tæŋgl] razmrsiti
disfigure [dis'figə] nagrditi
disgrace [dis'greis] nemilost; sramota; baciti u nemilost; osramotiti; **~ful** sramotan
disguise [dis'gaiz] prerušiti; zakrabuljiti; prikriti; maska, krinka
disgust [dis'gʌst] odvratnost (***at, for***); ***~ed with*** osjećati ogorčenost (odvratnost) prema; **~ing** odvratan
dish [diʃ] zdjela; pojedino jelo; ***~ up*** (i *fig*) garnirati
dishearten [dis'ha:tn] obeshrabriti
dishonest [dis'ɔnist] nepošten; **~y** nepoštenje
dishonour [dis'ɔnə] beščasnost; sramota; osramotiti; ne prihvatiti (mjenicu); **~able** sramotan, nepošten
disillusion [disi'lu:ʒən] deziluziranost; razočaranje
disinclin|ation [disinkli'neiʃən] nesklonost (**for, to**); **~ed** ['~klaind] nesklon
disinfect ['disin'fekt] dezinficirati; **~ant** raskužno sredstvo; **~ion** dezinfekcija
disinherit [disin'herit] razbaštiniti
disinterested [dis'intristid] nezainteresiran
disk [disk] (okrugla) ploča; gramofonska ploča; **~ drive** pogon diska

dislike [dis'laik] antipatija; ne voljeti; **~d** omrznut
dislocate ['disləkeit] poremetiti; iščašiti
dismal ['dizməl] turoban
dismantle [dis'mæntl] demontirati
dismay [dis'mei] očaj; očajavati
dismember [dis'membə] raskomadati
dismiss [dis'mis] otpustiti; likvidirati sa; **~al** otpust
dismount [dis'maunt] sjahati; skinuti
disobedien|ce [disə'bi:djəns] neposluh; **~t** neposlušan (***to***)
disobey ['disə'bei] biti neposlušan
disobliging ['disə'blaidʒiŋ] nesusretljiv; neuljudan
disoder [dis'ɔ:də] nered; MED smetnja; poremetiti; **~ly** neuredan; izgrednički
disown [dis'oun] ne priznavati; odreći se
dispatch [dis'pætʃ] brzo rješenje; žurba; odaslati; **~er** otpremnik
dispens|able [dis'pensəbl] nevažan; **~ary** apoteka; **~e with** moći bez; biti bez
disperse [dis'pə:s] raspršiti (se)
displace [dis'pleis] premjestiti; pomaći; preseliti; potisnuti; **~d person** raseljeno lice
display [dis'plei] iznošenje; prikazivanje; aranžirana roba; izložiti; prikazati
displeas|e [dis'pli:z] ozlovoljiti; **~ure** [~'pleʒə] negodovanje
dispos|al [dis'pouzəl] raspolaganje; određenje; **~e** odrediti; ***~e of*** raspolagati nečim; primijeniti; likvidirati; **~ed** sklon; **~ition** [dispə'ziʃən] određivanje; *fig* sklonost; narav
disproportion ['disprə'pɔ:ʃən] nesrazmjer
dispute [dis'pju:t] spor; osporavati; raspravljati (***about***)
disqualif|ication [diskwɔlifi'keiʃən] diskvalifikacija; **~y** [~fai] diskvalificirati
dis|quiet [dis'kwaiət] nemir; briga; uznemiriti; **~regard** ignoriranje; ne obazirati se; zanemariti; **~reputable** na zlu glasu, ozloglašen; **~respectful** drzak
dissatis|faction ['dissætis'fækʃən] nezadovoljstvo; **~fy** ne zadovoljiti
dissemble [di'sembl] prikriti; pretvarati se
dissen|sion [di'senʃən] razmirica; **~t** razilaziti (se) (***from***); neslaganje
dissertation [disə:'teiʃən] (učena) rasprava (***on***)
dissimilar ['di'similə] različit
dissipat|e ['disipeit] razići se; rasuti; **~ed** razuzdan; **~ion** rastrošnost

dissociate [di'souʃieit] rastaviti
dissolv|able [di'zɔlvəbl] rastopiv; **~e** rastopiti
dissua|de [di'sweid] odvratiti od (***from***); **~sive** koji odvraća od
distan|ce ['distəns] daljina; razmak; uzdržanost; **~t** udaljen; dalek; uzdržan
distaste [dis'teist] nesklonost (***for a th***)
distend [dis'tend] napuhnuti (se)
distil [dis'til] destilirati; **~lation** destilacija; **~ler(y)** pecar(a)
distinct [dis'tiŋkt] različit; jasan; **~ion** razlikovanje; ***in ~ion from*** za razliku od; isticanje; **~ive** značajan; osebujan
distinguish [dis'tiŋgwiʃ] razlikovati; (***oneself***) istaknuti (se); **~ed** istaknut; odličan; otmjen
distort [dis'tɔːt] iskriviti; izvrnuti; izobličiti; izvrtanje; izobličenje (i RADIO, OPT)
distract [dis'trækt] odvratiti (pažnju); rastresti; **~ed** rastrojen; **~ion** odvraćanje; ludilo
distress [dis'tres] nevolja; ojaditi; **~ful** jadan
distribut|e [dis'tribjuːt] (raz-, po-)dijeliti; (robu) raspačavati; **~ion** raspodjela; distribucija; **~or** distributer; prodavač
district ['distrikt] općina, kotar, okrug; predio
distrust [dis'trʌst] nepovjerenje; nemati povjerenja u
disturb [dis'təːb] uznemiriti; ometati; **~ance** smetnja
disunion ['dis'juːnjən] nesloga
disuse ['dis'juːs] neupotreba
ditch [ditʃ] jarak
dive [daiv] skok naglavce; (u)roniti; (u)skočiti; AERO obrušavanje; **~r** ronilac
divers|e [dai'vəːs] različit; raznorodan; **~ion** skretanje; razonoda; **~ity** raznolikost
divert [dai'vəːt] odvratiti; zabaviti
divest [dai'vest] svući
divide [di'vaid] (po)dijeliti (se); razdijeliti (se); *Am* razvođe
divin|ation [divi'neiʃən] gatanje; **~e** [di'vain] božanski; **~ity** [di'viniti] božanstvo; teologija
division [di'viʒən] dioba; divizija
divorce [di'vɔːs] rastava (braka); rastaviti (se)
DIY [diːai'wai] = **do it yourself** uradi sam
dizz|iness ['dizinis] vrtoglavica; **~y** vrtoglav
do [duː] činiti; pripravljati, kuhati; (uslugu) učiniti; obaviti; osjećati se; odgovarati; ***that will ~*** dosta je; ***how ~ you ~?*** milo mi je; kako ste? ***~ you like London?***

— *I* ~ da li vam se sviđa London? Da; ***what is to be ~ne?*** što da se radi? ***I could ~ with*** ne bih imao ništa protiv; ***~ without*** moći i bez, biti bez; *Pitanje*: ***~ you see him?*** vidiš (viđaš) li ga? *Nijekanje*: ***we ~ not know*** ne znamo; *Pojačanje*: ***~ shut up!*** daj prestani već jednom !; ***I ~ feel better*** zaista se bolje osjećam
docile ['dousail] poslušan; povodljiv
dock [dɔk] dok; **~er** lučki radnik; **~yard** brodogradilište
doctor ['dɔktə] doktor; liječnik
document ['dɔkjumənt] dokument; **~ary** dokumentaran; **~ary film** dokumentarni film
dodge [dɔdʒ] izmicanje; trik; izmicati; **~r**: (***artful***) **~r** prepredenjak
dog pas; ***go to the ~s*** propasti; **~cart** jednoprežna dvokolica; **~-days** najvrući dani ljeta; **~ged** uporan; **~-tired** premoren
doing ['du:iŋ] djelovanje; čin; *pl* zbivanje, stvari
dole [doul] potpora za nezaposlenost; ***be on the ~*** primati potporu; **~ful** žalostan, turoban
doll [dɔl] lutka
dolphin ['dɔlfin] dupin
dome [doum] katedrala; kupola
domestic [də'mestik] kućni; sluga; **~s** *pl* služinčad
domicile ['dɔmisail] mjesto boravka; **~d** sa stalnim boravkom u
domination [dɔmi'neiʃən] (pre)vlast
domineer [dɔmi'niə] komandirati; **~ing** nasilan; bahat
dominion [də'minjən] vlast; ***the ~s*** *pl* dominioni (engleske kolonije sa samoupravom)
donation [dou'neiʃən] dar; prilog
done [dʌn] učinjen; iscrpljen; svršen; ***well ~*** dobro ispečen
donkey ['dɔŋki] magarac
donor ['dounə] darivatelj; davalac
doom [du:m] sudbina; kob; osuditi
door [dɔ:] vrata; ***next ~*** (***to***) susjedni; ***within ~s*** u kući; ***out of ~s*** vani; **~-handle** kvaka na vratima; **~-keeper**, *Am* **~-man** vratar; **~way** veža
dope [doup] *Am* droga; dopingovati
dormant ['dɔ:mənt] **partner** tajni kompanjon
dose [douz] doza; dozirati
dot tačka; mrlja; istočkati
dote [dout] (po)djetinjiti; ludovati (***on*** za)
double ['dʌbl] dvostruk; duplikat; dvojnik; SPORT igra parova; prepoloviti;

~-breasted dvoredni (sako); ~-click dvoklik; *you have to ~-click on this icon* morate dvaput kliknuti na ikonu; ~-entry dvostruko knjigovodstvo ~-faced dvoličan; ~-line dvostruki kolosjek
doubt [daut] sumnjati; sumnja; *no ~* nesumnjivo; ~ful sumnjiv
douche [du:ʃ] irigiranje; tuš; irigirati (se)
dough [dou] tijesto; ~nut uštipak
dove [dʌv] golub
dowager ['dauədʒə] udovica (plemkinja)
dower ['dauə] miraz
down [daun] paperje; *pl* brežuljkasta pustopoljina
down [daun] dolje; (is)pod; naniže; *~ the river* nizvodno; *~ platform* polazni peron; ~-hearted utučen; ~hill nizbrdo; ~load učitati; učitavanje; ~pour pljusak; ~right temeljito; ~right potpun (laž, besmisao); ~stairs dolje, u prizemlju; ~wards naniže
dowry ['dauəri] miraz
doze [douz] drijemati; drijemež
dozen ['dʌzn] tuce
Dr. = **debtor**; **doctor**
drab [dræb] mutnosmeđ; *fig* bezbojan; neugledan; monotonija
draft, **draught** [dra:ft] (trasirana) mjenica; sastaviti nacrt, koncipirati
drag povlačna mreža; smetnja; potezati; vući; ići tromo (poslovi)
dragon ['drægən] zmaj
dragoon [drə'gu:n] dragun
drain [drein] odvodni kanal; isušiti; oteći; ~age (uređaji za) isušivanje
dramatist ['dræmətist] dramatičar
draper ['dreipə] trgovac tekstilom; ~y trgovina tekstilom; tekstil; drapiranje
draught [dra:ft] vučenje; propuh; gutljaj; *pl* dama (igra); ~sman crtač; ~y izvrgnut propuhu
draw [drɔ:] (po-, na-, od-, raz-)vući; podići (novac); crtati; upijati (zrak); pomodni artikl; vučenje; *~ up* sastaviti, koncipirati; ~back nedostatak; smetnja; ~bridge most na dizanje; ~ee COM trasat
drawer ['drɔ:ə] crtač; COM trasant; ladica; ~s [drɔ:z] *pl*: *(pair of) ~s* gaće; *chest of ~s* komoda
drawing ['drɔ:iŋ] vučenje; crtanje; ~-board crtaća daska; ~-room soba za primanje, salon
dread [dred] strah; strava; plašiti se; ~ful strašan; grozan
dream [dri:m] san; sanjati; *I ~t* sanjao sam
dreary ['driəri] turoban, pust

dredge [dredʒ] bager; jaružati
drench [drentʃ] smočiti do kože; **~er** pljusak
dress odjeća; haljina; očistiti, prirediti; obući (se); povijati (rane); ***in full ~*** u svečanoj odjeći; **~-circle** THEAT mezzanin; **~-coat** frak; **~er** kredenc
dressing ['dresiŋ] priređivati; MED povoj; apretura; **~-case** neseser; **~-gown** kućni ogrtač; **~-table** toaletni stolić
dress|maker krojačica; **~-suit** večernje odijelo
drift tok misli; (sniježni) nanos; biti tjeran (nošen); **~-ice** ledene sante
drill svrdlo; bušilica; uvježbavanje; uvježbavati
drink [driŋk] piće; napitak; piti; **~able** pitak; **~ing glass** čaša
drip kapati; curiti; **~ping** mast od pečenja
drive [draiv] vožnja; MOT pogon; *fig* inicijativa; voziti; goniti; (na)tjerati; ***~ on*** natjerati; ***~ up to*** zaustaviti kola pred; **~r** vozač; šofer; kočijaš
driving ['draiviŋ] vožnja; **~ mirror** vozačko ogledalo; **~ school** auto škola; **~-wheel** pogonski kotač
drizzle ['drizl] kišica
droll [droul] smiješan
drone [droun] ZOOL trut (i *fig*)
droop [dru:p] objesiti se
drop kap; (o)pad(anje); kapati; ispustiti; ubaciti (pismo); baciti (bombe); ***~ in*** navratiti; ***~ a line*** napisati nekome par redaka; iskrcati putnika (iz kola); **~-scene** THEAT zastor; finale
dropsy ['drɔpsi] vodena bolest
drought [draut] suša
drown [draun] utopiti se; preplaviti; *fig* zaglušiti; ***be ~ed*** utopiti se
drows|e [drauz] drijemati; biti pospan; **~y** pospan
drug [drʌg] lijek; droga; **~gist** drogerist; *Am* ljekarnik; **~store** *Am* (velika) drogerija
drum [drʌm] bubanj; bubnjati; **~ head** strana bubnja s kožom
drunk [drʌŋk] pijan; **~ard** pijanica; **~enness** pijanstvo
dry [drai] suh; isušen; sušiti; ***~ up*** isušiti; **~-cleaning** kemijsko čišćenje; **~ goods** *Am* tekstil; **~ness** suhoća
dual carriage-way cesta s dvostrukim kolovozom
dubious ['dju:biəs] neizvjestan
ducal ['dju:kəl] vojvodski
duchess ['dʌtʃis] vojvotkinja
duchy ['dʌtʃi] vojvodstvo
duck [dʌk] patka; jedrenina; potopiti; zaroniti

ductile ['dʌktail] rastezljiv; kovan
due [dju:] dužan; dospio; ***in ~ time*** u svoje (pravo) vrijeme; ***the train is ~ at 5*** vlak treba doći u 5; što pripada; dug; **~s** *pl* pristojbe
duel ['dju:əl] dvoboj
dug-out ['dʌgaut] MIL zemunica
duke [dju:k] vojvoda; **~dom** vojvodstvo
dull [dʌl] tup (i *fig*); mutan; mukao; dosadan; trom; mlitav; otupiti; **~ness** tupost; dosada; jednoličnost
dumb [dʌm] nijem; *Am* glup; ***deaf and ~*** gluhonijem; **~ bell** bučice za gimnastiku; *Am* glupan; **~ waiter** okretni stolić za posluživanje; *Am* kuhinjski lift
dummy ['dʌmi] imitacija; krojačka lutka; *fig* prazna figura
dump [dʌmp] izbaciti; COM dempovati, baciti jeftinu robu na tržište; *fig pl* potištenost; **~ing** COM demping
dumpling ['dʌmpliŋ] valjušak
dung [dʌŋ] gnojivo; pognojiti
dungeon ['dʌndʒən] tamnica
dunghill ['dʌŋhil] gnojište
dupe [dju:p] prevarena (lakovjerna) osoba; nasamariti
duplicate ['dju:plikit] dvostruk; duplikat; ['-keit] kopirati; umnožiti
dura|bility [djuərə'biliti] trajnost; **~ble** trajan; **~tion** trajanje
during ['djuəriŋ] za vrijeme
dusk [dʌsk] sumrak
dust [dʌst] prašina; (is-, o-) prašiti; **~-bin** kanta za smeće; **~-cloak ~-coat** kuta, radni ogrtač; **~-proof** koji ne propušta prašinu; **~y** prašnjav
Dutch [dʌtʃ] holandski; ***the ~*** Holanđani; **~man** Holandez; **~-woman** Holanđanka
dutiable ['dju:tiəbl] što podliježe carini
dutiful ['dju:tiful] poslušan; **~ness** poslušnost; pokornost
duty ['dju:ti] dužnost; carina; služba; ***on ~*** u službi, dežuran; ***off ~*** koji nije u službi; ***pay (the) ~ on*** platiti carinu na; **~-free** slobodan od carine
DVD [di:vi:'di:] DVD; **~-ROM** DVD-ROM
dwarf [dwɔ:f] patuljak
dwell stanovati; zadržati se na ([***up***]***on***)
dwelling ['dweliŋ] stan; **~-house** stambena kuća
dye [dai] boja; bojati; **~r** bojadisač; **~-works** bojadisaonica
dying ['daiiŋ] umirući; umiranje
dynam|ic [dai'næmik], **~ical** dinamičan; **~ics** dinamika
dynamite ['dainəmait] dina-

mit
dynamo ['dainəmou] dinamo
dysentery ['disntri] MED dizenterija

E

E. = **East(ern)**; **English**
each [iːtʃ] svaki; ~ ***other*** jedan drugoga, se
eager ['iːgə] željan (***after, for***); nestrpljiv; **~ness** želja; žudnja (***for***); nestrpljivost
eagle ['iːgl] orao
ear [iə] uho; sluh; klas; ručka (na peharu i sl.); **~-ache** uhobolja; **~-drum** ANAT bubnjić
earl [əːl] grof (u Engleskoj)
earliness ['əːlinis] ranost
early ['əːli] ran(o); uskoro; ~ ***in the morning*** rano ujutro; ~ ***in May*** početkom svibnja; ***as*** ~ ***as*** još, već
earn [əːn] zaraditi; **~*ed income*** osobna zarada
earnest ['əːnist] ozbiljan; ***be in*** ~ ozbiljno misliti
earnings ['əːniŋz] *pl* zarada; prihod
ear|-pendant privjesak za uho; **~-ring** naušnica; **~-splitting** zaglušan; **~-trumpet** rog za nagluhe; **~-wax** ušna mast; **~wig** uholaža
earth [əːθ] zemlja; svijet; tlo; RADIO uzemljiti; **~en** zemljan; **~enware** zemljano posuđe; **~ly** zemaljski; **~quake** potres; **~-worm** glista
eas|e [iːz] ugodnost; udobnost; spokojnost; neusiljenost; olakšati; (bol) ublažiti; ***at*** **~*e*** mirno, ležerno; **~iness** lakoća; neusiljenost
east [iːst] istok; Orijent; istočni
Easter ['iːstə] Uskrs
eastwards ['iːstwəd(z)] prema istoku
easy ['iːzi] lak; udoban; trom (tržište); ***make your mind*** ~ ***about that!*** o tom ne brini; ***take it*** ~***!*** ne uzrujavaj se! bez žurbe! **~-chair** naslonjač; **~-going** bezbrižan
eat [iːt] jesti; žderati; *fig* gristi; ~ ***up*** pojesti; **~ables** ['iːtəblz] *pl* jestvine; **~er**: ***poor*** (***great***) **~*er*** osoba koja malo (puno) jede; **~ing** jedenje; **~*ing-house*** gostionica
eaves ['iːvz] *pl* streha
ebb oseka (i **~*-tide***); opadati (i *fig*)
ebony ['ebəni] ebanovina
e-book ['iːbuk] e-knjiga
E. C. = **Eastern Central** (poštanski distrikt Londona)
eccentric(al) [ik'sentrik(əl)] ekscentričan
ecclesiastical [ikliːzi'æstikl] crkveni

echo ['ekou] jeka
eclipse [i'klips] pomrčina
economic [i:kə'nɔmik] ekonomski; ~ ***crisis*** kriza; ~ ***policy*** privredna politika; **~al** ekonomičan, štedljiv
economy [i:'kɔ'nəmi] štedljivost; ***political*** ~ politička ekonomija
ecstasy ['ekstəsi] zanos
ed. = **edition**, **editor**
edge [edʒ] oštrina; rub; ivica; brid; britkost; ***she is on ~ today*** danas je napeta; oštriti; porubiti; **~ways**, **~wise** pobočke
edging ['edʒiŋ] oštrenje; rub; opšav
edible ['edibl] jestivo
edifice ['edifis] građevina
edify ['edifai] *fig* izgrađivati; **~ing** poučan
edit ['edit] (knjigu) urediti; **~ion** izdanje; naklada
editor ['editə] urednik; **~ial** uvodni članak; **~ship** uredništvo
educat|e ['edju:keit] odgajati; podučavati; obrazovati; **~ion** odgoj; obrazovanje; ***Board of* ~*ion*** ministarstvo prosvjete
eel [i:l] jegulja
efface [i'feis] izbrisati; *fig* uništiti
effect [i'fekt] učinak; posljedica; djelovanje; TECH kapacitet; ***~s*** *pl* vrijednosni papiri; imovina; ***take*** ~ djelovati, stupiti na snagu; ***of no*** ~ bez učinka; ***in*** ~ doista; izazvati; **~ive** djelotvoran; ***become*** ~ *Am* stupiti na snagu; ~ ***capacity*** korisni kapacitet; *ugl* MIL **~ives** aktivna vojska; **~uate** izvršiti
effeminate [i'feminit] ženskast
effervescent [efə'vesnt] pjenušav; ~ **powder** prašak za umjetna sodna pića
efficacious [efi'keiʃəs] efikasan
efficien|cy [i'fiʃənsi] djelotvornost; **~t** sposoban
effigy ['efidʒi] slika; lutka
effluence ['efluəns] istjecanje
effort ['efət] napor; nastojanje; **~less** bez muke (napora)
effuse [e'fju:z] izlijevati
effus|ion [e'fju:ʒən] izljev; prolijevanje; **~ive** pretjeran
e. g. = **exempli gratia** npr., na primjer
egg jaje; ***scrambled ~s*** *pl* kajgana; ***fried ~s*** jaja na oko; **~-cup** čašica za jaje; **~-shell** ljuska jajeta
ego|ism ['egouizəm] egoizam; **~ist** egoist; **~istic(al)** egoističan
Egypt ['i:dʒipt] Egipat; **~ian** egipatski; Egipćanin
eight [eit] osam; osmica; **~een** osamnaest; **~eenth** osamnaesti; **~fold** osmerostruko; **~h** osmi; osmina; **~ieth** osamdeseti; **~some reel**

škotsko kolo za osmero; **~y** osamdeset

either ['aiðə] jedan od dvojice; oba; bilo koji (od dvojice); ***~ ... or*** ili ... ili, bilo ... ili

ejaculation [idʒækju'leiʃən] uzvik

eject [i'dʒekt] izbaciti

eke [i:k]: ***~ out*** dopuniti, "skrpati"; *fig* kuburiti

elaborate [i'læbərit] fino izrađen; razrađen; složen; [~reit] razraditi; opširno iznositi; **~ness** pažljiva obrada

elapse [i'læps] proteći (vrijeme)

elastic [i'læstik] elastičan, rastezljiv; elastika; **~ity** *fig* elastičnost

elbow ['elbou] lakat; ***at one's ~*** pri ruci; na dohvat; ***~ one's way through (a crowd)*** progurati se; **~-room** slobodan prostor

elder ['eldə] stariji; bazga; **~ly** postariji

eldest ['eldist] najstariji; ***the ~ born*** prvorođeni

elect [i'lekt] izabran; birati; **~ion** izbori

elector [i'lektə] izbornik

electri|c(al) [i'lektrikəl] električni; **~cal engineer** elektroinženjer; **~cian** električar; **~city** struja; **~fication** elektrifikacija; **~fy** elektrificirati; elektrizirati

electro|cution [ilektrə'kju:ʃən] smaknuće na električnoj stolici; **~type** galvanoplastični otisak (kliše)

elegan|ce ['eligəns] elegancija; **~t** elegantan

element ['elimənt] element; počelo; **~ary** elementaran; jednostavan; početni; **~ary school** osnovna škola

elephant ['elifənt] slon

elevat|e ['eliveit] podignuti; uzvisiti; ***~ed (railroad)*** *Am* nadzemna željeznica; **~ion** uzdignuće; uzvisivanje; uzvisina; **~or** *Am* lift

eleven [i'levn] jedanaest; jedanaestica; **~th** jedanaesti

eligibility [elidʒə'biliti] izberivost, prihvatljivost

eliminate [i'limineit] eliminirati; isključiti

elk evropski los

elm, **~-tree** brijest

elope [i'loup] pobjeći (s ljubavnikom)

eloquen|ce ['eləkwəns] rječitost; **~t** rječit

else [els] inače; ***anyone ~*** bilo tko drugi; ***what ~?*** šta drugo (još)?

eludicate [i'lu:sideit] razjasniti: rastumačiti

elu|de [i'lu:d] izbjegavati; izigrati; **~sive** [~siv] neuhvatljiv, lukav

emaciat|e [i'meiʃieit] smršaviti; **~ion** [~si'eiʃən] mršavljenje; mršavost

e-mail ['i:meil] e-pošta; poslati e-poštu; **~ address**

adresa e-pošte
emanate ['emәneit] izbijati (zračiti) iz
emancipate [i'mænsipeit] osloboditi
embalm [im'ba:m] balzamirati
embank [im'bæŋk] podići nasip; **~ment** nasip; kej
embargo [em'ba:gou] MAR embargo
embark [im'ba:k] ukrcati (se) (***for***); **~ation** ukrcavanje
embrrass [im'bærәs] smesti; dovesti u nezgodan položaj; **~ment** smetenost; zapreka
embassy ['embәsi] ambasada
emblish [im'beliʃ] ukrasiti; iskititi
embers ['embәz] *pl* žeravica, žar
embezzle [im'bezl] pronevjeriti; **~ment** pronevjera
embitter [im'bitә] ogorčiti
emblem ['emblәm] emblem
embod|iment [im'bɔdimәnt] utjelovljenje; **~y** utjeloviti
embrace [im'breis] zagrliti (se); zagrljaj
embroider [im'brɔidә] vesti; **~y** vezenje; vez
embroilment [im'brɔilmәnt] zapletaj; upletenost
emerald ['emәrәld] smaragd
emerge [i'mә:dʒ] izroniti; pojaviti se; proizaći (***from***); **~ncy** slučaj nužde; ***~ncy decree*** izvanredne odredbe; ***~ncy exit*** izlaz za nuždu
emery ['emәri] šmirak
emetic [i'metik] sredstvo za povraćanje
emigra|nt ['emigrәnt] iseljenik; **~te** iseliti se; **~tion** iseljenje
eminen|ce ['eminәns] visok položaj; istaknutost; eminencija (*titula*); **~t** *fig* istaknut
emit [i'mit] ispuštati, zračiti
emotion [i'mouʃәn] emocija; čuvstvo
emperor ['empәrә] car
empha|sis ['emfәsis] isticanje; **~size** naglasiti; **~tic** naglašen
empire ['empaiә] carstvo
employ [im'plɔi] upotrijebiti (***in***, ***for***, ***on***); zaposliti; ***in the ~ of*** namješten kod; **~ee** namještenik; **~er** poslodavac; **~ment** zaposlenost; namještenje; ***~ment agency*** zavod za zapošljavanje
empower [im'pauә] ovlastiti; opunomoćiti
empress ['empris] carica
empt|iness ['emptinis] praznina; ispraznost; **~y** prazan; *fig* isprazan, ništavan; (is)prazniti (se); **~ies** *pl* ambalaža
emulate ['emjuleit] takmičiti se sa; oponašati
enable [i'neibl] osposobiti; omogućiti; (***to do***) zakoniti
enact [i'nækt] uzakoniti; odrediti; THEAT glumiti
enamel [i'næml] emajl,

gleđa; caklina (zubna); emajlirati
enamour [i'næmə]: ***be ~ed of*** zaljubiti se u
encamp [in'kæmp] utaboriti (se)
encase [in'keis] zatvoriti (u kutiju)
encashment [in'kæʃmənt] inkaso; unovčenje
enchant [in'tʃa:nt] očarati; **~ing** čaroban
encircle [in'sə:kl] okružiti
enclos|e [in'klouz] ograditi; priložiti (u pismu); **~ure** ograđeno zemljište; prilog (pismu)
encore [ɔŋ'kɔ:] THEAT tražiti ponavljanje; dodatak (programu); ponavljanje
encounter [in'kauntə] susret; okršaj; sukobiti se sa; (teškoćama itd.); naići na
encourage [in'kʌridʒ] hrabriti; stimulirati; **~ment** hrabrenje; stimulacija
encroach [in'kroutʃ] dirnuti u nečija prava; prekoračiti (***[up]on***)
encumb|er [in'kʌmbə] opteretiti; ometati; **~rance** smetnja; ***without ~rance*** bez djece
end kraj; ***no ~ of*** bezbrojno; ***be at an ~*** biti pri kraju; ***in the ~*** konačno ***to*** (ili ***for***) ***this ~*** u tu svrhu; ***to no ~*** uzalud; ***my hair stood on ~*** kosa mi se naježila; dokrajčiti
endanger [in'deindʒə] ugroziti
endear [in'diə] omiliti
endeavour [in'devə] nastojanje; težnja; nastojati; težiti (***after***)
end|ing ['endiŋ] kraj; svršetak; **~less** beskrajan
endorse [in'dɔ:s] COM indorsirati; poduprijeti; **~e** žirant(ar); **~ment** žiro; podrška; **~r** indosant, žirant
endow [in'dau] obdariti; pokloniti zakladu
endur|able [in'djuərəbl] podnošljiv; **~ance** izdržljivost; ***past ~ance*** neizdržljiv; **~e** izdržati
enema ['enimə] klistir
enemy ['enimi] neprijatelj
energ|etic [enə'dʒetik] energičan; **~y** energija
enervate ['enə:veit] iscrpsti, istrošiti
enfeeble [in'fi:bl] oslabiti
enforce [in'fɔ:s] pojačati; nametnuti (***upon*** kome); provesti
enfranchise [in'fræntʃaiz] osloboditi; dati pravo glasa
engage [in'geidʒ] obavezati; angažirati; zaposliti; rezervirati; ***line ~d!*** linija je zauzeta; **~ment** angažman; obaveza; zaruke; namještenje
engine ['endʒin] stroj; lokomotiva; motor; **~-driver** strojovođa; **~-trouble** kvar (smetnje) na motoru, defekt
engineer [endʒi'niə] inže-

njer; stojar; *Am* strojovođa; *coll* udesiti; **~ing** tehnika
English ['iŋgliʃ] engleski; ***the ~*** Englezi; **~man** Englez; **~woman** Engleskinja
engrave [in'greiv] gravirati, urezati; **~r** graver
engross [in'grous] (potpuno) zaokupiti
enhance [in'ha:ns] povečati; **~ment** povećanje
enigma [i'nigmə] zagonetka
enjoin [in'dʒɔin] naložiti (***on a p***)
enjoy [in'dʒɔi] uživati; radovati se; ***I ~ my dinner*** prija mi ručak; **~able** zabavan; prijatan; **~ment** užitak
enlarge [in'la:dʒ] povećati (i PHOT); proširiti (se); **~ment** proširenje; rasprostranjenje
enlighten [in'laitn] *fig* prosvijetliti; razjasniti
enlist [in'list] zaverbovati; stupiti u
enliven [in'laivn] oživiti
enmity ['enmiti] neprijateljstvo
enorm|ity [i'nɔ:miti] golemost; **~ous** golem
enough [i'nʌf] dosta
enrage [in'reidʒ] razbijesniti
en|rapture [in'ræptʃə] zanijeti; **~rich** obogatiti; pojačati
ensign ['ensain] zastava
enslave [in'sleiv] zarobiti; **~ment** ropstvo
ensnare [in'snɛə] uhvatiti u zamku
ensue [in'sju:] slijediti, proizlaziti (***from, on***)
ensure [in'ʃuə] osigurati
entail [in'teil] povlačiti za sobom
entangle [in'tæŋgl] zaplesti
enter ['entə] ući; stupiti u; (pro)knjižiti; ***~ into*** stupiti u; spadati u
enteri|c [en'terik] **fever** trbušni tifus; **~tis** crijevni katar
enterpris|e ['entəpraiz] poduzeće; poduzetnost; **~ing** poduzetan
entertain [entə'tein] zabavljati; primati goste (***at***); **~ment** zabava; ***~ment tax*** porez kao dio ulaznice (sa zabavne priredbe)
enthusias|m [in'θju:ziæzəm] oduševljenje; **~t** zanesenjak; **~tic** ushićen
entic|e [in'tais] namamiti; **~ing** primamljiv
entire [in'taiə] cio; potpun; **~ly** potpuno, u cijelosti
entitle [in'taitl] dati ime (pravo) na (***to***)
entrails ['entreilz] *pl* utroba
entrance ['entrəns] ulaz; pristup
entreat [in'tri:t] zaklinjati; **~y** zaklinjanje, (usrdna) molba
entrust [in'trʌst] povjeriti
entry ['entri] ulaženje; ulaz; knjiženje, stavka; carinska deklaracija; **~ permit** dozvola ulaska
enumerate [in'] nabrojiti
envelop [in'veləp] okružiti;

umotati; **~e** ovoj; koverta
env|iable ['enviəbl] zavidan (uspjeh); **~ious** zavidan (čovjek); **~y** ['~vi] zavist, zloba
environment [in'vaiərənmənt] okolina; ***~ally friendly*** ekološki neškodljiv
epidemic [epi'demik] epidemički; epidemija
epilepsy ['epilepsi] padavica
episcopa|l [i'piskəpl] biskupski; **~te** biskupska čast
episode ['episoud] epizoda
epistle [i'pisl] poslanica
epitaph ['epita:f] nadgrobni natpis
epoch-making ['i:pɔk'meikiŋ] epohalan
equal ['i:kwəl] jednak; ravnopravan; ***~ to*** dorastao (čemu); premac; ***my ~s*** meni ravni; ***not to be ~led*** bez premca; **~ity** jednakost; ravnopravnost; **~ize** izjednačiti
equanimity [i:kwə'nimiti] staloženost
equat|ion [i'kweiʃən] MATH jednadžba; **~or** ekvator
equerry [i'kweri] konjušnik
equestrian [i'kwestriən] jahač(ki)
equilibrium [i:kwi'libriəm] ravnoteža
equinox ['i:kwinɔks] ekvinocij
equip [i'kwip] opremiti; **~ment** oprema; *fig* sprema
equitable ['ekwitəbl] pravedan; nepristran
equivalent [i'kwivələnt] istovrijedan; istoznačan (***to***)
equivocal [i'kwivəkəl] dvomislen
era ['iərə] era, doba
erase [i'reiz] izbrisati; *fig* iskorijeniti; **~r** strugač; *Am* gumica
erect [i'rekt] uspravan; uspraviti; **~ion** podizanje; zgrada; **~or** podizač; graditelj
eremite ['erimait] pustinjak
ermine ['ə:min] hermelin
erode [i'roud] istrošiti, podlokati
err [ə:] pogriješiti; upasti u bludnju
errand ['erənd] sitni posao (za obavljanje); **~-boy** dostavljač; teklić
erratum [i'reitəm], *pl* ***errata*** tiskarska pogreška
erroneous [i'rounjəs] pogrešan; u zabludi
error ['erə] pogreška
erudition [eru:'diʃən] učenost
eruption [i'rʌpʃən] provala (vulkana); osip
erysipelas [eri'sipiləs] MED vrbanac
escalator ['eskəleitə] pomične stepenice
escapade [eskə'peid] ispad; ludorija
escape [i'skeip] pobjeći, umaknuti; izbjeći; bijeg; ***have a narrow ~*** za dlaku umaknuti
escort ['eskɔ:t] pratnja;

[is'k~] pratiti
especial [is'peʃəl] naročit; poseban; **~ly** naročito
espy [is'pai] ugledati
esquire [is'kwaiə] niži plemić (posjednik); zemljoradnik
essay [e'sei] pokušati; ['esei] pokus; sastavak; esej
essential [i'senʃəl] bitan
establish [is'tæbliʃ] postaviti; ustanoviti; osnovati; **~ment** osnivanje; utemeljenje; tvrtka
estate [is'teit] POL stalež; posjed; imovina; ***personal ~*** pokretni imetak; ***real ~*** nekretnine; **~ duty** porez na ostavštinu
esteem [is'ti:m] štovanje (***with***); ugled; cijeniti
estimable ['estiməbl] vrijedan štovanja
estimat|e ['estimeit] (pro)cijeniti (***at***); ***rough ~e*** ['~mit] gruba procjena; **~ion** štovanje; sud, ocjena
estrange [is'treindʒ] otuđiti; **~ment** otuđenje
etern|al [i:'tə:nl] vječan; **~alize** ovjekovječiti; **~ity** vječnost
ether ['i:θə] eter; **~eal** [i:'θiəriəl] eteričan
ethics ['eθiks] *ugl sg* etika; ćudoređe
euphony ['ju:fəni] blagozvučje
Europe ['juərəp] Evropa; **~an** [juərə'piən] evropropski; Evropejac
evacuate [i'vækjueit] isprazniti; MIL povući se iz
evade [i'veid] izbjegavati; izigrati
evaluat|e [i'væljueit] procijeniti; vrednovati; **~ion** procjena
evaporat|e [i'væpəreit] ispariti (se); ishlapiti; **~ion** isparivanje
evasive [i'veisiv] koji okoliša; neodređen (***of***)
eve [i:v] predvečerje
even ['i:vən] baš; ravan; izjednačen; COM ***of ~ date*** istog datuma; čak; ***not ~*** čak ni; ***~ if, ~ though*** pa makar i
evening ['i:vniŋ] večer; **~ dress** večernje (svečano) odijelo (toaleta)
evenness ['i:vənnis] jednakost; mirnoća
event [i'vent] događaj; SPORT takmičenje; ***at all ~*** svakako; **~full** znamenit
eventuality [iventju'æliti] mogućnost
ever ['evə] ikada; ***~ so*** vrlo; makoliko; ***~ since*** otada; otkad; ***for ~*** zauvijek; **~lasting** neprestan; vječan; **~more** uvijek; vječno
every ['evri] svaki; ***~ few days*** svakih par dana; ***~ other day*** svaki drugi dan; ***~ bit as much*** sasvim jednako; **~one**, **~body** svatko; **~day** svakodnevni; **~thing** sve;

~where svagdje
eviden|ce ['evidəns] dokaz(i); svjedočanstvo; **~t** očit; jasan, vidljiv
evil ['i:vil] zao; loš; zlo
evince [i'vins] pokazivati; odavati
evolution [i:və'lu:ʃən] razvoj
ewer ['juə] vrč
ex: COM **~ *factory*** franko tvornica; **~-minister** bivši ministar
exact [ig'zækt] tačan; zahtijevati; iznuditi; **~itude**, **~ness** točnost
exaggerat|e [ig'zædʒəreit] pretjerivati; **~ion** pretjerivanje
exaltation [egzɔ:l'teiʃən] zanos
examin|ation [igzæmi'neiʃən] ispiti(vanje); pregled; **~e** ispit(iv)ati; pregledati; istražiti; **~er** ispitivač
example [ig'za:mpl] primjer(ak); uzor, ugled; ***for* ~** na primjer
exasperat|e [ig'za:spəreit] ogorčiti; pogoršati; **~ion** ogorčenje
excavat|e ['ekskəveit] iskopavati; izdupsti; **~ion** iskopavanje
exceed [ik'si:d] nadmašiti; pretjerati; **~ingly** izvanredno
excel [ik'sel] nadmašiti; isticati se (***in***, ***at***); **~lence** izvrsnost; odličnost; **~lency** titula ekscelencija; **~lent** izvrstan
except [ik'sept] izuzeti, isključiti; **~ion** izuzetak; **~ional** izuzetan
excess [ik'ses] prekoračenje; prekomjernost; **~ *fare*** nadoplata na voznu kartu; **~ *luggage*** prtljaga preko dozvoljene težine; **~ *postage*** nadoplata poštarine; **~ive** pretjeran; preko mjere
exchange [iks'tʃeindʒ] zamijeniti; razmijeniti (***for***); zamjena; razmjena (*novca*); burza; telefonska centrala; ***foreign* ~ *control office*** devizna uprava; **~able** zamjenljiv (***for***)
exchequer [iks'tʃekə] državna riznica (blagajna)
excise [ek'saiz] trošarina; oporezovati; izrezati
excit|able [ik'saitəbl] lako uzbudljiv; **~e** uzbuditi; nadražiti; **~ement** uzbuđenje
exclaim [iks'kleim] uzviknuti; glasno optužiti (***against***)
exclamation [eksklə'meiʃən] uzvik
exclu|de [iks'klu:d] isključiti; **~sion** isključenje; **~sive** isključiv; ekskluzivan
excrescence [iks'kresns] izraslina
excursion [iks'kə:ʃən] izlet; **~ *train*** izletnički vlak; **~ist** izletnik
excus|able [iks'kju:zəbl] oprostiv; opravdan; **~e** [~z] ispričati (se); [~s] isprika

execrate ['eksikreit] proklinjati; biti odvratan
execut|e ['eksikju:t] izvršiti; obaviti; MUS izvesti; **~ion** izvođenje; provođenje; MUS izvedba; smaknuće; **~ioner** krvnik; **~ive**: ***(the) ~ive*** egzekutiva, izvršni odbor; **~or** izvršitelj (oporuke)
exempl|ary [ig'zempləri] uzoran; **~ify** služiti kao primjer
exempt [ig'zempt] izuzet (***from***); osloboditi; poštediti; poštediti (***from***)
exercise ['eksəsaiz] vježba; kretanje; ***take ~*** razgibati se; vježbati; obučavati
exert [ig'zə:t]: ***~ oneself*** napregnuti se; nastojati; **~ion** napor
exhal|ation [ekshə'leiʃən] izdisanje; **~e** [eks'heil] izdahnuti
exhaust [ig'zɔ:st] iscrpsti; (zrak) ispumpati; TECH ispuh; ***~ gas*** ispušni plin; ***~ pipe*** ispušna cijev; **~ion** iscrpljenost; **~ive** *fig* iscrpan
exhibit [ig'zibit] izložiti; pokazati; ispoljiti; **~ion** izložba; stipendija; **~or** FILM prikazivač
exhilarate [ig'zilərait] razveseliti
exhort [ig'zɔ:t] opominjati; **~ation** opomena
exhumation [ekshju:'meiʃən] iskop
exile ['eksail] progonstvo; prognanik; prognati (***from***)
exist [ig'zist] postojati; živjeti; **~ence** postojanje; život; **~ent** postojeći
exit ['eksit] izlaz; smrt; odlazak; THEAT izlazi ("odlazi"); **~ permit** dozvola izlazka iz zemlje
exorbitan|ce [ig'zɔ:bitəns] pretjeranost; **~t** pretjeran
expan|d [iks'pænd] proširiti (se); raširiti (se); **~sion** širenje; **~sive** ekspanzivan; opsežan; širok
expect [iks'pekt] očekivati; **~ant** koji očekuje; **~ation** očekivanje
expectorat|e [iks'pektəreit] iskašljavati; **~ion** iskašljavanje
expedi|ency [iks'pi:diənsi] svrsishodnost; **~ent** sredstvo (u nuždi); **~te** pospješiti; **~tion** ekspedicija
expel [iks'pel] izbaciti; istjerati
expen|d [iks'pend] izdati; potrošiti; **~diture** izdaci; **~ses** *pl* troškovi; **~sive** skup
experience [iks'piəriəns] iskustvo; doživjeti; **~d** iskusan
experiment [iks'perimənt] pokus; [-ment] praviti pokuse
expert ['ekspə:t] stručan; stručnjak; **~ness** stručnost
expiation [ekspi'eiʃən] pokora
expir|ation [ekspaiə'reiʃən]

izdisanje; istek; **~e** izdisati; izdahnuti; isteći (rok)
expl|ain [iks'plein] objasniti, rastumačiti; protumačiti; **~anation** [eksplə'~] razjašnjenje, itd.; **~icable** ['eksplikəbl] razjašnjiv
explicit [iks'plisit] izričit
explode [iks'ploud] eksplodirati; detonirati
exploit ['eksplɔit] podvig
explor|ation [eksplɔ:'reiʃən] istraživanje; **~e** istraživati; **~er** istraživač
explosi|on [iks'plouʒən] eksplozija; provala; **~ve** eksplozivan; eksploziv
export [eks'pɔ:t] izvoziti; ['~] izvoz; **~ *licence*** izvozna dozvola; **~ *trade*** izvozništvo; **~s** *pl* izvoz (roba); **~ation** izvoz; **~er** izvoznik
expos|e [iks'pouz] izložiti (i *fig*); PHOT eksponirati; **~ure** [iks'pouʒə] izloženost (elementima); PHOT eksponaža; *fig* razotkrivanje
express [iks'pres] izričit; ekspresni; **~ (*train*)** brzi vlak; ekspresno; izraziti (misli); istisnuti; **~ion** izraz; istiskivanje
expropriat|e [eks'prouprieit] izvlastiti; **~ion** izvlaštenje
exquisite ['ekskwizit] izvrstan; delikatan; **~ness** profinjenost
extant [eks'tænt] postojeći
extemporize [iks'tempəraiz] improvizirati
extend [iks'tend] protegnuti (se); proširiti; produžiti (*rok*); pružati se (***to***)
extensi|bility [ikstensə'biliti] rastežljivost; **~ble** rastežljiv; **~on** proširenje; produbljenje; **~on *cord*** EL produžni kabl; **~on *table*** stol na razlačenje; **~ve** opsežan
extent [iks'tent] opseg; veličina; ***to a certain* ~** donekle
extenuate [eks'tenjueit] ublažiti; ispričati
exterior [eks'tiəriə] vanjski; vanjština; FILM eksterijer
exterminate [eks'tə:mineit] iskorijeniti; uništiti
external [eks'tə:nl] vanjski
extinct [iks'tiŋkt] ugasnuo; *fig* izumro; **~ion** gašenje (i *fig*)
extinguish [iks'tiŋgwiʃ] ugasiti; iskorijeniti; **~er** gasilo
extirpat|e ['ekstə:peit] iskorijeniti; **~ion** iskorijenjenje;
extort [iks'tɔ:t] iznuditi (***from***); **~ion** inuđivanje
extra ['ekstrə] dodatni; posebni; dodatak; **~ *special*** kasno izdanje; **~s** *pl* posebni troškovi
extract ['ekstrækt] ekstrakt; [iks'trækt] izvući; **~ion** porijeklo
extraneous [eks'treinjəs] vanjski; nebitan (***to***); tuđi
extraordinary [iks'trɔ:dnəri] izvanredan; neobičan
extravagan|ce [iks'trævigəns] pretjeranost; rasip-

nost; **~t** pretjeran; rasipan
extreme [iks'tri:m] krajnost; ekstrem; krajni
extremit|y [iks'tremiti] krajnja nužda; **~ies** *pl* udovi
exuberan|ce [ig'zju:bərəns] bujnost; **~t** bujan; pun života
exude [ig'zju:d] lučiti
exult [ig'zʌlt] veseliti se; **~ation** likovanje
eye [ai] oko (i *fig* i BOT); pogled; vid; ušica; (pažljivo) promatrati; **~ball** očna jabučica; **~brow** obrva; **~-catcher** nešto što privlači pažnju; **~-glass** monokl; **~glasses**: (***a pair of***) **~** naočale; **~lash** trepavica; **~lid** očni kapak; **~-opener** *fig* nešto što otvara oči; **~shot** vidokrug; **~sight** vid; *coll* **~-wash** obmana; **~-witness** očevidac

F

f. = **farthing**; **fathom**; **following**; **foot**
fable ['feibl] bajka
fabric ['fæbrik] tkivo; tkanina; **~ate** izmišljati; **~ation** izmišljotina
fabulous ['fæbjuləs] bajoslovan
face [feis] lice; obraz; izraz lica; površina; prednja strana; brojčanik sata; ***on the* ~ *of it*** na izgled; na prvi pogled; **~ value** nominalna vrijednost; stajati nasuprot; suočiti se sa; prkositi; prevući; opločiti
facetious [fə'si:ʃəs] šaljiv
facil|e ['fæsail] lagan; spretan; **~itate** olakšati; **~ity** lakoća, mogućnost; *pl* instalacije
facing ['feisiŋ] TECH prevlaka, oplata
fact [fækt] činjenica; **~s** *pl* (***of the case***) činjenično stanje; ***in*** (***point of***) **~** u stvari, zapravo
faction ['fækʃən] frakcija; **~ist** frakcionaš
factious ['fækʃəs] buntovan
factitious [fæk'tiʃəs] fiktivan
factor ['fæktə] činilac; **~y** tvornica; faktorija
faculty ['fækəlti] sposobnost; sila; *fig* nadarenost; fakultet
fad|e [feid] uvenuti; izblijediti; ***~e away*** postepeno iščezavati; **~ing** radio nestajanje tona
fag [fæg] *sl* cigareta
faggot ['fægət] svežanj pruća
fail [feil] (uz)manjkati; promašiti; zakazati (*glas*) propustiti; ne učiniti; propasti; srušiti (ispitanika); iznjeveriti; ***without* ~** neizostavno; **~ure** neuspjeh; propao (promašen) čovjek
faint [feint] slab; blijed; onesvjestiti se; **~-hearted** malo-

dušan; **~ness** slabost
fair [fɛə] lijep; ***the ~ sex*** krasni spol; čist; svjetao; plavokos; pošten (***with***); (vele)sajam; **~ copy** čist prijepis; **~ly** prilično; **~ness** ljepota; plava kosa (i bijela put); poštenje; **~ play** pošten postupak (igra); **~way** plovni dio (sredina) rijeke, kanala
fairy ['fɛəri] vila
faith [feiθ] vjera (***in***); vjernost; povjerenje; **~ful** vjeran; **~less** nevjeran
fake [feik] *sl* prevara; *Am* imitacija; *Am* varalica (i ***~r***); *Am* patvoriti (i ***up***)
falcon ['fɔːlkən] sokol
fall [fɔːl] pad; propast; opadanje (lišća, snijega, vode itd.); *Am* jesen; pad (cijena); (o-, ot-, is-)pasti; survati se; popustiti; utjecati (***into***); ***~ asleep*** zaspati; ***~ between two stools*** proigrati obje prilike; ***~ due*** dospjeti; ***~ ill*** (*Am* ***sick***) razboliti (se); ***~ in love with*** zaljubiti se u; ***~ in with*** slagati se sa; ***~ short of*** ne postići; podbaciti
fallow-deer ['fæloudiə] jelen lopataš
false [fɔːls] kriv; neiskren; lažan; **~ key** otpirač; **~hood** laž; neiskrenost
falsi|fication ['fɔːlsifi'keiʃən] falsifikat; **~fy** krivotvoriti ['~fai]
falter ['fɔːltə] pokolebati se; zapinjati (glas)
fame [feim] slava; glasovitost; **~d** glasovit (***for***)
familiar [fə'miljə] (dobro) poznat; upućen; prisan; **~ity** familijarnost; prisnost; **~ize** pobliže upoznati
family ['fæmili] obitelj
famine ['fæmin] glad(ovanje)
famous ['feiməs] slavan
fan [fæn] lepeza; AGR vijača (žita); ventilator; SPORT *coll* ljubitelj nečega: RADIO amater; hladiti (se) lepezom
fanatic [fə'nætik] fanatik; **~ism** [~sizm] fanatizam
fanciful ['fænsiful] maštovit
fancy ['fænsi] mašta; fantazija; sklonost; ljubav za; uobraziti; ***take a ~*** zavoljeti; **~ articles** *pl* galanterija; **~ dress** kostim za krabuljni ples; **~ goods** galanterija; **~-work** fini (ženski) ručni rad
fantastic [fæn'tæstik] fantastičan; **~ally** fantastično
fanzine ['fænziːn] fanzine
far [faː] daleko; ***~ the best*** daleko najbolji; ***by ~*** daleko, neusporedivo
farce [faːs] farsa; lakrdija (i THEAT)
fare [fɛə] prevoznina; putnik; **~well** zbogom!; ***~well party*** slavljenje rastanka
far-fetched ['faː'fetʃt] *fig* pretjeran, nategnut
farm [faːm] imanje; gazdin-

stvo; farma; baviti se seoskim gospodarstvom; **~er** seljak; farmer; **~ing** seosko gospodarstvo; **~yard** seosko dvorište
far-off ['fa:rɔf] dalek
farrier ['færiə] potkivač
far-sighted dalekovidan
farth|er ['fa:ðə] dalji(e); **~est** najdalji(e)
farthing ['fa:ðiŋ] 1/4 penija; *fig* para
fascinate ['fæsineit] očarati
fashion ['fæʃən] oblik; kroj; moda; oblikovati; **~able** moderan; modni; elegantan
fast [fa:st] čvrst; učvršćen; nepomičan; brz; koji ide naprijed (sat); koji ne pušta boju u pranju; "laka" (žena); ***be ~ asleep*** čvrsto spavati; ***it is raining ~*** kiša lijeva; **~ day** posni dan; **~ train** brzi vlak
fasten ['fa:sn] pričvrstiti; privezati; dobro zatvoriti (vrata); **~er** kopča; zatvarač; ***patent ~er*** druker
fastidious [fæs'tidiəs] izbirljiv
fastness ['fa:stnis] čvrstoća; brzina
fat [fæt] mastan; debeo; mast
fatal ['feitl] koban; smrtonosan; **~ity** kobnost; žrtva
fate [feit] sudbina; kob
fat free ['fætfri:] bez masti
father ['fa:ðə] otac; **~-in-law** svekar, punac; **~less** bez oca; **~ly** očinski
fathom ['fæðəm] hvat; MAR paš (1,8 m); dokučiti; **~less** nedokučiv
fatigue [fə'ti:g] umor; izmoriti
fat|ness ['fætnis] debljina; **~ty** debeo, usaljen
fatuity [fə'tjuiti] blesavost
fault [fɔ:lt] greška; mana; krivnja; ***find ~ with*** kuditi; **~iness** manjkavost; **~less** bez mane; **~y** pogrešan; neispravan
favour ['feivə] sklonost; usluga; favorizirati; popovoljan; **~ite** ljubimac; favorit
fawn [fɔ:n] lane; žućkasto-smeđ; puzati pred (***upon***)
fear [fiə] strah; bojati se; **~ful** strašan; strašljiv; **~less** neustrašiv
feasible ['fi:zəbl] ostvariv; izvediv
feast [fi:st] gozba; svetkovina; pogostiti; gostiti (se)
feat [fi:t] podvig
feather ['feðə] pero; ***that is a ~ in his cap*** time se može podičiti; **~ed** pernat
featur|e ['fi:tʃə] crta lica; značajka; ***a film ~ing N. N.*** film sa N. N. u glavnoj ulozi; **~e film** cjelovečernji film; imati kao značajku; uključivati
febrifuge ['febrifju:dʒ] sredstvo protiv groznice
February ['februəri] veljača, februar
federa|l ['fedərəl] savezni; **~l-**

ize, **~te** stupiti (okupiti) u savez; **~tion** federacija (strukovni) savez
fee [fiː] pristojba; honorar
feeble ['fiːbl] slab; **~-ness** slabost
feed [fiːd] hrana; (na-, ot-)hraniti; posluživati; (stroj); puniti; hraniti se pasti; **~ *up*** toviti; TECH dovodni uređaj; bočica s dudom
feeding ['fiːdiŋ] hranjenje; **~ bottle** bočica s dudom; **~ crane** RLW hidraulična pumpa; **~-trough** valov, korito
feel [fiːl] osjećati (se); pipati; ***I ~ like doing*** rado bih; **~er** ticalo *fig* ispitivanje terena; **~ing** osjećajan; osjećaj
feet [fiːt] *pl* od ***foot*** stopala
feign [fein] (i **~ *to do***) pretvarati se
felicitat|e [fi'lisiteit] čestitati; **~ion** čestitanje
felicity [fi'lisiti] sreća
fell oboriti; posjeći
fellow ['felou] drug; kolega; *coll* čovjek; **~-citizen** sugrađanin; **~-traveller** suputnik
felt filc; pokriti filcom
female ['fiːmeil] ženski; ženka
feminine ['feminin] ženski (i GRAM)
fen močvara
fenc|e [fens] ograda; plot; opasati; ograditi; mačevati; **~ing** ograđivanje; **~ing-foil** floret
fend: **~ *off*** odvratiti
fender ['fendə] niska ograda kamina; *Am* MOT blatobran
ferment ['fəːmənt] vrenje; [-'ment] vreti; **~ation** vrenje
fern [fəːn] paprat
ferocious [fə'rouʃəs] divlji
ferret ['ferit] afrički tvor; njuškati
ferrule ['feruːl] okov; prsten
ferry ['feri] skela; prevesti; **~-boat** trajekt; **~man** brodar, skelar
fertil|e ['fəːtail] plodan; **~ity** plodnost; **~ize** oploditi
ferv|ent ['fəːvənt], **~id** *fig* gorući; revan; **~our** žar; revnost
festiv|al ['festəvəl] svetkovina; **~e** svečan; **~ity** svečanost
festoon [fes'tuːn] girlanda
fetch [fetʃ] donijeti; postići (*cijenu*)
fetter ['fetə] lanac; sputati
feud [fjuːd] svađa; feud
fever ['fiːvə] groznica; **~ed**, **~ish** grozničav
few [fjuː] malo; ***a ~*** nekoliko
fibr|e ['faibə] vlakno; nit; **~ous** vlaknast
fickle ['fikl] prevrtljiv; **~ness** prevrtljivost
fiction ['fikʃən] izmišljotina; roman, pripovijest, beletristika
fiddle ['fidl] violina; guslati
fidelity [fi'deliti] vjernost (***to***)
fidget ['fidʒit] vrpoljenje; ***have the ~s*** vrpoljiti se; **~y** uzvrpoljen

field [fi:ld] polje; igralište; *fig* područje; doseg; **~-glass** dalekozor; **~-sports** *pl* lov i ribolov
fierce [fiəs] divlji, žestok; **~ness** žestina
fiery ['faiəri] vatren, žestok
fif|teen ['fif'ti:n] petnaest; **~teenth** petnaesti; **~th** peti; petina; **~thly** peto; **~tieth** pedeseti, pedesetina; **~ty** pedeset
fig smokva
fight [fait] borba; boriti se; tući se; ***show ~*** pružati otpor
figure ['figə] figura; stas; brojka; predstaviti (se); javljati se; ***cut a sorry ~*** ostaviti jadan dojam; ***~ up*** *ili* ***out*** izračunati; ***~ out at*** izlaziti na
filament ['filəmənt] vlakno; nit; prašnik; **~ resistance** ogrjevni otpornik
file [fail] fascikl; evidencija; turpija; evidentirati; odložiti (spis); turpijati
filial ['filjəl] sinovski; kćerinski
filigree ['filigri:] filigran
filings ['failiŋz] *pl* kovinske strugotine
fill (na-, is-)puniti; biti na (položaju); *Am* izvršiti (*nalog*); ***~ in*** *ili* ***up*** ispuniti (tiskanicu)
fillet ['filit] CUL pečenica (*riblji*) file; ARCHIT letva
filling ['filiŋ] nadjev; MOT **~ station** benzinska stanica
film kožica; opna; film; ***shoot*** (*ili* ***take***) ***a ~*** snimiti film; snimati
filter ['filtə] filter; filtrirati; procjeđivati
filth [filθ] prljavština; **~y** prljav; pornografski
fin peraja; *sl* ruka; AERO bočno kormilo; MOT (***radiator***) **~** rebro radijatora
final ['fainl] konačan; zaključan; SPORT finale
financ|e [fi'næns] financije; financirati; **~ial** [fai'nænʃəl] financijski
find [faind] naći; naići na; proglasiti (krivim); ***~ out*** otkriti; informirati se; **~er** nalaznik; OPT tražilac; **~ing** nalaženje; nalaz; **~ings** *pl Am* alat, potrepštine
fine fin; nježan; otmjen; lijep; ***cut it ~*** doći u zadnji čas; "knap" proračunati; globa; oglobiti; **~ness** finoća; **~ry** *fig* puna parada
finger ['fiŋgə] prst; ***have a ~ in the pie*** biti umješan; opipa(va)ti; **~post** putokaz na raskršću; **~-print** otisak prstiju; **~-stall** navlaka za prst
finish ['finiʃ] dokrajčiti; svršiti; prekinuti; ***~ing touch*** završno dotjerivanje; apretura
fir [fə:] jela; **~-cone** češer
fire ['faiə] vatra; požar; (za-, is-)paliti; *Am coll* otpustiti; ***on ~*** koji gori; **~-alarm** požarni alarm; **~-brigade**

vatrogasci; **~-curtain** THEAT željezna (protupožarna) zavjesa; **~-department** *Am* vatrogasci; **~-engine** vatrogasna kola; **~-escape** protupožarne ljestve; **~-fighter** *Am* vatrogasac; **~-insurance** osiguranje protiv požara; **~-irons** lopatica, klijesta i žarač uz kamin; **~-lighter** palilo za kamin; **~-man** vatrogasac; ložač; **~place** kamin; ognjište; **~plug** hidrant; **~proof** vatrostalan; **~screen** zaklon od vatre (kod kamina); **~-station** vatrogasna stanica; **~wood** ogrjevno drvo; **~works** vatromet

firing ['faiəriŋ] paljenje; loženje

firm [fə:m] čvrst; postojan; tvrtka, firma; **~ness** čvrstoća

first [fə:st] prvi; kao prvo; ***at ~*** s početka; isprva; ***~ of all*** prije svega; **~ly** u prvom redu; **~-rate** prvoklasan; izvrstan

firth [fə:θ] fjord; ušće

fish [fiʃ] riba; pecati; ribariti; **~-bone** riblja kost; **~(-plate)** RLW spojnica

fisher|man ['fiʃəmən] ribar; **~y** ribarstvo

fishing ['fiʃiŋ] ribarenje; **~-rod** štap za pecanje; **~-tackle** pribor za pecanje

fissure ['fiʃə] pukotina

fist šaka

fit [fit] pogodan; sposoban; odgovarati; namjestiti; probati (i ***~ on***); ***~ out*** opremiti; ***~ up*** podesiti namjestiti; napadaj; **~ness** sposobnost; **~ter** monter; instalater; **~ting** koji odgovara; montaža; **~tings** pribor; okovi; namještaj; rasvjetna tijela

five [faiv] pet; **~fold** petorostruk(o)

fix [fiks] učvrstiti; prikovati (pogled); utvrditi; odrediti (dan); ***~ up*** *Am* urediti; prirediti; *coll* ***be in a ~*** biti u neprilici; **~ed** čvrst; utvrđen; ukočen (pogled); fiksni (ideja); ***~ed star*** zvijezda stajačica

fizz pjenušati se, prštati

fl. = **florin**

flabbergast ['flæbəga:st] *coll* zapanjiti

flabby ['flæbi], **flaccid** ['flæksid] mlitav

flag [flæg] zastava; ploča; vodeni ljiljan; omlitavjeti

flake [fleik] pahuljica; otpadati u ljuskama

flame [fleim] plamen; plamsati, gorjeti (i *fig*)

flank [flæŋk] bok; stajati o boku

flannel ['flænl] flanel; **~s** *pl* odijelo (ili hlače) od flanelastog sukna

flap [flæp] ušna resa; preklop; lomatati

flapper ['flæpə] *sl fig* šiparica

flare [flɛə] blještati

flash [flæʃ] bljesak; bljesnuti; **~-light** PHOT "fleš" lampa; *Am* džepna lampa; **~ signal** svjetlosni signal
flask [fla:sk] demižon; džepna boca
flat [flæt] plosnat; plitak; bez sjaja; bezbojan; ravnica; stan; **~-foot** ravni tabani; **~ iron** pegla; **~ten** spljoštiti (se)
flatter ['flætə] laskati; **~er** laskavac; **~y** laskanje
flatulen|ce ['flætjuləns], **~cy** nadutost
flavour ['fleivə] okus; aroma; začiniti
flaw [flɔ:] pukotina, napuklina; mana
flax [flæks] lan
flea [fli:] buha
flee [fli:] bježati; **~ *from*** pobjeći, udaljivati se
fleec|e [fli:s] runo; ovčice (oblaci); *fig* operušati; **~y** runast
fleet [fli:t] flota; vozni park
flesh [fleʃ] meso; put
flex EL kabl; žica; **~ibility** savitljivost; **~ible** elastičan
flicker ['flikə] treptati; podrhtavati; treperiti
flier, flyer ['flaiə] letač
flight lijet; bijeg; stepenise (do prvog prekida)
flims|iness ['flimzinis] tankoća; **~y** tanak; loš
flinch [flintʃ] trgnuti se; ustuknuti
fling [fliŋ] bacanje; zavitlati; **~ *away*** (od)baciti
flint [flint] kremen; kresivo
flip udarac; kvrcaj; AERO *sl* let
flirt [flə:t] ljubakati; flertovati; **~ation** ljubakanje, flert
flit šmugnuti
flitch [flitʃ] pola slanine
flitter ['flitə] lepršati
float [flout] plovak (i AERO); lopata na kotaču; ospoposobiti (*brod*); pokrenuti; pustiti u opticaj; plutati; ploviti; lebdjeti
floating ['floutiŋ]: **~ bridge** pontonski most; **~ capital** obrtna glavnica; **~ debt** viseći dug; **~ ice** sante leda; **~ kidney** putujući bubreg
flock krdo; stado; pramen; jatiti se
flog šibati, bičevati; **~ging** batinanje, bičevanje
flood [flʌd] poplava; poplaviti; **~-disaster** katastrofalna poplava; **~-gate** ustanova; **~-light** reflektor; obasjati
floor [flɔ:] pod; kat; AGR guvno; *Am* PARL poslaničke klupe; ***take the* ~** *Am* uzeti riječ u debati; popoditi; **~-lamp** stajaća lampa; **~-walker** *Am* = **shopwalker**; **~-wax** laštilo za parkete
florin ['flɔrin] florin (dva šilinga)
florist ['flɔrist] cvjećar(ica)
flounce [flauns] volan
flounder ['flaundə] iverak (*riba*)
flour [flauə] brašno

flourish ['flʌriʃ] ukrasni zavoj (šara); slikoviti pokret; MUS tuš; biti u procvatu; mahati
flow [flou] tok; struja; izljev; teći; izlijevati se
flower [flauə] cvijet; cvat
flu [flu:] *coll* ***influenza*** gripa
fluctuat|e ['flʌktjueit] kolebati se; **~ion** fluktuiranje
fluen|cy ['flu:ənsi] tečnost, glatkoća; **~t** tečan, gladak
fluff [flʌf] pahuljica; **~y** pahuljičav; mek i našušuren
fluid ['flu:id] tekuć; tekućina
flurry ['flʌri] nalet; uzbuđenost; uznemiriti
flush [flʌʃ] crvenilo; mlaz; zarumeniti se; isplahnuti
flute [flu:t] flauta
flutter ['flʌtə] lepršati
flux [flʌks] MED TECH, *fig* tok
fly [flai] muha; THEAT *pl* ***flies*** sofita; letjeti; puštati (*zmaja*); prenositi (*avionski*); AERO pilotirati; **~ *into a passion*** razbjesniti se; **~ *open*** naglo se otvoriti
flying ['flaiiŋ] leteći; **~ boat** hidroavion (bez plovaka); **~ machine** letalo; **~ squad** leteća patrola; **~ visit** kratka iznenadna posjeta
foal [foul] ždrijebe
foam [foum] pjena; pjeniti se; **~y** pjenušav
f. o. b. = free on board
focus ['foukəs] žarište; OPT i *fig* izoštriti (sliku)
fog magla; **~gy** maglovito
fog-horn sirena za maglu
foil [fɔil] folija; metalna podloga ogledala; osujetiti
fold [fould] nabor; preklop; preklopiti; **~ *up*** složiti; sklopiti; sklopljivi prospekt; fascikl; nož za savijanje papira
folding ['fouldiŋ]: **~-boat** (sklopljivi) kajak; **~-chair** sklopljiva stolica; **~ door(s** *pl*) razvlačna (sklopljiva) vrata; **~-screen** sklopljivi paravan
foliage ['fouliidʒ] lišće, krošnja
folk [fouk] narod; ljudi; *Am coll* ***my ~s*** moja obitelj
follow ['fɔlou] slijediti; pratiti; **~ *up*** nastaviti iskoristiti; **~er** sljedbenik
folly ['fɔli] ludost
foment [fou'ment] poticati
fond odviše nježan; ***be ~ of*** voljeti; **~le** milovati; **~ness** nježnost
food [fu:d] hrana; jelo; **~-shortage** nestašica hrane; **~-stuffs** *pl coll* orehrambeni artikli; **~-value** hranljivost
fool [fu:l] budala; ludovati, zbijati šalu; **~hardy** smion; **~ish** nerazborit; **~proof** vrlo jednostavan; potpuno siguran
foot [fut], *pl* ***feet*** stopalo; MIL pješadija; ***on ~*** pješice; u toku; **~ball** nogomet; **~board** papuča; **~-gear** obuća; **~ing** osnova; *fig* uporište; **~lights** *pl* THEAT svjetla rampe;

~-man lakaj; ~-passenger pješak; ~-path pješačka staza; ~step korak, stopa; ~-wear *Am* = foot-gear
fop kicoš
for za; radi; u; ~ ***example*** *ili* ***instance*** na primjer
forbear [fɔ:'bɛə] uzdržati se; ~ance uzdržljivost
forbid [fə'bid] zabraniti
force [fɔ:s] sila; snaga; moć; ***the*** ~ policija; prisiliti; ~ ***on*** natjerati; ~ ***open*** razvaliti; ~d landing prisilno spuštanje; ~d loan prinudni zajam; ~d sale prinudna prodaja; ~-pump kompresiona pumpa
forcible ['fɔ:səbl] snažan, moćan
fore [fɔ:] sprijeda; prednji; ~bode nagovještati; ~cast prognoza; ~finger kažiprst; ~ground prvi plan; ~hand *tenis*; ~ (stroke) forhend; ~head ['fɔrid] čelo
foreign ['fɔrin] stran; tuđ; ***the*** ♀ ***Office*** ministarstvo vanjskih poslova; ~ policy vanjska politika; ~ trade vanjska trgovina; ~er stranac
fore|land rt; predzemlje; ~leg prednja noga; ~most najistaknutiji; ~man predsjednik (porote); predradnik; poslovođa; ~noon prijepodne; ~runner preteča; ~see predvidjeti; ~sight dalekovidnost; ~taste nagovještaj
forest ['fɔrist] šuma; ~er šumar
forfeit ['fɔ:fit] proigrati; pokora; globa; otkupnina; ~s *pl* igra zaloga; proigrati
forge [fɔ:dʒ] kovačnica; kovati; krivotvoriti; ~r kovač; krivotvorilac; ~ry krivotvorina
forget [fə'get] zaboraviti; ~fulness zaboravljivost; ~-me-not potočnica
forgive [fə'giv] oprostiti; ~ness oproštenje
fork [fɔ:k] viljuška; račvati se
form [fɔ:m] oblik; lik; forma; tiskanica; klupa; razred; oblikovati (se); formirati (se); SPORT ***be in*** ~ biti u formi; ~al formalan; ~ality formalnost; ***without formalities*** bez ceremonija
former ['fɔ:mə] prijašnji; bivši; prethodni; ~ly prije
formic acid ['fɔ:mikæsid] mravlja kiselina
formidable ['fɔ:midəbl] zastrašujući; velik; težak
formless ['fɔ:mlis] bezobličan
formul|a ['fɔ:mjulə] formula; pravilo; ~ate formulirati
forsake [fə'seik] napustiti
forswear [fɔ:'swɛə] odreći se
fort tvrđava
forth [fɔ:θ] dalje; odatle; ~-coming predstojeći; ~with smjesta
fortieth ['fɔ:tiiθ] četrdeseti
fortify ['fɔ:tifai] utvrditi;

fortieth ['fɔːtiiθ] četrdeseti
fortify ['fɔːtifai] utvrditi; pojačati
fortnight ['fɔːtnait] četrnaest dana; **~ly** polumjesečno
fortress ['fɔːtris] tvrđava
fortuitous [fɔː'tjuitəs] slučajan
fortunate ['fɔːtʃnit] sretan; **~ly** srećom
fortune ['fɔːtʃən] sreća; sudbina; slučaj; bogatstvo; **~-teller** gatara
forty ['fɔːti] četrdeset
forward ['fɔːwəd] prednji; bezobrazan; naprijed; SPORT navalni igrač; otpremati, slati dalje; **~ing agent** otpremnik
foster ['fɔstə] njegovati (i *fig*); **~-child** posvoj če; **~-parents** poočim i pomajka
foul [faul] odvratan, odbojan; zagađen; pokvaren; SPORT protupravilan; zaplesti; omesti
found [faund] osnovati; zasnivati (se); lijevati; **~ation** osnivanje; zaklada; temelj; **~er** osnivač; ljevač
foundling ['faundliŋ] nahoče (dijete)
foundry ['faundri] ljevaonica
fountain ['fauntin] česma; *fig* vrelo; **~-pen** naliv pero
four [fɔː] četiri; SPORT četverac; **~-cycle** *ili* **~stroke engine** četverotaktni motor; **~-engined** četveromotorni; **~-fold** četverostruko; **~-in-hand** četveropreg; **~-power talk** četvorni razgovori; **~-seater** MOT četverosjed; **~teen(th)** četrnaest(i); četrnaestina; **~th** četvrti(na); **~thly** četvrto; **~-wheel-drive** MOT auto s dvije pogonske osovine
fowl [faul] perad; kokoš; **~ing-piece** laka sačmarica (puška)
fox [fɔks] lisica
Fr = **France**; **French**; **Friday**
fraction ['frækʃən] mali dio; MATH razlomak
fracture ['fræktʃə] lom kosti
fragil|e ['frædʒail] loman; krhak; **~ity** krhkost
fragment ['frægmənt] odlomak
fragran|ce ['freigrəns] (ugodan) miris; **~t** mirisav
frail [freil] krhak, slabašan
frame [freim] (tjelesna) građa; stas; okvir; **~ of mind** raspoloženje; duševno stanje; sastaviti; zamisliti; uokviriti; *Am* potkopati; **~-up** *Am* smicalica; **~work** TECH okosnica, struktura
France [fraːns] Francuska
franchise ['fræntʃaiz] biračko pravo
frank ['fræŋk] iskren, otvoren; **~ness** otvorenost
frantic ['fræntik] lud; izvan sebe (***with***)
fratern|al [frə'təːnl] bratski; **~ity** bratstvo
fraud [frɔːd] prevara; **~ulent**

prevaran
fray [frei] izlizati (se); otrcati (se)
freckle ['frekl] sunčana pjega
free [fri:] slobodan; darežljiv; obilan; ***set ~*** osloboditi; **~dom** sloboda; neusiljenost; **~-kick** SPORT slobodni udarac; **~ trade** slobodna trgovina; osloboditi
freemason ['fri:meisn], **~ry** mason(stvo)
freez|e [fri:z] smrznuti (se); zepsti; **~ing point** ledište
freight [freit] teret; natovariti; **~er** teretni brod
French [frentʃ] francuski; francuski jezik; ***the ~*** Francuzi; **~man** Francuz; **~woman** Francuskinja
frequen|cy ['fri:kwənsi] učestalost; EL frekvencija; **~t** čest; [fri'kwent] pohađati
fresh [freʃ] svjež; nov; neiskusan; **~-frozen** svježe zaleđen; **~ness** svježina; novina; **~water** slatka voda (riječna)
fret uzrujavanje; briga; uzrujavati (se); gristi se
fret|-saw rezbarska pilica; **~-work** rezbarije (u šperploči)
friar ['fraiə] redovnik
friction ['frikʃən] trenje
Friday ['fraidi] petak; ***Good ~*** Veliki Petak
friend [frend] prijatelj(ica); **~ly** prijateljski; **~ship** prijateljstvo
frigate ['frigit] fregata
fright [frait] strah; **~en** uplašiti; **~ful** strašan
frigid ['fridʒid] leden, hladan
frill ukrasni nabor; ukrasiti
fringe [frindʒ] resa; šiška
frivol|ity [fri'vɔliti] frivolnost; **~ous** neozbiljan, frivolan
fro [frou]: ***to and ~*** amo tamo
frock [frɔk] ženska (dječja) haljina; **~-coat** kaput
frog žaba
frolic(some) ['frɔlik(səm)] vragoljanski; prpošan
from iz; od; sa; ***~ above*** odozgo
front [frʌnt] čelo; pročelje; fronta; ***in ~ of*** ispred; **~ier** državna granica; **~ispiece** naslovna ilustracija; **~ room** soba s ulične strane; **~ view** izgled s prednje strane; **~ wheel drive** prenos (pogon) na prednje kotače
frost mraz; inje; **~-bitten** promrzao; **~y** leden
froth [frɔθ] pjena; (za)pjeniti se
frown [fraun] (na)mrštiti se; mrko gledati
frozen ['frouzn] smrznut; zaleđen (kapital); **~ meat** smrznuto meso; **~ up** *ili* **over** zamrznut
frugal ['fru:gəl] umjeren; štedljiv
fruit [fru:t] voće; plod; **~arian** sljedbenik voćne dijete; **~erer** prodavač voća; **~ful** plo-

dan; **~less** besplodan
frustrate [frʌs'treit] osujetiti; razočarati
fry [frai] prženo jelo; pržiti
frying-pan tava; ***get out of the ~ into the fire*** zapasti iz zla u gore
ft. = **foot, feet**
fuel ['fjuəl] gorivo (i MOT)
fugitive ['fju:dʒitiv] prolazan; bjegunac
fulfil [ful'fil] ispuniti; izvršiti; **~ment** izvršenje
full pun; potpun; punopravan; opširan; **~-dress** svečani, paradni; **~-length** u naravnoj veličini
ful(l)ness ['fulnis] punoća
fumble ['fʌmbl] prtljati; šeprtljiti
fume [fju:m] dim; isparenje; (o)dimiti; *coll* bjesnjeti
fumigat|e ['fju:migeit] ciklonizirati; **~ion** ciklonizacija
fun [fʌn] šala; zabava
function ['fʌnkʃən] funkcija; funkcionirati; **~ary** funkcionar
fund [fʌnd] fond; *pl* sredstva
funeral ['fju:nərəl] sprovod
funicular [fju:'nikjulə]: **~ railway** uspinjača
funk [fʌŋk]:(***blue***) **~** *coll* smrtni strah
funnel ['fʌnl] lijevak; brodski dimnjak
funny ['fʌni] šaljiv, smiješan
fur [fə:] krzno; oblog (na jeziku); ***~s*** *pl* krznena odjeća (izrađevine); **~coat** krzneni kaput; **~-lined** postavljen krznom; **~red** obložen (jezik)
furious ['fjuəriəs] bijesan
furnace ['fə:nis] velika peć (talionice, centralnog grijanja)
furnish ['fə:niʃ] opremiti (***with***); namjestiti; opskrbiti
furniture ['fə:nitʃə] namještaj
furrier ['fʌriə] krznar
furrow ['fʌrou] brazda; brazdati
further ['fə:ðə] dalji(e); unapređivati; **~more** osim toga
furtive ['fə:tiv] potajan
fury ['fjuəri] bijes; gnjev
fus|e [fju:z] stopiti; EL osigurač; upaljač; **~ible** taljiv; **~ion** ['fju:ʒən] stapanje; PHYS fuzija
fuss [fʌs] buka; zbrka; uznemirivati se, komplicirati; *Am* udvarati
fustian ['fʌstiən] plijesniv; staromodan
futile ['fju:tail] uzaludan
future ['fju:tʃə] budućnost; budući

G

gab [gæb]: ***have the gift of the ~*** biti okretan na jeziku
gable ['geibl] zabat
gad [gæd]: ***~ about*** lunjati, dangubiti
gag [gæg] povez; začepiti usta; THEAT improvizirati
gage [geidʒ] zalog
gaiety ['geiəti] veselost
gain [gein] dobitak; dobiti; postići; **~ful employment** plaćeni radni odnos
gait [geit] hod; **~er** gamaša
gale [geil] jaki vjetar; *fig* provala
gall [gɔ:l] žuč; žučni mjehur; ranjavo mjesto
gallant ['gælənt] viteški; hrabar; galantan
gallery ['gæləri] galerija; MIN hodnik
gallivant [gæli'vænt] skitati se
gallon ['gælən] galon (4,54 litre)
gallows ['gælouz] vješala
galosh [gə'lɔʃ] kaljača
gambl|e ['gæmbl] kockati; **~ing-house** kockarnica
game [geim] igra; divljač; kockati; **~-licence** lovna dozvola
gander ['gændə] gusak
gang [gæŋ] družina; skupina
gangrene ['gæŋgri:n] MED gangrena
gangway ['gæŋwei] prolaz; MAR mostić za ulaz na brod
gap [gæp] otvor; prekid; ***(spark-) ~*** EL iskrište
gape [geip] blenuti; zjapiti
garage ['gæra:ʒ] garaža; garažirati (*auto*)
garden ['ga:dn] vrt; **~er** vrtlar
gargle ['ga:gl] grgljati; tekućina za grgljanje
garland ['ga:lənd] vijenac
garlic ['ga:lik] češnjak
garment ['ga:mənt] odjevni predmet
garnet ['ga:nit] granat
garnish ['ga:niʃ] garnirati; (na)kititi
garret ['gærət] sobica u potkrovlju
garrison ['gærisn] posada; garnizon
garter ['ga:tə] podvezica; *Am* muška podvezica; ***Order of the ~*** red podvezice
gas [gæs], *pl* **~es** plin; *Am* MOT benzin; MOT ***step on the ~*** dati gas; **~-bracket** plinska cijev s plamenikom; **~-burner** plinski plamenik; **~-fitter** uvoditelj plina
gash [gæʃ] duboka rana; duboko se porezati
gas|-lighter ['gæslaitə] plinski upaljač; **~metre** plinska ura; **~olene**, **~oline** *Am*

MOT benzin
gasp [ga:sp] teško disanje
gas|-stove plinska peć; **~-works** plinara
gate (velika) vrata; **~man** vratar perona; **~way** kolni prolaz; veža
gather ['gæðə] skupljati; ubirati; sazrijevati (i *fig*); **~ from** *fig* zaključivati prema
gaudy ['gɔ:di] kričav
gauge [geidʒ] mjera; šablona; RLW širina kolosjeka; baždariti
gauntlet ['gɔ:ntlit] rukavica s dugim suvratkom
gauze [gɔ:z] gaza
gay [gei] veseo; šaren; živahan
gaze [geiz] zuriti
gazette [gə'zet] službene novine; službeno objaviti
gear [giə] pribor; zupčanici; **~-box**, **~-case** mjenjačka kutija; **~-change** MOT mijenjanje brzina; **~ing** zupčanici; **~-lever**, *Am* **~-shift** poluga mjenjača
gem [dʒem] dragulj
gender ['dʒendə] GRAM rod
general ['dʒenərəl] općenit; glavni; general; **~ize** generalizirati; **~ly** općenito; obično
generation [dʒenə'reiʃən] rađanje; naraštaj
gener|osity [dʒenə'rɔsiti] velikodušnost; darežljivost; **~ous** velikodušan; darežljiv
genetic [dʒi'netik] genetski; **~ally engineered** genetski promijenjen; **~ally modified** genetski modificiran; **~ engineering** genetsko inženjerstvo; **~ fingerprinting** genetska identifikacija
Geneva [dʒi'ni:və] Ženeva
genial ['dʒi:njəl] srdačan
genius ['dʒi:njəs] genij; dobar duh
Geno|a ['dʒenouə] Đenova; **~ese** [-'i:z] Đenovežanin; đenoveški
gentian ['dʒenʃiən] BOT goreč
gentle ['dʒentl] blag; pitom; **~man** džentlmen; gospodin; **~manlike** džentlmenski; **~ness** blagost; nježnost; **~woman** plemkinja
gentry ['dʒentri] niže plemstvo, veleposjednici
genuine ['dʒenjuin] nepatvoren; pravi
geograph|er [dʒi'ɔgrəfə] zemljopisac, geograf; **~y** geografija, zemljopis
geolog|ist [dʒi'ɔlədʒist], **~y** geolog(ija)
geomet|er [dʒi'ɔmitə], **~rician** geometar; **~ry** geometrija
germ [dʒə:m] bacil, klica
German ['dʒə:mən] njemački; Nijemac; njemački jezik; **~ *Ocean*** Sjeverno more; **~y** Njemačka
germ|inate ['dʒə:mineit] klijati; **~-killing** koji ubija klice
gesture ['dʒestʃə] kretnja; gesta

get dobiti; nabaviti; postići, domoći se; doći, dospjeti; uhvatiti; razumjeti; postati; ***you have got to obey*** moraš slušati; ~ ***abroad*** pročuti se; ~ ***along with*** slagati se sa; ~ ***along*** *ili* ***on*** napredovati; ~ ***in*** ući; ~ ***off*** sići; ~ ***out*** izvući; izaći; ~ ***over*** preći; preboliti; ~ ***ready*** spremiti se; ~ ***through to*** *tel* dobiti vezu; ~ ***up*** ustati; **~-up** oprema
ghastly ['ga:stli] grozan; sablastan
ghost [goust] duh; prikaza
giant ['dʒaiənt] divovski; div
giblets ['dʒiblits] *pl* iznutrice od guske (peradi)
giddiness ['gidinis] vrtoglavica
giddy ['gidi] vrtoglav
gift [gift] (na)dar(enost); poklon; **~box** poklon pakovanje; **~ card** poklon-bon; **~ed** nadaren
gigantic [dʒai'gæntik] divovski
giggle ['gigl] hihotanje
gild pozlatiti
gilt-edged ['giltedʒd] sa zlatnim rezom; pupilarni (vrijednosni papiri)
gin [dʒin] džin
ginger ['dʒindʒə] đumbir; *coll* polet; živost; ~ (***up***) *coll* oživiti; **~-beer** pjenušavo piće; paprena soda; **~-bread** paprenjak, medenjak začinjen đumbirom
gipsy ['dʒipsi] ciganin
gird [gə:d] opasati; **~le** pojas
girl [gə:l] djevojka; **~hood** djevojaštvo; **~ish** djevojački
girth [gə:θ] kolan; obujam
give [giv] dati; pružiti; podijeliti; predati; navesti; pokloniti; popustiti; uvinuti se; ~ ***way*** (***to***) ustupiti; povući se; ~ ***away*** pokloniti; *coll* izdati; ~ ***back*** vratiti; ~ ***in to*** popustiti nekome; ~ ***out*** izdavati; iscrpsti se; ~ ***up*** odustati od
glaci|al ['gleisiəl] leden; **~er** ledenjak
glad [glæd] zadovoljan; veseo; **~ly** rado; **~ness** zadovoljstvo
glance [gla:ns] bljesak; letimičan pogled; ~ ***at*** pogledati
gland [glænd] žlijezda
glar|e [glɛə] zaslijepljivanje; bijesan pogled; zabliještiti; **~e at** zuriti u; **~ing** zasljepljujući; očit
glass [gla:s] staklo; čaša; dalekozor; barometar; ogledalo; **~es** *pl* naočale; **~-works** staklana; **~y** staklen
glaz|e [gleiz] glazura; glazirati; **~ier** staklar
gleam [gli:m] sjaj; sjati
glean [gli:n] pabirčiti (**i** *fig*)
glee [gli:] veselje
glen uska dolina
glid|e [glaid] klizanje; lebdenje; klizati; letjeti bez motora; **~er** (*i* **~ing boat**, **~ing machine**) jedrilica (zračna)

glimmer ['glimə] svjetlucanje; svjetlucati
glimpse [glimps] letimičan pogled (***of***); ***catch a ~ of*** načas opaziti
glitter ['glitə] blistati
gloaming ['gloumiŋ] suton
gloat [glout]: ***~ over*** uživati nad
global ['gloubl] globalni; **~ization** [~'zeiʃn] globalizacija; **~ warming** globalno zagrijavanje
globe [gloub] kugla; zemljina kugla; **~trotter** svjetski putnik
gloom [glu:m] polumrak; sumornost; **~y** tmuran; smrknut
glori|fication [glɔ:rifi'keiʃən] veličanje; **~fy** veličati; **~ous** sjajan; slavan
glory ['glɔ:ri] slava; blaženstvo; ***~ in*** uživati u
gloss sjaj; ulaštenost; ulaštiti; ***~ over*** uljepšati; **~y** sjajan; ulašten; izlizan (odijelo)
glove [glʌv] rukavica; **~r** rukavičar
glow [glou] žar; sjaj; žariti se; **~ worm** krijesnica
glue [glu:] ljepilo; lijepiti
glut [glʌt] zasićenost; zaititi; **~ton** proždrljivac
gnash [næʃ] škripati zubima
gnat [næt] komarac
gnaw [nɔ:] glodati
go [gou] ići; poći; otići; voziti se; putovati; biti u pokretu, raditi (stroj, sat); dopirati (***to***); postati; ***~ bad*** pokvariti se; ***~ mad*** poludjeti; ***~ wrong*** zalutati, zastraniti; ***just ~ and try*** pokušaj samo!; ***let ~*** (is)pustiti; ***~ about*** obilaziti; ***~ by*** proći mimo; ravnati se po; ***~ in for*** baviti (zanimati) se nečim; ***~ on*** ići dalje; nastaviti; ***~ through*** proći; pregledati; ***~ up*** popeti se; porasti
goal [goul] cilj; (nogomet); ***score a ~*** postići zgoditak; **~-keeper** vratar
goat [gout] koza; *sl* ***get a p 's ~*** razljutiti; **~ee** šiljata bradica
god REL bog; *fig* idol; **~child** kumče; **~dess** božica; **~father** krsni kum; **~like** bogu sličan
go-getter *Am* energičan i poduzetan čovjek (kome sve uspijeva)
goggle ['gɔgl] buljiti; (***a pair of***) **~s** *pl* zaštitne naočale
going ['gouiŋ]: ***be ~ to*** spremati se; upravo htjeti; ***keep ~*** održavati
gold [gould] zlato; zlatan
golf golf; **~er** igrač golfa; **~-links** *pl* igralište golfa
good [gud] dobar; drag; vrijedan; sposoban; prikladan; dobro; korist; ***for ~*** zauvijek; ***that's no ~*** to ne pomaže (vrijedi); ***no ~ talking about it*** nema smisla govoriti o tome; **~s** *pl* roba
good|-bye [gud'bai] zbo-

gom! do viđenja!; **~-for-nothing** ništarija; **~-natured** dobroćudan; **~ness** dobrota
goods|station, **~ train** teretni kolodvor, vlak
goodwill ['gud'wil] dobrohotnost; COM mušterije, uvedeno poslovanje
goose[gu:s], *pl* ***geese*** [gi:s] guska; **~berry** ogrozd
gorge [gɔ:dʒ] gudura; proždirati; nažderati se
gorgeous ['gɔ:dʒəs] divan
gormandize ['gɔ:məndaiz] žderati
gospel ['gɔspəl] evanđelje
gossip ['gɔsip] naklapanje; tračati
gourd [guəd] bundeva
gout [gaut] kostobolja; **~y** kostoboljan
govern ['gʌvən] vladati; upravljati; voditi; **~ess** guvernanta; **~ment** vlada(nje); **~or** namjesnik; guverner
gown [gaun] ženska duga haljina; talar
grace [greis] dražest; milost; vrlina; ***your ~*** Vaša milosti; **~ful** dražestan; graciozan
gracious ['greiʃəs] milostiv, dobrohotan; ***good ~!*** za boga miloga!
grade [greid] stupanj; nagib; stupnjevati
gradua|l ['grædjuəl] postupan; **~te** ['-eit] diplomirati; stupnjevati
graft [gra:ft] *Am* mito; kalem; ucijepiti; **~er** davalac (ili primalac) mita
grain [grein] žito; zrno; zrnce; mrviti (se)
grammar ['græmə] gramatika
gram(me) [græm] gram
gramophone ['græməfoun] gramofon; **~ disk** *ili* **record** gramofonska ploča
granary ['grænəri] ambar; žitnica
grand [grænd] velik; veličanstven; sjajan; **~daughter** unuka; **~eur** veličina, sjaj; **~father** djed; **~mother** baka; **~son** unuk
grange [greindʒ] majur
granite ['grænit] granit
grant [gra:nt] podjeljivanje; dotacija; dodijeliti; darovati; odobriti
granular ['grænjulə] zrnat
grape [greip] grožđe; **~fruit** grepfrut; **~-sugar** grožđani šećer
grapple ['græpl] pograbiti; ***~ with*** uhvatiti se u koštac sa
grasp [gra:sp] zahvat; stisak; zgrabiti; shvatiti
grass [gra:s] trava; pašnjak; **~hopper** skakavac; **~-widow(er)** *coll* slamnata udovica (-ac)
grate [greit] rešetka; roštilj; ribati (*sir*); škripati
grateful [greitful] zahvalan; **~ness** zahvalnost
grater ['greitə] ribež
grati|fy ['grætifai] udovoljiti;

zadovoljiti; **~tude** ['~tju:d] zahvalnost
gratuit|ous [grə'tju:itəs] besplatan; **~y** napojnica
grave [greiv] ozbiljan; težak; grob; **~-digger** grobar
gravel ['grævəl] šljunak; MED pijesak (u žući)
graveyard ['greivja:d] groblje
gravit|ation [grævi'teiʃən] sila teža; **~y** težina; ozbiljnost; važnost
gravy ['greivi] sok od pečenke
graze [greiz] pasti; napasti
grease [gri:s] mast; [~z] zamastiti; pomazati; **~proof** koji ne propušta masnoću; **~ paper** masni papir
greasy ['gri:zi] mastan; zamašćen
great [greit] velik; ***a ~ deal*** mnogo; **♀ Britain** Velika Britanija; **~grandchild** praunuk(a); **~ly** uvelike; **~ness** veličina
Greece [gri:s] Grčka
greed|iness ['gri:dinis] pohlepa; **~y** pohlepan
Greek [gri:k] grčki; Grk(inja); grčki jezik
green [gri:n] zelen; nezreo; zelenilo; *pl* zelenje; **~grocer** povrćar; **~horn** žutokljunac; **~ish** zelenkast; **~sward** tratina
greet [gri:t] pozdraviti; **~ing** pozdrav
grey [grei] siv; **~hound** hrt
grid RADIO rešetka; **~ iron** roštilj
grief [gri:f] žalost; tuga
griev|ance ['gri:vəns] pritužba; jadanje; **~e** žalostiti se
grill [gril] pržiti na roštilju; roštilj
grim ozbiljan; mračan
grimace [gri'meis] grimasa; praviti grimase
grimy ['graimi] prljav; čađav
grin cerenje; osmjeh; ceriti se (***at***)
grind [graind] mrviti; (sa)mljeti; brusiti; *sl* bubati; muka; škripati (zubima); **~er** kutnjak; brusač
grip zgrabiti; stisnuti; zahvat; **~sack** *Am* putna torba
grizzly ['grizli] (pro)sijed; **~ bear** sivi američki medvjed
groan [groun] jecaj; jecati; stenjati (***for***)
groats [grouts] *pl* zobena krupica
grocer ['grousə] trgovac mješovitom robom; **~ies** *pl* mješovita roba
grog grog
groin [grɔin] ANAT prepona
groom [grum] konjušar
groove [gru:v] žlijeb
gross [grous] tust; krupan; neotesan; brutto (težina); gros (12 tuceta)
ground [graund] tlo; pod; gradilište; ***~s*** *pl* talog; ***~s*** *pl* perivoj; nasadi; osnovati; EL uzemljiti; **~-floor** prizem-

lje; **~less** bestemeljan; **~-staff** neletačko (tehničko) osoblje
group [gru:p] grupa; grupirati se
grove [grouv] gaj; šumarak
grow [grou] rasti; posta(ja)ti; **~ *into fashion*** postati moderno; **~er** uzgajatelj; poljoprivrednik
growl [graul] režanje; režati
growth [grouθ] rast(enje); raslinstvo; izraslina
grudge [grʌdʒ] zamjerka; zamjerati
gruel [gruəl] zobena kaša
gruff [grʌf] otresit; zlovoljan
grumble ['grʌmbl] gunđati; **~r** gunđalo; nezadovoljnik
guarantee [gærən'ti:] garancija; garantirati (***for***)
guard [ga:d] straža; čuvar; gazda; stražariti; čuvati se (***against***); **~ian** zaštitnik; skrbnik
guess [ges] nagađati; pogađati; *Am* misliti, pretpostavljati
guest [gest] gost
guid|able ['gaidəbl] (po)vodljiv; **~ance** vodstvo
guide [gaid] vođa; voditi; **~-book** vodič (knjiga); **~-post** kažiprst
guild [gild] ceh; bratovština
guilt [gilt] krivnja; **~y** kriv; kažnjiv
guise [gaiz] *fig* krinka
guitar [gi'ta:] gitara
gulf [gʌlf] zaliv; bezdan
gullet ['gʌlit] ANAT jednjak; grlo
gully ['gʌli] vododerina; odvodni kanal
gulp gutljaj; gutanje
gum [gʌm] desni (i *sl* pl); guma; gumirati; **~boil** čir na desnima
gun [gʌn] top, puška; *Am* revolver; **~-licence** *Am* oružna dozvola; **~ner** topnik; **~ powder** barut
gust [gʌst] zapuh vjetra; **~y** vjetrovit
gut crijevo; izvaditi utrobu; *fig* isprazniti; **~ted** izgorio
gutter ['gʌtə] oluk; slivnik za pločnik; curiti (svijeća); **~-press** bulevarska štampa
gymnas|ium [dʒim'neizjəm] gimnastička dvorana; **~tics** [~'næstiks]: ***light ~tics*** *pl* slobodne vježbe
gyp [dʒip] *Am sl* prevariti
gypsum ['dʒipsəm] sadra

H

haberdasher ['hæbədæʃə] trgovac kratkom robom
habit ['hæbit] navika; ***be in the ~ of*** imati naviku; **~ation** prebivalište; **~ual** uobičajen
hack [hæk] zasjek; zasjeći
haddock ['hædək] kolja (*riba*)
haemorrh|age ['hemərid3] krvarenje; **~oids** *pl* hemeroidi
haft [ha:ft] držak
haggard ['hægəd] upalih očiju; mršav
haggle ['hægl]: **~** (***about***) cjenkati se
Hague [heig]: ***the ~*** Haag
hail [heil] tuča; padati (tuča); pozdraviti
hair [hɛə] kosa; **~-cut** šišanje; **~dresser** frizer; **~-dryer** fen za kosu; **~pin** ukosnica; **~y** dlakav
half [ha:f] pola; (*pl* ***halves***) polovica; ***a pound and a ~*** funta i pol; **~-moon** polumjesec; **~-time** SPORT poluvrijeme; **~-way** na pola puta
hall [hɔ:l] dvorana; predsoblje; vlastelinska kuća; **~-mark** znak čistoće (nepatvorenosti)
Hallowmas ['hæloumæs] Svi Sveti (blagdan)
halo ['heilou] ASTR kolut oko sunca (mjeseca)
halt [hɔ:lt] zastajanje, prekid; RLW stajalište; zaustaviti (se)
ham [hæm] šunka
hamlet ['hæmlit] zaselak
hammer ['hæmə] čekić; zabijati
hammock ['hæmək] mreža za spavanje
hamper ['hæmpə] košara za piknik; priječiti
ham-roll žemlja sa šunkom
hand [hænd] ruka; rukopis; kazaljka; čovjek, radnik; ***at ~*** pri ruci; ***on the one ~*** s jedne strane; ***on the other ~*** s druge strane; ***a good ~ at*** okretan u; ***be ~ and glove*** biti vrlo prisni; ***change ~s*** mijenjati vlasnika; ***come to ~*** dopasti u ruke (pismo); ***on ~*** pri ruci, postojeći; ***he can turn his ~ to anything*** u svakom poslu će se snaći; ***~ in*** predati; ***~ over*** izručiti; **~bag** torbica; taška; **~ful** pregršt
handi|craft ['hændikra:ft] obrt; **~ness** prikladnost, praktičnost
handkerchief ['hæŋkətʃif] džepni rupčić
handle ['hændl] ručka; ***fly off the ~*** *coll* razbjesniti se; **~-bar** upravljač, guvernal (na biciklu)
hands-free [,hændz'fri:] za

slobodne ruke
hand|some ['hænsəm] lijep; pristao; **~-writing** ['hændraitiŋ] rukopis; **~y** priručan, prikladan
hang [hæŋ] visjeti, objesiti (***on***); ***~ about*** dangubiti
hangar ['hæŋə] hangar
hangman ['hæŋmən] krvnik
happen ['hæpən] dogoditi se; ***~ to be*** slučajno biti
happ|ily ['hæpili] na sreću; **~iness** ['hæpinis] sreća; **~y** sretan
harras ['hærəs] mučiti; uznemirivati
harbour ['ha:bə] luka; pružiti zaklon; gajiti
hard [ha:d] tvrd; strog; neumoljiv; težak; ***the ~ facts*** neumoljive činjenice; ***~ of hearing*** nagluh; ***it is snowing ~*** pada gusti snijeg; ***work ~*** mnogo raditi; **~-boiled** tvrdo kuhan; *Am* trijezan; **~en** otvrdnuti; **~-hearted** tvrda srca; **~ly** jedva; **~ness** tvrdoća; neumoljivost; **~-shell** neumoljiv; *Am* ortodoksan; **~ship** tegoba; **~ware** metalna roba, željezarija; **~y** otporan; smion
hare [hɛə] zec; **~-brained** smušen; **~lip** ANAT zečja usna
hark [ha:k] osluškivati (***to***)
harm [ha:m] šteta; zlo; naškoditi; **~ful** štetan; **~less** neškodljiv
harness ['ha:nis] konjska orma; upregnuti
harp [ha:p] harfa; ***be always ~ing on the same string*** guditi uvijek istu pjesmu
harpoon [ha:'pu:n] harpuna; pogoditi harpunom
harrow ['hærou] drljača; drljati
harsh [ha:ʃ] hrapav; opor; neskladan
harum-scarum ['hɛərəm-'skɛərəm] *coll* brzopleta osoba
harvest ['ha:vist] žetva; (po)žeti; **~er** žetelica (i stroj)
hash [hæʃ] sjeckano meso; sasjeckati
hast|e [heist] žurba; hitnja; ***make ~e*** žuriti se; **~en** (po)žuriti; **~y** nagao, nepromišljen
hat [hæt] šešir
hatch [hætʃ] leglo; MAR grotlo; AERO otvor za krcanje
hatchet ['hætʃit] sjekirica
hatchway grotlo (nad hodnikom)
hate [heit] mrziti; **~ful** mrzak; odvratan
hatred ['heitrid] mržnja
hatter ['hætə] klobučar
haugt|iness ['hɔtinis] oholost; **~y** ohol; arogantan
haul [hɔ:l] ulov (ribe); vući
haunch [hɔ:ntʃ] bok; but
haunt [hɔ:nt] progoniti; posjećivati (duhovi)
have [hæv] imati; dobiti; posjedovati; ***~ to do*** morati učiniti; ***I had rather go*** bit

će bolje da odem; ***I would ~ you know*** želim da znate; ***~ about one*** imati kod sebe; ***~ it out with*** izvesti na čistac
havoc ['hævək]: ***make ~ of*** *ili* ***among*** opustošiti, poharati
hawk [hɔːk] jastreb; kobac; hrakati; torbariti; piljariti; **~er** ulični trgovac s kolicima
hay [hei] sijeno; **~ fever** peludna groznica; **~loft** sjenik
hazard ['hæzəd] slučaj; izvrgnuti se opasnosti; **~ous** opasan
haze [heiz] maglica
hazel-nut ['heizlnʌt] lješnjak
he [hiː] on; ***~ who*** onaj tko
head [hed] glava; razum; komad; glavar; vođa; direktor; voditi, biti na čelu; dati zaglavlje; *nogomet*: igrati glavom; ***~ for*** krenuti prema; ***come to a ~*** sazrijeti (*čir*) doći do kritičke tačke; ***make ~ against*** pružati uspješan otpor; ***I can't make ~ or tail of it*** ništa ja tu ne razumijem; **~ache** glavobolja; **~dress** ukras za glavu; frizura; **~er** skok naglavce; **~-gear** pokrivalo, šešir; **~ing** naslov, rubrika; **~land** (visoki) rt; **~less** bezglav; **~light** MOT glavno prednje svjetlo; **~-master** direktor škole; **~most** naistaknutiji; **~-phone**, **~-piece**, **~-receiver** RADIO slušalica; **~-quarters** *pl* glavni stan; centrala; **~way**: ***make ~way*** napredovati; imati uspjeha
heal [hiːl] liječiti; **~ (*up*)** zacijeliti
health [helθ] zdravlje; **~-resort** lječilište; **~y** zdrav
heap [hiːp] gomila; nagomilati
hear [hiə] čuti; saslušati; uslišati; **~ing** sluh; preslušavanje; audijencija; domet sluha
hearken ['haːkən] čuti; oslušķivati (***to***)
hearse [həːs] mrtvačka kola
heart [haːt] srce; *fig* hrabrost; duša; jezgro; ***by ~*** napamet; ***out of ~*** snužden; **~-beat** kucanje srca; **~-breaking** koji para srce; **~burn** žgaravica; **~en** ohrabriti
hearth [haːθ] ognjište
heart|iness ['haːtinis] srdačnost; srčanost; **~less** bez srca; **~y** srdačan, srčan
heat [hiːt] vrućina; žar; zagrijati; ražariti; ***dead ~*** neodlučna utrka
heath [hiːθ] ledina
heathen ['hiːðəŋ] poganin; poganski
heating ['hiːtiŋ] grijanje; **~ cushion**, **~ pad** električni termofor
heat|-stroke sunčanica; **~-value** ogrjevna moć; **~ wave** val vrućine
heave [hiːv] dignuti; nadimati se; ***~ the anchor*** podići sidro
heaven ['hevn] nebo; **~ly** ne-

beski
heaviness ['hevinis] težina
heavy ['hevi] težak (i *fig*); tmuran; glomazan; **~ current** jaka struja; **~weight** *boks*: teške kategorije
Hebrew ['hi:bru:] hebrejski; Hebrej, Židov
hectic ['hektik] grozničav; *coll* uzbudljiv
hedge [hedʒ] živica; ograditi živicom; **~hog** jež
heed [hi:d] obzir; uzimati u obzir; ***take ~ of*** čuvati se nečega; **~ful** koji se osvrće na (***of***); **~less** koji zanemaruje
heel [hi:l] peta; ***take to one's ~s*** pobjeći
height [hait] visina; uzvisina; vrhunac; **~en** povisiti; povećati
heir [ɛə] nasljednik; **~ess** nasljednica
hell pakao; **~ish** paklenski
helm rudo kormila
helmet šljem (i MOT, AERO)
help [help] pomoć; (pomoćno) sredstvo; *Am* kućna pomoćnica; ***lady ~*** pomagačica domaćice; ***mother's ~*** dječja paziteljica; pomagati; posluživati; ***~ o. s.*** poslužiti se; ***I can't ~ saying*** ne mogu a da ne kažem; **~er, ~mate** pomagač(ica); **~ful** koristan; susretljiv; **~ing** porcija; **~less** bespomoćan
hem (po)rub; (po)rubiti; nakašljati se
he-man *Am* pravi muškarac
hemisphere ['hemisfiə] hemisfera
hemlock ['hemlɔk] kukuta
hemp konoplja
hemstitch ažur; raditi ažur
hen kokoš
hence [hens] odavle; odsada; zato; **~forth** ubuduće
hen|-party *coll* žensko društvo (zabava); **~-pecked** koji je pod papučom
her [hə:] njen, njezin; nje, njoj, nju, njom
herald ['herəld] glasnik, najaviti
herb [hə:b] (kulinarska, ljekovita) biljka
herd [hə:d] krdo; okupljati se u krdo; **~sman** pastir
here [hiə] ovdje; ovamo; **~about(s)** tu negdje; **~by** ovime, na temelju toga
hereditary [hi'reditəri] nasljedan
heresy ['herəsi] krivovjerje
here|upon nato; **~with** ovime
heritage ['heritidʒ] baština
hermit ['hə:mit] pustinjak
hernia ['hə:njə] MED kila
hero ['hiərou], *pl* **~es** heroj; **~ic** herojski; **~ine** junakinja; **~ism** junaštvo
herring ['heriŋ] sleđ; **~-bone pattern** uzorak "riblja kost"
hers [hə:z] njezin
herself [hə:'self] ona sama; nju samu
hesitat|e ['heziteit] oklijevati; **~ion** oklijevanje; neodlučnost

hew [hjuː] sjeckati, sjeći
hiccup ['hikʌp] štucavica; štucati
hide [haid] koža (velikih životinja); sakriti se (***from a p***)
hideous ['hidiəs] ružan; odvratan
hiding ['haidiŋ] skrivanje; batine; **~-place** skrovište
high [hai] visok; otmjen; ponosan; nadmen; skup; žestok; **~ spirits** dobro raspoloženje; **~diving** SPORT skakanje s tornja; **~ life** otmjeni krugovi i život; **~lights** *pl* ono najvažnije (najistaknutije); **~ tension** EL visoka napetost; **~-bred** plemićki; otmjen; **~-brow** *Am* intelektualac; **~-class** prvoklasan; **~-coloured** jako rumen; živopisan; **~lands** *pl* brda; **~-level railway** visinska željeznica; **~ly** vrlo; **~ness** *fig* visina; (naslov) Visost; **~-power station** velika centrala; **~-power radio** (*ili* **wireless**) **station** snažna radio stanica; **~-road** (*ili* **~-way**) cesta; **~-wayman** drumski razbojnik
hike [haik] *Am coll* izlet pješke
hilarious [hi'lɛəriəs] veseo; radostan
hill brežuljak; brijeg; **~y** brdovit
hilt balčak
him njega, njemu, njim
himself [him'self] sam, sama, sebe; ***of ~*** sam od sebe; ***by ~*** sam
hind [haind]: **~ leg** stražnja noga
hind|er ['hində] spriječiti (***from***); ometati; **~rance** zapreka
hinge [hindʒ] šarka, šarnir
hint mig; natuknuti;
hip bok; kuk; **~-bath** sjedeća kada; **~ped** iščašena (spuštena) kuka
hire ['haiə] najamnina; nadnica; uzeti u najam; **~-purchase** kupnja na otplatu
his [hiz] njegov
hiss psikanje; psikati
histor|ian [his'tɔːriən] povjesničar; **~ical** povijesni; **~y** ['histəri] povijest
hit udarac; pogodak; sretan slučaj; THEAT uspio komad; udariti; pogoditi
hitch [hitʃ] trzaj; *fig* smetnja; **~-hike** *Am coll* putovati autostopom
hither ['hiðə] ovamo; **~to** dosada
hive [haiv] košnica
H. M. S. = **His (Her) Majesty's Ship**
hoard [hɔːd] zaliha; tajno; zgrtati (novac, blago); **~er**: (***food***) ***~er*** onaj koji zgrće zalihe hrane; **~ing** visoka ograda oko gradnje; ***advertisement ~ing*** ograda za lijepljenje plakata
hoarfrost ['hɔːfrɔst] mraz, inje

hoarse [hɔ:s] promukao; **~ness** promuklost
hoax [houks] obmana; prevariti
hobble [hɔbl] šepati
hobby ['hɔbi] hobi
hobo ['houbou] *Am* skitnica
hock [hɔk] rajnsko vino
hockey ['hɔki] hokej
hog svinja; **~shead** velika (podrumska) bačva; **~skin** svinjska koža
hoist [hɔist] dizalo; dizati
hold [hould] držanje; zahvat; tovarni brodski prostor; ***catch*** (*ili* ***get, lay, take***) ***~ of*** uhvatiti; dohvatiti; (o-, za-, pri-, iz-)držati; smatrati; ***~ the line*** *tel* ostati na aparatu; ***~ good*** (*ili* ***true***) vrijediti; ***~ water*** ne curiti; biti logičan (argument); ***~ to*** držati se nečega; ***~ up*** držati se (uspravno); **~er** držalac; posjednik; ***~er of shares*** dioničar; **~ing** držanje; posjed; **~over** *Am* ostatak; **~-up** *Am* prepad; zastoj
hole rupa, udubina; izdupsti
holiday ['hɔlidei] praznik, slobodan dan; *pl* ferije
holiness ['houlinis] svetost
hollow ['hɔlou] šupalj, izduben; šupljina
holly ['hɔli] božikovina
holy ['houli] svet; ***☊ Week*** Veliki tjedan
homage ['hɔmidʒ] odavanje štovanje (priznanja)
home [houm] **1.** dom; domovina; ***at ~*** kod kuće; **2.** domaći; kućni; ***☊ Office*** Ministarstvo unutrašnjih poslova; ***~ trade*** unutarnja trgovina; ***bring ~ to*** razjasniti; ***hit*** (*ili* ***strike***) ***~*** pogoditi u pravo mjesto; ***see ~*** otpratiti do kuće; **~less** bez doma; **~ly** jednostavan; priprost; **~-made** domaći; **~-sick**: ***be ~-sick*** biti nostalgičan; **~-sickness** nostalgija; **~ward(s)** kući; **~-work** domaća zadaća
Hon. = **honorable**; **honorary**
honest ['ɔnist] pošten; **~y** poštenje
honey ['hʌni] med; **~-moon** medeni mjesec; **~suckle** kozja krv
honk MOT trubiti
honorary ['ɔnərəri] počastan
honour ['ɔnə] čast; počast; **~s** *pl* počasti; iskazivati počasti; **~able** častan; čestit; pohvalan
hood [hud] kukuljica; kapa (i TECH); MOT pokrov motora (hauba); pomični krov auta; **~lum** ['hu:dləm] *Am* huligan; **~wink** obmanuti, prevariti
hoof [hu:f] kopito; papak
hook [huk] kvaka; *coll* ***by ~ or*** (***by***) ***crook*** milom ili silom; zakvačiti kukom (udicom); **~ed** kukast; **~-up** RADIO: povezivanje stanica radi prenosa
hooligan ['hu:ligən] huligan

hoop [huːp] obruč
hooping-cough ['huːpiŋkɔf] hripavac
hoot [huːt] galamiti; MOT trubiti; **~er** sirena; MOT truba
hop skok; skakutanje; AERO etapa; skakutati; *sl* **~ it** odmagliti; **~ off** AERO *Am* uzletjeti
hope [houp] nada; nadati se; **~ful** pun nade; **~less** beznadan
horizon [hə'raizn] horizont; **~tal** [hɔri'zɔntl] horizontalan
horn [hɔːn] rog; megafon; MOT truba; **~ed** rogat
hornet ['hɔːnit] stršen
horri|ble ['hɔrəbl] strahovit; grozan; **~d** ['~id] grozan; strašan; **~fy** užasnuti
horror ['hɔrə] groza; užas; strava
horse [hɔːs] konj; **~back**: **on ~** na konju; **~-dealer** trgovac konjima; **~manship** jahačka vještina; **~power** konjska sila; **~-radish** hren; **~shoe** potkova; **~-whip** bič za konje
hose [houz] (duga) čarapa; crijevo (za polijevanje)
hosier ['houʒə] trgovac čarapama i pletenom robom; **~y** ['~ri] čarape i pletena roba
hospitable ['hɔspitəbl] gostoljubiv
hospital ['hɔspitl] bolnica; **~ity** [~'tæliti] gostoljubivost; **~ize** ['~təlaiz] *Am* smjestiti u bolnicu; liječiti u bolnici
host [houst] domaćin; krčmar; hostija; **~age** talac; **~el** đački (studentski) dom; ***youth ~el*** omladinsko prenoćište; **~ess** domaćica
hostil|e ['hɔstail] neprijateljski; **~ity** [~'tiliti] neprijateljstvo
hot vruć; oštar; žestok; strastven; ***go*** (*ili* ***sell***) ***like ~ cakes*** prodavati se na jagmu; **~ air** mlaćenje prazne slame; **~ dogs** *Am* hrenovke u žemlji
hotel [hou'tel] hotel
hot|head usijana glava; **~house** staklenik; **~spur** napržica; **~-water bottle** termofor; **~ heating** grijanje na vruću vodu; **~ supply** snabdjevanje toplom vodom
hound [haund] lovački pas
hour ['auə] sat; vrijeme; čas; *pl* radno vrijeme; **~ly** svaki sat
house [haus] kuća; [hauz] staviti (primiti) u kuću; smjestiti; **~breaker** *Am* provalnik; poduzetnik koji ruši stare kuće; **~hold** kućanstvo; **~-hunting** traženje kuće (stana); **~keeper** kućanica; **~-trained** (pas) koji ne vrši nuždu u kući
housing shortage stambeni problem
hovel ['hɔvəl] potlušica
hover ['hɔvə] lebdjeti; zadržavati se u blizini
how [hau] kako; **~ *about*** ...

šta mislite o ...? kako bi bilo da...?; **~ever** međutim
howl urlati; RADIO pištati; **~ing** urlanje; RADIO pištanje
h. p. = horse power
H. R. H. = His (Her) Royal Highness Njegovo kraljevsko visočanstvo
huckster ['hʌkstə] pokućarac; pokućariti
huddle ['hʌdl] nagomilati; **~ (*together*)** stisnuti se; ***~ on*** prebaciti (odjeću) na sebe
hue [hju:] boja; nijansa
huff [hʌf] grubo postupati; "pojesti" kamen (u igri Dame); **~y** *coll* razljućen
hug [hʌg] zagrljaj; zagrliti
huge [hju:dʒ] golem, ogroman
hugger-mugger ['hʌgə-'mʌgə] *coll* konspiracija; zbrka
hull [hʌl] komuška; mahuna; MAR korito broda; ljuštiti komuške
hullabaloo [hʌləbə'lu:] galama, strka
hum [hʌm] zujanje; zujati; *coll* ***make things ~*** živo pokrenuti posao, snažno aktivirati
human ['hju: mən] ljudski; **~e** human; **~ity** čovječanstvo; čovječnost
humble ['hʌmbl] čedan; ponizan; poniziti
humbug ['hʌmbʌg] obmana, varka
humdrum ['hʌmdrʌm] jednoličan; prozaičan
humid ['hju:mid] vlažan; **~ity** vlaga
humili|ate [hju:'milieit] poniziti; **~ation** poniženje; **~ty** poniznost
humorous ['hju:mərəs] humorističan; šaljiv
humour ['hju:mə] raspoloženje; humor; popuštati, ugađati
hump [hʌmp] grba
hunchback ['hʌntʃbæk] grbavac
hundred ['hʌndrəd] sto(-tina); stotica; **~fold** stostruki(o); **~th** stoti; **~weight** II2 funti (50,8 kg)
Hungar|ian [hʌŋ'gɛəriən] mađarski (jezik); Mađar; **~y** ['hʌŋgəri] Mađarska
hung|er ['hʌŋgə] glad; gladovati (***for, after***); **~ry** gladan
hunt [hʌnt] lov; loviti; **~er** lovac; **~ing**: ***go ~ing*** ići u lov
hurdle ['hə:dl] prepona; **~-race** trčanje (trka) s preponama
hurl [hə:l] bacanje; baciti
hurricane ['hʌrikən] orkan
hurr|ied ['hʌrid] žuran; na brzinu; **~y** žurba; hitnja; ***be in a ~y*** žuriti se (*i* ***~y up***)
hurt [hə:t] povreda; povrijediti; uvrijediti; ozlijediti; **~ful** štetan (***to***)
husband ['hʌzbənd] suprug; **~ry** seosko gospodarstvo
hush [hʌʃ] tišina!; utišati; ***~ up*** ušutkati; **~-money** plaća

za šutnju
husk [hʌsk] lupina; ljuska; ljuštiti
hussar [hu'zaː] husar
hustle ['hʌsl] gurati (se); *Am* živo raditi; *Am* radinost
hut [hʌt] koliba; baraka
hydro|-(aero)plane ['hai-drou-] hidroavion; **~-cloric acid** solna kiselina; **~gen** vodik; **~pathy** liječenje vodom; **~-phobia** strah od vode
hyena [hai'iːnə] hijena
hygien|e ['haidʒiːn] higijena; **~ic** higijenski
hygrometer [hai'grɔmitə] vlagomjer
hymn [him] crkvena pjesma; pjevati crkvene pjesme (ili hvalospjeve)
hyphen ['haifən] crtica (između riječi)
hypno|sis [hip'nousis] hipnoza; **~tist** ['hipnətist] hipnotizer
hypo|chondria [haipə'kɔndriə] hipohondrija; **~crite** licemjerac
hyster|ia [his'tiəriə] histerija; **~ical** histeričan

I

I [ai] ja
ib = **ibidem** [i'baidem] isto (mjesto)
ice led; sladoled; *Am* ***cut no ~*** nemati djelovanja; *coll* ne paliti; zalediti; rashladiti ledom; preliti šećernom glazurom; **~-axe** (alpinistički) cepin; **~-cream** sladoled; **Żland** Island
icicle ['aisikl] ledena svijeća (siga)
icy ['aisi] leden (i *fig*)
idea [ai'diə] ideja; misao, predožba; pojam
ideal [ai'diəl] ideal(an); **~ism** idealizam; **~ize** idealizirati
identi|cal [ai'dentikəl] identičan; **~fication (card)** *Am* legitimacija; **~fy** identificirati; **~ty card** legitimacija
ideology [aidi'ɔlədʒi] ideologija
idiom ['idiəm] idiom; narječje
idiot ['idiət] idiot
idle ['aidl] besposlen; lijen; isprazan; TECH ***run ~*** biti u praznom hodu; **~ness** besposlenost; **~r** lijenčina
idol ['aidl] idol, kumir; **~ize** obožavati
idyl ['aidil] idila; **~lic** idiličan
i. e. = **id est** (= **that is**) to jest
if ako; iako; da li
ignition [ig'niʃən] MOT paljenje
ignor|amus [ignə'reiməs] neznalica; **~ance** ['ignərəns] neznanje; **~ant** neuk; **~e**

[ig'nɔː] ignorirati; zanemariti
ill zao; loš; bolestan; nesretan; teško; zlo; nevolja; **~-advised** nerazborit; nesmotren; **~-bred** neodgojen
illegal [i'liːgəl] nezakonit
illegible [i'ledʒibl] nečitljiv
illegitima|cy [ili'dʒitiməsi] nezakonitost; **~te** nezakonit
ill|-fated ['il'feitid] zlokoban; **~-gotten** nepošteno stečen; **~iterate** nepismen; **~-matched** loše sparen; koji ne pristaje jedan uz drugog; **~-natured** mrzovoljan; **~ness** bolest; **~-tempered** zloćudan; **~-timed** u zao čas; **~-treat** zlostavljati
illuminat|e [i'ljuːmineit] rasvijetliti; **~ed advertising** svjetleća reklama; **~ion** rasvjeta
ill-use zlostavljati
illus|ion [i'luːʒən] iluzija; **~ive** [~siv] iluzoran
illustrat|e ['iləstreit] ilustracija, objašnjenje
illustrious [i'lʌstriəs] slavan
image ['imidʒ] slika; lik; slikom prikazati; odraziti
imagin|able [i'mædʒinəbl] zamisliv; **~ation** mašta; **~e** zamišljati
imitat|e ['imiteit] oponašati; **~ion** imitacija; ***~ion leather*** umjetna koža; **~ive** koji oponaša; **~or** imitator
immeasurable [i'meʒərəbl] nemjeriv, neizmjeran
immediate [i'miːdjət] neposredan; izravan; trenutan; **~ly** odmah
immense [i'mens] beskrajan
immers|e [i'məːs] zaroniti; **~ion heater** EL ogrjevno ronilo
immigra|nt ['imigrənt] doseljenik; **~te** doseliti; **~tion** doseljenje
imminent ['iminənt] predstojeći; neizbježan
immoderate [i'mɔdərit] neumjeren
immodest [i'mɔdist] nečedan; neskroman
immoral [i'mɔrəl] nemoralan; **~ity** nemoralnost
immortal [i'mɔːtl] besmrtan; **~ity** besmrtnost
immovable [i'muːvəbl] nepokretan; nepokolebiv
immun|e [i'mjuːn] imun (***from***); **~ity**: ***~ity from*** oslobođenje od, neosjetljivost na; **~ize** imunizirati
impair [im'pɛə] oštetiti; naškoditi
impalpable [im'pælpəbl] neopipljiv; *fig* nedokučiv
impart [im'paːt] pružati, davati
im|partial [im'paːʃəl] nepristran; **~passable** neprohodan; **~passive** bešćutan
impatien|ce [im'peiʃəns] nestrpljivost; **~t** nestrpljiv (***of***); željan nečega (***for***)
impeach [im'piːtʃ] optužiti; okriviti; naškoditi

impediment [im'pedimənt] zapreka; ~ ***in one's speech*** govorna mana
impel [im'pel] nagnati; prisiliti
impend [im'pend] lebdjeti (***over***); predstojati; prijetiti
impenetrable [im'penitrəbl] neprobojan (***to***, ***by***)
imperative [im'perətiv] zapovjedni; neodložan
imperceptible [impə'septəbl] nezamjetljiv
imperfect [im'pə:fikt] nesavršen; nepotpun; manjkav
imperial [im'piəriəl] carski
imperious [im'piəriəs] zapovjednički; prijeko potreban
imperishable [im'periʃəbl] neuništiv
imperson|al [im'pə:snl] bezličan; **~ate** utjelovljai; THEAT predstavljati; **~ation** utjelovljavanje; THEAT predstavljanje; imitiranje
impertinen|ce [im'pə:tinəns] drskost; **~t** drzak
imperturbable [impə'tə:bə:bl] koga ništa ne uzbuđuje
impervious [im'pə:viəs] nepristupačan; neprobojan (***to***)
impetuous [im'petjuəs] nagao, neobuzdan
implacable [im'plækəbl] nepomirljiv
implant [im'pla:nt] *fig* usaditi
implement ['implimənt] oruđe, pribor
implicat|e ['implikeit] uplesti (***in***); **~ion** upletenost; ono što proizlazi
implicit [im'plisit] koji se podrazumijeva; bezuvjetan
implore [im'plɔ:] zaklinjati
imply [im'plai] podrazumijevati; uključivati; dati naslutiti
impolite [impə'lait] nepristojan
imponderable [im'pɔndərəbl] koji se ne može odvagnuti (ocijeniti)
import ['impɔ:t] uvoz; značenje; smisao; [im'pɔ:t] uvoziti; **~ance** važnost; **~ant** važan
importunate [im'pɔ:tjunit] nametljiv, dosadan
impos|e [im'pouz] nametnuti; odrediti; ***~e upon*** prevariti; nametnuti; **~ing** impozantan; **~ition** nametanje; zadatak (kao kazna); prevara
impossib|ility [impɔsə'biliti] nemogućnost; **~le** nemoguć
impostor [im'pɔstə] varalica
impracticab|ility [imprækti-kə'biliti] neizvedivost; **~le** neizvediv
imprecation [impri'keiʃən] kletva
impregna|ble [im'pregnəbl] neosvojiv; **~te** ['~neit] oploditi; impregnirati; prožeti
impress ['impres] utisak; otisak; žig; [im'pres] impresio-

nirati; otisnuti; utisnuti; **~ion** dojam; otisak; izdanje; ***be under the ~ion that*** imati dojam da; **~ive** impresivan
imprint [im'print] utisnuti; usaditi
imprison [im'prizn] zatvoriti; **~ment** zatvor
improbab|ility [imprɔbə'biliti] nevjerojatnost; **~le** nevjerojatan
improper [im'prɔpə] nepristojan
improv|able [im'pru:vəbl] koji se može poboljšati; **~e** poboljšati (se), popraviti (se); **~ement** poboljšanje
improvi|dent [im'prɔvidənt] nesmotren; neštedljiv; **~se** improvizirati
impruden|ce [im'pru:dəns] nerazboritost; **~t** nerazuman
impud|ence ['impjudəns] drskost; **~ent** drzak
impulse ['impʌls] poziv; pobuda
im|punity [im'pju:niti] nekažnjivost; **~pure** [im'pjuə] nečist (i *fig*)
imput|ation [impju:'teiʃən] objeđivanje; **~e** pripisati
in u; na; kod; po; unutra; ***be ~*** **a**) biti kod kuće; **b**) sudjelovati u; biti na vlasti
in|ability [inə'biliti] nesposobnost; **~accessible** nepristupačan; **~accurate** netočan
inacti|on [in'ækʃən] nerad; **~ve** neaktivan
in|adequate [in'ædikwit] nedovoljan; neodgovarajući; **~admissible** nedopustiv; **~alienable** neotuđiv; **~alterable** nepromjenljiv; **~animate** neživ
inanition [inə'niʃən] MED iznurenost
in|applicable [in'æplikəbl] neprimjenljiv; **~appreciable** neprocjenjiv; neznatan; neprimjetan; **~approachable** nepristupačan, nedostiživ **~apt** nepodesan; **~articulate** nerazgovjetan
inasmuch [inəz'mʌtʃ]: ***~ as*** budući da
inattenti|on [inə'tenʃən] nepažnja; **~ve** nepažljiv
inaudible [in'ɔdəbl] nečujan
inaugurat|e [i'nɔ:gjureit] ustoličiti; svečano otvoriti; uvesti; **~ion** ustoličenje itd.
incalculable [in'kælkjuləbl] neizračunljiv; neprocjenljiv
incandescent [inkæn'desnt] užaren (do bjelila); **~ light** električno svjetlo
incapa|bility [inkeipə'biliti] nesposobnost; **~ble** nesposoban; **~city** nemoć
incautious [in'kɔ:ʃəs] neoprezan
incendiary [in'sendjəri] palikuća
incen|se ['insens] tamjan; [in'sens] razbjesniti; **~tive** poticaj; inicijativa
incessant [in'sesnt] neprestan

inch [intʃ] palac (2,54 cm); ***by ~es*** pedalj po pedalj
incident ['insidənt] slučaj; incident
incineration [insinə'reiʃən] spaljivanje
incis|e [in'saiz] zarezati; **~ion** (u)rez; **~or** sjekutić (zub)
incite [in'sait] dražiti; **~ment** poticanje; draženje
incivility [insi'viliti] neučtivost
inclin|ation [inkli'neiʃən] sklonost; **~e** [in'klain] biti nagnut; imati sklonost; nagib
inclu|de [in'klu:d] uključiti; **~sive** [~siv] uključiv
in|coherent [inkou'hiərənt] nesuvisao; **~combustible** neizgoriv
income ['inkəm] dohodak; **~ tax return** prijava poreza na dohodak
in|comparable [in'kəmpərəbl] neusporediv; **~compatible** nespojiv; **~competent** nesposoban; nenadležan; **~complete** nepotpun; **~comprehensible**, **~conceivable** neshvatljiv; **~congruous** koji se ne slaže; neskladan
inconsidera|ble [inkən'sidərəbl] neznatan; **~te** [~'sidərit] bezobziran
in|consistent [inkən'sistənt] nedosljedan; nespojiv; protuslovan; **~consolable** neutješan; **~constant** nepostojan; **~contestable** nepobitan; neosporan
incontinence [in'kɔntinəns] neobuzdanost; ***~ of urine*** nesposobnost zadržavanja mokraće
inconvenien|ce [inkən'vi:njəns] nezgodnost; smetnja; smetati; **~t** nezgodan
inconvertible [inkən'və:təbl] nepretvoriv; nezamjenljiv
incorporate [in'kɔ:pəreit] utjeloviti; pripojiti; **~d** utjelovljen; zakonski konstituiran
in|correct [inkə'rekt] netočan; **~corrigible** nepopravljiv; **~corruptible** nepokvarljiv
increase [in'kri:s] porasti (***in***); prirasti; umnožiti (se); ['inkri:s] porast; prirast; uvećanje
incred|ible [in'kredəbl] nevjerojatan; **~ulous** [~juləs] zapanjen; sumnjičav
increment ['inkrimənt] rast; dobitak; ***(unearned) ~ value*** nezarađeni višak
incriminate [in'krimineit] okriviti; inkriminirati
incubator ['inkjubeitə] inkubator
inculcate ['inkʌlkeit] usaditi, utuviti (u glavu)
inculpate ['inkʌlpeit] okriviti, optužiti
incur [in'kə:] izvrgnuti se; navući na sebe

incurab|ility [inkjuərə'biliti] neizlječivost; **~le** neizlječiv
indebted [in'detid] zadužen; obavezan (***to***)
indecen|cy [in'di:snsi] nepristojnost; **~t** nepristojan
indecision [indi'siʒən] neodlučnost
indeed [in'di:d] doista; zaista? nije moguće!
indefatigable [indi'fætigəbl] neumoran
indefensible [indi'fensəbl] neodrživ, neobranljiv
indefinite [in'definit] neodređen
indelible [in'delibl] neizbrisiv; neoperiv
indelicacy [in'delikəsi] bezobzirnost; prostota
indemni|fication [indemnifi'keiʃən] odšteta; **~fy** obeštetiti; **~ty** odšteta
indent [in'dent] ulupiti; naručiti; ['~] uleknina; **~ure** ugovor (o naukovanju)
independen|ce [indi'pendəns] nezavisnost; **~t** nezavisan
in|describable [indis'kraibəbl] neopisiv; **~destructable** neuništiv; **~determinable** neodrediv
index, *pl* ***indices*** ['indeks, '~isi:z] pokazatelj; kažiprst; kazalo; registrirati
India ['indjə] Indija; **~-rubber** guma, brisalo; **~n** indijski; indijanski; Indijac; Indijanac
indicat|e ['indikeit] (u-)kazivati; **~ion** upozorenje, znak
indict [in'dait] podići tužbu; **~ment** tužba
Indies ['indiz] *pl*: ***the ~*** Indija
indifferen|ce [in'difərəns] ravnodušnost (***to***); **~t** ravnodušan; osrednji
indigest|ible [indi'dʒestəbl] neprobavljiv; **~ion** probavne smetnje
indign|ant [in'dignənt] ogorčen; **~ation** ogorčenost
indiscernible [indi'sə:nəbl] nezamjetljiv
indiscre|te [indis'kri:t] indiskretan; nepromišljen; **~tion** [~'kreʃən] nerazborit postupak; indiskrecija
indiscriminate [indis'kriminit] bez odabiranja; nekritičan
indispensable [indis'pensəbl] neophodan, prijeko potreban, nezamjenjljiv
indispos|ed [indis'pouzd] neraspoložen; **~ition** neraspoloženje
indisputable [indis'pju:təbl] nepobitan
indissoluble [indi'səljubl] neraskidiv
indistinct [indis'tiŋkt] nejasan
indistinguishable [indis'tiŋgwiʃəbl] koji se ne može razlikovati
individual [indi'vidjuəl] osobni; pojedinačan; individua(lan)

indivisible [indi'vizəbl] nedjeljiv
indolen|ce ['indələns] nemar; **~t** nemaran, lijen
indoor ['indɔː]: **~ aerial** sobna antena; **~ gymnastics** sobna gimnastika; **~ swimming-bath** *Am* **~ swimming-pool** zatvoreni bazen; **~s** u kući, pod krovom
induce [in'djuːs] navesti; potaći; **~d current** inducirana struja
indulge [in'dʌldʒ] popuštati, udovoljavati; **~ *in*** sebi nešto dopustiti; **~nce** popuštanje; **~nt** popustljiv
industr|ial [in'dʌstriəl] industrijski; **~ialist** industrijalac; **~ialize** industrijalizirati; **~ious** marljiv, vrijedan; **~y** industrija; ***the heavy ~ies*** teška industrija
inebriate [i'niːbrieit] opiti; [~iit] opit; pijanica
ineffable [in'efəbl] neizreciv
ineffective [ini'fektiv],
inefficient neefikasan, neuspješan, nesposoban
inept [i'nept] neumjestan; nespretan
inequality [iniː'kwɔliti] nejednakost
inequitable [in'ekwitəbl] nepravedan
inert [i'nəːt] nepomičan, trom; **~ness** inercija
in|estimable [in'estiməbl] neprocjenjiv; **~evitable** neizbježan; **~excusable** neoprostiv; **~exhaustible** neiscrpan; **~exorable** neumoljiv; **~expedient** nesvrsishodan; **~expensive** jeftin; umjeren; **~experienced** neiskusan; **~explicable** neobjašnjiv
inexpress|ible [iniks'presəbl] neizreciv; **~ive** bezizražajan
inextinguishable [iniks'tiŋgwiʃəbl] neugasiv
infallible [in'fæləbl] nepogrešiv
infamous ['infəməs] sramotan
infan|cy ['infənsi] djetinjstvo (i *fig*); **~t** djetešce; ***~t welfare*** skrb za novorođenčad; **~ticide** čedomorstvo; čedomorka; **~tile** djetinjski; ***~tile paralysis*** dječja paraliza; **~try** pješadija
infatuate [in'fætjueit] zaluditi; ***~d with*** zaluđen kime
infect [in'fekt] zaraziti; okužiti; **~ion** zaraza; **~ious** zarazan
infelicitous [infi'lisitəs] nesretan; nepodesan
infer [in'fəː] zaključivati; **~ence** ['infərəns] zaključak, izvod
inferior [in'fiəriə] donji; podređeni; niži; manji (***to***); inferioran; ***be ~ to*** biti lošiji od; **~ity**: ***~ity complex*** osjećaj manje vrijednosti
infernal [in'fəːnl] paklenski

infest [in'fest] vrvjeti od
infiltrate ['infiltreit] pomalo prodirati; infiltrirati
infinit|e ['infinit] beskrajan; **~y** neizmjerno mnogo
infirm [in'fə:m] slab; **~ary** bolnica; **~ity** slabost; bolest
inflame [in'fleim] zapaliti (se)
inflamma|ble [in'flæməbl] upaljiv; **~tion** [inflə'meiʃən] upala
inflat|e [in'fleit] napuhnuti; **~ion** inflacija
inflexib|ility [infleksə'biliti] krutost; **~le** neelastičan; *fig* neumoljiv
inflict [in'flikt] zadati; nanijeti; odrediti (kaznu)
influence ['influəns] utjecaj (***with, up[on]***); utjecati
inform [in'fɔ:m] obavijestiti, saopćiti; **~al** neslužben; **~ation** saopćenje; vijest; znanje; informacija; ***gather ~ation*** prikupljati obavijesti; **~er** prokazivač
infringe [in'frindʒ] kršiti (zakon); **~ment** kršenje
infus|e [in'fju:z] ulijevati; **~ion** ulijevanje; *fig* prožimanje; **~oria** *pl* infuzorija
ingen|ious [in'dʒi:njəs] duhovit; **~uity** domišljatost; **~uous** [in'dʒenjuəs] iskren, prostodušan, naravan
inglorious [in'glɔ:riəs] neslavan; nečastan
ingratitude [in'grætitju:d] nezahvalnost
ingredient [in'gri:diənt] sastojak
inguinal [iŋgwinl]: ***~ rupture*** MED kila
inhabit [in'hæbit] stanovati; nastavati; **~able** prikladan za stanovanje; **~ant** stanovnik
inhale [in'heil] udisati; **~r** inhalator
inhere [in'hiə] biti sadržan u; pripadati
inherit [in'herit] naslijediti; **~ance** nasljedstvo
inhibit [in'hibit] spriječiti; zabraniti kome nešto (***a p from a th***); **~ion** [~'biʃən] sprečavanje; zabrana; "hemung"
inhospitable [in'hɔspitəbl] negostoljubiv
inhuman [in'hju:mən] neljudski
initia|l [i'niʃəl] početno slovo; **~te 1.** [~ʃiit] upućena osoba; **2.** [~ʃieit] uputiti u (***into***); **~tive** [~ʃiətiv] inicijativa
inject [in'dʒekt] uštrcati; **~ion** uštrcavanje
injunction [in'dʒʌŋkʃən] nalog; zabrana
injur|e ['indʒə] oštetiti, ozlijediti; **~ious** štetan; **~y** šteta; ozljeda
injustice [in'dʒʌstis] nepravda
ink [iŋk] tinta; **~-lines** podložak sa crtama; **~pot** tintarica; **~stand** stalak za tintarnicu

inland ['inlænd] unutrašnjost
inlay ['in'lei] praviti intarziju
inlet ['inlet] otvor; pripust; **~valve** pripusni ventil
inmate ['inmeit] stanar; ukućanin
inmost ['inmoust] najdublji
inn gostionica
innate ['i'neit] prirođen
inner ['inə] unutarnji; **~ life** duševni život; **~ tube** MOT zračnica, "šlauh"
innocen|ce ['inəsns] nevinost; **~t** nevin (***of***); bezazlen
innovation [inə'veiʃən] novotarija
innumerable [i'nju:mərəbl] bezbrojan
inoculate [i'nɔkjuleit] cijepiti; nakalamiti
inodorous [in'oudərəs] bezmirisan
inoffensive [inə'fensiv] bezazlen
inopportune [in'ɔpətju:n] u nezgodan čas
inquest ['inkwest] istraga
inquir|e [in'kwaiə] raspitati se; informirati se (***about, after, for***); **~e into** istražiti; **~ing** ispitivački; **~y** istraga, raspitivanje; **make ~ies** raspitivati se
inquisitive [in'kwizitiv] radoznao
inroad ['inroud] provala
insan|e [in'sein] umobolan; **~ity** [in'sæniti] ludilo
insatiable [in'seiʃiəbl] nezasitan
inscri|be [in'skraib] upisati; **~ption** [in'skripʃən] natpis; upis
insect ['insekt] kukac
insecure [insi'kjuə] nesiguran
insens|ibility [insensə'biliti] ravnodušnost; nesvjesnost; **~ible** neosjetljiv; ravnodušan (***of, to***); besmislen
inseparable [in'sepərəbl] nedjeljiv; nerazdruživ
insert [in'sə:t] umetnuti; uvrstiti; **~ion** umetanje; oglas
inside ['insaid] unutrašnjost; nutrina; unutra; *nogomet*: **~** (***left, right***) (lijeva, desna) spojka
insight ['insait] uvid (***into***)
insignificant [insig'nifikənt] nevažan
insincere [insin'siə] neiskren
insinuate [in'sinjueit] (zlobno) natuknuti; **~ *oneself*** ulaskati se
insipid [in'sipid] bljutav
insist [in'sist] **(up)on** insistirati; ne popuštati
insolen|ce ['insələns] drskost; **~t** drzak
insolven|cy [in'sɔlvənsi] nesposobnost plaćanja; **~t** insolventan; nesposoban da plati
insomnia [in'sɔmniə] nesanica
inspect [in'spekt] nadzirati; kontrolirati; razgledati; **~ion** nadziranje; kontrola; **~or** inspektor

inspir|ation [inspə'reiʃən] nadahnuće; **~e** [in'spaiə] nadahnuti; inspirirati
inst. = **instant** ['instənt] ovog mjeseca
install [in'stɔ:l] ustoličiti (***in***); instalirati
instalment [in'stɔ:lmənt] obrok (otplate), rata; ***by ~s*** na otplatu
instance ['instəns] usrdna molba; ***for ~*** na primjer
instant ['instənt] trenutan, neodložan; ***on the loth ~*** lo-og tekućeg mjeseca; **~aneous** trenutačan; **~ly** smjesta
instead [in'sted] **of** umjesto
instep ['instep] svod stopala, "rist"
instigat|e ['instigeit] podbadati; **~tion**: ***at ~tion of*** na poticaj
instinct ['instiŋkt] instikt; **~ive** instiktivan
institut|e ['institju:t] postaviti; institut; pokrenuti; **~ion** uvođenje; institut
instruct [in'strʌkt] poučavati, uputiti, dati razjašnjenje; **~ion** pouka; uputa; **~ive** poučan
instrument ['instrumənt] instrument; oruđe; dokument
in|subordinate [insə'bɔ:dnit] nepokoran; **~sufferable** nepodnošljiv; **~sufficient** nedovoljan
insula|r ['insjulə] otočni; **~te** izolirati; **~ting tape** traka za izoliranje; **~tor** izolator
insult ['insʌlt] uvreda; [in'sʌlt] uvrijediti; napasti
insuperable [in'sju:pərəbl] nesavladiv
insupportable [insə'pɔ:təbl] nepodnošljiv
insur|ance [in'ʃuərəns] osiguranje; **~ant** osiguranik; **~e** osigurati
insurgent [in'sə:dʒənt] ustanik
insurmountable [insə:'mauntəbl] nesavladiv
insurrection [insə'rekʃən] ustanak
intact [in'tækt] netaknut
integr|al ['intigrəl] cjelovit, nedjeljiv; **~ity** [in'tegriti] cjelovitost; poštenje
intellect ['intilekt] intelekt; **~ual** [~'lektʃuəl] intelektualan; intelektualac
intelligence [in'telidʒəns] inteligencija, razum; **~ department, ~ service** obavještajna služba; **~ office** *Am* obavještajni ured
intellig|ent [in'telidʒənt] inteligentan; **~ible** razumljiv (***to***)
intempera|nce [in'tempərəns] neumjerenost; **~te** neumjeren
intend [in'tend] namjeravati; ***~ for*** predvidjeti za; **~ed** odabranik(-ca), "budući(a)"
intense [in'tens] intenzivan, snažan

intensi|fication [intensifi'keiʃən] pojačanje; **~fy** pojačati (se); zaoštriti (se); **~ty** intenzitet, jačina; **~ve** intenzivan
intent [in'tent] napet, usredotočen ***(on)***; **~ion** namjera, nakana; **~ional** namjera(-va)n
interact ['intərækt] THEAT međučin
intercede [intə:'si:d] posredovati
intercept [intə:'sept] presresti, uhvatiti u kretanju
intercession [intə'seʃən] zagovor
interchange [intə:'tʃeindʒ] izmjenjivati; izmjenjivanje; **~able** zamjenljiv
intercourse ['intə:kɔ:s] općenje, ophođenje
interdict [intə:'dikt] zabraniti
interest ['intrist] interes, zanimanje; udio; kamate; zainteresirati za ***(in)***; ***be ~ed in*** zanimati se za; ***~ed party*** interesent; **~ing** zanimljiv
interfere [intə'fiə] upletati se; miješati se u; smetati ***(with)***; RADIO **~nce elimination** otklanjanje smetnji, **~nce suppressor** ublaživač smetnji
interior [in'tiəriə] unutrašnji; unutrašnjost; ***(art of) ~ decoration*** uređenje interijera
interlude ['intəlu:d] međuigra
intermedia|ry [intə'mi:diəri] posredan; posrednik; **~te** u sredini, među; ***~te landing*** AERO međuslijetanje
interminable [in'tə:minəbl] beskrajan, beskončan
intermission [intə'miʃən] prekid; *Am* THEAT pauza
intermit [intə'mit] (is)prekidati; **~tent fever** nastupna groznica
intern [in'tə:n] internirati; **~al** [in'tə:nl] unutarnji
international [intə:'næʃnl] međunarodni; **~ exhibition** svjetska izložba; **~ law** međunarodno pravo
Internet ['intənet] internet
interpellate [in'tə:peleit] interpelirati; postaviti pitanje
interpose [intə'pouz] staviti među; umiješati se
interpret [in'tə:prit] razjasniti; tumačiti; **~er** tumač
interrogat|e [in'terəgeit] preslušavati; **~ion** preslušavanje; ***note** ili **mark** ili **point of ~ion*** upitnik; **~ive** upitan; upitna riječ
interrupt [intə'rʌpt] prekidati; **~ion** prekid
interval ['intəvəl] interval; razmak; stanka
interven|e [intə'vi:n] intervenirati; **~tion** [~'venʃən] intervencija; uplitanje
interview ['intəvju:] intervju; razgovor; ispitivanje
intima|cy ['intiməsi] intimnost; **~te** intiman, prisan

intimation [inti'meiʃən] davanje na znanje
intimidate [in'timideit] zastrašiti
into ['intu] u
intolera|ble [in'tɔlərəbl] nepodnošljiv; **~nt** netrpeljiv
intoxicate [in'tɔksikeit] opiti
intractable [in'træktəbl] nepokoran, tvrdoglav; neukrotiv
intrepid [in'trepid] neustrašiv; **~ity** [intri'piditi] neustrašivost
intricate ['intrikit] zamršen
intrigue [in'tri:g] intriga; intrigirati
introduc|e [intrə'dju:s] uvesti; predstaviti (***to***); **~tion** [~'dʌkʃən] uvod, upoznavanje; ***letter of ~tion*** preporučno pismo
intrude [in'tru:d] nametati se (***into***); **~r** uljez; nezvan gost
intrusive [in'tru:siv] nametljiv
intuition [intju'iʃən] intuicija; pronicanje
inundat|e ['inʌndeit] poplaviti; **~ion** poplava
inure [i'njuə] priviknuti (se) (***to***)
invade [in'veid] provaliti, upasti u; **~r** napadač, osvajač
invalid [in'vælid] nepravomoćan; ['invəli:d] nesposoban za vojsku; bolestan; **~ate** proglasiti nepravovaljanim; **~ity** [invə'liditi] nepravovaljanost; nesposobnost
invaluable [in'væljuəbl] neprocjenjiv
invariable [in'vɛəriəbl] nepromjenljiv
invasion [in'veiʒən] invazija, provala u (***of***), napad
invective [in'vektiv] pogrda
inveigh [in'vei] grditi; ***~ against*** psovati (nekoga)
invent [in'vent] izumiti; **~ion** izum; **~or** izumitelj
inver|se ['in'və:s] obrnut; **~t** [in'və:t] okrenuti
invest [in'vest] zaodjenuti; uložiti (novac)
investigat|e [in'vestigeit] istražiti, ispitati; **~ion** istraga
investment [in'vestmənt] investicija
inveterate [in'vetərit] ukorijenjen, okorio
invidious [in'vidiəs] zavidan; zloban
invigorate [in'vigəreit] okrijepiti; ojačati; obodriti
invincible [in'vinsəbl] nepobjediv
inviolable [in'vaiələbl] nepovrediv
invisible [in'vizibl] nevidljiv
invit|ation [invi'teiʃən] poziv; **~e** [in'vait] pozvati u goste; izazivati; primamiti
invoice ['invɔis] faktura; fakturirati
invoke [in'vouk] zazivati; pozivati se na; dozivati (duha)

involuntary [in'vɔləntəri] nehotičan
involve [in'vɔlv] zamotati; uključivati; povlačiti za sobom, imati za posljedicu; uplesti ***(in)***
invulnerable [in'vʌlnərəbl] neranjiv
inward ['inwəd] nutarnji; **~s** (prema) unutra; **~ly** u sebi, u duši; **~ness** nutarnjost, bit
iodine ['aiədi:n] jod
IOU = **I owe you** zadužnica
Ireland ['aiələnd] Irska
Irish ['aiəriʃ] irski; ***the ~*** Irci
iron ['aiən] željezo; glačalo; ***~s*** *pl* okovi (i *fig*); glačati rublje; **~-bound** željezom okovan; vrlo strog; **~-clad** oklopljen; **~er** peglačica; **~-foundry** ljevaonica
ironic(al) [ai'rɔnik(əl)] ironičan
iron|ing ['aiəniŋ] glačanje; **~monger** željezar; **~-mould** mrlja od rđe; **~-works** željezara
irony ['aiərəni] ironija
irradiant [i'reidiənt] sjajan, koji baca zrake
irrational [i'ræʃnl] nerazuman, iracionalan
irreconcilable [i'rekənsailəbl] nepomirljiv
ir|recoverable [iri'kʌvərəbl] nenadoknadiv; **~redeemable** neotkupiv; **~refutable** nepobitan
irregular [i'regjulə] nepravilan; **~ity** [iregju'læriti] nepravilnost
irrelevan|ce [i'relivəns] irelevantnost; **~t** irelevantan ***(to)***
irremovable [iri'mu:vəbl] neukloniv; stalan
irreparable [i'repərəbl] nenadoknadiv
irreproachable [iri'proutʃəbl] besprijekoran
irresistible [iri'zistəbl] neodoljiv
ir|resolute [i'rezəlu:t] neodlučan; **~respective of** bez obzira na
irresponsib|ility ['irispɔnsə'biliti] neodgovornost; **~le** neodgovoran
irretrievable [iri'tri:vəbl] nenadoknadiv; nenadomjestiv
irreverence [i'revərəns] nepoštivanje; bez poštovanja
irrevocab|ility [irəvəkə'biliti] neopozivost; **~le** neopoziv
irrigat|e ['irigeit] navodnjavati; **~ion** navodnjavanje
irrita|bility [iritə'biliti] razdražljivost; **~ble** razdražljiv; **~te** dražiti; **~ting** koji razdražuje; **~tion** razdraživanje, razljućenost; razdraženost
is [iz] je, jest; ***that ~ to say*** to jest
island ['ailənd] otok; otok za pješake (usred ulice)
isn't ['iznt] = **is not**
isolate ['aisəleit] izolirati; osamiti

issue ['isjuː] istjecanje; izda(va)nje; broj (novina); potomstvo; sporna točka; problem; istjecati; objaviti; izdati; poteći od (***from***)
it to, ono
Italien [i'tæljən] talijanski; Talijan(ka); talijanski jezik
Italy ['itəli] Italija
itch [itʃ] svrbež; svrbiti
item ['aitəm] isto; stavka; točka
iterat|e ['itəreit] ponoviti; **~ion** ponavljanje
itinerary [ai'tinərəri] put; maršruta; dnevnik puta
its njegov, svoj
itself [it'self] ono samo; se, sebe; ***by ~*** sam(o) po sebi
ivory ['aivəri] slonovača
ivy ['aivi] bršljan

J

jack [dʒæk] dizalica (za kola)
jackal ['dʒækɔːl] šakal
jackdaw ['dʒækdɔː] čavka
jacket ['dʒækit] sako; kaput; TECH omotač; ovojnica (*knjige*)
jack-of-all-trades ['dʒækəv-'ɔːltreidz] majstor za sve
jail [dʒeil] zatvor; utamničiti; **~er** tamničar
jam [dʒæm] pekmez; gužva; nagurati (se); RADIO ometati prijem
January ['dʒænjuəri] siječanj, januar
Japan [dʒə'pæn] Japan; ♀ lak (na umjetninama); **~ese** japanski; Japanac
jar [dʒaː] vrč; škripati; tresti; ***~ upon*** vrijeđati, parati
jaundice ['dʒɔndis] žutica; **~d** žutičav
jaw [dʒɔː] čeljust; razglagoljati se; *pop* grditi; **~-bone** vilica, čeljust
jazz-band ['dʒæz'bænd] džez orkestar
jealous ['dʒeləs] ljubomoran (***of***); **~y** ljubomora
jeer [dʒiə] podrugivanje; podrugivati se
jelly ['dʒeli] hladetina, žele
jeopardize ['dʒepədaiz] staviti na kocku, ugroziti
jerk [dʒəːk] trzaj; ***by ~s*** u trzajima, isprekidano; **~y** trzav, grčevit
jersey ['dʒəːzi] džemper; žerse (materijal)
jest [dʒest] šala; šaliti se; **~er** šaljivčina
jet [dʒet] mlaz; mlazni avion; šiknuti mlazom; gagat, crni jantar
jet-black crn kao gagat
jet lag tegobe uzrokovane promjenom vremenskih zona
jet-plane mlazni avion
jetty ['dʒeti] lukobran

Jew [dʒu:] Židov
jewel ['dʒu:əl] dragulj; **~ler** draguljar; **~(le)ry** dragulji; nakit
Jew|ess ['dʒu:is] Židovka; **~ish** židovski
jingle ['dʒiŋgl] zveckanje; zveckati
jingo ['dʒiŋgou] šovinist
job [dʒɔb] posao; namještenje; ***by the ~*** na akord; **~ber** mešetar na burzi; **~ lot** partija razne lošije robe; **~-work** rad na akordu
jockey ['dʒɔki] džokej
Joe [dʒou] Josip
joggle ['dʒɔgl] drmati; tresti
John [dʒɔn] Ivan
join [dʒɔin] spojiti, združiti (***to***); pridružiti se
joiner ['dʒɔinə] stolar
joint [dʒɔint] spoj; sastavak; zglob; but; veliki komad mesa; **~-stock company** dioničko društvo
joke [dʒouk] šala; šaliti se
jolly ['dʒɔli] veseo
jolt [dʒoult] tresti, drmati; udarac
jostle ['dʒɔsl] gurati
jot [dʒɔt] mrva; malenkost
journal ['dʒə:nl] dnevnik; novine; časopis; **~ism** novinarstvo; **~ist** novinar
journey [dʒə:ni] put(ovanje); vožnja; putovati (kopnom)
jovial ['dʒouvjəl] veseo; društven
joy [dʒɔi] veselje; **~ful**, **~ous** veseo; **~-ride** "posudba" kola, besplatna vožnja
jubil|ate ['dʒu:bileit] klicati, bučno slaviti; **~ee** obljetnica; jubilej
judge [dʒʌdʒ] sudac; sudi ti (*ugl fig*)
judg(e)ment ['dʒʌdʒmənt] presuda; sud; mišljenje
judic|ature ['dʒu:dikətʃə] pravosuđe; **~ial** [~'diʃəl] sudski; **~ious** razborit, pametan
jug [dʒʌg] vrč
juggle ['dʒʌgl] žonglirati, izvoditi trikove; **~r** čarobnjak; **~ry** čarobnjaštvo
Jugoslav ['ju:gou'sla:v] *hist* jugoslavenski; Jugoslaven(-ka); **~ia** *hist* Jugoslavija
juic|e [dʒu:s] sok; **~y** sočan
July [dʒu:'lai] srpanj, juli
jump [dʒʌmp] skok; (pre-) skočiti; trgnuti se; ***~ at*** nasrnuti na; **~er** skakač; **~ing-pole** motka za skakanje
junction ['dʒʌŋkʃən] spoj; RLW čvorište
June [dʒu:n] lipanj, juni
jungle ['dʒʌŋgl] džungla, prašuma
junior ['dʒu:njə] mladi; junior
junk food ['dʒʌŋkfu:d] nezdrava hrana
juris|diction [dʒuəris'dikʃən] jurisdikcija; **~prudence** nauka o pravu
juror ['dʒuərə] porotnik
jury ['dʒuəri] porota; žiri
just [dʒʌst] pravedan; tačan;

upravo, tačno; ~ ***now*** upravo sada; ***but*** ~ malo prije
justice ['dʒʌstis] pravda; sudac; ***court of*** ~ sud
justification [dʒʌstifi'keiʃən] opravdanje
justify ['dʒʌstifai] opravdati
Jute [dʒu:t] juta; Jutlanđanin
juvenile ['dʒu:vinail] mladenački

K

Kate [keit] Kata
keel [ki:l] kobilica (broda)
keen [ki:n] oštar; revan; **~ness** oštrina; oštroumnost
keep [ki:p] (od-, uz-)držati; čuvati; voditi (*knjige*); uzdržavanje; ~ ***company*** praviti društvo; ~ ***time*** biti tačan (sat); ~ ***waiting*** pustiti nekoga da čeka; ~ ***away*** držati se podalje; ~ ***on*** zadržati (na sebi; u službi); ~ ***out*** isključiti; ~ ***in with*** održavati dobre odnose; ~ ***doing*** nastaviti; ~ ***on talking*** nastaviti govoriti; ~ ***up with*** ići u korak s; ~ ***to*** držati se čega
keep|er ['ki:pə] čuvar; upravitelj; lugar; **~ing** čuvanje; ***be out of ~ing with*** biti u neskladu s; **~sake** dar za uspomenu
kennel ['kenl] pasja kućica
kernel ['kə:nl] koštica; jezgra
kettle ['ketl] kotao; **~drum** veliki bubanj
key [ki:] ključ (i *fig*); tipka; taster; **~board** klavijatura; tastatura; **~hole** ključanica; **~-industry** ključna industrija; **~-note** temeljni ton; **~-position** ključni položaj
kick [kik] udarac nogom; udariti nogom; ritnuti se (*konj*)
kid jare; ~ **glove** glase rukavica
kidney ['kidni] bubreg; *coll* soj, vrsta
kill ubiti; zaklati; **~ing** ubilački; *coll* smiješan; **~-joy** kvaritelj veselja
kilo|cycle ['kiləsaikl] kiloherc; **~gramme** kilogram; **~metre** kilometar; **~watt** kilowat
kin srodstvo
kind [kaind] dobar; ljubazan; prijazan (***to***); vrsta; rod; ***value in*** ~ vrijednost u naturi
kindle ['kindl] zapaliti (se)
kindness ['kaindnis] dobrota; ljubaznost; prijaznost
kindred ['kindrid] srodan; rodbina
king [kiŋ] kralj; **~dom** kraljevstvo
kipper ['kipə] dimljeni slеđ
kiss poljubac; poljubiti; **~-proof** koji se ne skida (*ruž*)
kitchen ['kitʃin] kuhinja;

~-range štednjak
kite [kait] papirnati zmaj
kitten ['kitn] mače
knack [næk] vještina; trik
knag [næg] kvrga; **~gy** kvrgav
knapsack ['næpsæk] uprtnjača
knav|e [neiv] lopov; **~ery** lopovluk; **~ish** lopovski
knead [ni:d] mijesiti; masirati
knee [ni:] koljeno; **~-cap**, **~-pan** čaška, iver (koljena)
kneel [ni:l] klečati
knell [nel] pogrebno zvono
knicker|bockers ['nikəbɔkəz] *pl* (kratke) pumphlače; **~s** *pl* gaćice
knife, *pl* ***knives*** [naif, ~vz] nož; ubosti nožem; **~-battle** borba noževima; **~-grinder** brusač noževa
knight [nait] vitez; učiniti vitezom
knit [nit] plesti; tijesno (se) združiti; ~ ***the brows*** namrštiti čelo
knob [nɔb] kvrga; dugme
knock [nɔk] udarac; kucanje; udariti; kucati; ~ ***down***, ~ ***out*** nokautirati; **~er** alka (na vratima); **~-kneed** s "iksericama"; **~-out** *boks* nokaut
knot [nɔt] čvor; (i MAR uzao, morska milja); zauzlati
know [nou] znati; (pre)poznati; upoznati; ***make ~n*** objaviti; **~ing** bistar; pun razumijevanja; **~ledge** ['nɔlidʒ] poznavanje; znanje; ***to my ~ledge*** koliko ja znam
knuckle ['nʌkl] zglob prsta; **~-duster** (metalni) bokser

L

label ['leibl] naljepnica; etiketa; etiketirati
laboratory [lə'bɔrətəri] laboratorij
laborious [lə'bɔ:riəs] naporan; mučan; radin
labour ['leibə] rad; mučan posao; MED trudovi; radnici; radna snaga; ***Ministry of*** ~ Ministarstvo rada; ***hard*** ~ prisilan rad; ~ ***Exchange***, *Am* ***labor registry office*** burza rada; ~ ***Party*** Laburistička stranka; **~er**: ***heavy (manual)*** **~er** teški fizički radnik, nadničar
lace [leis] čipka; vrpca; vezati vrpcom; **~d boots** cipele na vezice
lack [læk] pomanjkanje; manjkati, nemati, nedostajati
lackey ['læki] lakaj
laconic [lə'kɔnik], **~ally** lakonski
lacquer ['lækə] lak; lakirati
lad [læd] dječak, momče
ladder ['lædə] ljestve; spu-

šteno očica; **~proof** kome ne bježe očice (čarapa)
lad|e [leid] natovariti; **~ing** krcanje; tovar
ladle ['leidl] kutlača; vaditi (dijeliti) kutlačom
lady ['leidi] gospođa, dama; plemkinja; gospodarica; ***~'s maid*** sobarica, komorkinja
lager (beer) ['la:gə] svijetlo (njemačko) pivo
lagoon [lə'gu:n] laguna
lake [leik] jezero; (grimizna) boja, lak
lamb [læm] janje
lame [leim] šepav; klimav; šepati; **~ness** šepavost
lament [lə'ment] jadikovka; jadikovati; **~able** žalostan; **~ation** jadikovka
lamp [læmp] svjetiljka; **~-post** stup ulične svjetiljke
lamprey ['læmpri] ZOOL paklara (*riba*), piškor
lance [la:ns] koplje; razrezati
land [lænd] kopno; zemlja, posjed; iskrcati se; **~holder** zemljoposjednik
landing ['lændiŋ] pristajanje; spuštanje; odmorište (stubišta); AERO **~ gear** stajni trap; **~ ground** uzletište; **~-stage** plovno pristanište
land|lady ['lændleidi] gazdarica, kućevlasnica; **~lord** gazda, kućevlasnik; **~mark** međaš; nešto upadljivo; značajan događaj; **~scape** krajobraz; **~slide** POL velika većina na izborima; **~-tax** zemljarina
lane [lein] uličica; prolaz kroz špalir
language ['læŋgwidʒ] jezik
langu|id ['læŋgwid] trom, mlitav; **~ish** venuti; čamiti; **~or** [~gə] klonulost; snenost
lank(y) ['læŋk(i)] mršav; visok, štrkljast
lantern ['læntən] fenjer; ***dark ~*** sljepica
lap [læp] krilo; oplakivanje (valova); (po)lokati
lapel [lə'pel] suvratak, rever
lapse [læps] odmicanje; tok (vremena); propust; odmicati; zapasti (***into***)
laptop ['læptɔp] prijenosno računalo
lard [la:d] svinjska mast; nadjevati slaninom; **~er** smočnica
large [la:dʒ] velik, opsežan; brojan; **~-ness** veličina; **~-minded** širokogrudan; **~-scale** velik, opsežan; **~-size(d)** velik; krupan
lark [la:k] ševa; šala; zbijati ludorije
laryn|x ['læriŋks], *pl* ***larynges*** [lə'rindʒi:z] grkljan
lash [læʃ] udarac bičem; remen biča (kandžije); bičevati; *fig* šibati; ***~ out*** ritnuti se
lass [læs] djevojka
lassitude ['læsitju:d] klonulost
last [la:st] posljednji; protekli, prošli; krajnji; trajati; doteći; izdržljivost; kalup; ~

but one predzadnji; ***at*** ~ konačno; **~ing** trajan; **~ly** konačno
latch [lætʃ] kvaka; zasun; **~-key** ključ patent brave
late [leit] kasni(o); preminuo; prijašnji; ***be*** ~ (za)kasniti; **~*r on*** kasnije; **~-comer** kasni dolaznik; prišipetlja; **~ly** u posljednje vrijeme
lateral ['lætərəl] pobočan
lath [la:θ] letva; obiti letvama
lathe [leið] tokarska klupa
lather ['la:ðə] sapunica; nasapunati; pjeniti se
Latin ['lætin] latinski; latinski jezik
latitude ['lætitju:d] širina (i GEOGR, *fig*)
latter ['lætə] noviji; drugi, potonji; **~ly** u posljednje vrijeme
lattice ['lætis] rešetka; staviti rešetku
laudable ['lɔ:dəbl] pohvalan
laugh [la:f] smijeh; smijati se; ~ ***at*** ismijavati; **~able** smiješan; **~ter** smijeh
launch [lɔ:ntʃ] porinuće; porinuti; pokrenuti; lansirati
laund|ress ['lɔ:ndris] pralja; **~ry** praonica; rublje
laurel ['lɔrəl] lovor
lavatory ['lævətəri] umivaonik; ***public*** ~ javni zahod
lavish ['læviʃ] vrlo darežljiv; raskošan; rasipati
law [lɔ:] zakon; ***go to*** ~ tužiti sudu; **~-court** sud(nica); **~ful** zakonit
lawn [lɔ:n] tratina; **~sprinkler** prskalo za polijevanje tratine
lawsuit ['lɔ:sju:t] parnica
lawyer ['lɔ:jə] pravnik; odvjetnik, advokat
lax [læks] mlitav; popustljiv; nemaran; **~ative** sredstvo za otvaranje; **~ity** mlitavost
lay [lei] položaj; smjer; *coll* zaposlenje; postaviti; položiti; nesti; kladiti se; prostrijeti; **~-by** malo parkiralište uz autoput; ~ **down** spustiti, odložiti; naložiti, odrediti; graditi (*ceste i sl*); ~ **on** provesti (plinske, vodovodne cijevi); ~ **out** izložiti; zasaditi (vrt)
layer ['leiə] naslaga; sloj
layman ['leimən] nestručnjak; laik
lay-out ['leiaut] plan; (tiskarski) prijelom
laz|iness ['leizinis] lijenost; **~y** lijen
lead [led] olovo; MAR dubinomjer; **~-pencil** olovka
lead [li:d] vodstvo; EL vod; remen za psa; voditi; navoditi; prvi bacati (kartu); ~ ***on*** zavesti, namamiti; ~ ***up to*** dovesti do
leaden ['ledn] olovan (i *fig*)
lead|er ['li:də] vođa; prvak; (konj) prednjak; uvodnik; **~ing** vodeći; vođenje; vodstvo
leaf [li:f] *pl* ***leaves*** list; krilo (vrata itd.); produžetak sto-

la na sklapanje; **~let** listak; letak; prospekt
league [li:g] savez; **ℒ *of Nations*** Liga Nacija; morska milja (4,8 km); udružiti se; **~-match** prvenstvena utakmica
leak [li:k] rupa (koja propušta vodu); propuštati; **~age** izbijanje na javu; propuštanje
lean [li:n] mršav; krt (meso); naslanjati (se); **~ness** mršavost
leap [li:p] skok; skočiti; **~-year** prestupna godina
learn [lə:n] učiti; saznati; ***~ from*** shvatiti iz; **~ed** ['~nid] učen; **~er** početnik, učenik
lease [li:s] najam, zakup; **~holder** zakupnik
least [li:st] najmanji(e); ***at (the) ~*** barem
leather ['leðə] koža; obložiti kožom; **~y** kožnat, žilav
leave [li:v] dopuštanje; dopust; odlazak; (na)pustiti; otići, otputovati; ***~ off*** prestati
lecture ['lektʃə] predavanje; korenje; predavati; očitati bukvicu; **~r** predavač; docent; lektor
ledge [ledʒ] izbočina; hrbat; podboj (prozora); **~r** COM glavna knjiga poslovanja
leech [li:tʃ] pijavica; *fig* krvopija
leer [liə] ceriti se (***at***)
lees [li:z] *pl* drožde, talog
left lijevi (-o); lijeva strana; **~-handed** ljevak
leg noga; but, plećka
legacy ['legəsi] baština, ostavština
legal ['li:gəl] zakonit; **~ization** ozakonjenje; **~ize** ozakoniti
legation [li'geiʃən] poslanstvo
legend ['ledʒənd] legenda; **~ary** legendaran
leggings ['legiŋz] *pl* sare; gležnjaci
legible ['ledʒəbl] čitljiv
legion ['li:dʒən] legija
legislat|ive ['ledʒisleitiv] zakonodavan; **~or** zakonodavac
legitima|cy [li'dʒitiməsi] zakonitost; **~te** [~meit] ozakoniti; [~mit] zakonit
leisure ['leʒə] slobodno vrijeme; dokolica; **~ly** bez žurbe
Leman ['lemən]: ***Lake ~*** Ženevsko jezero
lemon ['lemən] limun; **~-squash** limunada
lend posuditi; pružiti (pomoć)
length [leŋθ] dužina; trajanje; ***at ~*** konačno; **~en** produljiti (se); **~ways**, **~wise** po duljini
lenient ['li:niənt] blag; obziran
lens [lenz] leća (staklo)
Lent korizma
lentil ['lentil] BOT leća

leprosy ['leprəsi] MED guba
less manji, (-e); COM uz odbitak; **~en** smanjiti (se); ublažiti (se)
lesson ['lesn] zadaća; školski sat; **~s** *pl* poduka
lest da ne (bi)
let (do)pustiti; iznajmiti (***at, for***); **~ *alone*** a kamoli; pustiti na miru; **~ *down*** ostaviti na cjedilu, iznevjeriti; **~ *on*** odati tajnu; **~ *out*** ispustiti, izbrbljati; **~ *up*** *Am* prestati
letter ['letə] slovo; pismo; *pl* književnost; ***by* ~** pismom; pismeno; **~-box** poštanski ormarić; **~-carrier** *Am* pismonoša; **~-case** lisnica; **~gram** *Am* noćni brzojav, telegram
lettuce ['letis] zelena salata
level ['levl] vodoravan; ravan; izjednačen; razina; ***do one's* ~ *best*** dati sve od sebe; ***on a* ~ *with*** na istoj razini; **~ *of the sea*** morska razina; ***on the* ~** *coll Am* pošteno, otvoreno; izravnati; nivelirati; **~ *up*** povisiti; RLW **~ crossing** cestovni prijelaz preko pruge; libela; razina; nivo
lever ['li:və] poluga; **~-watch** sat s kotvenim zaporom
levy ['levi] raspisivanje (*poreza*); MIL podizanje vojske; raspisati (*porez*); podizati (*vojsku*)
liability [laiə'biliti] odgovornost; ***liabilities*** *pl* pasiva dugovanja
liable ['laiəbl] odgovoran; obavezan (***to***); sklon (***to***); **~ *to duty*** ocarinjiv
liar ['laiə] lažac
libel ['laibəl] kleveta
liberal ['libərəl] darežljiv (***of***), slobodouman; **~ity** darežljivost; širokogrudnost
liberate ['libəreit] osloboditi (***from***)
liberty ['libəti] sloboda; ***be at* ~** slobodno (činiti)
librarian [lai'brεəriən] knjižničar
licen|ce ['laisəns] licenca; dozvola; (***driving***) **~ce** vozačka dozvola; **~se** dozvoliti; dati licencu; **~see** korisnik dozvole; **~ser** izdavalac dozvole; **~tious** [~'senʃəs] raskalašen
lick (ob)lizati; *coll* pobijediti; **~ing** *coll* batine
lid poklopac; očni kapak
lie [lai] laž; položaj; ***tell a* ~** lagati
lien ['li:ən] JUR pravo zadržanja
lieu: ***in* ~ *of an oath*** umjesto zakletve
life [laif], *pl* ***lives*** [laivz] život; **~-annuity** doživotna renta; **~-belt**, **~-boat** pojas (čamac) za spasavanje; **~-insurance** životno osiguranje; **~-less** bez života; **~-sized** u prirodnoj veličini; **~ support** aparat za reanimaciju; **~time** trajanje života
lift dizalo; AERO uzgon; dizati

(se); uzdići (se); **~ing power** AERO uzgon

ligature ['ligətʃuə] povez; spojnica; MED podvez

light [lait] svjetlost (i *fig*); svjetiljka; prozor; zapaliti; rasvijetliti; lagan; plavokos; svijetao; ***come to ~*** izići na vidjelo; ***give a p a ~*** pripaliti nekome; ***~ on*** slučajno naći; **~en** sijevati; olakšati (se); **~er** upaljač; **~house** svjetionik; **~-minded** bezbrižan; **~ness** lakoća; neozbiljnost

lightning ['laitniŋ] munja; **~-conductor** gromobran; **~-strike** "divlji" štrajk

like [laik] sličan; poput, kao; ***~ that*** tako; ***what is he ~?*** kako izgleda?, kakav je?; voljeti; sviđati se; ***how do you ~ him?*** kako vam se sviđa?; **~lihood** vjerojatnost; **~ly**: ***he is ~ly to die*** vjerojatno će umrijeti; **~ness** sličnost; slika; **~wise** također

liking ['laikiŋ] sklonost; simpatija

lilac ['lailək] ljubičast; jorgovan

lily ['lili] ljiljan

limb [lim] udo; grana

lime vapno; lipa; **~light**: ***in the ~light*** biti u središtu pažnje

limit ['limit] granica; ***that's the ~!*** to je vrhunac!, tu prestaje sve!; ograničiti (***to***); **~ation** ograničenje; JUR zastara; **~ed company** društvo s ograničenim jamstvom

limp šepati; opušten, mlitav

line [lain] crta; redak; potez; RLW pruga; *tel* vod, žica; konopac; povraz; ***that's not my ~*** to nije moje područje (struka); *pl* **~s** smjernice; ***stand in ~s*** *Am* stajati (čekati) u redu; izvući crte; postaviti; napuniti (džepove); ***~s up*** *Am* postrojiti (se)

lineament ['li:niəmənt] crta (lica)

linen ['linin] platno; rublje; platnen; **~-draper** trgovac platnenom robom

liner ['lainə] veliki putnički brod (ili avion)

linger ['liŋgə] zadržavati se, otezati; vući se (*bolest*); **~ing** dugotrajan

lining ['lainiŋ] podstava

link [liŋk] karika; *fig*, *internet* veza; povezati

links [liŋks] *pl* obalne dine; igralište golfa

linseed ['linsi:d] laneno sjeme; **~ oil** laneno ulje

lion ['laiən] lav; **~ess** lavica

lip usna; **~-stick** ruž za usne

liposuction [,lipə'sʌkʃn] liposukcija

liqu|efy ['likwifai] (ras)topiti se; **~id** tekuć; bistar; tekućina; **~idate** ['~ideit] likvidirati

liquor ['likə] tekućina; **~ice** ['likəris] "crni" šećer

Lisbon ['lizbən] Lisabon

lisp šušljati (loše izgovarati "s")
list rub; popis; MAR nagib (broda); popisati
listen ['lisn] slušati; ~ ***to*** RADIO slušati; **~er** slušalac
listless ['listlis] bezvoljan
literal ['litərəl] doslovan
literature ['litəritʃə] književnost
litter ['litə] otpaci, smeće
little ['litl] malen; kratak (vrijeme); malo; sitnica; ~ ***by*** ~ malo po malo
live [liv] živjeti; stanovati; trajati; ~ ***on*** živjeti od (čega); ~ ***out*** preživjeti
livel|ihood ['laivlihud] zarada za život; **~iness** živahnost; **~y** živahan
liver ['livə] jetra; onaj koji živi
livery ['livəri] livreja
livid ['livid] sivomodar; blijed
living ['liviŋ] živ; stanovanje; način života; zarada za život; **~-room** dnevna soba
lizard ['lizəd] gušter
Lloyd's [lɔidz] Londonska tvrtka
load [loud] tovar; teret; TECH opterećenje; (na)tovariti; **~ing** krcanje; tovar
loaf [louf], *pl* ***loaves*** hljeb; glava šećera; skitati se, besposličiti
loafer ['loufə] besposličar
loam [loum] ilovača
loan [loun] zajam; ***on*** ~ na zajam
loath [louθ] nesklon; **~e** mrziti; **~ing** gnušanje; **~some** gnusan
lobby ['lɔbi] predvorje; THEAT foaje; kuloari
lobe [loub] **of the ear** ušna resica
lobster ['lɔbstə] jastog
local ['loukəl] mjesni; **~ity** mjesto; nalazište; **~ize** lokalizirati
locate [lou'keit] smjestiti; naći položaj (mjesto); ***be ~d*** *Am* biti smješten
lock brava; ustava; uvojak; zabraviti; zaključati; **~et** medaljon; **~-out** lokaut, prekid rada od strane poslodavca zbog neslaganja s radničkim zahtjevima; **~smith** bravar
locust ['loukəst] skakavac
lodg|e [lɔdʒ] smjestiti; spremiti; ***~e a complaint*** uložiti žalbu; stanovati; **~er** (pod-) stanar; **~ings** *pl* stan
loft potkrovlje; crkveni kor; **~iness** uzvišenost; plemenitost; **~y** visok; uznosit
log deblo; panj; ~ ***in***, ~ ***on*** pristupiti; ~ ***out*** odjaviti se
loggerheads ['lɔgəhedz]: ***be at*** (***come to***) ~ (***with***) (po-) svađati se
logic ['lɔdʒik] logika; **~al** logičan
loin [lɔin] slabine; bubrežnjak
loiter ['lɔitə] klatiti se; dangubiti

lonely ['lounli] osamljen
long [lɔŋ] dug(o); ***before ~*** uskoro; ***be ~*** dugo trajati, zadržati se; ***in the ~ run*** u konačnoj liniji; ***~ for*** čeznuti za; **~-dated** dugoročan; **~-distance call** međugradski razgovor; **~ing** čežnja; **~-sighted** dalekovidan (i *fig*)
look [luk] pogled; (***~s*** *pl*) vanjština; ***have a ~ at*** pogledati; gledati (***at, on***); izgledati; pripaziti; ***~ after*** brinuti se za; ***~ for*** očekivati; tražiti; ***~ forward to*** unaprijed se radovati; ***~ in*** navratiti; ***~ into*** ispitati; ***~ out!*** pazi(te)!; ***~ out*** izabrati; ***~ over*** pregledati; ***~ to*** pobrinuti se; ***~ up*** podići oči; popraviti se; ***~ up(on)*** smatrati (***as***); **~er-on** gledalac; **~ing-glass** ogledalo; **~-out** promatračnica; oprez; izgled
loom [luːm] tkalački stan; pojaviti se nejasno u daljini, ocrtavati se
loop [luːp] petlja; zavoj (rijeke); načiniti petlju; ***~ the ~*** AERO izvesti luping; **~hole** puškarnica; *fig* rupa; RLW **~-line** odvojak u obliku petlje
loose [luːs] labav, klimav; prostran; komotan; rahal; raspušten; ***be at a ~ end*** biti slobodan (neangažiran); razriješiti, olabaviti; **~n** razriješiti (se), olabaviti (se)
lop-sided ['lɔp'saidid] naheren
loquacious [lə'kweiʃəs] glagoljiv
lord [lɔːd] gospodin, lord
Lord [lɔːd] Bog, Gospod; **~'s Prayer** očenaš; **~'s Supper** pričest
lord|ly ['lɔːdli] gospodski; otmjen; **~ship** čast (naslov) lorda
Lorraine [lə'rein] Lotaringija
lorry ['lɔri] RLW laki plato vagon za popravak pruge; (***motor-***) ***~*** kamion, teretnjak
lose [luːz] izgubiti; potratiti; propustiti; kasniti (sat)
loss gubitak; ***at a ~*** na čudu, u neprilici
lot ždrijeb; udio; parcela; ***a ~ of people*** mnogo ljudi
lotion ['louʃən] losion
lottery ['lɔtəri] lutrija
loud [laud] glasan; bučan; **~-speaker** RADIO zvučnik
lounge [laundʒ] besposličiti; fotelja; društvena prostorija; foaje; **~ suit** dnevno odijelo
louse [laus] *pl* ***lice*** uš
lovable ['lʌvəbl] ljubak; drag
love [lʌv] ljubav; dragi, (-a); ***what a ~ of a hat!*** kakav krasan šešir!; ***give*** (*ili* ***send***) ***one's ~ to*** poslati pozdrave; ***make ~*** (***to***) voditi ljubav (sa); udvarati; **~ly** dražestan; divan; lijep; **~r** ljubavnik; dragi, (-a); ***pair of ~rs*** ljubavni par

loving ['lʌviŋ] pun ljubavi
low [lou] nizak; dubok(o); tiho; *fig* potišten; (pri)prost; **~-brow** *coll* priprosta osoba, poluinteligent; **~er** niži; donji; spustiti; prigušiti (*glas*); oboriti (*oči*); sniziti (*cijene*); **~-fat** niske masnoće; **~-necked** dekoltiran; **~-pressure** niski tlak (pritisak); **~-spirited** potišten, malodušan
loyal ['lɔiəl] vjeran; **~ty** vjernost
lozenge ['lɔzindʒ] pastila, tableta
Ltd = **limited**
lubricate ['lu:brikeit] podmazati, nauljiti
lucid: **~ *interval*** MED trenuci nepomračenog uma
luck [lʌk] sreća (sretan slučaj); ***bad* ~** nesreća; **~ily** srećom; **~y** sretan
lucrative ['lu:krətiv] unosan
ludicrous ['lu:dikrəs] smiješan
luge [lu:ʒ] sportske saonice; sanjkati se
luggage ['lʌgidʒ] prtljaga; **~-rack** polica za prtljagu
lukewarm ['lu:kwɔ:m] mlak; ravnodušan
lumbago [lʌm'beigou] lumbago, krstobolja, "heksnšus"
lumber ['lʌmbə] starudija; **~-room** ropotarnica
luminous ['lu:minəs] svijetao; svjetleći; blistav
lump [lʌmp] gruda; komad; ***in the* ~** u cijelome, poprijeko; **~ sugar** šećer u kockama; **~ sum** okrugao (paušalni) iznos
lunatic ['lu:nətik] lud; luđak; **~ asylum** ludnica
lunch(eon) ['lʌntʃən] ručak; ručati; **~time** vrijeme ručka, pauza za ručak
lungs [lʌŋz] pluća
lurch [lə:tʃ]: ***leave in the* ~** ostaviti na cjedilu
lure [ljuə] mamac; namamiti
lurk [lə:k] vrebati; ležati u busiji
luscious ['lʌʃəs] sočan, slastan
lustre ['lʌstə] sjaj; luster; **~less** bez sjaja; mutan
lute [lu:t] leut, lutnja; brtvilo, kit; zabrtviti
luxurious [lʌg'zjuəriəs] raskošan; **~ness** raskošnost
luxury ['lʌkʃəri] raskoš(nost); luksuz
lying-in ['laiiŋ'in] **hospital** rodilište
lynch [lintʃ] linčovati; **~-law** zakon linča
lynx [liŋks] ris
lyric ['lirik] lirski; lirska pjesma; **~s** *pl* lirika; riječi pjesme (šlagera)

M

M. A. = **Master of Arts**
ma'am [mæm] = **madam**
macaroon [mækə'ru:n] kolačić s mljevenim bademima
mace [meis] PARL žezlo
machine [mə'ʃi:n] stroj, mašina; **~-driven** na strojni pogon; **~ gun** (puško) mitraljez; **~ry** strojevi; mašinerija; **~-tool** alatni stroj
machinist [mə'ʃi:nist] strojar; upravljač strojem
mackerel ['mækrəl] lokarda, skuša; ovčice (oblak)
mackintosh ['mækintɔʃ] kišni ogrtač
mad [mæd] lud; ljut; ***drive* ~** natjerati u ludilo
madam ['mædəm] gospođo (kod oslovljavanja)
mad|den ['mædn] razbjesniti; **~house** ludnica; **~man** luđak; **~ness** ludost
magazine [mægə'zi:n] skladište; časopis
maggot ['mægət] crv(ić)
magic ['mædʒik], **~al** čaroban; čarolija; **~ian** [mə'dʒiʃən] čarobnjak; mađioničar
magist|racy ['mædʒistrəsi] položaj suca; **~rate** (policijski, niži) sudac
magnanimity [mægnə'nimiti] velikodušnost
magnet ['mægnit] magnet
magnificen|ce [mæg'nifisns] veličanstvenost; **~t** sjajan; divan
magnify ['mægnifai] poveća(va)ti; **~ing glass** povećalo
magnitude ['mægnitju:d] veličina; važnost
magpie ['mægpai] svraka
mahogany [mə'hɔgəni] mahagoni
maid [meid] djevojka; ***old* ~** usidjelica; **~en**, **~enly** djevojački; čedan; **~en name** djevojačko prezime; **~servant** sluškinja
mail [meil] pošta (pisma itd.); *Am* poslati poštom; **~-bag** poštanska torba; **~-boat** poštanski brod; **~-box** poštanski ormarić; **~-carrier** (*ili* **~-man**) *Am* poštar; **~-coach** poštanska kočija; **~-order house** *Am* robna kuća za narudžbe preko kataloga; **~-train** poštanski vlak; **~ed fist** *fig* gruba sila
maim [meim] osakatiti
main [mein] glavni; **~ point** ono glavno; **~ station** *tel* centrala; glavni vodovod; **~land** kopno
maintain [men'tein] podržavati; ostati kod svoga
maintenance ['meintinəns] (p)održavanje; uzdržavanje
maize [meiz] kukuruz

majest|ic, **~ically** [mə'dʒestik(əli)] veličanstven; **~y** ['mædʒisti] veličanstvo
major ['meidʒə] veći; važan; glavni; MUS dur; MIL major; *Am* glavni predmet studija
make [meik] (u-, na-)činit; (na)praviti; spremiti, pripraviti; obaviti; (tjelesna) građa; forma; marka; tip; **~ sure of** provjeriti; osigurati se; **~ way** prokrčiti sebi put; **~ out** razabrati; ispostaviti; sastaviti; **~ up** sastaviti; našminkati se; **~ up one's mind** odlučiti (se); **~ up for** nadoknaditi; **~r** proizvođač; **~shift** privremeno pomagalo; **~-up** ustrojstvo; struktura; šminka
malady ['mælədi] bolest
male [meil] muški; mužjak
malediction [mæli'dikʃən] proklinjanje
malevolen|ce [mə'levələns] zloba; **~t** zloban
malic|e ['mælis] zloba; **~ious** [mə'liʃəs] zloban
malign [mə'lain] poguban, štetan; klevetati; **~ant** [~'lignənt] zloban; MED zloćudan
malle|able ['mæliəbl] kovak; **~t** ['~it] TECH kladivo, bat
malnutrition ['mælnju'triʃən] neishranjenost
malt [mɔ:lt] slad; pretvarati (se) u slad
mammal ['mæməl] sisavac
man [mæn], *pl* **men** čovjek; muškarac; čovječanstvo; MIL snabdjeti posadom
manage ['mænidʒ] rukovati; upravljati; postupati; uspjeti; ravnati (držati u posluš-nosti); **~able** spretan za rukovanje; savitljiv; **~ment** upravljanje; uprava; **~r** upravitelj; direktor; menedžer; THEAT intendant
mane [mein] griva
manful ['mænful] muževan; srčan
manger ['meindʒə] jasle
mangle [mæŋgl] tijesak za rublje; izažimati rublje u tijesku; osakatiti; unakaziti
manhood ['mænhud] muževnost; svi muškarci
mania ['meiniə] manija; mahnitost; **~c** manijak
manicur|e ['mænikjuə] manikiranje; **~ist** manikirka
manifest ['mænifest] očit; ispoljiti; **~ation** manifestacija
manifold ['mænifould] mnogostruk; umnožiti
manipulate [mə'nipjuleit] manipulirati, rukovati
man|kind [mæn'kaind] čovječanstvo; **~ly** muževan
mannequin ['mænikin] maneken
manner ['mænə] način; manira; **~ism** manirizam; **~ly** uljudan
manoeuvre [mə'nu:və] manevar
man-of-war ratni brod
manor ['mænə] plemićki (go-

spodski) posjed; **~-house** plemićki (vlasteoski) dvorac
man-power sposobno muško stanovništvo; radna snaga (stanovništvo)
mansion ['mænʃən] velika kuća
manslaughter ['mænslɔːtə] ubojstvo (bez predumišljaja)
mantelpiece ['mæntlpiːs] polica nad kaminom
mantle ['mæntl] ogrtač; pokrov; zastrijeti; *fig* sakriti
mantrap ['mæntræp] stupica za ljude
manual ['mænjuəl] ručni; priručnik
manufactory [mænju'fæktəri] tvornica
manufactur|e [mænju'fæktʃə] fabrikat; prerađivati; proizvoditi (***into***); **~er** tvorničar
manure [mə'njuə] gnoj đubre; đubriti
many ['meni] mnogo; ***~ a*** mnogi (čovjek)
map [mæp] geografska karta; izraditi nacrt; ***~ out*** prikazati
maple ['meipl] javor
mar [maː] pokvariti
maraud [mə'rɔːd] pljačkati
marble ['maːbl] mramor; špekula; mramoran
March [maːtʃ] ožujak, mart
march [maːtʃ] marš; marširati; hodati
marchioness ['maːʃənis] markiza
marchpane ['maːtʃpein] marcipan
marconigram [maː'kounigræm] radiotelegram
mare [mεə] kobila
margin ['maːdʒin] rub; prostor za manevriranje; marža
marigold ['mærigould] neven
marine [mə'riːn] (po)morski; mornarica; **~r** mornar, pomorac
maritime ['mæritaim] pomorski; primorski; moreplovni
mark [maːk] znak; oznaka; biljeg; zaštitni znak; ožiljak; cilj; školska ocjena; označiti; upamtiti; ***be up to the ~*** ispuniti očekivanja; **~ed** izrazit
market ['maːkit] trg; tržnica; prodavati (kupovati) na tržištu; **~ing** tržišni poslovi
marking|-ink tuš za obilježavanje rublja; **~-iron** željezo za žigosanje
marmalade ['maːməleid] (gorak) pekmez od naranči
marplot ['maːplɔt] mutikaša; zabadalo
marqu|ess, **~is** ['maːkwis] markiz
marriage ['mæridʒ] ženidba; udaja; vjenčanje; brak; **~able** dorastao za brak; **~-certificate** *ili* **~-lines** vjenčani list
married ['mærid] oženjen, udata

marrow ['mærou] koštana moždina
marry ['mæri] oženiti se; udati se
marsh [maːʃ] močvara, močvarno tlo; **~ fever** močvarna groznica; **~ gas** barski plin; **~y** močvaran, barski
marshal ['maːʃəl] maršal; redati
marten ['maːtin] kuna
martial ['maːʃəl] ratni(čki); **~ law** prijeki sud, izvanredno stanje
martyr ['maːtə] mučenik; mučiti (na smrt)
marvel ['maːvəl] divota; čuđenje; čuditi (diviti) se; **~lous** čudesan, divan
mascot ['mæskət] maskota; talisman; MOT ***radiator ~*** figura na hladnjaku
masculine ['mæskjulin] muški, muževan
mash [mæʃ] kaša; **~ed potatoes** *pl* pire krumpir
mask [maːsk] maska; maskirati
mason [meisn] zidar; klesar
masquerade [mæskə'reid] maskerada, krabuljni ples
mass [mæs] REL misa; masa; **~ meeting** masovni sastanak; gomilati (se)
massacre ['mæsəkə] pokolj
massage ['mæsaːʒ] masaža; masirati
massive ['mæsiv] masivan; čvrst
mast [maːst] jarbol; opremiti jarbolom
master ['maːstə] gospodar; majstor; učitelj; **~ of Arts** magistar (akademski stupanj); savladati; temeljito naučiti; **~-builder** graditelj; **~ly** majstorski; **~piece** majstorsko djelo; **~ship** majstorstvo; služba učitelja; **~y** vlast; majstorstvo
masticate ['mæstikeit] žvakati
mat [mæt] rogožina; mat (bez sjaja)
match [mætʃ] žigica; utakmica; par (nekome); brak; pristajati nečemu; biti dorastao; ***well ~ed*** dobro usklađen; **~box** kutija žigica; **~less** bez premca
mate [meit] drug; suprug(a)
material [mə'tiəriəl] materijalan; tvaran, bitan; materijal; sukno; **~ize** ostvariti (se)
maternal [mə'təːnl] majčinski, po majci
maternity [mə'təːniti] majčinstvo; **~ hospital** rodilište; **~suit** trudnička haljina
mathematics [mæθi'mætiks] matematika
matrimony ['mætriməni] brak
matron ['meitrən] matrona; nadzornica; **~ly** matronski, staložen
matter ['mætə] materija, tvar; stvar; posao; predmet; MED gnoj; ***postal ~*** sve što

se može slati poštom; **printed ~** tiskanica; **in the ~ of** s obzirom na; **what's the ~ (with you)?** šta (ti) je?; **no ~** nije važno, ništa zato; **no ~ who** bilo tko; **~ of course** što se samo po sebi razumije; **~ of fact** činjenica; **~ of taste** stvar ukusa; biti važan; **it does not ~** nije važno

mattres ['mætris] madrac

matur|e [mə'tjuə] zreo; sazreti; dospjeti (mjenica); **~ity** zrelost; dospjeće

Maundy ['mɔːndi] **Thursday** Veliki Četvrtak

mauve [mouv] svijetloljubičast

maxim ['mæksim] načelo; **~um** maksimum; **~ output** maksimalna proizvodnja

may [mei] smjeti, moći

May [mei] svibanj, maj; **~-day** prvi svibnja

mayor [mɛə] gradonačelnik

maze [meiz] labirint

me mene, me; meni, mi; mnom

meadow ['medou] livada

meagre ['miːgə] mršav; štur

meal [miːl] obrok; grubo brašno; **~-time** vrijeme jela; **~y** brašnast

mean [miːn] podao; škrt; srednji; (ozbiljno) misliti; htjeti reći; sredina; **~s** sredstva, imetak; **by all ~** svakako; **by no ~** nikako; **by ~ of** pomoću; **~ing** smisao, značenje; **~ness** podlost; **~time** međuvrijeme; **~while** u međuvremenu, međutim

measles ['miːzlz] ospice

measurable ['meʒərəbl] izmjeriv

measure ['meʒə] mjera, takt; **~ of capacity** šuplja mjera; **in some ~** donekle; (od-, iz-)mjeriti; **~ment** mjerenje

meat [miːt] meso; **roast ~** pečeno meso; **~ tea** popodnevni čaj s mesom

mechan|ic [mi'kænik], **~ical** mehanički; mehaničar; obrtnik; **~ics** *ugl sg* mehanika; **~ism** ['mekənizəm] mehanizam; **~ize** mehanizirati

medal ['medl] medalja

meddle ['medl] miješati se

medial ['miːdiəl] srednji; prosječan

mediat|e ['miːdieit] posredovati; **~ion** posredovanje; **~or** posrednik

medica|l ['medikəl] medicinski; liječnički; **2l Superintendent** glavni liječnik; **~ment** lijek; **~te** liječiti

medicin|al [me'disinl] ljekovit; **~e** ['medsin] lijek; **~e chest** kućna apoteka

medieval [medi'iːvəl] srednjovjekovan

mediocr|e ['midioukə] osrednji; **~ity** [~'ɔkriti] mediokritet(nost)

meditat|e ['mediteit] razmišljati; snovati; **~ive** sklon razmišljanju

Mediterranean [meditə'reinjən] **Sea** Sredozemno more
medium ['mi:diəm], *pl* ***media*** sredina; medij; srednji; prosječni
meek [mi:k] krotak; **~ness** krotkost
meet [mi:t] (su)sresti (se), naći se; dočekati; ispuniti (obavezu); okupiti se; ***~ with*** naići na; ***~ with an accident*** doživjeti nesreću; **~ing** sastanak; zbor; zasjedanje
melancholy ['melənkəli] melankolija; melankoličan
mellow ['melou] mek; zreo; smekšati
melod|ious [mi'loudjəs] melodiozan; **~y** melodija
melon ['melən] dinja, lubenica
melt (o-, ras-)topiti (se); ***~ away*** rastopiti se; **~ing point** točka taljenja
member ['membə] udo; član; **~ship** članstvo
memor|able ['memərəbl] vrijedan spomena; **~andum** memorandum; zabilježba; **~ial** spomenik; **~ize** *Am* naučiti napamet; **~y** pamćenje; uspomena
menace ['menəs] prijetiti; prijetnja
mend popraviti; krpati
mendacious [men'deiʃəs] lažljiv
mental ['mentl] duševni; **~ arithmetic** računanje u glavi; **~ hospital** duševna bolnica; **~ity** mentalitet
mention ['menʃən] spominjanje; spomenuti; ***don't ~ it!*** nema na čemu!; ***not to ~*** a kamo li
mercantile ['mə:kəntail] trgovački
mercenary ['mə:sinəri] plaćenički; potkupljiv; plaćenik
mercer ['mə:sə] trgovac tkaninama; **~y** tkanina; trgovina tkaninama
merchan|dize ['mə:tʃəndaiz] roba; **~t** ['-t] trgovac na veliko (*Am* i na malo)
merc|iful ['mə:siful] milosrdan; **~iless** nemilosrdan; **~y** milosrđe; milost
mere [miə] puki; tek
merge [mə:dʒ] *fig* stopiti (se); **~r** *Am* fuzija
meridian [mə'ridiən] meridijan; podnevni
merit ['merit] zasluga; vrijednost; prednost
merry ['meri] veseo; radostan; ***make ~*** veseliti se
mesh [meʃ] oko (mreže), ***~es*** *pl* mreža
mess zbrka; nered; neprilika; pobrkati
mess|age ['mesidʒ] vijest; **~enger** glasnik
metal ['metl] kovina; tucanik; **~lic** kovan, od kovine; **~lurgy** metalurgija
meteorolog|ical [mi:tjərə'lɔdʒikəl] meteorološki; **~ist** meteorolog; **~y** meteorologija

method ['meθəd] metoda; postupak; **~ical** metodički
meticulous [mi'tikjuləs] vrlo tačan, pedantan
metre ['mi:tə] metar (i pjesnički)
metropolis [mi'trɔpəlis] metropola
mettle ['metl] kov; žar; **~some** vatren, odvažan
micro|chip ['maikrəʧip] mikročip; **~phone** mikrofon; **~scope** mikroskop
midday ['middei] podne
middle ['midl] sredina; srednji; **~ Ages** *pl* Srednji Vijek; **~ classes** srednji stalež; **~-aged** srednjih godina; **~-sized** srednje veličine
middling ['midliŋ] osrednji
midge [midʒ] mušica; **~t** patuljak
midnight ['midnait] ponoć
midship|man ['midʃipmən] stariji (mornarički) kadet; **~s** sredina broda
midst: ***in the ~ of*** usred
mid|summer ['midsʌmə] sredina ljeta; **~way** na pola puta
might [mait] moć; **~y** moćan, snažan
Milan [mi'læn] Milano
milch-cow ['miltʃ-] krava muzara
mild [maild] blag, krotak
mildew ['mildju:] snijet; plijesan
mildness ['maildnis] blagost
mile [mail] milja; **~age** daljina u miljama
military ['militəri] vojni(čki); vojska
militia [mi'liʃə] milicija
milk mlijeko; musti; **~er** muzar; **~-float** kola za mlijeko; **~man** mljekar
mill mlin; tvornica; mljeti; obrađivati na glodalici; valjati; **~er** mlinar
millet ['milit] proso
milliard ['milja:d] milijarda
milliner ['milinə] modistica, kitničarka; **~y** posao (roba) modistice
milt slezena; riblja mliječ
mime [maim] lakrdija
mimic ['mimik] mimičar; oponašati
mince [mins] kosati; ***not to ~ matters*** otvoreno reći; ***~d meat*** kosano meso; **~meat** nadjev od grožđica itd. (za kolač); **~-pie** kolač od grožđica
mind [maind] duh, pamet, um; mišljenje; sklonost; svijest; ***change one's ~*** predomisliti se; ***bear in ~*** imati na umu; ***have half a ~ to*** gotovo htjeti (što učiniti); paziti, brinuti se za; ***never ~*** ništa za to!; ***I don't ~*** nemam ništa protiv; ***do you ~ my smoking?*** da li bi vas smetalo ako zapušim?; ***would you ~ taking off your hat?*** biste li bili tako dobri da skinete šešir?; ***~ your own business!*** to se vas ne tiče!;

~ful obziran (***of***)
mine [main] moj; rudnik; MIL mina; rovati (kopati) u zemlji; MIN kopati rudu; potkopati;
miner ['mainə] rudar; MIL miner
mineral ['minərəl] ruda; rudni, mineralni
mingle ['miŋgl] miješati se, družiti se (***in***, ***with***)
miniature ['minjətʃə] minijatura
minimum ['miniməm] minimum; najmanji
mining ['mainiŋ] rudarenje; (*i* **~ *industry***) rudarstvo
minister ['ministə] svećenik; ministar; poslanik; pomagati; pružati (pomoć)
ministry ['ministri] ministarstvo
mink [miŋk] krzno kanadske kune zlatice ("nerc")
minor ['mainə] manji; nevažan; malodobnik; MUS mol; *Am* sporedan predmet studija
minster ['minstə] stolna crkva
mint metvica; kovnica; kovati novac; **~age** kovanje novca
mint-sauce umak od metvice
minuet [minju'et] menuet
minute ['minit] minuta; *coll* tren; zapis; **~s** *pl* zapisnik; službeno zapisati; **~-hand** minutna kazaljka
mirac|le ['mirəkl] čudo; **~ulous** čudesan
mirage ['mira:ʒ] fatamorgana
mire ['maiə] blato, glib
mirror ['mirə] ogledalo; zrcaliti se
mirth [mə:θ] veselje; **~ful** veseo
misadventure ['misəd'ventʃə] nezgoda
misanthrop|ist, **~y** [mi'zænθrəpist, ‿i] mizantrop(ija)
misappl|ication ['misæpli'keiʃən] kriva primjena; zlouporaba; **~y** krivo upotrebiti
mis|apprehension ['misæpri'henʃən] krivo shvaćanje; **~behaviour** loše vladanje; **~belief** krivovjerje, pogrešno vjerovanje
miscalculat|e ['mis'kælkjuleit] krivo (iz)računati; **~ion** pogrešan račun
miscarriage [mis'kæridʒ] gubitak (pošiljke); pobačaj; **~ *of justice*** nepravedna, pogrešna osuda
miscellaneous [misi'leinjəs] mješovit; raznovrstan
mischance [mis'tʃa:ns] nezgoda, nesretan slučaj
mischie|f ['mistʃif] šteta; psina; zloćko; **~vous** ['‿vəs] štetan; zločest; vragoljast
misconduct [mis'kɔndəkt] loše vladanje; ['‿kən'dʌkt] loše upravljati
misdeed ['mis'di:d] zlodjelo
miser ['maizə] škrtac
miser|able ['mizərəbl] jadan;

bijedan; **~y** bijeda; nevolja
mis|fire ['mis'faiə] neuspjeh; zatajenje (oružja, motora); **~fortune** nesreća; **~give** ispunjati zlom slutnjom; **~govern** loše vladati; **~guide** zavesti; **~hap** nezgoda; **~interpret** krivo tumačiti (shvatiti); **~judge** krivo (pro)suditi; **~lay** zametnuti; **~lead** zavesti; **~print** pogrešno tiskati; tiskarska greška; **~rule** nered; loše upravljati
miss gospođica; promašaj; promašiti; propustiti
misshapen ['mis'ʃeipən] izobličen
missing ['misiŋ] odsutan; nestao (iz akcije)
mission ['miʃən] misija; zvanje; poziv; **~ary** misionar
mist magla
mistake [mis'teik] pogreška; zabuna; ***by ~*** greškom; krivo shvatiti; zamijeniti s kime (***for***); **~n**: ***be ~n*** pogriješiti; varati se
mister ['mistə] = **Mr.** gospodin
mistress ['mistris] gospodarica; domaćica; gospođa = **Mrs.** ['misiz]
mistrust ['mis'trʌst] nemati povjerenja u
misunderstand ['misʌndə'stænd] krivo razumjeti; **~ing** nesporazum
misuse ['mis'ju:z] krivo upotrebiti; zloupotrijebiti; ['~'ju:s] zloupotreba
mite [mait] crvić
mitigate ['mitigeit] ublažiti
mitten ['mitn] rukavica s jednim prstom
mix [miks] (po)miješati; ***~ed marriage*** mješoviti brak; ***be ~ed up with*** biti umiješan sa; **~ture** smjesa
moan [moun] stenjanje; stenjati
mob gomila; nasrnuti u gomili
mobil|ity [mou'biliti] pokretnost; **~ize** mobilizirati
mock ruganje; lažni; ismijavati se (***at***); imitirati; **~er** rugalac; **~ery** ruganje; sprdnja
mode [moud] način
model ['mɔdl] model; modelirati
moderat|e ['mɔdərit] umjeren; blag; osrednji; ['~reit] ublažiti; popustiti; **~ion** umjerenost
modern ['mɔdən] moderan; suvremen; **~ize** modernizirati (se)
modest ['mɔdist] skroman; **~y** skromnost
modi|fication [mɔdifı'keiʃən] preinačenje; **~fy** preinačiti; ublažiti
modulat|e ['mɔdjuleit] modulirati; **~or**: ***~or of tonality*** FILM tonska blenda
moist [mɔist] vlažan; **~en** ['mɔisn] navlažiti (se); **~ure** ['~tʃə] vlaga
molar ['moulə]: ***~ (tooth)*** kut-

njak
mole [moul] krtica; madež; lukobran
molest [mə'lest] dodijavati; **~ation** dodijavanje
moment ['moumənt] trenutak; važnost; **~ary** trenutačan; **~ous** važan
monarch ['mɔnək] monarh; **~y** monarhija
monastery ['mɔnəstri] samostan
Monday ['mʌndi] ponedjeljak
money ['mʌni] novac; ***ready* ~** gotovina; **~-changer** mjenjač; **~-order** novčana uputnica
mongrel ['mʌngrəl] križanac, mješanac
monk [mʌŋk] redovnik, monah
monkey ['mʌŋki] majmun; **~ business** *Am* podvala; glupost, neozbiljnost
mono|gram ['mɔnəgræm] monogram; **~polize** monopolizirati; **~poly** monopol (***of***); **~tonous** jednoličan
monst|er ['mɔnstə] čudovište; **~rosity** [~'trɔsiti] nakaznost, grozota; **~rous** nakazan, grozan
month [mʌnθ] mjesec; **~ly** mjesečni, (-o)
mood [mu:d] raspoloženje; ugođaj
moon [mu:n] mjesec; **~-light** mjesečina; **~-struck** luckast; smušen
Moor [muə] Maur; Crnac; **~** vriština; ledina
mop otirač, krpa za pranje poda (na dršku); obrisati (pokupiti) krpom
moral ['mɔrəl] ćudoredan; moral; pouka; **~s** *pl* (društveni) moral; **~ity** moralnost
morbid ['mɔ:bid] morbidan, bolestan
more više; ***once* ~** još jednom; ***no* ~** ne više; **~over** [~'rouvə] osim toga
morning ['mɔ:niŋ] jutro, prije podne; ***tomorrow* ~** sutra ujutru; ***in the* ~** ujutro
morose [mə'rous] mrzovoljan
mor|phia ['mɔ:fjə], **~phine** morfij
morsel ['mɔ:səl] zalogaj; komadić
mortal ['mɔ:tl] smrtan; smrtonosan; **~ity** [~'tæliti] smrtnost
mortar ['mɔ:tə] mužar; MIL minobacač; malter
mortgag|e ['mɔ:gidʒ] hipoteka; založiti; **~ee** hipotekarni vjerovnik; **~or** hipotekarni dužnik
mortif|ication [mɔ:tifı'keiʃən] MED trulenje živog tkiva; trapljenje; poniženje; **~y** trapiti (se); poniziti; MED obamirati, raspadati se
mortuary ['mɔ:tjuəri] mrtvačnica
Moselle [mə'zel] rijeka M.; **~**

francusko vino
mosque [mɔsk] džamija
moss mahovina; tresetište; **~y** obrastao mahovinom
most [moust] većina; većinom; vrlo; ***at (the) ~*** u najboljem slučaju; **~ly** većinom
moth [mɔθ] moljac; noćni leptir; **~eaten** izjeden od moljaca
mother ['mʌðɔ] majka; **~hood** majčinstvo; **~in-law** svekrva, punica; **~ly** majčinski; **~-of-pearl** sedef; **~-tongue** materinji jezik
motion ['mouʃən] kretanje; hod; PARL prijedlog; MED stolica; **~less** nepomičan
motive ['moutiv] pokretan; povod
motor ['moutə] motor; voziti automobil; **~ ambulance** bolnička kola; **~ boat** motorni čamac; **~ bus** autobus; **~ car** automobil; **~cycle** motorkotač; **~ school** vozačka škola; **~ing** voženje automobila, vožnja automobilom; automobilizam **~ist** automobilist; **~ization** motorizacija; **~-launch** veliki motorni čamac; **~-truck** *Am* kamion
mottled ['mɔtld] išaran; pjegast
mould [mould] zemlja crnica; plijesan; kalup; oblikovati; **~er** izradivač kalupa; raspadati se; **~y** pljesniv
moult [moult] linjanje; linjati se
mount [maunt] popeti se; uzjahati; montirati
mountain ['mauntin] planina; **~s** *pl* brda; **~eer** gorštak; planinar; **~ous** brdovit, planinski
mourn [mɔ:n] oplakivati; žaliti; **~er** ucviljenik; osoba na sprovodu; **~ful** žalostan; **~ing** tugovanje; crnina
mouse, *pl* ***mice*** [maus, mais] miš; loviti miševe
moustache [məs'ta:ʃ] brk
mouth [mauθ] usta; njuška; ušće; **~ful** zalogaj; **~-organ** usna harmonika; **~piece** pisak; *fig* govornik u ime drugih; **~-wash** tekućina za ispiranje usta i zubi
movable ['mu:vəbl] pokretan
move [mu:v] maknuti se; poticati; ganuti; predložiti; (iz-, pre-)seliti; potez (u šahu i sl.); (pre)seljenie; ***on the ~*** u pokretu; ***get a ~ on*** požuriti se; ***make a ~*** krenuti; poduzeti nešto; ***~ in*** useliti; ***~ on*** krenuti dalje; **~ment** kretanje; pokret
movies ['mu:viz] *pl* kino
moving ['mu:viŋ] koji pokreće; pokretan; ganutljiv
mow [mou] kositi
M.P. = **Member of Parliament**
Mr(.), Mrs(.) = **mister, mistress**
MS., *pl* = **MSS** = **manu-**

script(s)
much [mʌtʃ] mnogo; daleko, neusporedivo; ***as ~ as*** isto toliko kao; ***make ~ of*** mnogo se obazirati na; mnogo držati do
mucous ['mju:kəs] **membrane** sluznica
mud [mʌd] blato; prljavština; **~dle** pobrkati; prtljati; zbrka; **~dy** blatan; prljav; (u)prljati; **~-guard** blatobran
muffle ['mʌfl] umotati (*i* ***up***); prigušiti (*zvuk i sl.*); **~r** šal (*oko vrata*) boksačka rukavica; MOT ispušni lonac
mug [mʌg] vrč; pehar; **~gy** sparan
mulberry ['mʌlbəri] dud, murva
mule [mju:l] mazga; **~teer** mazgar
mulled [mʌld]: ***~ ale*** kuhano pivo; ***~ wine*** kuhano vino
multicultural [ˌmʌlti'kʌltʃərəl] multikulturalan
multi|ple ['mʌltipl] mnogostruk; **~plex** multipleks kino; **~plication** množenje, umnožavanje; **~ply** množiti
multitasking [ˌmʌlti'tɑ:skiŋ] višezadaćni rad
multitude ['mʌltitju:d] mnoštvo; ***the ~*** široki slojevi
mumble ['mʌmbl] mrmljati
mummy ['mʌmi] mumija
mumps [mʌmps] MED zaušnjaci
Munich ['mju:nik] München
municipal [mju:'nisipəl] gradski; općinski; **~ity** gradska općina (dio grada)
murder ['mə:də] umorstvo; umoriti; **~er** ubojica; **~ess** žena ubojica; **~ous** ubilački; *fig* krvav
muriatic [mjuəri'ætik] **acid** solna kiselina
murmur ['mə:mə] mrmljanje; žamor; mrmljati (***against***, ***at***); žamoriti
musc|le [mʌsl] mišić, mišica; **~ular** ['-kjulə] mišićav
muse [mju:z] razmišljati ([***up***]***on***); ♀ muza
museum [mju:'ziəm] muzej
mushroom ['mʌʃrum] gljiva, šampinjon
music ['mju:zik] glazba, melodija; note; **~al** muzikalan, melodičan; **~-hall** varijete; **~ian** [-'ziʃən] muzičar; **~-stand** stalak za note; **~-stool** stolac za glasovir
muslin ['mʌzlin] muslin
mussel ['mʌsl] dagnja (jestvina školjka)
must [mʌst] mošt; memla; morati; ***I ~ not*** ne smijem
mustard ['mʌstəd] senf
muster ['mʌstə] smotra; vršiti smotru; skupiti se
musty ['mʌsti] pljesniv, zagušljiv
muta|bility [mju:tə'biliti] promjenljivost: **~ble** promjenljiv; nestalan; **~tion** mijenjanje
mute [mju:t] nijem; statist

mutilat|e ['mju:tileit] osakatiti; **~ion** osakačenje
mutin|eer [mju:ti'niə] buntovnik; **~y** pobuna; pobuniti se
mutter ['mʌtə] gunđanje; gunđati, mrmljati
mutton ['mʌtn] ovčetina; **~-chop** kotlet ovčetine
mutual ['mju:tjuəl] uzajaman
muzzle ['mʌzl] njuška; brnjica; staviti brnjicu
my [mai] moj
myrtle ['mə:tl] mirta
myself [mai'self] ja sam; sebi; sebe; meni, mene
myster|ious [mis'tiəriəs] tajanstven; **~y** tajna; misterij
mysti|fication [mistifi'keiʃən] obmanjivanje; **~fy** obmanjivati
myth [miθ] mit, legenda

N

N. = **north**
N. A. = **North America(n)**
nacelle [nə'sel] trup (aviona)
nacre ['neikə] sedef
nag [næg] zanovijetati (***at a p***)
nail [neil] nokat; pandža; čavao; zabiti; prikovati
naive [na:'i:v] naivan, prostodušan
naked ['neikid] gol; nepokriven; nezaštićen; **~ness** golotinja; nezaštićenost
name [neim] ime; glas; ***call a p's ~*** (iz)grditi koga; imenovati; **~less** bezimen; **~ly** naime; **~plate** pločica *s* imenom; **~sake** imenjak
nap [næp] kratak san; prodrijemati
napkin ['næpkin] ubru *s* (*i **table~***); pelenice; mjesečni uložak
Naples ['neiplz] Napulj
narco|sis [na:'kousis] narkoza; **~tic** [~'kɔtik] narkotičan; narkotik, opojna droga
narrat|e [næ'reit] pripovijedati; **~ion** pripovijedanje; **~ive** ['nærətiv] narativan; pripovjetka; **~or** pripovjedač
narrow ['nærou] uzak, tijesan; ograničen; **~s** *pl* tijesnac, klanac; suziti (se); ograničiti; oduzimati (očice); **~-chested** uskih grudiju; **~-gauge** uskotračan; **~-minded** uskogrudan
nasty ['na:sti] gadan, ružan; nepristojan; neugodan (čovjek)
nation ['neiʃən] narod, nacija
national ['næʃnl] narodni; državljanin; državljanka; **~ity** narodnost; nacionalni osjećaj; **~ize** nacionalizirati, podržaviti

native ['neitiv] domaći, urođen; prirođen; ***a ~ of*** (koji je) rodom iz; **♀ American** indijanski; Indijanac, Indijanka; **~ country** domovina; **~ language** materinji jezik; domorodac, urođenik
natural ['nætʃrəl] naravan, prirodan; **~ history** prirodopis; **~ize** dati građanska prava; **~ science** prirodopis
nature ['neitʃə] priroda
naught [nɔːt] ništica; **~y** nepristojan, neodgojen
nause|a ['nɔːsiə] mučnina, gađenje; **~ous** ogavan
nautical ['nɔːtikəl] pomorski; **~ mile** nautička milja
naval ['neivəl] pomorski, mornarički; **~ affairs** *pl* pomorstvo; **~ base** mornarička baza; **~ forces** *pl* pomorske snage
nave [neiv] lađa (crkve); glavina (kotača)
navel ['neivəl] pupak
navig|able ['nævigəbl] plovan; **~ate** ploviti, broditi; upravljati; **~ation** plovidba, navigacija; **~ator** moreplovac, navigator
navvy ['nævi] radnik na zemljanim radovima
navy ['neivi] ratna mornarica
naze [neiz] rt
neap [niːp] **(tide)** najniža plima
near [niə] bliz, srodan; blizu; približavati se; ***~ at hand*** posve blizu; **~ly** skoro, gotovo; **~ness** blizina; tačnost; **~-sighted** kratkovidan
neat [niːt] uredan; skladan; čist; nerazriješen
necess|ary ['nesisəri] potreban; obavezan; **~aries** *pl*: ***~aries of life*** životne potrebe; **~itate** učiniti potrebnim; *Am* prisiliti; **~ity** potreba, nužda
neck [nek] vrat, šija; **~erchief** šal; **~lace** ogrlica; **~tie** kravata
need [niːd] nužda, potreba; trebati; **~ful** potreban
needle ['niːdl] igla
need|less ['niːdlis] nepotreban; **~s** *pl* nužno, bezuvjetno
negat|ion [ni'geiʃən] nijekanje; **~ive** ['negativ] niječan; GRAM niječan odgovor; PHOT negativ
neglect [ni'glekt] zanemarivanje, zapuštanje; zanemarivati; **~ful** nemaran
negligen|ce ['neglidʒəns] nemar; **~t**: ***~t of*** nehajan, nemaran (prema)
negotia|ble [ni'gouʃiəbl] prodajan; utrživ; unovčiv; **~te** [~eit] pregovarati; ugovarati; premostiti; **~tion** pregovaranje
negr|ess ['niːgris] *pej* crnkinja; **~o** *pl* ***~es*** ['~ou(z)] *pej* crnac
neigh [nei] rzati; rzanje
neighbour ['neibə] susjed(a); **~hood** susjedstvo; **~ing** su-

sjedan, koji graniči
neither ['naiðə] nijedan (od dva); ***~... nor*** niti ... niti
nephew ['nevju:] nećak
nerv|e [nə:v] živac; tetiva; snaga, hrabrost; ohrabriti; ***~e-racking*** koji uzrujava; **~ous** nervozan, razdražljiv
nest [nest] gnijezdo; gnijezditi se
nestle ['nesl] (u)gnijezditi se, priljubiti se (***to*** uz)
net [net] mreža; *Internet* mreža; neto, čist
Netherlands ['neðələndz] *pl*: ***the ~*** Nizozemska
nettle ['netl] kopriva; **~-rash** urtikarija
network ['netwə:k] mreža; splet
neur|algia [njuə'rældʒə] neuralgija; **~asthenia** živčana rastrojenost; **~osis** neuroza; **~otic** neurotičan; neurotik
neutral ['nju:trəl] neutralan; **~ity** neutralnost; **~ize** neutralizirati
never ['nevə] nikada; **~more** nikada više; **~theless** ipak, usprkos tome
new [nju:] nov; svjež; moderan; **~ly** novo; nedavno
news [nju:z] *pl i sg* novost(i), vijest(i); **~-agency** novinska agencija; **~-boy** ulični prodavač novina; **~paper** novine; **~print** novinski papir; **~-reel** (filmski) žurnal; **~-stall**, *Am* **~stand** kiosk za prodaju novina; **~-vendor** prodavač novina
New Year Nova Godina; **~'s Eve** Stara Godina, Silvestrovo
next [nekst] slijedeći; najbliži; zatim; ***what ~?*** što još?; **~ door**: ***~ to*** posve blizu
nib [nib] pero, šiljak pera
nibble ['nibl] griskati, nagristi
nice [nais] lijep, fin; ugodan; točan; **~ness**, **~ty** profinjenost; preciznost; ugodnost
niche [nitʃ] niša
nick [nik] (za)rez; ***in the ~ of time*** u pravi čas
nickel ['nikl] nikalj; *Am* (kovan novac od) 5 centa; poniklovati
nickname ['nikneim] nadimak
niece [ni:s] nećakinja
niggard ['nigəd] škrtac; **~ly** škrt, oskudan; škrto
night [nait] noć, veče; ***by ~, in the ~, at ~*** noću; ***~ out*** slobodna večer; **~cap** čašica alkoholnog pića prije spavanja; **~ club** noćni lokal; **~dress** (*ili* **~gown**) spavaćica; **~fall** sumrak; **~ingale** slavuj; **~ly** noću, svake noći; **~mare** (noćna) mora; **~shirt** (muška) noćna košulja
nimble ['nimbl] žustar, okretan
nine [nain] devet; devetica; **~fold** deveterostruk; **~pins** *pl* kuglanje s devet čunjeva;

~teen ['~'tiːn] devetnaest; **~tieth** devedeseti; **~ty** devedeset
ninth [nainθ] deveti; devetina; **~ly** deveto
nip [nip] uštip; ugriz; uštinuti; zagristi; ujedati (*o zimi*); ***~ in the bud*** ugušiti u zametku
nipple ['nipl] bradavica sise; TECH ispupčina
nitr|e ['naitə] salitra; **~ogen** ['~tridʒən] dušik
no [nou] nikakav; ***in ~ time*** začas; ***~ man's land*** ničija zemlja; **~ one** nitko, nijedan; ne, ništa (pred komparativom); ne, glas protiv
nobility [nou'biliti] plemstvo
noble ['noubl] plemenit; otmjen; plemić; **~man** plemić
nobody ['noubədi] nitko
no-brainer ['noubreinə]: ***a real ~ of a decision*** vrlo jednostavna odluka; ***the math test was a real ~*** test iz matematike bio je vrlo lagan
nod [nɔd] kimnuti; drijemati; (glavom) potvrditi; kimanje; mig
nois|e [nɔiz] buka; štropot; **~eless** tih; **~y** bučan, glasan
nominal ['nɔminl] nominalan, po imenu; imenski
nominat|e ['nɔmineit] imenovati; **~ion** imenovanje
non [nɔn] ne, ne-
non|-agression pact pakt o nenepadanju; **~-alcoholic** bezalkoholni; **~-creasing** koji se ne gužva; **~-intervention** neposredovanje; **~-party** vanpartijski; **~-payment** neplaćanje
none [nʌn] nitko, nijedan; ništa; nipošto; **~theless** ipak, usprkos
nonsens|e ['nɔnsəns] besmislica; **~ical** [~'sensikəl] besmislen, smiješan
non|-skid (tyre) (guma) koja se ne skliže; **~-smoker** nepušač; **~-stop** RLW koji se ne zaustavlja; AERO koji ne slijeće
nook [nuk] kutić, ugao
noon [nuːn] podne; (*i* **~day**, **~tide**); podnevni
noose [nuːs] petlja
nor [nɔː] niti, također ne
norm [nɔːm] pravilo; **~al** normalan
north [nɔːθ] sjever; sjeverni; na sjever(u); **~-east** sjeveroistok; sjeveroistočni; **~erly** sjeverni; **~ern** sjeverni; **~ward(s)** sjeverni; prema sjeveru; **~-west** sjeverozapad
Norwegian [nɔː'wiːdʒən] norveški; Norvežanin, Norvežanka
nose [nouz] nos; njuška; vršak; njušiti; mirisati; tragati (***after***, ***for*** za); **~-dive** AERO obrušavanje; **~gay** kita cvikeća
nostril ['nɔstril] nosnica, nozdrva
not [nɔt] ne

notable ['noutəbl] značajan
notary ['noutəri] (javni) bilježnik
notation [nou'teiʃən] bilježenje
notch [nɔtʃ] zarez; urezati
note [nout] znak; oznaka; bilješka; opaska; pisamce; nota; obratiti pažnju; ~ ***down*** zabilježiti; **~d** slavan; ozloglašen (***for*** zbog); **~worthy** vrijedan pažnje; značajan
nothing ['nʌθiŋ] ništa; nikako; ***for*** ~ zabadava; ***good for*** ~ beskoristan
notice ['noutis] bilješka; obavijest; otkaz; ***until further*** ~ do dalje obavijesti; opaziti; obazirati se; **~able** zamjetljiv, vidljiv; **~-board** oglasna ploča
noti|fiable ['noutifaiəbl] koji treba prijaviti; **~fication** obavijest; **~fy** objaviti; obavijestiti; prijaviti; najaviti
notion ['nouʃən] pojam, predodžba; ***~s*** *pl Am* galanterijska roba
notorious [nou'tɔ:riəs] opće poznat; zloglasan
notwithstanding [nɔtwiθ'stændiŋ] ipak, usprkos
nought [nɔ:t] ništica
nourish ['nʌriʃ] hraniti; **~ing** hranjiv; **~ment** hrana, ishrana
novel ['nɔvəl] nov; roman; **~ist** romanopisac; **~ty** novost, novotarija
November [nə'vembə] studeni
novice ['nɔvis] početnik; novajlija
now [nau] sada; no; zatim; ***by*** ~ dosada; ***just*** ~ upravo; **~adays** (dan)danas
nowhere ['nouwɛə] nigdje
noxious ['nɔkʃəs] škodljiv; nezdrav
nozzle ['nɔzl] TECH vršak (cijevi); štrcalo
nude [nju:d] gol; PAINT akt
nuisance ['nju:sns] smetnja, muka; *fig* gnjavator
null [nʌl] ništetan; nevažeći; **~ify** poništiti
numb [nʌm] ukočen; obamro
number ['nʌmbə] broj, brojka; brojiti; **~less** bezbrojan; **~-plate** MOT registarska tablica
numer|al ['nju:mərəl] brojka; **~ical** brojčan; **~ous** brojan
nun [nʌn] opatica
nuptial ['nʌpʃəl] svadben, vjenčani, bračni; *pl* vjenčanje
nurse [nə:s] dadilja; bolničarka; dojiti; njegovati; **~ry** dječja soba; rasadnik
nursing home sanatorij
nut [nʌt] orah; matica vijka; **~cracker** kliješta za orahe
nutri|ment ['nju:trimənt] hrana; **~tious**, **~tive** hranjiv
nuts: ***drive*** ~ tjerati u ludilo
nut-shell: ***in a*** ~ jezgrovito, najsažetije

O

o/a = on account (of)
oak [ouk] hrast
oar [ɔ:] veslo; veslati; **~sman** veslač
oasis, *pl* ***oases*** [ou'eisis, -i:z] oaza
oat [out] (*ugl* **~s** *pl*) zob; ***sow one's wild~s*** izludovati se u mladosti
oath [ouθ] prisega, kletva; ***~ of manifestation*** zakletva očitovanja; ***take an~*** zakleti se (***on***, ***to*** na)
obduracy ['ɔbdjurəsi] okorjelost
obedien|ce [ə'bi:djəns] poslušnost; **~t** poslušan
obey [ə'bei] slušati
obituary [ə'bitjuəri] **(notice)** obavijest o smrti; nekrolog
object ['ɔbdʒikt] predmet; cilj; [əb'dʒekt] prigovarati (***to***); **~ion** prigovor; **~ionable** komu se može prigovoriti; nevaljao
obligat|ion [ɔbli'geiʃən] obaveza; dužnost; obveznica; **~ory** [ə'bligətəri] obvezatan
oblig|e [ə'blaidʒ] vezati, obvezati; primorati; ***much ~ed*** vrlo zahvalan; **~ing** uslužan, ljubazan
oblique [ə'bli:k] kos, nagnut; neiskren
obliterate [ə'blitəreit] odstraniti; izbrisati
oblivi|on [ə'bliviən] zaborav; **~ous** zaboravljiv
oblong ['ɔblɔŋ] dugoljast
obnoxious [əb'nɔkʃəs] škodljiv; neugodan; omražen
obscure [əb'skjuə] taman; nepoznat; zamračiti; prikriti
observ|able [əb'zə:vəbl] vidljiv; **~ant** pažljiv (***of***); **~ation** opažanje; primjedba; **~atory** zvjezdarnica
observe [əb'zə:v] promatrati; paziti; čuvati; slaviti (svečanost); držati se (zakona); napomenuti (***on***)
obsolete ['ɔbsəli:t] zastario
obstacle ['ɔbstəkl] zapreka
obstina|cy ['ɔbstinəsi] tvrdoglavost; **~te** tvrdoglav; svojeglav; tvrdokoran (bolest etc.)
obstruct [əb'strʌkt] začepiti; zakrčiti; sprečavati; **~ive** koji smeta
obtain [əb'tein] postići; **~able** koji se može dobiti; **~ment** postignuće
obtru|de [əb'tru:d] nametati (se) (***on***); **~sive** nametljiv
obtuse [əb'tju:s] tup; *fig* glup
obviate ['ɔbvieit] predusresti; odstraniti
obvious ['ɔbviəs] očit, jasan
occasion [ə'keiʒən] prilika; povod; prouzročiti; dati povoda; ***on the~ of*** prigodom;

~al povremen
occidental [ɔksi'dentl] zapadni
occup|ant ['ɔkjupənt] posjednik; **~ation** zauzeće, okupacija; zanimanje; zaposlenje; ***~ation disease*** profesionalna bolest; **~y** zaposjesti, zauzimati; vršiti (službu); stanovati; ***be ~ied with*** (*ili* ***in***) biti zaposlen s
occur [ə'kə:] dogoditi se; ***~ to*** pasti na pamet; **~rence** događaj; zgoda
ocean ['ouʃən] ocean, more
o'clock [ə'klɔk]: ***five ~*** pet sati
October [ɔk'touvə] listopad
oculist ['ɔkjulist] specijalista za oči
odd [ɔd] neparan; prekobrojan; pojedinačan; čudan
odds [ɔdz] razlika; nejednakost; nejednaka oklada; nadmoć; prednost; šansa; ***at ~*** nesložan
ode [oud] oda
odious ['oudjəs] mrzak, odvratan
odour ['oudə] miris; zadah; *fig* glas
of [ɔv] od, iz; zbog; o; po; na; s obzirom na; ***be proud ~*** ponositi se; ***the city ~ London*** grad London
off [ɔ:f] od, iz, odatle; dolje; dalje; izvan; udaljeno od; sporedan; slobodan; desni; odlazi!; ***well ~*** imućan; ***be ~*** otići, morati otići; biti zatvoren (*pipac etc.*)
offal ['ɔfəl] otpaci; smeće
offen|ce [ə'fens] napad; uvreda; prestupak; smutnja; ***no ~ce!*** bez uvrede! **~d** uvrijediti; povrijediti; razljutiti; pogriješiti; ogriješiti se (***against*** o); **~sive** uvredljiv; navalni; ofenziva
offer ['ɔfə] ponuda; nuđenje; prijedlog; ponuditi; pružiti (otpor); pridonijeti (žrtvu); nuditi se; pokušati; namjeravati; **~ing** ponuda; nuđenje; žrtva
office ['ɔfis] služba, ured, poslovnica; **♀** Ministarstvo; **~-appliances** uredske potrepštine; **~r** činovnik; oficir
official [ə'fiʃəl] služben; činovnik; **~ business** službeni posao
officious [ə'fiʃəs] nametljivo uslužan; poluslužben
offspring ['ɔ:fspriŋ] potomak; potomstvo
off-time ['ɔ:ftaim] slobodno vrijeme
often ['ɔ:fn] često
oil [ɔil] ulje; nauljiti; podmazati (*i fig*); **~cloth** voštano platno; **~ gauge** uljomjer; **~-painting** uljena slika; **~-well** izvor nafte; **~y** nauljen; *fig* gladak
ointment ['ɔintmənt] (po-)mast
O. K., okay ['ou'kei] *Am* u redu, dobro
old [ould] star; **~ age** starost;

~-**fashioned** staromodan
olive ['ɔliv] maslina
Olympi|an [ə'limpiən] olimpijski; ~**c games** olimpijske igre
omelet(te) ['ɔmlit] omlet
omen ['oumen] (koban) predznak
ominous ['ɔminəs] zloslutan
omission [ə'miʃən] ispuštanje
omit [ə'mit] izostaviti; propustiti
omnibus ['ɔmnibəs] omnibus; ~ **order** skupna narudžba; ~ **train** osobni vlak
on [ɔn] na; kod; o; uz; dalje; naprijed; ***be*** ~ biti u toku; biti na redu; THEAT davat se; biti otvoren (*pipac*); upaljen (*svijetlo*)
once [wʌns] jedamput; jednom; nekada; ***at*** ~ odmah
one [wʌn] jedan; jedini; neki; netko; čovjek; ~ ***day*** jednog dana; ***every*** ~ svatko; ~ ***another*** jedan drugoga, međusobno; ~**self** se(be), sâm; ~-**way street** jednosmjerna ulica
onion ['ʌnjən] luk
online ['onlain] online; ~ **banking** internetsko bankarstvo; ~ **dating** internetsko upoznavanje; ~ **shopping** kupnja na internetu
only ['ounli] jedini; samo; ~ ***yesterday*** tek jučer
onward ['ɔnwəd] dalje; naprijed
ooze [u:z] mulj; ~ ***out*** procuriti
opaque [ou'peik] neproziran
open ['oupən] otvoren; slobodan; javan; pristupačan; ***in the*** ~ ***air*** pod vedrim nebom; napolju; otvoriti (se); ~**ing** otvaranje, otvor; prilika; izgled
opera ['ɔpərə] opera; ~-**dancer** baletni plesač; ~-**glass(es)** kazališni dalekozor; ~-**hat** sklopiv cilindar; ~-**house** opera (zgrada)
operat|e ['ɔpəreit] djelovati; *Am* funkcionirati; operirati; *Am* staviti u pogon; rukovati (strojem); ~**ing expenses** pogonski troškovi; ~**ion** operacija; djelovanje; ***come into*** ~***ion*** stupiti na snagu; ~**ive** djelotvoran; operativan; tvornički radnik; ~**or** operator, kirurg; FILM operater; telefonist
ophthalmic [ɔf'θælmik] **hospital** očna klinika
opinion [ə'pinjən] mišljenje; nazor; uvjerenje
opponent [ə'pounənt] protivnik
opportun|e ['ɔpətju:n] pravodoban; povoljan; podesan; ~**ity** povoljna prilika
oppose [ə'pouz] suprotstaviti se; staviti nasuprot; opirati se
opposit|e ['ɔpəzit] suprotan; oprečan; nasuprot; suprot-

nost; **~ion** suprotnost; protivljenje; opozicija
oppress [ə'pres] tlačiti; tištati; **~ion** tlačenje; pritisak; ugnjetavanje; bijeda; **~ive** koji tišti; sparan
optic|ian [ɔp'tiʃən] optičar; **~s** optika
option ['ɔpʃən] slobodan izbor
opulen|ce ['ɔpjuləns] bogatstvo; **~t** vrlo bogat
or [ɔː] ili; ***either ... ~*** ili ... ili; ***~ else*** inače
oral ['ɔːrəl] usmen
orange ['ɔrindʒ] naranča
orator ['ɔrətə] govornik
orchard ['ɔːtʃəd] voćnjak
orchestra ['ɔːkistrə] orkestar
ordain [ɔː'dein] odrediti; zarediti
order ['ɔːdə] red; poredak; zapovijed, nalog; narudžba; stalež; čin; orden; ***alphabetical ~*** abecedni red; ***put in ~*** staviti u red; ***in ~ to*** (zato) da; COM ***be on ~*** biti naručen; ***make to ~*** izraditi po narudžbi; zapovijediti; odrediti; naručiti; **~ly** uredan; redovit; miran; učtiv; kurir
ordinance ['ɔːdinəns] naredba
ordinary ['ɔːdnəri] običan
ore [ɔː] rudača
organ ['ɔːgən] orgulje; organ; **~-grinder** ulični svirač na orguljicama; **~ic** organski; **~ism** organizam; **~ist** orguljaš; **~ize** organizirati; **~izer** organizator
orifice ['ɔrifis] otvor
origin ['ɔridʒin] porijeklo; početak; **~al** izvorni; originalan; original; **~ate** proizvesti; vući porijeklo (***from***, ***in***); nastati; **~ator** začetnik
ornament ['ɔːnəmənt] ukras; ['~ment] ukrasiti; **~al** ukrasni
orphan ['ɔːfən] siroče; osiročen
orthography [ɔː'θɔgrəfi] pravopis
oscillat|e ['ɔsileit] titrati; **~ion** titranje
ostensible [ɔs'tensəbl] tobožnji; navodni
ostenta|tion [ɔsten'teiʃən] razmetanje; **~tious** hvalisav
ostler ['ɔslə] konjušar
ostrich ['ɔstritʃ] ZOOL noj
other ['ʌðə] drugi; drugačije; ***the ~ day*** neki dan; ***each ~*** jedan drugoga, međusobno; **~wise** inače; drugačije
ought [ɔːt] morao bih; ***I ~ to do it*** trebao bih to učiniti
ounce [auns] jaguar; unča (*28,35 g*)
our [auə] naš; **~s** *pron* naš; **~selves** mi (sami); se
out [aut] van(i), napolje; izvan; vanjski; ***~ of*** iz, izvan; ***voyage ~*** putovanje izvan države; ***way ~*** izlaz; **~bid** više nuditi; **~board motor** lagani motor na krmi čamca; **~-break**, **~-burst** provala;

~cast izopćenik; **~cry** graja, vika; **~distance** preteći, odmaći; **~do** nadmašiti; **~door dress** sportska odjeća; **~doors** vani, napolju

outer ['autə] vanjski; **~most** krajnji

out|fit ['autfıt] oprema; pribor; **~grow** prerasti; **~ing** izlet; **~last** preživjeti; **~lay** izdatak (novca); **~let** izlaz, otvor; TECH izljev, odušak; **~line** obris, skica; skicirati; izložiti; **~look** izgled; vidik; **~number** nadmašiti brojem; **~put** prirod; utržak; proizvodnja (količina proizvedenog)

outrage ['autreidʒ] nasilje; uvreda; povrijediti; **~ous** pretjeran; odvratan

out|right ['aut'rait] izravan; **~run** prestići; **~side** vanjska strana; vani; **~sider** osoba koja ostaje po strani; **~size** specijalna veličina; **~skirts** *pl* predgrađe; rub; **~source** eksternalizirati; **~standing** koji iskače; izvanredan; **~strip** prestići; nadmašiti; **~ward** vanjski; van; **~wards** prema vani; **~weigh** pretegnuti; **~wit** nadmudriti; **~worker** radnik, koji radi kod kuće za tvornicu

oven ['ʌvn] pećnica

over ['ouvə] preko, nad, iznad; na drugu stranu; više; ***(all) ~ again*** iznova, još jedamput; ***all ~*** potpuno, sasvim; *Am* posvuda; ***~ there*** tamo preko; ***~ a glass of wine*** uz čašu vina; ***all ~ the world***, *Am* ***all the world ~*** po cijelom svijetu; ***~ the way*** preko puta; ***read ~*** pročitati; **~all** radni kombinezon; **~burden** preopteretiti; **~cast** prekriven oblacima; **~charge** EL preopteretiti; prejako nabiti; **~-coat** ogrtač; **~come** svladati; **~crowd** prenatrpati; **~do** pretjerati; **~draft** COM prekoračenje bankovnog računa; **~draw** prekoračiti svoj bankovni račun; **~due** zakasnio; **~flow** preplaviti; poplava; **~grow** prerasti; obrasti; **~head wire** EL nadzemni vod; **~head(s)** opći, režijski troškovi; **~heat** pregrijati; **~lap** preklapati se; ukrštavati se; **~load** pretovariti, preopteretiti; **~look** previdjeti; **~ night** preko noći; **~power** nadvladati; **~production** prevelika proizvodnja; **~rate** precijeniti; **~run** prestići; **~sea(s)** prekomorski; **~seas**: ***go ~seas*** ići preko mora; **~seer** nadglednik; **~sight** propust; **~sleep** predugo spavati; **~stock** prenatrpati; **~strain** prenapeti; **~take** prestići; **~throw** srušiti; rušenje; **~time** prekovremen; **~tired** premoren; **~train** pretrenirati

overture ['ouvətjuə] uvertira

over|turn [ouvə'tə:n] prevrnuti; **~value** precijeniti; **~weight** prevaga; pretezati težinom; **~whelm** obasuti; **~work** izmoriti (se) radom
owe [ou] dugovati; biti obvezan; SPORT dati prednost
owing ['ouiŋ] koji se duguje; ***~ to*** zbog, radi
owl [aul] sova
own [oun] vlastit; poseban; istinski; ***a house of my ~*** moja vlastita kuća; posjedovati; priznati; dopuštati; ***~ (up) to*** otvoreno priznati
owner ['ounə] vlasnik; **~driver** vozač amater; **~ship** vlasništvo
ox, *pl* ***oxen*** vol; go vedo
oxygen ['ɔksidʒən] kisik
oyster ['ɔistə] oštriga
oz. = ounce (*mjera za težinu*) unca
ozone ['ouzoun] ozon

P

pa [pa:] tata
pace [peis] korak; način hoda; stupati; SPORT određivati korak (tempo); **~-maker** određivač koraka (tempa)
Pacific [pə'sifik] **Ocean** Tihi ocean
pacify ['pæsifai] umiriti
pack [pæk] svežanj; bala; "špil" (karata); MED oblog; ***a ~ of lies*** hrpa laži; pakovati; ***~ up*** spakovati; **~age** paket; zamatanje; **~er** zamatač(ica); **~et** paket(ić); **~et-boat** poštanski brod; **~ing** pakovanje, zamatanje
pact [pækt] ugovor
pad [pæd] jastuk; podložiti; tapecirati; **~ded room** soba s meko obloženim zidovima; **~ding** punjenje
paddle ['pædl] kratko veslo; veslati kratkim veslom; **~-steamer** brod na točak
padlock ['pæklɔk] lokot
page [peidʒ] stranica (knjige); paž; paginirati
pail [peil] kabao
pain [pein] bol; *pl* patnja; mučiti; ***be in ~*** trpjeti; ***take ~s*** truditi se; **~ful** bolan; mučan
paint [peint] boja; ličilo; šminka; (o)bojiti; slikati; šminkati; ***wet ~!*** svježe oličeno!; **~er** slikar; ličilac; **~ing** slikanje; ličenje
pair [pɛə] par; (s)pariti (se); ***a ~ of scissors*** škare
palace ['pælis] palača
palat|able ['pælətəbl] tečan; **~e** ['-lit] nepce
pale [peil] blijed; svijetao; problijediti; kolac; **~ness** bljedilo
Palestine ['pælistain] Palestina
palette ['pælit] paleta
palliat|e ['pælieit] ublažiti;

ispričati; **~ive** lijek za ublaživanje boli
palm [pa:m] dlan; palma
palpable ['pælpəbl] opipljiv; *fig* očigledan
palpitat|e ['pælpiteit] kucati (*srce*); **~ion** lupanje (*srca*)
paltry ['pɔ:ltri] jadan; bezvrijedan
pamphlet ['pæmflit] pamflet; brošura
pan [pæn] tava; **~cake** palačinka
pane [pein] staklo, okno
panel ['pænl] ARCHIT ploča; oplata (*zida*); TECH polje; umetak; popis porotnika; popis liječnika socijalnog osiguranja; **~ doctor** liječnik socijalnog osiguranja
pang [pæŋ] oštra bol; *fig* tjeskoba, muka
panic ['pænik] paničan; panika
pansy ['pænzi] BOT maćuhica
pant [pænt] dahtati; teško disati
pant|aloon [pæntə'lu:n] lakrdijaš; *pl* (*ugl Am*) uske hlače; **~ies**['~iz] *pl*: (***a pair of***) **~*ies*** *Am* (*ženske*) gaćice
pantry ['pæntri] smočnica
pants [pænts] *pl Am* hlače; (muške) gaće
pap [pæp] kaša
papal ['peipəl] papinski
paparazzo [pæpə'rætsəu] paparazzo
paper ['peipə] papir; (***news***)**~** novine; (***wall***)**~** tapete; *pl* spisi; dokumenti; obložiti tapetama; **~-hanger** ljepilac tapeta; **~-mill** tvornica papira; **~-weight** pritiskivač za papire
par [pa:] jednakost; COM temeljna vrijednost
parachute ['pærəʃu:t] padobran
parade [pə'reid] svečanost, parada; držati paradu; ***make a ~ of*** hvalisati se
paradise ['pærədaiz] raj
paradoxical [pærə'dɔksikəl] paradoksan
paraly|se ['pærəlaiz] paralizirati; **~sis** uzetost; **~tic** uzet čovjek
paramount ['pærəmaunt] vrhovni; važniji (***to***)
parapet ['pærəpit] prsobran; ograda
paraphrase ['pærəfreiz] prepričavanje; prepričavati
para|sol [pærə'sɔl] suncobran; **~troops** *pl* padobranske jedinice
parboil ['pa:bɔil] napola skuhati
parcel ['pa:sl] paket; parcela; COM pošiljka; **~post** paketna pošta
parch [pa:tʃ] isušiti (se); **~ment** pergament
pardon ['pa:dn] oproštenje; oprost; oprostiti; **~able** oprostiv
pare [pɛə] podrezati (*nokte*); guliti (*jabuke etc*)
parent|age ['pɛərəntidʒ]

podrijetlo; srodstvo; **~al** roditeljski; **~s** *pl* roditelji;
parings ['pɛəriŋz] *pl* lupine; strugotine; otpaci
parish ['pæriʃ] župa; župni
Parisian [pə'rizjən] Parižanin; pariški
parity ['pæriti] jednakost
park [pa:k] park; nasadi; poređati; parkirati
parliament ['pa:ləmənt] parlament; **~arian** [pa:ləmen'tɛəriən] parlamentarac; **~ary** [pa:lə'mentəri] parlamentaran; ***~ary train*** jeftin vlak trećeg razreda
parlour ['pa:lə] soba za primanje; salon; *Am* lokal; **~-maid** služavka, sobarica
parquet ['pa:kei] parket; **~ry** parketarija
parrot ['pærət] papiga
parsimonious [pa:si'mounjəs] štedljiv; škrt
parsley ['pa:sli] peršin
parson ['pa:sn] župnik; **~age** župni dvor
part [pa:t] komad, dio, udio; svezak; područje; (THEAT i *fig*) uloga; MUS glas; partitura; ***~s*** *pl* okolica; ***be ~ and parcel of*** činiti bitni dio nečega; ***for my ~*** što se mene tiče; ***take ~ in*** sudjelovati; rastaviti; dijeliti (*kosu*); rastati se (***from***); raskinuti (***with***)
partake [pa:'teik] imati udjela; prisustvovati (***in, of***)
partial ['pa:ʃəl] djelomičan; pristran; **~ity** pristranost
participate [pa:'tisipeit] sudjelovati; imati udjela (***in***)
particle ['pa:tikl] čestica; malen dio
particular [pə'tikjulə] naročit; pojedinačan; neobičan; potanki; lični; izbirljiv (***in, about***); pojedinost; ***~s*** *pl* pojedinosti; **~ity** osobitost; potankost
parting ['pa:tiŋ] dijeljenje; rastanak; razdjeljak (*kose*)
partisan [pa:ti'zæn] pristaša (*stranke*), partizan
partition [pa:'tiʃən] podjela; pregrada; (po)dijeliti
partly ['pa:tli] djelomice; donekle
partner ['pa:tnə] dionik; partner; ***sleeping*** (*Am* ***silent***) ***~*** tihi kompanjon; **~ship** udruženost
part-payment djelomična otplata; kapara
partridge ['pa:tridʒ] jarebica
part-time ne puno radno vrijeme; **~ worker** radnik koji ne radi puno radno vrijeme
party ['pa:ti] partija, stranka; društvo; ***follow the ~ line*** slijediti partijsku liniju; **~boss** stranački vođa
pass [pa:s] klanac; propusnica; proći; prijeći; ***~ as*** vrijediti, prolaziti; položiti (*ispit*); desiti se; prekoračiti; propustiti; ***~ one's hand over one's face*** prijeći rukom preko lica; dodati; pro-

tjecati; provesti (*vrijeme*); proživjeti; preminuti; trpjeti; ~ ***away*** prolaziti; nestati; umrijeti; **~able** prolazan; podnošljiv
passage ['pæsidʒ] prolaz; prijelaz; hodnik; odlomak
passenger ['pæsindʒə] putnik; **~-train** putnički vlak
passer-by ['pa:sə'bai] prolaznik
passion ['pæʃən] strast; gnjev; **~ate** strastven
passive ['pæsiv] pasivan; koji podnosi; pasiv ~ **smoking** pasivno pušenje
pass|-key ['pa:ski:] otpirač; **~port** pasoš; **~word** MIL lozinka
past [pa:st] prošli; mimo, kraj; preko; izvan; prošlost; ***for some time*** ~ prije nekog vremena; ***half*** ~ ***two*** pola tri
paste [peist] tijesto; ljepilo; zalijepiti; **~board** ljepenka
pastime ['pa:staim] razonoda
pastry ['peistri] kolači; fino pecivo (tijesto)
pasture ['pa:stʃə] paša; pasti (se)
pat [pæt] tapšanje; tapšati
patch [pætʃ] mrlja; zakrpa; ~ (***up***) (za)krpati (*i fig*); **~work** krparija
patent ['peitənt] očit; patent; ~ **fastener** "druker"; ~ **leather** lakirana koža; patentirati; ~ **office** patentni ured; **~ee** vlasnik patenta
patern|al [pə'tə:nl] očinski; **~ity** očinstvo
path [pa:θ] staza, put; **~way** put (*i fig*)
pathological [pæθə'lɔdʒikəl] patološki
patien|ce ['peiʃəns] strpljenje; **~t** strpljiv; pacijent
patriot ['pætriət] rodoljub; **~ic** rodoljuban; **~ism** rodoljublje
patrol [pə'troul] patrola; patrolirati
patron ['peitrən] zaštitnik; **~ize** (pot)pomagati; zaštićivati
pattern ['pætən] uzor; uzorak; model
pause [pɔ:z] stanka; zastati; pauzirati; oklijevati (***upon***)
pave [peiv] popločiti; *fig* utrti; **~ment** pločnik
paw [pɔ:] šapa, capa; kopkati
pawn [pɔ:n] zalog; založiti; **~broker** vlasnik zalagaonice; **~shop** zalagaonica
pay [pei] plaća; isplata; platiti; ~ ***for*** platiti (*kupljeno*); namiriti; ~ ***in*** uplatiti; ~ ***off*** isplatiti; ~ ***out*** isplatiti; ~ ***attention*** pripaziti na; ~ ***a visit*** posjetiti; **~able** plativ; **~-day** dan isplate; **~-envelope** kuverta s plaćom; **~ing** koji plaća; unosan; **~ment** isplata; plaćanje; plaća
pea [pi:] grašak
peace [pi:s] mir; **~able** miran; miroljubiv; **~ful** miran; tih

peach [pi:tʃ] breskva
peacock ['pi:kɔk] paun
peak [pi:k] vrh; vrhunac; zaslon na kapi; ~ **load** najveće opterećenje maksimala; ~**season** glavna sezona;
peal [pi:l] zvonjava; tutnjava; zvoniti; brujiti; oriti se
pear [pɛə] kruška
pearl [pə:l] biser
peasant ['pezənt] seljak; ~**ry** seljaštvo
peat [pi:t] treset; ~**-moss** tresetina
pebble ['pebl] šljunak
peck [pek] jedinica za mjerenje žita (*oko 9 l*); kljucati; zanovijetati (***at***)
peculiar [pi'kju:liə] osebujan; čudan; ~**ity** [pikju:li'æriti] osebujnost
pedal ['pedl] pedal; gaziti pedal; voziti bicikl
pedestal ['pedistl] podnožje; pijedestal
pedestrian [pi'destriən] pješak
pedigree ['pedigri:] rodoslovlje
pedlar ['pedlə] pokućarac
peel [pi:l] lupina, ljuska; guliti; ljuštiti (se)
peep [pi:p] pijukatik; kradomičan pogled; viriti (***at***)
peer [piə] zuriti; proviriti; per, plemić; ~**age** položaj višeg plemića; visoko plemstvo; ~**less** bez premca
peev|ed [pi:vd] ozlojeđen; ~**ish** zlovoljan; razdražljiv
peg [peg] kolac; klin; kuka; ***take a p down a*** ~ učiniti poniznijim, skromnijim
pelt [pelt] bacati; obasipati; sručiti se
pen [pen] pero
penal ['pi:nl] kazneni; ~ **servitude** robija; ~**ty** ['penəlti] kazna; SPORT penal
penance ['penəns] pokora
pencil ['pensl] olovka; ~**-sharpener** šiljilo
pend|ant ['pendənt] privjesak; naušnica; pandan; ~**ing** viseći, još u toku; nekonačan; ~**ulum** ['-julәm] njihalo (*ure*)
penetrate ['penitreit] prodrijeti; doprijeti; spoznati
penholder ['penhouldə] držalo
peninsula [pi'ninsjulə] poluotok
penitent ['penitənt] pokajnički; pokajnik
penniless ['penilis] bez prebite pare; siromašan
penny ['peni] *pl* ***pence*** (pojedini novčići: ***pennies***) peni; ~**-dreadful** uzbudljiv roman; ~**worth** što se dobije za jedan peni; jeftina kupovina
pension ['penʃən] penzija; umiroviti
pensive ['pensiv] zamišljen
penthouse ['penthaus] nadstrešnica; dogradnja s kosim krovom
people [pi:pl] narod; ljudi;

my ~ moja obitelj; napučiti
pep *Am* krepkost; polet; **~per** papar; papriti; **~permint** mentol
perambulator ['præmbjuleitə] dječja kolica
perceive [pə'siːv] opaziti; osjetiti; razumjeti
percentage [pə'sentidʒ] postotak; provizija
perception [pə'sepʃən] zamjećivanje
percussion [pəː'kʌʃən] udarac; potres; **~instruments** udaraljke
peremptory [pə'remptəri] odlučan; bezuvjetan
perfect ['pəːfikt] savršen; perfektan; [pə'fekt] usavršiti; svršiti; **~ion** savršenost; usavršavanje; svršetak
perfidious [pəː'fidiəs] izdajnički; nevjeran (***to***)
perforat|e ['pəːfəreit] probušiti; **~or** bušilo
perform [pə'fɔːm] izvršiti; obaviti; THEAT predstavljati; izvoditi; **~ance** izvođenje; predstava
perfume ['pəːfjuːm] miomiris; **~ry** parfimerija
perhaps [pə'hæps] možda
peril ['peril] opasnost; **~ous** opasan
period ['piəriəd] period; doba; **~ic(al)** periodičan; **~ical** časopis
perish ['periʃ] poginuti; propasti; **~able** pokvarljiv
perjur|e ['pəːdʒə] krivo se zakleti; **~er** krivokletnik; **~y** krivokletstvo
perm [pəːm] trajna ondulacija; ***have one's hair ~ed*** dati učiniti trajnu ondulaciju
permanence ['pəːməməns] trajnost
permanent ['pəːməmənt] trajan; stalan; **~ (wave)** trajna ondulacija; RLW **~ way** željeznički nasip
permi|ssion [pə'miʃən] dozvola; **~t** dozvoliti; ***weather ~tting*** ako vremenske prilike budu dopuštale; ['pəːmit] dozvola; odobrenje
pernicious [pəː'niʃəs] štetan
perpendicular [pəːpən'dikjulə] okomit
perpetrate ['pəːpitreit] počiniti (nedjelo)
perpetua|l [pə'petjuəl] neprekidan; vječan; **~te** [~eit] ovjekovječiti
perplex [pə'pleks] zbuniti; **~ity** zbunjenost
persecut|e ['pəːsikjuːt] progoniti; dodijavati; **~ion** proganjanje; **~or** progonitelj
persever|ance [pəːsi'viərəns] ustrajnost; **~e** ustrajati (***in***, ***with***); **~ing** ustrajan
Persia ['pəːʃə] Perzija
persist [pə'sist] ustrajati; ne popuštati (***in***); **~ent** ustrajan
person ['pəːsn] osoba; ***in ~*** osobno; **~age** (ugledna) ličnost; **~al** ličan; uvredljiv; **~ate** prikazivati; izdavati se za drugoga; **~ify** personifici-

rati
perspective [pə'spektiv] perspektiva; vidik; perspektivan
perspir|ation [pə:spə'reiʃən] znoj; **~e** znojiti se
persua|de [pə'sweid] nagovoriti; uvjeriti; **~sion** nagovaranje; uvjeravanje; **~sive** uvjerljiv
pert [pə:t] drzak, bezobrazan; jezičav
pertinacious [pə:ti'neiʃəs] tvrdoglav
pertinent ['pə:tinənt] koji se odnosi na; umjestan; ispravan
pertness ['pə:tnis] drskost
perturbation [pə:tə:'beiʃən] smetnja; nemir
perus|al [pə'ru:zəl] pomno čitanje; tačan pregled; **~e** pomno pročitati; ispitati
pervade [pə:'veid] prožimati
pervert [pə'və:t] izopačiti; pokvariti koga
pervious ['pə:viəs] pristupačan; propustan (***to***)
pessimis|m ['pesimizəm] pesimizam; **~t** pesimist
pest pošast; kuga; **~er** dodijavati; mučiti
pet zlovolja; ljubimac (životinja); maza; **~-name** ime od milja
petition [pi'tiʃən] (pismena) molba; zahtjev; uputiti molbu (***for***); **~er** podnosilac molbe
petrify ['petrifai] okameniti
petrol ['petrəl] MOT benzin
petticoat ['petikout] podsuknja
pettifogger ['petifɔgə] nadriodvjetnik
pett|iness ['petinis] sitničavost; **~ist** osjetljiv; hirovit; **~y** malen; sitan
pew [pju:] klupa u crkvi
pewter ['pju:tə] kositar; kositreno suđe
phantasm ['fæntæzəm] utvara
phantom ['fæntəm] prikaza, fantom
pheasant ['feznt] fazan
phenomenon [fı'nɔminən], *pl* ***phenomena*** fenomen; čudo
phial ['faiəl] staklena bočica
philanthropist [fı'lænθrəpist] dobrotvor; filantrop
philatel|ist [fı'lætəlist] sakupljač maraka; **~y** filatelija
philolog|ical [fılə'lɔdʒikəl] filološki; **~ist** [fı'lolədʒist] filolog; **~y** [fı'lɔlədʒi] filologija
philosoph|er [fı'lɔsəfə] filozof; **~ize** filozofirati; **~y** filozofija
phone [foun] telefon; telefonski; **~-card** telefonska kartica
phonetic [fə'netik] **spelling** fonetski pravopis
phonograph ['founəgra:f] fonograf; gramofon
photo(graph) ['foutə(gra:f)] fotografija; ***have one's ~***

taken slikati se
photograph ['foutəgra:f] fotografirati; **~er** [fə'tɔgrəfə] fotograf; **~y** fotografiranje
phrase [freiz] fraza; izraziti se, opisati
physic|s ['fiziks] *sg* fizika; **~al** fizički; fizikalni; **~culture** fiskultura; **~ian** liječnik; **~ist** fizičar
piano ['pjænou], **~forte** glasovir; ***grand~*** koncertni klavir
pick [pik] pijuk (*i* ***~axe***); kopati; kljuvati; glodati; brati; ***~ (out)*** izvaditi; izabrati; raspoznati; ***~ up*** pokupiti; podići; prihvatiti; otkriti; uzeti (*koga sa sobom*); MOT povesti (*koga*)
picket ['pikit] kolac; kolcima ograditi
pickle ['pikl] rasol, *pl* ukiseljeno povrće; ukiseliti; **~d herring** usoljena haringa
pick|pocket ['pikpɔkit] džepar; **~-up** naprava za prenošenje zvuka s električnog gramofona na zvučnik
pictorial [pik'tɔ:riəl] slikovni; ilustriran časopis
picture ['piktʃə] slika; ***the ~s*** *pl* kino; slikati; opisivati; **~ (post)card** razglednica; **~book** slikovnica
pie [pai] pašteta; kolač s voćem
piece [pi:s] komad; sastaviti; ***~ out*** dopuniti; ***~ of advice*** savjet; ***in ~s*** razbijen; **~-work** posao plaćen po komadu
pier [piə] stup; MAR molo
pierc|e [piəs] probosti; prodrijeti; **~ing** prodoran (*i fig*)
piety ['paiəti] pobožnost
pig [pig] svinja, prase; ***buy a ~ in a poke*** kupiti mačka u vreći
pigeon ['pidʒin] golub; **~-hole** pretinac (*za pisma i sl.*); spremiti u pretinac
pike [paik] šiljak; koplje
pile [pail] hrpa; stup; gomila (*drva*); ***~ up*** (***on***) nagomilati; naslagati; natovariti
pilgrim ['pilgrim] hodočasnik; **~age** hodočašće
pill pilula
pillage ['pilidʒ] pljačkanje; pljačkati
pillar ['pilə] stup; **~-box** poštanski sandučić (*u obliku stupa*)
pillion ['piliən] MOT stražnje sjedalo na motociklu
pillory ['piləri] sramotni stup
pillow ['pilou] jastuk; **~-case**, **~-slip** jastučnica
pilot ['pailət] pilot, kormilar; vodič; pilotirati; voditi
pimple ['pimpl] bubuljica, prištić
pin pribadača; klin(ac); probosti; iglom pričvrstiti
pincers ['pinsəz] *pl* kliješta
pinch [pintʃ] štipanje; mala količina (*duhana*); koliko se uhvati s dva prsta; štipati; tištiti; *coll* ukrasti; ***at a ~*** u

škripcu

pine [pain] bor; ginuti; venuti; čeznuti (***for, after***); **~-apple** ananas

ping-pong ['piŋpɔŋ] stolni tenis

pink BOT karanfil; ružičaste boje; MOT lupati; ***in the ~*** u odličnom stanju

pinnacle ['pinəkl] tornjić; vrhunac (*brda*); *fig* vrh

PIN number [pin] = **personal identification number** PIN broj

pint [paint] pinta (*mjera za tekućinu, 0,47 l*)

pin-up girl *Am* slika privlačne djevojke koja se prikuca na zid

pioneer [paiə'niə] pionir

pious ['paiəs] pobožan

pipe [paip] lula; cijev; svirala; zviždati; **~-line** cjevovod; naftovod

pirate ['paiərit] gusar; štampati bez autorova odobrenja

pistol ['pistl] pištolj

piston ['pistən] klip

pit jama; THEAT parket; **~ted** kozičav

pitch [pitʃ] smola; bacanje (lopte); stupanj; stepenica; nagib; visina (glasa); podići (šator); baciti; smjestiti se; mazati smolom; **~fork** vile (*za sijeno ili đubre*)

pitfall ['pitfɔ:l] stupica (jama)

pit|iless ['pitilis] nemilosrdan; **~y** samilost; žaliti; ***it's a ~y*** šteta je

pivot ['pivət] stožer; središnja tačka; vrtjeti se oko nečega

placard ['plæka:d] plakat; oglas; oblijepiti plakatima

place [pleis] mjesto; položaj; namještenje; stan, dom; ***out of ~*** neumjesno, nezgodno; (po)staviti; položiti; smjestiti; namjestiti

placid ['plæsid] blag; miran; **~ity** blagost; mirnoća

plague [pleig] kuga; pošast; nevolja; mučiti

plaice [pleis] list (*riba*)

plaid [plæd] vunen pokrivač

plain [plein] ravan; jasan; jednostavan; otvoren; jednobojan; **~ *clothes*** civilno odijelo; ravnica; ravna površina; **~ness** jednostavnost; otvorenost

plaint [pleint] tužba; **~ive** tugaljiv

plait [plæt] pletenica; plesti

plan [plæn] plan; nacrt; planirati

plane [plein] ravan; blanjati; voziti se u avionu, jedrilici; ravnica; razina; blanja; avion; platana

planet ['plænit] planet

plank [plæŋk] daska; planka

plant [pla:nt] biljka; pogon; (po)saditi; **~ation** plantaža; **~er** vlasnik plantaže

plaster ['pla:stə] flaster; žbuka; staviti flaster; žbukati

plate [pleit] ploča; tanjur;

oklop; suđe od srebra; prevući metalom; posrebriti
platform ['plætfɔ:m] peron; podij
platinum ['plætinəm] platina
play [plei] igra; THEAT kazališni komad; TECH polje rada; igrati (se); **~bill** kazališni oglas, program; **~ground** igralište; **~ing card** igraća karta
plea [pli:] obrana; isprika; **~d** zagovarati; ***~d guilty*** priznati se krivim; **~der** branitelj
pleasant ['pleznt] ugodan
pleas|e [pli:z] svidjeti se; ugoditi; molim; **~ing** prijazan; ugodan; **~ure** ['pleʒə] užitak; veselje; dopadanje
pleat [pli:t] nabor (na haljini), plise
pledge [pledʒ] zalog; svečano obećanje; založiti
plent|iful ['plentiful] obilan; **~y** obilje; mnoštvo; ***~y of*** mnogo
pleurisy ['pluərisi] upala porebrice
pliable ['plaiəbl] gibak; prilagodljiv
plight [plait] stanje; neugodan položaj
plot urota; radnja (*drame etc*); spletkariti; urotiti se; **~** (***of land***) parcela
plough [plau] plug; orati
pluck [plʌk] čupanje; odvažnost; trgati; perušati; čupati; ***~ up courage*** skupiti hrabrost; **~y** odvažan, smion
plug [plʌg] klin; čep; EL utikač; plomba; svjećica (*motora*); EL ***~ in*** utaknuti; uštekati; **~ socket** utičnica; začepiti; zatrpati
plum [plʌm] šljiva; grožđica
plumage ['plʌmidʒ] perje
plumb [plʌm] okomit; olovo; raditi limarske radove; **~er** limar, vodoinstalater
plunder ['plʌndə] pljačka; pljačkati
plunge[plʌndʒ] uroniti, zaroniti (***into***)
plural ['pluərəl] množina; **~ity** brojnost
plush [plʌʃ] pliš
plywood [plaiwud] šperploča
p. m. = **post meridiem** popodne
pneumatic [nju:'mætik] zračni; tjeran zrakom; **~ tire** zrakom punjena guma
pneumonia [nju:'mounjə] upala pluća
poach [poutʃ] krasti divljač; **~er** zvjerokradica; **~ing** nedozvoljen lov divljači
pocket ['pɔkit] džep; staviti u džep (*i fig*); **~ful** pun džep nečega; **~lighter** džepni upaljač
pod komuška, mahuna
poem ['pouim] pjesma
poet ['pouit] pjesnik; **~ic(al)** pjesnički; **~ry** pjesništvo
point [pɔint] šiljak; tačka; stupanj; ***~ of view*** gledište; stanovište; ***the ~ is that...*** stvar je u tome da...; ***make***

a ~ of nastojati; smatrati što za važno; ***in ~ of*** što se tiče; ***off the ~*** što ne spada na stvar; ***be on the ~ of*** upravo htjeti; ***to the ~*** konkretno; naoštriti; ***~ out*** istaknuti (***to***); **~ed** šiljast; **~er** pokazivač, kazaljka; prepeličar; **~sman** skretničar; saobraćajac
poise [pɔiz] ravnoteža; držanje (*tijela*)
poison ['pɔizn] otrov; otrovati; **~ous** otrovan
poker ['poukə] žarač; poker; **~ face** *Am coll* bezizražajno lice
pole [poul] motka; rudo; pol
Pole [poul] Poljak
pole-jump skok s motkom
police [pə'li:s] policija, milicija; **~man** policajac, milicioner; **~-station** policijska (milicijska) stanica
policy ['pɔlisi] politika; lukavost; polica
poliomyelitis [pɔliəmaiə'laitis] dječja paraliza
polish ['pɔliʃ] ulaštenost; sjaj; (u)laštiti
polite [pə'lait] učtiv; **~ness** uljudnost
politic|al [pə'litikəl] politički; ***~al science*** političke nauke; **~ian** političar; **~s** ['~iks] *pl* politika; ***talk ~s*** politizirati
pomp raskoš; **~ous** naduven; pompozan
pond ribnjak
ponder ['pɔndə] duboko razmišljati (***on***, ***over***); **~ous** težak (*fig*)
pontoon-bridge [pɔn'tu:nbridʒ] pontonski most
P. O. O. = **post-office order** poštanska uputnica
poodle ['pu:dl] pudl (*vrsta psa*)
pool [pu:l] ribnjak; mlaka; ulog (*u igri*); COM kartel
poor [puə] siromašan; oskudan; ***~ health*** slabo zdravlje; **~ness** siromaštvo; oskudica
pop prasak; koncert popularne glazbe; ***~ the question*** nenadano zaprositi; (*s adverbom*) šmugnuti; ***~ in*** upasti; svratiti; ***~ up*** pojaviti se, skočiti
pope [poup] papa
poplar ['pɔplə] jablan
poppy ['pɔpi] mak
popular ['pɔpjulə] narodni; popularan; **~ity** popularnost; **~ize** popularizirati; prikazati na lako shvatljiv način
populat|e ['pɔpjuleit] napučiti; **~ion** stanovništvo
populous ['pɔpjuləs] jako napučen
porcelain ['pɔ:slin] porculan
porch [pɔ:tʃ] trijem; veranda
pore [pɔ:] pora; ***~ over*** pohlepno čitati
pork [pɔ:k] svinjetina
porous ['pɔ:rəs] porozan
porridge ['pɔridʒ] zobena kaša
port [pɔ:t] luka; ***~ of tran-***

shipment luka za pretovar; porto (crno portugalsko vino)
portable ['pɔːtəbl] prenosiv; **~ typewriter** portabl pisaći stroj
portal ['pɔːtl] portal
portentous [pɔːtentəs] koban
porter ['pɔːtə] vratar; nosač; crno pivo
portfolio [pɔːt'fouljou] mapa; ministarski portfelj (položaj)
portion ['pɔːʃən] dio; dio baštine; porcija; miraz; dati miraz
port|liness ['pɔːtlinis] dostojanstvenost; krupnoća; **~ly** dostojanstven; krupan
portmanteau [pɔːt'mæntou] ručni kovčeg (od kože)
portrait ['pɔːtrit] portret; **~ure** portretiranje
pose [pouz] poza; pozirati
position [pə'ziʃən] položaj; služba; gledište; ***be in a ~ to*** biti u stanju da
positive ['pɔzətiv] siguran; pozitivan
possess [pə'zes] posjedovati; **~ed** opsjednut (***with***); **~ion** vlasništvo; **~or** posjednik, vlasnik
possib|ility [pɔsə'biliti] mogućnost; **~le** moguć; **~ly** moguće, možda; ***if I ~ly can*** ako ikako mogu; ***I cannot ~ly do it*** ne mogu to nikako učiniti
post [poust] stup; kolac; služba, namještenje; ured; pošta; poštirati; poslati poštom; **~age** poštarina; **~age stamp** poštanska marka; **~al cheque** poštanski ček; **~box** poštanski sandučić; **~card** dopisnica; **~date** staviti kasniji datum; **~er** plakat
posteri|or [pɔs'tiəriə] kasniji; **~ty** potomstvo
post|man ['poustmən] poštar; **~mark** poštanski žig; **~-office** pošta, poštanski ured; **~-paid** frankirano
postpone [poust'poun] odgoditi; **~ment** odgoda; zapostavljanje
postscript ['pousskript] dodatak pismu
posture ['pɔstʃə] položaj; držanje (*tijela*); postaviti u izvjestan položaj
post-war ['poust'wɔː] poslijeratni
pot lonac; staviti u lonac
potato [pə'teitou], *pl* ***~es*** krumpir
poten|cy ['poutənsi] jakost; moć; **~t** moćan
pot-hole MOT rupa; uleknina
potter ['pɔtə] lončar; **~y** lončarstvo
pouch [pautʃ] kesa, vrečica
poultice ['poultis] topao oblog
poultry ['poultri] perad
pounce [pauns] zaskočiti; baciti se na ([***up***]***on***); napad; skok

pound [paund] funta; zatvoriti u tor; udarati; tucati
pour [pɔ:] lijevati; sipati; ~ ***out*** (*piće*) natočiti; izlijevati (*i fig*)
pout [paut] naprćiti (*usne*); duriti se
poverty ['pɔvəti] siromaštvo
powder ['paudə] prah; puder; napudrati (se)
power ['pauə] snaga; jakost, moć; MATH potencija; **~ful** moćan; djelotvoran; **~ station** električna centrala
practica|ble ['præktikəbl] izvediv; moguć; **~l** praktičan
practi|ce ['præktis] praksa; vježba; **~se** vježbati (se); vršiti (*zvanje*); prakticirati
practitioner [præk'tiʃnə] liječnik opće prakse
praise [preiz] pohvala, hvaljenje; **~worthy** hvalevrijedan
pram [præm] *coll* = **perambulator** dječja kolica
prank [præŋk] obijesna šala; jogunstvo
prattle ['prætl] brbljati
pray [prei] moliti; prositi; **~er** [prɛə] molitva; zaklinjanje
preach [pri:tʃ] propovijedati; **~er** propovjednik
precarious [pri'kɛəriəs] neizvjestan
precaution [pri'kɔ:ʃən] oprez; mjera predostrožnosti
precede [pri'si:d] prethoditi; **~nce** prednost; prvenstvo; **~nt** ['presidənt] presedan
precept ['pri:sept] propis
precinct ['pri:siŋkt] kvart, rajon (u gradu)
precious ['preʃəs] dragocjen; plemenit (*kamen etc*)
precipi|ce ['presipis] ponor; **~tate** strmoglaviti (se); **~tation** survavanje; **~tous** strm; nagao
precis|e [pri'sais] tačan; ***~ely!*** tačno!; **~ion** [~'siʒən] tačnost
preconception ['pri:kən'sepʃən] unaprijed stvoren zaključak
pre|cursor [pri:'kə:sə] prethodnik, preteča; **~decessor** prethodnik; **~destinate** unaprijed odrediti
predict [pri'dikt] proreći; **~ion** proricanje
pre|dilection [pri:di'lekʃən] sklonost (***for***); **~dominant** premoćan; **~-eminent** istaknut; **~-emption** pravo prve kupnje
preface ['prefıs] predgovor; staviti predgovor
prefer [pri'fə:] više voljeti; **~able**: ***~able*** (***to***) što se više voli; **~ence** prednost; **~ment** unapređenje
pregnant ['pregnənt] trudna
prejudic|e ['predʒudis] predrasuda; šteta; **~ial** škodljiv
preliminar|ies [pri'liminəriz] *pl* pripreme; **~y** uvodni, prethodni
prelude ['prelju:d] MUS pred-

igra
premature [premə'tjuə] preran
premier ['premjə] ministar predsjednik
premises ['premisiz] *pl* kuća sa zemljištem; prostorije; ***on the ~*** u kući (zgradi, prostorijama)
premium ['pri:mjəm] premija
preoccupied [pri:'ɔkjupaid] zaokupljen mišlju
prepar|ation [prepə'reiʃən] pripremanje; **~e** [pri'pɛə] pripraviti
pre|pay ['pri:'pei] unaprijed platiti; platiti poštarinu unaprijed; **~ponderate** prevagnuti
prepossess [pri:pə'zes] zaokupiti, obuzeti; **~ion** predrasuda
prescri|be [pris'kraib] propisati (***for a p***); **~ption** [~'kripʃən] propis; pravilo; recept
presen|ce ['prezns] prisutnost; pojava; ***~ce of mind*** prisutnost duha; **~t** prisutan; sadašnji; koji postoji; sadašnje vrijeme; ***at ~t*** sada; ***for the ~t*** za sada; ovaj čas; poklon; [pri'zent] predstaviti; pružati; uručiti; prikazati; pokloniti; **~tation** predstavljanje; podnošenje; predočenje; **~timent** predosjećaj, slutnja
preservation [prezə:'veiʃən] čuvanje; održavanje
preserve [pri'zə:v] (sa)čuvati; obraniti (***from***); (*voće*) ukuhati; konzervirati; **~s** ukuhano voće ili povrće
preside [pri'zaid] predsjedati
president ['prezidənt] predsjednik
press preša; štampa; gužva; ormar; (pri)tiskati; glačati; gnječiti; **~-button** dugme (*na stroju, aparatu*); **~-gallery** galerija za novinare; **~ing** hitan; **~-stud** dugme (*na aparatu*); **~ure** pritisak; **~ure-gauge** sprava za mjerenje tlaka
prestige [pres'ti:ʒ] ugled
presum|e [pri'zju:m] pretstaviti; usuditi se; **~ing** drzak
presumpt|ion [pri'zʌmpʃən] pretpostavka; drskost; **~ive** vjerojatan; **~uous** preuzetan
preten|ce [pri'tens] pretvaranje; izlika; ***false ~ce*** tobožnji razlog; lažni navod; **~d** tvrditi; ***~d to*** pretvarati se da; zahtijevati; pretendirati (***to***); **~sion** svojatanje (***to***); pretenzija
pretext ['pri:tekst] izlika
pretty ['priti] zgodan; dražestan; prilično; ***~ much the same*** gotovo isto
prevail [pri'veil] prevladati
prevalent ['prevələnt] nadmoćan
prevent [pri'vent] spriječiti, predusresti (***from***); **~ion** sprečavanje; **~ive** preventi-

van; zaštitni; zaštitno sredstvo; *~ive arrest* pritvor
previous ['pri:vjəs] prijašnji; prethodan; *~ to* prije; *~ly* prije
pre-war ['pri:'wɔ:] predratni
prey [prei] plijen; pljačka; *~ (up)on* vrebati; pljačkati
price [prais] cijena; COM odrediti cijenu; *~less* neprocjenjiv; vrlo vrijedan
prick ubod; (pro)bosti; *~ up one's ears* naćuliti uši; *~ly* bodljikav
pride [praid] ponos
priest [pri:st] svećenik
prim ukočen; uredan
prima|cy ['praiməsi] prvenstvo; primat; *~ry* prvobitan; početni
prime [praim] prvi; glavni; napon; zrelost; *fig* cvat; *~r* početnica
primitive ['primitiv] primitivan; prvobitan; jednostavan
prim|ness ['primnis] ukočenost; *~rose* jaglac
prince [prins] knez; princ, kraljević; *~ly* kneževski; *~ss* kneginja; kraljevna
principal ['prinsəpəl] glavni; najvažniji; šef; glavnica; kapital; *~ity* kneževina
principle ['prinsəpl] princip; *on ~* principijelno
print tisak; PHOT kopija; štampana pamučna tkanina; *out of ~* rasprodan; štampati; tiskati; PHOT kopirati; *~er* štampar; *~er's ink* tiskarsko crnilo
printing ['printiŋ] štampanje; *~-frame* PHOT okvir za kopiranje; *~-office*, *Am ~-plant* štamparija
prior ['praiə] prije (*to*); nadstojnik samostana; *~ity* prioritet; prvenstvo
prism ['prizəm] prizma
prison ['prizn] zatvor; *~er* zatvorenik
priva|cy ['praivəsi] povučenost; *~te* ['~vit] privatan; osobni; tajni; redov; *in ~te* privatno, u četiri oka; *~te parts* spolni organi; *~tion* [~'veiʃən] oskudnica
privilege ['privilidʒ] povlastica; dati povlasticu
prize [praiz] nagrada; zgoditak; premija; vrlo cijeniti; *~ (open)* razvaliti; *~-winner* dobitnik nagrade
probab|ility [prɔbə'biliti] vjerojatnost; *~le* vjerojatan
probation [prə'beiʃən] kušnja; pokusni staž; uslovna sloboda
probity ['proubiti] poštenje
problem ['prɔbləm] problem
procedure [prə'si:dʒə] procedura
proceed [prə'si:d] poći dalje; nastaviti (*with*); potjecati (*from*); događati se; poduzeti sudske korake (*against*); postupati; *~ings pl* postupak; izvještaji učenih društava; *~s* ['prousi:dz] dohodak, prihod

process ['prouses] tok; proces; ***in ~ of construction*** u toku gradnje; **~ion** povorka
procla|im [prə'kleim] proglasiti; **~mation** [prɔklə'meiʃən] proklamacija; proglašenje
procur|ation [prɔkjuə'reiʃən] punomoć; **~e** pribaviti; priskrbiti; **~ement** nabavljanje; posredovanje
prodig|ious [prə'didʒəs] izvanredan; **~y**: ***infant ~y*** čudo od djeteta
produce [prə'djuːs] proizvesti; iznijeti; izvaditi; davati ploda; ['prɔ~] proizvod; zemaljske plodine; prinos; **~s** proizvođač; producent; režiser
product ['prɔdəkt] proizvod; **~ion** proizvodnja; **~ive** produktivan; plodan
profane [prə'fein] svjetovan, profan; obeščastiti; profanirati
profess [prə'fes] ispovijedati (*vjeru*); obavljati (*zvanje*); **~ion** ispovijedanje; zanimanje; **~ional** profesionalan; stručnjak; profesionalac (*i* SPORT)
proffer ['prɔfə] (po)nuditi
proficien|cy [prə'fɪʃənsi] vještina; stručnost; **~t** vješt (***in, at***)
profile ['proufɪːl] profil
profit ['prɔfɪt] korist; dobitak; profit; **~ *by*** (o)koristiti (se); **~able** koristan; probitačan; **~eer** nepošteno zarađivati; profiter; ratni dobitnik; **~eering** nepošteno zarađivanje
profligate ['prɔfligit] razuzdan
profound [prə'faund] dubok; temeljit
profuse [prə'fjuːs] rasipan
prognos|is [prɔg'nousis], *pl* ***prognoses*** prognoza; **~ticate** [prəg'nɔstikeit] predskazivati
progress ['prougres] napredak; [prə'~] napredovati; **~ive** napredan; progresivan
prohibit [prə'hibit] zabraniti; spriječiti; **~ion** zabrana (proizvodnje, prodaje alkoholnih pića)
project ['prɔdʒekt] projekt; [prə'~] (iz)baciti; planirati; **~ion** projekcija; nacrt; izbočina
proletarian [proule'tɛəriən] proleterski; proleter
prologue ['proulɔg] prolog
prolong [prə'lɔŋ] produžiti
prominent ['prɔminənt] istaknut
promis|e ['prɔmis] obećanje; obećati; **~ing** koji mnogo obećava; **~sory note** obveznica; zadužnica
promot|e [prə'mout] unaprijediti; osnovati; **~ion** unapređenje; osnivanje
prompt brz; bez odlaganja; smjesta; THEAT šaptati; **~-box** šaptačeva kabina;

~er šakptalac
promulgate ['prɔməlgeit] (javno) objaviti
prong [prɔŋ] vile; šiljak
pronounce [prə'nauns] izgovoriti; proglasiti
pronunciation [prənʌnsi'eiʃən] izgovor
proof [pru:f] dokaz; pokus; PHOT negativ; otisak; ~ (***sheet***) korektura, otisak za korekturu; čvrst; otporan (***against***); (*u slož.*) nepromočiv, otporan
prop potporanj; ~ (***up***) poduprijeti
propaga|te ['prɔpəgeit] množiti (se); širiti (se); propagirati; **~tion** širenje
propeller [prə'pelə] propeler
proper ['prɔpə] vlastit; pravi; prikladan; pristojan; **~ty** vlasništvo; imanje; nekretnine; svojstvo; imetak; THEAT **~ties** *pl* rekviziti
prophe|cy ['prɔfısi] proročanstvo; **~sy** ['~sai] proricati; **~t** prorok; **~tess** proročica
prophylactic [prɔfı'læktik] MED profilaktično sredstvo
propitious [prə'piʃəs] povoljan
proportion [prə'pɔ:ʃən] razmjer; omjer; **~al** razmjeran; **~ate** razmjeran; prikladan
propos|al [prə'pouzəl] prijedlog; (*bračna*) ponuda; **~e** predložiti; namjeravati; **~ition** prijedlog izjava; *Am* stvar; posao
propriet|ary [prə'praiətəri] vlasnički; **~or** vlasnik; **~y** ispravnost; pristojnost; ***the ~ies*** pristojnost
prose [prouz] proza; prozaičan
prosecut|e ['prɔsikju:t] progoniti (*i* JUR); **~ion** sudski progon; ***witness for the ~ion*** svjedok optužbe; **~or** tužitelj; ***public ~or*** javni tužilac
prospect ['prɔspekt] izgled(i); ***have in ~*** imati u izgledu; **~ive** očekivan; budući
prosper ['prɔspə] napredovati; uspijevati; **~ity** uspjeh; blagostanje; **~ous** uspješan, bogat
prostrate ['prɔstreit] oboren; ispružen; [prɔs'~] srušiti
protect [prə'tekt] (za)štititi (***from***); **~ion** zaštita; **~ive duty** zaštitna carina; **~or** zaštitnik
protest ['proutest] protest; [prə'~] uvjeravati; protestirati; **~ant** ['prɔtistənt] protestantski; protestant
protract [prə'trækt] odugovlačiti
proud [praud] ponosan; **~ flesh** MED divlje meso
prov|able ['pru:vəbl] koji se može dokazati; **~e** (is)kušati; dokazati; pokazati se (kao)
proverb ['prɔvəb] poslovica;

~ial [prə'vəːbjəl] poslovičan
provide [prə'vaid] (po)brinuti se (***for***); nabaviti; opskrbiti (***with***); **~d** (***that***) pod uvjetom; ukoliko
providen|ce ['prɔvidəns] predviđanje; providnost; **~t** brižljiv; oprezan
province ['prɔvins] pokrajiva; *fig* područje
provision [prə'viʒən] nabava; priprema; zaliha; opskrbljivanje; JUR odredba; **~s** *pl* živežne namirnice; **~al** privremen; provizoran
provocat|ion [prɔvə'keiʃən] izazivanje; **~ive** izazovan
provoke [prə'vouk] izazivati; uzbuditi
prowl [praul] šuljati se (*za plijenom*)
proxim|ate ['prɔksimit] najbliži; **~ity** blizina
proxy ['prɔksi] opunomoćenik; punomoć; zastupanje
pruden|ce ['pruːdəns] razboritost; oprez; **~t** razborit
prud|ery ['pruːdəri] tobožnja stidljivost; **~ish** prividno stidljiv
prune [pruːn] suha šljiva; obrezivati; *fig* čistiti
Prussia ['prʌʃə] Prusija; **~n** pruski; Prus
prussic ['prʌsik]: **~ acid** cianovodična kiselina
P. S. = **postscript**
psalm [saːm] psalm
psychiatr|ist [sai'kaiətrist] psihijatar; **~y** psihijatrija
psycholog|ical [saikə'lɔdʒikəl] psihološki; **~ist** psiholog
psychosis [sai'kousis] psihoza
pub [pʌb] *coll* krčma
puberty ['pjuːbəti] pubertet
public ['pʌblik] javni; državni; **~ation** objava; izdanje; opći; **♀ Health** narodno zdravstvo; **~ house** krčma; **~ity** publicitet; reklama; **~ spirit** smisao za zajednicu
publish ['pʌbliʃ] objaviti; objelodaniti; (*knjigu*) izdati; **~er** izdavač, nakladnik; **~ing-house** izdavačko poduzeće
pudding ['pudiŋ] puding; ***black* ~** krvavica
puddle ['pʌdl] mlaka, bara
puff [pʌf] dašak; jastučić za pudranje; reklama; puhati; otpuhnuti; dahtati; sukljati; preuveličavati; **~er** onaj koji diže cijene (*na dražbi*)
puff-paste lisnato tijesto
pull vučenje; trzaj; zahvat; (po)vući; trzati; (iš)čupati; veslati; **~ *down*** srušiti; **~ *off*** skinuti; odlaziti; **~ *through*** preboljeti; izvući (se); **~ *oneself together*** sabrati se; **~ *one's leg*** zafrkavati
pulley ['puli] TECH kolotur
pulp [pʌlp] meso (*voća, ploda*); kaša (*za papir*); pretvoriti (se) u kašu
pulpit ['pulpit] propovjedao-

nica
puls|ate [pʌl'seit] kucati (*srce, bilo*); **~e** puls, bilo; kucati (*srce*); udarati
pulverize ['pʌlvəraiz] drobiti (se) u prah; smrviti
pumice(-stone) ['pʌmis] kamen plavučac
pump [pʌmp] pumpati; pumpa; cipela (za ples); **~kin** bundeva; **~-room** prostorija toplica, u kojoj se pije mineralna voda
pun [pʌn] igra riječi; igrati se riječima
Punch [pʌntʃ] **and Judy show** ulično kazalište lutaka
punch [pʌntʃ] (pro)bušiti; udarati; udarac (*Šakom*); *coll Am* snaga; punč; **~ing-ball** kožnata lopta po kojoj boksači udaraju za vježbu
punctual ['pʌŋktjuəl] tačan; **~ity** tačnost
puncture ['pʌŋktʃə] gumidefekt; probušiti (se) (*o gumi*)
punish ['pʌniʃ] kazniti; **~able** kažnjiv; **~ment** kazna
pupil ['pju:pl] zjenica; učenik; štićenik
puppy ['pʌpi] štene; *fig* uobražen mladić, kicoš
purchas|e ['pə:tʃəs] kupnja; kupljena roba; kupiti; nabaviti; **~er** kupac; **~ing power** kupovna moć
pure [pjuə] čist; sam; **~-bred** čistokrvan
purgat|ive ['pə:gətiv] sredstvo za čišćenje; **~ory** čistilište
purge [pə:dʒ] POL čistka; POL provesti čistku; MED očistiti (*stolica*)
puri|fy ['pjuərifai] (o)čistiti (se); razbistriti (se); **~ty** čistoća
purple ['pə:pl] ljubičast; ljubičasta boja
purpose ['pə:pəs] svrha; namjera; ***for the ~ of*** u svrhu, radi; ***on ~*** namjerno; ***to no ~*** uzalud; bez smisla; ***play with a ~*** drama s tendencijom; namjeravati; **~ful** svrsishodan; **~less** bezkoristan, bez svrhe; **~ly** namjerno
purr [pə:] presti (*mačka*)
purse [pə:s] novčarka; novčana sredstva; skupiti usta
pursu|ance [pə'sju:əns]: ***in ~ance of*** slijedeći (nešto); **~e** slijediti; baviti se; **~it** proganjanje; nastojanje
purvey [pə:'vei] opskrbljavati; nabavljati (**for**); **~ance** snabdijevanje; **~or** nabavljač (živežnih namirnica)
push [puʃ] guranje; udarac; energija; poduzetnost; *sl* ***get the ~*** dobiti otkaz; ***give a p the ~*** otpustiti (koga); gurati; tjerati; poticati; **~-button** EL dugme kojim se pokreće mehanizam; **~ing** nasilan; poduzetan; laktaški
pussy-foot(er) ['pusifut(ə)] *Am* onaj koji se šulja

put staviti, položiti; postaviti (***on***, ***to***); izreći; ~ ***away*** skloniti; odložiti; ~ ***back*** vratiti natrag (kazalo); ~ ***by*** štedjeti (novac); ~ ***down*** metnuti; položiti; ugušiti; napisati; ~ ***in*** umetnuti; uvrstiti; upasti u riječ; uložiti; ~ ***off*** svući; skinuti (šešir); odgoditi; zavarati (obećanjima); odvratiti (***from***); ~ ***on*** obući, navući, staviti na sebe; ~ ***on airs*** afektirati; ~ ***it on*** postaviti komad na scenu; ~ ***out*** istjerati, izbaciti; ugasiti; smesti; ~ ***through*** *tel* dati vezu, spojiti; ~ ***up*** postaviti; otvoriti (*kišobran*); podići (*prozor*); ~ ***up*** (***at***) smjestiti koga; dati komustan; ~ ***up with*** podnositi

putr|efaction [pju:tri'fækʃən] trulež; **~efy** gnjiti; **~id** ['~id] gnjio

puttee ['pʌti] ovijač

putty ['pʌti]: (***glazier's***) ~ staklarski kit

put-up job namještena igra

puzzle ['pʌzl] zagonetka; zabuna; zbrka; zbuniti

pyjamas [pə'dʒa:məz] *pl* pidžama

pyramid ['pirəmid] piramida

pyre ['paiə] lomača

Pyrenees [pirə'ni:z] *pl* Pirineji

pyrotechnics [pairou'tekniks] *pl* vatromet(i)

python ['paiθən] udav

Q

Q. = **Queen**

quack [kwæk] gakanje; nadriliječnik; gakati

quadrangle [kwɔ'dræŋgl] četverokut

quadrup|ed ['kwɔdruped] četveronožac; **~le** četverostruk; početverostručiti (se); **~lets** *pl* četvorci

quail [kweil] prepelica; klonuti

quaint [kweint] neobičan

quake [kweik] tresti se (***with***, ***for***); **⁀r** Kveker (vjerska sekta)

quali|fication [kwɔlifi'keiʃən] kvalifikacija; **~fy** osposobiti (se); kvalificirati (se); ograničiti; ublažiti; razrijediti (piće); **~ty** svojstvo; kvaliteta

quantity ['kwɔntiti] količina

quarantine ['kwɔrəntain] karantena

quarrel ['kwɔrəl] svađa; prepirka; svađati se; **~some** svadljiv

quarry ['kwɔri] kamenolom; lomiti (kamen)

quart [kwɔ:t] mjera za tekućinu (*1,136 l*)

quarter ['kwɔ:tə] četvrtina,

(gradska) četvrt; tromjesečje; *pl* stan; nastaniti; ***from all ~s*** sa svih strana; **~-day** dan u tromjesečju kad se plaća stanarina i sl.; **~ly** tromjesečni
quartz [kwɔ:ts] kremen
quaver ['kweivə] triler; drhtavo pjevati
quay [ki:] kej, pristanište
queen [kwi:n] kraljica
queer [kwiə] čudan, neobičan; ***I feel ~*** nije mi dobro
quench [kwentʃ] ugasiti (*ugl žeđ*); zatomiti
question ['kwestʃən] pitanje; ispitivati; sumnjati; ***ask a p a ~, put a ~ to a p*** postaviti nekome pitanje; ***the ~ is*** radi se o; ***the person in ~*** čovjek, o kom se radi; **~able** dvojben, prijeporan; **~naire** upitni arak
queue [kju:] red; ***~ up*** stati u red
quick [kwik] brz; okretan; bistar; oštar (*sluh, etc*); ***cut to the ~*** pogoditi koga u živo; **~en** oživiti; požuriti; ubrzati; pokrenuti (se); **~ness** živahnost; brzina; oštrina (*sluha, etc*); **~silver** živa; **~-witted** dosjetljiv
quiet ['kwaiət] miran, tih; mir; **~ness**, **~ude** tišina
quill [kwil] pero (iz krila)
quilt [kwilt] poplun; prošiti
quince [kwins] dunja
quinine [kwi'ni:n] kinin
quinsy ['kwinzi] grlobolja; upala krajnika
quintuplets ['kwintjuplits] *pl* petorci
quit [kwit] ostaviti; otići iz; slobodan (***of***); riješen
quite [kwait] sasvim; potpuno; ***~ (so)!*** baš tako, zaista; ***~ another story*** sasvim nešto drugo
quiver ['kwivə] drhtaj; tobolac (*za strijele*); drhtati; treptati
quota ['kwoutə] kvota; (u)dio
quotation [kwou'teiʃən] citat; navedena cijena; **~-marks** *pl* navodnici
quote [kwout] citirati, navoditi; označiti cijene; notirati (***at***)
quotidian [kwɔ'tidiən] svakodnevan

R

R. A. = **Royal Academy**
rabbet ['ræbit] žlijeb; užlijebiti; utoriti
rabbi ['ræbai] rabin
rabbit ['ræbit] kunić
rabble ['ræbl] rulja
rabid ['ræbid] mahnit; bijesan (*životinja*)
race [reis] rod; pleme; rasa; trka; utrkivanje; struja(nje);

~s *pl* (*konjske etc*) trke; **~-course** trkalište; **~-crew** ekipa veslača; **~r** trkaći konj; trkaći čamac; trkaća kola
racing ['reisiŋ] trkaći sport; **~ car** trkaća kola
rack [ræk] stalak; vješalica za odijela; mučilište; ***luggage* ~** polica za prtljagu; raspinjati; mučiti; **~ *one's brains*** razbijati si glavu
racket ['rækit] (*tenis*) reket; buka; graja; *Am* ucjenjivanje; **~eer** *Am* ucjenjivač
rack-railway zupčana željeznica
racy ['reisi] rasan; iskonski; aromatičan; jak
radar ['reida:] radar; **~ set** radarski uređaj
radia|nt ['reidiənt] sjajan, blistav; **~te** isijavati; **~tion** zračenje; **~tor** radijator; MOT hladnjak
radical ['rædikəl] korijenski; osnovni; radikal
radio ['reidiou] radio; *Am* radiotelegrafska vijest; rentgenski snimak; rentgensko zračenje; **~ drama, ~ play** radio drama; osvijetliti rentgenskim zrakama; zračiti (*radijem*); **~gram** radiogram; rentgenski snimak; **~graph** rentgenska slika; načiniti rentgensku sliku; **~scopy** zračenje (rentgenskim zrakama); **~telegram** radiotelegram
radish ['rædiʃ] rotkva
radium ['reidiəm] radij(um)
radius ['reidiəs] radijus, polumjer; područje
raffle ['ræfl] (i)ždrijebati
raft [ra:ft] splav; splavariti
rag [ræg] prnja; krpa; dronjak; *sl* zlurado se našaliti s kim
rage [reidʒ] bijes; oduševljenje; žudnja (***for***); bjesnjeti; ***it is all the ~ now*** to je u velikoj modi
ragged ['rægid] grub; rutav; nazupčan
rag-time ['rægtaim] crnačka glazba
raid [reid] prepad; racija; provaliti
rail [reil] zasun; tračnica; ograditi; ***run off the ~s*** iskočiti s tračnica; **~-car** motorna kola; **~ing** ograda, rešetka; **~road** *Am* željeznica; **~way** željeznica; **~wayman** željezničar
rain [rein] kiša; kišiti; **~bow** duga; **~coat** kišni kaput; **~y** kišovit
raise [reiz] dizati, (po)dignuti; uzvisiti; utjerati novac; uzeti zajam; prouzročiti; uzbuditi; pobuniti; uzgajati; utemeljiti
raisin ['reizn] rozina
rake [reik] grablje; nagib; razvratnik; grabljati
rally ['ræli] okupiti (se); oporaviti se; skupljanje; zbor
ram [ræm] ovan; kljun (za udar pramcem); malj; nabi-

jati maljem
ramble ['ræmbl] lutati
ramify ['ræmifai] račvati (se)
ramp [ræmp] rampa
ranch [ræntʃ] *Am* ranč, stočarska farma
rancid ['rænsid] užežen, pokvaren
rancour ['ræŋkə] pakost
random ['rændəm]: ***at ~*** nasumce, slijepo
range [reindʒ] red; (gorski) lanac; COM kolekcija; asortiman; štednjak; područje; opseg; domet; ređati, svrstati; prokrstariti; pružati se; tumarati
rank [ræŋk] red; čin, rang; položaj; (po)ređati se; ubrajati se (***with***, ***among***); biti u položaju (***above***); mastan; užežen, pokvaren; odvratan
ransack ['rænsæk] pretražiti
ransom ['rænsəm] otkupnina; otkup; otkupiti, osloboditi
rap [ræp] kucanje; *music* rap; kucati
rapac|ious [rə'peiʃəs] lakom; **~ity** grabežljivost
rape [reip] grabež; silovanje; ***~ and murder*** umorstvo iz pohote
rapid ['ræpid] brz, nagao; strm; ***~s*** *pl* brzica; **~ity** brzina
rapt [ræpt] zanesen; ushićen; **~ure** ['~tʃə] zanos
rare [rɛə] rijedak (*i fig* dragocjen); PHYS razrijeđen; **~fy** razrijediti (se); **~ness**, **rarity** rijetkost; finoća
rascal ['ra:skəl] lupež
rash [ræʃ] nagao; osip
rasp [ra:sp] turpija; turpijati
raspberry ['ra:zbəri] malina
rat [ræt] štakor; ***smell a ~*** nanjušiti opasnost
rate [reit] omjer; stopa; cijena; tarifa; (općinski) porez; brzina; ***~ of exchange*** devizni tečaj; ***~ of interest*** kamatna stopa; ***~ of wages*** plaća, nagrada; ***at any ~*** svakako; (pr)ocijeniti; oporezovati (***at***)
rather ['ra:ðə] radije; prije; prilično
rati|fication [rætifi'keiʃən] potvrda; **~fy** potvrditi
ration ['ræʃən] obrok; porcija; racionirati; **~-card** karta za racionirane živežne namirnice
rational ['ræʃnl] razuman; racionalan; **~ization** racionalizacija; **~ize** racionalizirati
ratten ['rætn] sabotirati
rattle ['rætl] štropot(anje); čegrtati; štropotati; klepetati; **~snake** (zmija) čegrtuša
ravage ['rævidʒ] (o)pustošiti
rave [reiv] bjesnjeti; bulazniti
raven ['reivn] gavran; **~ous** proždrljiv; izgladnio
ravine [rə'vi:n] usjek; gudura
ravish ['ræviʃ] ushititi; **~ing** koji ushićuje
raw [rɔ:] sirov; ranjav; neiskusan

ray [rei] zraka; ~ **treatment** MED zračenje
rayon ['reiən] umjetna svila
razor ['reizə] britva; ~**strap** brijački remen
reach [ri:tʃ] (do)sezanje; domet; opseg; ***out of*** ~ nedokučiv; ***within easy*** ~ na dohvat, u blizini; posegnuti, dosezati; prispjeti
react [ri'ækt] reagirati
reaction [ri'ækʃən] reakcija, protivno djelovanje; ~**ary** reakcionaran
read [ri:d] (pro)čitati; pokazati; ~ ***off*** očitati; ~**er** čitatelj; predavač, izvanredni profesor; korektor
readi|ly ['redili] spremno; rado; ~**ness** spremnost, voljnost
reading ['ri:diŋ] čitanje; predavanje; načitanost; lektira; tumačenje
readjust ['ri:ə'dʒʌst] preudesiti
ready ['redi] gotov; spreman; voljan; sklon (***to***); brz; pri ruci; ***get*** ~ pripremiti (se); ~**-made** konfekcijski
real [riəl] stvaran; realan; pravi; ~ **estate**, ~ **property** nekretnina; ~**ity** stvarnost
realiz|ation [riəlai'zeiʃən] ostvarenje; predočivanje; ~**e** ostvariti; spoznati; uvidjeti; realizirati; unovčiti
really ['riəli] zaista, stvarno
realm [relm] kraljevstvo
realtor ['riəltə] *Am* posrednik za prodaju nekretnina
reap [ri:p] žeti; požnjeti (*i fig*); ~**er** žetelac; žetelica (*masina*)
reappear ['ri:ə'piə] ponovo se pojaviti
rear [riə] uzgojiti, odgojiti; pozadina; ~**most** zadnji
rearrange ['ri:ə'reindʒ] preurediti
reason ['ri:zn] razum; pravo; razlog; povod; razumno razmišljati, rasuđivati; ***by*** ~ ***of*** zbog; ~**able** razborit; umjeren
reass|emble ['ri:ə'sembl] ponovo (se) sakupiti; ~**ure** ponovo osigurati; umiriti
rebel ['rebl] pobunjenik; [ri'bel] (po)buniti se; ~**lion** (po)buna
rebound [ri'baund] odskočiti
rebuild ['ri:'bild] ponovo (iz-) graditi
rebuke [ri'bju:k] ukor, prijekor; (u)koriti, kuditi
recall [ri'kɔ:l] opoziv; poricanje; THEAT pozvati natrag; opozvati; sjećati se; otkazati (*kapital*)
recast ['ri:'ka:st] pretopiti
receipt [ri'si:t] priznanica; primitak; kuhinjski recept; potvrditi primitak
receiv|e [ri'si:v] primiti; dobiti; uzeti; prihvatiti; ~**er** primalac (*i* RADIO); *tel* slušalica; ~**ing set** radio-prijemnik
recent ['ri:snt] nov; nedavni; ~**ly** nedavno, u posljednje

vrijeme
receptacle [ri'septəkl] posuda
reception [ri'sepʃən] primanje; (radio-)prijem; **~ist** činovnik recepcije
receptive [ri'septiv] sposoban da prima, receptivan (***of***)
recess [ri'ses] udubina, niša
reciprocal [ri'siprəkəl] uzajaman; obostran
recit|al [ri'saitl] pripovijedanje; izvještaj; solistički nastup; **~e** predavati; recitirati
reckless ['reklis] bezobziran; nesmotren (***of***)
reckon ['rekən] računati s ([***up***]***on***) (*i fig*); zbrojiti; (o)cijeniti; smatrati; ***~ up*** sračunati; ***be out in one's ~ing*** prevariti se u računu
reclaim [ri:'kleim] popraviti koga; obratiti; tražiti natrag; meliorirati
recline [ri'klain] nasloniti se
recogni|tion [rekəg'niʃən] prepoznavanje; priznanje; **~ze** prepoznati; priznati
recoil [ri'kɔil] odskočiti
recollect [rekə'lekt] sjetiti se; **~ion** sjećanje
recommend [rekə'mend] preporučiti; **~ation** preporuka
recompense ['rekəmpens] nagrada; naknada; nagraditi; nadoknaditi (štetu), nadomjestiti
reconcil|e ['rekənsail] pomiriti; uskladiti; **~iation** pomirenje; poravnanje
reconsider ['ri:kən'sidə] ponovo razmisliti; **~ation** ponovno razmišljanje
reconstruct ['ri:kən'strʌkt] rekonstruirati; ponovo izgraditi; **~ion** ponovna izgradnja; rekonstrukcija
reconver|sion ['ri:kən'vɜ:ʃən] preorijentacija na mirnodopsku industriju; **~t** preorijentirati
record ['rekɔ:d] zapis; bilježenje; protokol; gramofonska ploča; rekord; [ri'~] zabilježiti; registrirati; ***beat the ~*** oboriti rekord; **~er** [ri'kɔ:də] zapisničar; registrator
recourse [ri'kɔ:s] utočište
recover [ri'kʌvə] ponovo steći; nadoknaditi; oporaviti se
rectangle ['rektæŋgl] pravokutnik
rectif|ier ['rektifaiə] radio ispravljač; **~y** ['~fai] ispraviti; poboljšati
rector ['rektə] župnik; **~y** župa
recur [ri'kɜ:] vratiti se (***to***); ponavljati se; ***~ to a p's mind*** vratiti se komu u sjećanje; **~rence** povratak, vraćanje
red crven; ***see ~*** razbjesniti se; **~ herring** dimljeni sleđ; **~-tape** birokracija; **~-tapism** birokracija
redact [ri'dækt] uređivati; iz-

davati
red|breast crvendać; **~den** (po)crveniti; **~dish** crvenkast
redecorate ['ri:'dekəreit] ponovo ličiti (*sobu*)
redeem [ri'di:m] otkupiti, izbaviti; nadoknaditi; **~able** otkupiv; koji se da popraviti, spasiti; **Ser** Spasitelj
redemption [ri'dempʃən] otkupljivanje; spas(enje)
red-hot užaren
redirect ['ri:di'rekt] ponovo adresirati
redress [ri'dres] naknada; nadoknaditi
reduc|e [ri'dju:s] umanjiti; reducirati; sniziti (*cijene*); *fig* skinuti; **~tion** sniženje; ***~tion of 5 per cent*** 5 posto popusta
reef [ri:f] greben
reek [ri:k] smrdjeti (***of***)
reel [ri:l] špula; svitak; rola (*filma*); namatati; okretati se; teturati; zanjihati se
re-|elect ['ri:i'lekt] ponovo izabrati; **~engage** ponovo namjestiti koga; **~enter** ponovo ući; **~establish** ponovo osnovati
refer [ri'fə:] uputiti na (***to***); odnositi se (***to***); **~ee** arbitar; nogometni sudac
reference ['refrəns] odnos; upućivanje na; preporuka; ***terms of ~*** smjernice; ***make ~ to*** upućivati na; **~-book** priručnik; **~ number** broj spisa
refill ['ri:'fil] uložak; ponovo napuniti
refine [ri'fain] (pro)čistiti; oplemeniti (se); **~ment** finoća; dotjeranost; uglađenost; **~ry** rafinerija
refit ['ri:fit] popraviti
reflect [ri'flekt] odraziti se; razmišljati (**[*up*]*on***); ***~ on*** nepovoljno se izraziti o; **~ion** odraz; razmišljanje; primjedba; **~or** reflektor
reflux ['ri:flʌks] otjecanje; oseka
reform [ri'fɔ:m] poboljšanje; reforma; poboljšati (se); reformirati; preinačiti (*ugl* **re-form**); **~ation** [refə'meiʃən] preinačenje; **~er** reformator
refract|ion [ri'frækʃən] prelamanje svjetlosti; **~ory** tvrdoglav; TECH vatrostalan; CHEM židak
refrain [ri'frein] obuzdati (se) (***from***)
refresh [ri'freʃ] osvježiti (se); **~ment** osvježenje
refrigera|te [ri'fridʒəreit] (ras)hladiti; **~tor** hladnjak; frižider
refuel [ri:'fjuəl] MOT napuniti gorivom
refuge ['refju:dʒ] utočište; zaklonište; **~e** izbjeglica
refund [ri:'fʌnd] nadoknaditi; refundirati
refurnish ['ri:'fə:niʃ] nanovo meblirati
refus|al [ri'fju:zəl] odbijanje;

uskrata; **~e** [~z] odbiti; otkloniti; uskratiti; protiviti se; ['refju:s] otpaci, smeće; izmet
refut|ation [refju'teiʃən] opovrgavanje; **~e** opovrći
regain [ri'gein] opet (za)dobiti
regard [ri'ga:d] štovanje; obzir; ***with ~ to*** s obzirom na; ***with kind ~s*** uz srdačne pozdrave; smatrati (***as***); štovati; ***as ~s*** što se tiče; **~ful** pažljiv (***of***); **~ing** što se tiče; **~less** bezobziran; bez obzira na (***of***)
regenerate [ri'dʒenəreit] preporoditi (se)
regent ['ri:dʒənt] namjesnik
regimen ['redʒimən] režim; propisan način ishrane, života; **~t** puk
region ['ri:dʒən] predjel
register ['redʒistə] registar (MUS *i* TECH); popis; upisati (se); predati (*prtljagu*); preporučiti (*pismo*); **~ed** registriran; preporučen (*pismo*)
registr|ar [redʒi'stra:] matičar; **~ation fee** upisnina; **~y office** prijavni ured; matični ured
regret [ri'gret] žaljenje; žaliti; **~table** vrijedan žaljenja
regular ['regjulə] pravilan; pravi; redovan; tačan; **~ity** pravilnost
regulat|e ['regjuleit] urediti; regulirati; **~ion** uređivanje; uredba; ***~ions*** *pl* propisi; ***traffic ~ions*** saobraćajni propisi
rehears|al [ri'hə:səl] THEAT pokus, proba; **~e** ponoviti, uvježbati; THEAT održavati probu
reign [rein] vladavina; vladati
reimburse [ri:im'bə:s] nadoknaditi; odštetiti; **~ment** naknada
rein [rein] uzda; ***~ in*** obuzdati; **~deer** sob
reinforce [ri:in'fɔ:s] pojačati; **~d concrete** armirani beton; **~ment** TECH pojačanje (*i* MIL)
reinsurance ['ri:in'ʃuərəns] reosiguranje
reiterate [ri:'itəreit] (neprestano) ponavljati
reject [ri'dʒekt] odbaciti; otkloniti; povratiti; **~ion** odbijanje; ***~ions*** *pl* škart roba
rejoic|e [ri'dʒɔis] razveseliti; veseliti se (***at***, ***in***); **~ing** veselje
rejoin ['ri:'dʒɔin] ponovo (se) sjediniti; **~der** odgovor
re|juvenescence [ri:dʒu:vi'nesns] pomlađivanje; **~lapse** povraćaj (u staro stanje, bolesti); ponovo zapasti u staro stanje
relate [ri'leit] izvijestiti; dovesti u vezu (***to***); **~d** srodan
relation [ri'leiʃən] pripovijetka; rođak; odnos; **~ship** srodstvo; odnos
relative ['relətiv] koji se odnosi (***to***); rođak

relax [ri'læks] olabaviti; ublažiti; otpustiti se; odmoriti se; **~ation** odmor
relay [ri'lei] smjena; nova zaprega; ['ri:'lei] relej; **~ race** štafeta
release [ri'li:s] osloboditi; odriješiti; ustupiti pravo; FILM dopustiti javno prikazivanje; oslobađanje (*fig*); premijera; PHOT okidač
relegate ['religeit] protjerati (***to***)
relent [ri'lent] umekšati se
relia|bility [rilaiə'biliti] pouzdanost; **~ble** pouzdan; **~nce** pouzdanje
relic ['relik] (pre)ostatak; relikvija
relief [ri'li:f] olakšanje; potpora; **~ works** *pl* javni radovi
relieve [ri'li:v] ublažiti; podupirati; izdići; ***~ nature*** obaviti nuždu
religi|on [ri'lidʒən] religija; **~ous** religiozan; vjerski
relinquish [ri'liŋkwiʃ] napustiti (namisao); odreći se; odstupiti
relish ['reliʃ] okus, tek; naläziti slast u
reluctant [ri'lʌktənt] nesklon; koji oklijeva
rely [ri'lai]: **~ (*on, upon*)** osloniti se, uzdati se
remain [ri'mein] (pre)ostati; **~der** ostatak; neprodano književno izdanje; **~s** *pl* ostaci
remark [ri'ma:k] primjedba; primijetiti; **~able** značajan
remedy ['remidi] lijek; pomoć; (iz)liječiti; pomoći
rememb|er [ri'membə] sjetiti se; ***~er me to him!*** izruči mu moje pozdrave!; **~rance** sjećanje; uspomena
remind [ri'maind] podsjetiti; opomenuti (of); **~er** opomena
remit [ri'mit] predati; doznačiti; popustiti; **~tance** (novčana) doznaka
remnant ['remnənt] ostatak (*tkanine*)
remonstra|nce [ri'mɔnstrəns] prigovor; **~te** prigovarati (***on***)
remorse [ri'mɔ:s] grižnja savjesti; **~ful** pokajnički
remote [ri'mout] dalek, udaljen; **~ control** daljinski upravljač
remov|al [ri'mu:vəl] uklanjanje; udaljavanje; otpuštanje; **~e** udaljiti; ukloniti; otpustiti; ***~e furniture*** (pre)seliti se; prijelaz u viši razred (*škole*)
remunerate [ri'mju:nəreit] nagraditi; platiti
render ['rendə] vratiti; pružati; izručiti; iskazati (*hvalu*); prevoditi; izvoditi; ***~ an account of*** položiti račun o
renew [ri'nju:] obnoviti; **~al** obnova
renounce [ri'nauns] okaniti se, odreći se; poricati
renovate ['renəveit] obnoviti

renown [ri'naun] slava; ugled; **~ed** slavan
rent pukotina; najam(nina); zakup(nina); iznajmiti, zakupiti; **~-free** koji je slobodan od zakupnine ili stanarine
renunciation [rinʌnsi'eiʃən] odricanje
reopen ['riː'oupən] ponovo otvoriti
reorganiz|ation ['riːɔːgənai'zeiʃən] preuređenje; **~e** reorganizirati; sanirati
repair [ri'pɛə] popravak; popraviti; **~ *to*** uputiti se; ***out of* ~** trošan
reparation [repə'reiʃən] odšteta; nadoknada
repartee [repaː'tiː] brz i duhovit odgovor
repast [ri'paːst] obrok
repatriat|e [riː'pætrieit] vratiti (se) u domovinu; [~iit] povratnik; **~ion** povratak u domovinu
repay [riː'pei] vratiti dug; **~ment** otplata
repeat [ri'piːt] ponoviti; **~ed** ponovljen; **~er** ponavljač; ura koja odbija sate; **~-order** ponovljena narudžba
repel [ri'pel] odbiti; potisnuti; suzbiti (*i fig*)
repent [ri'pent] (po)kajati se; **~ance** kajanje
repetition [repi'tiʃən] ponavljanje
replace [riː'pleis] opet (po-) staviti; nadomjestiti
replenish [ri'pleniʃ] nadopuniti
replete [riː'pliːt] napunjen, pun
reply [ri'plai] odgovoriti; odgovor; **~ postcard** dopisnica s odgovorom
report [ri'pɔːt] izvještaj; glasina; prasak; pucanj; izvijestiti **([up]on)**; (pri)javiti se; **~er** izvjestitelj
repose [ri'pouz] mir; počinak; odmoriti se
reprehen|d [repri'hend] koriti; **~sible** pokudan; **~sion** prijekor
represent [repri'zent] predstaviti; THEAT prikazivati; **~ation** predstavljanje; prikazivanje; zastupanje; **~ative** zastupnik; značajan; koji predstavlja; reprezentativan
repress [ri'pres] svladati; ugušiti; **~ion** obuzdavanje; zatomljivanje
reprieve [ri'priːv] odgoda
reprimand ['reprimaːnd] ukor
reprint ['riː'print] nanovo štampati; novo nepromijenjeno izdanje
reproach [ri'proutʃ] predbacivanje; predbacivati; **~ful** prijekoran
reproduc|e [riːprə'djuːs] ponovo proizvesti; reproducirati; **~tion** ponovo izvođenje; reprodukcija; reproduciranje
repro|of [ri'pruːf] predbaci-

vanje; **~ve** [~v] kuditi; koriti
reptile ['reptail] gmizavac
republic [ri'pʌblik] republika; **~an** republički; republikanac
republi|cation ['ri:pʌbli'keiʃən] novo izdanje; **~sh** ponovo izdati
repugnan|ce [ri'pʌgnəns] nesklad (***to***); **~t** protuslovan; odvratan
repuls|e [ri'pʌls] odbiti; **~ive** odbojan; odvratan
reput|able ['repjutəbl] čestit; ugledan; **~ation** (dobar) glas; ugled; **~e** ugled; smatrati za
request [ri'kwest] zahtjev; molba; potražnja; (za)moliti; ***at a p's ~*** na čije traženje; ***by ~*** na zahtjev
require [ri'kwaiə] tražiti; zahtjevati; trebati; **~ment** zahtjev; uvjet; potreba
requisite ['rekwizit] potreban; zahtjev; potrepština
requite [ri'kwait] naplatiti
rescue ['reskju:] spasenje; oslobođenje; spasiti; osloboditi
research [ri'sə:tʃ] (naučno) istraživanje
resembl|ance [ri'zembləns] sličnost; **~e** sličiti, biti nalik na
resent [ri'zent] zamjerati; **~ful** uvredljiv; kivan; **~ment** ogorčenost
reservation [rezə'veiʃən] rezervacija
reserve [ri'zə:v] zaliha (*i fig*); zadržati; sačuvati; rezervirati; **~d** uzdržljiv; rezerviran
reshuffle ['ri:'ʃʌfl] pregrupirati; promiješati (*karte*)
reside [ri'zaid] stanovati; počivati
residen|ce ['rezidəns] prebivalište; **~ce *permit*** dozvola boravka; **~t** koji stalno boravi, koji stanuje
resign [ri'zain] napustiti; odreći se; dati ostavku; **~ation** [rezig'neiʃən] ostavka; rezignacija; **~ed** odan, predan
resist [ri'zist] oprijeti se; **~ance** otpor(nost) (*i* EL)
resolut|e ['rezəlu:t] odlučan; **~eness** odlučnost; **~ion** odluka, odlučnost; *fig* rješenje
resolve [ri'zɔlv] rješiti; rastvoriti
resort [ri'zɔ:t] utočište; ***health ~*** lječilište; ***summer ~*** ljetovalište; često pohađati
resound [ri'zaund] odjekivati
resource [ri'sɔ:s] pomoćno sredstvo; vrelo; **~ful** snalažljiv
respect [ris'pekt] obzir; poštovanje; ***in this ~*** u tom pogledu; ***pay one's ~s to a p*** izraziti poštovanje kome; lijepo pozdraviti koga; (po)štovati; cijeniti; ticati se; **~able** ugledan; poštovan; **~ful** pun poštovanja; uljudan;

~ing u vezi sa; **~ive** koji se odnosi na svakog pojedinog; **~ively** odnosno
respiration [respə'reiʃən] disanje
respite ['respait] odgoda
resplendent [ris'plendənt] sjajan
respond [ris'pɔnd] odgovoriti; reagirati (***to***)
responsi|bility [rispɔnsə'biliti] odgovornost; **~ble** odgovoran; **~ve** prijemljiv (***to***)
rest mir; počinak; pauza; **~** (***up***)***on*** osnivati se na; počivati na; **~ cure** liječenje; odmaranje; odmor; ostatak; ostali; odmarati se; osloniti se
restitution [resti'tju:ʃən] uspostavljanje; vraćanje
restless ['restlis] uznemiren; nemiran; **~ness** uznemirenost, nemir
restor|ation [restə'reiʃən] obnova; uspostava; **~e** [ris'tɔ:] uspostaviti; vratiti na prijašnji položaj (***to***); nadoknaditi; ***~e to health*** ozdraviti; **~er**: ***hair ~er*** sredstvo za porast kose
restrain [ris'trein] zadržati; zatomiti; **~t** obuzdavanje; pritvor
restrict [ris'trikt] ograničiti; **~ion** ograničenje; restrikcija
result [ri'zʌlt] rezultat; proizlaziti (***from***); **~ *in*** imati za posljedicu
resume [ri'zju:m] ponovo dobiti; zauzeti; rezimirati
retail ['ri:teil] trgovina na malo; **~er** trgovac na malo
retain [ri'tein] zadržati; sačuvati
retard [ri'ta:d] otezati; zakasniti
retch [ri:tʃ] dolaziti na povraćanje, podrigivati se
retire [ri'taiə] povući (se); poći u mirovinu; **~ment** povlačenje; povučenost; mirovina
retort [ri'tɔ:t] oštar (duhovit) odgovor; odgovoriti; odbrusiti kome
retouch ['ri:'tʌtʃ] preraditi; PHOT retuširati
retrace [ri'treis] vratiti se istim putem
retract [ri'trækt] opozvati; **~able** koji se može opozvati; uvlačiv
retreat [ri'tri:t] povlačenje; povući se
retribution [retri'bju:ʃən] odmazda
retrieve [ri'tri:v] ponovo dobiti
retro|active [retrou'æktiv] koji djeluje unatrag; **~spective view** pogled unazad
return [ri'tə:n] povratak; (uz)vraćanje; dobitak; izvještaj; izborni rezultat; vratiti (se); odgovoriti; donijeti prihod; ***by ~*** (***of post***) obratnom (prvom) poštom; ***many happy ~s*** (***of the day***) sretan rođendan (doživio još mnogo rođendana); **~ ticket** po-

vratna karta
Rev. = **Reverend**
reval|orization ['riːvælərai'zeiʃən], **~uation** revalorizacija
reveal [ri'viːl] otkriti; objaviti
revel ['revl] naslađivati se (*in*); **~ry** bančenje; razuzdana zabava
revenge [ri'vendʒ] osveta; revanš (kod igre); osvetiti (se); **~ful** osvetljiv
revenue ['revinjuː] dohodak
revere [ri'viə] (po)štovati; **~nce** ['revərəns] (po)štovanje; strahopoštovanje; (po)štovati; **~nd** častan
rever|se [ri'vəːs] protivnost; naličje; poraz; obrnut; ***~se gear*** MOT unazadni hod; obrnuti, okrenuti; **~sible** koji se može okrenuti; poništiv; **~t** okrenuti (se) natrag; vratiti se (*to*)
review [ri'vjuː] ponovo ispitivanje; pregled; napisati prikaz; vršiti smotru; **~er** recenzent, kritičar
revis|e [ri'vaiz] revidirati; ponovni pregled; revizija; **~ion** [ri'viʒən] revizija; preispitivanje
reviv|al [ri'vaivəl] oživljenje; preporod; **~e** oživjeti
revocation [revə'keiʃən] opoziv
revoke [ri'vouk] opozvati
revolt [ri'voult] (po)buna; (po)buniti se
revolution [revə'luːʃən] okretanje; prevrat; revolucija; **~ary** revolucionaran; **~ist** revolucionar; **~ize** radikalno izmijeniti, revolucionirati; pobuniti
revolve [ri'vɔlv] okretati se
revulsion [ri'vʌlʃən] preokret (osjećaja)
reward [ri'wɔːd] nagrada; nagraditi
rheumat|ic [ruː'mætik] reumatičan; **~ism** ['ruːmətizəm] reumatizam
Rhine [rain] Rajna
rhubarb ['ruːbaːb] rabarbara
rhyme [raim] rima; srok; rimovati (se)
rhythm ['riðm] ritam
rib rebro
ribbon ['ribən] vrpca, traka; pruga
rice [rais] riža
rich [ritʃ] bogat (*in*); skupocjen; pun (*glas*); mastan, težak (*jelo*); **~es** *pl* bogatstvo
rickets ['rikits] rahitis
rid osloboditi; ***get ~ of*** riješiti se
riddle ['ridl] zagonetka; grubo sito; odgonetati; prosijati
ride [raid] jahanje; vožnja; jahati; voziti se; **~r** jahač
ridge [ridʒ] hrbat; lanac brda
ridicul|e ['ridikjuːl] ismijavati; **~ous** smiješan; **~ousness** smiješnost
riding-habit ['raidiŋhæbit] odijelo za jahanje
rifle ['raifl] puška; opljačkati
rift pukotina; jaz

rigging ['rigiŋ] MAR snast
right [rait] pravo; desna strana; ispravan; tačan; desni; ***be ~*** biti u pravu; ***on the ~ side of 50*** još ispod 50 godina; ***~ on*** ravno; **~eous** ['-tʃəs] pravedan
rigid ['ridʒid] ukočen; strog
rigo|rous ['rigərəs] strog; **~ur** strogost
rim rub, ivica
rind [raind] kora; lupina; koža slanine
ring [riŋ] prsten; kolut; krug; boksački ring; zvonjava; ***the ~*** boksači; zvoniti; zvečati; ***~ the bell*** pozvoniti; ***~ off*** *tel* objesiti slušalicu; ***~ up*** *tel* nazvati; **~-leader** kolovođa
rink [riŋk] klizalište (i umjetno)
rinse [rins] ispirati
riot ['raiət] metež; buna; orgijanje; činiti izgrede; **~er** izgrednik
rip (raz)derati; ***~ up*** rasparati
ripe [raip] zreo; **~n** (sa)zreti; **~ness** zrelost
ripple ['ripl] mreškati (se)
rise [raiz] dizanje; povišenje; (po)rast; dizati se; ustati; pobuniti se; izlaziti (*sunce*); nabujati
rising ['raiziŋ] ustanak
risk opasnost, rizik; stavljati na kocku; ***run the ~*** izlagati se opasnosti; riskirati; **~y** riskantan
rival ['raivəl] suparnik (***in***); takmičiti se; **~ry** rivalstvo
river ['rivə] rijeka; potok
rivet ['rivit] zakovica; prikovati
rivulet ['rivjulit] rječica
road [roud] cesta; ***~s*** *pl* sidrište; **~ster** običan bicikl; otvoren dvosjed (*automobil*); **~way** kolnik
roar [rɔː] rikati; tutnjeti
roast [roust] peći; (is)pržiti; pečen; pržen
rob orobiti; **~ber** razbojnik; **~bery** razbojstvo
robe [roub] službena odjeća; talar
robust [rə'bʌst] krepak; snažan
rock [rɔk] hrid, stijena; ljuljati; tresti; **~-bottom** najniži (*cijena*)
rocket ['rɔkit] raketa; **~ plane** raketni avion; **~ propulsion** raketni pogon
rocking-chair stolica za ljuljanje
rocky ['rɔki] kamenit; pun pećina
rod prut; šipka
roe [rou] ikra; srna; **~buck** srndać
rogu|e [roug] lupež; vragoljan; **~ish** lopovski; vragoljast
roll [roul] smotak; TECH valjak; zemička; popis; valjati; (za)motati; saviti (*cigaretu*); vrtjeti se; talasati se; ***~ up*** smotati (se); **~-call** prozivka; **~er** valjak; **~er-skate** koturaljka

rolling|-mill valjaonica; **~-stock** *rly* vozni park
roll-top desk rolo pisaći stol
Roman ['roumən] rimski; Rimljanin
romantic [rə'mæntik] romantičan
romp nestaško; ludovati; **~ers** *pl* dječja odjeća za igru
röntgeno|gram [rɔnt'genəgræm] rentgenogram; **~graphy** rentgenografija; **~scopy** rentgenoskopija
roof [ru:f] krov; pokriti krovom; **~ *of the mouth*** nepce; **~ing felt** krovna ljepenka
room [rum] prostor; soba; mjesto; *pl* stan
root [ru:t] korijen; ukorijeniti; prerovati; **~ *out*** iščupati
rope [roup] uže, konop; konopcem svezati; **~-dancer** plesač na užetu; **~-ladder** ljestve od užeta
ros|e [rouz] ruža; **~y** ružičast
rot trulež; trunuti
rotary ['routəri] obrtni; rotacioni
rotate [rou'teit] vrtjeti (se)
rotten ['rɔtn] gnjio, truo; odvratan
rouble ['ru:bl] rubalj
rouge [ru:ʒ] rumenilo; ruž
rough [rʌf] grub; surov; neotesan; **~ *it*** mučno se probijati; **~-neck** *Am sl* siledžija; **~ness** surovost; neotesanost
Roumania [ru:'meinjə] Rumunjska; **~n** rumunjski; Rumunj
round [raund] okrugao; pun; okružiti; obilaziti; unaokolo; krug; runda; prečka ljestava; ***all the year* ~** kroz cijelu godinu; **~ *off*** zaokružiti; **~ trip** kružno putovanje
roundabout ['raundəbaut]: **~ *way*** zaobilazan put; **~ *traffic*** kružni saobraćaj
round|-table conference konferencija za okruglim stolom; **~-up** *Am* racija
rouse [rauz] probuditi; pobuditi
route [ru:t] put; maršruta
rove [rouv] skitati se; švrljati
row [rou] red, niz; veslanje; veslati
row [rau] gungula; svađa; ***kick up a* ~** dići galamu
rowdy ['raudi] kavgadžija
row|er ['rouə] veslač; **~ing-boat** čamac na vesla
royal ['rɔiəl] kraljevski; **~ty** kraljevstvo; kraljevska osoba; tantijema, autorski honorar
rub [rʌb] trljati; **~ *in*** utrljati; **~ *off*** istrti
rubber ['rʌbə] guma; gumica; **~s** *pl* galoše; **~neck** *Am sl* radoznala osoba
rubbish ['rʌbiʃ] smeće; besmislica
ruby ['ru:bi] rubin
rudder ['rʌdə] kormilo
rude [ru:d] grub; sirov; neotesan; neizrađen; **~ness** grubost
rudiments ['ru:dimənts] *pl*

osnovni elementi
ruff [rʌf] nabran ovratnik
ruffian ['rʌfjən] lupež
rug [rʌg] debeo vunen pokrivač; sag
ruin [ruin] ruševina; *ugl* **~s** ruševine; uništiti; **~ous** ruševan; srušen; štetan
rule [ru:l] pravilo; ***as a ~*** u pravilu; propis; ***~ of the road*** saobraćajni propis; vladavina; ravnalo; odrediti; vladati; upravljati; linirati papir; **~r** vladar; ravnalo
rumble ['rʌmbl] tutnjeti
ruminant ['ru:minənt] preživač
rumour ['ru:mə] glasina
run [rʌn] trčati; juriti; teći; biti u pogonu; kružiti; THEAT davati se; glasiti (*tekst*); kolati (*glasine*); voditi (*posao*); trčanje; trka; navala; ***the common ~*** prosjek; običan tip; ***~ down*** isteći; prestati ići (*ura*); iscrpsti se; grditi koga; ***I have ~ out of tobacco*** ponestalo mi je duhana; ***~ short*** ostati bez čega; ***~ up to*** popeti se do; **~about (car)** mali automobil; **~away** bjegunac; **~ner** trkač, teklić; **~ner-up** SPORT onaj koji se je plasirao na drugo mjesto; **~ning board** MOT RLW papuča
rupture ['rʌptʃə] raskid; kila
rural ['ruərəl] seoski
rush [rʌʃ] navala; jurnjava; ***~ at*** nasrnuti na; ***~ through*** požurivati; **~ hours** satovi najvećeg prometa; navaliti; jurnuti; srljati
Russia ['rʌʃə] Rusija; **~n** ruski; Rus
rust [rʌst] rđa; rđati
rustic ['rʌstik] seoski; ladanjski
rustle ['rʌsl] šuštati
rusty ['rʌsti] rđav
rut [rʌt] kolotečina
ruthless ['ru:θlis] nemilosrdan
rutted ['rʌtid] utrt (*put*)
rye [rai] raž

S

S. = **Saint**; **South**; **s.** = **second(s)**; **shilling(s)**
S. A. = **South Africa** *ili* **America**; **Salvation Army**
sable ['seibl] samur(ovina) (krzno)
sabre ['seibə] sablja
sack [sæk] vreća; kratak kaput; pljačka; pljačkati; ***give (get) the ~*** dati (dobiti) otkaz; **~cloth** tkanina za vreće
sacred ['seikrid] svet
sacri|fice ['sækrifais] žrtva; žrtvovati; **~lege** ['-lidʒ] svetogrđe; **~sty** ['-sti] sakristija
sad [sæd] žalostan; tmuran;

~den (ra)žalostiti (se)
saddle ['sædl] sedlo; osedlati; **~r** sedlar
sadness ['sædnis] žalost
safe [seif] siguran; zdrav; bezopasan; ormarić za hranu; željezna blagajna; sef (*u banci*)
safety ['seifti] sigurnost; **~-pin** pribadača; **~-razor** brijaći aparat
saffron ['sæfrən] šafran
sagacious [sə'geiʃəs] oštrouman
sail [seil] jedro; jedriti; ploviti; **~ing-ship** jedrilica; **~or** mornar; ***be a good (bad) ~or*** dobro (slabo) podnositi more
saint [seint] svetac
sake [seik]: ***for the ~ of*** za volju; ***for my ~*** mene radi
salad ['sæləd] salata
salary ['sæləri] (mjesečna) plaća; davati plaću
sale [seil] (ras)prodaja; prodja; ***public ~*** dražba; **~able** koji se lako prodaje; **~sman**, **~swoman** prodavač(ica)
salient ['seiljənt] izbočen
saline ['seilain] slan
saliva [sə'laivə] slina
sallow ['sælou] blijed; žućkast
salmon ['sæmən] losos
saloon [sə'lu:n] salon; *Am* krčma
salt [sɔ:lt] sol; slan; (po)soliti; **~-cellar** soljenka; **~petre** salitra; **~-works** solana
salutary ['sæljutəri] ljekovit; zdrav
salute [sə'lu:t] pozdrav; počasna paljba; pozdraviti; salutirati
salvage ['sælvidʒ] spasavanje; spasiti
salvation [sæl'veiʃən] spas (*duše*); **♀ Army** Armija spasa
salve [sælv] spasiti
same [seim]: ***the ~*** isti; spomenuti; ***it is all the ~ to me*** svejedno mi je
sample ['sa:mpl] uzorak; uzeti *ili* dati uzorak
sanct|ify ['sæŋktifai] proglasiti svecem; posvetiti; **~imonious** licemjeran; **~ion** sankcija; potvrda; odobriti; **~uary** svetište
sand [sænd] pijesak; **~s** *pl* pješčani prud; **~blast** pješčani mlaz; **~-glass** pješčana ura; **~-shoes** cipele za plažu
sandwich ['sænwidʒ] sendvič; **~-man** (*ulični*) nosač plakata (reklama)
sane [sein] razborit
sanguinary ['sæŋgwinəri] krvoločan
sanitary ['sænitəri] zdravstven; **~ towel** mjesečni uložak
sanit|ation [sæni'teiʃən] zdravstvo; sanitarni uređaji; **~y** zdrav razum
sap [sæp] sok (*drveća etc*).
sapphire ['sæfaiə] safir
sarcasm ['sa:kæzəm] sarka-

zam
sardine [sa:'di:n] sardina
sash [sæʃ] ešarpa; **~ window** engleski prozor (*za dizanje i spuštanje*)
satchel ['sætʃəl] školska torbica
sateen ['sæti:n] atlas (*tkanina*)
satellite ['sætəlait] satelit; **~ dish** satelitska antena
sati|ate ['seiʃieit] (pre)zasititi; **~ation** prezasićenost; **~ety** [sə'taiəti] zasićenost
satin ['sætin] atlas (*tkanina*)
satirist ['sætərist] satiričar
satis|faction [sætis'fækʃən] zadovoljenje; zadovoljstvo; **~factory** zavoljavajući, dovoljan; **~fied** zadovoljan; **~fy** zadovoljiti; udovoljiti; uvjeriti
saturate ['sætʃəreit] CHEM zasititi
Saturday ['sætədi] subota
sauce [sɔ:s] umak; sok; **~-boat** zdjelica za umak; **~r** tanjurić
saucy ['sɔ:si] *coll* drzak; obijestan
saunter ['sɔ:ntə] tumarati; besposličiti
sausage ['sɔsidʒ] kobasica
savage ['sævidʒ] divlji; divljak
save [seiv] spasiti; poštedjeti (***from***); (u)štedjeti; ***~ that*** osim ako
saveloy ['sævilɔi] safalada
saving ['seiviŋ] štedljiv; ***~s*** *pl* uštedjevina; **~s-bank** štedionica
saviour ['seivjə] spasilac; ♀ Spasitelj
savour ['seivə] tek, okus; imati tek, mirisati (***of***); **~y** ukusan
savoy [sə'vɔi] BOT bijela vrzina; ♀ Savoja
saw [sɔ:] pila; piliti; **~dust** piljevina; **~-mill** pilana
Saxon ['sæksən] (anglo)saski; Sas; **~y** Saska
say [sei] reći; ***that is to ~*** to jest; ***I ~!*** hej! čujte!; ***you don't ~ so*** što govorite! je li moguće!; ***he is said to be*** govori se da je on; ***have a ~ in*** reći što se misli o; **~ing** govor; izreka
scab [skæb] krasta; svrab; štrajkolomac
scaffold ['skæfəld] skele; stratište; **~ing** skele (*za gradnju*)
scald [skɔ:ld] (po)pariti; prekuhati (*mlijeko*)
scale [skeil] ljuska (*ribe etc.*); korice džepnog noža; zdjelica vage; mjerilo; ljuštiti (se); ostrugati; vagati
scamp [skæmp] protuha
scan [skæn] pretraživanje; pretražiti; **~ner** pretražnik
scandal ['skændl] skandal; **~ize** užasnuti koga; **~ous** sramotan; sablažnjiv
Scandinavia [skændi'neivjə] Skandinavija; **~n** skandinavski; Skandinavac

scant|iness ['skæntinis] oskudnost; **~y** oskudan
scape|goat ['skeipgout] onaj koji ispašta tuđe grijehe; **~grace** nitkov
scar [ska:] ožiljak; ljaga; litica; načiniti brazgotinu; zacijeliti
scarc|e [skɛəs] rijedak; oskudan; **~ely** jedva; **~ity** oskudnost; nestašica (***of***)
scare [skɛə] (pre)plašiti; **~-crow** strašilo za ptice (*i fig*); **~monger** paničar
scarf [ska:f] ešarpa; marama; kravata; TECH spojnica; **~-pin** igla za kravatu
scarlet ['ska:lit] grimizan; **~ fever** šarlah
scarred [ska:d] pun brazgotina
scatter ['skætə] rasuti (se); raštrkati
scavenger ['skævindʒə] pometač ulica
scene [si:n] scena; mjesto radnje; pozornica; *pl* kulise; **~ry** krajobraz; dekoracije pozornice
scent [sent] (mio)miris; parfem; njuh; trag; namirisati; nanjušiti
sceptic ['skeptik] skeptik; **~al** skeptičan
sceptre ['septə] žezlo
schedule ['ʃedju:l] tabela; *Am* vozni red; napraviti raspored; odrediti; **~d** *Am* predviđen
scheme [ski:m] shema; plan; planirati
scholar ['skɔlə] učenik; učenjak; **~ship** naobrazba; stipendija
school [sku:l] škola; ***at ~*** u školi; **~fellow** školski drug; **~ing** školovanje
sciatica [sai'ætikə] išijas
scien|ce ['saiəns] znanost; prirodne nauke; **~tific** [~'tifik] (prirodo)znanstven
scissors ['sizəz] *pl* škare
scoff [skɔf] poruga; rugati se
scold [skould] (iz)grditi; **~ing** grđenje
scoop [sku:p] lopatica; kutljača; ***~ out*** (iz)grabiti; izdupsti
scooter ['sku:tə] romobil; skuter
scope [skoup] vidokrug; djelokrug
scorch [skɔ:tʃ] opržiti; opaliti; *coll* juriti najvećom brzinom
score [skɔ:] rovaš; račun; dvadeset (*komada*); SPORT bod; partitura; (o)bilježiti rezovima; SPORT postići bodove; pobijediti
scorn [skɔ:n] prezir; prezirati; **~ful** preziran
Scotch [skɔtʃ] Škotski; ***the ~*** škoti; **~man** Škot
scot-free ['skɔt'fri:] nekažnjen
Scotland ['skɔtlənd] Škotska; **~ Yard** glavni stan londonske policije
Scot|sman ['skɔtsmən] Škot;

~tish škotski
scoundrel ['skaundrəl] hulja
scourge [skə:dʒ] bič (*i fig*); bičevati
scout [skaut] izviđati; izviđač; uhoda; ***Boy ~s*** izviđači
scrabble ['skræbl] (po)šarati; črčkati; škrabati
scramble ['skræmbl] verati se; otimati se (***for***); **~d eggs** kajgana
scrap [skræp] komadić; izrezak (*iz novina*); ***~ of paper*** komad papira; baciti u staro željezo; **~iron** staro željezo
scrape [skreip] struganje; grebenje; grepsti; (o)strugati; **~r** strugalo
scratch [skrætʃ] ogrebotina; struganje; (iz)grepsti
scrawl [skrɔ:l] črčkati; **~ing** črčkanje
scream [skri:m] vrisak; ***it was a ~*** bilo je da prasneš; vrisnuti;**~ing** vrištav; vrlo smiješan
screen [skri:n] zaslon; FILM ekran; platno; zaklanjati; zasjeniti; štititi
screw [skru:] vijak; (za)šarafiti; **~-driver** odvijač; **~-propeller** brodski vijak; **~-steamer** parobrod na vijak
scribble ['skribl] črčkanje; (na)črčkati
script [skript] rukopis; pismo; FILM knjiga snimanja; **~ure** ['-tʃə] Sveto pismo
scrofula ['skrɔfjulə] škrofule
scrounge [skraundʒ] ukrasti; užicati
scrub [skrʌb] šikara; ribati; trljati; **~ber** četka za ribanje (od žice)
scruple ['skru:pl] skrupula; dvoumica
scrupulous ['skru:pjuləs] skrupulozan; brižljiv
scrutin|eer [skru:ti'niə] brojitelj glasova; **~ize** pomno ispitati
scuffle ['skʌfl] tučnjava; rvanje; tući se
sculp|tor ['skʌlptə] kipar; **~ture** kiparstvo
scum [skʌm] pjena; *fig* talog
scurf [skə:f] prhut; perut
scurry ['skʌri] juriti; trčkarati
scurvy ['skə:vi] MED skorbut
scuttle ['skʌtl] posuda za ugljen
scythe [saið] kosa; (po)kositi
sea [si:] more; veliki val; ***at ~*** na moru
seal [si:l] tuljan; pečat; žig; (za)pečatiti; TECH zabrtviti; plombirati (*i* ***~ up***)
sea-level morska razina
sealing-wax ['si:liŋwæks] pečatni vosak
seam [si:m] šav; porub
seaman ['si:mən] pomorac
seamstress ['semstris] švelja
sea|-piece PAINT morski pejsaž; **~plane** hidroplan
search [sə:tʃ] (pre)tražiti; sondirati; istraživati (***for***);

in ~ of u potrazi za; **~light** reflektor
seasick ['si:sik] bolestan od morske bolesti
seaside ['si:'said] obalno područje; **~ resort** morsko kupalište
season ['si:zn] godišnje doba; ***height of the ~*** glavna sezona; ***cherries are in ~*** sada je vrijeme trešanja; ostaviti da dozrije; odležati; začiniti; prekaliti (***to***); **~able** pravodoban; primjeren; **~ing** začin; **~-ticket** mjesečna (godišnja) karta; pretplatna karta
seat [si:t] sjedalo; sjedište; mjesto; boravište; (po)sjesti; ***be ~ed*** sjediti; ležati (naselje)
sea|weed ['si:wi:d] morska trava; **~worthy** sposoban za plovidbu morem
seclude [si'klu:d] odijeliti
second ['sekənd] drugi; slijedeći; sekunda; **~ary** sekundaran; sporedan; **~-hand** rabljen; antikvaran; **~-rate** drugorazredan
secre|cy ['si:krisi] tajnovitost; šutnja; **~t** (po)tajan; šutljiv; tajna; **~tary** ['sekrətri] tajnik
secret|e [si'kri:t] izlučivati; **~ion** izlučivanje
sect [sekt] sekta
section ['sekʃən] sekcija; presjek; odio; *Am* **~ manager** šef odjela
secular ['sekjulə] svjetovni; stoljetni
secure [si'kjuə] siguran; osigurati; (za)štititi (***from, against***)
security [si'kjuəriti] sigurnost; bezbrižnost; kaucija; ***securities*** *pl* vrijednosni papiri
sedan [si'dæn] nosiljka (*i* ***~ chair***); limuzina
sedate [si'deit] staložen
sedative ['sedətiv] sredstvo za umirenje
sedentary ['sedntəri] **life** sjedilački način života
sediment ['sedimənt] talog
seduce [si'dju:s] zavesti; **~r** zavodnik
see [si:] vidjeti; ***I ~*** razumijem; promatrati; posjećivati; ***wish to ~ a p*** željeti s nekim razgovarati; ***~ a th done*** brinuti da se što učini; ***~ a p off*** otpratiti koga; ***~ out*** ispratiti koga; ***~ a th through*** provesti što do kraja
seed [si:d] sjeme, sjemenka; klica
seeing ['si:iŋ]: ***worth ~*** vrijedan da se vidi; ***~ that*** budući da
seek [si:k] tražiti; nastojati (oko)
seem [si:m] činiti se; **~ing** prividan; **~ly** doličan
seesaw ['si:'sɔ:] ljuljačka; ljuljati se
seethe [si:ð] kipjeti
segregate ['segrigeit] odije-

liti
seiz|e [si:z] zgrabiti; prisvojiti; oteti; **~ure** otimanje
seldom ['seldəm] rijetko
select [si'lekt] odabrati; izabirati; **~ion** selekcija; **~ive** RADIO selektivan; **~ivity** selektivnost
self, *pl* ***selves*** sam; **~-acting** koji radi sam od sebe; **~-centred** egocentričan; **~-command** samosvladavanje; **~-conceit** uobražavanje; **~-contained** odijeljen; povučen; **~-control** vladanje samim sobom; **~-deception** varanje sama sebe; **~-defense** samoobrana; **~-government** samoupravljanje; **~-interest** koristoljublje; **~ish** sebičan; **~preservation** samoodržanje; **~-starter** MOT elektropokretač; **~-willed** samovoljan
sell [sel] prodavati, prodati; imati prođu (roba); ***~ off, ~ out*** (iz)vršiti rasprodaju; **~er** prodavač; ***best ~er*** bestseler (knjiga); **~ing staff** prodavači; **~ing price** prodajna cijena
seltzer ['seltsə] vrst mineralne vode
semblance ['sembləns] sličnost; lik
semi ... ['semi] polu ...; **~-final** polufinale; **~-manufactured product** polufinalni proizvod
semolina [semə'li:nə] pšenična krupica
senate ['senit] senat
send (po)slati, otpremiti; ***~ word*** poručiti; ***~ for*** poslati po
senile ['si:nail] senilan
senior ['si:njə] stariji; pretpostavljeni
sensation [sen'seiʃən] osjet; dojam; uzbuđenje; senzacija; **~al report** senzacionalan izvještaj
sense [sens] smisao; osjet; razum; značenje; **~less** besmislen; nerazuman; beščutan
sensi|bility [sensi'biliti] osjećajnost; osjetljivost (***to***); **~ble** osjetan; razuman; osjetljiv; ***be ~ble of*** imati osjećaj za; **~tive** osjetljiv; osjećajan
sensual ['sensjuəl] čulni; **~ity** putenost
sentence ['sentəns] JUR osuda; GRAM rečenica; izreći osudu
sentiment ['sentimənt] osjećaj; mišljenje; **~al** sentimentalan, osjećajan
sentinel ['sentinl], **sentry** straža
separat|e ['seprit] poseban; odvojen; ['~reit] odvojiti; rastati se; **~ion** rastava; **~or** separator
September [səp'tembə] rujan, septembar
septic ['septik] septičan
sepulchre ['sepəlkə] grob-

nica
seque|l ['si:kwəl] nastavak priče; zaključak; **~nce** slijed; tok; sekvenca
sequestrat|e [si'kwestreit] zaplijeniti; **~or** upravljač imovine koja je stavljena pod sekvestar
serene [si'ri:n] vedar; miran; *kao naslov* ♀ prejasan
seri|al ['siəriəl] serijski; koji izlazi u nastavcima; **~es** *pl* red, serija; **~es connexion** serijsko povezivanje
serious ['siəriəs] ozbiljan
sermon ['sə:mən] propovijed
serpent ['sə:pənt] zmija
servant ['sə:vənt] sluga, sluškinja; *pl* služinčad
serve [sə:v] (po)služiti; podvoriti; dobro postupati; postići svrhu; TENNIS servirati; ***(it)* ~s *him right*** pravo mu budi
service ['sə:vis] služba; služba božja; pogon; promet; korist; jedaći pribor; TENNIS servis; **~able** koristan; uslužan
servi|le ['sə:vail] ropski; servilan; **~tude** ['~vitju:d] ropstvo
session ['seʃən] zasjedanje
set (po)staviti; položiti; namjestiti; udesiti; (po)saditi; zaći (*sunce*); utvrđen; ustaljen; propisan; nir; serija; garnitura; pribor za jelo; TENNIS set; kroj (*odjeće*); RADIO aparat; ***~ at ease*** umiriti; ***~ forth*** dokazati; poredati; razložiti; ***~ out*** krenuti (*na put*); uputiti (se); ***~ up with*** obračunati sa; **~back** *fig* pogoršanje; **~ting** postavljanje; zalazak; usađivanje dragulja; THEAT inscenacija; kompozicija
settle ['setl] ustanoviti; nastaniti (se); smjestiti (se); namjestiti; urediti; zaključiti (*posao*); opskrbiti; riješiti (*pitanje*); namiriti (*račun*); staložiti se; ustaliti se (*vrijeme*); odležati (*pivo, duhan*); ***~ down*** smjestiti se; naseliti se; **~d** određen; stalan (*vrijeme, etc.*); **~ment** osnutak; određenje; naredba; pogodba; zavičajnost; COM izravnanje; naseljenje; naselje; **~r** naseljenik
seven ['sevn] sedam; **~fold** sedmerostruk; **~teen(th)** sedamnaest(i); **~th** sedmi; sedmina; **~tieth** sedamdeseti; **~ty** sedamdeset
sever ['sevə] odijeliti (se)
several ['sevrəl] nekoliko; različan
severe [si'viə] strog; žestok; oštar; ozbiljan; krut
severity [si'veriti] strogost; žestina
sew [sou] šivati; prošivati (*knjigu*); **~er** šivač(ica); ['sjuə] odvodni kanal
sex [seks] spol
sexton ['sekstən] crkvenjak; grobar

sexual ['seksjuəl] spolni; seksualni; **~ desire** spolni nagon; **~ intercourse** spolno općenje
shabby ['ʃæbi] otrcan
shade [ʃeid] hlad(ovina); sjenilo (*svjetiljke*); zaslon; nijansa; zasjeniti; štititi (*od svjetla*); potamniti; šatirati
shadow ['ʃædou] sjena; sjenka; zasjeniti; **~y** hladovit
shady ['ʃeidi] sjenovit; taman; ***on the ~ side of 40*** preko 40 godina star
shaft [ʃa:ft] koplje; motka; TECH vreteno; os; rudo; MIN rov, šaht
shaggy ['ʃægi] čupav, rutav
shake [ʃeik] (pro)drmati; tresti; drhtati; potresanje; ***~ hands*** rukovati se
shaky ['ʃeiki] klimav; drhtav
shall [ʃæl] treba da; ću, ćemo (za tvorbu futura)
shallow ['ʃælou] plitak; plićak
sham [ʃæm] neprav; lažan; pretvarati se
shame [ʃeim] stid; sramota; posramiti; **~faced** stidljiv; **~less** besraman
shampoo [ʃæm'pu:] prati glavu
shank [ʃæŋk] goljenica
shape [ʃeip] oblik, lik; ***in bad ~*** u lošem stanju; oblikovati; **~less** bezobličan; **~ly** skladan; lijep
share [ʃɛə] dio; dionica; dijeliti (***amongst***); ***have a ~ in*** sudjelovati u; **~holder** dioničar
shark [ʃa:k] morski pas
sharp [ʃa:p] oštar; nabrušen; rezak; lukav; ***at 10 ~*** tačno u 10; ***look ~*** pazi! brzo! **~en** (na)oštriti; **~ener** brus za noževe; šiljilo za olovke; **~ness** oštrina; žestina; oštroumnost; **~-shooter** vješt strijelac; **~-sighted** oštrovidan
shatter ['ʃætə] razmrskati (se); rastrojiti (*živce etc.*)
shav|e [ʃeiv] brijati (se); okrznuti; brijanje; **~ing** brijanje; *pl* blanjevina; **~ing-brush** četkica za brijanje
shawl [ʃɔ:l] šal, marama
she [ʃi:] ona; žensko; **she- ...** ženka životinje
sheaf [ʃi:f] snop, svežanj
shear [ʃiə] šišati; (***a pair of***) ***~s*** *pl* velike škare
shed [ʃed] (pro)lijevati; bacati (*svijetlo*); širiti; šupa, suša
sheep [ʃi:p] ovca (*i pl*)
sheer [ʃiə] puki; ***~ nonsense*** čista glupost
sheet [ʃi:t] ploča; arak (*papira*); plahta; ploha; **~-glass** staklo u pločama; **~-iron** cinčani lim; **~-lighting** bljeskavica
shelf, *pl* ***shelves*** [ʃelf, ~vz] polica, pretinac; greben u moru; ***on the ~*** odbačen; ***get on the ~*** ostati usidjelica
shell [ʃel] ljuska; školjka; granata; ljuštiti; skinuti koru;

~-fish ljuskar
shelter ['ʃeltə] nadstrešnica; sklonište; zakloniti
shelve [ʃelv] *fig* staviti ad acta
shepherd ['ʃepəd] pastir
sheriff ['ʃerif] šerif
sherry ['ʃeri] šeri (vino)
shield [ʃi:ld] štit; štititi (***from***)
shift [ʃift] promjena; lukavština; trik; smjena (radnika); ***make ~*** snaći se; ***make ~ to live*** životariti; pomicari; mijenjati položaj; preseliti (se); skretati (*vjetar*); snaći se; **~y** lukav; nepostojan
shilling ['ʃiliŋ] šiling
shin(-bone) ['ʃin(boun)] goljenica (kost)
shine [ʃain] sjaj, blistanje; svijetliti; blistati
shingle ['ʃiŋgl] šindra; **~d hair** kratka, podrezana ženska kosa
shiny ['ʃaini] sjajan
ship [ʃip] brod; ukrcati na brod; **~ment** otprema; pošiljka; **~-owner** brodovlasnik; **~ping** otprema; brodovlje; **~wreck** brodolom; **~wright** brodograditelj; **~yard** brodogradilište
shire ['ʃaiə] grofovija
shirt [ʃə:t] muška košulja; **~ing** materijal za košulje
shiver ['ʃivə] trijeska, krhotina; razbiti (se) u komade; drhtati; **~y** drhtav
shock [ʃɔk] udarac; sukob; duševni potres; ***be ~ed at*** zgražati se nad; **~-absorber** amortizer; **~er** *coll* jeftin uzbudljivi roman; **~ing** uvredljiv; sablažnjiv; **~-troops** udarne trupe
shoddy ['ʃɔdi] šund; jeftin; patvoren
shoe [ʃu:] cipela; obuti; okovati; **~blacking** crno laštilo za cipele; **~horn** žlica za cipele; **~maker** postolar; **~string** *Am* vezica za cipele
shoot [ʃu:t] munjevita kretnja; mladica; oluk; opaliti; pucati; nicati; snimati (FILM); povući zasun
shooting ['ʃu:tiŋ] pucanje; koji probada (*bol*); ***go ~*** ići u lov; **~ star** meteor
shop [ʃɔp] dućan; radionica; pogon; ***talk ~*** razgovarati o stručnim stvarima, o svom poslu; **~keeper** trgovac (na malo); **~lifter** kradljivac po dućanima; **~ping**: ***~ping centre*** trgovačka četvrt grada; ***go ~ping*** ići kupovati; **~walker** nadglednik odjela robne kuće; **~-window** izlog
shore [ʃɔ:] obala; žal
short [ʃɔ:t] kratak; nizak (*stas*); oskudan, nedovoljan; ***in ~*** ukratko; **~age** manjak; nestašica; **~coming** nedostatak; mana; nedovoljnost; **~dated** kratkoročan; **~en** skratiti; **~hand** stenografija; **~ly** nedavno; uskoro; **~ness**

kratkoća; **~s** *pl* kratke hlače; **~-sighted** kratkovidan; **~ wave** kratki val
shot [ʃɔt] hitac; sačma; strijelac; PHOT snimak; ***within (out of) ~*** na domet (izvan dometa)
shoulder ['ʃouldə] rame; (*i fig*) uzeti na se; staviti o rame; ***put one's ~ to the wheel*** dobro prionuti uz posao
shout [ʃaut] vika; vikati; vrištati
shove [ʃʌv] guranje; gurati
shovel ['ʃʌvl] lopata; lopatom grabiti
show [ʃou] pokazati; izložiti; ukazati; izložba; predstava; ***~ off*** isticati se; producirati se; ***run the ~*** *Am* imati glavnu riječ; **~case** vitrina
shower ['ʃauə] pljusak; tuš; **~-bath** kupaonica s tušem; tuš; pljuštati; politi; obasuti; **~y** kišovit
show|room izložbeni salon; **~-window** izlog; **~y** napadan
shrewd [ʃru:d] oštrouman
shriek [ʃri:k] vrisak; zvižduk; vrištati
shrill [ʃril] vrištav; prodoran
shrimp [ʃrimp] rak; skamp
shrink [ʃriŋk] smanjiti se; skupiti se (*tkanina*); ustuknuti (***from, at***)
Shrove|tide ['ʃrouvtaid] poklade; **~ Tuesday** pokladni utorak
shrub [ʃrʌb] grm
shrug [ʃrʌg] slijeganje ramenima; slegnuti ramenima
shudder ['ʃʌdə] drhtati; protrnuti; drhtaj; trnci
shuffle ['ʃʌfl] guati; miješati (*karte*); strugati nogama
shun [ʃʌn] izbjegavati
shunt [ʃʌnt] ranžiranje; EL odvod; ranžirati
shut [ʃʌt] zatvoriti (se); opkoliti; ***~ up!*** šuti! **~-down** obustava rada; **~ter** kapak prozora; rolo; PHOT zatvor (blenda)
shuttle ['ʃʌtl] tkalački čunac; čunčić šivaćeg stroja; neprekidan lokalni saobraćaj u oba smjera
shy [ʃai] plah; baciti; **~ness** plahost
Sicily ['sisili] Sicilija
sick [sik] bolestan (***of***); koji osjeća mučninu; sit (***of***); **~-bed** bolesnički krevet; **~en** oboljeti; **~-fund** bolesnička blagajna
sickle ['sikl] srp
sick|-leave bolovanje; **~ly** bolešljiv; slabašan; odvratan; **~ness** bolest
side [said] strana; obala; stranka; **~board** kredenc; **~-car** prikolica motocikla; **~-light** bočno svijetlo; *fig* slučajno objašnjenje; **~-slip** MOT zanašati se; AERO bočno se spuštati; **~-splitting** koji tjera na smijeh; **~walk** *Am* pločnik; **~ways**, **~wise** postrance

siege [siːdʒ] opsada
sieve [siv] sito
sift [sift] prosijati; prorešetati
sigh [sai] uzdah; uzdisati
sight [sait] vid; vidik; pogled; prizor; ***catch ~ of*** ugledati; ***out of ~*** izvan vidokruga; **~seeing** razgledavanje znamenitosti
sign [sain] znak; mig; cimer; potpisati
signal ['signəl] signal; osobit; signalizirati; **~ box** *rail* skretničarska kućica
signat|ory ['signətəri] **powers** *pl* sile potpisnice; **~ure** potpis
signboard ['sainbɔːd] natpis nad dućanom, cimer
significan|ce [sig'nifıkəns], **~cy** značenje; **~t** značajan; karakterističan (***of***)
signify ['signifai] naznačiti; značiti; ***it does not ~ to*** nema nikakve važnosti
signpost ['sainpoust] putokaz
silen|ce ['sailəns] šutnja; ***~ce!*** tišina!; **~cer** prigušivač; MOT izduvni lonac; **~t** tih; šutljiv
Silesia [sai'liːziə] Šlezija
silk [silk] svila; svilen; **~en** svilenast; **~y** poput svile; svilenast
sill [sil] prag; daska prozora
sill|iness ['silinis] glupost; **~y** glup; luckast
silver ['silvə] srebro; srebrni novac; srebrnina; posrebriti
similar ['similə] sličan
simmer ['simə] ključati; pomalo vreti
simple ['simpl] jednostavan; bezazlen
simpli|city [sim'plisiti] jednostavnost; jasnoća; **~fication** pojednostavljenje; **~fy** pojednostaviti
simply ['simpli] jednostavno; samo
simulate ['simjuleit] hiniti; simulirati
simultaneous [siməl'teinjəs] istodoban
sin [sin] grijeh; (sa)griješiti
since [sins] od; odonda; otkako; budući da; ***long ~*** odavna
sincer|e [sin'siə] iskren; **~ity** iskrenost
sinew ['sinjuː] tetiva; *pl* snaga; žilavost; **~y** žilav; mišičav; jak
sing [siŋ] pjevati
singe [sindʒ] opržiti
singer ['siŋə] pjevač(ica)
single ['siŋgl] jedan; jedini; pojedinačan; neoženjen; neudata; **~ combat** dvoboj; TENNIS igra pojedinaca; **~-breasted** jednoredan (*kaput*)
singular ['siŋgjulə] neobičan; osobit; GRAM jednina
sinister ['sinistə] koban; zlosutan
sink [siŋk] (po)tonuti; uleknuti se; spustiti se; izljev, sudoper; **~ing** malaksalost;

~ing fund fond za otplatu dugova
sinner ['sinə] grešnik
sip [sip] gutljaj; pijuckati
siphon ['saifən] sifon(ska) boca
sir [sə:] gospodine
siren ['saiərin] sirena
sirloin ['sə:lɔin] bubrežnjak
sister ['sistə] sestra; **~-in-law** šurjakinja
sit [sit] sjediti; zasjedati; **~ *down*** sjesti; **~ *up*** ostati budan, ne leći; **~-down strike** štrajk kod kojeg radnici ne napuštaju radno mjesto
site [sait] položaj; gradilište
sitting ['sitiŋ] sjednica; **~-room** soba za dnevni boravak
situat|ed ['sitjueitid] smješten; **~ion** položaj; služba; situacija
six [siks] šest; šestica; **~fold** šesterostruk; **~teen** šesnaest; **~teenth** šesnaesti; šesnaestina; **~th** šesti; šestina; **~thly** šesto; **~tieth** šezdeseti; **~ty** šezdeset, šezdesetica
size [saiz] veličina; obujam; format; broj (*cipela, etc*)
skat|e [skeit] klizaljka; klizati se; **~ing-rink** klizalište
skeleton ['skelitn] kostur; trkaće saonice
sketch [sketʃ] skica; skicirati
ski [ski:] skija; skijati se
skid zavor; kočnica; AERO saonice aviona; kočiti; MOT klizati; zanašati
ski|er ['ski:ə] skijaš; **~ing** skijanje
skilful [skilful] vješt, spretan
skill [skil] vještina; spretnost; **~ed** vješt; kvalificiran
skim| **(off)** skidati vrhnje; obirati (mlijeko); **~ milk** obrano mlijeko
skin koža; krzno; ljuska; oderati kožu; oguliti; **~-deep** površan, plitak
skip skok; (pre)skočiti; **~per** kapetan (i vlasnik) broda; SPORT kapetan momčadi; **~ping-rope** uže za preskakivanje
skirmish ['skə:miʃ] okršaj; ogledati se u okršaju
skirt [skə:t] suknja; (ob)rub; obrubiti
skittle ['skitl] čunj; ***play (at) ~s*** kuglati se; **~-alley** kuglana
skulk [skʌlk] skrivati se; **~er** kukavica (na frontu)
skull [skʌl] lubanja
sky [skai] nebo; **~light** prozor na krovu; **~-line advertising** zračna reklama; **~scraper** neboder
slab [slæb] kamena ploča
slack [slæk] labav; nenapet; **~en** popustiti; usporiti (se); **~er** zabušant; lijenčina
slag [slæg] šljaka
slake [sleik] gasiti vapno
slam [slæm] zalupiti (vrata); tresnuti
slander ['sla:ndə] kleveta(-nje); (o)klevetati; **~er** kle-

vetnik
slang [slæŋ] slang; šatrovački jezik
slant [sla:nt] kosina; koso položiti; nakriviti; **~(ing)** kos; nakriv
slap [slæp] pljuska; udariti
slash [slæʃ] udarac; (pro)rez
slate [sleit] pločica ili crijep od škriljevca; **~-pencil** pisaljka od škriljevca; **~r** pokrivač krovova škriljevcem
slattern ['slætə:n] žena neuredne vanjštine
slaughter ['slɔ:tə] pokolj; (po)klati; **~house** klaonica
slave [sleiv] rob; **~ry** ropstvo
sled(ge) [sled(ʒ)] saonice; sanjkati se
sledge(-hammer) kovački bat
sleek [sli:k] gladak; ugladiti
sleep [sli:p] san; spavati; **~ away** (*vrijeme*) prespavati; **~ on** (*ili* **over**) prespavati; **~ off** odspavati (*mamurluk*); **~er** spavač; *rail* prag; spavaća kola; **~iness** pospanost
sleeping| bag vreća za spavanje; **~ car** spavaća kola; **~ sickness** bolest spavanja
sleep|less ['sli:plis] besan; **~lessness** besanica; **~-walker** mjesečar; **~y** pospan
sleet [sli:t] solika
sleeve [sli:v] rukav
sleigh [slei] = **sled**
slender ['slendə] vitak; nježan; **~ness** vitkost
slice [slais] kriška; komad
slide [slaid] klizati; sklizati se; ***let things* ~** ostaviti da stvari idu svojim tokom; tobogan; TECH šiber; **~ rule** logaritamsko računalo
sliding ['slaidiŋ] klizanje; **~ scale** pomična skrižaljka cijena; **~ seat** pomično sjedalo (*u sportskom čamcu*)
slight [slait] slab(ašan); neznatan; lagan; omalovažavati; omalovažavanje
slim vitak; slabašan
slime [slaim] sluz
sling [sliŋ] omča; petlja; povoj; zavitlati; prebaciti preko
slip (po)skliznuti se; omaknuti se; **~ on** (**off**) baciti na se (odbaciti) (*odjeću*); *fig* pogriješiti; **~ of paper** ceduljica; kombine; jastučnica; **~ of a girl** slabašno djevojče; **~per** papuča; **~pery** sklizav; *fig* škakljiv
slit razrez, šlic; rasporiti
slogan ['slougən] lozinka; parola
sloop [slu:p] MAR šalupa
slop lokva *pl* spirine; proliti; **~-basin** posuda za izlijevanje ostataka čaja
slope [sloup] obronak; padina; nagib; nagnuti; učiniti kosim
slot [slɔt] prorez, otvor za ubacivanje novca na automatu; **~machine** automat
slouch [slautʃ]: **~ (along)** gu-

ravo (mlitavo) hodati; ~ **hat** mekan šešir
slovenly ['slʌvnli] prljav, neuredan
slow [slou] polagan, trom; ***my watch is ten minutes*** ~ moj sat zaostaje 10 minuta; **~-motion picture** FILM usporena snimka
slugg|ard ['slʌgəd] lijenčina; **~ish** trom, lijen
sluice [slu:s] brana
slumber ['slʌmbə] drijem; drijemati
slump [slʌmp] *burza*: (naglo) padati; pad (*tečaja, cijena*)
slums [slʌmz] *pl* prljava gradska četvrt
slush [slʌʃ] bljuzgavica
slut [slʌt] prljava (neuredna) žena
sly [slai] lukav, prepreden; **~-boots** prefriganac
smack [smæk] udarac; okus; imati tek (***of***); pljusnuti; cmoknuti (*usnama*)
small [smɔ:l] malen; slab; neznatan; ~ **arms** *pl* streljačko oružje; **~pox** boginje
smart [sma:t] oštar; žestok; žustar; spretan; pametan; lukav; elegantan; ***he shall ~ for it*** pokajat će se on za to
smash [smæʃ] smrskati; *fig* uništiti
smattering ['smætəriŋ] površno poznavanje
smear [smiə] (raz)mazati; mrlja
smell miris; mirisati
smelt taliti
smile [smail] smiješak; (na-) smiješiti se
smith [smiθ] kovač
smithy ['smiði] kovačnica
smitten ['smitn] **with** pogođen
smoke [smouk] dim; ***have a ~*** (za)pušiti; **~(*s*** *pl*) duhan; pušiti; **~-free** *building* (zgrada) gdje je pušenje zabranjeno; **~r** pušač *rail* kola (kupe) za pušače
smoking ['smoukiŋ]: ***no ~!*** pušenje zabranjeno!; ~ **carriage** kola za pušače; ~ **compartment** kupe za pušače
smoky ['smouki] koji se dimi; zadimljen
smooth [smu:ð] gladak; mekan; izgladiti (***~ out, down***); ***~ a p's path*** *fig* utrti kome put; ublažiti (*i* ***~ down***); ***~ away, ~ over*** ukloniti teškoće; ***things are going on ~ly with him*** sve mu ide glatko
smoulder ['smouldə] tinjati
smuggle ['smʌgl] krijumčariti; **~r** krijumčar
smut [smʌt] prljavština; mrlja (*od čađe*); ***talk ~*** bestidno govoriti; **~ty** prljav; nepristojan
snack [snæk] zalogaj
snail [sneil] puž
snake [sneik] zmija
snap [snæp] ugriz; škljocaj; ***cold ~*** val hladnoće; naglo

posegnuti (***at***); **~-fastener** druker (*na haljini*); **~shot** PHOT snimka, fotografija; snimiti
snare [snɛə] zamka
snarl [sna:l] režati
snatch [snætʃ] zgrabiti; nagli zahvat; komadić; čas; **~ *at*** posegnuti za
sneak [sni:k] (od)šuljati se; ukrasti
sneer [sniə] poruga; podrugivati se
sneeze [sni:z] kihati
sniff [snif] njušiti; frkati nosom (***at***)
snipe [snaip] ZOOL šljuka
snob [snɔb] snob; **~bish** snobovski; **~bery** snobizam
snooze [snu:z] dremuckanje
snor|e [snɔ:] hrkanje; hrkati; **~t** dahtati
snout [snaut] njuška
snow [snou] snijeg; sniježiti; **~drop** visibaba
snub [snʌb] ukoriti; otresti se
snub-nose frntast nos
snuff [snʌf] burmut; šmrkati (*burmut*)
snug [snʌg] udoban; zaklonjen
so [sou] tako; dakle; ***you are tired, ~ am I*** ti si umoran, i ja također
soak [souk] kvasiti, (na)močiti; prodrijeti (***into***); namakanje
soap [soup] sapun; (na)sapunati
soar [sɔ:] uzvinuti se
sob [sɔb] jecaj; jecati
sober ['soubə] trijezan (*i fig*); ***sleep oneself ~*** otrijezniti se spavanjem; otrijezniti (se)
sob-stuff ['sɔbstʌf] *Am coll* sentimentalna literatura
so-called ['sou kɔ:ld] takozvan
sociab|ility [souʃə'biliti] društvenost; **~le** društven; vrsta kočije
social ['souʃəl] društven; socijalan; **~ gathering** društvance; **~ insurance** socijalno osiguranje; **~ism** socijalizam; **~ist** socijalist
society [sə'saiəti] društvo
sock [sɔk] kratka čarapa; uložak za cipelu
socket ['sɔkit] tuljac; očna (zubna) šupljina; TECH naglavak; EL utikačka kutija
socle ['sɔkl] postolje; sokl
soda ['soudə] soda; **~ (*water*)** soda voda
sodden ['sɔdn] promočen; raskvašen
sofa ['soufə] sofa
soft [sɔft] mekan; blag; tih; nježan; **~en** umekšati (se); ublažiti; **~ness** mekoća; blagost; nježnost
soil [sɔil] tlo; zemlja; uprljati
solder ['souldə] lem; lemiti; **~ing iron** lemilo
soldier ['souldʒə] vojnik; **~y** vojska; soldateska
sole [soul] jedini; đon; pođoniti; ZOOL list; **~ agent** is-

ključivi zastupnik
solemn ['sɔləm] svečan; ozbiljan; **~ity** svečanost
solicit [sə'lisit] moliti; nagovarati; tražiti; **~or** odvjetnik
solid ['sɔlid] čvrst; trajan; masivan; pouzdan; **~ *leather*** jedra koža; **~ity** čvrstoća; pouzdanost
solit|ary ['sɔlitəri] osamljen; **~ude** osamljenost
solstice ['sɔlstis] solsticij
solub|ility [sɔlju'biliti] topivost; **~le** topiv
solution [sə'luːʃən] otopina; rješenje
solve [sɔlv] (raz)riješiti; **~ncy** sposobnost plaćanja; **~nt** solventan
some [sʌm] neki; nekakav; nešto; **~body** netko; **~how** nekako; **~thing** nešto; **~time** nekad; **~times** katkada; **~what** nešto; prilično; **~where** negdje; bilo kamo
son [sʌn] sin
song [sɔŋ] pjesma; pjev(anje)
son-in-law zet
sonor|ous [sə'nɔːrəs] zvučan; **~ity** zvučnost
soon [suːn] skoro; (u)brzo; rado; **~er** prije; ***no ~er said than done*** rečeno, učinjeno
soot [sut] čađa
soothe [suːð] (u)miriti; ublažiti
sooty ['suti] čađav
sorcer|er ['sɔːsərə] čarobnjak; **~ess** čarobnica; **~y** čarobnjaštvo
sore [sɔː] ranjav; bolan; osjetljiv; ranjavo mjesto; **~ness** osjetljivost; **~ throat** grlobolja
sorrow ['sɔrou] žalost; jad
sorry ['sɔri] žalostan; zabrinut; ***(I am) so ~!*** žao mi je!; oprostite!; ***I am ~ for you*** žao mi vas je
sort [sɔːt] vrsta; kakvoća; način; razvrstati
S. O. S. radiotelegrafski poziv u pomoć brodu (ili avionu) u nevolji
soul [soul] duša; **~less** bezdušan
sound [saund] zdrav; neoštećen; čvrst (*san*); zvuk; glas; sonda; zvučati; ječati; sondirati; MAR mjeriti dubinu; **~-box** zvučna kutija (*gramofona*); **~(ing)-board** rezonator; **~ film** zvučni film; **~less** bezvučan; **~ news** zvučne novosti; **~-proof**, **~-tight** neprobojan za zvuk; **~ wave** zvučni val
soup [suːp] juha
sour ['sauə] kiseo; ogorčen; ogorćiti
source [sɔːs] izvor; podrijetlo
souse [saus] (u)soliti
south [sauθ] jug; južni; južno; **~-east** jugoistok
souther|ly ['sʌðəli], **~n** južni; **~ner** južnjak; *Am* stanovnik južnih država
south-west jugozapad; jugo-

zapadni
sovereign ['sɔvrin] vrhovni; nenadmašiv; suveren; zlatnik od jedne funte sterlinga
Soviet ['souviət] *hist* Sovjet
sow [sau] krmača; [sou] (za-) sijati
spa [spaː] ljekovito kupalište
spac|e [speis] prostor; razmak; svemir; **~ious** prostran
spade [speid] lopata
Spain [spein] Španija
spam [spæm] *mail* spam
span [spæn] razmak; ARCHIT, AERO raspon; luk; premostiti
spangle ['spæŋgl] "fliter"
Spani|ard ['spænjəd] Španjolac; **~sh** španjolski
spanner ['spænə] ključ za matice
spare [spɛə] oskudan; mršav; rezervni; ***to ~*** suvišan; **~(bed-)room** soba za gosta; **~ (part)** rezervni dio; **~ time** slobodno vrijeme; štedjeti; odstupiti; biti bez čega; pregorjeti što
spark [spaːk] bljesak; iskra; iskriti se; **~le** blistati se; iskriti se; pjenušati se; **~ling wine** pjenušavo vino; **~ plug**, *Br* **~ing-plug** svjećica
sparrow ['spærou] vrabac
spasm [spæzəm] grč; **~odic(al)** grčevit
spatter ['spætə] (po)prskati
spatula ['spætjulə] lopatica
speak [spiːk] govoriti (***to***); ***~ out*** glasno govoriti; **~er** govornik; predsjedatelj
speaking ['spiːkiŋ] koji govori; izražajan; ***to be on ~ terms with*** imati s kim površno poznanstvo; *tel* ***Brown ~*** ovdje Brown
spear [spiə] koplje; sulica
special ['speʃəl] osobit; posebno izdanje; posebni vlak; **~ist** stručnjak; specijalist; **~ize** specijalizirati se (***in***, *Am* ***on***)
specif|ic [spi'sifik] specifičan; **~ication** specifikacija; **~y** pobliže označiti
specimen ['spesimin] uzorak, primjerak
speck [spek] mrlja; posuti mrljicama
specs [speks] *pl coll* naočale
spectacle ['spektəkl] prizor; **~s** *pl*: (***a pair of***) **~s** naočale
spectator [spek'teitə] gledalac
speculate ['spekjuleit] mozgati ([***up***]***on***); spekulirati
speech [spiːtʃ] govor; **~less** zanijemio
speed [spiːd] brzina; žurba; MOT brzina; žuriti se; ***~ up*** ubrzati; **~-dial button** tipka za brzo biranje; **~-limit** najveća dopuštena brzina; **~ometer** MOT brzinomjer; **~y** brz
spell vrijeme (rada); časak; čarolija; razdoblje; sricati, izgovarati slovo po slovo; **~-bound** *fig* začaran
spelling ['speliŋ] pravopis; **~-book** početnica

spend (po)trošiti (novac); provoditi (vrijeme); potratiti; **~thrift** rasipnik
sphere [sfiə] zemaljska kugla; sfera
spice [spais] mirodija; začin; začiniti
spick and span ['spikən-'spæn] nov novcat; vrlo uredan
spider ['spaidə] pauk
spike [spaik] klin; šiljak; BOT klas; pribosti
spill proliti; prosuti
spin presti; vrtjeti; okretati se; AERO strmoglaviti se okrećući se oko svoje osi
spinach ['spinidʒ] špinat
spinal ['spainl] hrptenični; **~ cord (marrow)** kičmena moždina
spindle ['spindl] vreteno
spine [spain] kičma; trn
spinning|-mill predionica; **~-wheel** kolovrat
spinster ['spinstə] usidjelica
spirit ['spirit] duh; duša; raspoloženje; temperament; (*motor* **~**) benzin; *pl* alkoholna pića; ***in high (low) ~s*** dobro (loše) raspoložen; **~ed** živahan; temperamentan; **~ism** spiritizam; **~ist** spiritist; **~ual** duševni; duhovni; **~ualize** produhoviti
spirt [spə:t] šiknuti
spit ražanj; pljuvačka; nabosti na ražanj; pljuvati; puhati (*mačka*)
spite [spait] pakost; ***in ~ of*** usprkos; **~ful** zloban; pakostan
spitt|le ['spitl] pljuvačka; **~oon** [~'tu:n] pljuvačnica
splash [splæʃ] štrcaj; mrlja (*od blata etc*); (po)prskati; **~-board** blatobran
spleen [spli:n] slezena; sjeta
splend|id ['splendid] sjajan, divan; **~our** sjaj; veličanstvenost
splint MED šinja; **~er** iver; krhotina
split pukotina; raskol; raskoliti (se); odcijepiti; podijeliti; ***~ one's sides*** pucati od smijeha; **~ting** jak, žestok
splutter ['splʌtə] pljuckati; pištati; MOT kašljati
spoil [spɔil] plijen; **~s system** POL sistem, po kojem mjesta u upravi dobivaju članovi stranke koja je pobijedila na izborima; (o)pljačkati; porobiti; pokvariti; razmaziti; **~sport** kvarilac raspoloženja
spoke [spouk] žbica
sponge [spʌndʒ] spužva; (o)čistiti spužvom; muktašiti; **~ cake** meki kolač, biskvit
sponsor ['spɔnsə] jamac; *Am* pokrovitelj; kumovati; financirati
spontaneous [spən'teinjəs] spontan; dobrovoljan
spool [spu:l] kalem; špula; namatati na kalem
spoon [spu:n] žlica; grabiti

žlicom; **~ful** žlica, količina koja stane u žlicu

sport [spɔ:t] sport; zabava; šala; (***good***) **~** zgodan momak; igrati se; **~ing** sportski; **~sman** sportaš; lovac; **~swear** sportska odjeća; **~swoman** sportašica

spot [spɔt] mrlja; mjesto; tačka; (za)mrljati; **~less** bez mrlje; **~-light** THEAT MOT reflektor; *fig* ***in the ~-light*** u središtu pažnje; **~ted fever** pjegavac

spout [spaut] njuška; kljun (*posude*); briznuti

sprain [sprein] iščašenje; iščašiti

sprat [spræt] ZOOL sledjica

sprawl [sprɔ:l] izvaliti se

spray [sprei] raspršiti; **~er** štrcalo; raspršivač

spread [spred] (*i* **~** ***out***) (ra)širiti; protezati (se); presvući; prekriti; (na)mazati; pružanje; raspon; jelo za mazanje (*na kruh*)

sprig grančica; izdanak; čavlić; klin

sprightly ['spraitli] živahan

spring [spriŋ] (od)skok; opruga; izvor; proljeće; (po)skočiti; proizlaziti (***from***); **~board** odskočna daska; **~-mattress** madrac na opruge; **~ tide** plima (*za mlađa i uštapa*); proljeće; **~y** TECH elastičan

sprinkle ['spriŋkl] (po)škropiti; **~r** prskalica; kanta za zalijevanje

sprint sprint; sprintati; **~er** kratkoprugaš

sprout [spraut] nicati; klica

spur [spə:] ostruga; podbosti (*konja*)

spurt [spə:t] napregnuti sve sile; kratak napor; ubrzavanje

spy [spai] špijun; uhoditi, špijunirati; **~glass** dalekozor

squabble ['skwɔbl] prepirka; prepirati se; **~r** svadljivac

squadron ['skwɔdrən] odred; eskadra

squall [skwɔ:l] vrisak; udar vjetra; vrisnuti; **~y** olujan

squander ['skwɔndə] tratiti, rasipati

square [skwɛə] četverokutan; pošten; namiren; koji se izravnao (***with***); kvadrat, četverokut; trg; izravnati; namiriti; **~built** plećat; **~ mile** kvadratna milja

squash [skwɔʃ] kaša; voćni sok; zgnječiti

squat [skwɔt] čučati; koji čuči

squeak [skwi:k] cičati; škripiti

squeeze [skwi:z] stisnuti (se); gnječiti; stisak; stiska

squib [skwib] *vatromet*: žabica; rugalica

squint [skwint] škiljiti

squire ['skwaiə] posjednik

squirrel ['skwirəl] vjeverica

squirt [skwə:t] štrcaljka; mlaz

S. S. = **steamship**
St. = **Saint**; **street**
stab [stæb] (u)bod; (u)bosti
stabili|ty [stə'biliti] stabilnost; **~zation** stabilizacija; **~ze** stabilizirati; **~zer** stabilizator
stabl|e ['steibl] stabilan; postojan; staja; **~ing** smještanje u staju
stack [stæk] stog; hrpa; skladište; složiti u hrpu
staff [sta:f] štap; štab; osoblje
stag [stæg] ZOOL jelen
stage [steidʒ] pozornica; mjesto zbivanja; stadij; **~ box** proscenijska loža; **~ fright** trema; **~ manager** režiser
stagger ['stægə] teturati; posrtati
stagnant ['stægnənt] ustajao; koji stagnira
stag-party muško društvo
stain [stein] mrlja; (za)mrljati; obojiti; **~less** neokaljan; koji ne rđa (*čelik*)
stair [stɛə] stepenica; *pl* stube; **~case**, *Am* **~way** stubište
stake [steik] kolac; uložak (*u igri*); uložiti novac (*u igru*); ***be at ~*** biti na kocki
stale [steil] star (*ne svjež*); ustajao; zagušljiv; istrošen
stalk [stɔ:k] stabljika; stalak čaše; šepiriti se
stall [stɔ:l] štand; sajamski šator; THEAT sjedalo u parketu
stammer ['stæmə] mucati; mucanje
stamp [stæmp] žig; marka; otisak; biljeg; (z)gaziti; tapkati; žigosati; frankirati; **~ duty** biljegovina
stand [stænd] stajati; nalaziti se; izdržati; zastoj; stajalište; stalak; štand; ***it ~s to reason that ...*** logično je da...; ***~ up*** ustati; ***~ up for*** zauzeti se za; ***~ one's ground*** zadržati svoj stav; ***~ a p a th*** častiti koga nečim
standard ['stændəd] stijeg; zastava; valuta; norma; jedinstvena mjera; standard; standardan; ***~ of living*** životni standard; **~ization** normiranje; **~ize** normirati; **~ lamp** stojeća lampa
standpoint stajalište
standstill mirovanje
stand-up ['stændʌp]: ***~ collar*** uspravan ovratnik; ***~ fight*** poštena borba
star [sta:] zvijezda; THEAT star; **℞s and stripes** zastava SAD; THEAT igrati glavnu ulogu; gostovati
starboard ['sta:bəd] desna strana (*broda*)
starch [sta:tʃ] škrob; škrobiti
stare [stɛə] ukočen pogled; buljiti ***(at)***
starling ['sta:liŋ] ZOOL čvorak
start [sta:t] polazak, start; početak; prednost; skočiti; krenuti, poći; početi; pokre-

nuti (*mašinu*); **~er** SPORT onaj koji daje znak za početak natjecanja; MOT pokretač; anlaser; **~ing point** polazna tačka

startl|e ['sta:tl] preplašiti; **~ing** koji zapanjuje

starv|ation [sta:'veiʃən] gladovanje, smrt od gladi; **~e** izgladnjeti

state [steit] stanje; prilike; država; navoditi; ustanoviti; izjaviti; **~liness** dostojanstvo; **~ly** svečan, dostojanstven; **~ment** izjava; prikaz; konstatacija; ***~ment (of account)*** izvadak (iz računa); **~room** luksuzna kabina; **~sman** državnik

station ['steiʃən] stajalište; mjesto; stanica; **~ary** nepokretan; stacioniran; **~er** trgovac pisaćim priborom; **~ery** papirnata roba i pisaći pribor; **~ master** šef stanice; **~ waggon** *Am* MOT karavan

statistic|al [stə'tistikəl] statistički; **~s** *pl* statistika

statue ['stætju:] kip, statua

stature ['stætʃə] stas, uzrast

statute ['stætju:t] statut, zakon

stave [steiv] dužica (*bačve*); strofa

stay [stei] boravak; (***a pair of***) ***~s*** *pl* steznik; ostati; boraviti; **~ *away*** izostati; **~-at-home** čovjek koji stalno sjedi kod kuće; **~er** SPORT konj, koji izdrži trku do kraja; **~ing power** izdržljivost

stead [sted] mjesto; ***in his ~*** namjesto njega; **~fast** postojan; čvrst; **~iness** stalnost; **~y** stalan; čvrst; stabilan; pouzdan; nepokolebljiv

steak [steik] odrezak; šnicla

steal [sti:l] (u)krasti; šuljati se; **~ *into*** ušuljati se

stealth [stelθ]: ***by ~*** kradomice; **~y** kradomičan

steam [sti:m] para; ispustiti paru; pušiti se; **~-boiler** parni kotao; **~-engine** parni stroj; **~er**, **~ship** parobrod; **~-tug** parni tegljač

steel [sti:l] čelik; (o)čeličiti; **~ engraving** čelikorez; **~-clad** opkoljen čelikom

steep [sti:p] strm; pretjeran; namakati; močiti; *fig* zadubiti se

steeple ['sti:pl] (šiljast) toranj; **~chase** utrka sa preprekama

steepness ['sti:pnis] strmina

steer [stiə] kormilariti; **~able** koji se dade upravljati; **~age** međupalublje; **~ing (gear)** uređaj za pokretanje kormila

stem deblo; stabljika; MAR pramac broda; suprostaviti se

stench [stentʃ] smrad

stencil ['stensl] matrica

stenographer [ste'nɔgrəfə] stenograf

step korak; stepenica; stupati; koračiti; **~-father** očuh

stepney ['stepni] MOT rezervni točak
sterile ['sterail] neplodan, sterilan
sterling ['stə:liŋ]: ***a pound ~*** funta sterlinga
stern [stə:n] ozbiljan; mrk; krma; **~ness** ozbiljnost; strogost
stevedore ['sti:vidɔ:] MAR lučki radnik
stew [stju:] pirjati, dinstati
steward ['stjuəd] upravitelj imanja; konobar; stjuard; redatelj kod priredbi; **~ess** stjuardesa
stick [stik] štap, palica; šipka pečatnog voska; zapeti; zalijepiti (se) (***to***); **~ing plaster** flaster; **~y** ljepljiv; odvratan
stiff ukočen; krut; naporan; jak (*piće*); **~en** ukočiti (se), ukrutiti (se)
stifle ['staifl] ugušiti (se)
still miran; još (uvijek); ipak; umiriti; **~ness** tišina
stimul|ant ['stimjulənt] stimulativan; stimulans; **~ation** poticanje; podražaj
sting [stiŋ] žalac; ubod; ubosti; *fig* zaboljeti
stingy ['stindʒi] škrt; oskudan
stink [stiŋk] smrad; smrdjeti (***of***)
stint ograničenje; škrtariti čime; stegnuti koga
stipulat|e ['stipjuleit] ugovoriti; uglaviti; **~ion** pogodba; klauzula
stir [stə:] kretanje; *fig* živahnost; (po)kretati (se); miješati; ***~ up*** uzbuditi
stirrup ['stirəp] stremen
stitch [stitʃ] (u)bod iglom; očica; šiti; prošiti
stock panj; deblo; rod; zaliha; (temeljna) glavnica; *pl* dionice; državni papiri; ***in ~*** na zalihi; na skladištu; **~breeder** stočar; **~broker** burzovni mešetar; **~ exchange** efektna burza; **~holder** *Am* dioničar
stockinette [stɔki'net] triko
stocking ['stɔkiŋ] čarapa; **~ weaver** čarapar
stock|-jobber ['stɔkdʒɔbə] burzovni mešetar; **~taking** inventura
stoic ['stouik] stoički; stoik
stoke [stouk] poticati vatru; **~r** ložač
stolid ['stɔlid] ravnodušan; tup
stomach ['stʌmək] želudac
stone [stoun] kamen; koštica; kamenovati; vaditi koštice; **~ blind** posve slijep; **~ dead** posve mrtav; **~mason** klesar
stony ['stouni] kamenit; *fig* od kamena
stool [stu:l] stolac bez naslona; stolica
stoop [stu:p] sagnuti se
stop [stɔp] zapušiti; zaustaviti; zatvoriti; (s)priječiti; obustaviti (*isplatu*); stati; prestati; zastoj; pauza; prestanak;

~gap pomoć u nuždi; zakrpa; **~page** začepljenje; zaustavljanje; obustava; zadržavanje; prekid; ***~page of current*** prekid struje; **~ping** plomba; **~-press (news)** vijesti ubačene nakon zaključene redakcije lista; **~watch** štoperica
storage ['stɔːridʒ] pohrana; skladišnina; **~ battery** akumulator
store [stɔː] zaliha; *i pl*: skladište; žitnica; *Am* dućan; (*pl*) robna kuća; ***~ up*** nagomilati; **~house** skladište; **~keeper** skladištar; *Am* vlasnik dućana; **~room** magazin
storied ['stɔːrid] s ... katova
stork [stɔːk] ZOOL roda
storm [stɔːm] oluja; juriš; bjesnjeti; **~y** olujni
story ['stɔːri] povijest; pripovijetka; kat, sprat; ***short ~*** novela; **~teller** pripovjedač; lažljivac
stout [staut] jak; krupan, debeo; hrabar; **~hearted** odvažan; **~ness** snaga; SPORT izdržljivost
stove [stouv] peć
stow [stou] tovariti; ***~away*** slijepi putnik
straight [streit] ravan; ispravan; ***~ on*** ravno naprijed; ***put ~*** dovesti u red; **~en (out)** izravnati; ispraviti; **~forward** pošten; izravan
strain [strein] naprezanje; napor; podrijetlo; (pre)napeti; naprezati; MED iščašiti; procjeđivati; **~er** cjedilo; filter
strait [streit] tjesnac; *pl* škripac; **~en** ograničiti; **~jacket** luđačka košulja; **~laced** uskogrudan; puritanski
strand [strænd] obala, žal; nasukati se
strange [streindʒ] stran; čudan; **~r** stranac
strangle ['stræŋgl] (za)daviti
strap [stræp] remen; pojas; kožna omča; pričvrstiti remenom; **~-hanger** putnik koji stoji držeći se za remen (*u tramvaju etc*)
stratagem ['strætidʒəm] (ratna) lukavština
strateg|ic(ally) [strə'tiːdʒik(əli)] strateški; **~y** ['strætidʒi] strategija
straw [strɔː] slama; **~berry** jagoda; **~ hat** slamnat šešir
stray [strei] (za)lutati; zastraniti
streak [striːk] pruga, trak; isprugati; **~y** isprugan mesom (*o slanini*)
stream [striːm] potok; rječica; rijeka; struja(nje); strujati; teći, curiti; lepršati; **~er:** ***paper ~er*** papirnata zmija (vrpca); **~lined** koji ima aerodinamičnu liniju
street [striːt] ulica
strength [streŋθ] snaga, moć; ***on the ~ of*** na osnovu čega; **~en** (po)jačati; (pot)krijepi-

ti

strenuous ['strenjuəs] neumoran; naporan

stress pritisak, naglasak; naglasiti

stretch [stretʃ] ispružiti (se); protezati (se); rastegnuti; rastezanje; komad puta; **~er** rastezalo; nosila

strew [stru:] (po)sipati

stricken ['strikən] udaren; pogođen; obolio (***with***)

strict [strikt] strog; tačan

stride [straid] prekoračiti; (dugačak) korak

strike [straik] pogoditi; udariti; tući; spustiti jedro; složiti šator; štrajkati; zapaliti šibicu; pasti u oči; ~ ***home*** pogoditi cilj (*i fig*); ~ ***out*** precrtati; ~ ***up*** zasvirati; štrajk; ***be*** (***go***) ***on*** ~ štrajkati; **~breaker** štrajkolomac

striking ['straikiŋ] napadan; izrazit; dojmljiv

string [striŋ] vrpca; uzica; konopac; ***the ~s*** gudački instrumenti; gudači; ***pull the ~s*** biti nevidljivi pokretač; napeti; (na)nizati (*bisere etc*); **~-band** gudački orkestar; **~y** vlaknat; žilav

strip svući (se); lišiti (***of***); TECH rastaviti

stripe [straip] pruga; isprugati

strive [straiv] težiti (***after, for***); truditi se; boriti se (***against***)

stroke [strouk] udarac; kap; hod klipa; potez (*perom, kistom*); odbijanje sata; (po-) gladiti

stroll [stroul] lutati; šetati; šetnja

strong [strɔŋ] jak; snažan; energičan; težak; **~box** čelična blagajna; **~hold** tvrđava *fig* uporište

structure ['strʌktʃə] građa; struktura

struggle ['strʌgl] boriti se; naprezati se; otimati se; borba; otimanje

strut [strʌt] šepiriti se; šepirenje; kosi potporanj

stubble ['stʌbl] strn; strnište

stubborn ['stʌbən] tvrdoglav; nepopustljiv

stuck-up ['stʌk'ʌp] uobražen

stud [stʌd] dugme ovratnika ili manšete

student ['stju:dənt] student; **~ship** stipendija

studied ['stʌdid] usiljen; promišljen

studio ['stju:diou] atelje

studious ['stju:djəs] marljiv; brižan; revnosan (***to***)

study ['stʌdi] studij; radna soba; PAINT *etc* studija; studirati

stuff [stʌf] građa; tvar; sukno; glupa stvar; (na)trpati; **~ing** punjenje; nadjev; materijal za tapeciranje; **~y** zagušljiv; sparan

stumble ['stʌmbl] spotaknuti se; ~ ***upon*** nabasati na

stump [stʌmp] panj; batrljak; *Am* držati predizborne govore; *coll* zbuniti; teško gaziti; **~y** zdepast; ***~y umbrella*** kratak kišobran (koji se može složiti)
stun [stʌn] zaglušiti
stunt [stʌnt] *Am* majstorija; ekshibicija; novinska senzacija; akrobacija
stupe|faction [stju:pi'fækʃən] zaprepašćenje; **~fy** zapanjiti; zaglupiti
stupendous [stju:'pendəs] koji zapanjuje
stupid ['stju:pid] glup; tup; **~ity** glupost
sturdy ['stə:di] krepak; jak; krupan
sturgeon ['stə:dʒən] ZOOL jesetra
stutter ['stʌtə] mucati
sty [stai] svinjac; ječmenac na oku
styl|e [stail] stil; način života; ***under the ~e of*** pod firmom; osloviti; titulirati; **~ish** stilski; elegantan
subaltern ['sʌbltən] niži oficir
sub|committee ['sʌbkəmiti] pododbor; **~consciousness** podsvijest
subdivi|de [sʌbdi'vaid] još (se) dalje dijeliti; **~sion** podvrsta
subdue [səb'dju:] podvrgnuti; obuzdati; prigušiti (*svijetlo*)
subhead(ing) ['sʌbhed(iŋ)] podnaslov
subject ['sʌbdʒikt] podanik; subjekt; sadržaj; predmet; podložan; ***~ to change without notice*** pridržano pravo promjene; [səb'dʒekt] podvrgnuti; izložiti
sublime [sə'blaim] uzvišen
sub|machine gun [sʌbmə'ʃi:n gʌn] automat (ručna strojna puška); **~marine** podmorski; podmornica
submerge [səb'mə:dʒ] uroniti
submiss|ion [səb'miʃən] pokornost; podnošenje na uvid; **~ive** pokoran
submit [səb'mit] podvrći (se) pokoriti se; predložiti; trpjeti
subordinate [səb'ɔ:dnit] podređen
subscribe [səb'skraib] potpisati; upisati prilog u novcu; pretplatiti se (***for***); **~r** potpisnik; *tel* pretplatnik
subscription [səb'skripʃən] potpis(ivanje); pretplata
subsequent ['sʌbsikwənt] slijedeći; kasniji (***to***); **~ly** kasnije
subsid|e [səb'said] utonuti; spustiti se; staložiti se; **~iary** dopunski; pomoćni; ***~iary company*** podružnica; **~ize** subvencionirati; **~y** novčana potpora
subsist [səb'sist] postojati; živjeti; **~ence** postojanje; sredstva za život

substance ['sʌbstəns] supstanca; bit
substantial [səb'stænʃəl] bitan; hranjiv; krepak; znatan
substitute ['sʌbstitju:t] nadomjestiti (***for***); zamijeniti; nadomjestak; zamjenik
sub|structure ['sʌbstrʌktʃə] podgradnja; **~tenant** podstanar; **~terfuge** izlika
subterranean [sʌbtə'reinjən] podzeman
subtle ['sʌtl] fin; nježan
subtract [sʌb'trækt] oduzimati; odbijati
suburb ['sʌbə:b] predgrađe; **~an** [sə'bə:bən] predgradski
subversion [sʌb'və:ʃən] prevrat; subvezija
subway ['sʌbwei] podvožnjak; *Am* podzemna željeznica
succeed [sək'si:d] slijediti; uspjeti; poći za rukom
success [sək'ses] uspjeh; **~ful** uspješan; **~ion** slijed; nasljedstvo; **~ive** uzastopan; **~or** nasljednik
succulent ['sʌkjulənt] sočan
succumb [sə'kʌm] podleći
such [sʌtʃ] takav; taj; ***~ a man*** takav čovjek; ***no ~ thing*** ništa takva; ***~ is life*** takav je već život
suck [sʌk] (u)sisati; ***~ in*** usisati; ***~ out*** isisati; **~ing pig** odojak; **~le** dojiti
suction ['sʌkʃən] **pump** sisaljka (pumpa za vodu)
sudden ['sʌdn] iznenadan; (***all***) ***of a ~*** (sasvim) iznenada
suds [sʌdz] *pl* sapunica
sue [sju:] tužiti sudu (***for***); (iz)moliti (***for***)
suède [sweid] fini antilop
suet [sjuit] loj
suffer ['sʌfə] trpjeti (***from***); pretrpjeti; podnositi; **~ance** patnja; **~er** patnik; **~ing** patnja
suffice [sə'fais] dostajati
sufficien|cy [sə'fiʃənsi] dostatnost; **~t** dostatan
suffocat|e ['sʌfəkeit] (u)gušiti (se); **~ive** zagušljiv
suffrage ['sʌfridʒ] pravo glasa
sugar ['ʃugə] šećer; (za)šećeriti
suggest [sə'dʒest] predložiti; sugerirati; **~ion** poticaj; prijedlog; savjet; **~ive** koji ukazuje (***of***); sugestivan; dvomislen (*Šala*)
suicide ['sjuisaid] samoubojstvo; samoubojica
suit [sju:t] odijelo; kostim; parnica; *kartanje*: boja; pristajati; dobro stajati; ***~ed*** pogodan; **~able** prikladan (***to, for***); **~case** (ručni) kovčeg; **~e** [swi:t] (redo)slijed; ***~e of rooms*** apartman; **~or** prosac; tužitelj
sulky ['sʌlki] SPORT kola za kasačke trke; mrzovoljan
sullen ['sʌlən] mrk; zlovoljan; prkosan
sulphur ['sʌlfə] sumpor

sult|riness ['sʌltrinis] sparina; **~ry** sparan
sum [sʌm] suma; svota; bit; sadržaj; zbrajati
summar|ize ['sʌməraiz] ukratko prikazati; **~y** rezime
summer ['sʌmə] ljeto
summit ['sʌmit] vrh(unac)
summon ['sʌmən] pozvati; sazvati; **~s** poziv; poziv na sud
sun [sʌn] sunce; sunčati (se); **~beam** sunčana zraka; **~burn** opeklina od sunca; **~burnt** opaljen od sunca; **℞day** ['~di] nedjelja; **~dial** sunčana ura; **~down** *Am* zalaz sunca
sundries ['sʌndriz] *pl* razna roba; izvanredni izdaci
sun|glasses naočale protiv sunca; **~ helmet** tropski šljem
sunken ['sʌŋkən] uleknut; upao (*obrazi, etc.*)
sun|rise ['sʌnraiz] izlazak sunca; **~set** zalazak sunca; **~shade** suncobran; **~shine** sunčev sjaj; **~stroke** sunčanica; **~-up** izlazak sunca
super|abundant [sju:pərə'bʌndənt] preobilan; **~annuation** starosna penzija
superb [sju:'pə:b] sjajan
super|ficial [sju:pə'fiʃəl] površan; **~fluous** suvišan; **~human** nadčovječni; **~intend** nadzirati; **~intendence** nadziranje
superior [sju:'piəriə] gornji; viši; nadmoćniji; bolji po kakvoći; pretpostavljeni; **~ity** nadmoćnost
super|man ['sju:pəmən] nadčovjek; **~numerary** prekobrojan; **~scription** natpis; naslov; **~stition** praznovjerje; **~-structure** nadgradnja; **~tax** dodatni porez (*na dohodak*); **~vision** nadzor
supper ['sʌpə] večera; ***the (Lord's)* ℞** pričest
supplant [sə'pla:nt] istisnuti; izgurati
supple ['sʌpl] gibak; savitljiv; **~ness** gipkost
supplement ['sʌplimənt] dopuna, dodatak; **~ary** dopunski; naknadni; ***take a ~ary ticket*** nadoplatiti voznu kartu
suppl|ier [sə'plaiə] opskrbljivač; **~y** dovoz; zaliha; COM ponuda; **~y** opskrbljivati (***with***); nadoknaditi (*nedostatak*); dobavljati
support [sə'pɔ:t] potpora (*i fig*); TECH potporanj; uložak (*za cipele*); oslonac; podupirati (*i fig*); uzdržavati; podnositi; **~able** podnošljiv
suppos|e [sə'pouz] smatrati; pretpostavljati; **~ition** pretpostavka
suppress [sə'pres] ugušiti; **~ion** ugušenje
suprem|acy [sju'preməsi] nadmoć; prevlast; **~e** vrhovni, najviši
surcharge [sə:'tʃa:dʒ] pre-

opteretiti; nadoplata; porto
sure [ʃuə] siguran; pouzdan; ***make ~*** uvjeriti se (***of***); **~ly** sigurno; **~ness** sigurnost; **~ty** jamac
surf [sɜ:f]: **~ *the net*** surfati na internetu
surface ['sə:fis] površina
surge [sə:dʒ] velik talas; talasati se
surge|on ['sə:dʒən] kirurg; **~ry** kirurgija; ordinacija
surly ['sə:li] mrzovoljan
surmise [sə:'maiz] nagađati; slutiti
surmount [sə:'maunt] prijeći; svladati
surplus ['sə:pləs] (su)višak
surprise [sə'praiz] iznenađenje; iznenaditi; prepasti
surrender [sə'rendə] predaja; predati (se); izručiti
surround [sə'raund] okruživati; **~ings** *pl* okolina
surtax ['sə:tæks] dodatni porez (na dohodak)
survey [sə:'vei] pregledati; razgledati; izmjeriti (*zemlju*); ['~] pregled; **~or** nadglednik; geometar
surviv|e [sə'vaiv] preživjeti; **~or** onaj koji je preživio
susceptibility [səseptə'biliti] osjetljivost
suspect [səs'pekt] sumnjati; osumnjičiti; slutiti; ['sʌs~] sumnjivac
suspend [səs'pend] objesiti; obustaviti isplatu; suspendirati; **~ers** *pl* podvezice (halteri) za čarape; *Am* naramenice za hlače
suspense [səs'pens] neizvjesnost
suspension [səs'penʃən] vješanje; odgoda; **~ bridge** viseći most
suspic|ion [səs'piʃən] sumnja; **~ious** sumnjičav; sumnjiv
sust|ain [səs'tein] podupirati; izdržati; podnositi gubitak; **~enance** ['sʌstinəns] uzdržavanje; hranjenje
SUV [esju:'vi:] = **sport utility vehicle** SUV
swaddling ['swɔdliŋ] **clothes** *pl* pelene, povoji
swagger ['swægə] šepiriti se; razmetati se; hvalisati se
swallow ['swɔlou] ZOOL lastavica; ždrijelo; gutljaj; (pro)gutati; opozvati izjavu
swamp [swɔmp] močvara
swan [swɔn] ZOOL labud
swarm [swɔ:m] roj; vrvjeti (***with***)
sway [swei] njihanje; upliv; (pre)vlast; njihati; (pre)vladati
swear [swɛə] kleti (se); **~ *in*** zaprisegnuti
sweat [swet] znoj; znojiti se; **~er** džemper; **~ing system** sistem iskorišćavanja (*radnika*)
Swed|en ['swi:dn] Švedska; **~ish** švedski
sweep [swi:p] (po)mesti; goniti; ***make a clean ~ of*** pot-

puno se osloboditi koga ili čega; dimnjačar; **~er** pometač; stroj za metenje ulica; **~ing** dalekosežan; poletan; **~ings** *pl* smeće
sweet [swi:t] sladak; ugodan; ljubak; ***have a ~ tooth*** biti sladokusac; **~en** zasladiti; **~heart** dragi, draga; **~ish** slatkast; **~ness** slatkoća; dražest; svježina; **~s** *pl* slastice, bonboni
swell [swel] oticati; elegantan; otmjen; fin; veliki gospodin; dama; **~ing** oteklina
swerve [swə:v] skrenuti; zastraniti
swift [swift] brz; **~ness** brzina
swim [swim] plivati; **~ming** plivanje; **~ming-pool** bazen za plivanje
swindle ['swindl] prevariti (***out of***); prijevara; **~r** varalica
swine [swain] svinja
swing [swiŋ] njihati (se); visjeti; okretati se; zamah; njihanje; ***in full ~*** u punom zamahu
swirl [swə:l] kovitlati se; vrtlog; vir
swish [swiʃ] zviždati; šibati
Swiss [swis] švicarski; Švicarac, Švicarka; ***the ~*** *pl* Švicarci
switch [switʃ] RLW skretnica; EL prekidač; RLW skrenuti na drugi kolosijek; EL **~ *on*** uključiti; **~ *off*** isključiti; **~ *over*** prebaciti se na; promijeniti smjer; **~-board** razvodna ploča; kućna telefonska centrala
Switzerland ['switsələnd] Švicarska
swoon [swu:n] nesvjestica; onesvijestiti se
sword [sɔ:d] mač
syllable ['siləbl] slog
symbol ['simbəl] simbol; **~ic(al)** simboličan
symmetry ['simitri] simetrija
sympath|etic [simpə'θetik] suosjećajan; **~ize** suojećati; slagati se; **~y** sućut
symphony ['simfəni] simfonija
symptom ['simptəm] simptom
synagougue ['sinəgɔg] sinagoga
synchronize ['siŋkrənaiz] vremenski uskladiti; sinhronizirati
syndicate ['sindikit] sindikat
synonymous [si'nɔniməs] istog značenja, sinoniman
synthes|is ['sinθisis] sinteza; **~ize** TECH umjetno proizvesti
syringe ['sirindʒ] štrcaljka; (u)štrcati
syrup ['sirəp] sirup
system ['sistim] sistem; **~atic(al)** sistematski; planski

T

table ['teibl] ploča; stol; tabela; **~-cloth** stolnjak; **~-spoon** velika žlica
tablet ['tæblit] pločica; tableta; komadić (*sapuna*)
tacit ['tæsit] šutljiv; **~urn** mučaljiv
tack [tæk] klinac; čavlić; ***on the wrong ~*** na krivu putu; pribadati; lavirati
tackle ['tækl] pribor; koloturnik; latiti se
tact [tækt]; obzirnost; **~ical** taktičan
taffeta ['tæfıtə] taft
tag [tæg] privjesak; etiketa; staviti privjesak; nadovezati (***to***)
tail [teil] rep; povlaka; **~coat** frak
tailor ['teilə] krojač; krojiti; **~-made** načinjen po mjeri
taint [teint] mrlja; ljaga; okaljati; MED zatrovati
take [teik] uzeti; oduzeti; preuzeti; uhvatiti; odnijeti; odvesti; snimati; trebati; trajati; smatrati (***for***); ***~ the air*** izići na svježi zrak; AERO uzletjeti; ***~ place*** dogoditi se; ***~ a drive*** (***a walk***) ići na vožnju (šetnju); ***~ in*** uzeti; suziti odjeću; biti pretplaćen na novine; ***~ off*** skinuti (*šešir*); svući (*haljinu*); AERO uzletjeti; ***~ out*** izvaditi; odstraniti (*mrlju*); ***~ up*** (po)dići; prihvatiti se posla; ***be ~n ill*** oboliti; **~-off** AERO uzlijetanje; odskok; karikatura
tale [teil] pripovjetka; bajka
talent ['tælənt] talent; **~ed** darovit
talk [tɔːk] razgovor; govoriti; čavrljati; **~ative** razgovorljiv; **~ie** *coll* (= ***~ing film***) zvučni film
tall [tɔːl] visok; velik
tallow ['tælou] loj
tame [teim] pitom; pripitomiti; (u)krotiti; **~ness** krotkost; **~r** krotitelj
tan [tæn] trijeslovina; stroj (za učinjanje kože); žutosmeđ; strojiti (*kožu*)
tangible ['tæŋdʒəbl] opipljiv (*i fig*)
tangle ['tæŋgl] zbrka; zamrsiti (se)
tank [tæŋk] cisterna; tank; **~age** spremanje tekućine u cisternama; **~ard** vrč; **~er** tanker
tanner ['tænə] štavljač
tantalize ['tæntəlaiz] mučiti
tap [tæp] slavina, pipa; (po-)tapšati; kuckati; točiti (*iz bačve*); *tel* prisluškivati
tape [teip] traka,vrpca; SPORT vrpca na cilju; **~worm** trakavica
taper ['teipə] zašiljiti

tapestry ['tæpistri] zidni sag, tapiserija
tap-room točionica
tar [ta:] katran; namazati katranom; **~-board** krovna ljepenka
tardy ['ta:di] spor; zakasnio
tare [tεə] COM tara
target ['ta:git] meta; *fig* cilj
tariff ['tærif] (carinska) tarifa
tarnish ['ta:niʃ] izgubiti sjaj; potamnjeti
tart [ta:t] trpak; kiseo; (voćni) kolač; drolja
tartar ['ta:tə] birsa; zubni kamenac
task [ta:sk] zadaća, zadatak; ***take to ~*** pozvati na odgovornost
tassel ['tæsəl] kita, resa
taste [teist] okus; ukus; kušati; imati okus; **~ful** ukusan; **~less** neukusan
tatter ['tætə] razderati; **~s** *pl* dronjci
tattoo [tə'tu:] mirozov; tetoviranje; tetovirati
taunt [tɔ:nt] podrugivanje
tax [tæks] porez; oporezovati; procijeniti troškove; **~ collector** poreznik
taxi(cab) ['tæksi(kæb)] (auto) taksi; voziti se taksijem
tea [ti:] čaj
teach [ti:tʃ] poučavati; **~er** nastavnik
teagown ['ti:gaun] poslijepodnevna haljina
team [ti:m] zaprega; SPORT momčad; **~ spirit** osjećaj solidarnosti
teapot ['ti:pɔt] čajnik
tear [tεə] (po)derati; razderati; poderotina; [tiə] suza; **~ gas** plin suzavac
tease [ti:z] grebenati (*vunu*); zadirkivati
technical ['teknikəl] tehnički
technicolor ['teknikʌlə] film u boji
tedious ['ti:diəs] dosadan; zamoran; razvučen
tee [ti:] cilj; meta
teem [ti:m] vrvjeti (***with***)
teenager ['ti:neidʒə] mladić ili djevojka od 13 do 19 godina
teens [ti:nz] *pl* godine starosti od 13 do 19
teetotal(l)er [ti:'toutlə] trezvenjak
telegram ['teligræm] telegram, brzojav
telegraph ['teligra:f] telegraf, brzojav; brzojaviti; **~ist** telegrafist
telephone ['telifoun] telefon; ***be on the ~*** imati telefon; telefonirati
tele|printer ['teli'printə] teleprinter; **~scope** teleskop; sklopiti se; **~typer** dalekopisač
television ['teli'viʒən] televizija; **~ set** televizor
tell [tel] reći; izjaviti; raspoznati; ***I have been told*** rekoše mi; ***~ a p to do a th*** naložiti kome da što učini; **~tale** izdajnički

temper ['tempə] ublažiti; umanjiti; ćud; raspoloženje; ***lose one's ~*** uzrujati se; **~ance** umjerenost; **~ature** temperatura; **~ature-chart** bolesnička tabla s diagramom temperature

tempest ['tempist] oluja; **~uous** buran; žestok

temple ['templ] hram; sljepočica

tempor|al ['tempərəl] vremenski; **~ary** privremen; ***~ary work*** prigodan posao; **~ize** nastojati dobiti na vremenu

tempt iskušavati koga; mamiti; **~ation** napast

ten deset; desetica

tenac|ious [ti'neiʃəs] uporan; žilav; **~ity** [~'næsiti] upornost; žilavost

tenant ['tenənt] zakupnik; (pod)stanar

tend smjerati; naginjati; težiti (***to***); njegovati; čuvati; posluživati stroj

tenden|cy ['tendənsi] sklonost, tendencija; namjera; **~tious** tendenciozan

tender ['tendə] nježan; mek; osjetljiv; škakljiv; slabašan; ponuda; MAR tender; **~ness** nježnost

tenement ['tenimənt] nastamba; stan

tenfold ['tenfould] deseterostruk

tennis ['tenis] tenis; **~-court** tenisko igralište

tenor ['tenə] tok; sadržaj; tenor

tens|e [tens] napet; krut; GRAM vrijeme; **~ion** napetost; ***high ~ion*** EL visoki napon

tent šator

tenth [tenθ] deseti; desetina; **~ly** deseto

tenu|ity [te'njuiti] rjetkoća; **~ous** nježan, fin

tepid ['tepid] mlačan

term [tə:m] rok, termin; semestar; (stručni) izraz; ***~s*** *pl* uvjeti; odnosi; (na)zvati; ***be on good*** (***bad***) ***~s with*** biti u dobrim (lošim) odnosima sa

termin|al ['tə:minl] EL pol; stega; kraj; **~ate** svršiti (se); **~us** krajnja postaja

terrace ['terəs] terasa

terri|ble ['terəbl] strašan; **~fic** strahovit; **~fy** (pre)strašiti

territor|ial [teri'tɔ:riəl]: ***~ial waters*** teritorijalne vode; **~y** područje

terror ['terə] strava; **~ize** terorizirati

test pokus; testirati

testator [tes'teitə] oporučitelj

test-case školski primjer

testify ['testifai] (po)svjedočiti

testimon|ial [testi'mounjəl] svjedodžba; **~y** svjedočanstvo (***to***)

test|-paper reagens papir; **~ pilot** pilot za pokusne le-

tove; ~ **tube** epruveta
text [tekst] tekst; slanje poruke; poslati poruku; ~**book** priručnik
textile ['tekstail] tekstilni; *pl* tekstil
text message tekstovna poruka
texture ['tekstʃə] tkivo
Thames [temz] Temza
than [ðæn] nego, od
thank [θæŋk] zahvaliti; ~**ful** zahvalan; ~**less** nezahvalan; ~**s** *pl* hvala; ~***s to*** zahvaljujući; ~**sgiving (Day)** svetkovina zahvalnosti *(posljednji četvrtak u studenom)*
that [ðæt, ðət] onaj; ona; ono; taj, ta, to; da; usto; pošto; koji, koja, koje
thaw [θɔː] jugovina; topljenje; topiti (se)
the [ðə] određen član; ~ ... ~ što ... to
theatre ['θiətə] kazalište, teatar
theft [θeft] krađa
their [ðɛə] njihov, -a, -o; ~**s** njihov, -a, -o
them [ðem] njih; njima; ~**selves** (oni) sami; sebe, sebi, se
theme [θiːm] tema
then [ðen] onda, tada; dakle; prema tome; tadašnji
theologian [θiə'loudʒiən] teolog
theology [θi'ɔlədʒi] teologija
theory ['θiəri] teorija
there [ðɛə] tamo, onamo; u tome; ~ ***is***, ~ ***are*** ima, nalazi se, nalaze se; ~ ***you are!*** eto vidiš!
there|about(s) ['ðɛərəbauts] tu negdje; ~**after** zatim; ~**by** uslijed toga; ~**fore** zato; ~**upon** nato, zatim
thermo|meter [θə'mɔmitə] termometar; ~**s flask**, ~**s bottle** termos boca
these [ðiːz] (*pl od **this***) ovi, ove, ova
they [ðei] oni, one, ona
thick [θik] debeo; gust; promukao (*glas*); mutan (*tekućina*); ~**en** udebeliti; zgusnuti; ~**et** guštara; ~**ness** debljina; gustoća
thief [θiːf], *pl **thieves*** kradljivac
thieve [θiːv] krasti
thigh [θai] bedro
thimble ['θimbl] napršnjak
thin [θin] tanak, lagan; mršav; istanjiti; razrijediti
thing [θiŋ] stvar; predmet; biće; stvor; *pl* stvari; roba; odjeća; ~***s are going better*** stvari su se popravile
think [θiŋk] misliti (***of***); razmišljati (***about***, ***over***); vjerovati; smatrati za; ~ ***a th over*** razmisliti
third [θəːd] treći; trećina; ~**ly** treće
thirst [θəːst] žeđ; žeđati (***for***, ***after***); ~**y** žedan
thir|teen ['θəː'tiːn] trinaest; ~**teenth** trinaesti; ~**tieth** trideseti; ~**ty** trideset

this [ðis] ovaj, ova, ovo; **~ *day* (*week*)** danas (tjedan dana)
thistle ['θisl] čičak
thorn [θɔ:n] trn; **~y** trnovit
thorough ['θʌrə] potpun; temeljit; **~bred** punokrvan; **~fare** glavna prometna arterija
those [ðouz] oni, one, ona
though [ðou] iako, premda; makar; ***as ~*** kao da
thought [θɔ:t] misao; **~ful** zamišljen; pažljiv (***of***); **~fulness** zamišljenost; obzirnost; **~less** nepromišljen, lakomislen, bezobziran; **~-reader** čitalac misli
thousand ['θauzənd] tisuću; tisuća; **~th** tisući
thrash [θræʃ] (iz)mlatiti; ***a sound ~ing*** poštene batine
thread [θred] konac, nit; loza zavrtnja; provući; **~bare** iznošen
threat [θret] prijetnja; **~en** prijetiti; ugrožavati
three [θri:] tri; trojka; **~fold** trostruk; **~pence** novčić ili svota od 3 penija
thresh [θreʃ] mlatiti žito
threshold ['θreʃould] prag
thrifty ['θrifti] štedljiv
thrill [θril] prodrijeti, prožeti; obuzeti; biti dirnut; ganuće; jeza
thrive [θraiv] uspijevati, napredovati
throat [θrout] ždrijelo, grlo, vrat; ***clear one's ~*** iskašljati se
throb [θrɔb] kucati, udarati (*srce*); kucanje; bi;lo
throne [θroun] prijesto(lje)
throng [θrɔŋ] vreva; mnoštvo; gurati se
throttle ['θrɔtl] (za)daviti; **~-valve** TECH leptirica
through [θru:] kroz; izravan; **~out** kroz sve; diljem; skroz naskroz
throw [θrou] bacanje; baciti; ***~ dust in a p's eyes*** bacati kome prašinu u oči; ***~ over*** prebaciti; napustiti; ***~ up one's cards*** baciti karte (*i fig*)
thrush [θrʌʃ] ZOOL drozd
thrust [θrʌst] udarac; gurati
thumb [θʌm] palac; zaprljati palcem (*knjigu etc*); *Am* ***~ one's nose*** (***to a p***) pokazati kome dugi nos; **~-print** otisak palca
thump [θʌmp] mukao udarac; tresnuti
thunder ['θʌndə] grmljavina; grmjeti; **~storm** oluja s grmljavinom
Thursday ['θə:zdi] četvrtak
thus [ðʌs] tako; prema tome
thyroid ['θairɔid] **gland** štitna žlijezda
tick [tik] inlet presvlaka; ZOOL krpelj; kucanje; (*ure*); kuckati
ticket ['tikit] (*vozna, kazališna etc*) karta; ceduljica; ***on ~ of leave*** pod policijskim nadzorom; **~ inspector** kontrolor voznih karata; **~**

office blagajna za prodaju voznih karata vozni red
ticklish ['tikliʃ] škakljiv
tide [taid] morske mijene; struja
tidings ['taidiŋz] vijesti
tidy ['taidi] uredan; urediti
tie [tai] veza (*i fig*); kravata; čvor; (pri)vezati
tier [tiə] red (*sjedala*)
tiger ['taigə] ZOOL tigar
tight [tait] koji ne propušta (*vodu etc*); čvrst; tijesan; napet; nakresan; **~en** nategnuti, stegnuti; napeti; **~-fisted** škrt; **~s** *pl* triko
tigress ['taigris] ZOOL tigrica
tile [tail] crijep; pločica za oblaganje zida, etc; pokriti crijepom; opločiti
till [til] dućanska blagajna (ladica); dok, do; obrađivati (*zemlju*); **~er** rudo kormila
tilt platneni krov (*na kolima etc*); nagib, kosina; nasrtaj; nagnuti se
timber ['timbə] (*građevno*) drvo
time [taim] vrijeme; puta; takt; ***at ~s*** s vremena na vrijeme; ***at the same ~*** istovremeno; ***by that ~*** do tog vremena; ***in ~*** na vrijeme; ***for the ~ being*** zasada; ***have a good ~*** dobro se zabavljati; odrediti vrijeme za; učiniti u pravo vrijeme; **~keeper** metronom; **~piece** ura, sat; **~ signal** RADIO znak tačnog vremena; **~table** satnica; vozni red
timid ['timid] plah, bojažljiv
tin kositar; bijeli lim; limenka, konzerva; pokositriti; stavljati u limenke; ***~ned meat*** mesna konzerva
tincture ['tiŋktʃə] boja; primjesa; tinktura; (o)bojiti
tinfoil ['tin'fɔil] staniol
tinge [tindʒ] boja; obojenje; (o)bojiti
tingle ['tiŋgl] zvoniti; brujiti
tin|man ['tinmən] limar; **~ny** limen (*zvuk*); **~ opener** otvarač za limenke; **~plate** bijeli lim
tinsel ['tinsəl] šljoka; lažno blistavilo
tint nijansa; osjenjivanje; obojiti; šatirati
tiny [taini] sićušan
tip vrh; usnik cigarete; napojnica; mig; savjet; izvrnuti; dati napojnicu; dati kome mit; **~-off** *Am* mig, savjet; **~sy** pripit; **~toe**: ***on ~toe*** na vršacima prstiju
tire [taiə] umoriti (se); guma (*na kotaču*); **~d** umoran; **~some** dosadan
tissue ['tisju:] tkivo; **~ paper** svileni papir
tit|bit ['titbit] poslastica; **~ for tat** milo za drago
title ['taitl] naslov; titula; zahtjev; nasloviti; nazvati; **~d** koji ima (plemićki) naslov
to [tu:] u, k, prema, na, za, sve do
toad [toud] ZOOL žaba kra-

stača; **~stool** (otrovna) gljiva; **~y** ulizica
toast [toust] prepečenac; zdravica; pržiti
tobacco [tə'bækou] duhan; **~nist** trafikant
toboggan [tə'bɔgən] saonice; sanjkati se
today [tə'dei] danas
toe [tou] nožni prst; vrh
together [tə'geðə] zajedno; odjednom
toil [tɔil] težak rad; **~s** mreža; mučiti se
toilet ['tɔilit] toaleta (*odjeća; zahod*); **~-set** toaletni pribor
token ['toukən] znak; uspomena; dar
tolera|ble ['tɔlərəbl] snošljiv; podnošljiv; **~nce** snošljivost; **~nt** tolerantan (***of***); **~te** podnositi; **~tion** snošljivost
toll [toul] daća; cestarina; mostarina
tomato [tə'ma:tou], *pl* ***~es*** rajčica
tomb [tu:m] grob(nica)
tomboy ['tɔmbɔi] nestašno djevojče
tomcat ['tɔmkæt] mačak
tomorrow [tə'mɔrou] sutra
ton [tʌn] tona
tone [toun] ton; zvuk
tongs [tʌŋz] *pl*: (***a pair of***) **~** kliješta
tongue [tʌŋ] jezik; govor
tonic ['tɔnik] tonikum
tonight [tə'nait] večeras
tonnage ['tʌnidʒ] tonaža
tonsil ['tɔnsl] ANAT krajnik; **~litis** upala krajnika
tonsure ['tɔnʃə] tonzura
too [tu:] pre(više); također
tool [tu:l] alat; oruđe; **~ kit** torba za alat
tooth [tu:θ], *pl* ***teeth*** zub; **~ache** zubobolja; **~brush** četkica za zube
top [tɔp] najgornji dio; vrh, vršak; krošnja; pročelje; čigra; najgornji; **~-boots** *pl* visoke čizme sa suvratkom
topic ['tɔpik] predmet; tema; **~al talk** aktuelna tema
top-notch ['tɔp'nɔtʃ] prvoklasan
topography [tə'pɔgrəfi] topografija
topsyturvy ['tɔpsi'tə:vi] pobrkan, naopak
torch [tɔ:tʃ] baklja; ***electric*** **~** džepna lampa
torment ['tɔ:ment] muka; [tɔ:'–] mučiti
torpedo [tɔ:'pi:dou], *pl* ***~es*** torpedo; MAR mina; torpedirati; **~(-boat)-destroyer** razarač
torpid ['tɔ:pid] ukočen; apatičan
torrent ['tɔrənt] bujica (*i fig*)
torrid ['tɔrid] ispržen; žarki
tortoise ['tɔ:təs] kornjača; **~shell** kornjačevina, kornjačin oklop
torture ['tɔ:tʃə] mučenje; mučiti
toss [tɔs] bacanje (uvis); ***~ up*** baciti uvis; ždrijebati (***for***)

total ['toutl] cjelokupan; ukupan; suma; zbrojiti; ~ (***up to***) iznositi; **~ity** ukupnost
totter ['tɔtə] teturati
touch [tʌtʃ] (do)dirnuti; ~ ***off*** *tel* objesiti (*slušalicu*); dodir; napadaj bolesti; crta; ***get in ~ with*** stupiti u vezu sa
tough [tʌf] žilav; **~ness** žilavost
tour [tuə] (kružno) putovanje; turneja; (pro)putovati; **~ing** putni
tourist ['tuərist] turist; **~ agency**, **~ office**, **~ bureau** turistička agencija; **~ industry** turistička industrija; **~ season** turistička sezona
tout [taut] domamljivač mušterija; mamiti mušterije
tow [tou] tegljenje; tegliti; ***take in ~*** tegliti
toward(s) [tə'wɔːdz] k, ka, prema; za
towel ['tauəl] ručnik
tower ['tauə] toranj; dizati se (uvis); **~ing** koji se visoko diže
town [taun] grad; **~ council** gradsko vijeće; **~ hall** gradska vijećnica; **~-planning** urbanistika; **~sman** građanin; **~swoman** građanka
toy [tɔi] igračka
trace [treis] trag; slijediti; (pro)naći; utvrditi; nabaciti
track [træk] trag; kolotečina; SPORT staza; pruga; tragati
tractable ['træktəbl] gibak; povodljiv
tract|ion ['trækʃən] **engine** vučni stroj; **~or** traktor
trade [treid] trgovina; zanat; trgovački; **~mark** trgovački znak; **~r** trgovac; trgovački brod; **~(s) union** sindikat
tradition [trə'diʃən] tradicija
traffic ['træfɪk] trgovina; promet; **~ jam** zastoj prometa; trgovati
trag|edy ['trædʒidi] tragedija; **~ic(al)** tragičan
trail [treil] povlaka; trag; put; povlačiti; **~er** prikolica
train [trein] niz; vlak; pratnja; povlaka (haljine); odgojiti; izobraziti; trenirati; ***by ~*** vlakom; **~ accident**, **~ disaster** željeznička nesreća; **~er** trener; **~ing** vježbanje; trening; **~ing-college** učiteljska (pedagoška) škola
trait [trei] osobina; crta; **~or** izdajica (***to***); **~orous** izdajnički
trajectory ['trædʒiktəri] putanja
tram(-car) [træm(kaː)] tramvajska kola
tramp [træmp] topot(anje); skitnja; skitnica; (pro)pješačiti
tramway ['træmwei] tramvajska pruga, tramvaj
trance [trаːns] trans, zanos
tranquil ['træŋkwil] miran
transact [træn'zækt] obavljati, izvesti; **~ion** (trgovački) posao; transakcija; **~or**

ugovarač
trans|cribe [træns'kraib] prepisati; transkribirati; **~fer** [~'fəː] prenijeti; premjestiti; prenositi; prelaziti; ['~] prijenos; transfer doznaka; premještaj; otisak; prijelazna karta; **~ferable** prenosiv
transfiguration [trænsfıgjuə'reiʃən] preobražaj
transform [træns'fɔːm] preobraziti; preinačiti; pretvoriti; **~ation** promjena; transformacija; **~er** EL transformator
trans|fuse [træns'fjuːz] pretočiti; izvesti transfuziju; **~gression** [~'greʃən] prekršaj
tranship [træn'ʃip] prekrcati
transient ['trænziənt] prolazan; kratkotrajan; *Am* prolazni putnik
transit ['trænsit] prolaz; tranzit; **~ion** prijelaz
translat|able [traːns'leitəbl] prevediv; **~e** prevesti, prevoditi; **~ion** prijevod; **~or** prevodilac
transmarine [trænzmə'riːn] prekomorski
transmi|ssion [trænz'miʃən] TECH, PHYS, RADIO prenošenje; prijenos; **~t** otpremiti, poslati; odašiljati; prenositi; **~tter** odašiljač
trans|parent [træns'peərənt] proziran; **~pire** [~'paiə] isparivati se; pročuti se; **~plant** presaditi; **~port** [~'pɔːt] (pre)voziti; ['~] prijevoz; transport; zanos
trap [træp] zamka; **~door** poklopna vrata; THEAT jama
trapeze [trə'piːz] trapez
trash [træʃ] smeće; besmislica; **~y** bezvrijedan, loš
travel ['trævl] putovati; putovanje; **~ler** putnik; **~ling crane** TECH mosna dizalica
traverse ['trævəːs] ukrstiti; prijeći poprijeko; ići poprijeko
trawl [trɔːl] koča (mreža)
tray [trei] poslužavnik, taca; plitica; umetak kovčega
treacher|ous ['tretʃərəs] izdajnički; **~y** izdaja
treacle [triːkl] sirup
tread [tred] stupiti; gaziti; korak; **~le** pedal; gaziti pedal; **~mill** točak pokretan gaženjem
treason ['triːzn] izdaja
treasur|e ['treʒə] blago; sakupljati; gomilati blago; **~er** rizničar; blagajnik; **~y** riznica; državna blagajna; ***~y bill*** državna kratkoročna obveznica; ***Ꞩy Department*** *Am* ministarstvo financija
treat [triːt] postupati; tretirati; častiti; veliki užitak; ***~ with*** ugovarati s; **~ise** rasprava; **~ment** postupak; obrada; **~y** međunarodni ugovor; ***be in ~y with*** pregovarati s kim
treble ['trebl] trostruk; so-

pran, diskant
tree [tri:] drvo
trellis ['trelis] sjenica; rešetka; uzgajati u špaliru
tremble ['trembl] drhtati (***at***)
tremendous [tri'mendəs] strašan; ogroman
trem|or ['tremə] drhtanje, potres; **~ulous** drhtav
trench [trentʃ] jarak; izbrazditi; **~ coat** trenčkot
trend smjer, tok
tress [tres] uvojak kose, pletenica
trial ['traiəl] pokus, ispitivanje; proces; ***on ~*** na pokus
triangle ['traiæŋgl] trokut
tribe [traib] pleme, rod
tribunal [tri'bju:nl] sudsko sjedište
tribut|ary ['tribjutəri] podvrgnut porezu; pritoka; **~e** porez; priznanje
trick [trik] lukavština; trik; prevariti (***out of***)
trickle ['trikl] kapati; prokapljivati
trick(s)y ['trik(s)i] prepreden
triplets ['triplits] *pl* trojci
troop [tru:p] trupa; mnoštvo; jato; *pl* trupe; sakupljati se; sjatiti se
trophy ['troufı] trofej
tropic|al ['trɔpikəl] tropski; **~s** *pl* tropi
trot [trɔt] kas(anje); kasati; **~ters** *pl* životinjske noge kao jelo
trouble ['trʌbl] nemir; smetnja; (*i* TECH); nevolja; jad; muka, patnja; smetati, uznemirivati; dosađivati; (po-) truditi se; **~some** neugodan, dosadan
trough [trɔf] korito
trousers ['trauzəz] *pl* hlače
trout [traut] pastrva
troy(-weight) ['trɔi(weit)] težinska mjera za plemenite kovine i dragulje
truant ['truənt] dokon; koji dangubi; ***play ~*** markirati; izbivati s obuke
truce [tru:s] primirje
truck [trʌk] (ručna) kolica; teretna kola; *Am* kamion
true [tru:] istinit; prav; vjeran; ispravan; ***come ~*** obistiniti se; ***be ~ of*** vrijediti za
truffle ['trʌfl] gomoljika
truism ['truizəm] očevidna istina
truly ['tru:li] istinito; zaista
trump [trʌmp] *kartanje*: adut; tući adutom; ***~ up*** izmisliti
trumpet ['trʌmpit] truba; zvučnik; **~er** trubač
truncheon ['trʌntʃən] (policijska) palica; (maršalski) štap
trunk [trʌŋk] deblo; trup; surla (*slona*); veliki kovčeg
trust [trʌst] povjerenje (***in***); ***on ~*** na povjerenje; ***in ~*** u pohrani; polog; trust; vjerovati; povjeriti
trust|ee [trʌs'ti:] upravitelj; skrbnik; **~ful**, **~ing** pun povjerenja
trustworth|iness ['trʌstwə:-

ðinis] pouzdanost; **~y** pouzdan
truth [tru:θ] istina; **~ful** istinit
try [trai] (po)kušati; ispitivati; voditi istragu (***for***); ***~ on*** probati odjeću; **~ing** naporan; **~-on** proba odjeće
tub [tʌb] bure; kaca; kada; kupelj (*u kadi*); *coll* želudac
tube [tju:b] cijev; (*Am katodna*) cijev; tuba; zračnica; podzemna željeznica (*osobito u Londonu*)
tuberculosis [tju:bə:kju'lousis] tuberkuloza
tuck [tʌk] nabor; *sl* poslastice; ***~ up*** porubiti; (u)turiti
Tuesday ['tju:zdi] utorak
tug [tʌg] tegljač; trzaj; vući, potezati (***at***); tegliti
tuition [tju'iʃən] poučavanje, nastava
tulip ['tju:lip] BOT tulipan
tumble ['tʌmbl] pasti; prebacivati se; prevrnuti se; ispremlatiti; **~r** čaša za vodu
tumour ['tju:mə] tumor
tumult ['tju:məlt] buka, metež
tun [tʌn] bačva; sud
tune [tju:n] melodija; ***out of ~*** neusklađen; RADIO ***~ in*** namjestiti na; ***~ out*** isključiti
tunnel ['tʌnl] tunel
turbine ['tə:bin] turbina
turbot ['tə:bət] ZOOL obliš, iverak (*riba*)
turbulent ['tə:bjulənt] nemiran; buran
tureen [tə'ri:n] zdjela za juhu
turf [tə:f] tratina; tresetište; trkalište; **~y** pokriven tratinom; koji se tiče trkačkog sporta
Turkey ['tə:ki] Turska; **♀** puran
Turkish ['tə:kiʃ] turski; ***~ towel*** frotir ručnik
turmoil ['tə:mɔil] buna; metež
turn [tə:n] vrtjeti; okrenuti (se); usmjeriti; pretvoriti (***into***); svratiti (***from***); tokariti; postati; ***~ a corner*** skrenuti iza ugla; ***~ down*** zavrnuti (*plin, etc*); otkloniti (*prijedlog*); dati kome košaricu; ***~ off, on*** zatvoriti, otvoriti slavinu; ***~ out*** proizvoditi robu; otjerati; ispasti; ugasiti (*plin, etc*); ***~ up*** dići uvis; zasukati; odvrnuti (*plin, etc*); izroniti; pojaviti se; okret(anje); zavoj; prekretnica; promjena; šetnja; oblik; tačka programa; usluga; ***by*** (*ili* ***in***) **~s** naizmjence; ***it is my ~*** na meni je red; **~coat** prevrtljivac; **~-down collar** presavinut ovratnik; **~er** tokar
turnip ['tə:nip] (bijela) repa
turn|-out ['tə:n'aut] oprema; proizvodnja; **~over** prodaja; promet; **~pike** brklja (*na mitnici*); mitnica; **~-table** RLW okretnica; **~-up** suvratak na hlačama
turpentine ['tə:pəntain] terpentin
turquoise ['tə:kwa:z] tirkiz

turtle ['tə:tl] ZOOL kornjača
tusk [tʌsk] kljova; zub derač
tutor ['tju:tə] skrbnik; privatni učitelj
tuxedo [tʌk'si:dou] *Am* smoking
tweezers ['twi:zəz] *pl* pinceta
twelfth [twelfθ] dvanaesti; dvanaestina
twelve [twelv] dvanaest; **~fold** dvanaesterostruk
twice [twais] dvaput
twig [twig] grančica; *coll* shvatiti
twilight ['twailait] sumrak; **~ *of the gods*** suton bogova
twin [twin] dvostruk; blizanac
twine [twain] dretva; konac; (u)sukati; (is)prepletati
twinkle ['twiŋkl] svjetlucati; treptati; ***in the twinkling of a eye*** u tren oka
twirl [twə:l] vitlanje
twist [twist] okretanje, uvijanje; konac; okretati; iskriviti
twitch [twitʃ] trgnuti, trzati; čupkati; trzanje; štipanje
twitter ['twitə] cvrkutati
two [tu:] dva; **~fold** dvostruk; **~pence** ['tʌpəns] (iznos od) dva penija (*2d*)
tycoon [tai'ku:n] *Am coll* industrijski magnat
type [taip] tip; uzor(ak); štamparsko slovo; **~writer** pisaći stroj
typhoon [tai'fu:n] tajfun
typical ['tipikəl] tipičan (***of***)
typist ['taipist] daktilograf
tyranny ['tirəni] tiranija
tyrant ['taiərənt] tiranin

U

udder ['ʌdə] vime
ugl|iness ['ʌglinis] ružnoća; **~y** ružan, gadan
U. K. = United Kingdom
ulcer ['ʌlsə] čir
ulterior [ʌl'tiəriə] onostran; daljnji
ultimate ['ʌltimit] konačan; krajnji
umbrella [ʌm'brelə] kišobran
umpire ['ʌmpaiə] (*arbitražni ili sportski*) sudac
un|abashed ['ʌnə'bæʃt] drzak; smion; **~able** nesposoban; **~abridged** neskraćen; **~acceptable** neprihvatljiv
unaccustomed ['ʌnə'kʌstəmd] neuobičajen; **~ *to*** nenavikao na
un|acquainted ['ʌnə'kweintid] neupoznat s; **~affected** nepromijenjen; neizvještačen; **~alterable** nepromjenljiv; **~amiable** neljubezan
unanimity [ju:nə'nimiti] jednodušnost
un|answerable [ʌn'a:nsər-

əbl] nepobitan; **~appalled** neustrašiv; **~approachable** nepristupačan; **~apt** nesposoban; neprikladan; **~armed** nenaoružan; **~assuming** skroman; **~attainable** nedokučiv; **~attended** nepraćen; **~available** neraspoloživ; neupotrebljiv; beskoristan; **~avoidable** neizbježiv

unaware ['ʌnə'wɛə] nesvjestan; **~s** nehotice

un|balanced ['ʌn'bælənst] neuravnotežen; **~bar** otkračunati; **~bearable** nepodnošljiv; **~becoming** nepristao; **~beknown** nepoznat; **~believing** koji ne vjeruje; **~bend** olabaviti (se); **~biassed** nepristran; **~bid(den)** nepozvan; **~bind** odriješiti

unbolt ['ʌn'boult] otkračunati; **~ed** otkračunan

unbound ['ʌn'baund] nevezan; **~ed** neograničen; neobuzdan

un|broken ['ʌn'broukən] neslomljen; **~burden** oteretiti (*fig*); **~button** otkopčati; **~ceasing** neprestan; **~certain** nesiguran; neizvjestan; **~changeable** nepromjenljiv; **~checked** nesmetan; neispitan; **~civil** neučtiv; **~claimed** netražen; nepodignut (*pismo*)

uncle ['ʌŋkl] ujak

un|comfortable [ʌn'kʌmfətəbl] neudoban; **~common** neobičan; **~concerned** ravnodušan; nezainteresiran; **~conscientious**, **~conscionable** nesavjestan

unconscious [ʌn'kɔnʃəs] nesvjestan; bez svijesti; ***be ~ of*** ne slutiti

un|contested ['ʌnkən'testid] neosporen; **~convinced** neuvjeren; **~couple** iskopčati; **~cover** (raz)otkriti; **~damaged** neoštećen; **~daunted** neustrašen; **~deceive** otvoriti kome oči; objasniti; **~decided** neodlučan; **~defined** neodređen; **~deniable** neosporan

under ['ʌndə] dolje; ispod; niže; pod; **~bid** (po)nuditi nižu cijenu; **~clothing** rublje; **~-developed** nerazvijen; nedovoljno razvijen; **~done** nedopečen; **~expose** prekratko osvijetliti (FILM); **~fed** neishranjen; **~go** pretrpjeti; **~graduate** student(ica); **~ground railway** podzemna željeznica; **~line** podcrtati; **~-linen** donje rublje; **~mine** minirati; potkopati; **~most** najniži; **~neath** (is)pod; **~pin** poduprijeti (*i fig*); podzidati; **~signed** potpisnik; **~sized** koji je ispod normalne veličine; **~stand** razumjeti; uvidjeti; *fig* čuti; **~take** poduzeti; **~taker** vlasnik pogrebnog zavoda; **~value** podcijeniti; **~-wear** donje rublje

un|deserved ['ʌndi'zəːvd]

nezaslužen; ~**desirable** nepoželjan; ~**developed** nerazvijen; ~**digested** neprobavljen; ~**diminished** nesmanjen; ~**disturbed** nesmetan; ~**do** otvoriti; otkopčati; popraviti učinjeno; ~**doubted** nesumnjiv; ~**dress** skinuti (se); kućna haljina; ~**dutiful** neposlušan; koji zaboravlja na dužnost; ~**earthly** nezemaljski; strašno ran; ~**easiness** nemir; tjeskoba; ~**eatable** nejestiv; ~**educated** neobrazovan

unemploy|ed ['ʌnim'plɔid] nezaposlen; neupotrebljiv; ~**ment benefit** potpora za nezaposlene

un|equal ['ʌn'i:kwəl] nejednak; ~**equivocal** nedvomislen; ~**essential** nevažan; ~**even** nejednak; ~**exampled** besprimjeran; ~**expected** neočekivan; ~**explored** neistražen; ~**fading** stalan (*boja*); ~**failing** nepogrešiv; ~**fair** nepošten; nepravedan; ~**faltering** nepokolebljiv; koji ne tetura; ~**fashionable** nemoderan; ~**fasten** otvoriti; odvezati; ~**fathomable** nedokučiv; ~**favourable** nepovoljan; ~**feeling** bezosjećajan; ~**finished** nesvršen; ~**fit** neprikladan; nesposoban; ~**fold** razviti (se), otvoriti (se); ~**foreseen** nepredviđen; ~**forgiving** nepomirljiv; ~**forgot(ten)** nezaboravljen; ~**fortunate** nesretan; jadan; ~**furnished** nemebliran; ~**gentlemanly** negospodski; neodgojen; ~**graceful** nezgrapan; ~**gracious** neprijazan; ~**grateful** nezahvalan; ~**guarded** neoprezan; nezaštićen; ~**happy** nesretan; ~**healthy** nezdrav; ~**heard-of** nečuven; ~**hook** otkvačiti; ~**hoped-for** neočekivan; ~**hurt** neozlijeđen

uniform ['ju:nifɔ:m] jednoličan; ujednačen; uniforma

un|impaired ['ʌnim'pɛəd] neoslabljen; ~**injured** neozlijeđen; ~**insured** neosiguran; ~**intelligible** nerazumljiv; ~**intentional** nenamjeran

union ['ju:njən] savez; unija; brak; ujedinjenje; sloga; jedinstvo; udruženje; ~**ist** sindikalist; ♀ **Jack** britanska nacionalna zastava; ~ **suit** *Am* potkošulja i gaće u jednom komadu

unique [ju:'ni:k] jedinstven

unit ['ju:nit] jedinica

unit|e [ju:'nait] ujediniti (se); ♀**ed States** Sjedinjene Države Amerike; ~**y** ['~niti] jedinstvo; jedinica

univers|al [ju:ni'və:səl] (sve)opći; univerzalan; svjetski; ~**ality** mnogostranost; ~**e** svemir; ~**ity** sveučilište, univerzitet

un|just ['ʌn'dʒʌst] nepravedan; **~kind** neljubezan; **~known** nepoznat; **~lace** odvezati; **~ladylike** koji ne dolikuje dami; **~lawful** nezakonit; **~learned** neškolovan, neuk

unless [ən'les] ako ne; osim da

un|like ['ʌn'laik] ne nalik; različit; **~limited** neograničen; **~load** istovariti

unlock ['ʌn'lɔk] otključati; **~ed** otključan

un|looked-for neočekivan; **~manageable** neposlušan; nepodatan; teško savladiv; **~manly** nemuževan; **~mannerly** neodgojen; **~matched** neusporediv; **~meaning** beznačajan; **~mentionable** koji se ne može spomenuti; **~merciful** nemilosrdan; **~mindful** bezobziran; **~mistakable** očevidan

unmoved ['ʌn'mu:vd] nedirnut; nepomičan

un|natural [ʌn'nætʃrəl] neprirodan; **~nerve** oslabiti živce; **~noticed** neprimjećen; **~observant** nepažljiv; **~obtrusive** nenametljiv

unoffending ['ʌnə'fendiŋ] bezazlen; koji ne vrijeđa

un|pack ['ʌn'pæk] ispakovati; **~palatable** neukusan; **~perceived** neopažen; **~pleasant** neugodan; **~popularity** neomiljenost; **~practised** neuvježban; **~precedented** besprimjeran; **~prejudiced** nepristran; **~prepared** nepripravan; **~pretending**, **~pretentious** skroman; **~promising** koji ne obećava mnogo; **~proved** nedokazan; **~provoked** bezrazložan; **~questionable** neosporan; nesumnjiv; **~ravel** razmr(se); riješiti; **~reasonable** nerazuman; pretjeran; **~redeemed** neotkupljen; neiskupljen

unrefined ['ʌnri'faind] nepročišćen; *fig* neobrazovan

un|relenting ['ʌnri'lentiŋ] nepopustljiv; **~reliable** nepouzdan; **~rewarded** nenagrađen; **~rivalled** neusporediv; **~ruled** neupravljen, neliniran (*papir*); **~safe** nesiguran; **~satisfactory** koji ne zadovoljava; **~screw** odviti; odšarafiti (se); **~scrupulous** besavjestan; neskrupulozan; **~seasonable** neumjestan; **~seen** neviđen; **~selfish** nesebičan; **~serviceable** neupotrebljiv

unsettle ['ʌn'setl] poremetiti; **~d** nesiguran; poremećen; kolebljiv; nesmiren

unshapely ['ʌn'ʃeipli] neskladan; ružan

unshrink|able ['ʌn'ʃriŋkəbl] koji se ne skuplja (*tkanina*); **~ing** neustrašiv

un|sightly [ʌn'saitli] ružan; **~skilled** nevješt; nekvalificiran; **~sociable** nedruštven;

~sound nezdrav; **~spent** nepotrošen; neiscrpljen; **~sportsmanlike** nesportski; nelovački; **~steady** nestalan; nesiguran; **~studied** neupućen; prirodan; **~suitable** neprikladan; **~surpassable** nenadmašiv; **~suspicious** nesumnjičav; **~sworn** nezaprisegnut; nezaklet; **~thinkable** nezamisliv; **~tidy** neuredan; **~tie** odvezati

until [ən'til] (sve) do; dok (ne)

un|timely [ʌn'taimli] prijevremen; nepravodoban; nezgodan; **~tiring** neumoran; **~touched** netaknut; **~travelled** koji nije putovao; neproputovan (*kraj*); **~tried** neokušan; neisproban; nepresuđen; **~true** neistinit; **~trustworthy** nepouzdan; **~truth** neistina; **~usual** neobičan; **~utterable** neizreciv; **~varied** nepromijenjen; **~veil** skinuti veo; **~versed** neupućen; **~warranted** neovlašten; nezajamčen; **~welcome** koji nije dobro došao; **~wholesome** nezdrav; štetan; **~wieldy** nespretan; nezgrapan; **~willing** nesklon; nerad; **~wise** nerazuman; **~womanly** neženski; **~wonted** nenaviknut (*to*); **~worthy** nedostojan; **~wrap** odmotati; razmotati; **~written** nepisan; neispisan; **~yielding** nepopustljiv

up [ʌp] gore; naviše; prema gore; na nogama; izišao (*sunce*); istekao (*vrijeme*); ***be hard ~*** biti u teškim prilikama; ***~ to*** (sve) do; ***be ~ to a th*** biti dorastao čemu; ***it's to me to do*** na meni je da učinim; ***what are you ~ to there?*** što vi tamo radite?; ***what's ~?*** što se tu zbiva?; ***it's all ~ with him*** s njim je gotovo

up|-country (koji je) u unutrašnjosti zemlje; **~hill** uzbrdo; **~hold** držati uspravno; poduprijeti

upholster [ʌp'houlstə] tapecirati; **~er** tapetar; dekorater

upkeep ['ʌpki:p] troškovi održavanja; uzdržavanje

upon [ə'pɔn] na

upper ['ʌpə] gornji; ***the ~ ten (thousand)*** gornjih deset tisuća; **~s** *pl* gornja koža; **~cut** *boks* udarac odozdo

upright ['ʌp'rait] uspravan (*i fig*); stup; pianino

uproar ['ʌprɔ:] buka; metež

upset [ʌp'set] izvrnuti; poremetiti

upside ['ʌpsaid]: ***~ down*** obrnuto; u neredu

upstairs ['ʌp'stɛəz] gore; u gornjem katu

upstart ['ʌpsta:t] skorojević

uptake ['ʌpteik]: ***be slow in the ~*** sporo shvaćati

upward ['ʌpwəd] okrenut uvis

urge [ə:dʒ] goniti; požurivati;

nagovarati; uporno tražiti; **~ncy** hitnost; požurivanje; **~nt** hitan; uporan
urn [ə:n] urna
us [ʌs] nama; nas; sebe; ***of ~*** naš
U. S. (A.) = United States (of America)
usage ['ju:zidʒ] navika; jezični običaj; upotreba (*riječi*)
use [ju:s] upotreba; primjena; običaj; korisnost; [~z] upotrebljavati; služiti se; primijeniti; ***it is (of) no ~*** uzaludno je; ***I ~d to do*** običavao sam činiti; ***~d to*** naviknut na; ***~ up*** potrošiti; istrošiti; **~ful** upotrebiv; koristan; **~less** beskoristan; neupotrebiv
usher ['ʌʃə] vratar; sudski sluga; ***~ (in)*** uvesti; najaviti
usual ['ju:ʒuəl] običan; uobičajen
usufruct ['ju:sju:frʌkt] uživanje prava
usur|er ['ju:ʒərə] lihvar; **~y** lihvarstvo
utensil [ju:'tensl] alat
utili|ty [ju:'tiliti] korisnost; ***public ~ty*** komunalne usluge; **~zation** korišćenje; **~ze** koristiti se; iskoristiti
utmost ['ʌtmoust] krajnji
utter ['ʌtə] *fig* krajnji; izreći; **~ance** izražavanje; izraz; **~most** krajnji
uvula ['ju:vjulə] ANAT jezičac, resica

V

vacan|cy ['veikənsi] praznina; nepopunjeno radno mjesto; ***gaze into ~cy*** buljiti u prazno; **~t** prazan; slobodan
vacation [və'keiʃən] praznici
vaccinat|e ['væksineit] cijepiti; **~ion** cijepljenje
vacillat|e ['væsileit] kolebati se; **~ion** kolebanje
vacuum ['vækjuəm] **cleaner** usisivač prašine
vagabond ['vægəbənd] skitnica
vague [veig] neodređen; mutan
vain [vein] tašt (***of***); isprazan; ništav; ***in ~*** uzalud
valerian [və'liəriən] valerijana
valet ['vælit] sobar
valient ['væljənt] hrabar
valid ['vælid] (puno)valjan; **~ity** pravomoćnost
valley ['væli] dolina
valorize ['væləraiz] valorizirati
valu|able ['væljuəbl] vrijedan; **~ables** *pl* dragocjenosti; **~e** ['~ju:] vrijednost; valuta; (pro)cijeniti
valve [vælv] zalistak; ventil;

RADIO cijev
vamp [væmp] naglavak cipele; zavodnica
van [væn] (zatvorena) kola za prijevoz pokućtva; (zatvoren) teretni vagon
vane [vein] vjetrenica; krilo (vjetrenjače, propelera)
vanilla [və'nilə] vanilija
vanish ['væniʃ] nestati
vanity ['væniti] taština; ispraznost; ~ **bag** ručna torbica; ~ **case** kutijica za puder s ogledalcem
vapo|rize ['veipəraiz] isparivati; ~**ur** maglica, para; ***~ur-bath*** parna kupelj
varia|ble ['vɛəriəbl] promjenljiv; ~**nce** promjena; neslaganje; ~**tion** promjena; kolebanje; varijacija
varicose ['værikous] **vein** proširena vena
variety [və'raiəti] raznolikost; (pod)vrsta; ~ **show** varijetetska predstava
various ['vɛəriəs] različit; raznolik
varnish ['va:niʃ] firnis; lak; lakirati
vary ['vɛəri] mijenjati; promijeniti; razlikovati se (***from***)
vase [va:z] vaza
vast [va:st] ogroman; golem; beskrajan
vault [vɔ:lt] svod; trezor; grobnica; skok; nadsvoditi; (pre)skočiti
veal [vi:l] teletina; ***roast*** ~ teleće pečenje
vegeta|ble(s) ['vedʒitəbl(z)] povrće; ~**rian** vegetarijanac; ~**tion** vegetacija
vehemen|ce ['vi:iməns] žestina; ~**t** nagao; žestok
vehicle ['vi:ikl] vozilo; sredstvo
veil [veil] veo; zastrti (se) velom
vein [vein] vena; sklonost
velocity [vi'lɔsiti] brzina
velvet ['velvit] baršun; ~**een** pamučni baršun
vend prodavati; ~**er**, ~**or** prodavač; ~**ible** koji se može prodati; ~**ing machine** prodajni automat
venerat|e ['venəreit] (po)štovati; ~**ion** (po)štovanje
venereal [vi'niəriəl] **disease** spolna bolest
Venetian [vi'ni:ʃən] venecijanski; ~ **blind** žaluzija
vengeance ['vendʒəns] osveta
Venice ['venis] Venecija
venison ['venizn] divljač; srnetina
vent otvor; ispuh; odvod; ***give ~ to*** dati oduška
ventilat|e ['ventileit] ventilirati; ~**ion** ventilacija; ~**or** ventilator
ventriloquist [ven'triləkwist] trbuhozborac
venture ['ventʃə] smion pothvat; spekulacija; staviti na kocku; usuditi se; ***at a ~*** na sreću; ~**some** odvažan
veracious [və'reiʃəs] istinit

verb [və:b] GRAM glagol; **~al** verbalan; usmen; GRAM glagolski
verdict ['və:dikt] pravorijek
verd|igris ['və:digris] bakreni acetat; **~ure** zelenilo
verge [və:dʒ] rub; naginjati se
verify ['verifai] provjeriti; dokazati; potvrditi
vermicelli [və:mi'seli] fidelini (*tjestenina*)
vermin ['və:min] gamad
vers|e [və:s] stih; **~ed** verziran; vješt (***in***); **~ion** ['-ʃən] verzija
verve [vɛəv] zanos; žar
very ['veri] vrlo; ***the ~ best*** (baš) ono najbolje; ***the ~ same*** baš taj isti; ***in the ~ act*** na samom činu; ***the ~ thought*** već i sama pomisao
vessel ['vesl] posuda; brod
vest potkošulja; maja; prsluk; ***~ed rights*** stečena prava
vestibule ['vestibju:l] predvorje; pretsoblje; trijem; *Am* **~ train** vlak s vagonima spojenim natkritim hodnicima
vestige ['vestidʒ] trag
vestry ['vestri] sakristija
vet [vet] *coll* veterinar; *Am* veteran
veteran ['vetərən] veteran
veterinary ['vetnri] **surgeon** veterinar
veto ['vi:tou], *pl* **~es** veto
vex [veks] dosađivati mučiti; šikanirati; **~ation** dodijavanje; šikaniranje; **~atious** neugodan; dosadan
vibrat|e [vai'breit] vibrirati; **~ion** vibracija
vicar ['vikə] vikar
vice [vais] porok; mana; škrip
vice... ['vais-]: **~-consul** vicekonzul; **~roy** potkralj
vice versa ['vaisi'və:sə] obrnuto
vicinity [vi'siniti] blizina; susjedstvo
vicious ['viʃəs] pokvaren; opak
victim ['viktim] žrtva
victor ['viktə] pobjednik; **~ious** pobjednički; **~y** pobjeda
victuals ['vitlz] *pl* živežne namirnice
Vienna [vi'enə] Beč
view [vju:] vidik; pogled; prizor; razgledati; motriti; prosuđivati; ***in ~ of*** s obzirom na; ***in my ~*** po mom shvaćanju; ***with a ~ to*** u svrhu; s ciljem; ***have*** (***keep***) ***in ~*** imati na umu; držati na oku; **~finder** PHOT tražilo, vizir; **~point** gledište, stanovište
vigilance ['vidʒiləns] budnost
vigorous ['vigərəs] snažan
vigour ['vigə] snaga; energija
vile [vail] podao; prost
village ['vilidʒ] selo
villain ['vilən] nitkov; hulja; **~y** lupeštvo
vindicate ['vindikeit] (o)braniti; opravdati

vine [vain] (vinova) loza
vin|egar ['vinigə] (vinski) ocat; **~tage** berba
viol|ate ['vaiəleit] povrijediti; prekršiti; silovati; **~ence** nasilje; silovitost; **~ent** silovit; žestok
violet ['vaiəlit] ljubičica
violin ['vaiəlin] violina
viper ['vaipə] zmija otrovnica
virgin ['və:dʒin] djevica; **~(al)** djevičanski; nevin; netaknut
virtue ['və:tju:] vrlina; krepost; ***in ~ of*** pomoću; uslijed
virtuous ['və:tjuəs] krepostan
virus ['vaiərəs] *computer* virus
visa ['vi:zə] viza
viscount ['vaikaunt] vikont (*engleski plemićki naslov*)
visé ['vi:zei] *vidi* **visa**
visib|ility [vizi'biliti] vidljivost; **~le** vidljiv; očit
vision ['viʒən] vid; vizija
visit ['vizit] posjetiti; razgledati; posjet; **~or** posjetilac; ***~ors' book*** knjiga gostiju
visual ['vizjuəl] vidni, vizuelan
vital ['vaitl] životni; vitalan; **~ity** životna snaga; vitalnost
vitamin(e) ['vitəmin] vitamin
vivaci|ous [vi'veiʃəs] živ(ahan); **~ty** živahnost
vivid ['vivid] živ(ahan)
vocal ['voukəl] glasovni; zvučan; glasan; **~ chord** glasnica
vocation [vou'keiʃən] nutarnji nagon; poziv; zvanje; **~al guidance** savjetovanje za izbor zvanja
vogue [voug] omiljelost; moda;
voice [vɔis] glas; **~ mail** telefonska sekretarica
void [vɔid] prazan; JUR bez zakonske vrijednosti; praznina; rupa; ***~ of*** koji nema; bez
volcano [vɔl'keinou], *pl* ***~es*** vulkan
volley ['vɔli] salva; *tenis* volej; ispaliti salvu; *tenis* odbiti loptu u zraku; **~ball** odbojka
voltage ['voultidʒ] EL napon
voluble ['vɔljubl] brbljav; blagoglagoljiv
volume ['vɔljum] svezak knjige; opseg (*glasa*); **~-control, ~ regulator** regulator jakosti glasa
volunt|ary ['vɔləntəri] dobrovoljan; **~eer** dobrovoljac; dobrovoljno služiti
voluptuous [və'lʌptjuəs] razbludan; obilan
vomit ['vɔmit] povraćati
voracious [və'reiʃəs] proždrljiv
vot|ary ['voutəri] poklonik; **~e** glas(anje); pravo glasa; (iz)glasati; ***~e of (non-)confidence*** izglašavanje (ne-)povjerenja; **~er** glasač, birač
voting-booth glasačka kabina; **~-box** glasačka kutija
vouch [vautʃ]: ***~ (for)*** jamčiti za; **~er** namira; dokaz

vow [vau] zavjet; zavjetovati se
vowel ['vauəl] vokal
voyage [vɔidʒ] dugo putovanje (*morem, zrakom*); putovati
vulcani|te ['vʌlkənait] ebonit (tvrda guma); **~red fibre** vulkanizirano vlakno
vulgar ['vʌlgə] prost; običan; vulgaran; **~ity** prostota; **~ize** popularizirati
vulnerable ['vʌlnərəbl] ranjiv

W

wadding ['wɔdiŋ] podstava od vate; vata
waddle ['wɔdl] gegati se
wade [weid] gaziti (*vodu*); **~rs** *pl* visoke čizme za vodu
wafer ['weifə] vafli, oblata
wag [wæg] kimati; tresti repom; šaljivčina
wage-earner ['weidʒəːnə] zarađivač
wages ['weidʒiz] *pl* nadnica
wag(g)on ['wægən] (teretna) kola; **~er** vozar
wail [weil] jadikovka; jadikovati
wainscot(ing) ['weinskət(iŋ)] drvena oplata
waist [weist] struk; **~coat** prsluk
wait [weit] čekati (***for***); posluživati (***on***); ***keep ~ing*** pustiti koga da čeka; **~er** konobar; **~ing-room** čekaonica; **~ress** konobarica
wake [weik] brazda za brodom; zračni vir; bdjeti; probuditi (se); ***~ up*** probuditi (se); **~n** (pro)buditi se; *fig* prodrmati
walk [wɔːk] hodati; šetati; obilaziti; vodati; šetnja; **~er** pješak; šetač; SPORT hodač
walking ['wɔːkiŋ]: ***~ tour*** pješačenje; ***~ stick*** štap za šetnju; *Am* ***give a p his ~ papers*** otpustiti koga
walk|-out ['wɔːkaut] *Am* štrajk; **~-over** laka pobjeda
wall [wɔːl] zid, stijena; obzidati; ***~ up*** zazidati; **~et** lisnica; **~flower** BOT šeboj; *fig* djevojka bez plesača
wallow ['wɔlou] valjati se
wall|-paper (zidna) tapeta; **~-socket** EL priključnica
walnut ['wɔːlnət] orah(ovina)
waltz [wɔːls] valcer; plesati valcer
wand [wɔnd] (dirigentski, čarobni) štapić
wander ['wɔndə] (za)lutati; udaljiti se (***from***); bulazniti; **~er** putnik
wangle ['wæŋgl] *sl* spletkariti; "udesiti"; **~r** spletkar
want [wɔnt] oskudica; potreba; nedostajati; trebati;

tražiti; željeti; ***for ~ of*** u pomanjkanju
war [wɔː] rat; ♀ ***Office*** ministarstvo rata
ward [wɔːd] zaštita; starateljstvo; štićenik; odjel (*u bolnici*); gradski kvart; ***~ off*** odbiti; **~er** čuvar; tamničar
wardrobe ['wɔːdroub] garderoba; ormar za odijela; **~-trunk** kovčeg za odijela
ware [wɛə] roba; **~house** skladište; robna kuća; uskladištiti
war|like ['wɔːlaik] ratnički; ratoboran; **~-loan** ratni zajam; **~-monger** ratni huškač
warm [wɔːm] topao; ugrijati (se); **~th** toplina
warn [wɔːn] upozoriti (***of, against***); opomenuti (***to do***); **~ing** upozorenje; opomena
warp [wɔːp] iskriviti (se); svinuti se (*drvo*)
war-profiteer ['wɔːprɔfɪ'tiə] ratni dobitnik
warrant ['wɔrənt] punomoć; (***dock-, warehouse***) ~ skladišni list; ~ (***of apprehension***) tjeralica; ~ ***of arrest*** nalog za hapšenje; ovlastiti; jamčiti
warrior ['wɔriə] ratnik
Warsaw ['wɔːsɔː] Varšava
wart [wɔːt] bradavica
war|-wedding brak sklopljen za vrijeme rata; ~ **zone** ratna zona
was [wɔz] I. & 3. *lice sg pret. od* **be**
wash [wɔʃ] prati (se); isprati; ***~ up*** prati suđe; ***~ed out*** ispran; pranje; umivanje; **~er** stroj za pranje; brtveni prsten; **~erwoman** pralja; **~ing** pranje; rublje za pranje, **~ingpowder** prašak za pranje; ~ **out** neuspjeh; fiasko; ~ **rag** *Am* krpica za pranje; ~ **stand** stalak s umivaonikom
wasp [wɔsp] osa
waste [weist] pust; jalov; neupotrebiv; otpadni; rasipavanje; (o)pustošiti; rasipati; propadati (*bolesnik*); **~paper basket** košara za papir
watch [wɔtʃ] straža; džepni ili ručni sat; stražiti; promatrati; **~bracelet** narukvica za ručni sat; ~ **case** okućje sata; **~ful** oprezan; **~maker** urar; **~man** (noćni) čuvar
water ['wɔːtə] voda; navodnjavati; zalijevati; ***high ~*** plima; ***low ~*** oseka; ***drink the ~s*** liječiti se mineralnom vodom; ***make a p's mouth ~*** učiniti da kome rastu zazubice; **~-cart** kola za polijevanje ceste; **~colour** akvarel; vodena boja; **~-cooled** hlađen vodom; **~cress** BOT potočarka; **~-gauge** vodomjer; **~ing-pot** kanta za zalijevanje; **~ing-place** napajalište; toplice; morsko kupalište; **~plane** hidroavion; **~proof**

nepromočiv; kišni kaput; **~works** (*i pl*) vodovod; **~y** razvodnjen (*i fig*)
wave [weiv] val; ondulacija; učiniti valovitim; ondulirati; mahati; vitlati; **~-range** RADIO valno područje; **~trap** zaporni krug
waver ['weivə] posrtati; kolebati se
wax [wæks] vosak; navoštiti; rasti (*mjesec*)
way [wei] put; pruga; smjer; kurs; sredstvo; način; stanje; zanimanje; **~ *in*** ulaz; **~ *out*** izlaz; ***by the* ~** usput; ***by* ~ *of*** kroz; umjesto; ***out of the* ~** zabitan; neobičan; ***have one's* ~** raditi po svojoj volji; ***see one's* ~ *to*** (*inf*) znati kako što učiniti; **~lay** dočekati u zasjedi; **~side** rub puta, ceste; **~ward** mušičav; samovoljan
we [wi:] mi
weak [wi:k] slab(ašan); nejak; **~en** (o)slabiti; **~ly** slabunjav; **~ness** slabost
wealth [welθ] blagostanje; bogatstvo; **~y** bogat
weapon ['wepən] oružje
wear [wɛə] nositi na sebi; držati se dobro; **~ *away*** (***off, out***) istrošiti; iznositi; izmoriti; nošenje; trošenje; ***for hard* ~** za štrapac
weariness ['wiərinis] umor
weary ['wiəri] umoran; zamoran
weather ['weðə] vrijeme (*atmosfersko*); **~-beaten** od vremena oštećen; otvrdnuo; **~-bureau** *Am* metereološki ured; **~-forecast** prognoza vremena; **~-proof**, **~-tight** otporan prema (ne)vremenu; nepropustan za vjetar; **~-worn** trošan od vremena
weave [wi:v] tkati; isplesti; *fig* snovati; tkanje
web [web] tkivo; paučina; **~site** internetska stranica
wed [wed] vjenčati (se); *fig* sjediniti
wedding ['wediŋ] vjenčanje; **~ dress** vjenčana haljina; **~ present** svadbeni dar; **~ ring** vjenčani prsten
wedge [wedʒ] klin; pričvrstiti klinom; **~ *in*** ugurati (*i fig*)
Wednesday ['wenzdi] srijeda
weed [wi:d] korov; plijeviti
week [wi:k] tjedan; ***cut working* ~** skraćeni radni tjedan; **~day**: ***on* ~*days*** radnim danom; **~-end** vikend; kraj tjedna; provesti vikend; **~-end-ticket** vikend vozna karta
weep [wi:p] plakati
weigh [wei] (iz)vagati; **~ *anchor*** podići sidro; **~ *upon*** tištiti koga; **~t** težina; teret; **~ty** težak
welcome ['welkəm] dobrodošao; zaželjeti dobrodošlicu; *fig* pozdraviti
weld [weld] zavarivati

welfare ['welfɛə] dobrobit; ~ **centre** ured za socijalno staranje; ~ **work** socijalno staranje
well [wel] zdenac; (jamsko) okno; dobro; ***as ~ as*** tako kao; i … i; ***I am not ~*** nijemi dobro; **~-advised** promišljen; **~-bred** dobro odgojen; **~-intentioned** dobronamjeran; **~-known** poznat; ~ **off**, **~-to-do** imućan
Welsh [welʃ] velški; **~man** Velšanin
welter-weight ['weltəweit] *boks* velter kategorija
were [wəː] *pl pret od* **be**
west [west] zapad; zapadni; zapadno; **~ern** zapadni; **~ern(er)** zapadnjak; **~ward(s)** prema zapadu
wet [wet] mokar; vlažan; ***~ through*** promočen; mokrina; smočiti; navlažiti; zaliti; proslaviti pićem
whale [weil] ZOOL kit; **~-bone** kitova kost; **~-oil** kitovo ulje
wharf [wɔːf] lučka obala; kej; **~age** pristojba za vezanje broda
what [wɔt] što; koje; kako?; koliko?; koji?; kakav?; ***~ about …?*** što je s…?; **~(so)ever** koji mu drago; svaki koji
wheat [wiːt] pšenica
wheel [wiːl] kotač; kotrljati; gurati; *Am sl* voziti bicikl; **~barrow** tačke; **~wright** kolar
when [wen] kada, čim, dok; **~ce** [wens] odakle; prema tome; **~(so)ever** ma kada, bilo kada
where [wɛə] gdje; kuda; **~about(s)** gdje otprilike; boravište; **~as** međutim; **~upon** našto; **~ver** gdje god; kud god
whet [wet] brusiti; oštriti
whether ['weðə] da li
which [witʃ] koji, koja, koje; što
whiff [wif] dašak; jedan dim (*cigarete*)
while [wail] časak; dok; ***~ away*** provoditi (*vrijeme*)
whim [wim] hir
whimper ['wimpə] cmizdriti; plakati
whimsical ['wimzikəl] hirovit; ekscentričan
whine [wain] cviljeti; cmizdriti
whip [wip] bičevati; tući (*vrhnje*); bič
whirl [wəːl] vrtjeti; **~pool** vrtlog; **~wind** vihor; zračni vrtlog
whisk [wisk] peruška; (po-) mesti; obrisati; tući snijeg; ***~ away*** obrisati
whisper ['wispə] šaptati; **~*(ing)*** šaptanje
whistle ['wisl] zviždati; zviždaljka; zvižduk
white [wait] bijel; čist; **~-hot** usijan; **~ lie** laž iz nužde; **~n** pobijeliti; **~ness** bjelina; bljedoća; **~smith** limar;

~wash kreč za bijeljenje; krečiti
Whitsuntide ['witsntaid] Duhovi
whiz [wiz] zujati; hujati
who [hu:] tko; koji, koja, koje
whole [houl] cijeli; potpun; zdrav; cjelina; ***on the ~*** u cjelosti; **~-meal bread** kruh s mekinjama; **~sale trade** trgovina na veliko; **~some** zdrav
whoop [hu:p] vikati; urlati; **~ing-cough** hripavac
whortleberry ['wə:tlberi] borovnica
whose [hu:z] čiji
whosoever [hu:sou'evə] tko god, koji god
why [wai] zašto; čemu
wick [wik] stijenj, fitilj
wicked ['wikid] zločest; zao; **~ness** zloća
wicker ['wikə]: **~ basket** pletena košara; **~ chair** stolica od pletera
wide [waid] širok, prostran; ***~ awake*** sasvim budan; **~n** proširiti (se)
widow ['widou] udovica; **~er** udovac
width [widθ] širina; daljina
wife [waif] žena, supruga
wig [wig] perika; *sl* ukor; izgrditi
wild [waild] divlji; ***run ~*** podivljati; **~ cat** divlja mačka; *Am* prijevarno poduzeće; **~erness** ['wildənis] divljina; **~fire**: ***like ~fire*** munjevito; kao razbuktali požar; **~ness** divljina
wilful ['wilful] svojevoljan
will [wil] volja; oporuka; htjeti; pomoćni glagol za futur; ***with a ~*** snažno i s poletom
willing ['wiliŋ] voljan, pripravan (***to do***)
willow ['wilou] vrba
win [win] dobiti; postići; pobijediti
wince [wins] trgnuti (se)
wind [wind] vjetar; nadimanje; ***be in good ~*** imati dobra pluća; ***get one's second ~*** izduhati se; odahnuti; ***there is something in the ~*** nešto je u toku, u zraku; *sl* ***raise the ~*** prikupiti novac; ***get the ~ up*** prepasti se; [waind] ***~ up*** namotati; naviti uru; zaključiti posao; **~bag** vjetropir; brbljavac; **~fall** otpalo voće; (neočekivana) sreća
winding ['waindiŋ] ovoj; namatanje; **~ stairs** *pl* zavojite stepenice; **~-up** likvidacija
windlass ['windləs] motovilo; vitlo
window ['windou] prozor; **~dressing** aranžiranje izloga; pokazivanje lijepe strane; obmana; **~-frame** okvir prozora; **~-ledge**, **~-sill** prozorska daska; **~-shutter** prozorski kapak
wind|pipe ['windpaip] ANAT dušnik; **~screen**, *Am* **~shield** MOT vjetrobran;

prednje staklo automobila; **~screen wiper** MOT brisač vjetrobrana; **~y** vjetrovit (*i fig*)
wine [wain] vino; **~press** preša za vino
wing [wiŋ] krilo; snabdjeti krilima; dati krila
wink [wiŋk] mig; žmirkanje; treptati
winner ['winə] dobitnik; SPORT pobjednik
winning ['winiŋ] koji dobiva; pobjednički; **~post** SPORT cilj
winter ['wintə] zima; prezimiti
wintry ['wintri] zimski
wipe [waip] (o)brisati; (o)čistiti; ***~ dry*** osušiti; ***~ off*** otrti; ***~ out*** izbrisati; uništiti
wire [waiə] žica; telegram; pričvrstiti žicom; brzojaviti
wireless ['waiəlis] bežičan; radio; **~ message** radiogram; **~ operator** radio-telegrafist; **~ phone** bežični telefon; **~ set** radioaparat; **~ station** radio stanica
wire|-netting ['waiə'netiŋ] žičana mreža; **~-puller** pokretač marioneta
wisdom ['wizdəm] mudrost
wise [waiz] mudar; razborit; *Am* ***put a p ~*** uputiti koga (***about***); **~crack** *Am* duhovita primjedba
wish [wiʃ] (za)željeti; želja; ***~ for*** čeznuti za
wistful ['wistful] zamišljen; čeznutljiv
wit [wit] duhovitost; ***be at one's ~'s end*** ne moći se više snaći
witch [witʃ] vještica; čarobnica
with [wið] s, sa; pokraj; kod; zbog; ***it is just so ~ me*** meni je upravo isto tako; **~draw** povući (se) (***from***); **~drawal** povlačenje
wither ['wiðə] (u)venuti; usahnuti; osušiti se
with|hold [wið'hould] zadržati; **~in** unutra; iznutra; unutar; ***~in doors*** u kući; **~out** izvana; bez; a da ne; **~stand** odoljeti
witness ['witnis] svjedok; svjedočiti; **~-box** mjesto (*u sudnici*) za svjedoke
witty ['witi] duhovit; šaljiv
wives [waivz] *pl od* **wife**
wold [wulf], *pl* ***wolves*** vuk
woman ['wumən], *pl* ***women*** ['wimin] žena; ženska; ***young ~*** djevojka; **~ doctor** liječnica; **~ student** studentica; **~kind** ženski svijet; **~like** ženski; ženstven; **~ly** ženski
wonder ['wʌndə] čudo; čudesno djelo; čuditi se; htjeti znati (***whether, if***)
woo [wu:] snubiti (*djevojku*); zaprositi
wood [wud] šuma; drvo; **~-cutter** drvosječa; **~ed** pošumljen; šumovit; **~en** drven; **~work** drvena građa;

stolarski radovi

wool [wul] vuna; **~len** vunen

word [wə:d] riječ; obavijest; lozinka; ***by ~ of mouth*** usmeno; ***have ~s*** posvađati se (***with***); **~ing** izražavanje; stilizacija

work [wə:k] posao, rad; *pl* pogon; tvornica; ***public ~s*** javni radovi; ***make short ~ of*** brzo likvidirati; raditi; djelovati; držati u pogonu (*tvornicu*); staviti u pokret; posluživati stroj; ***at ~*** pri poslu; u pogonu; ***~ out*** izraditi; izračunati; riješiti; ***~ up*** podići; uzbuditi (*živce, osjećaje*); **~day** radni dan; **~er** radnik; **~ers** *pl* radni kolektiv; **~house** ubožnica

working ['wə:kiŋ]: ***in ~ order*** u stanju sposobnom za pogon; **~ association, ~ cooperation** radna zajednica; **~ capital** obrtni, poslovni kapital

workman ['wə:kmən] radnik; obrtnik; **~like** spretan; stručan; **~ship** spretnost; vještina; izradba

work|shop ['wə:kʃɔp] radionica; **~woman** radnica

world [wə:ld] svijet; ***~'s championship*** svjetsko prvenstvo; ***~ly innocent*** koji ne poznaje svijet; neiskusan; **~-power** velesila; **~-renowned firm** svjetska firma; **~-wide** rasprostranjen širom svijeta; svjetski

worm [wə:m] crv; **~-eaten** crvotočan

worn-out ['wɔ:n'aut] istrošen; otrcan

worry ['wʌri] zabrinjavati se; ***don't ~ about it!*** ne brini o tome

worse [wə:s] gori; lošiji

worship ['wə:ʃip] štovanje; obožavanje; kult; služba božja; obožavati

worst [wə:st] najgori; najlošiji; ***get the ~ of it*** izvući kraći kraj

worsted ['wustid] kamgarn tkanina

worth [wə:θ] vrijedan; vrijednost; **~-while** vrijedan (*truda*); koji se isplati; **~y** ['wə:ði] vrijedan; ugledan

would [wud] *pret od* **will**; **~-be** navodni; takozvani; **~-be politician** politikant

wound [wu:nd] rana; raniti

wrap [ræp] (**up**) zamotati; uplesti; ***~ped up in*** sasvim zaokupljen čime; ogrtač; plašt; **~per** omot; (ženski) kućni kaput; ovojni list duhana na cigari; (***postal***) ***~per*** unakrsni omot na poštanskoj pošiljci; **~ping-paper** papir za zamatanje; "pakpapir"

wreath [ri:θ] vijenac; girlanda

wreck [rek] olupina (*i fig*); propast; ***be ~ed*** razbiti se; **~ing service** *Am* služba pomoći i teglenja na cesti

wrench [rentʃ] izvinuti; uganuti
wrest [rest] istrgnuti; iskriviti
wrestle ['resl] hrvati se; **~r** hrvač
wretched ['retʃid] bijedan; nesretan
wriggle ['rigl] koprcati se; vijugati se
wring [riŋ] stiskati; izažimati
wrinkle ['riŋkl] bora; naborati (se)
wrist [rist] ručni zglob; **~(let)-watch** ručni sat
writ [rit] sudbeni nalog; spis; naredba
write [rait] pisati; **~r** pisac; pisar
writing ['raitiŋ] pisanje; rukopis; stil; **~-case** mapa za pisanje
wrong [rɔŋ] neprav; kriv; neispravan; nepravda; učiniti krivo; nanijeti nepravdu; ***be ~*** biti u krivu; pogrešno ići (*sat*); ***there is something ~*** nešto nije u redu; ***on the ~ side of 60*** preko 60 godina star
wry [rai] kriv; nakrivljen

X

X, Xt = Christ
Xmas = Christmas
X-ray ['eks'rei]: **~s** rentgenske zrake; zračiti x-zrakama; rentgenizirati

Y

yacht [jɔt] jahta; sportska jedrilica; voziti se na jahti; **~ing** jedrenje
Yankee ['jæŋki] Jenki (Sjeveroamerikanin)
yard [ja:d] jard (*mjera za duljinu = 0,914 m*); dvorište
yarn [ja:n] pređa; MAR uže; uzica
yawn [jɔ:n] zijevati
year [jə:] godina; **~ly** godišnji
yearn [jə:n] čeznuti (***for***)
yeast [ji:st] kvas(ac)
yell [jel] vikati; vrištati; vrisak
yellow ['jelou] žut; **~ish** žućkast; **~ press** senzacionalistička štampa
yelp [jelp] štektanje; štektati
yes [jes] da, jest; jesni odgovor
yesterday ['jestədi] jučer
yet [jet] još; dosad; ipak; čak; ***as ~*** dosad(a); ***not ~*** još ne
yield [ji:ld] donijeti plod (prihod); dati rezultat; proizvesti; dopustiti; popustiti; predati se; plod; prihod; **~ing**

popustljiv
yoke [jouk] jaram; ujarmiti
yolk [jouk] žumanjak
you [juː] vi, vas, vam(a); ti, te(be), tebi; se
young [jʌŋ] mlad (*fig*), svjež, neiskusan
your [jɔː] vaš, tvoj; **~s** vaš, tvoj; **~self**, *pl* **~selves** se, sebe; ti sam
youth [juːθ] mladić; mladost; mladež; **~ful** mladenački
Yugoslav ['juːgou'slaːv] *hist* Jugoslaven; jugoslavenski
Yugoslavia ['juːgou'slaːviə] *hist* Jugoslavija

Z

zap [zæp] izbrisati; otpucati; pogoditi; poslati
zeal [ziːl] revnost; **~ous** ['zeləs] revan; gorljiv
Zealand ['ziːlənd] Zelandija
zenith ['zeniθ] zenit
zero ['ziərou] ništica; ništa
zest [zest] začin; polet; zanos; veselje (***for***); užitak
zigzag ['zigzæg] cikcak
zinc [ziŋk] cink
zip [zip] **fastener** patentni zatvarač
zone [zoun] zona; zemaljski pojas; *fig* područje
Zoo [zuː] zoološki vrt
zoolog|ist [zou'ɔlədʒist] zoolog; **~y** zoologija
zoom [zuːm] AERO strmo i naglo se uspeti

Appendices

Numbers

Cardinal Numbers

0 ništa *zero, nought*
1 jedan *one*
2 dva *two*
3 tri *three*
4 četiri *four*
5 pet *five*
6 šest *six*
7 sedam *seven*
8 osam *eight*
9 devet *nine*
10 deset *ten*
11 jedanaest *eleven*
12 dvanaest *twelve*
13 trinaest *thirteen*
14 četrnaest *fourteen*
15 petnaest *fifteen*
16 šesnaest *sixteen*
17 sedamnaest *seventeen*
18 osamnaest *eighteen*
19 devetnaest *nineteen*
20 dvadeset *twenty*
21 dvadeset i jedan *twenty-one*
22 dvadeset i dva *twenty-two*
23 dvadeset i tri *twenty-three*
30 trideset *thirty*
31 trideset i jedan *thirty-one*
40 četrdeset *forty*
41 četrdeset i jedan *forty-one*
50 pedeset *fifty*
51 pedeset i jedan *fifty-one*
60 šezdeset *sixty*
61 šezdeset i jedan *sixty-one*
70 sedamdeset *seventy*
71 sedamdeset i jedan *seventy-one*
80 osamdeset *eighty*
81 osamdeset i jedan *eighty-one*
90 devedeset *ninety*
91 devedeset i jedan *ninety-one*
100 sto *a* (ili *one*) *hundred*
101 sto i jedan *a hundred and one*
200 dvjesto *two hundred*
572 petstosedamdesetdva *five hundred and seventy-two*
1000 tisuću *a* (ili *one*) *thousand*
1956 tisućudevetstopedeset-šest *nineteen (hundred and) fifty-six*
2000 dvije tisuće *two thousand*
1 000 000 jedan milion *a* (ili *one*) *million*
2 000 000 dva miliona *two million*
1 000 000 000 jedna milijarda *a* (ili *one*) *billion*

Ordinal Numbers

1. prvi *first*
2. drugi *second*
3. treći *third*
4. četvrti *fourth*
5. peti *fifth*
6. šesti *sixth*
7. sedmi *seventh*
8. osmi *eighth*
9. deveti *ninth*
10. deseti *tenth*
11. jedanaesti *eleventh*
12. dvanaesti *twelfth*
13. trinaesti *thirteenth*
14. četrnaesti *fourteenth*
15. petnaesti *fifteenth*
16. šesnaesti *sixteenth*
17. sedamnaesti *seventeenth*
18. osamnaesti *eighteenth*
19. devetnaesti *nineteenth*
20. dvadeseti *twentieth*
21. dvadesetprvi *twenty-first*
22. dvadesetdrugi *twenty-second*
23. dvadesettreći *twenty-third*
30. trideseti *thirtieth*
31. tridesetprvi *thirty-first*
40. četrdeseti *fortieth*
41. četrdesetprvi *forty-first*
50. pedeseti *fiftieth*
51. pedesetprvi *fifty-first*
60. šezdeseti *sixtieth*
61. šezdesetprvi *sixty-first*
70. sedamdeseti *seventieth*
71. sedamdesetprvi *seventy-first*
80. osamdeseti *eightieth*
81. osamdesetprvi *eighty-first*
90. devedeseti *ninetieth*
100. stoti *(one) hundredth*
101. sto i prvi *(one) hundred and first*
200. dvjestoti *two hundredth*
300. tristoti *three hundredth*
572. petstosedamdesetdrugi *five hundred and seventy-second*
1000. tisući *(one) thousandth*
1950. tisućudevetstopedeseti *nineteen hundred and fiftieth*
2000. dvijetisući *two thousandth*
1 000 000. milionti *(one) millionth*
2 000 000. dvamilionti *two millionth*

Fractions, decimals and mathematical calculation methods

$\frac{1}{2}$ pola *one/a half*
$1\frac{1}{2}$ jedan i po *one and a half*
$2\frac{1}{2}$ dva i po *two and a half*
$\frac{1}{2}$ milje *half a mile*
$\frac{1}{3}$ jedna trećine *one/a third*
$\frac{2}{3}$ dvije trećine *two thirds*
$\frac{1}{4}$ jedna četvrtina *one fourth, one/a quarter*
$\frac{3}{4}$ tri četvrtine *three fourths, three quarters*
$\frac{1}{5}$ jedna petina *one/a fifth*
$3\frac{4}{5}$ tri cijela i četiri petine *three and four fifths*
$\frac{12}{20}$ dvanaest dvadesetina *twelve twentieths*
$\frac{75}{100}$ sedamdesetpet stotina *seventy-five hundredths*
0,4 ništa zarez četiri *point four (.4)*
2,5 dva zarez pet *two point five (2.5)*
jednostruko *single*
dvostruko *double*
trostruko *treble, triple, threefold*
četverostruko *fourfold, quadruple*
peterostruko *fivefold etc.*

1x jedamput *once*
2x dvaput *twice*
3x,4x,5x triput, četiriput, pet puta itd. *three, four, five times*
dvaput toliko *twice as much (many)*
još jednom *once more*
u prvom redu, u drugom redu, u trećem redu itd. *firstly, secondly, thirdly, in the first (second, third) place*
$2 \times 3 = 6$ dvaput tri je šest *two times three is six/two multiplied by three is six*
$7 + 8 = 15$ sedam i osam je petnaest *seven plus eight is fifteen*
$10 - 3 = 7$ deset manje tri je sedam *ten minus three is seven*
$20 : 5 = 4$ dvadeset podijeljeno sa pet je četiri *twenty divided by five is four*